Lise Pearlman's account of the tinderbox setting enveloping the trial of Huey Newton perfectly captures how much can be at stake for an entire community—even a nation—in a single trial and the exceptional role played by twelve everyday men and women we trust to decide each case. For those, like myself, who recall this case from our youth, Lise has done a wonderful job in both capturing a movement and its historical context. But anyone interested in history, courtroom drama or criminal justice should read this gripping account of an all too often forgotten chapter of the 20th Century.

Barry Scheck, PROFESSOR OF LAW, BENJAMIN N. CARDOZO SCHOOL OF LAW, CO-DIRECTOR, THE INNOCENCE PROJECT

I was born in Oakland a generation before the mass migration of African-American families to the Bay Area from the South during World War II. I later experienced the highly polarizing 1968 prosecution of Black Panther Huey Newton. Lise Pearlman has written a powerful account of both that trial and its place in our country's political history. I truly believe that had Newton received a death sentence, we would not have Obama in the White House today. Read this wonderful book.

Morrie Turner, AWARD-WINNING CREATOR OF "WEE PALS," THE FIRST INTEGRATED COMIC STRIP

Lise Pearlman's book about the trial of Huey Newton captures the tumultuous times, the personalities, the fighting defense lawyers, including Charles Garry, in a way that makes it eminently worth reading. Garry's jury selection dealing with race was one of the best pieces of trial work done by anyone. Loved the book.

James Brosnahan, SENIOR PARTNER, MORRISON FOERSTER, RATED AMONG THE TOP 30 TRIAL LAWYERS IN THE U.S.

I began my long career as a criminal defense lawyer in the mid-60s in Oakland, California and witnessed many of the legal events Lise Pearlman describes. I find her account of the 1968 Newton murder trial and its political context accurate and fascinating. Fans of famous trials will thoroughly enjoy this fast-paced, well-researched book. If "THE" trial of the 20th century can be measured, her argument for People v. Newton *heading the list is a strong one.*

Penny Cooper, MEMBER OF THE STATE BAR OF CALIFORNIA TRIAL LAWYERS HALL OF FAME

THE SKY'S THE LIMIT

PEOPLE v. NEWTON

THE REAL *TRIAL OF THE 20TH CENTURY?*

LISE PEARLMAN

REGENT PRESS
BERKELEY, CALIFORNIA

PAPERBACK:
ISBN 13: 978-1-58790-220-8
ISBN 10:1-58790-220-6
Library of Congress Control Number: 2011926517

E-BOOK
ISBN 13: 978-1-58790-185-0
ISBN 10: 1-58790-185-4

Cover photos of the Panthers © Ilka Hartmann 2012
Front: "All the leaders are in jail" Left: Posters of Huey Newton, Center and right, Eldridge Cleaver;
Back: "Huey Newton at the press conference after his release" with his lawyer, Fay Stender, behind him.

Author photo © 2012 Victoria Friend

Alameda Courthouse Photo © 2012 Lise Pearlman

Printed in the USA
REGENT PRESS
Berkeley, California
www.regentpress.net
regentpress@mindspring.com

Dedication

This book is dedicated to the memory of
Ed Johnson, Leo Frank, Joe Kahahawai, Bruno Richard Hauptmann,
and all other defendants whom our system of justice has grievously failed.
Hopefully, the lessons from our past will make similar outcomes
increasingly less likely as we go forward in the 21st century.

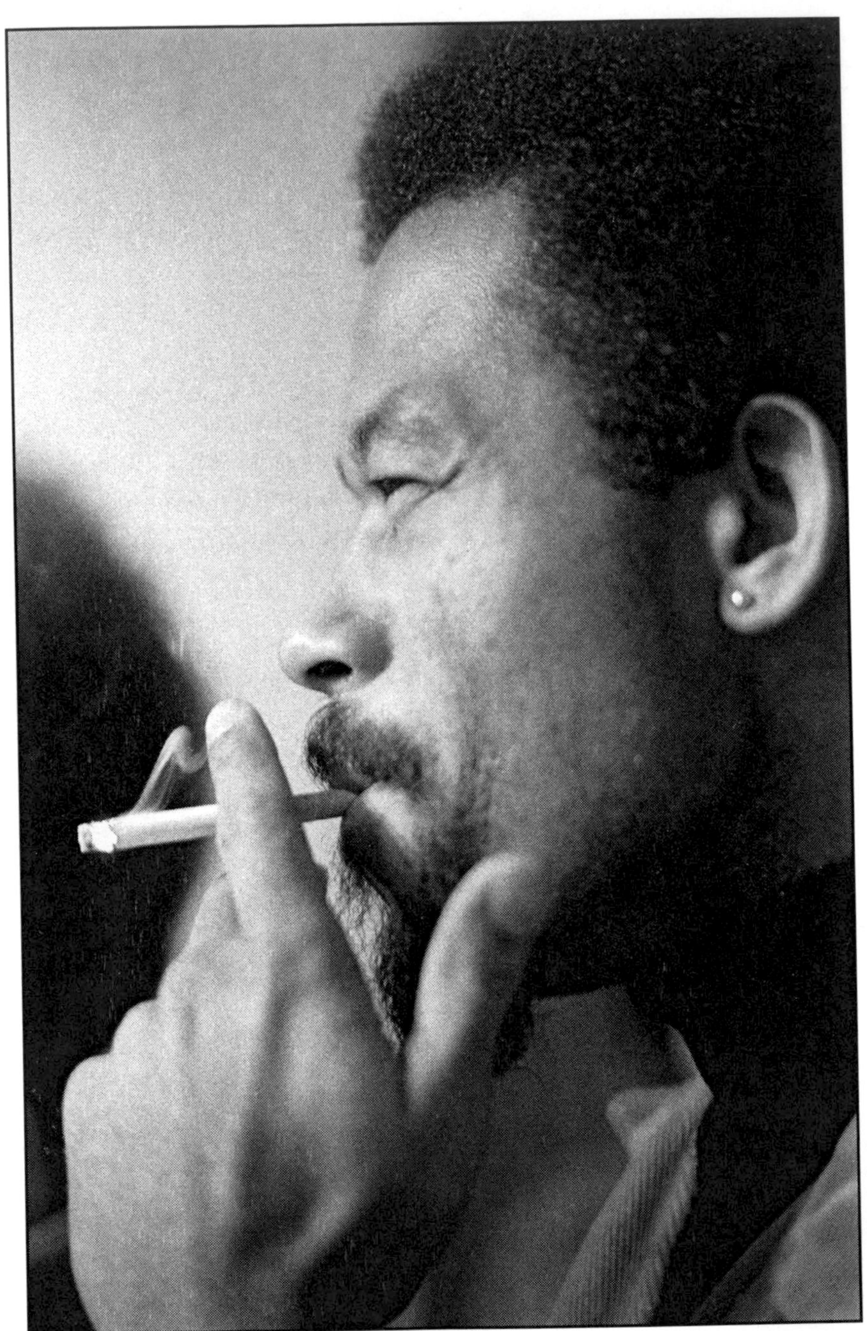

ELDRIDGE CLEAVER

FOREWORD

Talking shit is the iron in a young nigger's blood.

ELDRIDGE CLEAVER

The FBI could not help but take notice when militant black leaders converged on Oakland, California, from all across the nation in mid-February 1968 to meet with 10,000 local activists. It was a fund-raising birthday party for Huey P. Newton, the Black Panther Party's Minister of Defense. For almost a year, the Panther Party's popular biweekly newspaper featured Newton seated on a wicker throne with a rifle in one hand and a spear in the other. Now the empty throne stood in for Newton. The honoree paced back and forth in an isolation cell in the Alameda County jail just a few miles to the north. Newton was charged with murdering a police officer, wounding another and kidnapping a bystander at gunpoint—all while on parole that prohibited him from even carrying a firearm.

Most people gathered in the Oakland Arena on February 17, 1968, expected the twenty-six-year-old, self-proclaimed revolutionary to be convicted and sentenced to death for shooting the officer. Militant Malcolm X disciples joined white radicals and nervous local black community members on common ground—a rally to raise some of the anticipated $100,000 defense costs for the Newton murder trial. His lawyers cultivated grassroots support to prevent the outspoken critic of police brutality from going to the gas chamber. Comrades like Panther spokesman Eldridge Cleaver did not believe the pretrial publicity portraying Newton as a victim, but thought it useful propaganda; while conservative and mainstream newspapers denounced Newton as a cop killer, his militant followers celebrated the shooting death of a racist "pig." For many of them, his guilt was never in question, but it didn't matter; in fact, some considered the shooting a long-awaited signal from the revolutionary leader.

The air crackled with anticipation as a capacity crowd poured in for an experience of a lifetime. The featured speakers headed the Student Nonviolent Coordinating Committee ("SNCC"). Despite keeping the name, SNCC had turned its back on peaceful protest in 1966. The rally speakers included the incendiary H. Rap Brown, "black power" champion Stokely Carmichael, and SNCC organizer James Forman. By February of 1968 the chant "black power" had taken hold as "both a rallying cry and a declaration of war."[1] The theme of this kick-off rally for Huey Newton was unity, which was why the black separatists suppressed their mistrust and tolerated the inclusion of leaders of the white radical Peace and Freedom Party, who had forged an alliance with the Black Panthers. In exchange, Forman insisted that Panther co-founder Bobby Seale invite Maulana Ron Karenga, the head of the Organization US ("US") from Los Angeles, where the Panthers had just opened a second branch. At the gathering, the Panthers and US held their bitter rivalry in check.

The Panthers owed some of their countercultural clout to the fame of ex-felon Eldridge Cleaver, basking in the success of his recently published, best-selling prison essays—*Soul on Ice*—and his new platform as a journalist for the Leftist political magazine *Ramparts*. A self-educated Marxist, Cleaver had won parole from prison in December of 1966. By the time Cleaver walked out of Folsom Prison he had committed himself to becoming a professional revolutionary, as he envisioned his idol Che Guevara: "a cold, calculating killing machine, able to slit a throat at the drop of a hat and walk away without looking back."[2] Huey Newton impressed Cleaver at first sight in February of 1967. By daring a San Francisco cop to draw a gun on him in a street confrontation, Newton proved he was no paper Panther.

Cleaver dubbed the birthday rally "the biggest line-up of revolutionary leaders that had ever come together under one roof in the history of America."[3] As Air Force veteran James Forman took his turn at the podium near Newton's empty throne, he was similarly inspired. Though Forman had the least militant track record of the SNCC representatives who spoke, he electrified the gathering with his call for retaliation if Newton were executed: "The sky is the limit."[4] This did not sound like empty boasting coming off a year marked by race riots. After two political assassinations that spring and growing unrest over the Vietnam War, the Newton trial became a cause célèbre for radical groups and anti-war activists. In mid-July, when the proceedings began, one underground newspaper ran a blaring headline proclaiming "Nation's Life at Stake." The article explained:

> History has its pivotal points. This trial is one of them. America on Monday placed itself on trial [by prosecuting Huey Newton]. . . The Black Panthers are the most militant black organization in this nation. They are growing rapidly. They are not playing games. And they are but the visible part of a vast, black iceberg. The issue is not the alleged killing of an Oakland cop. The issue is racism. Racism can destroy America in swift flames. Oppression. Revolt. Suppression. Revolution. Determined black and brown and white men are watching what happens to Huey Newton. What they do depends on what the white man's courts do to Huey. Most who watch with the keenest interest are already convinced that he cannot get a fair trial.[5]

For a full year before the trial began, the FBI's twenty-year-old Counter Intelligence Program ("COINTELPRO") had been focusing on broadly defined black radicals and various ways to eliminate them. By the summer of 1968, COINTELPRO was bent on destroying the Black Panther Party, but the threat of government persecution could not stop the Panthers from ramping up their rhetoric. Taking his cue from the inflammatory language of both Newton and SNCC leaders, "El Rage" Cleaver challenged the government to instigate a second American revolution. In early July of 1968, the Panther spokesman held a press conference in New York City predicting open warfare in the streets of California if Huey Newton were sentenced to death. Cleaver expected the carnage to spread across country. The day Newton testified on his own behalf, crowds started lining up before dawn and broke the courthouse doors as they pushed against each other, vying for access. Gov. Reagan took keen interest in the proceedings from Sacramento, while J. Edgar Hoover elevated the Panthers to the number one internal threat to the country's security.

Following Newton's trial, Panther Party co-founder Bobby Seale faced conspiracy charges accusing him of a leadership role in the battle between Chicago police and demonstrators that had exploded onto the floor of the 1968 Democratic Convention. Soon far more serious allegations confronted Seale. He was extradited to New Haven, Connecticut, for allegedly ordering the torture and murder of Alex Rackley, a suspected government plant in the local Panther office. By 1969, the FBI was targeting members of the Panther Party in nearly eighty percent of 295 authorized "Black Nationalist" COINTELPRO missions nationwide. Among these raids was a widely condemned, predawn invasion in December of 1969 by plainclothes policemen who stormed the apartment of charismatic young Panther leader Fred Hampton. The police riddled Hampton's front door with bullets and killed the twenty-one-year-old community organizer as he lay in bed. The largely white anarchist Weathermen retaliated by bombing police cars. To far greater political effect, 5,000 people gathered in Chicago from across the nation to attend Hampton's funeral. Reverends Ralph Abernathy and Jesse Jackson led the eulogies. Jackson proclaimed, "When Fred was shot in Chicago, black people in particular, and decent people in general, bled everywhere."[6] Just six months before his death, Hampton had negotiated a truce among the city's rival gangs, the first "rainbow coalition" that Jackson would later popularize in his own 1984 historic campaign for the presidency. As reporters revealed cover-ups and discrepancies in the police account of the Hampton apartment raid, the Panthers and their outraged supporters launched a public relations campaign decrying governmental persecution and demanded a probe into COINTELPRO.

In April of 1970, tens of thousands of demonstrators descended on New Haven, Connecticut, from across the country to protest Seale's upcoming trial. The instigators were Youth International Party ("Yippie") leaders Abbie Hoffman and Jerry Rubin, joined by other "Chicago Seven" defendants. They wanted to show solidarity with Seale, who was the eighth co-defendant in their highly publicized Chicago conspiracy trial until Judge Julius Hoffman ordered Seale bound and gagged for backtalk and severed his prosecution from the others. In response to the Yippie-led pilgrimage to New Haven, President Nixon mobilized armed

National Guardsmen from as far away as Virginia, who came prepared to spray tear gas on demonstrators and students alike. Yale's President Kingman Brewster sized up the impending confrontation and decided to shut down the Ivy League University for a week to let students and professors who were so inclined to take part in voluntary teach-ins. In comments to the faculty that were quickly leaked to the press, Brewster created a storm of controversy that instantly put the Mayflower Pilgrim descendant on President Nixon's growing "Enemies List." Angry editorials throughout the nation reinforced Vice President Agnew's demand that Brewster resign for daring to say that "I am appalled and ashamed that things should have come to such a pass in this country that I am skeptical of the ability of black revolutionaries to achieve a fair trial anywhere in the United States."[7]

Articulating the opposite concern, Los Angeles Police Chief Ed Davis viewed the national situation in the same dire light as did J. Edgar Hoover. Testifying before a Senate committee, Davis asserted, "we have revolution on the installment plan . . . going on every day now."[8] But that was Brewster's point: something far greater is lost when we rationalize the abandonment of our core values as a society. Brewster, and those who rallied to his defense, echoed what Yale Law School's dean had noted eight years earlier: "The quality of a civilization is largely determined by the fairness of its criminal trials. . . ."[9] So was Brewster's skepticism justified?

Under intense pressure, an effort by a trial judge, prosecutor, and jury to provide a fair trial to a black revolutionary had in fact been undertaken in the summer of 1968. As Newton's lead lawyer Charles Garry questioned his final witnesses, the feisty Leftist knew that most of the packed courtroom had just seen shocking video footage of Mayor Daley's police force in Chicago cracking heads of both demonstrators and mainstream reporters during the Democratic Convention. Garry referred to the Chicago debacle in his highly emotional closing argument as another example of entrenched racism that infected Oakland's police force as well. In contrast, prosecutor D. Lowell Jensen tried to sell the jury on a matter-of-fact account of a dedicated local peace officer murdered in the line of duty. The city of Oakland seemed to hold its breath during the four days the Newton jury stayed out over Labor Day weekend. After two dramatic returns to the courtroom for rereading of testimony and further instruction, the sequestered Newton jury—led by a black middle-class foreman—did their best to reach a just result. The outcome greatly surprised both sides, as well as the myriad outside observers who had followed every development in the case.

The highly anticipated first-degree murder conviction and ensuing national conflagration never happened. Why not? What did that diverse Oakland jury of five men and seven women do with the prosecution claim of a police officer martyred by an itchy-fingered black revolutionary? How did they respond to the defense argument that the early morning shootout was just one more example in a long history of racist police brutality? And why, with the extraordinarily high tension surrounding the trial, did no urban violence erupt in its wake, as had occurred so often in the prior year? Even more puzzling, in light of the enormous stakes—why in the years to come did this particular "trial of the century" slip from general public consciousness? Why did it wind up all but forgotten by most experts who make a practice of analyzing such trials? How could they ignore *The People v. Huey P. Newton* while writing about trials whose only claim to fame is that they involved celebrity defendants? Isn't it time *People v. Newton* made everyone's list of pivotal trials of the 20th century?

CONTENTS

FOREWORD vii

Part One

INTRODUCTION 1

1. THE PLAYING FIELD:
   Sometimes the Fix Is In 9
2. DEMENTIA AMERICANA:
   The Murder of Stanford White 35
3. UNDESIRABLE CITIZENS:
   The Murder Trial of Big Bill Haywood 55
4. SHOWDOWN WITH THE SUPREME COURT:
   The Contempt Trial of Sheriff Joseph Shipp 76
5. LABOR V. CAPITAL REDUX:
   The Los Angeles Times Bombing Case 99
6. MURDER BEGETS MURDER:
   The Tragic Deaths of Mary Phagan and Leo Frank 107
7. ANARCHIST SCARE:
   The Trial of Sacco and Vanzetti 130
8. LEOPOLD AND LOEB:
   Murder for the Thrill of It 145
9. THE SCOPES MONKEY TRIAL:
   The Staged Battle of Evolution v. Creationism 163

10. EVEN A BLACK MAN'S HOME IS HIS CASTLE:
Pyrrhic Victory in the Sweet Murder Trials 180

11. SOUTHERN JUSTICE REVISITED:
The Railroading of the Scottsboro Boys 203

12. THE EXPLOSIVE MASSIE AFFAIR:
Truth Battles Raw Power 214

13. NATIONAL FRENZY:
The Lindbergh Baby Killing 242

14. SHAMELESS HASTE:
The Rosenberg Espionage Trial 267

15. DEATH OF INNOCENCE:
Hate Crimes and the Civil Rights Movement 281

16. BEYOND CIVIL RIGHTS:
Other Movement Cases 290

PART TWO

1. FREE HUEY NOW! 305

2. THE PANTHERS' ROOTS 313

3. TAKIN' CARE OF BUSINESS 323

4. THE DEFENSE TEAM 331

5. WHO DO YOU TRUST? 345

6. HONKIES FOR HUEY 351

7. THE SMELL OF REVOLUTION 356

8. CLIENT OR COMRADE? 360

9. POWER TO THE PEOPLE 366

10. THE QUEST FOR A JURY OF HIS PEERS 385

11. A MINORITY OF ONE 411

12. ON TRIAL — NEWTON OR AMERICAN SOCIETY? 425
13. THE DAY OF RECKONING ARRIVES 446
14. AFTERMATH 475

Part Three

1. THE "FREE HUEY" CAMPAIGN EXPANDS TO BURSTING 487
2. ECLIPSED 539
3. VISIONS OF APOCALYPTIC RACE WAR 549
4. TRIPLE JEOPARDY— BLACK, FEMALE, AND COMMUNIST 560
5. WATERGATE OVERSHADOWS THE COBRA 605
6. DOWNWARD SPIRAL 616
7. A CLOSER LOOK AT THE COMPETITION 646
8. THE PRECARIOUS PATH TO A BI-RACIAL PRESIDENT 676

Endnotes 717

Sources 762

Index 779

Acknowledgments 805

Part One

INTRODUCTION

You can jail a Revolutionary,
but you can't jail the Revolution.

— Huey Newton

In the last decade of the 20th century, Pulitzer Prize–winning journalist J. Anthony Lukas captured the essence of what to look for in evaluating a candidate for "THE" trial of the century: "a spectacular show trial, a great national drama in which the stakes [are] nothing less than the soul of the American people."[1] One would expect such a trial to involve top-notch lawyers wrangling over highly charged issues that polarize observers. One would also anticipate a packed courtroom, many hundreds of demonstrators, media from across the continent and beyond clamoring for press passes, riveting arguments, skewering cross-examination, some elements of mystery, and dramatic touches including, hopefully, a charismatic defendant taking the stand and putting the victim on trial, leaving serious doubt about the outcome.

A deeply politicized death penalty case that involves countercharges of racism against the police and prosecution witnesses promises great division among spectators. Throw in both counsel receiving death threats and extraordinary precautions taken to safeguard the courtroom and the deliberating jury. Assume that hordes of police and National Guardsmen must be put on alert to quell anticipated riots. Assume that the defendant heads a militant group viewed by the FBI as the most dangerous threat to American security, in a year already characterized by political assassinations and widespread urban unrest; that he is media savvy, well-read, highly articulate and persuasive; and that leaders of other radical groups have already declared that a revolution would begin if he were convicted. Assume the defendant is already a folk hero capturing the imagination not only of downtrodden members of his own race but athletes, singers and songwriters, Liberal professionals, college students and anti-war activists who have adopted him as a Leftist icon. The 1968 trial of twenty-six-year-old Huey Newton was just such a case. It well deserves recognition among the top handful of contenders for American trials of the 20th century—perhaps even at the top of the list. Even skeptics should question why the Newton case has fallen off most conventional radar screens in the past forty years. Indeed, the absence of *People v. Newton* from so many recently circulated lists of the most famous and controversial trials of the 20th century speaks volumes, given the media frenzy it created at the time.

Named for assassinated Southern demagogue Huey Pierce Long, Huey P. Newton was born in Louisiana and raised in Oakland, California. By the fall of 1967, he and co-founder Bobby Seale and a few hand-picked, armed associates had been following local Oakland police around on their beats for many months. Newton and Seale had agreed that Seale, more than five years older than Newton, should be named Party Chairman and Newton would take the title of Minister of Defense. They called themselves the Black Panther Party for Self-Defense because the panther fiercely defends itself, but only when provoked. After decades of suffering police abuse, many poor black residents of Oakland's flatlands welcomed the political "Ten Point Program" of the Black Panthers. The Panthers began to hound and shadow the nearly all-white police force, with Newton pulling out his criminal law book and reading arrestees their rights. Newton got a kick out of confronting those he considered racist "pigs," a term the Panthers popularized.

Students of Leftist philosophy, Newton and Seale modeled their Ten Point Program on the Nation of Islam's "What We Believe." Both had been inspired by the recent Cuban revolution and the overthrow of colonial governments in Africa. Newton particularly admired intellectual revolutionaries Frantz Fanon and Che Guevara. At the same time, unlike traditional Marxists, Newton welcomed other street toughs who, like him, had a criminal record and a reckless streak—what Communists called the *lumpenproletariat*.

The Panthers had a distinctive black leather uniform, logo, and clenched-fist salute that inspired a wide array of followers. Who among those watching the 1968 Mexican Olympics could forget Tommie Smith and John Carlos, the two African-American track medalists who raised their fists in a classic "Power to the People" salute and were promptly banned from the Olympics for life?[2] The new militant group first grabbed the international spotlight in the spring of 1967 when an entourage led by Party Chairman Bobby Seale marched into the California State Capitol bearing rifles. Following Newton's directive, they never aimed their guns at anyone, but their appearance made a bold public statement, challenging a proposed new law against carrying weapons in public places. Seale read a proclamation Newton had written, condemning racist colonialism in America's domestic and foreign policies. That summer of 1967, the *New York Times* magazine profiled Newton. The article characterized him as an alarming new radical leader who promoted anti-establishment violence. "Every time you execute a white racist Gestapo cop, you are defending yourselves," he told the reporter. Anticipating that a time for revolution would soon come, Newton expressed his willingness to kill and to die as part of a national revolt.[3] The Oakland police were already on high alert. They kept a list of known Panther vehicles and stopped them frequently. Both sides fully expected a bloody standoff to take place; it was just a question of when.

Even so, FBI head J. Edgar Hoover did not yet consider the Panthers a threat. In the 1950s, the FBI had created COINTELPRO, a secretive squad of counter intelligence personnel dedicated to destroying radical organizations. In August of 1967, Hoover instructed COINTELPRO to focus on Black Nationalist "hate groups." The Panthers did not surface on that list at the time. Among other targets, the FBI had been focused for several years on SNCC and tracing its Communist ties. By the early fall of 1967, SNCC leader H. Rap Brown faced criminal charges for making a fiery speech in Maryland in July following urban riots across the country. In Detroit alone, over forty people had been killed and hundreds wounded when, a short time later, Brown incited a rowdy audience in Baltimore: "If America don't come around, we're gonna burn it down."[4] Rioters set fire to local stores and began a looting rampage. Unrepentant,

Brown electrified the press by announcing that America was "on the eve of a black revolution."[5] President Lyndon Johnson grew so concerned about the escalating urban violence since 1964 that he appointed a blue ribbon National Advisory Commission on Civil Disorders. In the fall of 1967, the group began a comprehensive analysis of the bitter racial divide in America's cities that resulted in the "Kerner Report," which ascribed urban blight directly to white racism.

America was on edge long before the early morning of October 28, 1967, when Newton barely survived a shootout with two policemen in West Oakland's red light district, leaving him hospitalized with a bullet wound in his abdomen, one policeman wounded and another dead. Soon afterward, in spite of bitter criticism from local African-American lawyers, Newton accepted a high-powered team led by two white lawyers to defend him—radical San Francisco lawyer Charles Garry and his female associate Fay Stender. The soft-spoken former California Supreme Court clerk had no prior felony trial experience, but turned herself into a monomaniacal force of nature on Newton's behalf. The odd team worked wonders: Stender's thorough research and brief-writing skills honed as an appellate lawyer complemented her Armenian mentor's street-fighter-in-the-courtroom theatrics. Garry was famous among members of the criminal defense bar for his role in developing California's diminished capacity defense to murder charges. He and his gentlemanly partner Barney Dreyfus were also well known for their longstanding Communist ties; American Communist Party President William Patterson offered to raise money to help pay the Garry firm's legal bills when the Panthers agreed to accept the white radical as Newton's counsel.

By the spring of 1968, just before Newton's trial was first scheduled to take place, racial tensions had grown to explosive levels. It started on the afternoon of April 4 when Rev. Martin Luther King, Jr. was assassinated in Memphis, Tennessee. Riots again broke out in cities across the country. Bobby Seale took a leadership role in keeping the peace in the East Bay. He brought two vans of Panthers to patrol North Richmond and to chase looters and vandals off the streets. But Eldridge Cleaver had other ideas. In Oakland, two days after King's assassination, Cleaver led three vans filled with armed Black Panthers on a cruise through the flatlands looking for action. The Panther convoy wound up in a bloody confrontation with local police, which ended with Cleaver limping naked from a house where he had holed up. Cleaver knew that otherwise the police might claim he was still armed. His self-conscious companion, seventeen-year-old Bobby Hutton, emerged clothed behind Cleaver. The police shot him dead on the street. When they frisked the body, they discovered no weapon. The police arrested Cleaver for parole violation and accused the Panthers of attempting to ambush the cops; the Panthers accused the police of Hutton's cold-blooded murder. The publicity had the community taking sides and forced a postponement of Newton's impending trial. The trial had to be postponed yet again in early June, days after Senator Bobby Kennedy's assassination shocked the already reeling nation.

By the second week of June, Eldridge Cleaver was free again on bail. The Peace and Freedom Party named him their 1968 candidate for President, endorsed as well by the American Communist Party—its first such endorsement in many years. Cleaver and his young wife Kathleen helped Seale and Hilliard rally thousands of Panther supporters and anti-war activists to protest the upcoming Newton trial as an attack on a Movement hero, whom many now viewed as America's Che Guevara. For months, long-haired white "honkies for Huey" had joined forces with the Panthers. As the trial started, far larger multi-racial crowds of Movement supporters surrounded the courthouse, chanting "Free Huey" and raising signs that repeated Forman's angry rallying cry: "The Sky's the Limit." The Newton defense team thrived on all the Movement support. Garry had embraced from day one the Panther leader's desire to put four hundred years of racism in America on trial. That included the Vietnam War, in which young black men were disproportionally drafted, only to have many of them return permanently injured, emotionally scarred or in body bags. By the spring of 1967, SNCC's bellicose new chairman Stokely Carmichael — the Black Panthers' honorary field marshal — had derisively boiled the war down to: "white people sending black people to make war on yellow people in order to defend the land they stole from red people."[6]

Garry put on quite a show. Like Clarence Darrow, the Armenian streetfighter had a reputation for never having lost a client to the death penalty. A former tailor, Garry dressed with flair. He had a dazzling courtroom style and an instinct for ferreting out bias—his examination of potential jurors in the Newton case would later make its way into law school textbooks. Opposing him was the county's top prosecutor, future federal judge Delwen Lowell Jensen, well-known for his thorough preparation and success rate in the county's most intensely followed and controversial cases. The Newton trial would be the highest profile case of Jensen's career. The case also capped the judicial career of Presiding Judge Monroe Friedman, one of the county's most seasoned judges.

Media coverage was intense, with the local daily papers covering every development. Bay Area television and radio stations broadcasted the highlights along with national magazines and international papers. Yet in the extraordinarily volatile year of 1968 the message of black militant leaders—decrying police brutality and linking it to racism in general and the quagmire of the Vietnam War—resonated the most with those outside the establishment who got their news from the underground press. The hordes of counterculture reporters who flocked to Oakland to cover the trial served an audience of impoverished urban blacks, the Old and New Left, college students, and a growing coalition of war opponents. These were "the people" Newton was talking about when he proclaimed, "I have the people behind me, and the people are my strength."[7]

Of course, the Panthers alienated and threatened far more Americans than they attracted to their cause. They castigated Supreme Court Justice Thurgood Marshall as an "Uncle Tom" and included Rev. Martin Luther King, Jr. in that same derisive category while he was still alive. They strong-armed local middle class blacks for contributions, all the while ridiculing them as part of the hated capitalist structure. But Newton's message also inspired a surprising number of black professionals. Gilbert Moore, a Harlem-born investigative reporter, covered the murder trial daily for *Life* magazine. Moore, the first black reporter ever hired by *Life*, experienced an epiphany watching Newton on the stand: "conditioned by history, both sides blinded by myth and images, moved by rage and fear . . . each in their own blind way incapable of seeing each other as human beings . . . was a tragedy in the making."[8]

Moore soon quit his prestigious job to write a book about the newly discovered rage inside him that Newton and the Panthers had tapped into. *The Los Angeles Times* hailed Moore's insightful chronicle as "a classic document in the literature of the black-white experience in the 20th century."[9] Twenty-five years later, Moore's observations were still deemed equally relevant:

> The Panthers represented something new on the American political landscape. Lionized by the liberal cultural elite, spied on, shot at, and jailed by the police, they brought hope to some Americans and frightened many others. Revolutionaries, outlaws, pawns, they were a cultural bridge between urban street gangs and organized civil rights groups. They filled a dangerous void. They were the militant, articulate expression of the anger and aspirations of poor young black men. That critical void exists as much today as it did in the late 1960s.[10]

When armed Panthers first surfaced in California's Capitol in early May of 1967, they caught Gov. Ronald Reagan by surprise. That daring Sacramento debut increased pressure on the Oakland police to stop this gang at all costs. By the summer's end, the local African-American community had elevated the militant Panthers to heroic defenders, infuriating the city's official guardians of the peace even more. The Panthers were itching for action. They dogged patrol cars on their rounds. Some Oakland police were looking to provoke a confrontation, too. Among them was Officer John Frey, who told the radio dispatcher he was stopping "a known Panther vehicle" one early morning in late October 1967.

* * * * *

In *One Man's Freedom,* Washington super lawyer Edward Bennett Williams describes how the individual civil liberties we so cherish in the United States evolved in our criminal courtrooms, where the government often prosecutes "the weak and friendless, the scorned and degraded, or the nonconformist and the unorthodox."[11] These guarantees emerged because so many innocents were wrongly convicted without such protections and too often paid with their lives. Investigative journalist Mark Curriden restates Williams' observation more graphically: "the liberties and prerogatives we so frequently take for granted were written in blood."[12]

People v. Newton involved one of the most scorned revolutionaries of his day in an extremely volatile and bloody era. Was he guilty of murder as charged, or set up for a failed police ambush? By the late sixties, juries in mixed-race communities were ready to consider either possibility. At trial, Newton also benefited from key Supreme Court rulings that could have changed the outcomes of other high profile trials in earlier decades.

A member of O. J. Simpson's Dream Team noted that "The most remarkable aspect of every 'trial of the century' . . . has been the insight it provides into the tenor of the times in which it occurred. It is as though each of these trials was responding to some public appetite or civic need of the era in which it took place."[13] Looking back at pivotal cases from 1901 to 1999, the question remains: which one provides the most insight into the American 20th century as a whole—which is the real "trial of the century?"

1. THE PLAYING FIELD: Sometimes The Fix Is In

Every time I turn around,
there's a new trial of the century.

F. LEE BAILEY

Just as the World Series has always referred to an American baseball championship (Canadian teams now permitted), when American journalists promote "the trial of the century" they generally refer to a trial held in the United States. For this reason, most lists leave out famous and influential foreign proceedings, such as the marathon Philippine corruption trials of "the Steel Butterfly" Imelda Marcos, wealthy widow of dictator Ferdinand Marcos (1991–2011). List-makers often omit trials for crimes against humanity: the historic Nazi War Crimes Trials in Nuremberg (1945–46); the 1961 trial of Adolf Eichmann in Israel; the 1987 filmed French jury trial of Klaus Barbie ("the butcher of Lyon"); and the televised Romanian court martial of Nicolae Ceausescu in 1989. Like the 21st century war crimes trials of Slobodan Milosevic and Saddam Hussein, all of these international trials drew global interest. The Nuremberg trials trump all the others because they established the Nuremberg Principles, which separate the customary horrors of war from inhumane outrages—evils so extreme that the "just following orders" defense makes civilized people cringe.

But limiting the playing field to America still leaves a formidable number of choices. Perhaps because of our short public memory, national reporters never tire of promoting a new "trial of the century" every few years. *The Washington Post* once described this exercise as "a traditional bit of American hyperbole, like calling a circus 'The Greatest Show on Earth.'"[1] Some consider the category a childish game of superlatives, then favor contests they participated in or covered. Trials, like professional sports, have spectators—and many trial watchers and avid sports fans aren't afraid to reveal their prejudices. Americans are much more likely to hail a trial as a "trial of the century" if they lived through the era when the event took place.

Only talented trivia players recall that the 1921–22 San Francisco rape and manslaughter trials of silent movie megastar Roscoe "Fatty" Arbuckle ruined his acting career just after the obese comedian had signed an unprecedented million-dollar contract. Over Labor Day weekend in 1920—the first year of Prohibition—Arbuckle seldom changed out of his pajamas as he hosted a three-day drinking binge at San Francisco's St. Francis Hotel. The revelers included Virginia Rappe, an unemployed actress in her mid-twenties, who fell violently ill and died a few days later of a ruptured bladder and peritonitis. When the hotel physician arrived, another guest, Maude Delmont, told him Arbuckle had attacked Rappe, which Delmont later repeated to the police.

It looked like an open and shut case against the pie-throwing Keystone Kop. Hollywood already faced threats of federal censorship for its new focus on sex as a movie draw. For more than a year, tabloids had been scandalizing the public with revelations that performers with staid screen images had private lives rife with drug abuse and adultery. Outraged society women demanded that the San Francisco District Attorney's office take action to avenge the tragic death of the raven-haired beauty. Newly elected prosecutor Matthew Brady envisioned a murder conviction against Arbuckle as his ticket to the governor's office.

The only problem with targeting Arbuckle was that the allegations were patently false. The complaining witness, known also as Madame Black, was a blackmailer and bigamist, incapable of telling the same story twice. Rappe herself had told the hotel doctor that the shy comedian had made no advances whatsoever. Rappe did not arrive at the party in good health as Delmont claimed, but was feeling poorly, with symptoms similar to prior illnesses. Down and out, she came to borrow money from her old friend Arbuckle for an abortion—her sixth. Two doctors who examined Rappe confirmed she had advanced gonorrhea and died of natural causes with no signs of violence.

Before trial, the Hearst newspapers, which boasted a circulation of twenty million people in eighteen cities, piled on to destroy Arbuckle's reputation. Aside from his penchant for yellow journalism, publisher William Randolph Hearst had a personal motive: to distract people from rumors that the married father of five himself was keeping Hollywood leading lady Marion Davies as his own mistress. Theaters nationwide stopped showing Arbuckle's movies. Yet no witness at trial ever testified to seeing or hearing Arbuckle assault Rappe. Recognizing how poor a witness Delmont would make, District Attorney Brady never called her to the stand. Instead, he pressured two other women at the hotel party to swear they heard Rappe accuse Arbuckle of hurting her, contrary to their original statements when interviewed by the police.

After two hung juries, Arbuckle was officially banned from the movies by Hollywood's new censorship czar, lawyer Will Hays, President Harding's former campaign manager and Postmaster General. The third trial established Arbuckle's innocence. The jury met for only a few minutes, just long enough to record their acquittal and pen a rare written apology for the great injustice done in besmirching Arbuckle's name without "the slightest proof . . . to connect him in any way with the commission of a crime."[2] Though Hays rescinded the ban against Arbuckle, it came too late to save his career. Unrepentant, Hearst boasted that the three trials "sold more newspapers than any event since the sinking of the Lusitania."[3] By the summer of 1922, Hays blacklisted from the movie industry close to two hundred other reputed sinners. Hollywood soon developed a new morality code for movies by which it censored itself for decades.

Ironically in late 1924 Hearst himself was the subject of rampant rumors that he accidentally shot and killed Hollywood's pioneering Western filmmaker Thomas Ince aboard Hearst's yacht (supposedly while aiming at Charlie Chaplin, whom Hearst suspected of having an affair with his mistress Marion Davies). But the official medical report was that Ince died of a heart attack; his body was immediately cremated and the District Attorney quickly dropped the investigation.[4] Recently, *Hollywood Crime* reporter Denise Noe reviewed the Arbuckle case and suggested that Rappe may have actually died from complications of a hushed-up illegal abortion.[5] Brady never did attain higher office. In 1943, Edmund G. "Pat" Brown—the current governor's father—defeated Brady for reelection and the position became Pat Brown's stepping stone to California's governorship.

* * * * *

In contrast to the irresponsible newspaper coverage of the Fatty Arbuckle trials, in April of 1922 *The Wall Street Journal* broke a real scandal—secret leases of Navy oil reserves at Teapot Ridge in Wyoming by President Warren Harding's new Secretary of the Interior, Albert Fall. The former New Mexican Senator was a Republican crony of Ohio political boss Harry Daugherty, who had engineered Harding's improbable presidential campaign and his own appointment as Attorney General. Key Democrats in the Senate, with the support of Progressive Republican leader Robert "Fighting Bob" La Follette, called for investigation of the suspicious, no-bid Teapot Dome contracts.

In the spring of 1923, Harding tried to curb a related scandal by ordering the dismissal of Daugherty's aide Jess Smith, who then committed suicide. Harding himself died suddenly in August of 1923. The Senate probes continued after President Calvin Coolidge took office. Wisconsin's Senator La Follette then launched his own presidential campaign as a third party candidate—the short-lived Progressive Party of 1924—which garnered the Wisconsin reformer 17 percent of the vote. In the spring of 1924, Attorney General Daugherty resigned amid accusations of another major scandal—that he and his deceased pal Jess Smith had received large bribes from bootleggers buying immunity from prosecution under Prohibition's Volstead Act. In late 1924, investigators finally found evidence that Albert Fall had been bribed to permit the secret oil leases with a $100,000 interest free loan—about $1.2 million today—and lied to a Senate Committee to cover it up. The Teapot Dome Scandal established both the right of Congress to compel testimony and Albert Fall's dubious place in history as the first cabinet member ever imprisoned for his official actions.

* * * * *

People today know Gloria Vanderbilt for her designer jeans and as the mother of CNN news anchor Anderson Cooper. Some senior citizens may remember the 1934 custody battle between the aunt of the ten-year-old heiress and her beautiful mother that delved into the young widow's exotic love life in Europe. Though the court kept both the press and members of the public from attending the trial, headline stories and pictures emerged anyway from late night interviews of the warring principals.

Others of advanced age may recall the scandalous paternity trial of international superstar and filmmaker Charlie Chaplin. Targeted by the FBI as a political Leftist, the fifty-five-year-old British comedian defeated the Mann Act charge of transporting one of his many flames, aspiring actress Joan Barry, across state lines for immoral purposes. Blood tests also showed that Chaplin was not the father of the twenty-three-year-old ingénue's baby. Yet, after two civil jury trials sensationalized once again by the Hearst newspapers, a California judge ordered Chaplin to pay child support, convinced by Barry's lawyer that the blood test was unreliable. The outcome prompted changes in California law authorizing admission of such scientific evidence in all future paternity suits.

* * * * *

A far more quintessential "trial of the century" arose from events that took place on a real playing field back in 1919, when Chaplin reigned as the comic Little Tramp of silent film. That same year Prohibition became the law of the land and Congress sent the controversial women's suffrage amendment to the states for ratification. It was also a year of record strikes, bloody racial strife, and the world's deadliest flu pandemic. President Wilson spent most of the first half of 1919 in France, negotiating the Treaty of Versailles, hoping that his plan for a League of Nations would prevent another global war. By the time the World War I peace conference started, the Irish had already started a guerrilla war for independence from the British.

A month before Wilson's voyage back from France, radicals who called themselves "The Anarchist Fighters" set off bombs in seven American cities, leaving flyers warning of class war and bloodshed to "rid the world of your tyrannical institutions."[6] On the President's return, the isolationist Congress embarrassed him by refusing to ratify the treaty he had negotiated. The ailing President then crisscrossed the country by train in a doomed effort to convince the American public to support the Utopian plan that won him the 1919 Peace Prize.

In the first week of February, labor and management conflicts broke out from coast to coast, starting with the nation's first citywide general strike in Seattle. On September 9, Boston police made history when three-quarters of the mostly Irish-American force walked off their jobs to protest unmet demands, including the right to unionize. When gangs temporarily took control of its city streets, President Wilson accused the 1,100 underpaid peace officers of "an intolerable crime against civilization."[7] The police lost their jobs to returning soldiers. The city offered their replacements pay raises, free uniforms, and more time off.

Stagnating wages exacerbated by post-war inflation and outrage at corporate war profiteering had set off the strikes. Anger reached historic levels among steel workers after a Federal Trade Commission report issued in the summer of 1918 blamed the steel, oil, and gas industries for acts of "inordinate greed, barefaced fraud, deceptive accounting practices and artificial price inflation."[8] President Wilson tried to broker a deal with the intractable owners. On September 22, after the President's efforts failed, strikers shut down half the steel industry. Broken in spirit and health, back in Washington, D.C. on October 2, the President collapsed with a massive stroke—the same day that the best team in baseball appeared to be throwing the World Series.

The scandal took place at a time when baseball was still trying to shed its vulgar reputation—with half-hearted efforts and spotty results. In April of 1909, fans in Washington, D.C., had cheered when they recognized their three-hundred-pound, mustachioed President, William Howard Taft, arriving to watch the national pastime. The former sandlot catcher was the first sitting President to honor the sport with his presence. The next year, he started the tradition of throwing out a ceremonial first pitch. Taft, whose half-brother would soon buy the Chicago Cubs, called it a "clean, straight game."[9] But baseball, from its inception, was far from clean. The owners treated the players like slaves, the conditions were dangerous, and the rough-hewn teams came largely from the ranks of illiterate, hard-drinking coal miners, factory workers, and farm boys.

Yet President Taft had reason to applaud the improvements instituted by baseball's first unofficial czar, Byron Bancroft "Ban" Johnson. Johnson was almost as enormous as Taft. In his three-piece suit with his hair neatly combed, Johnson looked every bit the stern, determined businessman he was, except when he sidled up to a bar. The son of a professor, Johnson had started law school, but found himself drawn like a magnet to baseball, first as a college player and then a sports writer. At twenty-eight, Johnson took over a low-budget minor league franchise out West and made a go of it. At the turn of the century, Johnson ambitiously renamed his franchise the American League, aiming to challenge the National League's monopoly. Johnson believed baseball could draw far more spectators if priced affordably in a setting without on-site gambling and alcohol, crude behavior, and foul-mouthed fans as then characterized National League games. *The Sporting News* described major league owners as "a malodorous gang" often engaged in "mudslinging, brawling, corruption, breaches of confidence, dishonorable conspiracies [and] threats of personal violence."[10] The time was ripe for fresh leadership. At first, National League owners refused to give Johnson an audience. Then his new American League started outdrawing their games by luring key athletes like ace pitcher Cy Young. This wasn't hard to do, with salaries capped at a chintzy $2,400 a year. After battling in the courts for two years, the two leagues declared a truce and set up a three-man National Commission to oversee owner and player disputes, minimizing public scrutiny of any internal problems. The dictatorial Johnson would dominate the Commission and the sport for nearly two decades.

In an era rife with corruption, Johnson's changes were largely cosmetic. No one balked at players betting on their own teams to win. Baseball executives, including Johnson, sometimes wagered on the outcomes. Chicago reporter Hugh Fullerton—then regarded as one of the best sports analysts in the country—strongly suspected fixes in at least four early World Series, though no solid proof emerged. It was also an era of exclusion. The American establishment considered white supremacy a given; chapters of the revived Ku Klux Klan were opening across the country. Though more than fifty blacks had endured ridicule and abuse to play on some of the early professional baseball teams, by the late 1880s white athletes increasingly threatened boycotts of integrated match-ups. Faced with overwhelming pressure, the owners made a gentlemen's agreement banning all African-Americans from organized baseball. For the next six decades, though Native Americans could play, blacks had to be light-skinned enough to pass for white or Hispanic. If their ancestry became public, owners kicked them off the team. Almost all ball players were white and overtly, and sometimes violently, racist.

Above all, it was an era of rank hypocrisy—when society's leaders championed lofty ideals as they ignored blatant double standards in the courts and on the playing field. Detroit Tigers superstar Ty Cobb was among the most notorious. What Ty Cobb got away with over his career puts the 1919 White Sox Scandal into some perspective. In April of 1907, the twenty-year-old rising star attacked a black groundskeeper at a ball field in Augusta, Georgia, who made the mistake of offering a friendly backslap. When the man's wife came to her husband's aid, Cobb tried to choke her. He didn't let the woman go until a Tiger catcher tackled him. Two years later toward the end of the season in Cleveland, Cobb slapped an elevator operator for acting "uppity."[11] When a black night watchman intervened, Cobb wrestled him to the ground and knifed him. A little over a week before, during a game, Cobb had spiked a Philadelphia A's player in his bare hand. On owner Connie Mack's complaint that Cobb was the dirtiest player he had ever seen, Ban Johnson issued a warning to Cobb for unsportsmanlike conduct. Cobb finished the season by winning his third straight batting championship and first Triple Crown by also leading the American League in runs batted in and home runs. After the season ended, the Tigers' attorneys resolved the attempted murder charge and civil claim by having Cobb plead guilty to assault and battery, pay a $100 fine, and cover the night watchman's hospital costs.

On May 15, 1912, Cobb made the mistake of allowing his explosive temper to go out of control right before Ban Johnson's eyes. Johnson came to

Hilltop Park in Washington Heights to watch the Detroit Tigers finish their first series of the year against the New York Highlanders. The Highlanders looked spiffy in their new pinstripe uniforms. The following year, the team would officially become the Yankees, as they were sometimes called already. Claude Lueker was a regular Highlander fan who came to Tigers' games just to heckle Ty Cobb, then the reigning MVP. The disabled spectator sat twelve rows up behind home plate. (He had lost one hand and three fingers of the other in a printing press accident.) From Cobb's first time at bat, Lueker shouted insults, hoping, perhaps, to help the Highlanders even the series. Cobb threw insults back, but each time Cobb came to bat the heckler grew bolder. He called Cobb's mother a murderer, using ammunition available from old newspaper stories. When Cobb was a rookie in Detroit in August of 1905, his mother killed his father, who had sneaked home trying to surprise his wife in bed with another man. Mrs. Cobb was acquitted of murder, claiming she shot her husband in self-defense when she mistook his shadow for a burglar. Cobb looked for the Highlanders' owner to get Lueker evicted, but had no luck.

In the third inning, Lueker called Cobb a "half-nigger." This time, Cobb's teammate "Wahoo" Sam Crawford pressed Cobb to retaliate. As players switched sides for the fourth inning, the misnamed "Georgia Peach" instead clambered up the stands behind home plate. Detroit manager Hughie "Eeyah" Jennings, known for his own outbursts, did nothing to stop Cobb, rationalizing that "When Ty's Southern blood is aroused, he's a bad man to handle." Cobb tackled Lueker, viciously stomping on the New York fan with his spiked shoes, even as shocked onlookers screamed that the man had no hands to defend himself.[12] Johnson suspended Cobb pending investigation of the attack, prompting the first ever major league players' strike in defense of Cobb's reaction. His teammates claimed "no one could stand such personal abuse."[13] Each striker was fined $100; Cobb's suspension ended in eight days with a $50 fine. He remained unapologetic: "I would not take from the United States Army what that man said to me."[14]

Cobb's ability to set record after record on the playing field demonstrated the raw power of unrestrained ruthlessness, mirroring the success of unregulated industrial cutthroats. Not even the fact the surly superstar packed a gun alienated his huge fan base. Only at his career's end—when evidence emerged that he once bet on a game—did a charge of misbehavior jeopardize his chances for baseball immortality. In his case, timing was everything. So it was for his rival Shoeless Joe Jackson. The man who controlled both their destinies was a judge with the improbable name of Kenesaw Mountain Landis.

American League and National League team owners got to know Judge Landis when the Theodore Roosevelt appointee presided over a major antitrust suit against them in 1914. Some wealthy businessmen formed a new Federal League and sued to get the reserve clause declared illegal to allow players to change teams. The Federal League offered pay raises and a right to free agency that attracted 81 players. Judge Landis had a reputation as a strong-minded judge. He had even entered a whopping $29 million judgment against Standard Oil, later reversed on appeal, like many of his other rulings. Critics said Judge Landis "condemned or exonerated according to whim."[15] As it turned out, the Federal League folded while waiting for Landis to make the tough baseball call. In 1922, the Supreme Court would resolve the antitrust issue in a related case, holding that baseball was primarily local entertainment not covered by the Sherman Act—the only sport or business ever given the thumbs up to enter into agreements in restraint of trade.

Baseball owners began to assume that special treatment was their due. During World War I, they drew severe criticism by seeking to exempt players from the draft as members of an essential war-time industry. Since President Wilson had played center field himself in college and remained a devoted enthusiast, they must have assumed it was worth a try. Meanwhile, attendance sank to an all-time low. It was hard to draw fans when so many were out on the Western Front or heeded public health signs, posted all over public buildings, warning against spreading influenza. Yet, throughout the summer of 1918, baseball gambling continued unabated. Cincinnati Reds star Hal Chase was so well known for padding his income with payments for thrown games that fans often shouted, "what's the odds" when he took the field.[16] But some power players were counted on to remain clean. Straight arrow pitcher turned manager Christy Mathewson gave critics hope for reform when he suspended "Prince Hal" for bribery in early August only to have their cynicism renewed when National League President John Heydler later overturned Chase's suspension.

The 1918 season ended abruptly after the War Department told all players to report for the draft or obtain war-related employment by September 1, 1918. When the boys "Over There" let it be known how much they would enjoy the World Series, the owners negotiated a special exemption for a September match-up between the teams then leading their respective leagues—the Boston Red Sox and the Chicago Cubs. Ironically, this series took place in the same arena as would the 1919 scandal. The Cubs borrowed Comiskey Park because it was nearly double the capacity of their own home field on Chicago's North Side. The million-dollar structure replaced an old South Side dump. It was dubbed "The Baseball Palace of the World" for its impressive two-story steel and concrete grandstand, free-standing roofed-pavilions, and large outfield bleachers. During the 1917 World Series, Comiskey Park had sold out; now the combination of war-time travel restrictions and the Spanish Flu left nearly 13,000 seats empty. The absent fans had good reason to fear infection. An estimated 20,000 Chicagoans died in that epidemic, which killed at least fifty million people worldwide. The South Side near the stockyards was highly unsanitary, smelling of fresh animal blood, rotting carcasses, and manure. Yet many genteel Cubs fans may have stayed home because they feared rowdy Sox boosters. Back in 1906, the two teams had faced each other in the first cross-town World Series. The White Sox "Hitless Wonders" had embarrassed the favored Cubs with an upset that neither set of loyal fans would ever forget.

Chicago's neighborhoods were self-segregated by race and ethnicity. Its large Jewish population lived on the West Side, Germans and Scandinavians settled to the North, Irish and blacks divided the South, and pockets of Bohemians and Poles lived closer to the middle. Built in 1910 just north of the Stockyards, Comiskey Park stood between two tough neighborhoods. To its East was a ghetto called the "Black Metropolis." To the West was Bridgeport, a rough-and-tumble district of white Catholic immigrants. Bridgeport contained the heart of the Democratic machine that clashed with Republican Protestants, who formed the Cubs' fan base on the North Side. Diehard White Sox boosters included Bridgeport's athletic clubs, which had their own sports leagues. They also served as political clubs and enforcers of neighborhood boundaries; these glorified street gangs had names like the "Canaryville bunch," the "Hamburgs," "Ragen's Colts," and "Our Flag." Gang members might easily erupt against any Cubs' fan with a heavy German accent. The Wilson administration had recently launched a propaganda campaign demonizing both written and spoken German as evidence of disloyalty.

As game one started, Red Sox ace pitcher Babe Ruth shut out the Cubs in a one-run game, scattering six hits. The heavily favored home team played lackluster defense, fostering suspicion that the Fall Classic was fixed yet again. The game's highlight came in the seventh inning stretch, when the Navy band surprised everyone by striking up Francis Scott Key's the "Defence of Fort McHenry," later renamed "The Star-Spangled Banner." Back in 1916, President Wilson had ordered the war song played at all military ceremonies. Players and spectators now doffed their hats to join in a spontaneous burst of patriotism. It was a graphic demonstration of baseball as a great equalizer, emphasizing the common bonds of a people often divided by class and ethnic differences. The band struck up the song again in each remaining game. It became the official national anthem in 1931; by World War II, the song led off all games.

By the time the Series ended in Boston, the Red Sox had scored only nine runs in six games, the fewest ever for a winning World Series team. The Red Sox had help from five Cubs' fielding errors and a slew of base-running mistakes. Rumors circulated, but no official investigation took place. Later, two Cubs and one Red Sox player in that Series were banned from baseball for fixing other games. The stage was now set for the 1919 fiasco. Back in 1918, national attention focused on the War. By the summer of 1919, baseball's fan base returned, but the air crackled with new tension, particularly on Chicago's South Side. Since 1910, the Illinois metropolis had experienced a "Great Migration" of blacks fleeing persecution in the South. African-American publisher Robert Abbott's widely circulated *Chicago Defender* encouraged the newcomers with glowing descriptions of job opportunities in the Windy City. By the end of World War I, the "Black Belt" could no longer hold all the newly-arriving families, who then began to encroach on neighboring white districts.

When local veterans returned from overseas, they found many thousands of black co-workers at the stockyards and meat packing plants. Owners had fanned racial tension in recent years by hiring blacks as strikebreakers. Chicago's leading dailies inflamed their readers even more by exaggerating the rates of crime and disease in the black community. Politics added to the growing difficulties. Republican Mayor Big Bill Thompson, who would go down in history as one of the country's most corrupt mayors, had just been reelected in February of 1919, by a combination of German-American supporters and his lock on the black vote. That loss prompted ugly revenge. On the evening of June 21, 1919, police found two badly beaten black corpses on Chicago's South Side. The likely suspects were not arrested. A Bridgeport gang egged on by its sponsor, Democratic Alderman Big Joe McDonough, was trying to start a race riot and then "exploit the chaos."[17] The object was to drive colored families from the city and win back control of the mayor's office. The temperature hit 96 degrees on Sunday, July 27, 1919, drawing many Chicagoans to the lakefront. Whites threw stones at blacks encroaching on the 29th Street beach on Chicago's South Side, which was unofficially segregated. One rock hit Eugene Williams, a black seventeen-year-old who had drifted into the area on a rubber raft. Williams fell into the water and drowned.

Soon full-scale riots erupted—the worst racial violence the city had ever seen. The Bridgeport gangs attacked blacks in mixed neighborhoods. They burned houses, beat pedestrians, and perpetrated the first drive-by shootings recorded by Chicago police. They blocked streets to stop fire trucks from dousing the blazes. In the Loop, whites pulled colored workers off trolleys and beat them. Some blacks defended their homes with guns, fought back in the streets, or attacked whites in mostly black neighborhoods. Locals blamed blacks for torching several blocks of Lithuanian homes, leaving 950 homeless. It took 6,000 National Guardsmen to restore order. By August 3, when the violence ended, 38 men and boys were dead, including 23 blacks and 15 whites. Over 500 were injured, of whom two-thirds were black. Yet most men arrested were black and only blacks were indicted for murder. Many black families fled the area to return to the South. In 1922, the chief of police admitted to a grand jury that his officers "shut their eyes to offenses committed by white men while they were very vigorous in getting all the colored men they could get." By then, the fire department had concluded that blacks had not committed the devastating arson. The grand jury assumed that white gangs started the fire to incite "race feeling by blaming same on the blacks."[18]

Similar incidents of beatings, torture, lynching, and arson occurred across the country during that "Red Summer" of 1919, which history recorded as "the greatest period of interracial strife the nation had ever witnessed."[19] But the violence in Chicago was the worst of all. A formal commission report in 1922 blamed the Irish Hamburg Athletic Club of Bridgeport for instigating the mayhem. Its active members included seventeen-year-old future Democratic Mayor Richard Daley. With powerful Alderman Big Joe McDonough as his mentor, Daley would rise to become the club's president in 1924. In 1968, as the last of the old-time big city bosses, Daley oversaw the Chicago police, whose heavy-handed treatment of anti-war demonstrators, reporters and bystanders during the Democratic Convention became etched into American history as one of that violence-marked year's most indelible images.

When the neighborhood of Comiskey Park erupted in carnage on the night of July 27, 1919, the White Sox had just finished a homestead and were headed to New York on a long road trip. By the time they returned to their Chicago field on August 14, relative calm had been restored to the battered community. The team had its own problems with internal feuds and simmering resentment of owner Charles "The Old Roman" Comiskey for his imperious ways and miserly payroll. The Chicago native was the son of an Irish ward boss in Holy Family Parish. For several years, Comiskey was a first baseman on the St. Louis Browns, the club that became notorious as "a saloon with a baseball attachment."[20] Comiskey had fit right in with the gutter-mouth crowd. Later as an owner, Comiskey proved a master at public relations. He especially endeared himself to his base in South Chicago by building the majestic White Sox arena. Comiskey also made sure to treat the traveling press like royalty, while stinting players on fringe benefits. The only gladiator paid handsomely was pitcher Eddie Collins, whom his teammates widely despised. Unhappiness on the team did not interfere with its playing success. It won the 1919 American League pennant, fielding the almost identical team that had won the 1917 World Series. Its poor finish in 1918 was chalked up to a number of key players having enlisted or taken war-related jobs. With Shoeless Joe Jackson back, the Sox were heavily favored to win.

The two-hundred-pound, six-foot-one superstar had just turned thirty-one and was in his eleventh year in the majors. A native of Pickings, South Carolina, Jackson had worked in the mills as a child and had little formal education; he never even learned to read. But Jackson had played organized ball since he was thirteen and gained fame as the best natural hitter ever. He picked up his nickname in the minors when he batted in his socks because of a blister from new shoes. "Shoeless" Joe stuck because the big-eared Southerner with the boyish grin never lost his country boy naïveté. By 1919, millions of boys idolized Joe. Babe Ruth claimed he modeled his own batting technique after the White Sox outfielder, who hit .408 the season Ruth turned sixteen. Shoeless Joe had no idea that 1919 would end his extraordinary career in ignominy.

Sports reporters became suspicious when they noticed unusual betting patterns leading up to the nine-game 1919 series, lengthened to increase revenues as the fan base returned. Hugh Fullerton even warned his readers ahead of time not to bet on any games. More eyebrows rose when White Sox starting pitcher Eddie Cicotte, who had won a phenomenal 29 games during the season, hit the lead-off Cincinnati batter in the back. The favored Sox lost the first game nine to one. The catcher was not in on the fix and cursed out Cicotte for shaking off so many signs. Manager Kid Gleason was furious. Shoeless Joe Jackson had come to Comiskey before the Series started, begging to be benched, but Comiskey refused. Comiskey raised the obvious signs of a fix with Ban Johnson the night after the second game, but Johnson brusquely dismissed any concerns. Once friends, the strong-willed pair had often locked horns over the last fourteen years and no longer respected each other.

By game five, with the Reds up three games to one, Fullerton reported "more ugly talk and more suspicion among the fans then there ever has been in any World Series. The rumors of crookedness, of fixed games and plots, are thick."[21] By now, the White Sox conspirators doubted they would get their promised payments. The team rallied and won games six and seven, bringing the Series to four and three. Then, the game-eight pitcher, Lefty Williams, received a late night visit from a Chicago gangster who threatened to kill him and his wife. The next day, Williams yielded three runs in the first inning before the manager pulled him out. The Series ended with the White Sox committing a total of twelve errors, helping Cincinnati clinch its fifth win in eight games. After the game, Comiskey consulted with his corporate lawyer, Alfred Austrian, who advised Comiskey to hire a detective to collect evidence. Comiskey also held up on paying the suspected players their World Series bonuses and instructed the private eye to gather dirt on other teams as leverage against his own ouster from baseball should a scandal erupt. Without revealing what he already knew, Comiskey then met with his muck-raking friend Hugh Fullerton and suggested that the two pool any incriminating information they found before going public with it. Comiskey convinced Fullerton that his pal Commy was as interested in cleaning up baseball as Fullerton was.

Late in the Series, Shoeless Joe Jackson had tried once more to talk to Comiskey, but the owner remained unavailable. Afterward, the Old Roman made a show of publicly defending his players' honesty and offered a $20,000 reward for anyone with information to the contrary. Comiskey later reneged on the offer—even when Jackson's wife sent him a letter describing some of the sordid details. While Comiskey dreaded exposure of his players' misconduct, he had cause to worry about his own reputation. In 1917, the owner reportedly authorized gratitude payments to the Detroit Tigers for letting the White Sox steal bases at will in a key series when the White Sox faced a tough pennant race with the Boston Red Sox.[22]

That winter following the Series, Hugh Fullerton published an exposé of the unholy relationship between gamblers and ball players and urged that Judge Landis be appointed to investigate the corruption. Fullerton predicted that there would be no more World Series contests if the gambling problem remained unaddressed. Millionaire New York vice kingpin

Arnold "the Brain" Rothstein—the real-life model for Nathan Detroit in *Guys and Dolls*—reputedly bankrolled the 1919 scheme. *The Sporting News* backed up the owners' denial of any wrongdoing and attributed the dark rumors to "dirty, long-nosed, thick-lipped" immigrant Jewish gamblers trying to subvert the American pastime.[23] By July of 1920, White Sox manager Kid Gleason privately confirmed his own suspicions.

The following month ushered in the worst days in the history of the dead ball era. On August 20, Yankee pitcher Carl Mays killed a Cleveland Indians batter with a blackened spitball—leading to a ban on the common practice of altering baseballs with foreign substances (and a new era dominated by home runs). A week and a half later, Cubs owner Bill Veeck hired the famous Burns Detective Agency to check out rumors his players had just conspired with gamblers to throw a home game against the last place Philadelphia Phillies. After the story hit the headlines, state attorney Maclay Hoyne convened a Cook County grand jury. When a player mentioned that the White Sox had thrown the 1919 Series, the inquiry shifted to a far bigger target. Days later, a small-time gambler publicly claimed he'd been double-crossed after the first two games of the 1919 Series were fixed for $100,000. The scandal exploded. Pitcher Cicotte, and then Jackson, told Comiskey about the fix. He referred the two players to Austrian to prepare them to testify before the grand jury. Austrian assured the two everything would work out if they just signed immunity waivers and statements implicating themselves and the six other players. They followed his advice, with no clue about Austrian's hidden agenda to protect Comiskey.[24]

Arnold Rothstein also volunteered to testify before the grand jury. He arrived with his own lawyer and in his customary natty dress. The race-track and casino kingpin was no stranger to baseball's elite; he had several baseball executives among his wealthy clientele. Though rumor had it that Rothstein had sent the enforcer who threatened Lefty Williams, Rothstein adamantly denied any part in the scheme, claiming low level bookies had used his name without his say so. In fact, Rothstein had profited quite nicely from more than a quarter of a million dollars in bets placed on the Reds through intermediaries.[25] Rothstein emerged from the grand jury unscathed. Austrian proclaimed that the wealthy gangster "had proved himself guiltless."[26] (Seven years later a rival gangster gunned Rothstein down in a revenge killing. Rothstein's records revealed that he had indeed financed the World Series fix.) The Cook County grand jury then indicted ten professional gamblers and all eight players, who faced up to five years in jail and a fine of $10,000 each for accepting bribes to defraud the public. The foreman noted the grave symbolism of the crime: "Baseball is more than a national game, it is an American institution, [our great teacher of] respect for proper authority, self-confidence, fair-mindedness, quick judgment and self-control."[27]

That day, Comiskey suspended all seven players still on his team, pending the outcome of the criminal case, with the promise that they would be reinstated if acquitted. It was three days before the season ended; the White Sox were tied with the Cleveland Indians for first place in the American League. The suspensions handed the Indians the pennant. A stunned headline captured the White Sox fans' dashed faith: "Say It Ain't So, Joe." They needed to believe their hero played for the love of the game; that their idol was as irreproachable as their sainted mothers. Some heartbroken boys in the neighborhood boycotted baseball for years. The shocking story ranked as the most serious scandal in sports history, until the century ended with a mammoth steroid scandal which culminated in over eighty baseball players being named as abusers.

What the public did not learn for almost another ninety years is that Cicotte's sworn testimony before the grand jury in September of 1920 included the claim that he and several other White Sox players came up with the idea to throw the 1919 Series from seeing the Cubs get away with fixing the Series the year before.[28] Later that fall of 1920, as a cloud of corruption threatened baseball, the owners worried most about the future of self-regulation. They realized that posting signs outlawing gambling in their parks and ejecting known bookies hadn't worked to restore their credibility. Yet, with Babe Ruth whacking a record-smashing 54 homeruns, the 1920 season had drawn unprecedented crowds. Over Ban Johnson's strong objections, the desperate owners hit upon a new plan for damage control. They voted to accept an investor's proposal to replace the National Commission with a body of outsiders to oversee the sport and repair its tattered reputation. For members of this august new body, the owners flirted with asking luminaries like former President Taft and General Pershing of World War I fame. But one of the first people they spoke with was fifty-four-year-old Judge Kenesaw Mountain Landis. The white-haired jurist seemed typecast for the role and already had muck-raking journalist Hugh Fullerton's endorsement. A longtime fan of the game, Landis had been sickened by its association with gamblers and fixers. He made a counterproposal: he would accept a lifetime appointment if the owners empowered him as the sole Commissioner, retained no right of appeal, and waived access to the courts. Only these conditions would guarantee his independence. The owners remembered his hands-off approach to the antitrust suit that fizzled three years before and acceded to the free hand the bantam-weight, five-foot-seven-inch judge demanded.

Landis later told an interviewer that he took up the challenge with his own son in mind: "Baseball is something more than a game to an American boy; it is his training field for life work. Destroy his faith in its squareness and honesty and you have destroyed something more; you have planted suspicion of all things in his heart."[29] After the owners acquiesced to his terms, the sitting federal judge moonlighted as the first Commissioner of Baseball. He would endure a year of severe criticism for taking on this mammoth private job while still serving on the federal bench. Only when several members of Congress moved for his impeachment did Landis retire from his judgeship.[30]

Before trial, Jackson recanted the confession that Austrian had tricked him into giving. He claimed that he had only accepted $5,000 thrust upon him after the Series was over, but had not conspired with the others and did not participate in the fix.[31] Comiskey risked becoming embroiled in the scandal. He paid top dollar for the players' criminal defense counsel. By the time of their 1921 trial, Jackson's and Cicotte's damning grand jury testimony somehow went missing from the court records. Ban Johnson accused Arnold Rothstein of orchestrating the theft. (Years later, the records turned up in Austrian's office.)[32]

The trial proceeded against seven of the eight players originally accused of the fix. All seven looked out of their element dressed up in suits and ties. It took two weeks to select a jury from a panel of 600 men.

Almost all jurors chosen were in their twenties or early thirties. Cicotte and Johnson and one other player who had signed a confession never took the stand; the other four players denied any criminal conduct. The judge instructed the jury that it was not enough to prove games were thrown. There had to be evidence of a conspiracy against the public. The sympathetic jury acquitted both the players and the accused gamblers. Some jurors even hoisted the Sox players on their shoulders as spectators tossed their hats and threw confetti in the air. The gleeful players partied much of the night, anticipating that their suspension would be lifted. As usual, Jackson waited for others to order first so he could ask for the same plate as one of his friends and not expose his inability to read the menu.

The celebration turned out to be premature. The real impact came the next day when Landis, just a fortnight after taking office, established himself as a merciless guardian of the sport's purity—at least when it came to game-fixing. As a judge, Landis had already sent legendary black boxer Jack Johnson to Leavenworth for taking a white "sporting girl" across state lines for immoral purposes. (In 2009, Congress passed a resolution calling for Johnson's posthumous pardon—to date not acted upon). As Commissioner, Landis would never crack down on whoring and illegal boozing at speakeasies by married white players like the Yankees' notorious new "Sultan of Swat" Babe Ruth. Yet, with a missionary's zeal, the Commissioner's first act banned all eight accused White Sox players, including Joe Jackson, from the major leagues for life. As a warning to all current players, Landis issued this stiff pronouncement: "Regardless of the verdict of juries, no player who throws a ball game, no player who undertakes or promises to throw a ball game, no player who sits in confidence with a bunch of crooked gamblers and does not promptly tell his club about it, will ever play professional baseball."[33]

The Draconian decision was less dramatic than it appeared. By the time Landis made his move, the owners had already ostracized all eight players. Comiskey had fired them in the spring. Landis had held no hearing and ignored individual pleas for reconsideration. Historians Robert Grant and Joseph Katz note that there was precedent for a lifetime ban in the rare instance fixing had been found but none "for lesser offenses, for agreeing to throw a game and then double-crossing the conspirators by playing honestly, or for keeping silent about a known fix."[34] Nor was Landis inclined to create any such distinctions on his own. In 1924, Jackson sued Comiskey for payments due under his five-year contract and won a substantial jury verdict, only to see the judge overturn the award when Austrian magically produced Jackson's confession to participating in the 1919 fix. Austrian unethically used the stolen court document to protect Comiskey against the very person who relied on Austrian's advice to sign it in the first place.

Though Jackson admitted keeping $5,000 offered to him after the fix went down, sports historians still debate the extent of his involvement. In *Eight Men Out*, Eliot Asinof blames all eight players equally for conspiring with gamblers to fix the Series, but asserts that Comiskey set the stage by being such a skinflint. Jackson, regardless of his superstar status, only made $6,000 in 1919 while players on other teams earned as much as $10,000. Asinof's conclusions have since been disputed.[35] In *Say It Ain't So Joe! The True Story of Shoeless Joe Jackson,* author Donald Gropman argues that the South Carolinian was the only accused player who did not join in teammates' efforts to throw the series. Though his fielding was somewhat sluggish, Jackson had not committed any official errors and no one could deny his performance at the plate, wielding "Black Betsy" to bat an impressive .375 for the series.

Connie Mack, long-time owner of the Philadelphia Athletics, where Jackson started his major league career, called Jackson's fate "one of the real tragedies of baseball. I always thought he was more sinned against than sinning."[36] Commissioner Happy Chandler, who succeeded Landis as the second official czar of baseball, issued a far stronger statement: "I never in my life believed him to be guilty of a single thing."[37] Harvard professor and baseball fan Alan Dershowitz contends that "The real villain was Charles Comiskey. It was he who abused the game for money" and callously used his political power to sacrifice Jackson's career to protect his own reputation.[38] While Landis did get Comiskey to pay his players better wages, Landis never faulted "The Old Roman" for his cover-up, leaving Comiskey eligible for the Hall of Fame.

Looking back, most baseball insiders praise Landis for preserving public faith in America's most cherished game by his swift, punitive action against the eight Chicago White Sox players. Landis later ousted many other players of "undesirable reputation and character" who tarnished the game's image by throwing games or by hanging out with gamblers, including the infamous "Prince Hal" Chase. In 1943, Landis even tossed Phillies owner William D. Cox out of baseball after Cox admitted betting on his team. But Landis clearly played favorites. Aside from giving Comiskey a free pass in 1920, he let three Giants stars finish the season four years later while banning two lesser teammates for life for a bribery scheme to clinch the tight pennant race against the Dodgers. Ban Johnson blasted Landis for allowing the Giants to cheat their way into the World Series, which the Giants won.[39]

Landis showed his double standards again two years later when Ty Cobb was once more at the center of controversy. In 1926, Ty Cobb, as manager of the Tigers, mistreated Detroit pitcher Dutch Leonard. In retaliation, Leonard confessed to Commissioner Landis that he and Cobb had conspired with two Cleveland Indians players back in 1919 to have the Indians throw a late season game to Detroit, after which they bet heavily on Detroit to win. Just before the scandalous story surfaced, Cobb suddenly retired. By then, he had become a millionaire pitchman and investor in Coca Cola. Cobb disputed the charges and claimed that in his 22 years of baseball he had never been guilty of any "dishonorable thought or act." Congressmen, industrialists, and judges wrote letters of support, lauding Cobb's honesty and integrity and long "record in baseball . . . without a blemish."[40] Over the strenuous objections of American League President Ban Johnson—their second battle royal—Landis chose to ignore evidence implicating the superstar. Instead, Landis exonerated him with language supplied by Cobb's lawyers and convinced the owners to force Johnson out for criticizing Landis's leniency.[41]

Landis had started out aspiring to clean the game up to give Little Leaguers role models for life. But he employed selective whitewashes where he felt the truth would demoralize the public. President of the International Baseball Federation Dr. Robert Smith noted that Landis never was willing "to dig much more deeply than a finger's length into any baseball scandal." Baseball writer Glenn Stout compared Landis to a seamstress afraid to pull out a loose string because the whole garment might unraveled.[42] Ty Cobb's case showed just how far Landis fell short of his own lofty goal. Cobb biographer Don Rhodes laid bare the ugly side of the man who set ninety baseball records: "His legendary temper wasn't limited to the baseball field: at home he would beat his wife and children." His oldest daughter considered him a psychopathic Southern version of Dr. Jekyll and Mr. Hyde, claiming, "I never spent five seconds with that man that I wasn't scared pea green."[43]

Once Landis swept aside the game-fixing allegations against the superstar, it paved the way for Cobb to take his place among the first five men inducted into Baseball's Hall of Fame in 1936—with more votes than anyone else. Meanwhile, Josh Gibson, the undisputed home run king of the Negro Leagues, wound up bashing far more round-trippers than Hall-of-Famer Babe Ruth and had a better slugging percentage than Ty Cobb. He and strikeout phenomenon Satchel Paige humiliated Dizzy Dean's Major League All-Stars of 1934 in a winter exhibition game. Hall-of-Fame pitcher Walter Johnson later said it was "too bad" Gibson wasn't white. "He can do everything."[44] In 1937, Cum Posey, co-owner of the Homestead Grays Gibson played for, claimed that Gibson was "the best ballplayer, white or colored, that we have seen in all our years of following baseball."[45] Unfortunately, the "Black Babe Ruth" never got the chance to compete in "the Bigs."

On December 3, 1943, sports writers were abuzz as they covered the annual meeting of baseball owners and general managers of all sixteen major league clubs at the Hotel Roosevelt in New York. It included an historic meeting with African-American publishers, who had chosen as their spokesman Broadway star and political activist Paul Robeson. The extraordinarily versatile singer/actor had been a former All-American football player at Rutgers University, where he graduated first in his class. Robeson had followed that up with a law degree from Columbia University, where the ambitious son of a slave helped pay his tuition playing professional football. Commissioner Landis effusively presented the six-foot-two Renaissance man to the gathering as a man who needed no introduction, "Everybody knows him or what he's done as an athlete and an artist. I want to introduce him to you as a man of great common sense." Then Landis prefaced Robeson's comments with his own assurance to their black visitors: "I want to make it clear that there is not, never has been, and, as long as I am connected with baseball, there never will be any agreement among the teams or between any two teams, preventing Negroes from participating in organized baseball. Each manager is free to choose players regardless of race, color or any other condition."[46]

Robeson had just opened at the Shubert two months earlier to rave reviews as the first black man to play the Moor Othello in an American production of Shakespeare's tragedy. He told the gathering of baseball's management that his exceptionally enthusiastic reception by largely white audiences made him realize "the time has come that you must change your attitude toward Negroes and keep it consistent with the attitude of the entire country." The two-hundred-pound former athlete had experienced a number of death threats, but claimed they dropped off when he proved himself. He recalled his playing days at Rutgers when Southern teams warned they would cancel games if he was in the lineup. That was just bluster. "I can understand the owners' fears that there would be trouble if Negroes were to play in the big leagues, but my football experience showed me such fears are groundless. Because baseball is a national game, it is up to baseball to see that discrimination does not become the American pattern."[47] With the country engaged in another world war to defend its democratic ideals, Robeson urged the owners to let players in "this very season" to reflect "the best in the American spirit."[48]

After the meeting, Robeson directly challenged Commissioner Landis: if there was no barrier, why were there no Negroes in baseball like there were in all other professional sports? Landis claimed there was no prohibition, just the owners' free choice.[49] Landis' successor, Happy Chandler, unmasked Landis as a liar. Chandler read through Landis's files and reported that, "for twenty-four years Landis consistently blocked any attempts to put blacks and whites together on a big league field."[50] Newspaper editors had early on noted the absurdity of baseball's standards that excluded all blacks while allowing white "men of low birth and poor breeding" to become "the idols of the rich and cultured," with rosters including many "men of churlish disposition and coarse habits." One suggested that the owners instead "make character and personal habits the test. Weed out the toughs and intemperate men first" before drawing a color line.[51] Landis was deaf to such pleas; it was no coincidence that the Brooklyn Dodgers hired the first black player in the modern era a year after Landis died.

In retrospect, we reject Landis's system of values that tolerated racist brutes and adulterous sots while excluding all African-Americans for the "purity" of the game. Yet he was right about one thing. Destroy faith in the "squareness and honesty" of baseball and you may have "planted suspicion of all things" in the hearts and minds of the American people. Certainly the year 1919 had put faith in law and order to the test. Even scientific truth turned topsy-turvy when, late in the year, confirmation of Einstein's theory of relativity made startling headlines challenging Newton's long-accepted theory of the universe.

In the first two decades of the 20th century and for many years to come, on the field and in the courts, the rich and powerful wrote the rules of the game. The landslide election in 1920 of Warren Harding illustrates their successful strategy. From a smoke-filled Chicago hotel room at the June 1920 Republican Convention, the handsome dark-horse candidate emerged as the Party's tenth round choice for two essential attributes: his willingness to do the bidding of financiers and industrialists and his likely appeal to new women voters. Only after his nomination did Harding confess to Party insiders a longtime adulterous relationship with a married lover that the Party reportedly then covered up with hush money.[52] In the first modern campaign with a media blitz and Hollywood movie stars, the Republicans capitalized on Wilson's unpopularity to crush Democrat James Cox by promising war-weary Americans a "return to normalcy." (In *They Also Ran* author Irving Stone made the case that on every objective measure Cox was the far superior candidate). Meanwhile, New York's politically savvy Arnold Rothstein was among the first gangsters to recognize the golden opportunity Prohibition presented. When he established his bootleg empire, Rothstein hired the son of new Attorney General Harry Daugherty as insurance. Historian Rich Cohen likened the gambling kingpin to society's more traditional robber barons of his day. The key players all appreciated "the truths of early century capitalism"—"hypocrisy, exclusion [and] greed."[53]

Sometimes, before play started, "the fix" was in. Judges appointed through their ties to politicians often applied stiff penalties to scapegoats or outcasts and carved unwritten exceptions for those with connections. It is thus not surprising that the very first "trial of the century" hawked by corner newsies had ordinary Americans questioning whether murder charges would stick when one wealthy scoundrel killed another in full view of a large crowd.

2. DEMENTIA AMERICANA: The Murder of Stanford White

He had it coming to him!

Harry Thaw

Harry Thaw must have played the scene out in his head many times before. He could not have picked a more theatrical moment to kill the fifty-two-year-old premiere architect of the Gilded Age. The setting was a crowded performance of an open-air musical atop the city's tallest building—a landmark Stanford White himself had designed. The delusional Thaw saw himself as God's emissary to avenge the many teenage girls White had abused and to save countless others. At first, he appeared a hero upholding old-fashioned values against the decadent new era. Yet Thaw was a Dr. Jekyll and Mr. Hyde whose history of sadistic outbursts made White's predatory behavior pale in comparison. By the time the saga played out, the tarnished Gilded Age was history, as was public respect for the superiority of the sophisticated high society that harbored such tuxedo-clad vultures.

The object of both men's desire was Evelyn Nesbit. The wide-eyed Gibson Girl with lush chestnut curls and an enigmatic Mona Lisa smile was instantly recognizable everywhere. Her face sold products from soup to sewing machines, toothpaste to playing cards. The former model and Broadway chorine personified the "It" girl before America ever thought to apply the term to a sex symbol.[1] Like the dream of many showgirls, at twenty, Nesbit traded her career for a handsome millionaire. She married Thaw in April of 1905, disappearing from the limelight to the Thaw family mansion in Pittsburgh, ruled with an iron hand by Thaw's deeply religious and disapproving mother, Mary Copley Thaw.

As the public would soon learn, thirty-five-year-old Harry Thaw and his celebrity wife had only returned to Manhattan for a few days' stay before heading on a luxury cruise to England for a vacation with Thaw's family—one they never got to take. On the evening of June 25, 1906, Evelyn looked as spectacular as ever as her maid fastened the pearl buttons on her white satin, black-trimmed gown. Evelyn completed her fashion statement with matching black accessories, long gloves and an oversized hat with a bow. As usual, Harry had done all the planning. Later that night Evelyn's heart sunk when she realized her husband had arranged for dinner and a show at two of Stanford White's known haunts. Evelyn knew how obsessed Thaw was with "the beast" as he insisted they both call White. Ever since Thaw learned that White had deflowered Evelyn at sixteen, Thaw became preoccupied with the subject, making Evelyn repeat the details ad nauseam. He started having White followed by private detectives and made Evelyn report to him whenever she saw "the beast" passing on the street. Though she still had a soft spot in her heart for White, Evelyn always complied, realizing Thaw had spies tracking her, too.

Florence Evelyn Nesbit was the most celebrated beauty of her day. Hers was a Cinderella story with a twist. In Evelyn's case, she exchanged a life of poverty for one with a dangerous loon in a gilded cage. She started out a small town Pennsylvania girl, the daughter of a doting lawyer who paid for music and dance lessons and encouraged her interest in literature. Then in 1895, shortly after the family moved to Pittsburgh, Winfield Nesbit died suddenly, leaving his wife and two children nearly destitute. When the sheriff put them out on the street, Mrs. Nesbit sent her children to stay with relatives and friends, but eventually scraped by with money she borrowed to run a boarding house. Evelyn, her mother, and her younger brother Howard shared one bedroom while the rest were rented out.

A professional photographer first spotted the twelve-year-old naïf sweating in the August sun on the boarding house stoop, wearing a fetching homemade blue dress. Soon the family was again evicted. Evelyn and Howard stayed once more with relatives while Mrs. Nesbit found work in Philadelphia as a seamstress. After the family reunited, Evelyn obtained steady work as an artist and photographers' model. In the summer of 1900, Mrs. Nesbit again sent her children to live with friends and relatives while she spent months looking for work as a dress designer in New York. In December of 1900, both teenagers rejoined their still unemployed mother in Manhattan. Letters of introduction from Philadelphia artists led to Evelyn being hired to pose for a prominent portrait painter. Word spread to others of the "perfectly formed nymph" and the sixteen-year-old's modeling work quickly became the small family's principal source of income.[2] The days of making do with sometimes only bread to eat were now behind them.

Several months later, a newspaper interview with alluring photographs of "The Little Sphinx" prompted a theatrical agent to contact Mrs. Nesbit. He arranged for Evelyn to join Broadway's most popular show, "Florodora." The new five-foot-tall, childlike beauty in the chorus quickly caught the eye of one of its regular patrons, Stanford White, the most sought-after architect of an era when America's superrich favored ostentatious displays of their wealth. White asked an older chorine to introduce him to Evelyn, whose first impression was of an ugly old man. He was a contemporary of her deceased father. But unlike the quiet and unassuming Win Nesbit, White was large and gregarious with close-cropped red hair, an untamed moustache, and a huge appetite for delicacies from gourmet food to new sexual conquests. White was willing to bide his time. He ingratiated himself with Mrs. Nesbit and became Evelyn's benefactor. He sent her flowers, paid for an upscale apartment with the luxury of its own private bathroom, and sent her to the dentist at his expense. He suggested books for Evelyn to read to expand her cultural awareness as her father had done, indulged her sweet tooth, and invited her to taste exotic foods at private lunch and dinner parties with other guests. White never let her drink more than one glass of champagne or stay up too late as he encouraged mother and daughter to depend on his continued largesse.

After two months, White had completely won their trust and

convinced Mrs. Nesbit that it was safe for her to take a trip back to Pittsburgh and leave Evelyn in his charge. In November of 1901, White lured Evelyn to his love nest on 24th Street on the pretense of another dinner party, plied her with champagne, and led her to his bedroom. Over the next several months the two became lovers, which they kept secret from her mother. Though White considered his adorable "Kittens" quite extraordinary, she was only one of many under-aged chorines the married lecher turned into temporary concubines. Rumors of his debauchery thoroughly scandalized old-fashioned guardians of female purity. The President of the Society for the Suppression of Vice fumed even more when White placed an oversized, spot-lit statue of a nude Goddess Diana atop Madison Square Garden, higher than any other feature of the cityscape. It was a slap in the face of traditional morality, a tension that underscored life in the newly emerged metropolis, rapidly on its way to becoming a center of world trade.

Harry Thaw's enmity toward White had a different source, dating back at least a year before Evelyn Nesbit first arrived in New York. Thaw envied White as a charter member of the elite New York social circle to which Thaw had been denied entry. White hobnobbed with the Vanderbilts and the Astors, whose Fifth Avenue mansions he designed, and socialized with other millionaires in exclusive clubs which White also designed. Thaw was convinced White had badmouthed him to prevent Thaw's acceptance by the New York "Four Hundred." What fueled Thaw's fury even more was White's interference when Thaw tried to pick up chorus girls at Broadway shows. For their own protection, White persuaded a number of dancers to steer clear of the baby-faced younger Lothario with the glazed expression and weird giggle. Thaw had developed a reputation as a dope fiend with a violent temper. His mother used hush money to quash his prior bouts of scandal—with the exception of a publicized incident that occurred during the brief time the family's influence got the below-average prep school student enrolled at Harvard.

The peccadillo that hit the newspapers was a striking example of Thaw's often erratic behavior. At a bar he might leave a hundred dollar bill for a three-dollar tab. Yet Thaw had run after a Cambridge cab driver, waving an empty shotgun because he thought the man had stiffed him out of ten cents' change. Soon afterward, Thaw got expelled for unspecified "immoral practices" and threats to fellow students and staff.[3] He later bragged that, while at Harvard, he had spent more time playing poker than attending class; he divided his remaining time among women, cockfights, and benders. Since his expulsion, Thaw had been publicly charged with whipping a woman he had been dating in New York. Thaw made frequent use of laudanum and carried a special silver case filled with syringes for injecting his own drug cocktails, which reportedly included the original "speedball" mixing cocaine, morphine and heroin.

In courting Nesbit, Thaw kept his inner demons well hidden and even disguised his identity at first, sending her flowers and other gifts under an assumed name. In 1902, White still took a strong paternalistic interest in seventeen-year-old Evelyn, maintaining close ties with her mother and paying for her brother's schooling, while he added other young chorines to his list of conquests. At Mrs. Nesbit's urging, White broke up a budding romance between Evelyn and twenty-one-year-old John Barrymore by getting Evelyn admitted to a New Jersey boarding school. White also warned her against Thaw. Evelyn remained at the school through the spring of 1903, visited occasionally by White, but also receiving presents and correspondence from Thaw, who kept proposing. In April, when Evelyn fell ill with appendicitis, it was Harry Thaw who rushed to her side oozing solicitude for the girl he nicknamed his "Boofuls."

When doctors suggested that Evelyn convalesce following surgery, Thaw offered to pay for Evelyn and her mother to take a cruise to Europe, not revealing that he planned to join them in England. Once in Europe, the three traveled together to Paris in June. Thaw again proposed and Evelyn emphatically turned him down, convinced that he would not want her. At Thaw's insistence, she tearfully confessed her reasons. Stanford White had taken her virginity when she was sixteen and kept her as his mistress. Soon after, Thaw succeeded in alienating Mrs. Nesbit and sending her home on his promise to hire a chaperone to take her place. Instead, Thaw isolated Evelyn in a rented Austrian castle where he barged into her bedroom naked in a wild-eyed, drug-induced frenzy. He then beat her legs bloody with a whip, tore off her nightgown, and raped the terrified teenager, saying it was retribution for her past sins.

After they returned to America, Evelyn's mother and Stanford White persuaded Evelyn to avoid all contact with Thaw as she resumed her career in New York. White also had Evelyn sign an affidavit accusing Thaw of abducting and attacking her. White's lawyer kept it safe. Thaw's detectives then gathered dirt on White, and White hired his own men to trace Thaw's gum shoes to their source. Evelyn stayed under White's strong influence for a time, but ultimately chafed at neither being the sole love of White's life, nor in a position to marry anyone else. Thaw resumed the role of solicitous lover. He apologized for his attack on Evelyn and focused his anger instead solely on White. After being showered with gifts and love letters, Evelyn succumbed to Thaw's incessant pressure and married him in April of 1905, much to Stanford White's horror and the dismay of Mother Thaw, a woman devoted to religious salvation who forbade any mention of Evelyn's shameless past. Evelyn soon lamented her decision, trapped in a household of Presbyterian piety that treated her with disdain. Harry Thaw's obsessive jealousy continued unabated. He sent Evelyn to his own dentist to have every bit of dental work White had paid for removed and replaced. She was now his trophy, not White's.

Back in Manhattan at a mid-town luxury hotel on the evening of June 25, 1906, Thaw dressed in his tuxedo and asked Evelyn to meet him at a nearby high-end restaurant for drinks and dinner. He wore a long coat which easily concealed the hand gun he packed. They would be joined by Tommy McCaleb, an old friend who accompanied them to New York from Pittsburgh, and Thaw's new friend, Truxton Beale. Evelyn mistrusted Thaw's fascination with Beale, who was rumored to have committed an honor killing in California. It fit in too much with Thaw's morbid preoccupation with Stanford White. Yet Evelyn did not attach significance to Thaw's first choice of Sherry's for drinks and dinner, a showplace designed by White's architectural firm. The evening took a different turn when Beale came dressed too casually for Sherry's. Thaw then suggested the foursome go instead to another popular eatery, the Café Martin. By the time they left Sherry's, Thaw had already consumed several drinks.

Evelyn spotted Stanford White entering Café Martin and tried not to react visibly. It now occurred to her that her husband was deliberately trying to force a confrontation. White headed to the restaurant's porch with his son and a friend who were down visiting from Harvard, unaware he was about to enjoy his very last meal. Soon, Evelyn realized she could not disguise her angst. Evelyn borrowed a pencil from one of their dinner companions and wrote a brief note to her husband that "the B" had come and gone. Thaw was livid that he had not seen his quarry.

After dinner, they headed for the new musical "Mamzelle Champagne" at the open-air theater atop Madison Square Garden. Thaw had purchased the tickets that same afternoon. He knew White had a regular table five rows from the stage and may have heard from his detectives that White was expected there that evening. The foursome were seated at a table further back in the crowd. They drank more champagne. Evelyn's anxiety lessened when she saw that White's table remained empty. But many people noticed how agitated Thaw appeared as he repeatedly got up during the show, paced, and looked around before sitting back down. Just before 11 p.m., Thaw was once again out of his chair when Evelyn noticed that White had just arrived. White spoke briefly with the manager to remind him he wanted an introduction to the latest seventeen-year-old ingénue. The architect then headed for his table to catch the last few minutes of the show. When her husband came back to his seat, Evelyn nervously suggested they leave. Thaw and their two guests agreed. The show was painfully amateurish. Evelyn was relieved that Thaw apparently had not seen White enter. The couple headed out to the elevators with their two companions. Then Evelyn noticed her husband was gone; he had darted back into the theater.

By the time Thaw spotted him, White had been served a glass of wine and had his elbow on the table and his chin cupped in his right hand, apparently deep in thought. A male vocalist was just starting to sing "I Could Love a Million Girls." Thaw looked pale as a ghost as he approached White, who likely did not see him coming. Thaw pulled the pistol from under his coat and came within two feet of White's face. Thaw fired three quick shots. One entered through White's left eye; one broke his jaw; and a third penetrated his arm. White's elbow slipped and the table overturned, breaking his glass as White thudded to the floor. The singer stopped. Thaw raised his gun high in the air and attempted to reassure everyone he posed no further danger. Thaw said, "He had it coming to him."[4] Then Thaw left for the exit, holding the barrel of the gun, looking for someone to whom he could hand it over.

It took a couple of minutes for the audience to realize this was not part of the show. As blood pooled around White's body, a woman leapt up and became hysterical. Others rose in panic as well. The manager jumped on a table, urging the performers to resume the musical, but the chorines were far too horrified. Then the manager announced that a terrible accident had occurred and asked people to try to leave in an orderly fashion. As they rushed for the exits, Evelyn Thaw hurried to White's body and then ran back to her husband by the elevators, crying: "My God, Harry, you've killed him." He asked her for a kiss, and they embraced.

A policeman responding to the sound of gunfire arrived to see White's body on the floor and a woman who had fainted nearby. The officer asked Thaw if he had shot the man lying on the theater floor and Thaw said, "Yes, he ruined my wife." Thaw then asked, "Is he dead?" The policeman told him that he was. Thaw said "Well, I made a good job of it, and I'm glad."

Evelyn gave him another hug and kiss, whispering, "I didn't think you would do it in this way."[5]

Having killed the "Beast" who had deflowered his wife, Thaw seemed inordinately calm, some thought dazed. He gave his name to police as Mr. John Smith, though he carried calling cards which revealed his true identity. At the police station, he asked to have his lawyer notified and lit up a cigarette. A doorman familiar with White's many young conquests told a *New York Times* reporter that the shooting came as no shock. He later testified at trial that the only surprise was that White was killed by a husband: "Everyone always figured it would be a father."[6]

Publisher William Randolph Hearst instantly realized that the Thaw murder story was a gold mine—a beautiful girl, illicit sex, wealthy degenerates, and overpowering jealousy. Before moving to Manhattan to pursue his political ambitions, Hearst had transformed his father's *San Francisco Examiner* into the top-selling local paper. He developed a winning formula that he could replicate elsewhere: court the masses by letting them know he was on their side on key political issues and then fill the paper with wildly entertaining stories, comics, and pictures—the print world equivalent of a P. T. Barnum circus. So Hearst railed against vested interests like the powerful railroads and utilities, championed the eight-hour day and the income tax. Hearst could count on the popularity of taking such stances. Over 30,000 strikes had taken place in the past three decades throughout the nation, with the eight-hour day as the primary objective. Hearst also fed his readers a steady diet of sports, gossip, the funnies, and sensationalized crime, instructing his staff to use their imaginations to embellish and stretch the facts: whatever sold papers. Flushed with success, in 1896 Hearst bought *The New York Journal* to start a cut-throat readership battle with his role model, Joseph Pulitzer of *The New York World.* Staid competing papers invented the put-down "yellow journalism" to describe how the two-penny tabloids hawked colored cartoon supplements and ran oversized banner headlines to vie for the loyalty of the city's teeming numbers of recent immigrants.

Neither publisher viewed truth as an essential ingredient so long as attention-grabbing stories sped from the hands of corner newsies. This rivalry motivated Hearst to exploit the sinking of the battleship U.S.S. Maine in Havana Harbor on February 15, 1898, as a secret enemy attack. No proof of the charge would ever surface. With his repeated warmongering headlines, Hearst induced Pulitzer's paper to do the same, coining the term "Remember the Maine!" Together they created such public clamor they helped pressure President McKinley into precipitating the Spanish-American War. What Hearst cared most about was that circulation for *The Journal* rose fifty percent.

The United States emerged as a world power following the Spanish-American War. Rapid industrialization and consolidation of power in trusts fueled its rise while workers grew increasingly dissatisfied with rampant exploitation of labor. In editorial cartoons, Hearst's *New York Journal* characterized President McKinley as a tool of the money-hungry trusts. One of his editors called the President "the most hated creature on the American continent" and another Hearst journalist suggested that the President deserved killing.[7] The governor-elect of Kentucky had just been assassinated. In the past two decades anarchists had felled Russian Czar Alexander II, French President Sadi Carnot, Spanish Premier Antonio Canovas del Castillo, Empress Elizabeth of Austria, and most recently King Umberto of Italy.

Hatred of President McKinley among exploited manual laborers was intense. Few were surprised on September 5, 1901, at the news that someone shot him as he shook hands with well-wishers at an international exposition in Buffalo, New York. When Leon Czolgosz pulled out his mail-order gun from Sears Roebuck, it was not Hearst's paper that the young Polish-American worker drew inspiration from, but the revolutionary speeches of anarchist Emma Goldman. The Secret Service Agents guarding the President paid little attention to the innocuous-looking radical because they had their eyes on a suspicious, six-foot-six "colored man" with a black moustache who was next in line.[8]

James "Big Jim" Parker reacted quickly when the African-American saw Czolgosz get off two quick gunshots. The former slave knocked the weapon from Czolgosz's hand before he could fire again and tackled him as others joined in the fracas. Parker later boasted that if police hadn't rescued Czolgosz from his grasp, Parker was bent on cutting the assailant's throat on the spot like the vigilante justice he witnessed so often growing up in Georgia. Parker enjoyed national publicity for a short while as a quick-thinking hero, but soon the government supplanted that account with a new version giving an Irish Secret Service agent complete credit for capturing Czolgosz and eliminating all reference to Parker's heroism.

Though McKinley at first appeared to be recovering, he took a sudden turn for the worse a week after the shooting and died of gangrene from botched emergency medical care. Shocked readers blamed Hearst for the President's assassination because his paper suggested the revolutionary act. They burned him in effigy and boycotted *The New York Journal* for months. Reformer Jane Addams later wrote, "It is impossible to overstate the public excitement of the moment and the unfathomable sense of horror with which the community regarded an attack upon the chief executive of the nation, as a crime against government itself which compels an instinctive recoil from all law-abiding citizens."[9] Much ridiculed during his tenure, McKinley instantly became a martyr about whom few were willing to speak ill. Axe-wielding Prohibition crusader Carrie Nation was an exception, claiming "he got what he deserved."[10] Emma Goldman also voiced her dissent. She publicly praised Czolgosz as a modern-day Brutus for killing a 20th century Caesar—the "president of the money kings and trust magnates."[11]

Locals in upstate New York stormed the jail twice looking to lynch the assassin for his assault on the social order. Booker T. Washington took the frenzied response as a teaching moment to argue that even treasonous villains deserved their day in court. At the time, a black man was lynched somewhere in the South every few days. But, as Big Jim Parker bragged to the newspapers, whites were not alone in thirsting for immediate vengeance. Just the week before, African-American residents in a Kentucky town made headlines for storming a jail without interference from white jailers to hang several black men arrested for the murder of one of their community's respected elders. Buffalo officials sought to appease both those calling on them to set a civilized example in handling Czolgosz, and the mobs impatient for a hanging. (No jurisdiction had as yet adopted the 1893 proposal of pioneering woman lawyer Clara Foltz to create salaried public defenders for indigent defendants.) The district attorney put the despised social outcast on trial for his life just nine days after President McKinley died. The judge rejected Czolgosz's attempt to plead guilty. The prosecution presented all of its testimony in two days, and Czolgosz's court-appointed defense lawyer called no witnesses to back up a defense of not guilty by reason of insanity. Half an hour later, the jury came back with the expected conviction. Czolgosz was quickly electrocuted after which his body was dissolved in acid to prevent doctors from second-guessing the post mortem and to dissuade souvenir hunters from digging up his remains.

Like Czolgosz, Thaw pleaded insanity as a defense to gunning down his victim in front of hundreds of witnesses. Yet the public reaction to the crime, the nature of the trial, and its outcome were vastly different—a reflection obviously of the magnitude of Czolgosz's crime, but also of the difference in their class, their wealth, and their rationale. In a later era, a jury determined that John Hinckley, Jr. was insane when he attempted to assassinate President Reagan. In the first decade of the century, national outrage against Czolgosz would permit no such dispassionate analysis even had he been provided a meaningful opportunity to prepare for his death penalty trial. Defendants without status or resources commonly received short shrift in the courts. In contrast, with Mother Thaw footing the bill, Thaw had the best defense they could buy. In an era when so many Americans openly supported vigilante justice, Thaw invoked an age-old chauvinistic code of ethics that reinforced traditional community values vilifying debauchers of young virgins. His crime was not perceived to threaten society; it provided an entertaining lesson in morals.

Within a week of White's shooting, inventor Thomas Edison's New York movie studio churned out a short, dramatic reenactment, *Rooftop Murder,* which instantly attracted the most nickels in thousands of arcades across the country. By then, the new art of silent picture shows was well on its way to drawing 30 million fascinated people a week. Postcards of Evelyn Nesbit sold out so quickly, printers kept their presses going round the clock, generating millions more. As voyeurs flocked to nickelodeons and souvenir vendors, moralists on and off the pulpit, appalled by the city's sexual permissiveness, applauded Thaw's defense of his wife's honor, agreeing that monsters like White who ruined young girls deserved to be shot. When even Adolph Ochs' dignified *New York Times* played up the murder of Stanford White in effusive detail, a consensus was reached. The prosecution of millionaire Harry Thaw for killing high-society architect Stanford White would be the "trial of the century."[12] *The New York World*'s editor Frank Cobb drooled over the irresistible cast of characters: "rich old wasters, delectable young chorus girls and adolescent artists' models . . . artists and jaded debauchees. . . Bowery toughs, Harlem gangsters, Tenderloin panderers, Broadway leading men, Fifth Avenue clubmen, Wall Street manipulators, uptown voluptuaries and downtown thugs."[13]

The seamy side of the city's elite captivated everyone from housewives to professionals, society matrons, and political reformers. Most members of the public responded with gratitude to Thaw for the public service he performed. Exposure of the dirty linen of society leaders like White who did not follow rules of behavior expected of everyone else had great appeal to the disgruntled laboring class: Jews in the lower East Side, the denizens of Little Italy and Harlem, the Irish, and other European immigrants riding on the new subway system to and from their back-breaking, underpaid jobs and overcrowded slums.

In 1906 the desperate poverty and exhausting work schedules of millions of new immigrants caused simmering resentment but little concerted action. In 1909, a major strike known as the "Uprising of 20,000" commenced at the Triangle Shirtwaist Factory in Manhattan's garment district, protesting sixty to seventy-two hour work weeks for immigrant teenage girls earning just $7 per week. In March of 1911, nearly 150 garment workers lost their lives as the panicked girls vainly tried to escape the flames only to find the exit doors locked—the worst such disaster in New York City before September 11, 2001. Hearings on the seamstresses' brutal working conditions, including routine fourteen-hour days, helped galvanize support for reforms. Most employers accepted the eight-hour day for factory workers by 1912; the new norm would take until 1938 to be nationalized for businesses engaged in significant interstate commerce. But the eight-hour day seemed totally out of reach in 1906. Reformers had succeeded in getting some protective laws passed only to see victory snatched away by the United States Supreme Court in 1905. In *Lochner v. New York,* a bare majority of justices told the state legislature it had no power to limit the work week even to sixty hours. The high court said that laws to protect workers from exploitation violated both the purchaser's and seller's "liberty of contract."[14]

When anger at Hearst subsided following McKinley's assassination, the ambitious publisher again tapped into labor's ongoing resentment of perceived corporate abuses and misbehaving members of his class to win a seat in Congress as a populist Democrat. Yet the maverick millionaire's personal life differed little from the decadent circle of wealthy degenerates his readers loved to hate. Like Thaw, Hearst had been expelled from Harvard. In New York, the handsome transplanted Californian cultivated the backing of Tammany Hall's new top man, political fixer "Big Tim" Sullivan of the Lower East Side.

Hearst helped himself get elected to Congress in 1902 by offering free trips to Coney Island Amusement Park to every resident, recognizing that workers did not resent the wealthy when they shared their bounty with the public. He then celebrated with an extravaganza at Madison Square Garden, including fireworks that exploded prematurely and killed eighteen supporters. In 1903, the playboy forty-year-old bachelor married a twenty-one-year-old chorus girl whose mother ran a brothel protected by Sullivan. In 1905, Hearst took on Tammany Hall incumbent Mayor George McClellan (the Civil War General's son) and almost beat him. Hearst now had his eye on becoming governor of New York and ultimately President of the United States.

Both to generate sales and to enhance his own popularity, Hearst delighted in creating a wide audience for salacious details about White's immoral social circle of plutocrats, the sordid side of New York's theater life, and the "girl on the red velvet swing" that everyone soon learned White had hung from the ceiling of one of his Manhattan love nests. They read every horrifying detail of how the debaucher asked each of his young conquests to swing back and forth both in childlike innocence and in various states of undress while he looked on in lecherous anticipation of bedding his prey. By the time of trial in January of 1907, publicity had become so pervasive that the lawyers had to question six hundred men before they could agree on an unbiased jury. Women were not eligible for jury service at the time. The judge decided to sequester the jury to keep them from being tainted—reportedly a first. Journalists swarmed all over, including newly hired female reporters mockingly dubbed "The Pity Patrol" for their maudlin descriptions of Evelyn Nesbit's plight. Soon newswomen who appealed to their readers' sympathy would become known as sob sisters.

The prosecutor was a Republican, former judge William Travers Jerome, a talented district attorney with his eye—like Hearst—both on the governor's office and the White House, then occupied by New York's former Gov. Theodore Roosevelt. Though Jerome earned his reputation by routing out vice and corruption, Jerome did not let marriage impede him from dallying with a woman twenty years his junior. In fact, he traveled in the same social circles as White and should not have accepted the lead role in a trial involving so many friends as potential witnesses. Thaw's original trial counsel was veteran New York attorney Lewis Delafield. Delafield came highly recommended by the family's corporate lawyers, but soon lost Thaw's trust. Jerome had originally approached Delafield with a practical solution: to have Thaw sent to an asylum instead of an expensive trial for both sides where he might risk execution. The very idea of pleading insanity met with strong resistance from both Thaw and his mother. Thaw fired the man he called "the traitor." The family only agreed to try the case on a plea of temporary insanity based on provocation by White's conduct. Mrs. Thaw had no intention of airing family secrets, including her son's history of bizarre behavior.

The trial opened with Delafield's partner Gleason presenting a confused array of defenses that included—contrary to the Thaws' instructions—inherited tendencies toward mental instability. After a heated conference, Gleason volunteered his resignation. His replacement was renowned San Francisco criminal defense lawyer Delphin Delmas. "The legal Napoleon of San Francisco"[15] had never lost a case. His celebrated victories included a murder trial of a Californian who had similarly avenged the honor of a close female relative by killing her debaucher.

Delmas had a term for the defense he would present for Thaw, "Dementia Americana." The concept first surfaced in a United States courtroom shortly before the Civil War. Lawyers for New York Congressman (and future Union General) Daniel Sickles had used it successfully to exonerate Sickles for killing his wife's lover, the son of famed lawyer and poet Francis Scott Key. Unlike the Sickles case, by the time this trial ended, Mrs. Thaw would pour more than a million dollars into her son's defense, including $500,000 for Delmas and an equal amount on a dozen medical experts. The doctors would offer testimony on a new concept they called a "brain storm," by which they meant temporary interference with rational functions. Mrs. Thaw embraced the opportunity to avoid reference to her son's past behavior patterns as well as his feeble-minded uncles. Delmas focused on transforming Stanford White from victim to villain, the man whose lechery caused Thaw's brain storm. To accomplish that, Delmas turned to Evelyn Thaw as his star witness. He would leave his unpredictable client off the stand. With limited questions on direct examination they could avoid having Evelyn mention Harry's attack on her in Austria, his attempted suicide with laudanum, and other bizarre behavior. The risk was on cross-examination, but Evelyn gladly undertook to paint her husband in the best light possible. She did not want to see Harry executed; her own future support depended on doing her mother-in-law's bidding and saving Harry's life.

The day Evelyn Nesbit Thaw was called to the stand, thousands of would-be spectators tried to get in. But police and temporary barricades kept most of them out in the street. Dressed demurely in a long, navy blue suit and prim white blouse, Evelyn spoke in a soft, childish voice. The whole courtroom strained to hear her much-anticipated account. The basis for allowing Evelyn to tell her life story was that it had all been told to Harry Thaw and had motivated him to kill Stanford White. So Delmas started by having Evelyn explain how Thaw had proposed to her in Paris and how she had tearfully told Thaw that she could not marry him. Evelyn then revealed that she spent one long night explaining to Thaw why she would not make him a good wife. "He wanted every detail and I told him everything. He would sit and sob or walk up and down the room as I told him." At the defense table, Thaw became upset all over again. He sank down into his chair and shuddered. Evelyn described the poverty of her childhood after her father's death; her life as a model in Philadelphia and New York and the publicity that led to her getting selected as a chorine, giving all the money she earned to "momma." She had turned down the first invitation to a party at White's apartment as not proper, but was reassured by another chorus girl that the architect came from one of New York's best families.

The incredulous prosecutor periodically interrupted, "You told all this to Harry K. Thaw that night in Paris?" Evelyn said yes. White and another man took her and a girl friend to see his three-story apartment on West Twenty-Fourth Street. The two girls took turns being pushed on a red velvet swing. A Japanese paper parasol hung from the ceiling that they punctured with their feet. White let her sip champagne. He offered to have a dentist fix her teeth. Finally, Evelyn reached the crux of the story—the night in November of 1901 when White invited her to a party at his apartment on West Twenty-Fourth Street. She said that she almost left when she saw no one else, but White convinced her to stay for dinner, telling her perhaps the others had forgotten. He gave her a glass of champagne and after dinner took her up a back staircase to a sitting room filled with fine art and a piano. She played the piano briefly, and then he suggested she join him in the next room, a small bedroom all decorated in chintz. Another split of champagne sat on a bedside table from which he poured her a glass. She put it down after a sip, not liking the taste, but at White's urging she downed it all. Thaw hid his face behind his handkerchief. Evelyn said that her head began to buzz and she passed out. Thaw wept, his body heaving with emotion. The whole courtroom was otherwise still. Delmas paused for effect and then asked, "And, will you please, Madam, tell what happened when you regained consciousness?"

"I found myself in bed," Evelyn replied. White was naked beside her. The walls were covered with mirrors. Blood now stained her leg. She told the courtroom that she started screaming. White took her home and she cried through the night.

"And you told all of this to Harry Thaw that night in Paris after he had asked you to marry him?" Delmas finished with a flourish.

"Yes," Evelyn responded simply.[16]

Evelyn was forced to go through the whole story again under harsh cross-examination by Jerome. Jerome's strategy was to demolish both Evelyn Thaw's and Harry Thaw's character. His witness list included handsome young John Barrymore. But Barrymore left the state after being interviewed and declined to return, claiming he was ill with pneumonia. Jerome made do with a prize-winning 1901 photo of Evelyn sleeping on a bearskin rug, provocatively dressed in a loose kimono as the "Little Butterfly." As a surprise blow against both Evelyn and Harry, he produced the affidavit Evelyn had signed and given White's attorney, accusing Thaw of attacking her in Europe and of being a drug addict. The newspapers found that evidence sensational. Yet Jerome took the risk that he painted Harry Thaw as even crazier than the defense did.

In his argument to the jury after three months of trial, Jerome characterized Thaw as paranoid and dangerous, but technically sane. He knew right from wrong when he killed Stanford White. Delmas closed with his plea of insanity based on Dementia Americana:

> The species of insanity which makes every American man believe his home to be sacred; that is the species of insanity which makes him believe the honor of his daughter is sacred; that is the species of insanity which makes him believe the honor of his wife is sacred; that is the species of insanity which makes him believe that whosoever invades his home, that whosoever stains the virtue of this threshold,

> has violated the highest of human laws and must appeal to the mercy of God, if mercy there be for him anywhere in the universe.[17]

The jury took two full days before they returned deadlocked, with seven jurors convinced of Thaw's guilt and five convinced he was not guilty by reason of insanity. The standing-room-only courtroom erupted in a roar. Reporters rushed for the exits to write the result up for their papers. Thaw was deeply disappointed. He was headed back to jail pending a retrial when he had hoped to go free as the acclaimed defender of innocent girlhood.

The following January, in a less sensational retrial Thaw had a new chief defense counsel, Martin Littleton. Mrs. Thaw had finally realized that she could best save her son from conviction by giving far more ammunition to the temporary insanity defense. She offered up details of trauma experienced by Thaw in utero, serious illnesses he suffered as a child, and many instances of weird behavior. The tales his mother had done her best to keep private over the years included Thaw's history of writhing uncontrollably with a movement disorder (either from rheumatic fever or epilepsy); wild temper tantrums in which he threw china and heavy objects at servants; an attention-grabbing suicide attempt as a teenager; and his propensity for babbling like a baby even as a young man.

During the first trial, the names of White's friends and associates as well as chorus girls other than Evelyn were deliberately kept from public airing to protect their reputations. By the time of the second trial in 1908 no one involved came out unscathed. The public did not feel sorry for the victim, nor did they empathize much with his crazed, self-indulgent attacker. Evelyn Nesbit also was impugned as a gold digger with the spread of false rumors that she was paid a million dollars for her teary-eyed testimony. No faith remained in innocence as the 20th century emerged with a full-blown exposé of the immoral excesses of New York's moneyed class.

Thaw's tendency to lash out violently when angry and Evelyn's new testimony about his suicide attempt with laudanum made it far easier for the second jury to decide that Thaw was not guilty of murdering White by reason of insanity. The judge announced that Thaw was a danger to public safety and would be committed to an asylum. Thaw flew into a rage. He had expected to be set free. Seven years later, in 1915, Thaw was declared sane and released. He and Evelyn divorced soon afterward. By 1917, Thaw was rearrested for whipping a teenage boy and was sent back to an asylum for another seven years. Even after his final release, Thaw faced periodic civil claims from showgirls he dated, who claimed he whipped them, but none ever went to trial as his enormous inheritance came in handy yet again.

Evelyn Nesbit later penned two memoirs, one in 1934, *Prodigal Days: The Untold Story of Evelyn Nesbit,* and one twenty years earlier that would not be edited and published for ninety years—*Tragic Beauty: The Lost 1914 Memoirs of Evelyn Nesbit.* Harry Thaw wrote his own memoir, *The Traitor.* Stanford White's murder inspired several other books and movies. Among them, E. L. Doctorow's 1975 fictionalized *Ragtime* became the best known and was later adapted as a musical. In 2008, historian Paula Uruburu entranced audiences with her dramatic retelling of the tale—*American Eve: Evelyn Nesbit, Stanford White, The Birth of the "It" Girl and the Crime of the Century.*

* * * * *

The first "trial of the century" was practically a scripted melodrama. Audiences found compelling the rags-to-riches story that Evelyn Nesbit Thaw told; raged against the power imbalance that led to her deflowering; and applauded Thaw's revenge against the man who had "ruined" his wife. It gave new fodder to those who still viewed females as protected possessions of fathers and husbands to decry the decadence of big city life and agree the lecherous victim had it coming to him. Yet what gave ubiquitous coverage of Stanford White's murder its special oomph was how Thaw triggered new insights into the Gilded Age and permanently tarnished its most vaunted members.

As riveting as Thaw's first trial had been, it was eclipsed within a month by a political murder that had labor directly pitted against capital. The charges that radical labor leader Big Bill Haywood ordered the assassination of Idaho's ex-governor had obvious national implications.

Though far to the left of most Americans, Haywood had developed a large following in the previous decade as an outspoken champion of the eight-hour day. In June of 1905 he organized militant unions, Socialists and anarchists to a "Continental Congress of the working class." At that historic gathering, Haywood co-founded the International Workers of the World ("IWW")—also known as the "Wobblies"—dedicated, like *Mother Earth*'s Emma Goldman, to the overthrow of the capitalist structure. The potential for the IWW's radical message to rally millions of underpaid recent immigrants unnerved industrialists and Progressive reformers alike. President Roosevelt made it his personal mission to see Haywood executed and thereby decapitate his radical union. Socialist Party leader Eugene Debs called the upcoming confrontation the "greatest legal battle in American history."[18]

3. UNDESIRABLE CITIZENS: The Murder Trial of Big Bill Haywood

The solid column swept past—painters, carpenters, hod-carriers, masons, iron workers—every sort of trade-union, each with its own banners—and an extraordinary number of bands all playing the Marseillaise . . . an indescribable color of martial zest . . . Here were 40,000 men marching in New York City . . . because three labor leaders are on trial for murder in a state two thousand miles away. [E]ven a conservative like myself could see . . . how effective it was . . . a sort of contagious fervor.

NORMAN HAPGOOD, EDITOR OF COLLIER'S WEEKLY
DESCRIBING THE MAY 4, 1907, SOCIALIST PARADE DOWN FIFTH AVENUE

Big Bill Haywood had the intimidating look of a real life Cyclops. He was built like an ox and had lost an eye in a childhood whittling accident. Haywood never bothered to obtain a glass eye. He wore a tall cowboy hat to tower over companions. On the rare occasions he took off his Stetson, the two-hundred-pound spokesman for the Western Federation of Miners stood just under six feet tall. He was clean-shaven with neatly parted short brown hair, oversized features, and prominent jowls. When photographed, he presented a half-profile with only his good left eye facing the camera.

The "Lincoln of Labor" was born in 1869 in the Utah territory where his father was a Pony Express rider. He was three when his father died and nine when he lost his right eye, the same year he first started working in the mines. Violent confrontations over union demands for worker safety, a $3 minimum daily wage, and an eight-hour day were then common throughout the nation. Federal or state troops had to be called in to restore peace some five hundred times, almost always at the instigation of politically powerful industrialists.

Haywood was an impressionable seventeen when Chicago's infamous Haymarket Square riot broke out in May of 1886. He devoured newspaper accounts of how the mayhem started. First police and private detectives killed six strikers. The following day an unknown protestor threw a bomb at the police who responded by shooting into the crowd, some of whom returned gunfire. After the dust settled, seven policemen and three protesters were dead. About a hundred others were injured, most of them police officers. Eight leading anarchists and militant socialists who had addressed the May Day rally were tried for murder. All were convicted based solely on charges that the deaths were "the bloody fruit" of their "villainous teachings."[1] Four were hanged in 1887. The hysteria-driven executions turned the four Haymarket Square rally organizers into instant martyrs for their cause.

Local unions in frontier states were mired in similar bloody confrontations with owners of gold, silver, copper, lead, and coal mines. The horrendous working conditions of rough-hewn, poorly educated men, who drank too hard and seldom enjoyed civilizing female companionship, created an extremely volatile situation. Miners typically worked ten hours a day, six days a week down dangerous shafts. One third of all men who worked a decade in gold and silver mines wound up seriously injured from falling rocks or from inhaling clouds of silica dust sent up by new "widow-maker" compressed air drills; one out of eight died in the mines.[2] It was easy to hate the big businessmen back East who exploited them. Only able-bodied men were paid—there was no workers' compensation, no health benefits. Disabled workers simply lost their jobs and were replaced with others equally desperate for employment. The mining industry in the late 19th century made extensive use of dynamite as a new commercial blasting technique. By the mid-1880s, American anarchists and militant labor leaders had found other uses for Alfred Nobel's invention.

Banding together in unions that could cripple the mines with strikes was the mineworkers' only hope to improve their lot. But management of the mines infiltrated unions with spies and resorted to private armies who used brute force to break strikes and police the mining facilities with rifles, killing strikers with impunity. Union members fought back with sabotage and violence against scabs. In 1892, alarmed by the increasing class violence in Idaho, President Benjamin Harrison sent out federal troops to conduct mass arrests of union members. Then came the financial collapse of 1893—the worst the country had undergone. It caused a ripple effect of bankruptcies and a surplus of out-of-work laborers competing for jobs in the mines. Facing wage cuts, strikebreakers, armed company guards, and mass arrests, union members in Colorado, Montana, Idaho, Utah, and South Dakota merged to form the Western Federation of Miners ("WFM"). The WFM almost instantaneously developed a reputation as the most militant union in the country. By the turn of the century, pitched battles between the WFM and state-supported owners would become known as the Colorado Labor Wars: it was the closest the United States "has ever approached outright class warfare."[3]

Haywood was twenty-seven when he joined the WFM in 1896. An impassioned speaker, he rose quickly to national prominence as a champion of labor's goals, shouting to enthusiastic crowds, "Eight hours of work, eight hours of play, eight hours of sleep."[4] By May of 1907, the burly activist had served on the Executive Board of the WFM for seven years when he went on trial for his life, accused with two other WFM leaders of ordering the assassination of Idaho's former Gov. Frank Steunenberg. President Theodore Roosevelt took keen interest. The bombing death looked all too much like WFM payback for the governor having called in federal troops to impose martial law to end Idaho's labor wars. Executing the leadership of the WFM for that crime could throttle the revolutionary International Workers of the World in its infancy.

In 1896, Steunenberg had been nominated as both the Democratic and Populist candidate for Idaho's governor. Both groups enthusiastically endorsed a thirty-six year-old firebrand, Nebraskan William Jennings Bryan, for President that year on his pledge to take America off the "cross of gold" by freely coining silver to revitalize the nation's economy. Bryan lost to Ohio Republican and Civil War veteran William McKinley, the industrialists' candidate who supported retention of the gold standard.

Yet with labor union backers and the vote of "Silver" Republicans, Steunenberg had handily won the Idaho election. Steunenberg became the first non-Republican to hold that office since the rough and tumble remnant of Eastern "Oregon country" was admitted to the union in 1890, a year after its neighboring states of Montana and Washington.

Steunenberg was reelected two years later with a smaller majority, which still included the support of union men. During his second term, antagonism reached the boiling point between the WFM and the owners of the Bunker Hill concentrator, a $250,000 plant in Wardner, Idaho—recognized when built as the largest smelting facility on the planet. (It would be a multi-million dollar investment in today's dollars.) Unlike most other mine owners, the San Francisco owners of Bunker Hill still adamantly refused to recognize unions. The facility's president had recently gone a step further and begun purging Irish miners from his work force as un-American agitators. On April 29, 1899, local union members in Burke, Idaho, retaliated with a breathtakingly bold act of sabotage.

Scores of armed union men kept the employees of the Bunker Hill concentrator at bay while another couple hundred masked associates—armed with rifles, bats, and shotguns—commandeered a train. They brought the train to Wardner and unloaded sixty dynamite cartons, which a few volunteers then placed at strategic points under the concentrator. Then all of the men high-tailed it out of Wardner just before the explosives blew the concentrator and nearby buildings to smithereens. The union's extraordinary violence shocked Gov. Steunenberg. At the demands of the irate railroad and Coeur D'Alene mine owners, the governor surprised the union by reimposing martial law to restore order. With his own National Guard off serving in the Spanish-American War, Steunenberg asked President McKinley to deploy federal troops. Within days, the President purposely sent veteran black soldiers in the 24th Infantry Regiment to quell the uprising, knowing how insulted the miners would be.

The segregated soldiers of the 24th Infantry had been the true heroes of San Juan Hill, in the recent Spanish-American War, for which Assistant Secretary of War Teddy Roosevelt's Rough Riders had received most of the credit. But the regiment was bitter at the prejudice it suffered upon its return, increasingly fractious, and now under strict orders from its white officers to indiscriminately round up union members and sympathizing townsmen in the Coeur d'Alene region and lock them up without mercy. As expected, the French-Canadian, Irish, Welsh, and Cornish locals then arrested without charges especially resented being herded into filthy bullpens by "niggers" called in by the government at the behest of the hated mine owners.[5]

Meanwhile, Idaho's Attorney General Samuel Hays boasted to the press: "We have taken [the union] monster by the throat and we are going to choke the life out of it."[6] Hays was obviously speaking not just for himself but for the Populist governor the Democratic union had helped elect. Republican governors had previously authorized mass arrests, but this time the illegal round-up was followed by federal troops enforcing a new county permit requiring all mine workers to deny or renounce membership in any militant union. The illegal ordinance was squarely directed at the local branch of the WFM—all done with the approval of Steunenberg. Union men turned on him, calling him a "Benedict Arnold" to their cause.

Though the WFM had recently broken with Samuel Gompers' more collaborative American Federation of Labor in the East, the WFM and its supporters retained substantial national clout. Steunenberg was summoned to Washington to answer charges at a specially convened congressional committee hearing addressing his wholesale suspension of the constitutional rights of so many Idaho citizens in the Coeur D'Alene region. Though Democrats were livid, the Republican majority stood firmly behind Steunenberg's imposition of martial law. To the WFM, this was the final indignity. Steunenberg was condemned by its leaders, including Haywood, as an enemy of the working class. Death threats against Steunenberg followed. As the labor strife escalated, opposition to Steunenberg prevented his renomination. He retreated to private life as a farmer, banker, and real estate developer. Steunenberg may have thought he was safe on the sidelines, but in the escalating labor wars, it was getting harder to find any haven. In 1904, in just one incident, thirteen strikebreakers died in a bombing at a Colorado train station. Rumor had it that WFM's Big Bill Haywood ordered that hit, though the union claimed it had actually been set off at the behest of local mine owners. By then, use of agents provocateurs was well-documented, but so was murder and mayhem by mine workers, who again faced brutal retaliation.

Then in April of 1905 came the Supreme Court's highly controversial *Lochner v. New York* decision invalidating state limitation of bakers' hours as an interference with freedom of contract. Over a vigorous dissent, the court interpreted the Fourteenth Amendment to protect the right of business owners and workers to negotiate any hours of employment they agreed upon, explaining that the employee might want the extra money for longer hours. In reality, there were always workers desperate enough to take practically any job offered. The landmark ruling protected owners' property interests in imposing working conditions that Progressive legislatures deemed inhumane. The *Lochner* case foreshadowed the invalidation of a host of other new laws for worker protection, but its most immediate impact was to galvanize the founding of the revolutionary IWW in June 1905. Just six months later, former Gov. Steunenberg lost his life when he opened the booby-trapped side gate to his Caldwell, Idaho, farmhouse. The mine owners then secretly gave Idaho's current governor the funds to hire Pinkerton's chief of its Denver office, James McParland, to investigate the explosion. The assassination had all the earmarks of yet another violent episode in the ongoing class strife.

McParland was the most famous private eye in America. He already had substantial experience with the Colorado Labor Wars where mine owners kept him on retainer. The ace detective, now in his sixties, had catapulted to national fame almost thirty years before for his role in destroying another militant mine-workers' organization in Pennsylvania. The Molly Maguires had originated as a secret society in Ireland that retaliated against oppressive British landlords. In the 1870s they were rumored to have reemerged in the Scranton anthracite minefields, where some Irish emigrants had settled following the devastating mid-century potato famine in their homeland. Yet it was never clear how active the Molly Maguires were in the deadly guerrilla warfare between union organizers on one side and, on the other, a coalition of mine owners, local police, and judiciary whom the mine owners controlled.

It benefited management to label any ardent union man with that label, realizing that "The name of Molly Maguire being attached to a man's name is sufficient to hang him."[7]

The situation in Pennsylvania at the time differed little from that in the West at the turn of the century: "labor was at war with capital, Democrat with Republican, Protestant with Catholic, and immigrant with native."[8] By early 1875, a newly formed Irish union called a strike to challenge oppressive working conditions that ended when starving workers capitulated in June. Later that summer, the Molly Maguires reportedly started regaining strength. The Pinkerton Agency had already sent James McParland to Pennsylvania as an undercover agent using the pseudonym Jamie McKenna. He started out as a drinking buddy of Irish unionizers and eventually became secretary of the Molly Maguires. McParland succeeded in his charade for more than two years, all the while passing on information to Pinkerton. The Maguires suspected a spy in their midst when vigilantes organized by a mine owner raided a duplex where three members of the secret society resided, killing one of them and his pregnant sister. It did not take long for them to accuse the man they knew as McKenna, who, fleeing from a lynch mob, barely escaped with his life.

McKenna later emerged as Pinkerton Agent James McParland, the state's star witness against the gang. McParland's testimony helped clinch twenty hangings on "Black Thursday" of June 21, 1877—for the commission of revenge killings, many of which McParland likely knew about in advance and did nothing to prevent. Some of those who hanged may have only been found guilty by association. Labor historian Joseph G. Rayback credits that trial with "temporarily destroy[ing] the last vestiges of labor unionism in the anthracite area. More important, it gave the public the impression . . . that miners were by nature criminal in character."[9] McParland's nickname in the agency became "Pontius Pilate." Three decades later, Irish Catholics in his own community still scorned McParland as a traitor to his people.

By the time McParland arrived in Caldwell, Idaho, in January of 1906 an itinerant sheep dealer going by the name of Thomas Hogan had already been arrested for Steunenberg's murder. Hogan was found with incriminating evidence in his hotel room. When questioned by the sheriff, Hogan admitted his name was Harry Orchard, that he had once lived in the Coeur D'Alene mining region and knew the WFM leadership. McParland befriended the prisoner and obtained a confession by assuring Orchard the state was really after the WFM inner circle. Orchard then implicated WFM Secretary-Treasurer Big Bill Haywood, its President Charles Moyer, and former WFM executive board member George Pettibone. Orchard claimed the three men gave him instructions in Denver to go to Idaho to kill Steunenberg as an example to other political enemies that they could never escape revenge. Orchard said it was only the latest of many terrorist acts he performed for the WFM.

The Constitution did not permit extradition of the WFM leaders in Denver for ordering a murder in Idaho. Undaunted, McParland colluded with the governors of Idaho and Colorado, other state officials, and the Union Pacific Railroad to kidnap the three WFM leaders. To make the kidnapping look legal, they prepared traditional extradition warrants falsely claiming the three WFM leaders were in Idaho on the night of the murder and were fugitives from justice. On a cue from McParland, the three suspects—who were already under surveillance—were then arrested on unspecified charges without being given an opportunity to alert family or their lawyers. The trio were then handcuffed and placed in leg irons and spirited across state lines on a train later dubbed "the Pirate Special." The train arrived in Boise in record time and the three men were placed in cells on death row while awaiting trial for Steunenberg's murder. Meanwhile, the Governor of Idaho publicly asserted his belief in their guilt, and McParland boasted in a press release, "They will never leave Idaho alive."[10] Debs shot back, "If they don't, the governors of Idaho and Colorado and their masters from Wall Street, New York, to the Rocky Mountains had better prepare to follow them."[11]

Irate WFM lawyers challenged the unorthodox arrests and extradition all the way to the United States Supreme Court. But the political pressure was so intense, they stood no chance. At the justices' annual White House visit the Monday the high court began its 1906 fall term, Roosevelt weighed in by asserting his opinion that Moyer and Haywood were undesirable citizens—just three days before oral argument on the propriety of the labor leaders' forcible abduction from Colorado.

Roosevelt most likely assumed that the justices were already prepared to give short shrift to the radicals' appeal, but could not resist a heavy-handed hint as to how he hoped they'd rule. Two months later, the high court issued its opinion. It held—with only one dissenter—that any challenge to the illegality of the kidnapping had to be lodged in Colorado. Once the men were transported to Idaho, Idaho had authority to try them for conspiracy to assassinate its ex-governor. It is often said that possession is nine-tenths of the law. In this case, possession was ten-tenths of the law. The men had been spirited out of state without having an opportunity to challenge their kidnapping in Colorado. WFM supporters considered the bootstrap Supreme Court ruling as odious and unsupportable as the infamous 1857 *Dred Scott* decision that helped precipitate the Civil War.

Eugene Debs wasted no time excoriating McParland and the two governors, linking them with "the capitalist tyrants" who martyred the Haymarket speakers two decades before. Debs threatened all-out war from Socialists: "If they attempt to murder Moyer, Haywood and Pettibone and their brothers, a million revolutionists will meet them with guns."[12] At the same time, Debs called for a broader national labor strike than the crippling railroad strike he had orchestrated in 1894. Colorado's Socialist Party named Haywood its candidate for governor while he sat in his Idaho jail cell facing murder charges. Though he was not expected to win, Haywood amazed observers by quadrupling the party's last gubernatorial vote count.[13] In the meantime, radical union members and Socialists across the country angrily took to the streets with banners, torches, and flags, proclaiming Haywood's innocence. They were particularly incensed about the Pinkerton agency's underhanded role in the matter.

Labor had long considered Pinkerton men lowly spies for management and blamed the infamous May 4, 1886, Haymarket Square riots partly on the agency. The bloody riots had caused a severe setback to the growing eight-hour-day movement. The day before the bloodshed in Haymarket Square, Pinkerton detectives helped Chicago police end a violent confrontation between scabs and strikers locked out of the Cyrus McCormick Harvester Works by killing six strikers and wounding many more. That bloodshed in turn was the likely catalyst for the bombing of the local police that started the Haymarket riot. Though four of the speakers at the Haymarket rally had been hanged shortly afterward, three of the eight were still languishing in prison in 1898 when a new Democratic governor of Illinois pardoned them for lack of proof of their involvement in the bombing. The chief advocate of that pardon was Chicago labor lawyer Clarence Darrow, who had become Eugene Debs' lawyer four years before when Debs faced criminal conspiracy charges for leading a crippling railroad strike. Darrow had first made his mark as a corporate attorney for the city of Chicago and then as a railroad lawyer before he defected to the other side to defend Debs.

By 1907 when Debs asked Darrow to join the team representing the three accused WFM leaders, the accomplished fifty-year-old defense lawyer was not yet a household name, but had earned a formidable reputation as a passionate opponent of the death penalty and champion of labor and underdog causes. He liked to claim that he never lost a client to the death penalty, but that was only true if one didn't count the time Darrow argued a post-trial sanity motion in 1893 for the convicted assassin of Chicago's mayor. It was impressive enough that Darrow could boast that he had never lost a capital case to a jury. Darrow had never shed his down home mannerisms despite the insatiable appetite for knowledge he inherited from his parents, both of whose families hailed from New England but had migrated to rural Ohio. An accomplished orator, Darrow was destined from the cradle for a life of passionate advocacy. He was the fifth of eight children of the impoverished town undertaker in the hamlet of Kinsman, a stop on the Underground Railroad in which his father may have participated. Darrow recalled his father fondly as the "village infidel."[14] Amirus Darrow had first trained for the Unitarian ministry, then quit because he questioned faith in God. Yet he retained firm convictions about right and wrong and a hide impervious to ridicule—traits he also passed on to his famous son.

Darrow also mirrored his parents' abhorrence of slavery and admiration for the fiery John Brown, hanged when Darrow was two for his failed raid on a federal arsenal at Harper's Ferry, Maryland, to arm slaves so they could rebel against their Southern owners. Darrow's mother Emily, who died when he was fifteen, was the more practical of the two, but shared her husband's idealism and fondness for books. She was a passionate suffragette and advocate of other liberal causes, which her son would likewise embrace with fervor.

When Darrow reached manhood, he was taller than average and heavy set; he looked like someone used to manual labor. Actually, he loved to dance, but like his father, he was happiest with his nose in a challenging book. It took a number of tries before Darrow was admitted to the Ohio bar in 1878. Two years later, he married and settled down to law practice not far from his home town. By age thirty, he had found that life in Ohio lacked worldly stimulation and moved with his wife Jessie and young son Paul to the vibrant, sinful city of Chicago. Darrow found the company of avant-garde writers and painters irresistible. He admired free thinkers who disdained bourgeois relationships. By 1897, his magnetic personality had attracted a serious new lover. He divorced his wife and spent much of his spare time entertaining his new bohemian friends, reading, writing, and arguing philosophy. Darrow had a magnetic personality and handsome rectangular face with straight brown hair that flopped to one side of his high forehead. He mesmerized women with his piercing gray-green eyes, soft voice, and animated style. Over time, in court, he grew more careless of his appearance, wearing wrinkled, outdated suits and not bothering to keep his hair combed. By 1903, his dissolute life had sapped much of his vigor. Thankful for someone to look after his daily needs, he married Ruby Hamerstrom, a journalist a dozen years younger.

When Darrow accepted his friend Eugene Debs' invitation to help defend the three most militant union leaders in the country, he counted on Ruby to accompany him to Idaho's capital, where he'd never been. Darrow expected to face open hostility from Boise's citizens still grieving for their assassinated governor and openly antagonistic to the radical WFM, which they blamed for Steunenberg's death. Ironically, Darrow had just published a booklet on the virtues of turning the other cheek. Biographer Irving Stone notes that when Darrow agreed to join the defense team for this sensationalized murder, the veteran Chicago lawyer "knew that it would be the toughest case of his career, a knock-'em-down, and drag-'em-out brawl with no holds barred."[15]

In the spring of 1907, memory of the despised Pinkerton agency's role in precipitating the Haymarket Square massacre still loomed large. The widow of one of the martyrs was featured in a Chicago parade on behalf of the three WFM leaders. Some more conservative labor unions distanced themselves from the WFM for fear that its militant leaders were guilty as charged. But the issues championed by the WFM—grueling work shifts, safety, and living wages—remained top national concerns of conservative and radical unions alike. Close to a hundred thousand men and women gathered on Boston Common to protest the railroading of the champion of the eight-hour day. One reporter called it "the greatest demonstration the Hub has ever witnessed."[16] In Manhattan, an estimated forty thousand polyglot immigrant workers paraded down Fifth Avenue singing "The Marseillaise" and wore red arm bands or kerchiefs in support of the arrested WFM leaders.

Marchers nationwide were particularly angry at President Roosevelt's prejudicial use of his own bully pulpit to decry the three union men on trial for their lives as "undesirable citizens."[17] Tens of thousands of workers bought buttons proudly identifying themselves as "undesirable citizens," too, with the nickel cost of each button going to the defense fund. Other sympathizers hid their support for fear of being fired. Roosevelt ignored criticism from the press. The feisty President repeatedly characterized the WFM leaders as "thugs and murderers" whom he equated with the notorious Molly Maguires of Pennsylvania.[18]

The upcoming Idaho trial became the focal point of potential class warfare. In May of 1907, mainstream and Leftist media swarmed to cover what *The Boston Globe* called a "determined struggle between labor unions and capital" and Socialists deemed "the greatest trial of modern times."[19] Debs was eager to cover the trial himself for *The Appeal to Reason.* Darrow emphatically told Debs to stay away—it would be hard enough to defend the three WFM leaders without turning the trial into a referendum on Socialism. As the trial began, a reporter for the Boise *Statesman* claimed that "the eyes of the civilized world are on these great proceedings."[20]

Two of Idaho's ablest lawyers headed a team of four prosecutors—six-foot-four unsophisticated "I-dy-ho" bar leader James Hawley, and "Silver" Republican and newly-elected Senator William Borah. The renowned ladies' man was a generation younger than his rough-hewn colleague and had been a close friend of Steunenberg. Borah and Hawley had teamed up successfully before in prosecuting leaders of the mineworkers for the 1899 bombing in Coeur D'Alene. Both felt they now had an iron-clad case for hanging the WFM's national leaders, aided by McParland's detective work.

Neither side had any objections to the appointment of former U.S. Attorney Fremont Wood as the trial judge. The Republican jurist was an imposing Yankee from Maine, known for his even-handed rulings. Judge Wood first pleased the defense by granting their motion for change of venue to Boise from Steunenberg's inflamed hometown of Caldwell. The defense team then added to their table a prominent member of the Boise Bar who had once been Judge Wood's partner. Trying not to miss a trick, they also seated Haywood's crippled wife and freckle-faced nine-year-old daughter in the front row of spectators, along with his mother and older daughter. To the disappointment of the prosecution team, also looking for sympathy from the jury, Steunenberg's widow refused to attend. McParland fumed at how Haywood was being portrayed as such a model husband and father. When arrested in Denver, Haywood had been found "stripped naked in a room in an assignation house" with his young sister-in-law.[21]

For protection against assassination, Idaho's Gov. Gooding had law enforcement question all suspicious strangers and usher them out of town. He moved his own family to the same hotel as Pinkerton's McParland, both under armed guard. Gooding also succeeded in getting federal reinforcements stationed at Boise's edge and secretly encouraged armed vigilantes among local businessmen. For extra insurance, the prosecutor placed a sniper in the attic of a grocery store where he had a clear view of the courthouse. President Roosevelt was kept apprised of the situation, but the Secret Service doubted the WFM would be foolish enough to pull anything.

It took a month and a half just to select the twelve jurors. Darrow had limited choices in the relatively homogenous community that prohibited him from following his usual formula for success in Chicago trials: "Never take a German; they are bullheaded. Rarely take a Swede; they are stubborn. Always take an Irishman or a Jew; they are the easiest to move to emotional sympathy."[22] Among other subjects, Darrow inquired if they would vote to hang an anarchist. One candidate responded, "Yes, if I understand what an anarchist is, I would hang him on sight."[23]

The sheriff's handpicked jury pool was heavily skewed against wage earners, but the two sides ultimately agreed on twelve men. All of the jurors had started out as farmers or ranchers. One had since become a real estate agent, another a construction foreman, and one a building contractor. Eleven of the bewhiskered men were over fifty. (Darrow's other rule of thumb was: "Old men are generally more charitable and kindly disposed than young men; they have seen more of the world and understand it.")[24] Eight were Republicans, three Democrats, and one a Prohibitionist. Like the Thaw jury in New York earlier that year, the men were sequestered for the duration of the trial. They were permitted to read newspapers only after deputies cut out any coverage of the case. Of course, some of them had read slanted local articles against the WFM leadership before they were picked for the jury panel.

Both teams had secretly conducted extensive investigation of eligible jurors in advance. The defense team eventually discovered that their chief intelligence gatherer was a Pinkerton spy, who skewed his reports and copied them to the other side. The defense may have planted its own mole on the prosecution side. It was an era known for corrupt tactics, and this was an extraordinarily high stakes case. By the time the ten peremptory challenges for each side were used up, the prosecution was satisfied, but the defense hoped only for a hung jury, noting that most of the men had voted for, done business with, or otherwise had been familiar with Gov. Steunenberg, including one juror who boarded the governor in his Boise home for two years. Only one juror had ever been a member of a trade union. Socialist papers were even more pessimistic—they assumed the panel had already made up their minds to do the prosecution's bidding.

Prosecutor William Borah deliberately sought to inflame the jury with his claim that the trial was for a crime "a thousand times worse than murder"—it was "anarchy displaying its first bloody triumph in Idaho."[25] A parade of prosecution witnesses took the stand to describe Steunenberg's violent, agonizing death and the poorly groomed stranger spotted casing the farmhouse beforehand. The spectators in the packed courtroom were mesmerized when the confessed bomber finally took the stand. McParland had worked hard maintaining the good will of the assassin now known as Harry Orchard and in keeping him well-guarded from retaliation. Over the sixteen months since Orchard's arrest, McParland had also "transformed [him] from [an] unshaven, ill-kempt, shifty-eyed felon" to a "carefully attired" and "manicured" man who "might be a Sunday School superintendent."[26]

Orchard, a forty-year-old Canadian whose real name was Albert Horsley, had been accompanied into the courtroom by armed guards. The doors were then locked to keep out the overflow crowd of hundreds of men and women anxious to get a glimpse of the governor's assassin. Inside the courtroom, deputies and plainclothes detectives provided additional security. The remarkably composed star witness then testified in a low, credible monotone for several days, detailing his career as a union terrorist. He claimed that he had participated in the 1899 bombing of the compression mill in Wardner; set the bomb in 1904 at a Colorado train depot, killing thirteen scabs; and targeted several other political enemies of the WFM, including an aborted attempt on the life of Colorado's ex-governor and two members of its Supreme Court. Then came the damning testimony that was intended to seal the prosecutors' case: that Haywood, Moyer, and Pettibone promised Orchard several hundred dollars and a ranch if he assassinated Steunenberg to intimidate other WFM adversaries.

The newly beefed up Western Union office worked at a record pace to transmit the news to the nation from the hordes of mainstream and Socialist reporters who had descended on Boise to cover the story firsthand. *Collier's Weekly* magazine described Orchard as "the most remarkable witness that ever appeared in an American court of justice."[27] *New York Times* correspondent O. K. Davis proclaimed that the witness "upon whose testimony the whole case against Haywood, Moyer, and the other leaders of the Western Federation of Miners is based" told "a horrible, revolting, sickening story . . . as simply as the plainest . . . most ordinary incident . . . and as it went on, hour after hour, with multitudinous detail, clear and vivid here, half-forgotten and obscure there, gradually it forced home to the listener the conviction that it was the unmixed truth."[28] Though Judge Wood was incensed at the prosecution for permitting jailhouse interviews of Orchard to influence public opinion during the trial, Wood privately agreed with Davis's assessment of Orchard's credibility. Unbeknownst to the parties, the judge and the *New York Times* correspondent took several weekend fly fishing trips together during the pendency of the trial.

Meanwhile, observers could not help but notice that WFM's pompous Colorado counsel, Edmund Richardson, had difficulty sharing the leadership of the defense team with the equally egotistical Darrow. The two often disagreed vociferously on strategy, but Darrow reluctantly deferred to Richardson when he insisted on cross-examining Orchard. Though the veteran WFM lawyer brought considerable skills to his grilling of the state's star witness, most observers believed Orchard won that courtroom match-up handily. (In the next trial of WFM's George Pettibone, when Orchard was again the chief witness, Darrow conducted the cross-examination himself. He was credited with doing a masterful job of discrediting Orchard as a convicted felon, bigamist, company spy, and tool of Pinkerton's agency. The jury reportedly responded by recoiling from Orchard as if he were "the carcass of a dead animal.")[29]

Yet, in Haywood's trial, Richardson scored some points. Even after months of preparation, Orchard's story was confusing. He claimed to be a paid assassin of the union, but acknowledged that some of the misdeeds he committed were on his own initiative or that of the mine owners. None of the state's witnesses was able to corroborate the complicity of the WFM leader in Orchard's dastardly act in Caldwell. Before trial, one of Orchard's alleged collaborators had disappeared without a trace, and another, Steve Adams, retracted his own confession at the urging of Clarence Darrow. Detective McParland suspected that Darrow bribed Adams, but had no proof. The prosecution was forced to rely only on circumstantial evidence to support Orchard's conspiracy claim. The defense in the Haywood trial put on a hundred of its own witnesses, including Haywood, who denied all of Orchard's charges.

It was customary at the time for closing arguments to last up to a day and a half apiece. Judge Wood allowed all four veteran attorneys that privilege. The courtroom was filled to capacity with Gov. Gooding and James McParland showing up for the first time to lend their weight to the proceedings. Hawley went first, attributing Orchard's confession to "the saving power of divine grace."[30] He disavowed any effort by the state to make war on the WFM or that the mine owners had a role in financing the prosecution—statements that Hawley knew to be false, having taken a very active role himself in fund-raising to "rid the West entirely" of the WFM.[31]

Edmund Richardson went first for the defense. The meticulous, balding Denver lawyer in his three-piece suit stood and lectured the jury from a distance. Richardson suggested that Orchard might have acted out a personal grudge against the governor who had authorized the outrages committed by the "colored troops" against Orchard's fellow miners in Coeur D'Alene. "If you had been there, covered with vermin, . . . gentlemen of the jury, . . . you would have attained in your breast a righteous hatred for every person who had anything to do with causing your humiliation and suffering."[32] Alternatively, Richardson suggested that Pinkerton's agency used that lingering wrath as a cover for hiring Orchard to kill Steunenberg and for misdirecting blame on the WFM leadership.

Darrow sensed the jury had already made up its mind to convict Haywood and invested himself in an extraordinarily moving, closing argument attacking the prosecution as a conspiracy to behead the WFM. In stark contrast to Richardson, the unconventional, shaggy-haired Chicagoan doffed his jacket and thumbed his suspenders in animated conversational style within arm's length of the jury. For eleven hours, he alternately dared them to hang his client if he was guilty of such a heinous crime and pleaded with them to believe in Haywood's innocence as he did. He ended with a sterling defense of self-sacrifice in class struggle:

> [O]ther men have died in the same cause in which Bill Haywood has risked his life, men strong with devotion, men who love liberty, men who love their fellow men have raised their voices in defense of the poor, in defense of justice, have made their good fight and have met death on the scaffold, on the rack, in the flame and they will meet it again until the world grows old and gray. Bill Haywood

> is no better than the rest. He can die if die he needs, he can die if this jury decrees it; but, oh, gentlemen, don't think for a moment that if you hang him you will crucify the labor movement of the world . . . Think you there are no brave hearts, no other strong arms, no other devoted souls who will risk all in that great cause which has demanded martyrs in every land and age?[33]

Darrow's aim was to obtain a hung jury by convincing any doubter among them to hold out for acquittal. By the time he finished, he was drenched with perspiration and sobbing. At the very least, he had greatly impressed the motley WFM supporters gathered outside the courthouse. Yet Senator Borah drew the biggest crowd for his final argument. Boise's most prominent citizens turned out in full force. Widow Belle Steunenberg finally made an appearance, arriving from Caldwell with one of her sons. A thousand people remained outside, unable to get into the courtroom. It seemed that all of Boise could smell an historic hanging in the air. Prominent citizens had already begun planning a huge, multi-day picnic celebration. Still, Judge Wood reminded the jury that Orchard's testimony required corroborating evidence of Haywood's complicity in that specific crime. He instructed them that they should view Orchard's testimony with skepticism if they believed it resulted from promises of leniency by the prosecutor. When the jury left the courtroom, Darrow wearily confided to a newsman, "It only takes one," spawning rumors that Darrow, too, expected a conviction.[34]

After only four hours, the jury sent a note to the judge. A quick agreement on a verdict sounded like bad news for Haywood, but that turned out to be a false alarm. The panel only wanted to review some exhibits. As jury deliberations proceeded through the night, Darrow paced and listened to disheartening talk that the jury had gone from seven-to-five for acquittal to ten-to-two for conviction. Then shortly before dawn someone standing outside the jury's window overheard an eleven-to-one vote and ran to a newspaper office, which issued an exclusive within the hour. Darrow heard the raucous celebrants in the street and purchased his own copy hot off the press. When he read that only one juror still held out for acquittal his heart sank. At 6:30 a.m. the attorneys were summoned to court to hear the verdict read. Darrow passed women and men in the streets decked out in their Sunday best, giddy with excitement over the upcoming festivitics. In stark contrast, both Darrow and Richardson appeared lead-footed and downcast. When Haywood arrived from his cell, Darrow told his client to prepare for the worst.

To Haywood and his counsel's surprise and relief, the eavesdroppers got it backward—the jury had leaned all night toward a defense verdict. Early that morning, the last holdout for conviction changed his mind to make it unanimous. Hawley registered shock as Haywood won acquittal for lack of proof beyond a reasonable doubt. It was the miners who then declared a holiday, hoisting Darrow on their shoulders as they paraded around amid outraged locals who spread rumors the jury must have been bought off. Others, like President Roosevelt, speculated that the jurors feared reprisal if they convicted the hero of the violent labor union. Elated Socialists across the nation quickly proposed Haywood as their presidential candidate. Anarchist Emma Goldman sent President Roosevelt a telegram: "Undesirable citizens victorious. Rejoice!"[35]

Hawley and Borah blamed the result on the judge's careful jury instructions. Jurors themselves indicated that they focused on the need for corroboration of Orchard's testimony. The prosecutors figured Haywood only escaped the noose because Darrow somehow engineered Steve Adams' retraction of his confession that he acted as Orchard's accomplice. Hawley and Borah badly wanted to turn things around when they tried Pettibone. The prosecutors decided to go after Adams again to get him to turn state's evidence against Pettibone. Darrow had barely gotten back to Chicago to resume his practice when he was summoned back to defend both Adams and Pettibone. Doped up nightly fighting the flu and severe mastoiditis, Darrow won a hung jury in the Adams case. Then, appearing near death, he commenced a brilliant defense of Pettibone. When Darrow reached the point he could only make it to court in a wheel chair, his doctors ordered him off the case to recuperate in California. Co-counsel then completed the case and won Pettibone's acquittal. In jail, Pettibone had been stricken with cancer. He went back to Denver and died that summer following an unsuccessful operation.

By the time of Pettibone's acquittal, Steunenberg's reputation had suffered a severe setback. Borah himself faced federal charges that, when Steunenberg was governor, the two had conspired to perpetrate a series of fraudulent land deals. At this point, Idaho officials cut short their losses in attempting to destroy the WFM leadership. Charges against Moyer were dropped. Moyer, never one who favored violent tactics, soon afterward ousted the more aggressive Haywood from the WFM. Haywood went on to head major strikes over the next decade as a leader of the IWW. Yet some Socialists much preferred the boost their movement would have gotten had Haywood, Pettibone, and Moyer instead been martyred. They assumed Roosevelt would have faced far greater threats of mass strikes had the three labor leaders been hanged.

Roosevelt saw no benefit from Haywood's acquittal, which he called a "gross miscarriage of justice," from a jury he assumed had been terrorized.[36] Yet had the Supreme Court not given its blessing to the illegal extradition from Colorado, no Idaho murder trial could have taken place. Given the blatant due process violation that brought them to Idaho and the extremely prejudicial pretrial publicity, workers throughout the country would never have believed in the legitimacy of a guilty verdict. In contrast, Judge Wood's conscientious instructions, the jury's cautious deliberations, and the resulting acquittals showed workers everywhere that the fix was not in for conviction. The underdog prevailed, giving them hope their own situations would improve within the current political structure. One wonders how close the nation came to widespread violence, how much anger would have erupted in the streets and exacerbated pre-existing class, ethnic, and religious divisions had Boise's citizenry gotten their coveted hangings.

* * * * *

Ironically, at the same time Roosevelt was applying heavy pressure on the Supreme Court to let the questionable Idaho trials go forward against three "undesirable citizens," he was waging an unprecedented battle in the South for respect for the Supreme Court's authority. Just a month after the WFM leaders were kidnapped by Pinkerton agents, a lynch mob broke a black federal prisoner out of jail and hanged him to prevent Supreme Court review of his rape conviction. With President Roosevelt's full support, what followed was the one and only contempt trial the United States Supreme Court ever conducted.

4. SHOWDOWN WITH THE SUPREME COURT: The Contempt Trial of Sheriff Joseph Shipp

"To Justice Harlan. Come get your nigger now."

NOTE PINNED TO ED JOHNSON'S CORPSE

During the late 19th century, the national fad was to gather round the piano and sing "coon" songs. The public could not get enough of comic sheet music that portrayed Negro men as loose-living, watermelon-eating, ignorant buffoons; ridiculed them as lazy, shiftless gamblers and hustlers or drunks; or demonized them as razor-wielding street bullies. White women singers in black face gained followings as "coon shouters." Hundreds more coon songs fed an insatiable public appetite that lasted through the turn of the century.

In 1901, blacks and Progressives applauded President Theodore Roosevelt's historic invitation of *Up From Slavery* author Booker T. Washington to dine with the First Family at the White House. South Carolina Senator Benjamin Tillman was among the open racists appalled at that egalitarian gesture: "The action of President Roosevelt in entertaining that nigger will necessitate our killing a thousand niggers in the South before they learn their place again."[1] Novelist and playwright Thomas Dixon was then the nation's most popular lecturer. In the age before radio, he spoke to sold-out audiences across the country, waxing poetic on racial purity, the evils of Socialism, and the proper role of women—at home raising children. Belittling bi-racial intellectuals like

Tuskegee President Booker T. Washington and W. E. B. DuBois, Dixon repeatedly warned his audiences that Negroes were a race of savages: "[No] amount of education of any kind, industrial, classical or religious, can make a Negro a white man or bridge the chasm of centuries which separate him from the white man in the evolution of human nature."[2] (Dixon's anger may have been fueled by abhorrence of his own half-brother, the son of Dixon's father and the family cook.)[3]

In 1905, one out of six American households bought the sheet music for "If the Man in the Moon Were a Coon."[4] That same year Dixon published the best seller *The Clansman.* A decade later it would be turned into the blockbuster film *The Birth of a Nation.* In a key scene, Dixon reenacted the most frightening moment of his childhood when a Confederate widow got his father and his uncle—who headed the local Klan—to don their white robes and hoods and join other Klansmen in stringing up a former slave accused of attacking the woman's daughter. The Ku Klux Klan hanged the man in the center of town and shot him repeatedly for good measure. Dixon's mother reassured her young son, "They're our people—they're guarding us from harm."[5]

Chattanooga, Tennessee, had a significantly better civil rights record than most other Southern cities. It had not held a lynching since 1896—the year the Supreme Court of the United States decided the landmark case of *Plessy v. Ferguson,* putting its blessing behind enforced segregation of mixed-blood or Negro citizens so long as the accommodations were denominated "equal." Covered by that fig leaf, Jim Crow laws proliferated in the South and emboldened physical abuse of blacks throughout the land. Historian Eric Foner concludes that "By the early twentieth century [racism] had become more deeply embedded in the nation's culture and politics than at any time since the beginning of the antislavery crusade and perhaps in our nation's entire history."[6]

Chattanooga was an industrial city of 60,000 that included many transplanted Northerners as well as a substantial middle class among its 20,000 black residents. Back in 1886, Republicans had even elected a black lawyer, Styles Hutchins, to represent the district for one term in the state legislature. Progressive religious leaders fought bigotry and lobbied for peaceful resolution of all conflicts. In 1905, publisher Adolph

Ochs still owned *The Chattanooga Times*, though the Jewish philanthropist had already moved to Manhattan to oversee his more recent acquisition, *The New York Times*. Despite the city's progress, fifteen percent of Chattanooga's adults couldn't read. A large number of whites held dead-end, menial jobs and increasingly resented the growing prosperity of the city's black professionals. In Tennessee, new Jim Crow laws made race hatred far more contagious. It went viral in Chattanooga that winter.

Since early December of 1905, the papers had been reporting a wave of burglaries, rapes, and robberies by Negro men, including a girl attacked in her own bed in an orphanage and another on a downtown street. On Christmas Eve tension rose dramatically when a notorious black gambler, Floyd Westfield, barricaded himself in his house with a gun when a white constable headed a posse sent to arrest Westfield for disturbing the peace in his neighborhood by shooting off fireworks. When the constable and his men broke the door down, Westfield fired, killing the constable. The day after Christmas, Ochs' often Progressive *Chattanooga Times* captured the widespread fear: "Desperadoes Run Rampant in Chattanooga; Negro Thugs Reach Climax of Boldness." The paper blamed the climate of fear partly on the sheriff for not being tough enough. A month later, vigilantes impatiently waited for Westfield's murder trial to reach its foregone conclusion. Given their druthers, they would have already strung the gambler up to send the Negro community a strong message about respect for law and order.

When locals heard what happened after dark on Tuesday evening, January 23, 1906, to twenty-one-year-old Nevada Taylor, all many could think about was vengeance. Someone jumped the popular office worker from behind and brutally raped her as she approached the cemetery gate near her home in the city's St. Elmo District. The pretty blonde still lived with her widowed father, a groundskeeper at the Forest Hills Cemetery, and commuted daily by trolley to her job downtown. Whoever had assaulted her shortly after 6:30 p.m. had almost choked her with a leather strap around her throat and left her unconscious.

Hamilton County Sheriff Joseph Shipp jumped on the case Tuesday evening as soon as Nevada's father contacted him. The sixty-one-year-old diehard Rebel was tall and thin with receding white hair, moustache, and goatee. Though he only had a seventh grade education, since his arrival in Chattanooga from his home state of Georgia, the Civil War veteran had done quite well for himself in a furniture business and through real estate investments. After he and his wife raised their seven children, Shipp decided to run for sheriff. The Confederate veteran had all the qualities of a lawman the county's white male voters could trust—a hard-drinking, cigar-chomping, poker-playing champion of Southern womanhood.

Shipp's bloodhounds sniffed the scent from Nevada's torn dress and quickly found the abandoned black leather strap. City newspapers featured the shocking details on Wednesday together with a $50 reward, almost two months' wages for many workers. By day's end, the reward would grow to $375—a sum larger than many residents earned annually. Nevada had told the sheriff that she did not get a good look at the man who grabbed her from behind and threw her over the fence as she cried out for help. But she heard his oddly gentle voice. At first, she could not specify his race, but said he was dressed in black, wore a hat, was athletic and shorter than average. He might have been five-foot six. After talking with the sheriff, Nevada became convinced her attacker was Negro. Under the law, that made the rape a capital crime, which it was not if committed by a white man. Sheriff Shipp was up for reelection to a second two-year term at the end of March. He realized that if he identified the rapist quickly, he could get the suspect tried, convicted, and executed well before the election.

In a newspaper interview on Wednesday, the sheriff made a solemn promise to his constituents: "I know the people thirst for judgment of the Negro who did this. I can assure the people that all at the courthouse agree and will be satisfied with nothing less. I am confident we will find this beast and he will feel the vengeance of our community upon him."[7] Despite his boast, Shipp knew he could be thrown out of office if he did not quickly solve the sensational crime that had the city of Chattanooga in an uproar. That same day, the sheriff and his deputies arrested a twenty-five-year-old grocery deliveryman, James Broaden, who worked in the area and fit the general description of Nevada's assailant. Sheriff Shipp subjected Broaden to tough questioning, but kept the investigation open. The next morning, the sheriff was home eating breakfast when he received a call from a man named Will Hixson who worked near the cemetery. Hixson's first question was whether the reward was still available. When told it was, Hixson met with the sheriff and described a black man he claimed to have seen at the St. Elmo trolley stop ten minutes to six on Tuesday evening "twirling a leather strap around his finger."[8] Tuesday evening had been particularly dark and gloomy, but Hixson said he had offered the same man a light on Monday and believed he could identify the stranger if he saw him again.

Late Thursday morning, Hixson called the sheriff to say he spotted the man and learned his name, Ed Johnson. Shipp rushed over to the run-down colored neighborhood on Chattanooga's south side to the shack on Higley Row occupied by Skinbone Johnson and his wife. Their twenty-four-year-old son was not there. The sheriff ransacked his parents' home and that of Johnson's sister who lived nearby, but found no evidence relating to the crime. Shipp had no warrant. Under state law, he didn't need one. On a hunch, the sheriff hid around the corner and followed Johnson's sister a few minutes later. She flagged down her brother as he rode on the back of an ice wagon. Sheriff Shipp pounced. He had his deputies handcuff Johnson and take him to the county jail for questioning. Johnson asked the sheriff, "Why are you doing this?" but got no response.[9] At the jailhouse, the sheriff followed his usual methods. He tried to beat a confession out of Johnson.

Like many other colored kids, Johnson had left school in the fourth grade. The police never read him his rights. He was not yet offered an attorney—suspects would receive neither immediate protection for decades. Yet Johnson steadfastly maintained his innocence and gave the sheriff a sizeable list of alibi witnesses who had seen him working at the Last Chance Saloon—miles away from the crime—from late Tuesday afternoon through ten o'clock that night. The sheriff did not believe him. Shipp called the District Attorney. The two interrupted a trial then being conducted by criminal court Judge Samuel McReynolds to alert him that they had the rapist in custody. Word quickly spread.

Fearing that a lynch mob might assemble, the sheriff and judge decided to transfer Johnson to Knoxville temporarily. The jail had already been besieged twice before. Sure enough, that night, 1,500 men—

many wielding guns and ropes, bricks and rocks—descended on the Chattanooga jailhouse demanding "the Negro." They cut the telephone wires to prevent calls for reinforcements and shut off power. Refusing to believe Johnson had been transferred elsewhere, they stormed the building, smashed all the windows, and used a battering ram to try to break down the front door. Though police responded, they could not disperse the huge, angry crowd. Then Judge McReynolds showed up and called the governor to ask for National Guard reinforcements. The angry crowd stayed put. One man asked the judge: "Going to help us hang that Negro?" Another said, "The jury is in and we find him guilty and sentence him to hang by the neck until dead."[10]

McReynolds told them to go home, but did nothing to try to blunt their anger against a man who had not even been formally accused, let alone had his day in court. Instead, the former prosecutor explained, "We have laws we must follow." He then pledged that he would give the case the highest priority and told them, "I hope that before week's end, the rapist will be convicted, under sentence of death and executed according to law before the setting of Saturday's sun."[11] Such betrayal of bias should have forced McReynolds off the upcoming trial. Just over a decade earlier, the United States Supreme Court had traced back through Ancient Rome and Athenian Greece to the Old Testament the basic guarantee a free society promises all criminal defendants—the presumption of innocence.[12]

Not until Saturday did Sheriff Shipp bring Nevada Taylor to Nashville to view the two suspects then in custody—Broaden and Johnson. Shipp instructed them to speak so she could try to identify her assailant. Sheriff Shipp needed Nevada Taylor to pick the same man as Hixson. He was worried about more than the upcoming election; he was also concerned about his own safety and that of his staff, other prisoners and the jailhouse itself. When Johnson's voice sounded to Nevada different from the perpetrator's, Shipp assumed that the prisoner was just trying to disguise it. Soon Nevada told the sheriff what he wanted to hear—that Johnson was "like the man as I remember him." He "has the same soft, kind voice."[13] The sheriff immediately dispatched a wire to the prosecutor in Chattanooga. An all-white male grand jury indicted Johnson that afternoon, after which Judge McReynolds met with the sheriff and prosecutor to plan their joint trial strategy, which nowadays would be unethical but was then routine.

Tennessee was more advanced than many states in requiring trial judges to appoint a defense lawyer in all death penalty cases. But that was often an illusory right since the judge had discretion to choose any lawyer in his jurisdiction, even if he was clearly not up to the task. The trio thought about appointing a black defense lawyer, but decided that if Johnson somehow won acquittal, the mob would likely take revenge on the judge as well as defense counsel. McReynolds instead selected a known lightweight, lawyer Robert Cameron, who mostly earned his money finding cases for other lawyers. He had no criminal law experience and no contested civil trials under his belt.

On Saturday evening, January 27, former Circuit Judge Lewis Shepherd stopped by Judge McReynolds' home to offer his suggestions for the high profile case. Thirty-four-year-old McReynolds had only been on the bench three years, but was highly ambitious and pragmatic. He was open to ideas from the balding liberal, who at fifty was one of the leading lawyers in the state and a seasoned state politician as well. Shepherd was then defending gambler Floyd Westfield on the charge of murdering the constable. McReynolds surprised Shepherd by asking him to partner with Cameron as Johnson's lead counsel. Shepherd accepted on the condition that McReynolds would also name a prominent civil trial lawyer to serve as well.

The next morning before church, McReynolds summoned both Cameron and civil lawyer W. G. Thomas to his chambers. Thomas begged to be passed over, but McReynolds would not take no for an answer. McReynolds dumbfounded the pair by telling them he would not give them time to learn the facts and applicable law. The trial would start as soon as the Westfield trial ended, perhaps by the end of the week, when Judge Shepherd could join their team. As they left, Judge McReynolds reminded them they would not get paid, hinting broadly he expected little effort. Neighbors and clients immediately shunned both Thomas and Cameron and subjected them to ridicule. Thomas's secretary quit. Then rock-throwing hooligans attacked the home Thomas shared with his mother. Though Thomas moved her to a relative's for safety, she and Cameron's wife begged the two men to get off the case.

Johnson meanwhile stayed in the Nashville prison where he had been transferred for safe-keeping. On February 2, he gave a jailhouse interview to *The Nashville Banner* in which he protested his innocence and repeated the alibi he had told the sheriff. Johnson did not meet his lawyers until the following day when Shepherd and Thomas got him to review with them in detail his movements on January 23. Shepherd told Johnson how grim the situation looked because "the people of Chattanooga are very mad and they want someone to die for this crime."[14]

Johnson must have melted their hearts with his reply: "But I don't understand. I never done what they say. I swear to God I didn't. I've never seen the woman they brought up here before. I didn't even know where she lived. I just want to go home."[15] Shepherd embraced his client.

All three lawyers quickly scrambled to gather alibi evidence. Judge McReynolds had already held an improper private meeting with two of them, the sheriff, the mayor of Chattanooga, and District Attorney Whitaker. McReynolds warned the defense team against making a motion for change of venue or asking for a postponement of the trial until the situation calmed down. Contrary to his duty to decide how Johnson's case would proceed based on the arguments about to be presented in court, McReynolds had made up his mind in advance not to grant either form of relief for fear that it would only infuriate the mob and precipitate a lynching. McReynolds had already indicated to the sheriff and prosecutor that Johnson's acquittal would present the same serious political problem. The judge felt Johnson's life well worth sacrificing to preserve the façade of a law-abiding society. Let the defense lawyers try their best in an impossible time frame, the script was already written—Johnson had to die to satisfy the mob.

Shepherd was determined to succeed against all odds. For assistance, he had already approached the most gifted local African-American attorney for help, Noah Parden, the younger partner of black politician Styles Hutchins. Unlike Hutchins, forty-one-year-old Parden was scholarly and athletic. He had light skin, tight curly hair, a long straight nose, and bushy mustache. Parden had been raised in an orphanage since the age of six when his mother, a housecleaner, died of illness. He never knew his father, who likely was white. Among the few possessions Parden's mother left him was a Bible, perhaps explaining why he embraced his legal career like a religious calling. Like Hutchins, Parden was an impassioned champion of individual rights, but unlike his mentor, he was far more pragmatic. He did not dare offer help to Johnson publicly for fear of retribution from both the white and black communities, both of which wanted the alleged rapist quickly brought to justice and the whole ugly matter put behind them. Yet Parden helped Johnson's lawyers track down alibi witnesses and gave valuable behind-the-scenes advice. Thomas and Cameron worked day and night establishing that Johnson was at the saloon when he said he was from 4 p.m. until 10 p.m. the night of the rape. Yet they recognized that the bar's regulars were considered lowlife with little credibility.

The lawyers could do nothing with Parden's other lead. Two black residents in the neighborhood of the assault had told Parden that they had seen a white man washing off blackface on the street about 7 p.m. that fateful night. Burnt cork and greasepaint were then commonly used by whites in minstrel shows, and it would have been a smart move for a white rapist on a dark night to wear such makeup to reduce the chances of being caught. But the two potential defense witnesses realized the sheriff would never believe them; they refused to come forward.

The tabloids meanwhile kept the ire of impatient community avengers at fever pitch awaiting the trial's start. As a precaution, heavily armed guards brought Johnson back from Nashville in secrecy to the Chattanooga jail. When proceedings began on Tuesday morning, February 6, Judge McReynolds filled the courtroom with lawyers and newsmen strongly favoring the prosecutor; he refused admittance to Ed Johnson's parents and his pastor. McReynolds designated an all-white list of names for the jury panel, though such skewed practice was illegal. Two men who had qualms about the death penalty were dismissed. The defense excused others who admitted that they already believed Johnson guilty. When addressing the jury panel, Shepherd stood next to his slump-shouldered client and told them, "I ask but one thing of you. I ask that you treat this man throughout this trial and during your deliberations as you would a white man. He deserves no less. The law requires no less."[16]

During the three-day trial, the whole gallery openly cheered District Attorney Matt Whitaker and razzed the defense team at will without any reprimand from the judge. Johnson remained listless as both Hixson and Taylor identified him. Sheriff Shipp and his deputies testified that Johnson had told three inconsistent versions of his alibi when they were grilling him at the jail. It was almost dark when Johnson took the stand on his own behalf, but he suddenly perked up and explained to the jury his whole day Tuesday, January 23, in animated detail. Johnson reeled off the names of nine witnesses who saw him at the saloon. The judge kept the trial going late that night and reconvened early the next morning for another full day.

Aside from the alibi witnesses, the most compelling defense witness was an elderly black building supervisor of a nearby white church. His name was Harvey McConnell. McConnell accused Hixson of framing Johnson for the reward money. He testified that on Wednesday, January 24—the day after the rape—Hixson approached him to ask for a physical description of the roofer Hixson had seen recently working at the church and for the roofer's name. The defense argued that it was not based on Hixson's own observations Tuesday night but McConnell's description of Johnson that Hixson then went to the sheriff to collect his reward. Other defense witnesses testified that it was so dark Tuesday night before six p.m. that a pedestrian could not identify the race of a passerby at five feet, let alone the features of the stranger Hixson had claimed to have seen twirling a leather strap Tuesday night. Hixson took the stand and denied ever speaking to McConnell and reaffirmed his identification of Johnson.

On Thursday, Nevada Taylor retook the stand but was less sure now then she had been before: "I will not swear that he is the man, but I believe he is the Negro who assaulted me."[17] A juror then yelled, "If I could get at him, I'd tear his heart out right now."[18] Shepherd demanded a mistrial, which should have been declared, but Judge McReynolds had no such intention. After three hours of impassioned oral argument on both sides, it was after 5 p.m. when Judge McReynolds instructed the jury and nearly six when he ordered them to begin immediate deliberations. It was almost midnight when the exhausted jury came back to the courtroom. Much to the judge and sheriff's shock, the jury announced a deadlock. Even under intense pressure from the prosecutor to "send that black brute to the gallows," four jurors held out for acquittal. McReynolds ordered them to get some rest and return Friday morning. What happened next would only come out in a later federal investigation. "Long after everyone else had left the courthouse, McReynolds, prosecutor Whitaker, and Sheriff Shipp shared a bottle of whiskey in the judge's chambers. They all agreed that a 'not guilty' verdict could not be tolerated, nor could a mistrial—the city could not afford, financially or socially, a second trial."[19] How they followed up on that conspiratorial session never came to light.

Within an hour of when the jurors arrived Friday morning, they surprisingly announced they had reached agreement. Guards brought Ed Johnson into court handcuffed and in leg irons as a crowd quickly gathered to hear the jury verdict of guilty. Death was mandatory since the jury included no recommendation of leniency. Shepherd announced he would seek a new trial the next day, but his co-counsel Thomas disagreed and asked McReynolds to appoint three more attorneys to help resolve the defense team's impasse on what to do next. McReynolds then met again with District Attorney Whitaker—yet another breach of the judge's required neutrality—and let the prosecutor name two of the three defense consultants. Not surprisingly, the new lawyers joined forces with Thomas to try to pressure Shepherd and Cameron to forego requesting a new trial or appeal even though both men were convinced that the four jurors who changed their minds so quickly had been tampered with. The advisors told the defense team they had now completed all of their ethical responsibilities to Johnson and any further legal action would simply cause a few months' delay of the inevitable hanging. Thomas feared worse—that any further defense of Johnson's innocence might just incite the lynch mob to kill all of them and the sheriff would no longer get in the mob's way.

By the time the attorneys conferred with Ed Johnson in the jail Friday afternoon, they convinced the poor man he had only two choices, both ugly: to forego any further proceedings and die with relative dignity at the hands of the county hangman; to assert his rights and be lynched and mutilated by a rabid mob. With Shepherd now grudgingly silenced, Thomas talked Johnson into waiving his rights and throwing himself on the court's mercy. McReynolds showed none. He praised the jury as among the finest he had ever observed and announced his personal endorsement of their verdict that the defendant was the guilty party. McReynolds sentenced Johnson to be hanged on March 13—fulfilling his pretrial promise.

On Saturday, February 10, Skinbone Johnson arrived at Hutchins' and Parden's law firm desperate for help. He told Parden that his son did not want to die for a crime he had not committed and had only waived his appeal under duress. Styles Hutchins overheard their conversation and convinced Parden this was an historic occasion that cried out for their help. Money was not an issue; the two were used to poor black clients not being able to repay them with anything but gratitude and a home-cooked meal. Parden already believed Johnson was innocent and the trial a mockery of justice. He came to Shepherd's home on Sunday and enlisted the remorseful older lawyer's aid.

Ed Johnson's chances of regaining his freedom were slim to none in the Tennessee Supreme Court and not much better under federal law. The Bill of Rights guaranteed the right to trial by jury and the right not to be deprived of life, liberty, or property without due process of law, but those constitutional rights had been interpreted to apply only in federal courts. After the Civil War, the country enacted the Fourteenth Amendment declaring that "no state" shall "deprive any person of life, liberty, or property, without due process of law." But the Supreme Court had not yet determined whether that controversial Amendment was intended to enforce the Bill of Rights in state criminal trials.

The next five weeks would involve a race against the hangman's noose through four courts, including the highest in the land. On Monday morning, Parden and Hutchins surprised Judge McReynolds with a hastily prepared motion for a new trial. The judge told them to come back on Tuesday when the prosecutor would be available. The next morning, he denied the motion for a new trial as untimely, telling Parden that the three-day deadline had actually run on Monday. When Parden then requested a certified record to permit review by the Tennessee Supreme Court, McReynolds sneaked off on a week's unplanned vacation to stymie that process. Parden persisted anyway. On March 3, the Tennessee Supreme Court unanimously rejected the plea to delay Ed Johnson's execution. Four days later, Parden raced to the federal district court in Knoxville to challenge the trial. He cited a United States Supreme Court case on Sixth Amendment guarantees for a fair trial and pointed out the skewed handling of seventeen rape cases in the county over the past six years. Most of the victims were black, but only two of those cases resulted in convictions and the rapists got short jail terms. Three victims were white women who accused black men. All three of those cases resulted in convictions, with two of the three men sentenced to death.

By coincidence, Sheriff Shipp was on the same three-hour train to Knoxville as Parden, but traveling in first class the sheriff never saw the Chattanooga lawyer in the "coloreds" car. Shipp was planning to transfer Johnson back to Chattanooga, where he would likely be at the mercy of another lynch mob. Not in any particular hurry, Shipp ran other errands and spent time with old friends before he reached the prison. By the time he arrived, Shipp was shocked to find a marshal with an order signed by Judge Clark keeping Johnson in Knoxville pending a hearing on March 10. Shipp brought the judge and prosecutor to the unprecedented hearing, which lasted into the night. At lunch-time on March 11, Judge Clark issued his ruling on the merits of Parden's petition. The judge did not grant the requested relief, but issued a ten-day stay of Johnson's execution to allow for United States Supreme Court review. The Chattanooga officials immediately questioned Judge Clark's authority to change the execution date. Judge McReynolds suggested they might disregard the federal judge's ruling and go ahead with the execution on its prior schedule. Instead, the group asked Tennessee's Gov. William Cox to intercede. He postponed Johnson's execution just one week to March 20.

Ed Johnson resigned himself to death. His last wish was granted in the Knox County jail—he had experienced an epiphany and wanted to be baptized. Johnson no longer hated the white people persecuting him for a crime he hadn't committed. Instead of taking him to the church, officials allowed the black pastor into the prison. Over three hundred congregants crowded into the jail's cafeteria where Johnson joined in a full-throated rendition of "There's Power in The Blood" and "Amazing Grace." Johnson displayed such ecstasy that it enraptured the choir members, who ended with a wildly exuberant "In the Sweet By and By."[20]

Parden barely got any sleep as he prepared an emergency writ to file with the United States Supreme Court and booked a train to the nation's capital for the afternoon of March 15. That morning an arsonist set fire to his office building, but it was put out quickly. Parden found a seat in another "coloreds" car and had plenty of time to wonder if he was on a fool's errand as the train stopped at station after station with their segregated toilets and water fountains. Everywhere he looked were reminders of the Supreme Court's stamp of approval on these demeaning daily indignities in its 1896 decision in *Plessy v. Ferguson.* In Washington, D.C., Hutchins had arranged for Parden to meet first with Emanuel Hewlett, one of the few African-American lawyers already admitted to practice before the United States Supreme Court. Parden needed Hewlett to sponsor him to be sworn in, too.

Two days after Parden's arrival, the two men presented Parden's papers to Justice Harlan in the majestic Supreme Court conference room. Parden was hopeful. Harlan had been the lone dissenter in the *Plessy* case, arguing that the Constitution was color blind. It was their good fortune that the civil rights champion was assigned to review emergency requests from the Sixth Circuit, which encompassed Tennessee. The Kentucky-born jurist had himself been raised on a slaveholding plantation. Though Harlan had fought for the Union in the Civil War, he was then pro-slavery, like his father. In forty years, the six-foot-two-inch jurist had evolved from a svelte, brown-bearded Whig into a hefty, balding, and clean-shaven Republican. The Presbyterian's conversion to abolitionist had much to do with seeing his older half-brother Robert face so many painful experiences because Robert was one-eighth black.

Parden's urgency impressed Justice Harlan: Ed Johnson would hang in three days without Supreme Court intervention. The meeting lasted no more than ten minutes. Parden hoped he might hear something the next morning, but there was no news before he had to catch his train. On the long ride home he anxiously replayed in his mind the extraordinary session on March 17 with Justice Harlan, trying to decide if he had been convincing. Meanwhile, Harlan reviewed the papers and conferred with his brethren at the Chief Justice's home the morning of March 18. At Harlan's urging, the high court—for the first time in its history—agreed to review a state court conviction on constitutional grounds and gave Harlan authority to stay Johnson's execution pending a hearing. He immediately sent notice of the order by telegram.

Hutchins elatedly greeted Parden's return with the telegram in hand. The following day, March 19, the extraordinary relief ordered for the convicted rapist was all over the front pages of local newspapers. Ed Johnson had trouble realizing that a white-haired son of the South on the Supreme Court in Washington, D.C. gave a tinker's damn about a colored handyman in Chattanooga, Tennessee. Shepherd invited Parden and Hutchins to celebrate their historic victory at a dinner in his home. While they toasted their success, a lynch mob was already gathering to descend once more on the Chattanooga jail. This time, the sheriff was forewarned of the mob's plans and removed all but one other prisoner, a white woman moonshiner, from the third floor where Shipp had brought Johnson back for execution. Shipp then gave most of his deputies an unaccustomed night off.

Shipp's chances of reelection had taken a nosedive for not allowing the lynching in the first place. He was determined not to stand in the mob's way again. Instead, he went home to await the outcome, just a few blocks from the jail. Judge McReynolds still smarted from Shepherd's blistering attack on his judicial integrity and the deep personal affront the shocking federal intervention represented. He gave Adolph Ochs' brother at *The Chattanooga Times* a heads-up, but this time refrained from asking the governor to deploy the National Guard. The attack on the jail began around 8 p.m. McReynolds and Whitaker settled by a window overlooking the jail to watch the show.

As Johnson heard the ugly mob invading the Chattanooga jailhouse, he kept repeating to himself the 23d Psalm. During the three-hour siege, Judge McReynolds and District Attorney Whitaker never alerted the police, nor interceded with the crowd. Apparently, they also failed to take any notes of people they observed breaking into the jailhouse. When someone contacted Sheriff Shipp at home, he, too, neglected to ask for police support and failed to ask the governor to deploy the National Guard stationed nearby. Shipp arrived at the jailhouse well before the vigilantes found Johnson, but simply let the mob put him in an unlocked side room to stay out of their way.

It was close to eleven-thirty when the poorly executed siege of the almost undefended building finally succeeded. As the mob's leaders emerged triumphant pushing Johnson ahead of them with a rope around his neck, the crowd gained energy with shouts of "Kill him now!" and "Cut his heart out right here!" The men force-marched Johnson at the head of their ugly parade six blocks to the Walnut Street Bridge where the last lynching had occurred a decade before. Johnson shouted, "God bless you all. I am innocent" before they hanged him over the Tennessee River. Still unsure if he was dead, mob members repeatedly shot at his swinging body. Though no one tried to stop the hanging, there were policemen around. One was spotted bending over Johnson's bullet-ridden corpse to cut off a finger for a souvenir. Someone else pinned a note on what remained of Johnson's torso, "To Justice Harlan: Come get your nigger now."[21]

It was a classic reaffirmation of lynching as spectacular ritual—complete with torture after death—a joyous celebration of mob law and white supremacy that first became popular in the South in the mid-nineteenth century to intimidate the growing anti-slavery movement. To the rowdy crowd that participated—and those fellow citizens who were gleefully entertained—the macabre gathering constituted the fit "barbarous" end to a "barbarous criminal." The grotesque ceremony emphatically avenged the double indignity endured by a defiled white virgin who had been forced to testify in open court and undergo "the humiliation of having to relive the brutal crime."[22] Most importantly, devoted sons of the Confederacy wanted to send a strong message to the federal government that, regardless of what the detested Reconstruction Amendments purportedly dictated, the progeny of former slaves were not citizens entitled to trial by a jury of their peers, equal protection or due process rights afforded to the master race—period.

In shock the next day, but emboldened by the Supreme Court's unprecedented show of interest, Chattanooga's black community boycotted work, shutting down most factories and textile mills. Hardware stores were emptied of guns, knives, and ammunition as blacks and whites throughout the city geared up for race riots. Major stores closed early. Fearing an uprising, the sheriff imposed a curfew on blacks. The mayor closed bars that catered to blacks, while leaving open the ones white men frequented. Shipp deputized two hundred men to assist his regular staff; the mayor appointed some additional city policemen. The governor assigned fifty National Guardsmen as backup. Devastated as he was, Parden joined public efforts to maintain calm and focused instead on bringing the lynchers to justice.

President Roosevelt publicly condemned the open defiance of the Supreme Court as the Chief Justice convened the high court to determine what it should do. In an interview with reporters, Justice Oliver Wendell Holmes echoed Justice Harlan's outrage. The following day Ed Johnson received a martyr's funeral attended by his family, two thousand community members, and his three appellate lawyers. Undeterred by the fact that Sheriff Shipp and Judge McReynolds were big political supporters, President Roosevelt immediately met with Attorney General Moody to order an investigation of the lynching. Nor did the Commander-in-Chief back off when warned by leading Chattanooga citizens that "federal intervention in the matter would only incite a race war."[23] Their promises to deal severely with the lynchers themselves rang hollow.

Newspapers quoted the unrepentant sheriff, Judge McReynolds, District Attorney Whitaker, and Gov. Cox. All of them blamed Johnson's lynching on the United States Supreme Court for butting into purely state business by granting review of Johnson's conviction. Otherwise, they could have just gone ahead with the legal hanging on schedule. The city's leading white Baptist preacher lit into the lynch mob and its lawless supporters in his next sermon. They turned a deaf ear and listened instead to the editor of the influential *Chattanooga News,* who urged voters to reelect Sheriff Shipp by a wide margin to send a strong message to the "defenders of such fiends as Johnson." Appealing directly to "Anglo Saxon manhood," the newspaper had nothing but praise for the lawman who had just facilitated the lynching of his prisoner. Only a landslide would "show the whole country that this county proposes to stand by a sheriff who believes in protecting the womanhood of the South."[24] On March 27, an overwhelming majority reelected Sheriff Shipp. (Two years later black voter outrage helped galvanize his crushing defeat for a third term.)

Within days of the lynching, two Secret Service agents had quietly headed to Chattanooga to gather evidence. On the first day, no one would speak to them, but their purpose was whispered about, and three toughs attacked them on the street with pipes. Yet the two investigators refused to leave town. On April 5, local newspapers reported that Baptist minister Rev. Howard Jones had cooperated with the Secret Service men by revealing he had unsuccessfully urged the police to stop the lynch mob on March 19. That night, in retaliation, someone tried to burn down Rev. Jones' home.

The Secret Service agents completed their investigation on April 20, 1906, naming twenty-one co-conspirators in the lynching, including the sheriff and his deputies. Outraged at the murder, the local U.S. Attorney considered prosecution under federal law, but Attorney General William Moody rejected the idea, concluding that white Tennessee jurors would never convict anyone of conspiring to deprive Ed Johnson of his constitutional rights. Filing such proceedings would only exacerbate an already simmering situation. Not surprisingly, when District Attorney Whitaker convened his own state grand jury, it produced no indictments. Neither he nor Judge McReynolds, nor any of thirty-five witnesses Whitaker called, seemed to remember recognizing anyone who broke into the jail that night, even though many participants did not bother to wear masks.

As a protective shield enveloped the lynchers, Parden and Hutchins lost all their paying clients and faced ongoing death threats. Parden and his wife and Hutchins packed up and left the state, not knowing it was for good. Parden was already a much-coveted speaker in the North and hero to blacks elsewhere in the nation for his historic achievement in this case. He offered to assist in the federal prosecution of the sheriff and lynch mob.

By the end of May 1906, the United States Attorney General filed contempt charges against Sheriff Shipp and his co-defendants, the first and only such Supreme Court trial proceeding ever brought. Shipp was defiant. He publicly blamed the Supreme Court for Johnson's lynching and called the grant of review "the most unfortunate thing in the history of Tennessee."[25] By mid-October, the defendants would enter their not guilty pleas. Shepherd had now switched sides and vigorously represented several of the accused. The surprising move alienated Parden. With all of their bravado in Tennessee, before the Supreme Court the sheriff and his deputies defended themselves with lame alibis. None of them had any scruples about concocting a cover-up. Sheriff Shipp and Judge McReynolds also took time for an unannounced visit to the White House, where Roosevelt merely shook hands and exchanged awkward pleasantries.

The first round of arguments addressed the Southerners' claim that the lynching was none of the Supreme Court's business. There was plenty of precedent for its self-restraint. In the fall of 1875, the high court had reviewed the convictions of eight Ku Klux Klan members involved in gunning down a militia of 150 freedmen. The former slaves were protecting the Colfax, Louisiana, courthouse from a white supremacist revolt—it was the worst massacre in the Reconstruction Era. The Supreme Court reversed the convictions and held the federal law unconstitutional, declaring that the Fourteenth Amendment only protected citizens from official state action, not from lawless mobs.[26]

In 1883, the United States Supreme Court had played another key role in reducing all blacks nationwide to second class citizenship. The high court had on its docket several cases brought under the Civil Rights Act of 1875 banning discrimination both by government officials and by private citizens who ran public facilities. The Supreme Court issued a blanket ruling in five cases from coast to coast—New York, Tennessee, Missouri, Kansas, and California—that Congress exceeded its authority in passing the 1875 Civil Rights Act.[27] With a lone dissent by Justice Harlan, the high court said the Thirteenth Amendment meant only that Negroes were freed from literal bondage, not from blatant disregard of their civil rights. The Supreme Court's message reinforced its earlier rejection of federal protection of freedmen from mob violence. *The Wall Street Journal*'s Atlanta Bureau Chief Doug Blackmon sums up the result in his 2008 Pulitzer-Prize winning history, *Slavery by Another Name: The Re-Enslavement of Black Americans from the Civil War to World War II*: "In the wake of the [1883] Supreme Court ruling, the federal government adopted as policy that allegations of continuing slavery were matters whose prosecution should be left to local authorities only—a de facto acceptance that white southerners could do as they wished with the black people in their midst." [28]

Still, on December 4, 1906, the Supreme Court began two days of hearings on whether it had the right to entertain contempt charges against state lawmen for failure to protect a convicted black rapist who had been granted its review. Everyone knew that the Sixth Amendment right to a fair trial had never before been applied directly to state proceedings. Defense lawyers argued that the high court could not even consider the question whether the Fourteenth Amendment allowed such review. Otherwise, they would open the door to an enormous array of state criminal cases for potential federal oversight. Underlying this argument was the firm belief by Southern states' rights adherents that the Reconstruction Amendments were illegally ratified by pro-Union "rump" legislatures and ought to be considered null and void—a belief still held by many states' rights advocates to this day.[29] Notwithstanding this entrenched opposition, on Christmas Eve, the court unanimously declared that it did consider itself entitled to address whether Sixth Amendment guarantees applied in state courts via the Fourteenth Amendment.

The Supreme Court's historic ruling cleared the way for the contempt hearing. The high court then appointed a special magistrate to hear evidence. On Parden's advice, the Attorney General strongly urged that the hearing take place in Washington, D.C., to avoid witness intimidation. Defense counsel vigorously objected, claiming undue expense and no reason to worry about the safety of witnesses in Chattanooga. The Supreme Court compromised, letting the hearings proceed in Chattanooga with the proviso they could be moved if need be. Parden quit the team soon afterward. One of the very first white witnesses against the lynchers received a threat that his home would be dynamited if he did not flee the state. The federal agents took it seriously and relocated the man and his family to Georgia. Several other witnesses suddenly disappeared. After a continuance, testimony in Chattanooga concluded in June.

In both sessions, many witnesses braved community wrath by honoring the President's special subpoenas, others never surfaced. Sheriff Shipp's former black cook, Julia Wofford, came forward with key testimony that she heard Shipp tell his family he expected a mob if the Supreme Court delayed Johnson's execution. Wofford said she also heard Shipp on the afternoon before the lynching confirm he had heard that the Supreme Court had just granted Johnson a hearing. She quit the next day, disgusted with her employer. Shipp swore she was mistaken—he had no advance knowledge the mob was coming that night or that Johnson had just won Supreme Court review, making him a federal instead of a state prisoner. The special magistrate ultimately recommended dismissal of seventeen defendants for lack of evidence, but implicated nine of the men, including Sheriff Shipp, crediting Wofford's testimony over the lawman's.

In recognition of the extraordinary precedent being set, the Chief Justice authored the majority opinion himself. He ridiculed Sheriff Shipp's defense that he had no idea the lynching was planned for the night of March 19 and that he did nothing to assist in that lawless act. (Three justices would have found no fault with Shipp's conduct). The majority dismissed four defendants, but found Sheriff Shipp and four others acted in "utter disregard for this court's mandate" and were guilty of contempt of court by aiding and abetting the murder of a federal prisoner. Barkeeper Nick Nolan had been seen putting the noose around Johnson's neck; defendant Luther Williams had shot Johnson's swinging body five times.[30] An order was issued for the arrest of the five defendants. Shipp's political friends importuned President Roosevelt for a pardon to no avail.

The remaining question was the penalty to apply. The high court was again divided. Prosecution for conspiring to deprive a citizen of his federal rights permitted a sentence of up to ten years in prison. To discourage another such outrage, Justice Holmes suggested a year in jail and a $25,000 fine as the minimum sentence. The same three justices who believed Shipp had done no wrong, would have dismissed the contempt with a simple public reprimand. Instead, on November 15, 1909, the high court ordered the defiant sheriff, Williams, and Nolan to serve ninety days in jail; the other two defendants got sixty days. It was a sad commentary on the high court's perception of its own clout in avenging a major affront to its power and prestige—a lot of sound and fury signifying not so much in the short run. Even so, the ruling met with derision and anger among state officials in many parts of the country, particularly the Cotton Belt. The opposite result should have been unthinkable—that the United States Supreme Court might fail to hold state officials accountable for facilitating the murder of a prisoner to whom the high court had granted a hearing to address claimed violations of his constitutional rights.

Roosevelt's influence seemed quite evident in the manner in which Sheriff Shipp and the other defendants served out their brief sentence. They were held in comfortable quarters designed for women prisoners, where Shipp even got to bring his smoking jacket. Shipp was so impressed with the laxity of his punishment that he decided against asking to be transferred closer to home where his family could visit him. As it was, the men were released early—with time off for good behavior. On January 30, 1910, ten thousand celebrants welcomed Sheriff Shipp's arrival. As he stepped off the train, the band played "Dixie," and the patriotic Confederate crowd burst into song.

The Supreme Court's one major regret was that the Justice Department found no way to charge Judge McReynolds with contempt since he was not responsible for Johnson's safety pending federal review. They considered McReynolds' open disdain for the Supreme Court outrageous. Yet McReynolds' handling of the Johnson case played exceedingly well politically. The primary lesson he took from the landmark case was that criminal defendants had too much opportunity for appeal. He and Shipp lobbied to change Tennessee law to limit "criminal brutes" to just 30 days to seek to overturn any death sentence before the Tennessee Supreme Court.[31] Though that Draconian effort failed, McReynolds later parlayed his tough-on-crime and states' rights platform into nine terms in Congress, from 1922 through 1939. When he died, he was chair of the powerful House Committee on Foreign Affairs.

It took more than another half-century from its historic grant of a hearing to Ed Johnson for the United States Supreme Court to decide exactly which parts of the Bill of Rights were included in "due process of law" enforceable in every jurisdiction and exactly whose conduct besides state officials Congress could regulate under any theory. Diehard states' rightists have never acquiesced in controlling federal law. A movement is currently afoot to repeal that part of the Fourteenth Amendment which guarantees citizenship to all persons born in the United States.

Six decades after Johnson's conviction, the Supreme Court would bar as inherently unreliable jailhouse identifications conducted without a lineup that could be observed for fairness by the suspect's defense lawyer. Its rationale applied equally in 1906: "The influence of improper suggestion upon identifying witnesses probably accounts for more miscarriages of justice than any other single factor—perhaps it is responsible for more such errors than all other factors combined."[32] Witness identifications remain problematic to this day; the national Innocence Project reports that approximately three-quarters of wrongly imprisoned defendants later exonerated through DNA tests were convicted by mistaken eyewitness identification.[33]

Johnson was unfortunately like many hapless minorities denied their basic rights when hauled before a criminal justice system hell-bent on closing the books on high profile crimes. Johnson was different in that so many courageous people—black and white—made history in attempting to save the itinerant worker from the gallows, risking their own lives and careers in the process. In 2000, a judge in Hamilton County allowed the filing of a posthumous petition to clear Ed Johnson's name. The evidence was painstakingly dug up over ten years by Tennessee lawyer Leroy Phillips, Jr. and journalist Mark Curriden of *The Dallas Morning News.* The year before, the two had just published their acclaimed history, *Contempt of Court: The Turn-of-the-Century Lynching that Launched a Hundred Years of Federalism.* Ed Johnson finally got his fair trial and rightful dismissal of the unproven charges.

In the last thirty-five years since states began executing prisoners again after a four year national moratorium, over two-fifths of those executed have been either African-American or Hispanic. *From Lynch Mobs to the Killing State: Race and the Death Penalty in America* points out that, of all the death-row inmates exonerated in recent years through DNA testing, most were minorities[33]—not unlike Ed Johnson.

5. LABOR V. CAPITAL REDUX: *The Los Angeles Times* Bombing Case

They can kill our men and wreck our buildings, but by the God above they cannot kill The Times.

HARRY ANDREWS, MANAGING EDITOR OF *THE LOS ANGELES TIMES*, OCTOBER 1, 1910, SPECIAL EDITION

When Darrow's doctors wheeled him out of the Pettibone murder trial before it ended in January of 1908, neither the ailing champion of labor nor his wife Ruby counted on him surviving the agonizing train trip to Los Angeles. A few weeks later a surgeon performed a life-saving operation, draining a swollen mastoid behind his ear, after which Darrow still faced a long, uphill recovery. For months, Darrow did not speak and barely ate. Ruby kept all visitors at bay and shielded her husband from any business decisions, including frantic letters urging him to sell his investments. Darrow's convalescence in Los Angeles coincided with an economic depression that wound up bankrupting the successful lawyer from prolonged inattention to his affairs.

When doctors suggested that Darrow was well enough to absorb the news, Ruby told her husband all his savings were gone. He threatened never to forgive her for forcing him to go back into law practice and start all over building up a retirement fund. They barely scraped the train fare together to return to Chicago. Thoroughly demoralized, Darrow returned to his old law firm, vowing to concentrate on high-paying cases to quickly put together enough money to retire again. He had never even received all the fees promised him for disrupting his practice and jeopardizing his health to defend Haywood and Pettibone in Idaho. But Darrow did receive a solemn vow from grateful labor leaders after the unexpected victories in Boise—they would never ask him to defend a political murder trial again. With that promise still etched in his memory, Samuel Gompers, as head of the American Federation of Labor, personally showed up on Darrow's door step to beg Darrow to come West again in 1911 for an even bigger class confrontation than the Haywood murder trial. Darrow told Gompers an emphatic no. Ruby had threatened never to travel with him again for a labor trial, and he could not do it without her. Darrow's health wasn't up to it in any case, and the circumstances were dreadful.

The bombing of *The Los Angeles Times* building at one o'clock on Saturday morning, October 1, 1910, had shocked the nation. The building collapsed in flames. Twenty-one non-union employees died trying to escape. Somehow, on borrowed presses, key employees of *The Times* published the news in a one-page special edition the same day, placing the blame squarely on union men. The attack on the newspaper and an undetonated bomb found outside the owner's home had followed four months of escalating labor-capital confrontations.

Harry Otis, owner of *The Los Angeles Times*, was the self-proclaimed general of the movement to break the back of the unions, not only in Los Angeles but across the nation, through the militant Merchants and Manufacturers Association ("M & M"). Otis was also on a mission to destroy businesses that dared to support unions. Labor retaliated with equal fervor against non-unionized businesses. In June of 1910, iron workers had gone on strike for fifty cents an hour as their minimum wage. The M & M raised $350,000 to break the strike and used its clout to have the city council impose an ordinance banning picketing. Union members, strikebreakers, and police then came to blows. Local judges sided with management, issuing multiple restraining orders and jailing hundreds of strikers. To many labor supporters, the accusation that militant men were behind a retaliatory terrorist attack on *The Times* seemed too pat. The mass murder drew so much outrage that it dwarfed concerns over abusive labor practices and anti-union businesses. Why would union men be that short-sighted?

Coincidentally on the day of the bombing, William Burns, the celebrated sleuth who had already eclipsed Pinkerton as this generation's "Great Detective," arrived in Los Angeles to make a speech. Burns had rocketed to fame when President Theodore Roosevelt sent him to expose rampant political corruption in San Francisco after the city received unprecedented funds for rebuilding following the Great Earthquake and fire of April 1906. That investigation had prompted stunning indictments for graft and bribery against the mayor and entire board of supervisors, as well as political boss Abraham Ruef, the chief of police, officers of major utilities, and a railroad. Mayor Schmidt was forced to resign, and Ruef went to prison.

Harry Otis immediately asked Burns to head the investigation into the bombing of *The Times*. Burns soon realized that it bore similarities to suspicious bombings of non-union work sites his agency had investigated across the country. After six months of intensive national effort, detectives zeroed in on two brothers, James and John McNamara, as the key suspects. John McNamara was the national secretary of the AFL-affiliated Bridge and Structural Iron Workers Union. Like the Pinkerton men who illegally kidnapped the WFM leaders in Colorado in 1906 and whisked them to Idaho for trial, Burns' agents kidnapped the McNamara brothers in the Midwest and transported them to Los Angeles before anyone could challenge their extradition. Labor leaders smelled a frame-up and wanted to provide the McNamara brothers with their biggest legal guns. (It was, in any event, still more than two years before the city would be the first to employ a public defender.) AFL President Gompers joined Bill Haywood and Eugene Debs in rallying millions of union supporters nationwide—far broader support than for the Haywood trial—with charges that the McNamara brothers were being railroaded for murder. It was unquestionably the newest "crime of the century."

Gompers tried to convince Darrow that he was the only lawyer in the country with the skills to save the lives of the McNamara brothers and prevent labor from losing its war against closed shops. Darrow still declined. He could envision exactly what kind of a political nightmare he would be facing—much worse than in Boise. Back when Darrow had been recuperating in Los Angeles, he and Ruby had seen the polarized city first hand. Customers at local stores had to choose between union and "open" shops and expect to suffer retaliation for their partisanship. In its relatively short history, Los Angeles had developed a reputation as "the bloodiest arena in the Western World for Capital and Labor."[1] Business leaders in Los Angeles attributed the city's rapid rise to the much lower pay scale compared to the unionized city of San Francisco. Yet there seemed to be an unending supply of new job-seekers willing to work when management fired employees lobbying for higher pay and better working conditions. Darrow dreaded being thrust back into the center of the labor wars, but he did not want the McNamara brothers' deaths on his conscience. Going against his better judgment, Darrow ultimately yielded to Gompers' entreaties. He would live to regret that decision.

To counter the extraordinarily negative publicity, the union arranged for a movie biography to be filmed of John McNamara, proclaiming his innocence. The popular nickelodeon galvanized workers nationwide. But "Great Detective" William Burns was meanwhile systematically building a case that would trump all of the pre-trial propaganda. His agency uncovered irrefutable evidence from secret files in the Iron Workers' Union that the bombing was the end result of a five-year sabotage campaign carried out at the direction of union leaders on non-union sites.

In an early use of bugging devices, Darrow's visits to his clients in jail were recorded without their knowledge. With the array of witnesses and physical evidence against them, Darrow was astounded at the McNamaras' recklessness. John had bragged of the bombing in the presence of an undercover agent. Both were extremely remorseful. They told their lawyer that they had intended the bomb to go off at 4 a.m. when the building was empty. Yet as the two were privately confessing their guilt, the Socialist press kept promoting the McNamara brothers' innocence. Big Bill Haywood called for a general national strike to coincide with the first day of the McNamaras' trial. This time, Darrow expected his string of victories in keeping clients away from the gallows and the electric chair to end in ignominious defeat. Darrow became so depressed, he also began acting recklessly. He renewed an affair with a woman reporter from New York who came out to cover the trial. If the affair went public, it would have ruined his own reputation. Meanwhile, the police caught an investigator on his staff approaching two different jurors with bribe offers. Darrow could see no way that he could pull off an acquittal or a hung jury.

When muckraker Lincoln Steffens interviewed the McNamara brothers, their guilt was so manifest that Steffens strongly urged Darrow to have the brothers change their pleas. Darrow knew that labor leaders would vigorously oppose any such move. They would much rather claim the two men as martyrs. Yet Darrow told Steffens, "I can't stand it to have a man I am defending hang."[2] Darrow convinced the two brothers to save their lives by pleading guilty and publicly repenting the innocent deaths they caused. Darrow saved them from execution—and avoided a crushing defeat—but at the price of having organized labor turn on him. Union members had contributed hard-earned money to raise Darrow's legal fees only to watch the celebrated lawyer pocket the payment and eventually plead the brothers guilty.

As a consequence of the plea bargain that dramatically ended the McNamaras' trial, the labor movement suffered a huge blow to its credibility. The Los Angeles District Attorney then compounded Darrow's personal woes by prosecuting the famed lawyer on bribery charges—by far the worst legal fiasco of his career. Darrow contemplated suicide, but hired another giant in criminal defense, Los Angeles attorney Earl Rogers, to defend him. When Rogers kept showing up to court drunk, Darrow took over his own defense. For the first and only time, Darrow's emotional pleas asked jurors to salvage his own career. In one of the two attempted bribery trials, jury empathy won Darrow an acquittal; the other ended in a hung jury. To avoid a retrial, Darrow had to agree to forfeit his license to practice again in California. Fed up with labor, he headed back to Chicago.

So it was not Clarence Darrow that Bill Haywood asked to defend him in his next political trial in the spring of 1918—the longest criminal trial the United States had ever prosecuted. By then the coalition that had backed the WFM's defense in the 1907 murder trial had long since collapsed. Haywood and the IWW split from WFM leadership shortly after the Boise cases ended. In 1911, the IWW parted ways from Eugene Debs and the Socialists. Yet Haywood remained a formidable labor leader viewed by the business establishment as the "most hated and feared figure in America."[3] The "Wobblies" whom Haywood championed ultimately attracted three million factory, mill, and mine workers to their ranks, a coalition including non–English-speaking European immigrants, women, and African-Americans in an era when some unions expressly excluded blacks, while others took aggressive steps to block both African- and Asian-Americans from their own labor pools.

The IWW bore many similarities to the radical coalition that supported Huey Newton half a century later. Like the Black Panthers' strident opposition to the Vietnam War, the IWW strongly opposed America's entry into World War I as a rich man's war fought with the blood of the poor. Urging tactics that the Weathermen would later emulate, the IWW advocated industrial sabotage to undermine American war efforts. Unlike the bitter national divide generated by the Vietnam War, however, when the country joined World War I patriotic fervor spread across America. The IWW immediately began to feel the backlash as the federal government drafted harsh new laws blocking entry to revolutionaries and deporting radical immigrants. The war-time Espionage Act of 1917 included lengthy prison sentences for anyone whose speech or political activity encouraged draft resistance. In September of 1917, the Department of Justice raided four dozen IWW meeting halls and arrested 165 Wobblies for "conspiring to hinder the draft, encourage desertion, and intimidate others in connection with labor disputes."[4]

The raids resulted in a mass trial with more than a hundred defendants appearing before Judge Kenesaw Mountain Landis. The only evidence needed to convict them was proof they disseminated inflammatory IWW literature. All were found guilty and each sentenced to varying prison sentences, with Haywood receiving the twenty-year maximum. The following year, Debs was convicted for making an anti-war speech the Wilson administration deemed treasonous for use of "disloyal, profane, scurrilous, or abusive language" in violation of the 1918 Sedition Act. Debs was sentenced to ten years in prison; the perennial Socialist candidate for President was also disenfranchised. The United States Supreme Court later upheld Deb's conviction as a war-time necessity, through a narrow interpretation of First Amendment guarantees that has since been discredited.

Despite the Wilson administration's success in jailing radical labor leaders, strikes for increased wages and better working conditions escalated dramatically in 1919. Putting Haywood and Debs in prison made them into martyrs for a noble cause. Poet Carl Sandburg was then working as a journalist for a Socialist paper. He compared Haywood's vision for a worldwide labor uprising to that of John Brown's efforts to encourage slave rebellion and wondered, "Will there be marching songs written to Bill Haywood someday as the same kind of a 'traitor' as the John Brown who was legally indicted, legally tried, legally shot?"[5]

Government persecution only increased Haywood's stature among laborers. By 1920, Haywood made bail pending appeal and was out fundraising for fellow IWW inmates when America experienced the worst bomb attack so far in its history. The Wall Street bombing in front of J. P. Morgan's bank at noon on September 16, 1920, killed nearly forty people and injured ten times that number. The date coincided with a special election to fill the seats of five New York City Socialists ousted from the state legislature on the ground that Socialism itself was a treasonous cause. Was this payback from militant radicals?

The horrific bombing on Wall Street added fuel to "a nationwide antiradical hysteria provoked by a mounting fear and anxiety that a Bolshevik revolution in America was imminent—a revolution that would destroy property, church, home, marriage, civility, and the American way of life."[6] Haywood immediately became a prime suspect. Though he had long since publicly renounced violence as a useless tactic, he realized his appeal was doomed. Soon afterward, Haywood made plans to jump bail and escape with a fake passport to Russia to join Lenin's new government as a labor advisor. Haywood remained in exile for the last seven years of his life. Once settled in Russia, his naïve vision of a workers' utopia gave way as he observed the stark reality of the new Soviet dictatorship. He died utterly disillusioned, but the Soviets gave him a hero's funeral, keeping half of his ashes in the Kremlin and honoring his request to have the remainder sent back to Chicago to be buried near the Haymarket Square martyrs who had inspired his lifelong battle for worker rights.

Pulitzer Prize winner J. Anthony Lukas's epic history, *Big Trouble,* retells Haywood's story and notes the ironic difference in outcome of his trial for ordering Gov. Steunenberg's assassination from that of the accidental deaths caused by the McNamara brothers' sabotage. Several Socialist journalists close to both the WFM leadership and the militant Ironworkers Union privately shared the view in the fall of 1911 that the main difference between the two political crimes was that the two brothers got caught red-handed. A reporter who covered the McNamara trial for the Socialist paper *Appeal to Reason* wrote his publisher that "The McNamara brothers are not one bit more guilty of the crime charged against them than were Myer, Haywood and Pettibone . . . Trickery and audacity liberated the miners' officials." But *Appeal to Reason* refrained from publishing that story because of what it might do to the Socialist cause: to reveal the truth "would disgust hundreds of thousands of people" with their movement.[7] The rallying cry of innocence in each instance was a propaganda war fought against ruthless political adversaries. Neither the prosecutors nor the defense respected the law—these two "trials of the century" were merely cynical games in a deadly class struggle for power in which media on both sides were often complicit.

* * * * *

As class battle lines remained drawn between militant unions and management, Progressives gained slow headway as the more reasonable middle path. Yet rapid industrialization continued to take a heavy toll on exploited workers. In the city of Atlanta, smoldering resentment of Northern industrialists provided the fodder for demagogues and publishers to turn the murder of a young, teenage factory worker into a powerful political cause. With phenomenal success, yellow journalists focused local anger on the accused Jewish factory manager. The shocking case unleashed a torrent of anti-Semitism that both helped relaunch Georgia's Ku Klux Klan and prompted the formation of the Anti-Defamation League.

6. MURDER BEGETS MURDER: The Tragic Deaths of Mary Phagan and Leo Frank

I would rather be plowing in a field
than to feel that I had that blood on my hands.

GEORGIA GOV. JOHN SLATON

Four years after the historic *Shipp* contempt ruling, Leo Frank's murder trial once again focused national attention on Confederate hardliners rebelling against Northern interlopers. It would end the same tragic way—with local politicians and journalists brazenly inciting a lynch mob to bypass the rule of law. Yet in this case, Georgia's own governor was on the receiving end of widespread defiance orchestrated by a vengeful political rival. Muckraker William Randolph Hearst played a key role in both turning the original quest for justice into a firestorm and in vain efforts to break its destructive path before it became too late.

Still eyeing the White House in 1912, Hearst celebrated his fiftieth birthday and tenth wedding anniversary by purchasing a small Atlanta paper, *The Georgian.* He planned to transform the sleepy daily into yet another goldmine for his publishing empire—then at the pinnacle of its national influence—while creating a toehold for himself in the Deep South. He transferred to Atlanta a Kentucky-born managing editor with insights into what would play well with the locals. They made sure to fill the paper with lots of pictures, anticipating a lower literacy level than in his other markets.

As *The Georgian* began competing with the more widely read *Atlanta Constitution* and *Atlanta Journal,* one issue stood out as an easy target. Many children of Atlanta "crackers" (poor whites) were like Mary Phagan, who left school at ten to work in a mill and, at thirteen, averaged five dollars and fifty cents per week, working eleven-hour days in a monotonous dead-end job plugging erasers into pencils. Actually, Phagan clocked in less than the average work week in other factories, which included a full day on Saturday, too. Half of Atlanta's kids were malnourished or chronically ill, living in noisome slums that lacked plumbing and other basics taken for granted by the well-to-do. With only scant education, those who joined the work force at age ten had no realistic prospects of ever improving their situation. Social workers wrung their hands at this "awful curse."[1] Yet the President of Coca Cola expressed views typical of Atlanta's wealthy industrialists: "The most beautiful sight that we see is the child at labor; as early as he may get at labor the more beautiful, the more useful does his life get to be."[2] The city's movers and shakers realized how new business complexes and escalating property values owed their very existence to this replenishable resource. Factory workers up North could not be found for anything close to ten cents per hour.

Ever the opportunist, Hearst set his transplanted staff full throttle covering Atlanta's exploitation of child labor, joining reformers to point out that Georgia was "the only state that allows children ten years old to labor eleven hours a day in the mills and factories."[3] The maverick multimillionaire was characteristically uninhibited by his own past as a target of worse claims. For two weeks in July of 1899, thousands of homeless newsboys and girls as young as six went on strike against Hearst and his rival Pulitzer. Their cut-throat circulation wars depended primarily on independent street urchins hawking tabloids from dawn to long past dark to enrich the publishers' coffers. The newsies averaged thirty cents each per day, about two cents an hour.[4] Hearst hired strikebreakers to break up the rallies. Even after he and Pulitzer settled the strike, the exploited truants' situation remained dismal. Living in the biggest luxury apartment in all of New York City, Hearst had never developed much empathy for the orphans and beggars' children who made his empire possible. But he always knew a hot issue when he saw one, and "the Chief," as his staff referred to him, never let fear of hypocrisy get in the way of self-promotion. Crime journalist Herbert Asbury, who got his start working for Hearst, claimed that "Had not Hearst owned the *Georgian*, the story [of the Phagan murder] probably would have died a natural death."[5]

Hearst did not create this poisonous stew, he only stirred the pot. The ingredients already existed to explode the local cracker population into uncontrollable rage. Atlanta's business community promoted the city's exponential growth. They aimed to nearly triple the city's current size by the end of the decade despite already woeful lack of sanitation in the city's growing slums, poor public education, high crime, and disease. Turning the city into a modern metropolis meant luring ever more Northern capital investments. Unlike Atlanta's crackers, the city's elite had officially decided bygones were bygones: moneymaking was a common bond that, for dedicated capitalists, trumped their anger at cash-rich Yankees over the Civil War. A key selling point to investors was the opportunity to pay wages less than two-thirds of those paid in New England mills. By 1913, Jews owned many local factories. Atlanta's top echelon profited handsomely from their relationship with the Jewish middle class, but excluded them from the city's elite clubs and social circles. The Jews were otherwise largely assimilated in the business community and did not foresee their transformation into scapegoats.

The man who orchestrated the powerful backlash that followed was Georgia's kingmaker, 1904 Populist Party presidential candidate Thomas E. Watson. The lanky, red-headed lawyer born four years before the Civil War had actually co-founded Georgia's Populist Party in 1892 with black voter support. But after a disillusioning election loss, Watson did an about-face and became a rabid white supremacist. By the second decade of the 20th century, Watson was at his feistiest with a ready platform to spew venom against blacks, Catholics, and Jews—his own widely distributed *Jeffersonian Magazine*. Watson knew all along that for the multitude of Georgians the Civil War had never really ended, and he knew exactly how to galvanize that angry base.

* * * * *

With her sparkling blue eyes and auburn hair, Mary Phagan realized she was prettier than most girls her age. A big fan of the movies, Mary dreamed of escaping the tenements of "the bloody fifth" district where she lived with her mother and stepfather, who worked for the city's sanitation department. Her mother worried whenever Mary went about unchaperoned. The buxom thirteen-year-old had turned into quite a tease. On Saturday April 26, 1913, Mary put on an especially fetching outfit to attend the Confederate Memorial Day parade. She never arrived.

The prosecution of factory superintendent Leo Frank for the death of Mary Phagan became the perfect vehicle to focus the wrath of Atlanta crackers for their miserable working conditions. Displaced farmers still blamed carpetbaggers for the loss of their ante-bellum society. Significantly, local politicians did not start attacking the Jewish middle class until after they had succeeded in marginalizing black voters. Elder citizens in Georgia could vividly recall their sense of fear and anger when the state fell under martial law because its 1866 state legislature refused to ratify the Fourteenth Amendment. In Georgia, as elsewhere in the South, the vanquished Rebels abhorred universal male suffrage more than any other consequence of the Civil War. Georgia's 1868 constitution awarded blacks the vote only under duress. But intimidation kept many freedmen from exercising that right, while poll taxes adopted in the 1870s prevented poor people from voting, cutting black turnout in half.[6] Poor whites might expect a local politician to pick up the cost of their poll tax in exchange for their votes. Still concerned that blacks retained a voice in the electoral process, at the turn of the century white supremacists like Tom Watson successfully campaigned for new restrictions throughout the former Confederacy, including whites-only primaries.

To revitalize Atlanta, its civic leaders had already begun to coalesce around a "New South" philosophy predicated on renewed ties with the North, improved technology and education, and a broader based economy. In the first decade of the 20th century, Atlanta's population nearly doubled as impoverished tenant farmers relocated to the city in search of factory jobs. By then, blacks made up forty percent of the city's population and had developed a promising middle class, spurred by industrialist John D. Rockefeller's founding of three Negro colleges on the city's west side—Spelman (the maiden name of Rockefeller's wife), Clark, and Morehouse.

Class rivalry was easy to ignite. A racist gubernatorial campaign helped set off riots in 1906 by playing on fear that the rising black middle class would regain political clout. Journalists egged on local crackers with unverified newspaper accounts about drunken Negro workers emerging from downtown salons and molesting white women. Frenzied mobs then went on a rampage destroying black businesses. They injured hundreds of people and randomly killed over twenty black men. Georgia was second only to Mississippi in lynching.

Former Secretary of the Interior Hoke Smith, who made his fortune as publisher of the *Atlanta Journal,* won the 1906 governor's election. Smith obtained Watson's effusive endorsement on one principal condition: that, if elected, Smith would disenfranchise blacks to ensure they were kept "in their place."[7] As governor, Smith then forged a coalition that in 1908 adopted a state constitutional amendment to add a literacy test for voting with discretionary exceptions for those of "good character," i.e., illiterate whites.[8] By then, nine other Southern States had done the same. Through skewed literacy tests and poll taxes, they succeeded in preventing almost all blacks from voting for more than a half century.[9]

Watson thought Smith owed him personal favors as well. Watson had a long-time friend and supporter, a private detective named Arthur Glover, who shared Watson's devotion to the Confederacy. Glover's twenty-seven-year-old former lover, Maud Williamson, worked at an Augusta cotton mill. Glover showed up at the mill on October 19, 1906, bent on revenge for Williamson's infidelity. He shot Williamson four times in broad daylight in front of witnesses, not stopping even after she fell to the floor. Glover believed he had an absolute right to defend his honor, but the authorities saw it differently and convicted him of murder. Glover obtained no relief from appeals, but must have counted on Watson's clout with Gov. Smith when Glover cockily told the press he was certain he would not be hanged.[10] Despite Watson's personal plea, Smith did not commute the sentence. When Smith failed to deliver, Watson switched his allegiance to railroad commissioner "Little Joe" Brown, the son of Georgia's governor during the Civil War and got him elected instead. Watson still did not consider that he had evened the score against Smith. He would find that opportunity in the endgame of Leo Frank's tragedy.

In 1913, when the Mary Phagan murder story broke, Watson was otherwise occupied. He was busy fighting obscenity charges instigated by the Catholic Church for repeated scurrilous charges against the Pope. Watson was particularly perturbed about "the sinister portent of Negro priests."[11] The Catholic Church also imposed no ban on inter-racial marriage, a subject that greatly incensed the white supremacist. He absolutely abhorred the idea of black men having sex with white women. It was his book on the white slave trade that prompted passage of the federal Mann Act criminalizing the transportation of females across state lines for immoral purposes. Not surprisingly, the act was selectively enforced from day one. The first time it was ever invoked was against Jack Johnson, the reigning black heavyweight boxing champion. The handsome muscle man contributed enormously to the "Bad Nigger" image that drove this effort. In the 2005 PBS video, "Unforgivable Blackness, The Rise and Fall of Jack Johnson," film-maker Ken Burns describes how, in the early years of the 20th century, the bald, six-foot-five-inch Texan became "the most famous and the most notorious African-American on Earth."[12] The legendary boxer had a penchant for breaking social taboos, including flaunting his frequent sexual exploits with white women.[13]

Johnson was constantly in the sports news. In 1908 he shocked white boxing fans around the globe by beating the current World Heavy Weight Champion, Canadian-born Tommy Burns, in an historic match in Sydney, Australia. On Independence Day 1910, the world-renowned son of slaves—whom Muhammad Ali would later cite as his own role model—battled retired white heavy-weight champion James Jeffries in "The Fight of the Century." This marked the first inter-racial American match for that coveted title. Prominent sports writers like Jack London assumed that Jeffries, though long past his prime, would wipe the "smile from Johnson's face."[14]

The controversial contest was filmed in Reno, Nevada, before an all-white audience, whom security guards first checked for weapons. Energized by spectators' shouts urging Jeffries to "kill the nigger," Johnson won handily. Jubilant blacks took to the streets. Race riots followed in more than half the states across the country. Twenty-three people died—mostly black—and hundreds were injured. A feature-length movie of the historic fight was soon distributed across the country and internationally, though many cities prohibited its showing. (Church groups outraged at the moral depravity of the sport soon prompted Congress to ban interstate distribution of any boxing movies, a law that remained on the books for nearly three decades).

In January 1911, the hard-drinking Galveston Giant shocked America by marrying Etta Duryea, a white socialite divorcee from Long Island. It was when he openly cheated on his wife with a white prostitute that Johnson was targeted for the first Mann Act prosecution. Alienated from her family and depressed by Johnson's highly publicized sexual infidelities, his wife put a gun to her head and killed herself. Johnson then married the prostitute and the Mann Act charge had to be dropped. (Another one would later stick). Public outrage prompted Georgia Representative Seaborn Roddenberry to introduce a federal constitutional amendment in January of 1913 to ban inter-racial marriages in all states as it was already prohibited in Georgia.[16]

When Roddenberry launched this unsuccessful national campaign, the capital of his own state remained mired in poverty. Continued railing against uppity blacks by white supremacist politicians like Roddenberry and Tom Watson played to popular prejudice, but did nothing to address Atlanta crackers' own plight as indentured servants in the New South. By 1913, the fresh eyes of William Randolph Hearst's politically astute staff had already spotted the muckraking opportunity awaiting their relentless yellow journalism. Hearst's paper attacked factory owners (mostly Jewish) who helped kill a state bill to raise the minimum work age to fourteen. Newsboys hawked the latest edition of *The Georgian* deploring the horrors of child labor on the same Saturday in late April of 1913 that someone dumped Mary Phagan's battered body in a dark corner of the gloomy National Pencil Company basement.

Newly arrived country folk like Mary Phagan's mother and stepfather worried whenever they sent their daughters to work in factories that the girls might be attacked or subjected to moral degradation. Egged on by lurid newspaper photos and maudlin accounts of the teenager's death, Phagan's funeral attracted ten thousand angry locals who thirsted for retribution and demanded results. *The Atlanta Georgian* quoted Phagan's grandfather describing the victim as "the sweetest and purest thing on earth,"[17] an invented quote characteristic of Hearst newspapers. It was an obvious cross-reference to its readers' beloved antebellum South. By enflaming public opinion, all the leading papers put heavy pressure on the police to produce results.

The police department had an abysmal track record—hardly surprising when officers had little formal education and only a week's training on the force. Seventeen black women had been murdered in the previous two years with no one arrested for the crimes. The mayor warned the police chief that he would not tolerate such incompetence when the victim was a young white girl.[18] Starting on Sunday morning when first summoned to the pencil factory, the police had done a slipshod job in analyzing and preserving the crime scene. The basement's back door was covered with numerous bloody fingerprints that they never analyzed. They found two notes near the body, purportedly written by the dying young girl to describe the "long tall negro black,"[19] who assaulted her. Lax oversight allowed a journalist to borrow them. Once retrieved, the notes—no longer a useful source of prints—played a major, misleading role in the trial. Fingerprints on the victim's jacket were not sent out for analysis by the city's forensic analyst. Police and reporters trampled all the footprints in the factory basement that, if preserved, could have helped identify the perpetrator. Yet, if they did not find the brute who killed innocent Mary Phagan, the entire department might lose its badges.

Hearst offered a $500 reward for information leading to the arrest of the perpetrator—more than a year and a half's wages for many locals. Other papers chipped in, bringing the total to a whopping $1800. The extraordinary bounty resulted in a flood of suggestions, most of which proved useless. At first, the police focused on Newt Lee, the Negro night watchman who reported the crime immediately after he found Phagan's blood-caked corpse covered with sawdust near the colored toilet in the basement. The police grilled Lee mercilessly for three days—amid calls for his hanging—before police decided that Lee was telling the truth when he claimed no role in the girl's death. The murder occurred hours before Lee's shift started and his answers were so guileless he appeared incapable of having played any role in abetting the crime.

Leo Frank, the superintendent of the pencil factory, had been working that Saturday in his office. After police questioned the badly shaken superintendent, word got out that Frank was the last person who admitted seeing the young teen-ager alive. On her way to the parade, Phagan had stopped in Frank's office at mid-day on Saturday to collect $1.20 for part-time work that past week. Until Frank's arrest, he had been a rising star in Atlanta's Jewish community, the largest in the South. His wealthy wife, Lucille Selig Frank, descended from a co-founder of the first synagogue in the city two generations before. Both she and Leo had well-connected families. In 1912, at just twenty-eight, Frank was elected president of his local chapter of the B'nai Brith, a branch so prominent that they had just secured the organization's 1914 national convention for Atlanta. Frank stripped to show the police no signs of having engaged in a struggle. Their search of his home turned up no incriminating bloody shirt. Yet police found it suspicious that Frank had called in lawyers before he was officially arrested; they assumed it pointed to a guilty conscience. In fact, when officers first took Frank to headquarters for questioning, his uncle had sent for the lawyers on his own initiative.

The Georgian pounced on every suspect. Not having learned anything from having to retract the headline "LEE's GUILT PROVED," it printed Frank's picture with another banner headline, "POLICE HAVE THE STRANGLER."[20] Frank did not look like a son of the South, but the bantam-weight Hebrew number cruncher he was: impeccably dressed, five-foot-six, with neatly parted brown hair, a thin, angular face with a prominent, slightly hooked nose, and overgenerous mouth. He wore thick, wire-rimmed spectacles over his dark, protruding eyes. Though raised in Brooklyn, New York, Frank was actually born in Texas. Neither his birthplace nor Lucille's ante-bellum roots in Atlanta impressed Atlanta's crackers. As far as they were concerned, the tennis-playing opera buff with an engineering degree from Cornell was an elite Yankee Jew.

Leo Frank's uncle was a part-owner of the pencil factory, and Frank himself owned a small share. Frank's lack of warmth and sense of self-importance irritated many people who met him. Some girls who worked at the factory came forward to claim that Frank had harassed them on occasion. Much annoyance apparently stemmed from Frank sticking his head into the ladies' dressing room to warn dawdlers to get back to their stations. But being a boor was a far cry from committing a murder. Even had Frank done everything he was accused of—which was hotly disputed—his past behavior with other employees had no legitimate bearing on whether he killed Mary Phagan. Juries are not supposed to determine guilt based on prior bad acts or because they consider the defendant a bad person, but for proof beyond a reasonable doubt that the person committed the crime of which he is accused.

The Georgian's headline condemning Frank produced vehement protests to Hearst from Jewish advertisers both locally and in New York. That protest, in turn, prompted an editorial instructing readers not to rely on what they read in the newspapers. It by no means undid the damage, but from then on the Hearst paper would become increasingly skeptical of the case against Frank. Yet in the three months leading up to the July trial, local coverage in *The Georgian* and other city newspapers had prejudiced the Atlanta community beyond repair. A makeshift bed had been found in the basement storage area, which substantiated fears of the moral degradation associated with factory life, even if Frank had no knowledge of who put it there or used it. Rumors spread that Frank was a pervert with a history of improper advances toward young girls, and possibly boys too. The Jewish community rallied to Frank's defense, rejecting any such allegations out of hand. But the sensational gossip sold papers and enflamed a populace which had lynched many black men on far less provocation.

Forty-two-year-old prosecutor Hugh Dorsey badly needed a victory after two highly publicized prosecutions in which he failed to get a conviction. The owl-eyed son of a prominent Atlanta lawyer, Dorsey had high ambitions. Another embarrassing defeat like the one that had recently come at the hands of Frank's chief counsel Luther Rosser and Dorsey's political aspirations might be stymied. Fearful of being sabotaged by police incompetence, the shrewd prosecutor took the unusual step of seizing control of the investigation at the autopsy stage. Nothing was going to keep him from winning this conviction.

Although Rosser and his co-counsel were both prominent lawyers with accomplished track records, they severely misjudged the prejudice and rage being stirred up. Though later criticized for failing to request a change of venue, there may have been no city in Georgia where Frank stood a better chance of acquittal than its capital, where Jewish businessmen had long been valued members of the community. The grand jury that indicted Frank had included Jewish members who, at the time, believed there was enough evidence to indict Frank. The panel learned later that Dorsey had omitted key facts pointing to another suspect whose handwriting matched that of the notes found near the murdered girl.

The indictment of Frank depended on placing the murder on the second floor near Frank's office. Strands of hair found on a nearby lathe the Monday after the murder initially appeared to support this theory, but when analyzed under a microscope, they did not match others taken from Phagan's head. Dorsey suppressed the doctor's report and continued to assert that the hairs were Phagan's. A decade later a journalist reported another major discrepancy: the official files contained photographs and x-rays of Phagan's body that showed she had been bitten on her shoulder, leaving marks that "did not correspond with Leo Frank's set of teeth."[21] Today, prosecutors would be required to turn any potentially exculpatory evidence over to the defense before trial. Even under the prevailing standards at the time, Dorsey's concealment of key crime facts undermining his theory was indefensible.

The case went to trial in the scorching heat of July. Dubbed "the Greatest Legal Battle in the history of Dixie,"[22] it received the most press coverage of any case ever tried in Georgia. In preparation for trial, the defense team hired two Pinkerton detectives to ferret out exculpatory evidence. They were at the same time secretly reporting to the police, apparently concerned they would otherwise lose their privileges in Atlanta. One in particular made it his mission to prove Frank's guilt.

The proceedings took place in city hall with a huge crowd of partisan spectators. When the heat forced the windows open, the angry gathering outside could often be heard within the courtroom. Dorsey gambled his future career on the credibility of a part-time Negro janitor named Jim Conley as his chief witness against Frank. The stocky sweeper had a criminal record and reputation for hard drinking. The police had somehow waited three weeks before arresting him even though Conley had been seen attempting to wash his shirt shortly after the murder. Conley convinced the police that he was just an accessory-after-the-fact. He claimed that Leo Frank had paid him to transport the girl's dead body in the elevator to the basement from a room across from Frank's second-floor office. Conley explained that the reason his handwriting matched the two retrieved murder notes was because Frank dictated the murder notes to Conley to throw suspicion on the night watchman. All of this testimony was uncorroborated and inconsistent with Conley's earlier accounts. But Dorsey and the police erroneously considered Conley barely literate and incapable of inventing the last version of his story on his own initiative. They believed they had at last gotten to the bottom of the sordid tale. In any event, despite numerous false starts, Conley eventually told them exactly what they wanted to hear.

In preparation for trial, Conley was coached not only by Dorsey but by his own lawyer, William Smith, originally hired for Conley by *The Georgian*. But Smith refused to share confidential information with the newspaper and severed their relationship. Smith stayed on as Conley's lawyer because of his belief in Conley's innocence and concern the janitor might be scapegoated, a decision Smith would later regret. Even under Smith's tutelage, Conley changed his story, embellishing his final version with claims that Frank had secret trysts on a regular basis in his office on Saturdays with female employees, including oral sex. According to Conley, Frank had frequently trusted the alcoholic ex-convict to stand guard because his office otherwise afforded no real privacy. These tales outraged spectators, even though several factory employees on the premises most Saturdays testified that Conley was never seen standing guard for Frank and they considered the stories complete fabrications.

The defense, still confident of acquittal, presented two hundred witnesses on Frank's behalf, many attesting to Frank's good character. Given the poisonous accusations permeating the city, they may have felt they had no choice. But that tactic opened the door wide for Dorsey to assassinate Frank's character rather than stick just to the facts potentially implicating him in the murder. Dorsey presented a parade of former female employees who claimed Frank was a lecher. When he summed up, Dorsey simply told the jury to disregard all evidence of Frank's good character on the theory that Frank was a Dr. Jekyll and Mr. Hyde. Looking back after the trial, an editor of *The Atlanta Journal* observed that Dorsey appeared engaged in "a cynical bid for political notoriety and power."[23]

Frank's lawyers still thought they had a convincing defense. By painstakingly accounting for the superintendent's whereabouts on Saturday, April 26, they established that it would have been physically impossible for him to have completed detailed accounting chores, committed the murder, dictated the misleading notes, and helped transport the body as Conley asserted. Among the corroborating witnesses was a city trolley driver who testified that Mary Phagan had not yet arrived at the factory when Conley placed her there. Dorsey challenged key parts of the timeline, including browbeating the Franks' cook to sign an affidavit that her employer had cut short his lunch break—a statement she immediately repudiated.

Frank's wife Lucille was prohibited by law from taking the stand, but that did not prevent Dorsey from suggesting to the jury that Lucille's delay in visiting her husband a second time in jail evidenced her belief in his guilt. Dorsey also argued to the jury that having counsel at an early stage was further evidence of Frank's guilt. Frank's lawyers did not always raise timely objections, but even when they did, they were unable to convince the judge to declare a mistrial. The lawyers also failed to appreciate the significance of key physical evidence that would have completely disproved the prosecution's theory of where the murder took place. Worst of all, they failed to convince the trial judge to exclude the salacious charges of a history of sexual perversion. Once before the jury, these alleged outrages proved so powerful the jury never focused on gaping holes in the prosecutor's logic regarding the perpetration of the crime itself. Dorsey would then shamelessly indulge in Jew-bashing in his closing argument, even comparing Leo Frank to Judas Iscariot.

By the end of the trial, locals were so obviously out for blood against the Brooklyn-raised Jew that trial judge Leonard Roan convinced Leo Frank and his lawyers not to come to court when the verdict was read. The judge feared that if the jury acquitted Frank, the twenty courtroom deputies stationed outside could not prevent Frank and his counsel from being strung up on the spot. The judge and defense counsel had themselves been threatened with death if the "damned Jew" were not convicted; some of the jurors may have been as well.[24] Just before closing arguments, Gov. Slaton readied the National Guard for possible riots. After deliberating for four hours, the jury found Frank guilty as charged. As Dorsey exited the courthouse, men in the crowd hoisted their hero on their shoulders. The joyous multitude also applauded the judge and jurors for reaching the result they coveted and invited them all as guests of honor to a feast.

Racism played a significant but ironic role in the trial. The defense had stricken the only two blacks from the panel, leaving an all-white male jury. The ridicule heaped on a carefully groomed Conley by chief defense counsel Luther Rosser backfired. Carefully prepared by Dorsey and Smith, Conley remained unwavering on the details after sixteen hours of grueling cross-examination. Yet on any other subject he claimed lack of memory. He reeked of coaching. The jurors willingly accepted Dorsey's claim that Conley was simply too uneducated to have fabricated the detailed allegations for which he so convincingly confessed to being a paid accomplice. Conley instantly became a hero to the black community. No jury in America had to anyone's knowledge ever convicted a white man of murder solely on the word of a Negro. In some states, like California, such reliance was then prohibited by statute. But acceptance of Conley's charges constituted no sea change in Southern jurisprudence. As one spectator put it, "That wasn't a white man convicted by that Nigger's testimony. It was a [Yankee] Jew."[25] The implication was obvious. Had Frank been a local Protestant, he would have been acquitted in the extremely unlikely event that Dorsey prosecuted him based on Conley's word.

Judge Hoan was facing reelection the following year and could ill afford to have Tom Watson as a powerful political enemy. Some observers speculated that was the reason Hoan denied Frank a new trial even while taking the unusual step of expressing his personal doubt about Frank's guilt. The judge also privately opined that Dorsey's predecessor, known for his high standards, would never have brought the case to trial. When new evidence came to light implicating Conley, *The Atlanta Journal* tried its best to restore reason in the community. The *Journal* characterized the prior year as one that "unhinged" Atlanta to such a politically frenzied state that it suspended disbelief of the untrustworthy Conley to scapegoat Frank.[26]

The Journal's call for calm and a new trial brought Tom Watson out swinging. He considered the newspaper still the "personal organ" of his political enemy Senator Hoke Smith.[27] Watson joined the public debate with all the vituperation he had previously aimed at the Pope. Watson's editorials proclaimed Frank guilty because Jewish men, like blacks, all had a "ravenous appetite for the forbidden fruit." One could tell just by looking at "those bulging satyr eyes, the protruding fearfully sensual lips; and also the animal jaw."[28] Watson also attacked Adolph Ochs' *New York Times,* Hearst, and other Northern journalists for instigating a national uproar over Frank's trial. Ochs had abandoned all claim to objectivity in the campaign to save Frank's life. To Watson, that was all the more reason for Georgians to dig in their heels against all Yankee interference. Watson obtained more ammunition when Frank's supporters hired the "Sherlock Holmes of America," private detective William Burns, who promised to prove Frank innocent by exposing the true murderer. Burns' tactics had always been questionable, especially when his ego was on the line. His men were caught paying for false affidavits supporting Frank. The uproar over the compromised private investigation only fueled resentment of the Jews whose money kept the case alive. Burns lost his state license; the "Great Detective" was himself driven out of Georgia, barely escaping from incensed locals.

Frank's attorneys sought both state and federal review of the fairness of his trial all the way to the United States Supreme Court. They designated one hundred and three points of error, including affidavits that two jurors had expressed strong desire to hang Frank before they were chosen for the panel. Dorsey countered with sworn statements from eleven of the jurors that they had relied solely on the evidence presented. In February of 1915, two weeks before the Supreme Court heard oral argument, D. W. Griffiths premiered his three-hour-and-ten-minute epic film, *The Clansman,* soon to be renamed *Birth of a Nation.* The ambitious movie portrayed Ku Klux Klan lynch mobs as bands of heroes who reunited

America by putting an end to the horrors of the corrupt Reconstruction Era. The revisionist epic ends with Northern and Southern veterans of the Civil War recognizing their common bond of white supremacy under a beaming image of Christ, sending a powerful anti-Semitic message.

The celebrated author of *The Clansman*, Thomas Dixon, had been a college friend of President Woodrow Wilson, who himself was raised in Georgia. The President hosted a special showing of the controversial movie in the White House. It featured a quote from his own *History of the American People*, praising the Klan for its historic role in preserving the Southern homeland. A day after the White House showing, the novelist reportedly arranged another special viewing for the Supreme Court at the request of Chief Justice Edward D. White, a former Confederate soldier from Louisiana. White was raised on a plantation and was a veteran of the original Knights of the Ku Klux Klan. (In 1909, while still an associate justice, he had voted in the minority to absolve Sheriff Shipp of any wrongdoing in Ed Johnson's lynching.)

The film generated the largest attendance of any for a generation, aided no doubt by Dixon's claim that it was "federally endorsed."[29] In many cities the revisionist epic precipitated race riots. The anti-Semitism of Griffiths' movie could only have exacerbated the uphill battle that Frank's lawyers already faced in getting the Supreme Court to take a hard look at his politically charged conviction. Not surprisingly, in April of 1915, less than two months after oral argument, the Supreme Court rejected Frank's claim that he was denied his rights to a fair trial under the Fourteenth Amendment. Oliver Wendell Holmes wrote a scathing dissent, joined by Justice Charles Evans Hughes, that "mob law does not become due process of law by securing the assent of a terrorized jury."[30]

The three-man Georgia Prison Commission was the next tribunal standing between Leo Frank and the gallows. The record compiled by Frank's counsel now included affidavits from key prosecution witnesses that their testimony had been manufactured at the insistence of the police. Dorsey countered with new affidavits retracting these confessions, hopelessly muddling the case against Frank. Newly developed evidence further implicated Conley, including convincing signs that Phagan was killed downstairs. In a startling turnabout, Conley's own lawyer William

Smith went public with a detailed analysis of the murder notes, now convinced that Conley had authored the notes himself after he committed the murder and sought to blame it on another black janitor. When Smith first showed the evidence to Dorsey, Dorsey said it was too late.

After the trial, Leo Frank's cause had been taken up by advertising pioneer Albert Lasker, who orchestrated a powerful national campaign on Frank's behalf: "The Truth Is On The March." Nearly two million people eventually signed petitions on Frank's behalf. Unprecedented requests for commutation came from governors and legislatures of other states and prominent citizens throughout the country. Even trial judge Hoan joined in the writing campaign to commute Frank's sentence, but he died of cancer before he could testify before the prison commission, which refused to recommend clemency by a two-to-one vote.

One option still remained. Frank's fate was placed in the hands of popular outgoing Gov. Jack Slaton, who wanted to end his career with a stint in the Senate. Tom Watson made it clear to Slaton that Slaton would only get the nod for that coveted seat if Slaton did not interfere with Frank's execution. Slaton was a law partner of Luther Rosser and thus had a conflict of interest, which the governor could have invoked to avoid making the decision and preserve his own political career. Yet Slaton harbored serious doubts about Frank's guilt and the frenzied atmosphere in which he had been tried. At the urging of Lucille Frank and William Randolph Hearst, among others, the governor agreed to review the record. He received mountains of mail, divided between requests for clemency and letters urging him to leave the jury verdict alone. Some pointedly voiced threats that if he did not let Frank hang he would face death himself.

Slaton was particularly intrigued by evidence that Conley had admitted to police that he defecated earlier the day of the murder on the factory's basement floor under the elevator shaft. Yet Conley insisted that, later that day, at Frank's request, Conley transported Phagan's dead body down from the second floor using the elevator. An investigative reporter pointed out after the trial that the elevator had no mechanism for stopping at the bottom except by coming to a complete rest on the basement floor. If so, it would have had to land squarely on the excrement. Police reports showed that the excrement remained untouched until they used the elevator the day after the murder. When Slaton inquired about this point at the commutation hearing, Hugh Dorsey dismissed the argument, insisting that the elevator was capable of stopping a few inches above the floor. Gov. Slaton visited the crime scene to check for himself. Dorsey had misrepresented how the elevator worked. Slaton became convinced that Frank was the victim of a miscarriage of justice.

On June 20, 1915, Gov. Slaton had Leo Frank secretly transferred to a state prison farm before the governor announced his decision, which Slaton knew could both endanger Frank's life and possibly his own. Then Slaton issued a nearly thirty-page analysis of the case, upholding the conviction but exercising gubernatorial power to commute Frank's sentence to life imprisonment. Slaton told friends at the time that he believed Frank merited a full pardon, but it would be better to wait until the situation cooled off.[31] Mobs had to be kept by state troops from storming the governor's home. Less than a week later, Slaton would face cries of "lynch him" as the outgoing governor attended his successor's inauguration.[32] Slaton and his wife quickly fled the state for a three-month vacation, hoping that would be a sufficient cooling off period.

Incensed at the commutation, Tom Watson immediately called for Frank's lynching. He told his readers point blank that clemency was bought with Jew money—one law for the rich and one for the poor: "Let no man reproach the South with Lynch law . . . let him say whether Lynch law *is not better than no law at all.* What Rosser and Slaton have together done nullifies the Code, abolishes the courts and plunges us into administrative anarchy. Shall my soul not be avenged on such a nation as this? A WONDERFUL AND HORRIBLE THING IS COMMITTED IN THE LAND."[33] Of course the power of commutation Watson now ridiculed as lawless anarchy was the very act of clemency that Watson himself had asked Gov. Hoke Smith to exercise in 1907 to save Arthur Glover. With his enemy Hoke Smith allied with Slaton and Frank's supporters, Watson could now get two for one: eye for an eye revenge for Glover's death as well as Mary Phagan's—all wrapped in the Confederate battle flag.

In the next month, former Gov. Joseph Brown—still smarting from a lost bid to unseat Hoke Smith from the Senate in 1914—acted as Watson's liaison in organizing twenty-five prominent Georgians into a lynch mob. The vigilantes included two former state supreme court justices, a sitting judge, the son of a state senator, and the county prosecutor, among other prominent citizens. They called themselves the "Knights of Mary Phagan." They figured that, together with Watson, they had the political clout to engineer immunity from prosecution if they did Watson's bidding to kidnap Frank from the prison farm and hang him. Historian Steve Oney characterized the extensive battle plans as essentially "a rearguard action in the Civil War"—which to the participants it clearly was.[34]

Just about any politician in the overwhelmingly Protestant state who identified himself as a diehard son of the Old South could be trusted to support this reaffirmation of enmity for Yankees in general and Jews in particular. By now, thanks largely to Watson's relentless attacks on Frank's character, an estimated seventy-five percent of Georgians saw Frank as a monster who should die for Phagan's murder. Key members of the legislature cooperated in arranging a pretext for members of the lynch mob to visit the prison on an inspection tour. It gave them ample opportunity to scout out the premises. Given the lack of resistance they would later face, they likely informed the warden they were planning to come back for Frank and expected only token opposition.

Before the lynch mob returned, Frank had his throat slit by another inmate and almost died. Prompt medical care saved him. Frank had begun to recover by the evening of August 17, 1915, when the lynch mob carried out their mission. They cut the telephone lines and entered the prison farm without firing a shot. They knew just where to find Frank in a room near the warden's office. He was clad only in a night shirt. They forced him into one of their cars and transported him to a preselected location in Mary Phagan's hometown. The caravan arrived in Marietta early in the morning, by which time Frank's kidnapping was known all over the state. The self-appointed executioners were so proud of their role in defending Southern womanhood that none even bothered to wear masks. Before they strung him up, Frank impressed some of the vigilantes with his stoicism. His last request was that his lynchers deliver to his wife a letter and his wedding ring, telling them, "I think more of my wife and my mother than I do of my own life."[35] Then, the mob hanged him from a tree, slowly asphyxiating Frank with such horrible death throes that the healing knife wound on his throat reopened and bled down his shirt. He would be the only Jew in history ever recorded being lynched in the United States. Frank's body was left twisting for a growing crowd of onlookers to gawk at his partly exposed genitals and photograph their quarry for mementoes. That morning, nearly three thousand men, women, and children gathered from around Marietta and from Atlanta excited into a frenzy by what they had accomplished—in their view, true justice for Mary Phagan in killing the murderous, perverted Yankee Jew whom the governor had wrongly spared. Some of the lynchers gave interviews to local reporters as townsmen tore off pieces of Frank's clothing for souvenirs.

One of the key planners, Judge Newt Morris, retained some sense of propriety. He convinced the revelers to let Frank's body be returned to the undertaker for burial, but only after some of the men cut Frank's body down and dragged it on the ground. One rabid attacker, Robert E. Lee Howell, repeatedly stomped on Frank's face with his boot heels. The "Knights of Mary Phagan" had deliberately left Howell out of the planning stage for fear his lack of self-control might spoil their plot.

The lynching stunned the national media and shocked citizens throughout the land. Historian Steve Oney writes that "former President William Howard Taft might well have been speaking for the country as a whole when . . . he told reporters: 'The lynching of Leo Frank was a damnable outrage. There was no excuse, no mitigating circumstances to justify the action of the Georgia mob. An action like that makes a decent man sick.'"[36] Unabashed, Watson heaped praise on the lynching in *The Jeffersonian.* He blamed the nation's Jews for banding together in Frank's defense. It was the fault of people like Adolph Ochs that the lynching took place—much as Tennessee politicians blamed the United States Supreme Court for Ed Johnson's murder. The local Georgia paper took a similar tack, brashly lauding the hanging as the act of law-abiding citizens. The subsequent whitewash was easy to arrange. A conspiracy of silence enveloped the town of Marietta. Seven members of the lynch mob were appointed to the grand jury that, for appearances' sake, had to convene to investigate the lawless act. It held a perfunctory meeting in which witnesses said they could not identify a single member of the lynch mob. The grand jury then recorded the deed as having been perpetrated by persons unknown. No criminal proceedings were ever undertaken. Strangers coming to investigate from out of state were escorted out of town or met with stony silence. Federal charges against Watson for instigating the lynching were dropped following intense opposition from Georgia's Congressmen.

Not surprisingly, the anti-Semitism aroused in Atlanta and its environs resulted in extensive vandalism of Jewish stores. The Reform Jewish community retreated into scared silence, attempting to become as invisible as possible, leaving the Orthodox Jews as handier targets. This frightening display of lawless hatred prompted half the Jewish population of Georgia to flee the state. Of course, to Georgia blacks the stunned national reaction to Frank's kidnapping and death only underscored how little their own lives were valued. No similar outrage would have resulted if the case had ended abruptly at the outset with the lynching of innocent night watchman Newt Lee. He would have been just another sad casualty among hundreds of Negroes similarly dispatched in the South in the prior decade.

Among themselves, the perpetrators remained fiercely proud. Postcards of the illegal hanging would be sold in Marietta for the next two years.[37] After executing Leo Frank, the Knights of Mary Phagan regrouped as members of a renewed Ku Klux Klan that would grow to five million nationwide in the next decade, using terror and lynching as signature tools for implementing its white racist agenda. With the local Klan's enthusiastic support, and that of its instigator Tom Watson, prosecutor Hugh Dorsey twice won election as Georgia's governor. The voters rewarded Tom Watson himself with a seat in the United States Senate taken from his old nemesis Hoke Smith. As Prof. Alan Dershowitz notes with grim irony, "By any amoral criteria, the lynching of Leo Frank was a great success for those who incited it and for those who actually participated in it."[38]

Frightened into silence, American Jews discouraged reference to the case for many years. Yet the Frank lynching generated strong interest among writers and film makers in the '20s and '30s. It also spawned two widely read historical accounts in the '60s. An inmate in a federal penitentiary later told his attorney that he had been working in the pencil factory basement on April 26, 1913, and saw Conley grappling with a girl. Afterward, Conley gave him the girl's mesh purse for a gambling debt. Attorney William Smith had planned to write a book about the trial, but never completed it. By the time Smith lay on his death bed from Lou Gehrig's Disease in February of 1949, the remorseful lawyer had lost the use of his voice. He scratched out on a hospital pad a message to his family that had been tearing at him for decades: "IN ARTICLES OF DEATH, I BELIEVE IN THE INNOCENCE AND GOOD CHARACTER OF LEO M. FRANK. W. M. Smith."[39]

Nearly four decades later, a former office boy at the pencil factory, Alonzo Mann, came forward. Then in his eighties, Mann revealed that, as a thirteen-year-old, he had seen Conley carrying the limp body of Mary Phagan on the factory's main floor—contrary to Conley's story. At Frank's trial, Mann had kept silent about what he witnessed because he and his mother both feared Conley would kill him, too. Now Mann feared going to his grave with that knowledge on his conscience. This new evidence greatly helped the Anti-Defamation League and local volunteer attorneys obtain Frank's posthumous pardon in 1986. The pardon did not address Frank's guilt or innocence; the official records had long since disappeared and the Georgia Board of Pardons felt it could no longer review the fairness of the trial. Instead, it focused on the failure of the state government to safeguard Frank's life after his conviction, as well as the injustice of its willful failure to identify Frank's lynchers publicly or hold them in any way accountable.

Revived interest in the last twenty years of the century inspired a television docudrama, new chronicles, novels, and movies, including David Mamet's *The Old Religion* and the Broadway musical *Parade.* In 2003, journalist Steve Oney recounted the sorry details in *And the Dead Shall Rise: The Murder of Mary Phagan and the Lynching of Leo Frank,* winning the 2004 National Jewish Book Award for history. In 2008, the Jewish American Society for Historical Preservation and the Georgia Historical Society jointly engineered the placement of an official state marker near the site of the recently felled tree where Frank had been lynched. It explains briefly to all comers Frank's controversial trial for the murder of Mary

Phagan, the anti-Semitism that fueled it, his lynching, and the posthumous pardon. The formal dedication ceremony included state officials and a local rabbi from Cobb County's revitalized Jewish community as well as several current county officials, whose predecessors were now publicly acknowledged to have been complicit in the lynching.

* * * * *

The virulent anti-Semitism that surrounded the Frank trial drew comparisons at the time to the infamous French Dreyfus Affair, though it ended far differently. Jewish military officer Alfred Dreyfus, framed for treason in 1894 and exiled to the Devil's Island penal colony, had finally won exoneration in 1906 after polarizing press battles between French national security advocates and defenders of individual rights. Another high profile American case would soon also be compared to the Dreyfus Affair—a robbery murder committed in 1919 in the small town of South Braintree, Massachusetts. The trial of Nicola Sacco and Bartolomeo Vanzetti became more deeply embedded in the American psyche as a miscarriage of justice than probably any other case in the country's history.

7. ANARCHIST SCARE: The Trial of Sacco and Vanzetti

The time was on for two men
To march beyond blood into dust,
A time that comes to all men,
Some with a few loved ones at a bedside,
Some alone in the wilderness or the wide sea,
Some before a vast audience of all mankind.

CARL SANDBURG, EXCERPT FROM "LEGAL MIDNIGHT HOUR"

During World War I, Galleanists rivaled Big Bill Haywood and the IWW for designation as the country's most dangerous internal threat. Some radicals had ties to both militant groups. Of 25 million immigrants who had made the United States their new home between 1860 and 1920 many remained resident aliens. Others derisively called hyphenated-Americans either held dual citizenship or were naturalized citizens with strong ties to their native land and culture. Luigi Galleani was a resident alien. The Italian-born anarchist was already infamous in 1902 when he arrived in the United States at age forty-one. Galleani then made a beeline for the same community of Italian exiles in Paterson, New Jersey, from which Italian King Umberto's assassin, Gaetano Bresci, had emerged two years before. A government mole later infiltrated the radical cell and learned that several other world leaders were targeted by the Paterson group with would-be assassins.

Accused of inciting violence, Galleani soon fled to Canada and then resettled first in Vermont, among poor Italian marble cutters, and then in a similar immigrant community in Lowell, Massachusetts. From his base in these counterculture ghettos, Galleani traveled a lecture circuit to promote his revolutionary ideas of free love, atheism, and the overthrow of capitalism. His speeches met with great enthusiasm from Italian émigrés suffering from social ostracism and oppressive working conditions. Galleani published a widely read newsletter—*Cronaca Sovversiva* (Subversive Chronicle)—that advocated his revolutionary agenda. For an additional 25 cents, Galleani offered thousands of subscribers a revised version of the same how-to bomb manual that had circulated in Chicago shortly before the 1886 deadly dynamiting in Haymarket Square. Only now German anarchist Johann Most's "The Science of Revolutionary Warfare" went by the innocent title *La Salute è in voi* (Health Is in You).

Starting in 1914, Galleani's followers—like the Weathermen more than half a century later—claimed credit for planting bombs in a number of American cities. In 1915, police dramatically announced they had foiled a plot to blow up New York's St. Patrick's Cathedral by infiltrating another cell of Italian anarchists, one of whom reportedly had in his home a copy of Galleani's manual. In that case, the undercover agent had helped assemble the bomb and plan the audacious attack that sent his accomplices to prison. In 1916, an Italian chef in Chicago, who counted himself among the Galleanists, tried to poison with arsenic an entire banquet room gathered to honor Chicago's newly-appointed Archbishop. Other Galleanists exploded a bomb in a Boston police station; still more were suspected of planting a time bomb in San Francisco on July 22, 1916, at a parade in honor of Preparedness Day to build support for America's entrance into World War I. The bomb killed ten people and wounded forty more—the worst incident of violence San Francisco had ever seen. Prosecutors pinned it on labor leader Tom Mooney in a trial that drew widespread international criticism; Mooney won an eventual pardon based on evidence he had been framed.

In his much-quoted "Unification Speech," given on July 4, 1917—three months after Congress declared war on Germany—former President Teddy Roosevelt emphatically rejected hyphenated-Americans and conscientious objectors as unpatriotic: "There can be no 50-50 Americanism in this country. There is room here for only 100 percent Americanism, only for those who are Americans and nothing else."[1] That same year many Galleanists fled to Mexico to evade the draft and await European revolution. The group included resident aliens Ferdinando Nicola Sacco and Bartolomeo Vanzetti, who had barely known each other previously. When no widespread uprisings occurred, most of them returned to the United States. Bombings resumed in Milwaukee, Wisconsin, New York City, San Francisco, Washington, D.C., and Boston, but no criminal prosecutions resulted. The public demanded action and Congress echoed their outrage. In 1918, government agents forcibly shut down *Cronaca Sovversiva* and confiscated its mailing list. Congress passed the Anarchist Exclusion Act and Galleanists responded with anonymous threats to annihilate the ruling class "in blood and fire."[2] A series of new bomb attacks followed, including one in February 1919 that exploded too soon and killed four bombers trying to destroy a textile mill in Franklin, Massachusetts.

In late April of 1919, thirty neatly packaged bombs were addressed to political leaders, judges, and prominent businessmen across the nation. The intent was to set off a gruesome fireworks display to celebrate the international workers' holiday of May Day, the anniversary of the original deadline set for achieving the eight-hour work day. Lacking sufficient postage, most of the packages were discovered by mailmen before the bombs detonated. Some injuries resulted, but no deaths. In early June, eight more bombs exploded in the homes of political officials in seven cities, causing three deaths, including one anarchist with close ties to Galleani. At several sites investigators found a flyer signed "The Anarchist Fighters" threatening bloody class war. The bold June 1919 attack partially destroyed Attorney General Palmer's home in Washington, D.C. Palmer immediately embarked on a strategy of prevention that ignored past concerns for civil liberties. His new methods included warrantless wiretaps on thousands of presumed radicals, many of whose names surfaced only because they subscribed to anti-establishment periodicals. His protégé, J. Edgar Hoover, headed a new "Radical Division" where Hoover eagerly collected names of suspected subversives.

Palmer filled his fellow countrymen with panic that there were 60,000 terrorists in their midst poised "to bring the Russian revolution to America."[3] Working with the Immigration Department on "Palmer

Raids," the Justice Department aggressively invoked the new Anarchist Act to arrest and deport aliens, including Galleani and eight followers. Another, a printer named Andrea Salsedo, died in Manhattan while under interrogation for his connection to the publication of the anarchist threats. Officially, Salsedo's death was recorded as suicide for a fall from the high-rise building. Galleanists assumed he was pushed. In 1921, a congressional committee severely criticized Palmer's aggressive post-war strategy for exceeding his authority and trampling on basic constitutional guarantees. That same year, Congress repealed the war-time Sedition Act; labor leader Bill Haywood jumped bail on appeal of his Espionage Act conviction and fled to Russia; and a year-old robbery-murder of a payroll master and guard for a shoe company on the outskirts of Boston began to attract international attention.

The first break in solving the audacious daytime crime in South Braintree had come in early May of 1920, when a garage owner alerted police that four Italian-American men came to claim from storage the presumed get-away car for both that heist and an earlier attempted robbery in nearby Bridgewater. The heavily armed quartet were all members of *Il Gruppo Autonomo*—militant Boston anarchists with Mafia connections, also affiliated with the national Galleanist movement. Soon after their arrests, a new wave of bombings occurred, including the devastating Wall Street bombing in September 1920 that killed nearly forty people and injured hundreds more. Hand-stamped fliers found near the debris in lower Manhattan claimed they were authored by "American Anarchist fighters" and demanded, "Free the political prisoners or it will be sure death for all of you."[4]

Headlines then speculated that the Wall Street bombing was the work of Galleani's followers, renewing public fear that the same anarchists were responsible for the 1919 explosions. Yet that seemed too obvious a solution to state and federal officials who suspected the notes were intentionally misleading. J. P. Morgan's war profiteering had engendered so much Leftist outrage that the unsolved Wall Street crime had authorities also pointing the finger at labor leaders, Socialists, and Bolsheviks on the assumption the historic attack on Wall Street could have been a copycat's handiwork. Even the reference to political prisoners did not narrow the field; there were so many in 1920, no dissident group could be ruled out.

One of the four members of *Il Gruppo Autonomo* arrested in May of 1920 trying to collect the suspected get-away car from a local garage was thirty-two-year-old Bartolomeo Vanzetti. An itinerant bachelor with closely cropped, receding brown hair and a shaggy moustache, Vanzetti was a well-read intellectual who liked working outdoors with his hands. Since he arrived in America from Northern Italy in 1908, the wiry dreamer had handled various unskilled jobs while he committed himself increasingly to revolution. Vanzetti was friends with the recently deceased anarchist Salsedo. For the previous two years, Vanzetti had peddled fish in the Italian community around Plymouth, Massachusetts, as well as distributing anarchist literature.

Vanzetti first faced charges arising out of the aborted Christmas Eve robbery attempt in Bridgewater. *Il Gruppo Autonomo* anticipated strong local bias against Vanzetti for his extreme political views and hired a prominent Massachusetts politician and trial lawyer, James Vahey, to represent the Italian fish monger. Twenty-nine-year-old Ferdinando Nicola Sacco was one of the other arrestees, but the skilled shoe craftsman had produced a time card that convinced the prosecutor not to charge the clean-shaven family man with the Bridgewater attempted robbery. One of the other two men originally arrested also escaped prosecution by producing a time card; the fourth fled before he could be tried.

Judge Webster Thayer eagerly presided over Vanzetti's trial, proud of the many criminal cases he had already handled involving anarchist defendants. Vahey located eleven Italian alibi witnesses who swore that Vanzetti sold them eels in Plymouth on Christmas Eve when the Bridgewater holdup was in process, while prosecutor Frederick Katzmann found five Bridgewater witnesses who instead placed Vanzetti at the crime scene. By mutual agreement, the two lawyers kept Vanzetti's anarchist views out of the trial. Vahey warned his client that if he took the stand, he would open himself up to cross-examination that might alienate the jury. Vanzetti chose not to testify and was convicted after Katzmann cast doubt on the alibi witnesses' memory of when they made their purchases. When Vahey later joined the prosecutor's law firm, Vanzetti became livid with mistrust of his former lawyer and blamed Vahey for his imprisonment. The media paid scant attention to the case.

Meanwhile, police experts tested casings and shells of bullets from the South Braintree crime scene and the victims' bodies and compared them with the guns and bullets the suspects carried when arrested. The resulting evidence was inconclusive, but appeared to implicate Sacco's pistol as a murder weapon. Police also found a hat at the scene that they believed belonged to Sacco. The heavily guarded pair were then put on trial together in the wealthy Boston suburb of Dedham, Massachusetts, for the twin murders. Judge Thayer deliberately sought this assignment as well. The irascible jurist derided Sacco and Vanzetti to members of his club and the press as "Bolsheviki" and vowed he would "get those guys hanged."[5] This time veteran IWW lawyer Fred Moore came East to serve as Sacco's counsel. The relentless California labor champion had helped defend Big Bill Haywood in 1917. Moore had far too much baggage to benefit his new client. A Lothario and habitual cocaine user, he dressed flamboyantly and did not seem to care that he alienated both the judge and jury. Moore associated as local counsel a competent but excitable Irish-American attorney, Republican Jeremiah McAnarney, to represent Vanzetti.

Worry about bomb threats prompted reinforcements to the Dedham courtroom. It was fitted with sliding steel doors and cast-iron shutters painted to look like wood. Police patrolled the streets around the building on motorcycle and horseback. The immigrant anarchists drew no support from mainstream labor unions, and the case did not attract huge crowds. Those who did attend the trial each day were searched. An unusually large panel of five hundred potential jurors—more than five times that normally assembled—yielded only seven men deemed qualified to serve. Many had read about the sensational crime and already considered them guilty; others opposed the death penalty. After deputies scoured the county for another hundred and fifty worthy additional prospects—none of whom had Italian surnames—the judge finally seated five more men.

District Attorney Katzmann, again the chief prosecutor, focused on vilifying the two men as much for their lack of patriotism in avoiding war service as for their alleged role in the Braintree robbery. Though careful to minimize overtly biased statements in court, Judge Thayer likewise made his distaste for disloyal "arnuchists" like the defendants and their "long-haired" counsel so manifest that several prominent reporters covering the case later signed affidavits attesting to his prejudice.[6] Moore, in turn, told the press that an Italian had as little chance of receiving a fair trial in Boston as a Negro did in the South, an assessment with which Pulitzer Prize–winning columnist George Will would later heartily agree. Italians were at the time of the trial the most despised (and least assimilated) ethnic European group of immigrants in the Brahmin-controlled state.

The very first day of the trial came on the heels of Decoration Day (now Memorial Day) and started off on a bad footing. The prosecutor zeroed in on Sacco and Vanzetti's radicalism and avoidance of draft registration. He invited the jury's hatred of their politics to justify finding them both guilty of the robbery-murder. Moore repeatedly jumped up to object; the judge glared fiercely at him and overruled every objection. Attorney William Thompson—who had been a spectator—later described Thayer's belligerent attitude toward Moore as lead defense counsel: "It wasn't what [Judge Thayer] said, it was his manner of saying it. It looked perfectly straight on the record; he was too clever to do otherwise. I sat there for a while and I told John McAnarney, 'Your goose is cooked. You will never in this world get these two men acquitted. The judge is going to convict these two men . . . and keep his records straight . . . you have no chance."[7] (Expert studies have long since concluded that nonverbal cues from tone of voice and body language account for at least sixty percent of human communication.)[8]

The trial consumed thirty-five court days, during which the two reviled defendants were placed in a cage in the middle of the courtroom. Over forty witnesses had seen the robbery, but only a handful identified either of the two men as participants and only after having viewed them in prison without a lineup—a practice that has since been disallowed. At trial, both defendants testified in broken English with help from interpreters. They adamantly defended their radical politics, but denied any involvement in the robbery. On later review of the record, Harvard Professor (and future Supreme Court Justice) Felix Frankfurter noted how often the pair appeared to misunderstand questions put to them. Sacco claimed to have been in Boston on personal business obtaining a passport, and Vanzetti peddling fish, both of which alibis were supported by many defense witnesses, who disputed the prosecutor's eyewitnesses. Key eyewitnesses for the prosecutor grew far more positive at the time of trial than they had been before. Katzmann again claimed defense witnesses were wrong about their dates and pointed out that both men had lied about their activities when first arrested. Sacco and Vanzetti explained that they lied to protect themselves from deportation or persecution, as befell many colleagues who distributed anarchist literature.

The nearly seven-week trial produced conflicting testimony from nearly a hundred and sixty witnesses. In prosecutor Katzmann's zeal to see both men convicted, Katzmann claimed that the gun Vanzetti had in his possession when arrested had been lifted from the felled payroll guard. Historians Robert Grant and Joseph Katz assert that Katzmann had to know at the time that the assertion was false—the weapon was a different caliber than the guard carried.[9] Prof. Frankfurter later noted the judge's strong bias in skirting over the massive testimonial conflict when Judge Thayer summed up the evidence. Judge Thayer also overstated the state expert's opinion regarding Sacco's gun as the possible murder weapon and invited the jurors to dwell on the two men's behavior following arrest to assess whether it demonstrated "consciousness of guilt."[10] Most unprofessionally, Judge Thayer stressed loyalty as a virtue, which reinforced the prosecutor's focus on the defendants' lack of war service and had no legitimate bearing on their guilt or innocence of the charged crime. The judge then asked the jury members to do their civic duty as "soldiers" in reaching a verdict. The jury took less than a day to find the two anarchists guilty as charged. Judge Thayer was soon heard to brag, "Did you see what I did with those anarchistic bastards the other day?"[11]

Meanwhile, Moore and McAnarney worked day and night trying to publicize the case as the railroading of two innocent men based on ethnic bias and postwar anti-immigrant hysteria. The appeal resonated with prominent civil libertarians who had participated in a scathing 1920 report that condemned Palmer's 1919 raids. Additional reason for concern came to light in December of 1921 when newly appointed FBI Chief William Burns, aka "The Great Detective," triumphantly announced that the Wall Street bombing formerly attributed by the press to Italian anarchists had been planned and executed by Russian and Polish Bolsheviks. Burns was wrong. Unlike militant anarchists, Communist

Party officials shunned isolated acts of terrorism like the Wall Street bombing, which Lenin considered counterproductive to achieving true revolutionary conditions. Soon, much to Burns' embarrassment, newspapers discovered that the confessed co-conspirator was a former paid FBI informer. The tale he concocted was so unworthy of belief that Burns became a laughing stock. The Wall Street investigation was back at a standstill and discredited even further by a confession from another former paid informer, Albert Bailin, that Burns had directed him on a campaign of falsifying evidence to implicate Communists and labor leaders like Haywood in the Wall Street bombing. Bailin was himself caught threatening to bomb the Woolworth building in New York—using a note like the one found in a mailbox near the Wall Street bombing. He told police that Burns ordered the bogus bomb threat when he was still a private detective to convince bankers to increase funding for the Wall Street bombing investigation.

The entire fiasco underscored claims that Italian anarchists like Sacco and Vanzetti were being unfairly persecuted due to political scare tactics and ethnic prejudice. After Sacco and Vanzetti's conviction and death sentence, Moore gained traction in instigating international protests against the perceived injustice perpetrated by the world's new superpower. Moore's claim was bolstered by Palmer Raid opponent Louis Post, former acting Secretary of Labor, who wrote a 1923 memoir characterizing the American general public in 1920 as suffering from the same fear-driven "delirium" that had precipitated the 1886 Haymarket convictions—all out of proportion to any real threat to the country that the alleged revolutionaries posed.[12] Post also pointed to the huge state, federal, and private-banking resources that had been expended to no avail in bungled efforts to pin the Wall Street bombing on various radicals. He joined speculation that the Wall Street bombing might have been an isolated act (like that of President McKinley's assassin) or an industrial accident that had been recharacterized as a sinister plot solely to justify repressive governmental policies.

Media coverage of the Sacco and Vanzetti case in the United States remained spotty and protests elsewhere died down as the two Italian anarchists began to pursue fruitless motions for reconsideration and appeals. In 1924, the Justice Department made more embarrassing headlines by accusing a sitting Montana Senator of being a Communist in retaliation for his request that Congress investigate its recent abuses of power. When it came to light that the FBI had illegally searched Senator Burton Wheeler's office and put a tail on him, President Coolidge forced the resignation of both scandal-plagued Attorney General Daugherty and Bureau of Investigations Chief Burns.

Burns' ouster elevated his zealous assistant J. Edgar Hoover to head that office, though Hoover was not yet thirty. In securing the post, Hoover falsely assured the new reform-minded attorney general that he had played only an "unwilling part" in the "misguided raids and botched investigations."[12] The idea of rounding up thousands of immigrant Communist Party members and anarchists for deportation in 1919 had, in fact, been Hoover's own brainchild. Promising to avoid intrusion on civil liberties, Hoover agreed to stop the agency from gathering its own intelligence on radicals, but surreptitiously kept collecting information from other sources. He also kept alert for opportunities to obtain express authorization to "enable the federal authorities to deal vigorously with the ultra-radical elements."[13] Hoover would ultimately convince President Franklin Roosevelt to restore that power to the Bureau before America joined World War II. When Congress passed the peacetime Smith Loyalty Act, Hoover exulted in the opportunity to revive his official index file of suspected subversives.[14] Perceived radical threats to the government would remain Hoover's preoccupation throughout his long career.

Moore had never gotten along well with Sacco. The same year that Hoover assumed office as FBI Chief, Sacco fired Moore and replaced him with McAnarney and highly regarded Massachusetts lawyer William Thompson. Thompson proceeded to collect additional evidence in an effort to win a new trial for the two vilified radicals. Unfortunately, under Massachusetts law, these motions were all brought before Judge Thayer. French intellectuals analogized the prosecution to their own country's notorious Dreyfus Affair. Influential writers led by Nobel Prize–winner Anatole France fanned anti-American sentiment by citing the case as proof of the frightening "soullessness" of the new world superpower, which they decried as "mechanical, amoral, conformist and hypermaterialistic" with no regard for fundamental fairness or individual freedom of expression.[15] British author H. G. Wells, one of the most prominent international journalists to cover the Sacco and Vanzetti case, coined the term "Thayerism" to describe the "mental and moral obtuseness" he believed was all too prevalent in the United States.[16] Vanzetti aided his own cause with poignant letters from prison protesting persecution for his political beliefs. Meanwhile, Europeans increasingly demonstrated hostility toward American tourists amid anxiety about the consequences of the country's world dominance.

Across the political spectrum, Europeans were appalled at the extraordinary length of time the two men remained on death row pursuing apparently useless appeals. The post-trial delays allowed Communists the opportunity to exploit the travails of the two anarchists as a propaganda tool, collecting hundreds of thousands of dollars ostensibly for the cost of Sacco and Vanzetti's legal fees, much of which was used for other purposes. At the same time, Mussolini's new fascist government permitted only muted pleas for clemency to emerge from the Italian press. The new dictator did not want to unduly antagonize the United States by giving full vent to his compatriates' outrage.[17] (Neither Mussolini nor Joseph Stalin would have had any compunction about executing two more dissidents as they cemented their own control).

In 1925, Sacco and Vanzetti had begun receiving support from the newly formed International Labor Defense Committee ("ILD"). Comprised of Communist Party members, it included among its ranks William Patterson, a black attorney in his mid-thirties from Northern California. Its mission was to represent Communists and radical union members targeted for their politics. Wider support for the pair came after a belated confession in 1926 from a jailed member of a Rhode Island crime syndicate known as the Morelli gang, claiming, improbably, that the Morelli gang had actually perpetrated the South Braintree holdup. In early 1927, Frankfurter published a blistering attack on Judge Thayer's conduct of the trial and the doubtful evidence used to convict Sacco and Vanzetti. Ultimately, hundreds of thousands of people signed requests for clemency, possibly influenced by growing awareness of the unprecedented concentration of wealth among the top one percent of Americans, creating greater sympathy in the United States for the anarchists' political views at the same time that anarchism was on the wane.

Under intense pressure both from overseas and from domestic critics, Gov. Fuller took the unusual step of appointing a three-man commission headed by Harvard's President A. Lawrence Lowell to review the record of the two men's conviction and advise him of their opinion. The move was received with great relief by critics as a sign that the miscarriage of justice would soon be remedied. Trusting in Lowell's integrity, American intellectuals who considered the case a deplorable aberration pinned their hopes on his scholarly review of the record. Lowell had previously defended the freedom of speech of Harvard professors espousing unpopular views, including Jewish scholar Felix Frankfurter, whose published criticism of the Sacco and Vanzetti case had cost the venerable university over a million dollars in donations. But Lowell was also a prominent member of the Boston-based Immigration Restriction League, formed three decades earlier to curtail the influx of undesirable immigrants whom League members accused of debasing American society. In keeping with those views, Lowell enforced strict quotas on Jews admitted to Harvard. The seventy-one-year-old Brahmin was predisposed to reject claims of unfairness by two Italian working-class radicals. Lowell was also not blinded to the far more devastating economic impact on his beloved Harvard that could be expected if he vindicated a pair of admitted anarchists. Lowell steeled himself against threats of international repercussions against Americans abroad; he viewed such attempts to influence him as the equivalent of pressure from a lynch mob.

After three weeks of closed hearings, the Lowell Commission issued its much-anticipated report on July 27, 1927. Despite their own lack of legal training, the panelists had called in no experts to advise them. Nor did the panel consider it necessary to explain in detail the reasoning that led them to conclude that the two Italians were properly found guilty. The report even noted that the evidence against Vanzetti was less certain, but validated his conviction anyway. In reaching that result, the panel had a major hurdle to overcome—Judge Thayer's blatant misconduct. They solved it by noting that the jurist had engaged in "a grave breach of official decorum," but then simply refused to credit all the references to "Dagoes," "sons of bitches," and "anarchistic bastards" attributed to Judge Thayer. The report concluded that, in any event, the panel saw no signs that the jurist's out-of-court invective impugned the outcome. After all, the jurors who followed Judge Thayer's bidding thought he was fair.[18]

It is difficult to imagine a similar public whitewash occurring so readily today, particularly with heightened standards of judicial review like those instituted in Massachusetts as a direct result of this much-criticized case. Then the international outcry only reinforced mainstream support for carrying out the executions as an act in defiance of world opinion. Massachusetts Gov. Fuller had his eye on national office in 1928 and dared not accede to the demand for clemency. Last minute applications to the United States Supreme Court for stay of execution were also unavailing. That was unsurprising, given the extremely deferential standard of review of state proceedings then in effect and the conservative majority on the high court. Though both Justice Louis Brandeis and the "Great Dissenter" Oliver Wendell Holmes privately expressed their belief that Thayer had conducted a prejudiced trial, Brandeis recused himself from any official action because of his wife's personal involvement in assisting Sacco's family. Holmes resisted entreaties to grant a stay because he felt that federal interference in the state proceeding was unwarranted under existing law.

A few days before the scheduled execution, bombs exploded in several American cities. On the night the sentence was to be carried out in Charlestown, the Massachusetts prison was cordoned off and more than five hundred peace officers patrolled the thousands of Leftists and intellectuals who kept a grim vigil in the city square. President Coolidge absented himself on a Western vacation as extraordinary precautions against reprisals were taken throughout the country, including the nation's capital. Crowds gathered in protest in major cities throughout the world, some subdued, others incensed. In New York, conscience-pricking journalist Heywood Broun quipped, "What more can the immigrants from Italy expect? It is not every prisoner who has a President of Harvard throw the switch for him."[19] Workers walked off their jobs in South America; anarchists bombed the American Embassy and two American banks in Buenos Aires; others threatened the Embassy in Japan. Rioting caused deaths in Germany and Switzerland. In Paris, the American Embassy and the Moulin Rouge suffered extensive damage. The protests even extended as far away as Johannesburg, South Africa.

Thousands of mourners accompanied the remains of Sacco and Vanzetti on a march through Boston's North End. Not long after the pair's death, bombers targeted Judge Thayer's home and that of a juror and the executioner, among other prison officials, all causing damage but no fatalities. An unsuccessful effort had previously been made to bomb Gov. Fuller of Massachusetts, whose national ambitions were now history in the wake of the controversial executions. In 1928, a train transporting President Herbert Hoover on a trip through Argentina barely escaped bombing. Judge Thayer spent the rest of his own life living in his club under armed guard. Many American intellectuals lost faith in the establishment following the Lowell Commission's unexpected stamp of approval on Judge Thayer's biased conduct. The knee-jerk solidarity Brahmins had shown for Thayer's conduct of the trial proved a debilitating, self-inflicted wound that engendered decades of criticism. The executions gave momentum to growing alliances among disaffected Liberals, minority groups, and unions to support their own candidates and press for major reforms, many of which would be implemented in the next decade.

Ever since, the trial of Sacco and Vanzetti has become a source of reflection on the failings of the American justice system. It inspired an album by Woody Guthrie and Pete Seeger; an opera; numerous historical essays and books debating their guilt or innocence; movies; plays such as *Gods of the Lightning;* Sinclair Lewis's *Boston: A Novel;* Maxwell Anderson's *Winterset;* and poetry by Carl Sandburg and Edna St. Vincent Millay, among others. For decades in Russia, a state factory churned out Sacco and Vanzetti pencils and crayons for the nation's school children. In Italian towns, streets were renamed in the pair's honor. In the eyes of many around the world, Sacco and Vanzetti remain martyrs to this day, although the evidence was preserved and later, more exhaustive ballistics tests on Sacco's gun—as well as confirmation of his complicity by a fellow member of *Il Gruppo Autonomo*—convinced many skeptics that Sacco did in fact participate in the Braintree robbery-murder. His former lawyer, Moore, confessed to muckraker Upton Sinclair that he believed so too, prompting Sinclair to abandon a proposed exposé of the biased prosecution for a fictionalized account.

No similar proof of Vanzetti's participation ever emerged, though he might well have been an accessory after the fact. Controversy still surrounded the Sacco and Vanzetti case on the 50th anniversary of their execution, when Massachusetts Gov. Michael Dukakis proclaimed that the extreme prejudice surrounding the trial prompted him to decree that: "Any stigma and disgrace should be forever removed from the names of Nicola Sacco and Bartolomeo Vanzetti. We are not here to say whether these men are guilty or innocent. We are here to say that the high standards of justice, which we in Massachusetts take such pride in, failed Sacco and Vanzetti."[20]

More controversy followed twenty years later, on the 70th anniversary of their execution, when Boston's first Italian-American mayor presided over ceremonies at which the Boston Public Library finally accepted a fifty-year-old *bas-relief* artwork commemorating Sacco and Vanzetti that had been designed by the sculptor who created Mount Rushmore. By 1991, historian Paul Avrich had published his conclusion that both Sacco and Vanzetti were implicated in the April and June bombings of 1919 along with many other Galleanisti, including another suspect in the South Braintree robbery, Mario Buda, aka Mike Boda. Buda went into hiding in New England when Sacco and Vanzetti were arrested and never stood trial. But five days after Sacco and Vanzetti were indicted, Buda showed up in New York City where, as his nephew later told Avrich, Buda planned to retaliate for his revolutionary colleagues' arrest. On the fateful day of September 16, 1920, Buda loaded a horse and wagon with explosives, set a timer for noon and then fled Wall Street to Rhode Island, where he embarked for Sicily, never to be caught.[21]

* * * * *

As much as the general public vilified violent anarchists, at least their belief in a cause provided a rationale for robbery and murder that many could understand. The senseless murder of fourteen-year-old Bobby Franks in May of 1924 preoccupied people all over the globe. The case against teenagers Nathan Leopold and Richard Loeb provided ministers in their pulpits with fodder to condemn the godlessness and immorality of the new decade and intensified class rancor to a fever pitch.

8. LEOPOLD AND LOEB: Murder For The Thrill of It

This terrible crime was inherent in his organism, and it came from some ancestor. Is any blame attached because somebody took Nietzsche's philosophy seriously and fashioned his life upon it?

EXCERPT FROM CLARENCE DARROW'S CLOSING ARGUMENT

Public preoccupation with the Leopold and Loeb murder prosecution combined elements of both the 1913 Leo Frank trial and the 1907–08 Thaw murder prosecutions, updated through the prism of the Roaring Twenties. For Nativists who still believed Leo Frank was guilty, Leopold and Loeb proved once again their anti-Semitism was amply justified; these two Jewish intellectuals were perverts as well. The sooner they were hanged and made an example of the better. For those who had loudly protested that Leo Frank was framed, the sensationalized coverage of the Leopold and Loeb case silenced their voices. As in Thaw's case, the prosecution yielded voyeuristic glimpses into the decadent lives of two more spoiled rich boys with severe psychological problems. Yet, there was a new twist. The two teenagers were influenced most by Prussian nihilist Friedrich Nietzsche, whose dangerous views on Social Darwinism—survival of the fittest race—many Americans now blamed for inspiring the Germans in 1914 to instigate one of history's deadliest wars.

The question whether the two college students should live or die had millions of people at their kitchen tables outraged at the privileges of the rich. These youths had all the advantages normally associated with success. If they got off, what did that say about the poor nineteen-year-old Chicago boy then awaiting hanging for participating in a robbery in which his accomplice killed a policeman? It seemed like everyone who read newspapers and popular magazines was talking about the "new psychology" and Freudian concepts. What behaviors are human beings responsible for, and what in their nature is predetermined and beyond their control? Wasn't this just a question of how good a defense a perpetrator could afford?

Nathan Leopold was born November 19, 1904, into one of the wealthiest families in Chicago's Southside. By the turn of the century, his grandfather had established the biggest shipping company on the Great Lakes. Leopold's father magnified their wealth by launching a successful container-manufacturing business, spending little time in the process with his youngest son. The family soon realized the sickly "Babe" was a child prodigy; they bragged that he was walking and talking before he was six months old. More thought should have been given to the question of young Leopold's schooling. Small, flatfooted, and potbellied, with eyes that bulged out, the whiz kid went to two years of public elementary school where he endured constant hazing from other boys his age. What else but ridicule could his parents expect for a sensitive and unathletic mama's boy who was picked up each day after school by a governess?

In 1915, the family moved to a mansion in the city's upscale Kenwood District. Ten-year-old Nathan switched to the Harvard School for Boys. He still remained a loner raised largely by governesses, whom the other boys taunted as "Crazy Nathan" and "the flea," but his teachers fostered more avenues for escape into his own world. As a young teenager, Leopold developed a passion for dead languages and ornithology as well as a precocious interest in sex. By the time Leopold was twelve, it was common knowledge among the household staff that the family's thirty-year-old governess had embarked on a sexual relationship with him, just as she had already undertaken with his older brother.

Richard Loeb came from a similarly wealthy family that already lived in the same upscale Jewish neighborhood of Kenwood when the Leopolds arrived. Loeb's father was vice president of Sears, Roebuck; his mother was active in the Chicago Women's Club. The two boys were very unlike in many ways. As he matured, Leopold remained short, awkward, and sickly looking, with coarse, black hair and large, gray eyes; Richard Loeb was tall and athletic with sandy brown hair, blue eyes, and an engaging smile. Loeb made friends easily, though the relationships were often of short duration. He enthusiastically joined his classmates in extracurricular activities. Though he played baseball and football, he preferred tennis to contact sports for fear of injury. Like Leopold, Loeb was fragile. He had occasional fainting spells and a nervous tic. Both youths could behave quite recklessly despite their aversion to pain.

Loeb was no genius like Leopold, but a Canadian governess prodded him relentlessly to accelerate his studies at a record pace. Both Leopold and Loeb would finish college well ahead of their peers: Leopold emerged Phi Beta Kappa from the University of Chicago at eighteen, and Loeb would have the distinction of being the youngest person to ever graduate from the University of Michigan, though with an unremarkable record. Both planned to attend top law schools in the fall of 1924, presumably bound for successful legal careers like Loeb's Uncle Jacob, who had recently served as president of the Chicago Board of Education. The two friends had met after Leopold's junior year at the Harvard School for Boys when Loeb, though six months Leopold's junior, was already in college. The Leopold family then considered Loeb a good influence on their son. They had no idea he was an inveterate liar and corner-cutter, skating through school with as little effort as he could get away with while constantly plotting nasty bits of mischief. Nor did they realize that, at first sight, Leopold had developed a crush on Loeb.

Leopold greatly flattered Loeb with his slavish attention, and they became lovers, but then Loeb backed off and spent more time with other friends. Yet Loeb was an accomplished manipulator, intoxicated by the realization that Leopold would do anything for him. Loeb had been fascinated with crime novels and detective stories since he was a child—a secret he kept from his overbearing governess. He envisioned himself as a supercriminal and soon talked Leopold into joining him on a crime spree. The inducement was a formal pact that Loeb would agree to resume sex with Leopold three times a month, which evolved into once after each illicit adventure. For four years, the pair got away with a variety of crimes Loeb carefully planned, including arson, vandalism, and burglary. Loeb may have also accomplished a few more serious crimes on his own. His successful exploits with Leopold only whetted Loeb's appetite for attempting the perfect crime just for the thrill of getting away with it. The idea appealed to Leopold as well—he believed that would prove the two were Nietzschean supermen, unbound by laws applicable to mere ordinary mortals.

After several months of planning, the pair decided to rent a car under an assumed name and kidnap a child whose parents could afford $10,000 in ransom. They figured they had several suitable targets at the Harvard School for Boys, which Loeb's ten-year-old brother still attended. They prepared an elaborate scheme for collecting the ransom, which included a typed note that ended "should you carefully follow our instructions to the letter, we can assure you that your son will be safely returned to you within six hours of our receipt of the money."[1] This guarantee was designed to ensure payment of the ransom. The pair had already decided that, by the time the anxious parents delivered the money, the two would have jointly strangled the victim. That way neither could repent—since both would be complicit in the murder—and the victim could never identify his kidnappers to the police.

On the afternoon of the chosen day, May 21, 1924, Leopold picked up a green Willys-Knight touring car from a downtown rental agency, met up with Loeb, and the two cruised the school's neighborhood. They had almost given up hope of finding a boy walking alone when Loeb spotted his fourteen-year-old second cousin Bobby Franks headed home from umpiring a pickup baseball game. The two had just played tennis together the day before, and Franks showed little hesitation before he hopped in when offered a ride. As the unsuspecting youth settled into the front passenger seat, Leopold drove away. Then, before Franks realized he was not being dropped off as he expected, Loeb reached over from the back seat and stifled his cousin's surprised cry with one hand while, with the other, he clubbed Franks' head several times with the blunt end of a chisel. Blood streamed all over the front of the car. Franks continued to struggle and cry while Leopold somehow kept driving slowly through heavy traffic in the densely populated district. Loeb yanked Franks into the back, stuffed a rag down his cousin's throat, and taped his mouth shut, holding him until the boy went limp. Loeb then wrapped the body in a blanket.

Leopold drove for twenty miles. He had already picked out a remote spot near a forest preserve south of Chicago where he had often gone bird-watching. There, they would await darkness and hide Franks' body in a culvert. They made good time and decided to stop for hot dogs and root beer en route. In an effort to obscure Franks' identity if the body were found before it decomposed, Leopold poured hydrochloric acid on the boy's face and genitals. Back in the city, Leopold then made a call to Franks' frantic parents to tell them that their son was alive and well and being held for ransom. He penned their address on a generic ransom note he had typed before they selected the victim and posted it to arrive the next morning. Afterward, he parked the rental car on a side street near Loeb's home and the pair burned Franks' clothes in the Loebs' basement furnace. They hid the bloody blanket in the side yard and headed to Leopold's home where they played cards. Loeb forgot about the blood-soaked chisel still in his pocket until Leopold drove him home later that evening. Loeb tossed it out the window on the street where it was picked up by a night watchman, who got a good glimpse of the distinctive maroon sports car as it turned the corner.

The next morning, the Leopold family chauffeur was puzzled to observe the teenage boys in the driveway, hard at work at the unaccustomed chore of cleaning a car—the same one he had seen them drive off in the day before. The two made up a story about spilled wine and declined any help. They then set off to complete the rest of their perfect crime by collecting the ransom, unaware that an immigrant worker walking home from his night shift had spotted Franks' bare feet sticking out of the culvert that same morning. Meanwhile, Leopold called the drugstore he had designated as a rendezvous to ask if a Mr. Franks was there. By then, a family member had identified the naked, battered corpse, and Bobby Franks' father was at home with his shocked family meeting with the police.

The gruesome kidnap and murder of the popular, high-achieving student was the instant talk of the town. Whose child was safe if such a brazen crime in a good neighborhood could go unpunished? The police gave the matter the highest priority, a welcome diversion from the heat they got for allowing the widespread flouting of Prohibition. Law-abiding Chicagoans were scandalized at how corrupt police let gangsters like Al Capone flourish while the Volstead Act prohibited legitimate businesses from competing in the distribution and sale of liquor.

At first, police focused suspicion on two teachers at the Harvard School for Boys whom they attempted to beat into confessing—to no avail. The authorities then undertook a broad search for known perverts and harshly questioned the owners of gray Winton automobiles like the one seen by a playmate on the street just before Franks disappeared. With the attendant bad publicity, a couple of these early suspects lost their jobs, though they had done nothing wrong. A distinctive pair of horned-rimmed glasses had also been found near the site of Bobby Franks' corpse. Only one Chicago optometrist sold eyewear with that peculiar hinge. Through painstaking review of more than fifty thousand receipts, only three possible purchasers were found. The glasses were quickly identified as a pair sold to Nathan Leopold, Jr. in the fall of 1923. Police brought him in for questioning with the consent of his father and the family's lawyer Benjamin Bachrach. Neither suspected that Leopold had anything to do with the crime.

When Leopold was interviewed, he claimed to have just realized that he lost the glasses bird-watching the week before. He recited an alibi for the afternoon of the murder that he had concocted with Loeb. Soon police spoke to Loeb. Though vaguer on his whereabouts at the time of the crime, Loeb offered helpful suggestions to the police, appearing quite intrigued by the crime. Both sets of parents assumed the police had made a mistake as the two were subjected to close questioning for three days straight. The police had already found a gun in Leopold's room and a letter from Loeb that made it clear that the two were lovers. The boys' coordinated alibis seemed highly suspicious, especially when they claimed they had spent part of the afternoon cruising in Leopold's sports car looking for girls.

The Leopolds' chauffeur, Sven Englund, remembered an important piece of information which the family urged him to share with police. Nathan's sports car had been home the entire afternoon of May 21. How could Nathan have possibly committed the murder if his car remained at home? Englund had no idea the boys had told police they spent the afternoon driving Nathan's sports car. Apparently, until the police jogged his memory, Englund had also temporarily forgotten the green touring car the boys drove off in, which they had spent so much time cleaning the next morning. Their alibi in a shambles, Loeb confessed. Though disgusted with Loeb's cowardice, Leopold followed suit. Neither showed signs of remorse. The quick-thinking county prosecutor, Robert Crowe, immediately called in three top state psychiatrists to evaluate whether the pair knew right from wrong—the legal definition of sanity. Once both answered yes, Crowe announced to the reporters present that the murder had been solved. Crowe then dramatically formed a cavalcade of police cars and invited the press to follow along as Leopold and Loeb—without any legal counsel and flattered by all the attention—offered to retrace their steps the day of the murder, starting with the car rental agency.

Leopold's and Loeb's families were astounded to hear that their sons had just confessed to a capital crime. They immediately decided only the legendary Clarence Darrow could save the two from the gallows. Richard's Uncle Jacob had firsthand knowledge of Darrow's courtroom skills. Just a year before, Darrow had demolished the former school board president as the star witness for County Prosecutor Robert Crowe in a political corruption case. Jacob Loeb and Benjamin Bachrach arrived with two other family representatives by limousine unannounced early Sunday morning at Darrow's penthouse apartment near the University of Chicago. By persistent ringing of the doorbell, they succeeded in rousing Darrow's wife Ruby. The men then marched past her into the couple's bedroom and begged the aged libertarian for his help, assuring him that money was no object. Jacob Loeb sat next to the bed, explaining the dire situation to the barely awakened lawyer. Darrow had, of course, read of the brutal crime and felt torn between wanting to assist them and his visceral reaction to avoid such a "shocking and bizarre" case that already had so thoroughly alienated the public and press. At sixty-seven, his thinning hair was now all gray. His craggy face and loose jowls showed the ravages of time. The slump-shouldered lion of the Chicago bar was bone weary of "standing in the lean and lonely front line facing the greatest enemy that ever confronted man—public opinion."[2]

Darrow reluctantly got up and dressed to accompany his visitors down to the county jail in Loeb's limousine. As he contemplated how in the world he could keep the pair from being hanged for the abhorrent crime, prosecutor Crowe set out once more with Leopold and Loeb as his guides to locate further evidence. An even bigger media entourage accompanied the police procession. The large cavalcade attracted thousands of observers when they parked by the Jackson Park Harbor on Lake Michigan and dredged the water to retrieve the jettisoned Underwood Leopold had used to type the ransom note the night before the murder. During the time-consuming process, reporters had free access to both youths. Leopold and Loeb basked in the limelight.

Crowe had anticipated that the sensationalized media coverage would incense the public with details of the callous crime. So did Darrow. In his experience, unlike the English ban on inflammatory pretrial publicity, "in America, if the case is one of public interest, a campaign that reeks with venom is at once launched against the accused; columns of interviews and pictures are printed each day; . . . the stories grow lurid and appalling. Newspaper sales shoot up beyond belief."[3] So it immediately proved in the Leopold and Loeb case. Darrow had expected scorn from the public for switching from a passionate defense of the poor as victims of society to a paid mouthpiece of the rich, but perhaps did not realize that his own friends would desert him. Many reacted in disbelief at what they considered treachery to his calling, a disgrace to the nation's criminal defense bar. Rumors circulated that the champion of the oppressed had sold out for a million-dollar fee. A Nebraskan newspaperman close to Darrow ruefully observed that "The practice of criminal law fell into its greatest disfavor and disrepute in decades."[4] As public furor mounted, the Jewish community sat mute, while the Ku Klux Klan triumphantly added its powerful voice to the cacophony of calls for hanging the pair. Crowe exulted. He planned to use this case as a launching pad to run for mayor. Though he and Darrow remained cordial to each other, it would also be sweet revenge for losing the political corruption trial to Darrow when the two had opposed each other in June of 1923.

After the indictment issued, the arraignment on June 11, 1924—Loeb's nineteenth birthday—attracted the largest crowd in the history of the court, lining up hours ahead of time for standing room only. Gangster Al Capone's arrest that same day for a gangland execution garnered far less attention. Capone had counted on the public's distraction in choosing that day to surrender. He would later get the charges dismissed when his accusers developed sudden amnesia.[5] In a short hearing, Leopold and Loeb pleaded not guilty to the murder and kidnapping charges, and Chief Judge John Caverly set the trial date for early August in his own courtroom. Though time was short—the date was less than two months away—Darrow was greatly pleased with their draw. The judge had helped establish Chicago's pioneering juvenile court system, which gave judges discretion to treat youthful offenders less harshly than adults. "Fighting Bob" Crowe worried about all the resources available to his skilled adversary, but had faith any jury would vote for death.

In newspaper interviews, Darrow gave hints that insanity would be their defense. He sent co-counsel Walter Bachrach to a national convention of psychiatrists to hire some of the most highly respected authorities in the country on mental abnormality. Together with local experts, they questioned Leopold and Loeb at length and conducted a battery of medical tests. The media ridiculed the rich boys' proposed Freudian defense, comparing these expert witnesses to those used in the successful defense of Harry Thaw for Stanford White's murder twenty years earlier. Yet reveling in the prospect of stealing readers from *The Chicago Tribune,* Hearst contacted Sigmund Freud himself in Vienna and offered to charter a liner for the world's most renowned psychiatrist to come to Chicago to comment on the trial at whatever fee Dr. Freud named. *The Tribune* then cabled a counteroffer to Dr. Freud of $25,000 or more to psychoanalyze the two defendants. Feeling all of his sixty-eight years, Dr. Freud refused both offers, both for health reasons and because the circumstances would not permit any meaningful professional evaluation. As he probably anticipated, the newspapers harbored little or no respect for psychiatry. They happily substituted a phrenologist, astrologist, and character analyst to study the defendants' features and provide the public with pseudoscientific comments, such as that Leopold's left ear evinced a dynamic personality, while the curve of Loeb's jaw was "distinctly feminine."[6] The tongue-in-cheek publicity exacerbated populist outrage against the wealthy defendants.

Media representatives from Canada, Cuba, Argentina, Great Britain, Australia, and Italy all expressed interest in attending. To go one up on the Hearst papers and other competition, *The Chicago Daily Tribune* proposed to air the Leopold and Loeb trial over the radio—a battle that later in the century would be fought over the propriety of television broadcasts of murder trials. Hearst's *Evening American* derided that idea as appealing to morons and sarcastically suggested that the trial might as well take place in a baseball stadium.[7] Darrow vigorously objected—live radio coverage could only create even greater community prejudice against his clients. Shocked parents and clergy throughout the city voiced their strong opposition as well; they had already read innuendoes that the pair were homosexuals and wanted children in the city exposed to less coverage, not more. *The Tribune* offered to censor any lurid details, but then withdrew the proposed broadcast amid a torrent of criticism.

Darrow steered clear of his office most days to avoid harassment and the piles of hate mail. The few letters he read had been so vituperative he had no interest in the rest. It bothered him that the mere provision of a defense met with such anger and derision. Every defendant was entitled to representation, especially those most vilified. Darrow kept his defense strategy a closely guarded secret. By early July, every major paper in the country assigned a reporter to attend the trial in the 200-seat courtroom. As big a crowd as had shown up in June, it was dwarfed by the thousands of people waiting to swarm the courthouse for access to this hearing.

Crowe exuded self-assurance, striding buoyantly into the court smoking a cigar. At worst, he assumed that Darrow might challenge the two confessions, since the pair had no access to lawyers at the time. Of course, no one had read Leopold and Loeb their rights first—the law did not then require warnings. Crowe thought he had a pat hand. In contrast to the stylish prosecutor in his crisp black suit and lively bow tie, Darrow looked saggy and tired in an outdated blue suit, apparently bought when he was somewhat heavier. His younger co-counsel Benjamin Bachrach made a sharp contrast, well-tailored and exuding athletic vigor. But Darrow was playing possum. He had a surprise in store. When Leopold and Loeb arrived, Darrow shocked Crowe and the media. With his thumbs in his suspenders, he changed their pleas to guilty, avoiding any possibility of a jury. The bailiff had to call repeatedly for quiet in the courtroom. Darrow then employed a tactic he had successfully used a decade before in another case. The savvy trial lawyer asked Judge Caverly to agree to a sentencing hearing at which psychiatric evidence could be offered to justify a lesser penalty for the capital crime. Crowe immediately derided the change of plea as a ploy to substitute a "friendly judge" for a jury. Judge Caverly rebuked Crowe for "a cowardly and dastardly assault upon the integrity of this court" and ordered Crowe's comment removed from the stenographer's record.[8] Reporters fell over chairs running for telephones to make the afternoon paper. Could this daring move possibly preserve Darrow's track record of never losing a client to the death penalty?

Preparation for the hearing was grueling. The schedule had been a whirlwind of nonstop activity and heavy pressure since early June when Darrow first agreed to participate. At the August sentencing hearing, crowds overwhelmed the police at times in their efforts to gain access to the packed courtroom. Crowe put on eighty witnesses to describe the callous details of the murder plot. Darrow objected that Crowe simply wanted to inflame public opinion to pressure the judge into executing them. After all, the pair had already admitted their guilt. Judge Caverly disagreed. To Crowe's delight, the judge explained that he considered it appropriate to hear all the gory details of the kidnapping and murder. In deciding on the sentence, the judge wanted to consider all the aggravating circumstances of the crimes. But when Crowe tried to prevent any psychiatric testimony from coming in, the evenhanded judge overruled him, too. It was true that Leopold and Loeb had to be considered legally sane when they committed the crimes—that was established by their guilty pleas—but Judge Caverly was also interested in hearing how their mental state might cause him to reduce the penalty he might otherwise apply.

Darrow and his co-counsel proceeded with a parade of expert witnesses to show that tests of both Leopold and Loeb showed significant abnormalities. Both had long suffered from pathologically delusional fantasies—Loeb from schizophrenia and Leopold from paranoia. Each had contemplated suicide. Though they appeared normal or superior intellectually, they were emotionally immature. Loeb still talked to his teddy bear. Their courtroom demeanor bore that out. At times, the two smiled inappropriately, appearing to share inside jokes, and continued to demonstrate absolutely no remorse.

When his turn came, Crowe put on the stand the highly respected state psychiatrists who had previously vouched for the pair's sanity. But as eminent as these men were in their field, they had to admit their own examination of the two teenagers was hasty and exceedingly unorthodox. The trio had not seen the defendants privately, but only questioned them for a total of three hours in the presence of police, prosecutorial staff, and stenographers. The circumstances were hardly conducive to a probing inquiry.

As with the Leo Frank trial, throughout the proceedings the judge and defense lawyers received multiple death threats, as did at least one of the defense psychiatrists. As a precaution, all the participants had guards provided as they came and left the courthouse for various hearings. Anonymous notes threatened to blow up the courthouse and lynch Leopold and Loeb. More comparisons were made to the ghetto youth who was about to be hanged because his companion had killed a policeman the two accidentally encountered when pulling a robbery. Many people were incensed at the "poor little rich boys"[9] who premeditated a callous and arbitrary murder and sought a lesser penalty for their heinous crime. How fair was that?

With huge crowds outside the courtroom demanding vengeance, Darrow made an impassioned closing argument against capital punishment, weeping both for the victim and for the defendants, whom he claimed could not control their shocking behavior. Darrow went into such graphic detail of the hanging process that his clients lost all trace of their smirks. Loeb visibly shuddered and Leopold became hysterical. Many women in the courtroom were moved to tears. Darrow emphasized that the alternative punishment was life in prison. He argued that facing several decades behind bars would be an even harsher penalty for the youths to endure than execution. When Darrow ended, he was totally spent. He later described the strain as so extensive, "I could never do it again, even if I should try."[10]

Some observers considered Darrow's histrionics way over the top, but fans of the legendary lawyer believed he had just delivered the finest speech of his long career. Crowe still thought he held the trump card. He spent nearly two days in furious rebuttal. "Eyes blazing," he called the two a pair of "cowardly perverts" who had likely raped Franks after he died.[11] Crowe had not mentioned this sensational charge in his original presentation, probably because he knew how inconclusive the evidence was. He followed the claim of rape with unproved allegations that Loeb had committed four other serious crimes. Crowe argued that Leopold knew about Loeb's past criminal acts and that the joint murder of Bobby Franks was intended to buy Leopold's silence. Piling on every theory, Crowe also asserted that the ransom was a major motive. Loeb had gambling debts that greatly exceeded his allowance. Crowe saved his biggest zinger for Darrow, charging that the death penalty opponent's soft-hearted approach to law and order invited the court to "strike 'a greater blow . . . to our institutions' than a thousand murders."[12] Darrow made a quick, gloomy exit after the judge announced he would take ten days to reach his decision. Crowe reveled in the moment, smoking a cigar and accepting congratulations from colleagues for his masterful refutation of Darrow's plea for clemency.

The pressure was now all on the judge. Every day, he received stacks of letters urging him to impose the death penalty. Reporters fueled public ire with more interviews of Leopold and Loeb enjoying their celebrity status at the jail. They ate well, got plenty of sleep, played baseball in the yard, and entertained visitors, including a half dozen Chicago Cubs. Around the city, heavy bets were being placed on the outcome: Darrow's past record led odds-makers to favor a life sentence over the death penalty. The day before Judge Caverly announced his decision, the county took extraordinary security precautions. All other court business scheduled for Wednesday, September 10, 1924, was cancelled. Scores of sheriff's deputies and bailiffs were assigned to monitor the elevators and hallways. Nearly six dozen policemen on motorcycles would back up one hundred patrolmen encircling the Criminal Court Building. Another fifty mounted on horseback would patrol the street. Plainclothes men were instructed to mix into the crowds to spot any potential bomb throwers or gunmen.

On the day of the hearing, Judge Caverly's wife received a phone call that her husband had been killed. Unaware of the horrible prank, Judge Caverly arrived safely at the court building for his last case before retiring. To protect him from attack, he came in a limousine with an armed police escort. Accompanying him inside the car were two detectives carrying machine guns and revolvers. Crowds surged around the building into the street and up the stairs of the six-story building, but only media representatives and people connected with the case were allowed inside his courtroom. For the reading of his decision, the judge also permitted live radio coverage—score one victory for *The Chicago Tribune*'s station WGN (an acronym for the "World's Greatest Newspaper"). Throughout Chicago, people stopped whatever they were doing to congregate by radios to await his ruling.

Judge Caverly methodically addressed all three arguments for leniency argued by the defense team. First was the rarity of imposing the death penalty on a defendant who offered a guilty plea instead of forcing the prosecutor to prove his guilt. The elderly jurist rejected that argument out of hand. He noted that the evidence of guilt was so overwhelming, they would have been convicted anyway. They did not accommodate the prosecutor by pleading guilty; it was a surprise, unwelcomed, defense tactic. The second argument was based on the mountain of psychiatric evidence offered to convince the judge not to execute the pair for their compulsive crime. The judge was now convinced that Leopold and Loeb were quite abnormal, but he rejected the impact of their mental state on the sentence. "Similar analyses made of other persons accused of crime would probably reveal similar or different abnormalities,"[13] he said. By then, it seemed obvious to observers and those listening raptly to their radios that the pair would indeed be executed.

But Judge Caverly had not finished. He realized that it would be "the path of least resistance to impose the extreme penalty of the law."[14] He had saved until last the question of their age, noting that only two minors had been put to death in Illinois history by legal process. Falling in line with the thinking of modern criminologists, Judge Caverly reasoned that the penalty should never be used for minors. Despite the atrocity of the crime, he sentenced both Leopold and Loeb to life imprisonment for the murder and 99 years for the kidnap for ransom, expressing his strong opinion that the horrendous nature of their crime should render them permanently ineligible for parole.

Everyone was astounded. Darrow had salvaged his record and reinforced his amazing reputation. Crowe voiced his fury at the judge to the press, adding fuel to an already outraged public reaction by declaring the crime "unequaled in the criminal history of the state . . . an atrocious and cold blooded murder by [a pair with a history] of perversion . . . degenerates of the worst type [who] struck terror to the heart of every father and mother throughout the community."[15] Newspapers followed suit. The rich were judged by different standards. Money bought results. (Though most people believed newspaper accounts that Darrow had been paid a million-dollar fee, Darrow only wound up getting paid about thirty thousand dollars, the same amount as each of his two co-counsel and a fraction of the value he attributed to his services.) Some skeptics even speculated that Darrow bribed the judge, recalling the criminal charges on similar allegations for which Darrow had narrowly escaped conviction in California over a decade before in defending the McNamara brothers' bombing case.[16] Others wondered, if the judge's ruling was based simply on their age, why had the county been forced to waste huge amounts of taxpayers' money on a lengthy hearing entertaining psychiatric evidence? Leopold put it more succinctly. Couldn't they have achieved the same result by just offering their birth certificates into evidence?[17]

Historian Simon Baatz estimates that several thousand contemporaneous articles were written about the Leopold and Loeb proceedings.[18] The case soon spawned a highly successful London play, *Rope*, ironically adapted as one of Alfred Hitchcock's least-watched movies. Accounts of the case appeared prominently in Darrow biographies and inspired several novels, one of which was turned into another movie in 1959, *Compulsion*, with Orson Welles playing the aging legal giant. Interest revived in the story in the last decade of the century with films in 1992 and 2002; a 2003 musical, *Thrill Me: The Leopold and Loeb Story;* and, most recently, Baatz's own 2008 work *For the Thrill Of It: Leopold, Loeb, and the Murder That Shocked Chicago.* Throughout the 20th century and into our own, people remained captivated by the psychological motivation of two young men who threw away lives of great promise for a senseless act of extreme depravity.

One side benefit of all the publicity was that it raised awareness of the predicament of Bernard Grant, the other youthful defendant then on death row. Grant won a reprieve from the governor. Meanwhile, "Fighting Bob" Crowe's standing in the community plummeted due to his failure to stop bold gangland murders. Rumors began to circulate that Crowe must be on the take. Then in 1926, one of Crowe's chief assistants was gunned down by machine gun fire as he emerged from a Cicero bar with members of the O'Donnell gang. At the time, the Irish gang was known to be battling an Italian mob for the beer trade. The taint of corruption ruined Crowe's chances for future political office.

Leopold and Loeb helped update and expand the prison library and were permitted to start a correspondence school. Loeb also used family money to bribe his jailers for favors. In 1936, he was killed by another inmate, who claimed Loeb had made sexual advances and threatened him with a razor. The evidence suggested that Loeb was unarmed and attacked from behind, but the homicide was left unresolved. Leopold did his best to become a model prisoner. He compiled statistics to help officials evaluate parole risks and volunteered as a guinea pig for malaria testing on the promise that risking his life for that medical experiment would be taken into account when he came up for parole. Still, his release in 1958 after thirty-three years in prison—the second time he was eligible—brought severe criticism to the parole board. That same year Leopold published his autobiography *Life Plus 99 Years.* By then, he had moved to Puerto Rico where he began living off his substantial inheritance and started working with the local poor. Leopold spent the remaining decade of his life married to a doctor's widow and taking time to travel extensively throughout the world. He died of a heart attack in August of 1971, just a few months shy of his sixty-seventh birthday.

Darrow followed up on his defense of Leopold and Loeb with a spirited campaign to abolish the death penalty altogether. He would have been gratified to learn that in 2000 Republican Gov. George Ryan placed a moratorium on the Illinois death penalty pending recommendations for overhaul of the criminal justice system due to "grave concerns about our state's shameful record of convicting innocent people and putting them on death row."[19] The moratorium remained in effect until 2011, when Illinois officially abolished capital punishment, following recent bans enacted in New York, New Jersey and New Mexico. The federal government and thirty-four states still retain the death penalty for adults.

From the mid-1970s to 2005, though twenty states still permitted execution of minors, only ten in fact did so. Of the twenty-two youths executed in these states between 1976 and 2005, Texas alone accounted for thirteen, underscoring the mounting reluctance of most states to invoke capital punishment for juvenile offenders. In 1995, by a five-to-four vote in *Roper v. Simmons*, the United States Supreme Court concluded such an extreme penalty was cruel and unusual punishment. Writing for a bare majority, Justice Anthony Kennedy relied upon a national consensus supported by medical and social-science evidence that the immaturity of teenagers made it inappropriate to impose that ultimate sanction no matter how horrendous the circumstances. He noted that "instability and emotional imbalance of young people may often be a factor in the crime." Justice Kennedy concluded, "From a moral standpoint, it would be misguided to equate the failings of a minor with those of an adult, for a greater possibility exists that a minor's character deficiencies will be reformed . . . Our determination finds confirmation in the stark reality that the United States is the only country in the world that continues to give official sanction to the juvenile death penalty."[20] The Supreme Court's ruling spared 72 other juveniles on death row, 29 of them in Texas. The ruling applied only to those under 18 at the time of the crime. It would not have affected death sentences against teenage offenders like Leopold and Loeb, who were 19 and 18, respectively, on the date of Franks' murder.

* * * * *

History would not judge Darrow's astonishing performance in saving the lives of Leopold and Loeb as his most memorable case. In the summer of 1925, Darrow interrupted his lecture tour against capital punishment with an impromptu trip to Tennessee. The war horse who would spend much of his forty-five year career battling over issues of life and death would best be remembered for volunteering to defend a high school teacher for a minor infraction that involved a $100 fine. Yet everyone headed to Dayton, Tennessee, that July knew that the stakes were enormous. This show trial would engage Americans in a heated debate over the proper roles of science and religion in public education of their children on the most controversial subject then in dispute—the origins of mankind itself.

9. SCOPES: The Staged Battle of Evolution v. Creationism

I furnished the body that was needed to sit in the defendant's chair.

JOHN SCOPES

Darrow's most famous case was custom-designed to be an extraordinary spectacle. The Scopes "monkey" trial was, from start to finish, popular entertainment played out in an international arena. It capitalized on front-page clashes in newspapers and sold-out lecture halls that pitted Fundamentalist believers in the literal truth of Genesis against the consensus of established academia teaching Darwin's theory of evolution. Supporters of evolution included not only agnostics and atheists, but a growing number of liberal monotheists. Darwin also had most of the media on his side, both in the United States and abroad. Less widely remembered is the moral issue that underlay the debate—the growing worldwide Social Darwinism movement among white Christians embracing forced eugenics to accomplish racial purity, a movement that would soon reach its most frightening form in Nazi Germany.

In his Pulitzer Prize–winning book, *Summer for the Gods: The Scopes Trial and America's Continuing Debate over Science and Religion,* Prof. Edward Larson argues that the Scopes trial deserves the distinction of "THE" trial of the century: "The issues raised by the Scopes trial and legend endure precisely because they embody the characteristically American struggle between individual liberty and majoritarian democracy, and cast it in the timeless debate over science and religion."[1]

The issues do endure, but they preceded and post-dated the event in Dayton, Tennessee, that is more aptly described as an immensely entertaining political debate than a true trial. What made it so memorable is that it starred two men who stole the show: Darrow, the shaggy-haired legend in the twilight of his career against another aged American giant of even greater renown, perennial presidential candidate and orator William Jennings Bryan, trumpeting his very last cause. In the actual courtroom, the struggle between individual liberty and majoritarian democracy only surfaced in a pretrial motion to the judge. In the presence of the jury—which heard only a couple of hours of testimony—Scopes' lawyers never paid much attention to Scopes as an individual, nor did the jury ever consider any issue of his rights. The images imprinted in the memory of four generations of Americans—a jailed science teacher persecuted by a bombastic prosecutor who died fighting to impose creationism as the law of the land—are largely a media product of the McCarthy era.

It was not until its thirtieth anniversary in 1955 that the test case spawned a Broadway play, which has since been revived twice, in 1996 and again in 2007. In more than half a century, the play *Inherit the Wind* became a highly popular high school and community theater staple. Most indelibly, the trial was transformed into a classic 1960 movie, starring Oscar-winners Spencer Tracy and Fredric March as the two American titans. Since then, the movie with its irresistible lead roles was remade three more times with different actors, including the late George C. Scott as Darrow.

But the first time the *Scopes* trial was performed on stage was in the summer of 1925. Several leading townsmen of Dayton, Tennessee, including its part-time prosecutor, were excited by the prospect of a gimmick that would put their picturesque Cumberland Mountain town on a tourism map. The governor had just the month before signed the first law in the country forbidding the teaching in public schools of man's descent from primitive ancestors. One of the Dayton boosters then spotted an intriguing ad the ACLU ran in *The Chattanooga Times:* "We are looking for a Tennessee teacher who is willing to accept our services in testing [the new Tennessee anti-evolution] law in the courts. Our lawyers think a friendly test case can be arranged without costing a teacher his or her job. Distinguished counsel have volunteered their services. All we need now is a willing client."[2] What could bring renown and an influx of cash to Dayton better than hosting a summer debate on a national hot button issue? In Dayton, as elsewhere in Tennessee, almost everyone attended church. There were nine places of worship for a population of three thousand. But uncharacteristic of the South as a whole at that time, a majority of the local adults had a high school education. Dayton had established its own high school twenty years earlier. The town also boasted some Progressives who founded a library and met regularly in a readers' club.

As Larson points out, several recent developments had pushed the issue to the forefront of American public consciousness. More than a decade earlier a major archeological "find" was reported with much fanfare in England. The skeletal remains of what became known as "Piltdown man" were pronounced the missing link—a common ancestor of men and apes, just as Charles Darwin had posited in his 1859 book, *On the Origin of Species by Means of Natural Selection, or, The Preservation of Favoured Races in the Struggle for Life.*[3] Evolutionary theories predated Darwin by more than half a century, but many scientists did not find theories of evolution irreconcilable with their belief in God. They simply treated the Biblical account of creation as allegory. Charles Darwin considered himself an agnostic. But atheists began latching onto his assumption that, rather than springing into existence at God's command, species evolved as random variations passed on over millions of years simply by the principle of survival of the fittest. One of Darwin's most influential followers was Prussian philosopher Friedrich Nietzsche—who posited that the Christian God was dead—mankind, like other animals, only progressed through brutal battles for dominance. Nietzsche's theory—which included the concept of a race of supermen—gained wide support among white supremacists in the first two decades of the 20th century. Leopold and Loeb were but extreme examples of Nietzsche's many zealous followers.

Though Leopold and Loeb were not the only Jewish intellectuals to embrace Nietzsche, the prevailing view was that his super race would be achieved through breeding of homogenous Protestants of Northern European ancestry. Jews and Catholics were considered inferior, as were persons with inherited disabilities. Though Darwin considered Negroes part of the same species as whites, he firmly believed they were lower on the evolutionary chain than Caucasians. Growing numbers of Social Darwinists adhered to the views of influential New York lawyer Madison Grant, who advocated sterilization and anti-miscegenation laws to preserve the superior Nordic race from degradation.

Darwin's theory of evolution—supported by numerous archaeological discoveries—posed a direct threat to literalists who interpreted the Bible to mean that God created all life in six twenty-four hour days in or about 4004 B.C.[4] They firmly believed mankind was created by God in his own image, not as the result of gradual evolution from more primitive life forms. Yet for many years, these competing views occupied largely separate spheres. Fundamentalist farmers had little trouble accepting the pioneering work on plant hybrids by agriculturist Luther Burbank, though it was premised on Darwinian theory. There was also growing acceptance of the evolution of animals traceable through fossil remains. But the absence of evidence of modern man's own primitive ancestors left the issue of divine creation of humankind more debatable. That was why the discovery of "Piltdown man" in 1912 created such an uproar.

The Piltdown skull was much later exposed as a hoax: it combined an orangutan jaw with a modern human skull fragment. But at the time, world-renowned scientists were taken in, and reputable journalists turned the story into banner headlines. Its impact was compounded in 1916 when a new study of American religiosity rattled conservative Christians. The scholarly survey revealed that university students and professors now shared widespread disbelief in the fundamental Christian tenet of immortality. The author concluded that "Christianity, as a system of belief, has utterly broken down,"[5] a pronouncement that helped galvanize the foundation of the World's Christian Fundamentals Association ("WCFA") in 1919. It did not take long for the WCFA to focus on challenging the teaching of evolution in high schools as its primary focus. In the early 1920s, newspapers featured the growing controversy as leading Fundamentalist preachers across the nation condemned Darwin as an infidel and ridiculed as agents of the devil those who taught that man descended from prehistoric apelike ancestors.

In February of 1925, newspapers reported another missing link—a skull of a hominid more than two million years old, found in northern South Africa. Prodded by leaders of the national Fundamentalist movement, within a month, Tennessee's legislature made history by becoming the first to adopt a statute outlawing the teaching of evolution in the public schools. The 1925 Butler Act made it a finable offense "for any teacher in the public schools of the State which are supported in whole or in part by the public school funds of the State, to teach any theory that denies the Story of the Divine Creation of man as taught in the Bible, and to teach instead that man has descended from a lower order of animals."[6] In Tennessee, this was at the time simply considered good politics—few legislators in the majority assumed the new law would be rigorously enforced. Nor did the governor, who, like more than half of the state's adult population, was himself a Baptist. The ACLU had been following closely all the states considering such legislation and immediately set to work on challenging the new law. Its primary concern was the threat posed to academic freedom by religious fanatics whom many feared might not stop until the Biblical account of Genesis was enshrined in the Constitution.

Meeting at the local drugstore, the convivial Dayton plotters convinced a good-natured friend, young physics and math teacher, John Scopes, to volunteer for the proposed exhibition contest. The ACLU quickly accepted Scopes as the guinea pig and even offered a thousand dollars to each prosecutor. No one would expect a true legal contest to have one agency paying for both sides. Still, the ACLU Board assumed the case would likely be lost at trial and won on appeal on constitutional grounds in the United States Supreme Court. The ACLU was not focused on disproving Fundamentalism, but on preventing political curtailment of academic freedom. The broader issue was one of the original focuses of the ACLU almost a decade earlier, when the new organization was still called the National Civil Liberties Bureau and battled for the jobs of teachers who opposed World War I.

The local judge, John Raulston, was an eager participant in the scheme to lure new visitors to Dayton. If they wanted to attract summer vacationers and get the jump on every other Tennessee town, speed was essential. So Raulston specially convened the grand jury in late May with his eye on an early July trial date. Scopes coached his students what to say, and the indictment was issued within an hour. Word spread quickly. The Chamber of Commerce went to work on a brochure highlighting local industry, Dayton's shopkeepers stocked up on kitschy simian souvenirs, and the community weathered the scorn of neighboring townspeople for the publicity-seeking stunt. Daytonians figured other municipalities just wished they had thought of it first. They expected up to thirty thousand people to flock to their town.

The prosecutors were excited when one of the most prominent anti-evolutionists in the country, the "Silver-Tongued Orator" William Jennings Bryan, immediately volunteered his services. They gladly accepted, although Bryan had not practiced law in over thirty-five years. His job would primarily be to make speeches and attract media attention. Dayton hoped to entice British science fiction writer H. G. Wells to lead the defense team. The fact that Wells was not even a lawyer underscored just how little the spectacle was intended to resemble a real criminal trial. The most Scopes risked was being fined, and Bryan himself had generously offered to pay that fine for him, assuming Scopes was convicted. When Clarence Darrow read that Bryan had signed up, Darrow could not resist offering free assistance to the history-making effort, even though the ACLU felt Darrow's notoriety would do the case more harm than good. The chance to challenge his old friend Bryan directly in a courtroom in the heart of the Fundamentalist South was too tempting. Back in 1896, Darrow had vigorously campaigned for Bryan when the Populist first ran for President and Darrow ran unsuccessfully for Congress. Both had also supported the women's suffrage movement that had just succeeded in 1920 in passing the Nineteenth Amendment granting women the right to vote after more than seven decades of effort (though when it came to women lawyers in the courtroom, Darrow remained a confirmed misogynist).

The two men took opposite positions on the Eighteenth Amendment's installation of Prohibition. They also had parted ways over the recent world war. Bryan was a leading pacifist in the pre-war years and quit his post as Secretary of State in the Wilson administration to protest the impending entry of the United States into that war. Yet once war was declared, Bryan supported the Wilson administration's persecution of war opponents as unpatriotic. Always attracted to unpopular causes, Darrow was on the opposite side. He defended conscientious objectors, though he had personally come around to the view that the war was necessary. Yet the biggest issue that separated the two was the one that lured both aging giants to Dayton, Tennessee, in the summer of 1925.

Though Bryan was not as deep a thinker as Darrow, "The Great Commoner" was appalled by a newly published history book that described how Nietzsche and Darwin had influenced German war mongers. Nietzsche challenged the very premise of the Judeo-Christian ethic valuing charity and compassion to those less able. Nietzsche glorified war and ridiculed democracy as the refuge of weaklings. To Bryan, in contrast, the will of the majority was sacrosanct, as was the Biblical injunction to love thy neighbor as thyself. The horrific consequences of World War I reinforced Bryan's view that old time religion was a cure for what ailed the modern world. Though Darrow also prized democracy and compassion, he was, in contrast to Bryan, a confirmed agnostic and lifelong supporter of evolutionary theory. He had made it his own personal mission to challenge traditional Christianity as a "slave religion," tolerating injustice, mediocrity, and complacency.[7] In the early twenties, Bryan incorporated into his lectures the danger posed by Nietzsche's and Darwin's ideas. Bryan had new fodder from the widespread publicity surrounding the Leopold and Loeb murder trial in 1924. The God-fearing majority of Americans were horrified by the amoral consequences of Nietzsche's concept of supermen unbound by rules of behavior constraining ordinary mortals.

Fundamentalists' concern for the souls of the next generation found a ready audience among their alarmed congregations. Nationwide, public high schools had mushroomed over the past thirty years. In Tennessee, five times as many children attended high school in 1925 as had done so at the turn of the century. Didn't parents have the right to control what their children were being taught? In the 19th century, public schools had incorporated generalities from the Bible into their rudimentary science courses. But by the early 20th century, textbooks like that used in Tennessee routinely incorporated the growing scientific consensus supporting Darwin's theory of evolution, including the concept of survival of the fittest. Separation of church and state was interpreted to relegate religious teaching to private schools. Orators like Bryan argued that if the First Amendment prevented the teaching of the Bible in public schools, surely, it was improper to force-feed the nation's children with the notion that men and apes were cousins with common ancestors that evolved over millions of years. The very idea was contrary to everything Fundamentalists learned in Sunday school. Bryan was also greatly concerned by a more sinister aspect of teaching Social Darwinism.

George William Hunter—the author of the official textbook every public high school in Tennessee had been using for the past five years—was an ardent proponent of forced eugenics. After describing the evolution of man from races "much lower in their mental organization than the present inhabitants," his high school textbook, *A Civic Biology Presented in Problems,* states that:

> Even to-day the earth is not entirely civilized.
> The Races of Man. — At the present time there exist upon the earth five races or varieties of man, each very different from the other in instincts, social customs, and, to an extent, in structure. These are the Ethiopian or negro type, originating in Africa; the Malay or brown race, from the islands of the Pacific; The American Indian; the Mongolian or yellow race, including the natives of China, Japan, and the Eskimos; and finally, the highest type of all, the Caucasians, represented by the civilized white inhabitants of Europe and America.[8]

Bryan had no quarrel with Hunter's premise that "civilized white inhabitants from Europe and America" represented the highest form of life. But Hunter went much further: "If the stock of domesticated animals can be improved, it is not unfair to ask if the health and vigor of the future generations of men and women on the earth might not be improved by applying to them the laws of selection." Hunter and all those that approved the widespread use of his book had no qualms about including eugenics as the new gospel. Hunter argued that the "race should demand . . . freedom from germ diseases which might be handed down to the offspring. Tuberculosis, syphilis, that dread disease which cripples and kills hundreds of thousands of innocent children, epilepsy, and feeble-mindedness are handicaps which it is not only unfair but criminal to hand down to posterity." Then, in a section entitled "Parasitism and its Cost to Society," Hunter went much further:

> Hundreds of families . . . exist today, spreading disease, immorality, and crime to all parts of this country. The cost to society of such families is very severe. Just as certain animals or plants become parasitic on other plants or animals, these families have become parasitic on society. They not only do harm to others by corrupting, stealing, or spreading disease, but they are actually protected and cared for by the state out of public money. Largely for them the poorhouse and the asylum exist. They take from society, but they give nothing in return. They are true parasites."

Most chilling was Hunter's suggestion of "The Remedy." He asked his students:

> If such people were lower animals, we would probably kill them off to prevent them from spreading. Humanity will not allow this, but we do have the remedy of separating the sexes in asylums or other places and in various ways preventing intermarriage and the possibilities of perpetuating such a low and degenerate race. Remedies of this sort have been tried successfully in Europe and are now meeting with some success in this country.[9]

Bryan objected that Social Darwinists should pay for their own private schools and keep the public schools neutral. The taxpayers who funded educational institutions should have the right to prevent proselytizing atheists from advancing the theory of evolution as established fact. Bryan at least wanted Fundamentalist beliefs placed on an equal footing. Otherwise, the curriculum undermined the individual right of children raised as Fundamentalists to believe in an almighty God who created mankind directly in his own image just a few thousand years before the birth of Christ.

In the South, the question of how Darwin's theory would be presented in public schools was one whose direct impact was almost exclusively on white students. Schools remained strictly segregated. Evolution was not taught in elementary school, and virtually no black children anywhere in the state of Tennessee—as elsewhere in the South—had public schooling available to them after eighth grade. Although a few black preachers openly supported the Fundamentalist position, the NAACP and deans of black universities sided with evolutionary science as the more enlightened position. Darrow was a founding member of the NAACP and one of the leading civil rights advocates of his day. But acceptance of evolution still had Darrow and the NAACP at odds with Social Darwinists like Hunter who were indoctrinating impressionable high school students on the values of maintaining separation of the races and perpetuating belief in the inferiority of blacks.

Religious leaders were equally divided on the issue of white supremacy. Liberal ministers and rabbis had led the 19th century abolitionist movement. Their successors saw no conflict between evolutionary theory and belief in an almighty God, all of whose children were entitled to equal dignity and respect. In contrast, Fundamentalist preachers claimed blacks were a separate subhuman species or descendants of Ham cursed by God to eternal slavery or subservience. The revived Ku Klux Klan leaders were conservative ministers who strongly endorsed the anti-evolutionists. Though Bryan feared where Social Darwinists were headed with their glorification of racial purity, he believed that control of a peaceful world was the "white man's burden." Since 1896, Bryan had also allied himself with white supremacists in the South whose support was essential in getting "the Prairie Populist" nominated for President on the Democratic Party ticket. At the 1924 Democratic Convention, Bryan had just played a key role in preventing the Party platform from condemning the Ku Klux Klan.

When Darrow and his wife arrived in Dayton, they were quite surprised. It was already overflowing with competing factions, producing a carnival atmosphere, complete with live monkeys. Prominent signs throughout the town—including on the side of the courthouse itself—told all comers to "READ YOUR BIBLE." Hordes of reporters, atheists, scientists, and radicals overflowed the hotels and boarding houses, while poorer regional farmers and unemployed mineworkers created a tent city on the outskirts of town near where Pentecostal Christian "Holy Rollers" had decided to hold a revival meeting.

In anticipation of record crowds, brand new public toilets and phone banks were installed in the courthouse. The courtroom itself was redesigned to allow for five hundred more seats in the gallery, a platform for a movie camera, and telegraph wires. Few paying tourists actually ever arrived, but over 200 newspaper reporters did descend upon the town from across the country. London also sent two correspondents. "In a move symbolic of the trial itself," Larson noted that microphones displaced the jury box in the center of the courtroom so the proceedings could be heard simultaneously in four public halls elsewhere in Dayton and via loudspeakers for attendees on the court's own front lawn.[10] At a banquet in his honor, William Jennings Bryan called the upcoming debate, "a duel to the death." When Darrow got his chance to respond, he announced that "We will smother Mr. Bryan's influence under a mountain of scientific testimony."[11]

More than a score of telegraphers would cover the drama as if it were the World Series, disseminating play-by-play daily reports via the specially hung telegraph wires to over twenty-three hundred daily papers covering the trial. The media coverage exceeded that for any prior American event, including unprecedented transmissions during the trial to avidly interested European newspapers. The ACLU board had tried to get Darrow removed from the case as an unnecessary distraction, but did not succeed. So they sent their General Counsel Arthur Hays to make sure the defense stayed on track. Though Scopes had little to lose, the affable young bachelor from Kentucky liked having someone of Darrow's stature on his team. Nor was Scopes an ideal defendant for promoting the ACLU's agenda. He did not regularly conduct biology classes, but only occasionally taught the subject as a substitute. If called as a witness, he would likely have had trouble expounding articulately upon either evolutionary principles or academic freedom when faced with rigorous cross-examination. Indeed, his lack of substantial training in biology was the principal reason why Scopes assumed that his lawyers never asked him to testify.

Had Scopes been called to the stand, a major issue of criminal intent could have easily become dispositive of the trial's outcome. Before Scopes' friends asked him if he was game to submit to a symbolic arrest, Scopes had already brought to the attention of his principal that Hunter's *Civic Biology* violated the new Butler Act. With the short time left in the spring semester the principal—who normally taught the course himself—had told Scopes just to go ahead with teaching evolution the same as before. It was still the official textbook supplied by the state. No replacement had yet been put forward. In fact, Gov. Peary, in signing the Butler Act into law, had blithely stated that he did not believe that the textbooks currently in use contradicted the Bible and did not anticipate the law would be invoked any time soon. Nor did any of Scopes' students or their parents raise any issue when Scopes taught a class on Darwin's theory, which Scopes wasn't exactly sure he had really covered in any meaningful detail.

Had defending Scopes as an individual been the issue—as befits true criminal trials—the focus of the defense in seeking his acquittal should have been on Scopes's lack of criminal intent. Scopes was teaching from the legislatively preapproved Tennessee biology textbook at the express direction of the school's principal. But his lawyers had a different agenda and seemed almost to forget Scopes existed. On the afternoon that trial testimony was to commence, Scopes came back late. He had been cooling off with a swim at lunchtime, accompanied by a new member of the prosecution team, William Jennings Bryan, Jr. When Scopes wormed his way back to his seat, proceedings had already started without the ostensible defendant even in attendance!

Unlike the severe public reaction that had prevented radio broadcast of the Leopold and Loeb sentencing hearing, the radio station affiliated with *The Chicago Tribune* apparently had no difficulty obtaining permission to broadcast the entire Scopes trial live. *The Chicago Tribune* claimed the simultaneous broadcast was a first in the history of radio. It quashed criticism that such intrusion was unfair to Scopes with the observation that, "This is not a criminal trial as that term is ordinarily understood. It is more like the opening of a summer university. . . The defendant, Scopes, is . . . a negligible factor. Nothing serious can happen to him. The contest is entirely over ideas."[12]

In a gesture of equality, Darrow and Bryan had each been feted with consecutive banquets by the Chamber of Commerce before the trial commenced. But Darrow knew the deck was heavily stacked against the defense team. From what it appeared, the jury pool consisted mostly of conservative Christian men whose preachers warned them in Sunday sermons that those who questioned the literal truth of Genesis would be damned to Hell. The judge himself arrived in court with both a well-thumbed Bible and a statute book. Darrow soon began to wonder why the judge bothered at all with the latter. The very first day of trial set the tone with an invocation by a local minister that commenced, "We are conscious, our Father, that Thou art the source of our wisdom and of our power . . . . We come to Thee this morning, our divine Father, that we may seek from Thee that wisdom to so transact the business of this court in such a way and manner that Thy name may be honored and glorified among men."[13] Rev. Cartwright elicited amens from the gallery as he asked the Holy Spirit to "be with the jury and with the accused and with all the attorneys . . . [to] be loyal to God."[14]

Not surprisingly, the prosecution accepted every one of the panel of one hundred white men whose name was drawn from a hat for jury service. Darrow and his co-counsel realized they would do more harm than good by questioning the men extensively on their ability to be objective. Instead, they focused on just three basic issues. Did the jurors have preconceived ideas about evolution? Did they consider the Bible to be for or against evolution? Would they each make up their own minds based on evidence produced at the trial? It was clear from their answers that all the men relished having front-row seats at the spectacle. Only a few admitted to bias that forced their elimination. Though seasoned reporters like H. L. Mencken were highly critical of the jury's pro-Creationism bias, one East Coast African-American newspaper editor saw nothing unusual in the situation from his perspective: "The Scopes' jury is typical—typical of the judgment bar before which black men and women in the bourbon south must stand when charged with crime against members of the opposite group."[15]

The defense team primarily pinned its hopes for winning the case on pretrial arguments to the judge that the Butler Act was unconstitutional. They also intended to put on testimony from several leading scientists who believed both in God and in evolution, though not the literal truth of the Bible. Darrow and his co-counsel already had the upper hand in the court of public opinion. The scientists would cement that position. Secretly, Darrow planned to back that demonstration up by destroying Bryan's credibility. The defense would call Bryan himself to the stand and force him to answer under oath how much of Genesis he really took at face value. Though most reporters found Darrow extraordinarily effective in arguing the illegality of the Butler Act, he likely realized that he had made little headway with the conservative judge. In any event, the defense exhibited no surprise when Judge Raulston upheld the new law. Then the judge ruled out live testimony from scientific defense witnesses, upholding the prosecutors' position that the law precluded *any* teaching that men descended from lower animals even if it was consistent with theology.

The overcrowded courtroom was exceedingly hot. Judge Raulston also was concerned its floor could not hold all the extra weight. By Monday of the second week, Judge Raulston moved the proceedings to a specially built platform on the lawn in front of the courthouse where it could be viewed by thousands of spectators. As bottles of soft drinks were hawked to the thirsty crowd, the defense surprised the prosecution and spectators by calling Bryan to the stand. Bryan rose to the challenge, to the applause of many spectators. But, as Darrow had anticipated, Bryan floundered in answering pointed questions about his belief in the literal truth of the Bible, which ended with a shouting match between the two. *The New York Times* described Darrow's cross-examination of Bryan as "the most amazing courtroom scene in Anglo-American history."[16] Yet the next day, the trial judge ruled Darrow's examination of Bryan irrelevant and struck it from the record.

Back inside the courtroom, Darrow ended the proceedings abruptly. He explained to the jury that there was no factual issue for them to decide. Since the defense did not dispute what Scopes had taught, Darrow did not want to waste the court and jury's time. He considered Scopes' conviction a foregone conclusion. As Darrow had planned, the prosecutor was then also barred under Tennessee law from making a summation. The speech Bryan had prepared to rouse the faithful in the gallery and inspire the jury would have to await another forum. The jury retired for less than ten minutes and came back with their only choice: defendant John Thomas Scopes was found guilty of violating Tennessee's Butler Act. The judge then ordered Scopes to pay a $100 fine.

Constitutional scholar Douglas Linden describes the twelve-day Scope trial as "a symbolic struggle for America's culture between the forces of Traditionalism and the forces of Modernism . . . [T]he Scopes Trial was about what much of the twentieth century has been about."[17] Prof. Edward Gaffney, reviewing Prof. Larson's book for *The Los Angeles Times,* was more qualified in assessing the impact of that trial. He credited the Scopes trial with coming "close to meriting the designation 'trial of the century,' at least for its lasting impact on American culture."[18] The jury itself was never asked to grapple with either modernism versus traditionalism or individual rights versus majoritarian rule. As a consequence of the court's rulings and the defense strategy, the jury only heard about two hours of testimony, and almost no argument. In the end, it had no real decision-making role at all. The case ended anti-climactically with a conceded verdict of guilty that the ACLU could then appeal on constitutional grounds.

Bryan died while napping less than two weeks later, to be eulogized as a martyr to the cause. Darrow argued the appeal the following year before the Tennessee Supreme Court, which, much to the ACLU's dismay, reversed the conviction on a technicality that precluded further appeal of the constitutional issue to the United States Supreme Court.[19] The result in the case itself was thus a draw. In the meantime, Hunter's biology text was revised to delete the word "evolution" and almost all discussion of its related concepts. The book did mention that man was a vertebrate and a mammal and included Charles Darwin as one of the "Great Names in Biology." The category of Caucasians was expanded to include Hindus and Arabs of Asia, but was no longer described as "the highest type of all." What still remained largely unchanged was the advocacy of forced eugenics. To the passage on "Parasitism and its Cost to Society" was now added, "It is estimated that between 25% and 50% of all prisoners in penal institutions are feeble-minded."[20]

Creationists, buoyed by their successful defense of the Butler Act, were able to convince legislatures in a number of other states—mostly in the South—to pass similar laws against teaching evolution in the public schools. The Butler Act itself remained on the books for another forty years until the Supreme Court of the United States ultimately ruled in favor of the ACLU's original position—that state bans on teaching evolution were unconstitutional violations of the Establishment Clause of the First Amendment.[21]

Although Fundamentalists considered their crusade a holy war, the nation's fear of losing the Cold War won out. Creationists controlling public school curricula began to be perceived as undermining the country's standing as a world power. When the Russians launched Sputnik in the fall of 1957, concern that the Soviet Union was surpassing the United States in scientific advances prompted Congress to pass the National Defense Education Act. Among other changes, that 1958 law financed revised high school textbooks highlighting Darwin's theory of evolution as a key biological principle underlying the modern science of genetics. So, for the last half of the 20th century the actual issue tried in Dayton greatly diminished in real world significance just as the theatrical 1925 confrontation hit Broadway and began its enduring reincarnation in theaters and movies. Yet certain pockets of American school systems persisted in their strong resistance to Darwin's theory. Preachers in the pulpit, Sunday school teachers, home schooling parents, and conservative Christian religious schools continued to wage war against a scientific principle that they dismissed as untested. In the Deep South, local officials pasted disclaimers in the inside cover of some public school textbooks, disputing the scientific evidence that supported the theory of evolution.

* * * * *

The legendary criminal defense lawyer wanted to retire and vowed to take no more cases. Instead, he traveled the lecture circuit. But in October of 1925, Darrow could not resist returning to the forefront of the civil rights movement. A contingent from the NAACP begged him to come to Detroit to help defend a black doctor, his family, and friends—eleven people altogether—accused of murdering a spectator as a white mob tried to prevent the doctor's family from moving into their neighborhood. Darrow saw an extraordinary opportunity to expound upon the nation's sorry history of racial discrimination, with stakes as high as they could get. The challenge was to convince an all-white jury that a black man had the same right to occupy his own home in peace as the jurors themselves did.

10. EVEN A BLACK MAN'S HOME IS HIS CASTLE: Pyrrhic Victory In The Sweet Murder Trials

"The case is won or lost now.
The rest is window dressing."

CLARENCE DARROW'S WHISPERED ASIDE
AFTER SELECTING A JURY FOR THE FIRST SWEET MURDER TRIAL

Gladys Sweet spent the spring of 1925 scouring Detroit for a home for herself, her husband of three years and their toddler Marguerite, whom they called Iva. Her goal was to find an attractive bungalow at least as big as her parents' three-bedroom house on the city's northeast side. Like most young mothers, Gladys wanted a safe neighborhood, a decent school and a small yard where Iva could play. Housing prices had risen dramatically in the past year, but even so, if the family had been white, her quest would have posed little difficulty. Bungalows of the kind Gladys had in mind sold for around $12,000 to $13,000.

Gladys was a strikingly poised twenty-three-year-old, raised with impeccable manners and a fine appreciation for culture. She had long, dark hair with auburn highlights that she kept in a neat chignon, alluring brown eyes with dark lashes, and the bearing of a self-assured only child. Too thin and toothy to be considered beautiful, Gladys had about her a quiet sophistication and charm that disarmed most people, and which held her husband in awe.

Gladys and Ossian had just returned from a year abroad where he had the much-envied opportunity to study for a year with Nobel Prize–winner Dr. Marie Curie. The only discrimination they faced was when the American hospital in Paris had refused to allow Gladys to give birth there. Fortunately, Iva's health wasn't jeopardized. The Sweets had lost their first born, a premature baby son, in the summer of 1923. Back in Detroit in June of 1924, Dr. Sweet resumed his gynecology practice and took a position at Dunbar Hospital, the city's first black hospital. The couple and their daughter Iva then spent a cramped year living again with her parents.

Gladys was born in Pittsburgh when her mother was only seventeen; Gladys never knew her father. In Detroit, where they moved when Gladys was seven, her stepfather Benjamin Mitchell made a good living as a piano teacher and orchestra musician, enough to afford a car. Yet he and his wife Rosella had to take in a boarder to pay the mortgage. The family regularly attended St. Matthew's Church, the congregation to which the best black families belonged. Unlike her husband, Gladys was light-skinned. Her mother's father was white. Gladys could almost pass for white, too. In looking for her own home, Gladys checked out communities on the East Side and got repeatedly turned down. She did not shrink from being the first black family on the block. On the street where she grew up, there had been only one black couple besides her parents. Gladys had been the only black child in her elementary school class and among the few in her high school.

Ossian Sweet had spent many summers in Detroit as a bellhop and at other low-paying jobs before he returned to the city in 1921 with his long-sought medical degree. By age thirty, Dr. Sweet had saved enough and earned enough that, if he were white, he would have had no trouble making a down payment on their dream house and covering a bank mortgage. But banks would not lend to blacks trying to buy homes in white districts, and sellers quoted black buyers a hefty premium, if they made any proposal at all. Some newer developments had restrictive deeds preventing sales to Negroes. Gladys did not appreciate how racially charged the city had recently become. Her mistake turned out to be fatal.

In the late 19th century, Detroit had both thriving boat engine factories and high-quality carriage builders. The combination made it ideal turf for the new automobile industry. Since 1900, the city's population had grown almost fivefold, emerging as the country's fourth largest metropolis. Henry Ford's wildly popular Model T prompted the need for many thousand assembly line workers. His competitors Chrysler, General Motors, the Dodge brothers, and their suppliers also advertised widely for their ever-expanding labor requirements. Back in 1910, when Gladys was new to Detroit, white families did not feel threatened by their rare black neighbors. There were fewer than six thousand Negroes in the whole city, mostly living in three central districts near the railroad tracks where poor Russian Jews, Italians, Greeks, and Syrians had located. That area had long been called Black Bottom for the darkness of its soil. Starting in 1915, a surge of new employees, both black and white, migrated from the South, lured by Ford's offer of $5 per day—twice the going wage. By 1925, Detroit boasted 1,250,000 residents, including 82,000 Negroes. Most blacks new to Motor City crammed into the same three disease-plagued city districts where less than a tenth as many lived in 1910, with accommodations so scarce some fleabag hotels rented beds in eight-hour-shifts. Only half of Black Bottom had running water.

In 1921, when the Ku Klux Klan first organized in Detroit, just 3,000 people identified themselves as members. By the spring of 1923, there were 22,000 in the rapidly growing political movement. Most white Southerners had moved into Detroit's working class neighborhoods on the West Side, anxious to keep their women and daughters from mixing with black men and foreigners. The transplanted Fundamentalists found the urban culture of the Roaring Twenties particularly disturbing. They steered clear of the swarthy, Mafia-connected, Sicilian community and shunned Jewish bootleggers, Irish and Polish Catholics, Greeks, Russians, and other immigrants on the city's East Side. Indeed, as in Chicago and New York, ethnic and racial groups formed their own protective clusters where similarly self-identified newcomers commonly made their own home.

The newly arriving whites from the South mostly blamed Detroit's decadence on the influence of degenerate blacks. In fact, those looking to indulge in their favorite sin could find thousands of beer joints, drug sellers, prostitutes, and gambling dens throughout the city. Yet it was easier to focus on Black Bottom. It featured jazz and blues, speakeasies, gambling, pool halls, and rampant crime. Southern whites feared this loose behavior would spread if they did not remain vigilant; they joined forces with anxious Protestant locals to prevent any Negroes from moving onto their blocks.

Henry Ford had spearheaded a reform government in Detroit, which officially became a dry city two years before the Eighteenth Amendment went into effect. By the early '20s, the Ku Klux Klan—with its teetotaling, moralistic image and isolationist message—emerged as a powerful political machine, electing several city council members. Opponents got a frightening look at its sinister side in November of 1923, when members stormed an anti-Klan rally and 50,000 robed Klansmen gathered with flaming torches in nearby Dearborn. By 1925, the white supremacist organization boasted that Detroit had become its largest urban base in the nation. In the fall of 1924, the KKK sponsored a hand-picked unknown, Charles Bowles, as the write-in "American values" candidate for mayor. Bowles barely lost out in a three-way race to Johnny Smith, the street-smart Polish Catholic candidate supported by immigrants, Catholics, and blacks. Had misspelled ballots been counted, Bowles would have won. The KKK was bent on revenge. Its marketing tool was neighborhood improvement associations, a civic-sounding name for racial exclusion. The KKK argued that black neighbors drove down property values and should be forced out by any means, legal or not.

Gladys Sweet's exhaustive search included small black middle-class neighborhoods on the East Side which would pose a long commute for her husband. She found real-estate agents resistant to showing her anything in white neighborhoods, but she remained determined to succeed. By late May, Gladys thought she had found an excellent choice. It was a well-built brick cottage on Garland Avenue at the intersection of Charlevoix, a major boulevard with a streetcar line on the East Side, four miles from the city's center. Gladys noticed that across Charlevoix were an elementary school and a grocery store, several two-story flats, and an apartment house. The neighborhood was a mix of renters and owners of diverse Northern European ethnicity. The men mostly held high-level blue collar jobs. Some had spent many generations in Detroit. Others had moved recently from other cities in the north. The women were housewives or ran boarding houses. Many men who owned their own homes were barely hanging on with two or three mortgages, fearful of what would happen if they missed a paycheck.

Gladys enjoyed at first sight the shaded front porch of the arts-and-crafts style bungalow and appreciated how well-kept it looked with its newly painted shingles. The narrow lot was 125 feet deep, with a small, fenced-in backyard for Iva. Once inside, Gladys fell in love with the special touches that the Belgian builder had created for his family. The living room was trimmed in polished oak and had leaded glass windows along one wall. It also included a fireplace with inlaid Dutch tiles. The dining room was trimmed in matching oak and had an attractive chandelier, a handsome, built-in china cabinet on one end and bookcases on the other. Best of all, Gladys noticed that an adjacent alcove could later fit a piano. Upstairs, there were four bedrooms so Iva could have her own, even if they rented out two to boarders.

Though Gladys took heart from the fact that the sellers were an inter-racial couple, Mr. Smith was so light-skinned he normally passed for white. He had taken advantage of his appearance to establish a thriving real estate practice where no other black agents were permitted to compete. His neighbors had never been sure of his pigmentation. It appeared that the appraisers and banks had not either. If a new black family moved in, property values could easily plummet and the chance of refinancing any house on the block evaporate.

Though Ossian liked the idea of owning the best house on the block with its own attached garage, unlike Gladys he remained quite nervous about the transaction. He tried not to show the fear that gnawed at him. Gladys had heard her cousins' account of the bloody Chicago riots of 1919, targeting mainly blacks who moved into white neighborhoods. Ossian had been appalled at the New Year's Day 1923 murders and destruction of Rosewood, Florida, by a white mob searching for a black rapist. Rosewood was like the Florida town in which he had been raised. In recent years, he had seen plastered over the front pages of *The Chicago Defender* many other gory stories of race violence, each of which sent chills down his spine.

For Gladys, these events happened to other people. Unlike his wife, when Ossian was in medical school in Washington, D.C., in the Red

Summer of 1919, he had witnessed men in uniform pull a black man from a trolley and club him senseless. Ossian still vividly recalled with horror the scene he had witnessed as a five-year-old child hiding in a bush by a bridge in Bartow, Florida. A frenzied mob of whites lynched and set fire to his neighbor's sixteen-year-old son, accused of raping and murdering a white woman. Ossian could still hear the teenager's shrieks of agony and picture the laughing crowd of respectable white townspeople taking Fred Rochelle's charred bones home as mementoes.

In March of 1925, a black woman who moved with her baby into a white neighborhood in Detroit had her house stoned. When she fired a shotgun over the assailants' heads, she was arrested, though charges were later dropped. Other black families long ensconced in white communities suddenly faced harassment. But Gladys wanted Iva to grow up in a decent neighborhood like the one Gladys had enjoyed. She convinced Ossian that he had earned that right. Most Detroit physicians lived in even better neighborhoods than the one Gladys coveted. Ossian did feel self-righteous. When he was just thirteen, his parents had sent him North from his segregated Florida hometown on a scholarship to a black Methodist school in Xenia, Ohio. The scholarship never materialized. Rather than admit defeat, he had taken backbreaking menial jobs to pay his way while pursuing an almost unheard-of college degree and professional career. Ossian's parents had drilled in him the duty to lead by example. It was second nature to help his next brother Otis become a dentist and assist Henry with college. Ossian's training placed him among the "Talented Tenth" that W. E. B. Dubois encouraged to advance the Negro race with their coattails.

The two-story brick house Gladys found was only a few miles from where she had been raised and presented a short commute for Ossian Sweet. Dr. Sweet was cautiously optimistic after he sat with the sellers several times on their porch and no neighbors seemed to take offense. He had deliberately taken over negotiations because Gladys was so light-skinned. Wearing his tailored suit and tie, pressed shirt, horn-rimmed glasses, and a well-trimmed moustache, he probably thought he reassured his neighbors. Mr. Smith said he believed that his neighbors knew that he was black; none had ever bothered him. His wife swore that no Klansmen lived in the area. Ossian felt better. The negotiations were extremely lopsided. Mr. Smith took advantage of the Sweets' lack of options and priced the bungalow about fifty percent higher than it would have sold to a white buyer. At $18,500, Ossian could just barely afford it. The Smiths further gouged the Sweets by insisting on eighteen percent interest. They would retain title to the property for ten years while Dr. Sweet paid off the balance. Ossian saw little choice but to accept the harsh terms. His brother Otis, a dentist, could rent one bedroom and the Sweets could find another boarder. Ossian Sweet swallowed his fears and decided to embrace the challenge—he closed the deal on June 7. The Smiths would vacate by the end of July.

In late June, a mob attacked the new home of Dunbar's chief of surgery in an upscale white neighborhood. Dr. Turner was one of the city's most venerated physicians, who treated both white and black patients, but that mattered not a whit to the hooligans who stormed his house, pulled out the telephone lines, and destroyed his furnishings. Fearful for his life, Dr. Turner deeded his house to a KKK-backed neighborhood association that same night. Dr. Sweet now agonized over his decision. Although he disliked confrontation, he knew that blacks had fought back in Washington, D.C., in 1919. Emboldened black newspapers touted "The NEW NEGRO" for whom the "time for cringing is over."[1] Ossian was not part of the movement for a separatist African Black Brotherhood or, for that matter, a member of Detroit's NAACP. He simply embraced the principles of the NAACP's Talented Tenth to achieve integration by persistence and example.

Before the summer of 1925, Ossian's only public protest consisted of joining the lone table of black professionals at a banquet for Detroit superstar Ty Cobb. Their aim had been to discomfit the white supremacists in attendance and perhaps get a rise out of baseball's most virulent racist. Dr. Sweet now spent long hours talking to Dr. Turner and other colleagues. Most encouraged him to go ahead. More than pride was at stake, Dr. Sweet had already paid the down payment. But he knew what standing his ground meant. Guns were the only equalizer. He had received weapons training in the Student Army Training Corps in medical school during WW I and kept a .38 Smith and Wesson a patient had traded him for medical care.

The atmosphere got even uglier in early July, when 10,000 members of the KKK rallied under a burning cross on Detroit's West Side to lobby for a proposed law limiting the districts where black residents could live—an ordinance that might well run afoul of the Constitution. The United States Supreme Court had handed the NAACP a victory in 1917 by unanimously striking down a Kentucky segregation ordinance for violating the Fourteenth Amendment. But the high court ruling did not apply to discrimination by private citizens. Direct action felt far more satisfying to KKK members anyway. Several hundred armed men stormed the home of another Negro who moved into an all-white neighborhood. On July 10, thousands of whites wielding bricks and stones forced yet another colored man and his family to flee his new home amid cries of "lynch him."[2] Mayor Smith responded by warning against riots, which only spurred the KKK to further defiance.

By early July, the neighbors of 2905 Garland Avenue all knew about the Sweets' impending arrival. On July 12, posters appeared throughout the neighborhood announcing a meeting on July 14 for "self-defense" at the Howe elementary school. More than six hundred white residents—many only renters—came to the auditorium to join the new Waterworks Park Home Improvement Association. The guest speaker was the same man who had spearheaded the assault on Dr. Turner's residence. His biggest applause line was "Where the nigger shows his head, the white must shoot."[3] Dr. Sweet told his two brothers, "I have to die like a man or live a coward."[4] So he prepared as best he could. He postponed the move to September 8, the first day of school. His brother Otis contacted the police for protection. He and Henry agreed to join Ossian in defending the home for the first several nights. Twenty-one-year-old Henry was in Detroit only for the summer before entering his senior year in college. Dr. Sweet also pleaded with a few other good friends and business associates to help him ward off any invasion. The Sweets left Iva with her grandparents for the time being.

Dr. Sweet had hired a driver and handyman to help with the moving van It did not take long to settle in because the Sweets had not yet accumulated much furniture. Within an hour of their arrival, a policeman knocked on the door and let them know he and four other officers were stationed outside to protect them. Dr. Sweet did not tell the officer that he had brought into the home a satchel full of newly purchased guns and rounds of ammunition. More than a hundred people gathered outside the first night, surprised to see police protecting the sidewalk in front of the Sweets' property, wondering whose side they were on. The Detroit police force included many Klansmen, for whom such an assignment would have been anathema. A few rocks hit the house around 3 a.m., but otherwise the night was eerily quiet. The Sweets and their guests ate an uncomfortable dinner that lasted past dark, not daring to turn on lights when they had no curtains yet. They spent a sleepless night with the guns by their sides in case of attack. The next morning a neighbor warned that the Sweets better abandon their home before dark because an even bigger crowd was coming back. Ossian again asked his brothers and friends to join him the night of September 9.

That morning, Gladys and Ossian Sweet optimistically went furniture shopping, but returned to hear more warnings that neighbors intended to force the "niggers" out that night. As promised, a dozen police were stationed outside, but they never tried to disperse the menacing gathering on the street corner. Around 8 p.m., Otis arrived in a taxi with a friend. Someone shouted, "Here's niggers! There they go! Get them! Get them!"[5] The pair made it safely into the dark house as someone began throwing stones. Then others joined in, breaking a window. The police did not stop the hailstorm of rocks. Inside the house, panic reigned. Ossian again passed the guns out among the men. As the pelting continued, shots rang out from the second floor window and back porch. Outside, a man screamed in pain, shot through the back. Another sustained a minor leg injury. Officers called for reinforcements. Then they arrested all eleven people in the Sweets' home, marching them out a back alley and into a paddy wagon while waving their guns to hold back the seething crowd, now growing into the thousands.

The Sweets realized their situation was dire; someone had died. The men called their lawyers at the first opportunity. Detroit cops were notorious for beating confessions out of arrested black men, keeping them from access to lawyers and sometimes killing them with impunity. This time, the chief prosecutor sent an assistant to ensure a civilized interrogation. Yet the lawyers were denied access to their clients. As questioning proceeded into the night, the Sweets learned that a neighbor named Leon Breiner had died. He was a member of the new neighborhood association, but had only stopped to watch the goings on. At first, all of the defendants denied that they had gathered in the house in anticipation of violence, but a friend of Ossian's soon confessed the truth in hopes of leniency. Henry then admitted that he had fired a rifle from the second floor window. He was aiming just over the heads of the mob to get them to leave the family alone. A policeman later said he had also emptied his gun. More shots had been fired, but it was unclear by whom.

A reporter for *The Detroit News* had happened on the scene. He saw the large, menacing crowd, the rain of stones pelting the cottage, and the shooting. After taking his family home, he raced to the office with his story, which *The Detroit News* never printed. Instead, all three leading Detroit papers, including William Randolph Hearst's recently purchased *Detroit Times,* filed lock step accounts that exonerated the neighbors and the police. The police inspector on site had been adamant: no mob had gathered; no stones were hurled; the black occupants opened fire without provocation upon peacefully clustered neighbors. Other details emerged. The blacks had moved in with almost no furnishings, but plenty of ammo, ready to precipitate trouble. The story became an angry rallying cry as threats of race violence unnerved the city. The KKK held a huge rally and demanded murder prosecutions—it looked like the issue that could clinch them the mayor's office. The next day the district attorney's office announced first degree murder charges against all eleven people in the house since it could not tell who fired the fatal bullet. Gladys had never even held a gun.

By Saturday, the Detroit NAACP had agreed to defend the case, and the lawyers actually met with their clients. A three-day preliminary hearing was scheduled for the following week. As rumors spread of impending race war, Mayor Smith spoke out for the first time since the shooting. Rather than criticize the police in any way, he lambasted both the Invisible Empire and black people who moved into white neighborhoods. He accused people like the Sweets of being tools of the KKK and urged all Negroes to remain voluntarily segregated rather than insist on a right to move into "districts in which their presence would cause a disturbance."[6] The NAACP was furious to see their white allies beating a hasty retreat for fear of violence.

The NAACP brought five hundred supporters to the preliminary hearing. Police in plainclothes spread out through the crowded gallery in case any trouble broke out, but there was none. Rather than focus on the behavior of the defendants, Assistant Prosecutor Lester Moll brought witness after witness to describe in similar coached fashion how peaceful the folks on the street had been at the time a Negro in the newly purchased house shot and killed a neighbor. It worked. The judge ordered all of the defendants to stand trial for murder without bail. The new Presiding Judge, thirty-four-year-old Democrat Frank Murphy, assigned himself to try the politically explosive case. He drew the KKK's wrath when he released Gladys Sweet from the women's ward on October 2 on $10,000 bail. It was none too soon; the shocking ordeal of jail had destroyed her appetite. The KKK held another giant rally the next day. On Tuesday, October 6 its candidates for city council won the primary by a huge margin. The KKK expected to take over the entire city government in November, riding high on these murder prosecutions.

Trial was set to begin in mid-October. The men remained in the Wayne County Jail with pimps and burglars, drug addicts and thugs. Hearing bets among the jailers overwhelmingly favoring conviction beat down their spirits. At the same time, a turf battle raged between the local NAACP and its national office. With over three hundred branches, the powerful organization could cherry pick the few cases each year that framed race issues most dramatically. The Sweet prosecution focused on the most widespread problem blacks faced in the North—the perfect vehicle for a national campaign to create a NAACP Legal Defense Fund. The national office wanted to replace the three black lawyers already on the case with a high-powered white attorney.

An impasse had been reached before Henry Sweet, Sr. arrived from Florida to visit his three sons behind bars and reassure them how proud he was of their principled stand. Otis Sweet then sent telegrams to both the Detroit and national NAACP offices urging the national office to take the case over: "This is a case in which more is involved than the liberties of the eleven persons concerned; it is a case that boldly challenges the liberties, the hopes, and the aspirations of fifteen million colored Americans . . . to live without molestation and prosecution."[7] Soon word came to the defendants that the national NAACP leadership had talked Clarence Darrow into taking over the lead role for the defense team.

Darrow had frequently defended impoverished blacks and agreed to handle this case for a steep discount. He and his wife Ruby were themselves charter members of the NAACP, though he made Board members apprehensive by sitting with black students in a segregated train car and giving speeches advocating miscegenation. Some feared his radical views would backfire, but the publicity the most famous lawyer in America would bring outweighed the risks. Darrow was now sixty-eight years old and semi-retired. Yet he sensed an unparalleled opportunity for a full-bore attack on the history of racism. He made his dramatic public debut in the case at a hearing to request a two week continuance of the trial.

Darrow's first pleasant surprise was Judge Frank Murphy, a red-headed, teetotaling bachelor. The ambitious Irish lawyer had run as a reform candidate on a slate against entrenched conservatives. His 1922 campaign emphasized that the current criminal justice system benefited "political grafters, exploiters of the poor, and profiteers" and left "the friendless and the penniless" with "less than an equal chance of justice." Murphy vowed that, upon election, he would "try to have a temple of justice, not a butcher shop."[8] He had taken the Sweet case himself because every other judge was afraid to handle it. Prosecutor Robert Toms also impressed Darrow with his civility. Toms was a good-natured public servant, several years older than the judge. Toms normally prided himself on not chasing convictions as a numbers game. He felt honor-bound only to prosecute those cases where he felt he had solid evidence of guilt. But then again the Republican did not want to commit political suicide, which was what facing down the KKK would have meant in 1925, particularly on the eve of the hotly contested mayoral election.

Coincident with naming Darrow, the NAACP's chief publicist Walter White released to major newspapers the Sweets' version of the assault. It resulted in a wave of favorable front-page press. Suddenly, the Sweets were celebrities and the betting odds changed. Yet only the black press continued to follow the case closely as one affecting "every Negro in America;" it raised the "question whether prejudice and hatred shall rule our nation or whether a pure democracy shall prevail." *The Chicago Defender* warned "if the police cannot protect us from mob violence, then we must be prepared to protect ourselves." *The Amsterdam News* trumpeted it as "possibly the most important court case the Negro has ever figured in."[9] W. E. B. DuBois lauded Ossian Sweet as a role model.

The trial began on October 30, 1925. As in the Scopes trial, Darrow worked with ACLU General Counsel Arthur Hays. Darrow kept the original three attorneys as a support team and added another white Detroit attorney, for a total of six lawyers. Darrow was never one for handling the nuts and bolts. He liked to focus on the big picture, the critical work of jury selection, and the closing argument. He filled many evenings with speech engagements and political discussions over drinks, leaving most trial preparation to his co-counsel. Unlike his laid-back appearance in the heat of Dayton, Tennessee, Darrow came neatly groomed with his suit freshly pressed. The risk of life imprisonment demanded formality. Picking the jury for eleven defendants in a murder case gave the defense counsel thirty challenges per defendant, 330 opportunities to strike jurors. It was the main reason they opted to have all eleven defendants tried together. Yet Darrow left most of the challenges unused.

It was easy to get the judge to excuse for cause three admitted members of the KKK. Neither Darrow nor the prosecutor wanted the few women who showed up—a new phenomenon since the passage of the Nineteenth Amendment. Darrow said women took their role too seriously. He also avoided rich men, Presbyterians, Prohibitionists, and Baptists. Seven of the twelve selected were Catholics. Most were fathers with minor children, but the defense included one man past seventy and one just twenty-one, who had not yet left home. The jurors resided all over Detroit; some owned their own homes; some were tenants. Darrow's selections mostly favored workers with family ties to foreigners—a sign that they more likely supported Detroit's mayor than the Invisible Empire. By the time they finished, Toms had been far more choosy. To observers, Darrow seemed to be gambling that it was better to set the panel at ease than to give them the impression that only persons of a particular background would see the case his way. He conveyed the notion that all men with reasonably open minds were acceptable, while risking failure to discover entrenched prejudice. Some observers feared Darrow had been too hasty.

Hays opened the trial by reminding the jury of the age-old British right to self-defense: "The poorest man may in his cottage bid defiance to all the forces of the Crown; it may be frail, its roof may shake, the wind may blow through it; the storm may enter, the ram may enter; but the King of England cannot enter; all his forces dare not cross the threshold of that ruined tenement."[10] Michigan law favored the defense. If the Sweets had good reason to fear imminent danger, they could protect their home with deadly force even if no invasion was actually contemplated. Justifiable belief that a dangerous mob was about to descend upon them was enough. Under state law, a mob could be proved in one of two ways: a dozen or more armed persons or thirty unarmed persons gathered to intimidate or cause harm. The minimum standard of harm was $25, which the window breakage easily met.

Toms had his work cut out for him to deny the existence of a mob. Yet the jury could be expected to blame the Sweets for deliberately forcing the issue, arriving heavily armed and firing into the crowd even though they had police protection. When examined by the defense, some of the neighbors reluctantly admitted to a crowd far in excess of thirty, which kept growing larger and more ominous. Then a thirteen-year-old boy admitted what the adults would not—that four or five teens started throwing stones and broke at least one window before the shooting happened.

Fortunately for the defense, by the time of trial, KKK influence had already passed its peak. Liberal supporters rallied to the incumbent mayor's defense with backing from William Randolph Hearst's *Detroit Times* and the far more conservative *Detroit Free Press.* Three days into the trial, Mayor Smith won reelection by a thirty-thousand-vote margin in his rematch with KKK candidate Bowles. In fact, KKK influence nationwide had just taken a major blow due to a front-page scandal that enveloped one of its two most powerful leaders, Grand Dragon David Stephenson. Stephenson, who referred to himself as "the law in Indiana," was so influential in other states that he had his sights on securing nomination as the

1928 Republican presidential candidate. That was before the thirty-four-year-old demagogue's wild private life caught up with him.

Stephenson had been indicted in Indiana in the spring following the death of a twenty-seven-year-old state employee named Madge Oberholtzer. His murder trial started on October 12, 1925, spreading salacious details over the front pages based largely on a sworn statement Oberholtzer had made shortly before she died. With the help of two aides, the drunken Grand Dragon had lured her from her parents' home under false pretenses, abducted and drugged Oberholtzer, then raped and bit her so savagely that doctors who examined her afterward said she looked like she had been "chewed by a cannibal."[11] Oberholtzer had then attempted suicide, but recovered and died a few weeks later from infections in her left breast. On November 14, Stephenson's murder trial ended with a second-degree-murder conviction and life sentence, just before Ossian Sweet took the stand in Detroit. By then, the crowded gallery was filled with mostly black spectators, though when the trial began many more whites had flocked to the proceedings.

Though it is always risky for a defendant to testify in a criminal case, the benefits here far outweighed the downside. Dr. Sweet had a golden opportunity on the stand to educate the all-white jury about his Horatio Alger life story and, most particularly, all of the fear factors that affected his state of mind as he holed up with his wife, brothers, and other recruits to defend his new home. When Dr. Sweet began to describe the neighbor he saw burnt alive when he was a child in Florida twenty-five years earlier, Toms jumped up to object to its relevance. Darrow rose to respond: "What we learn as children we remember—it gets fastened to the mind . . . this defendant's actions were predicated on the psychology of the past . . ."[12] It was a variation on Darrow's Leopold and Loeb defense the year before. Here, the difference between judges like Samuel McReynolds and Webster Thayer, on the one hand, and Chicago's Judge Caverly and Detroit's Frank Murphy, on the other, was quite evident. Judge Murphy overruled Toms' objection.

Darrow then ceded the floor to Hays, who elicited from Dr. Sweet one horrid event etched in his mind after another: the trolley passenger he saw beaten in Washington, D.C.; the murder of a black surgeon in Tulsa, Oklahoma; the killing of two Negro professionals in Arkansas; the destruction of the town of Rosewood; and other acts of race violence, culminating in the June and July attacks on black home owners in Detroit. All formed the context in which Dr. Sweet acted to defend his family from the menacing crowd stoning his home September 9, 1925. Journalists noted the whole courtroom's silence at the riveting details.

In his closing argument, Darrow invited the jury to take a close look at the eleven defendants, including demure Gladys Sweet and the well-groomed professional men who had come to the aid of her beleaguered husband. They presented a stark contrast to the inarticulate neighbors the prosecution had placed on the stand, who fidgeted in response to questions whether they harbored any ill will toward their new black neighbors, why they joined the neighborhood protection association, and exactly what such a huge number of them were doing on the street that night. Darrow challenged the all-white jury to put themselves in his clients' shoes. "I know that if these defendants had been a white group defending themselves from a colored mob, they never would have been arrested or tried. My clients are charged with murder, but they are really charged with being black. . . . You are facing a problem of two races, a problem that will take centuries to solve. . . . Every policeman knew that the crowd was after the Negroes. But no one batted an eye. . . . Draw upon your imagination and think how you would feel if you fired at some black man in a black community, and then had to be tried by them. . ."[13]

When the jury retired to deliberate on November 25 the aged war horse was exhausted. The jurors' muffled voices carried outside the room as they argued with each other into the night until 2 a.m. They resumed all Thanksgiving Day, except for a break ordered by the judge for an elaborate turkey dinner. At 11 p.m. they reported they were deadlocked; the judge ordered them to deliberate again the next day. Darrow and a few close friends shared some Scotch while they waited. By his side was Josephine Gomon, a married local activist less than half his age whose friendship Darrow had cultivated when Ruby wasn't looking. By the trial's end, the irrepressible flirt had decided Jo Gomon was a kindred spirit. (Gomon would win recognition as "the City's Conscience" during the Depression, when she turned Detroit's welfare system into a model of compassionate efficiency.) After forty-six hours, the jurors came back to court bedraggled and exhausted, unable to reach a verdict. Judge Murphy declared a mistrial on November 27 and the following day ordered the defendants released on bail. Word had it that ten jurors voted for acquittal of all the defendants except Ossian and Henry Sweet, and five would have acquitted them as well. Seven jurors had voted to convict both brothers of second degree murder or manslaughter. None voted for first degree murder.

During the fall, police had guarded the Sweets' home from vandalism. A week before the trial ended, an officer saw someone running away after throwing rags soaked in gasoline into the Sweets' garage. The fire was extinguished with only minor damage. Yet no arrest followed. The police inspector announced plans to withdraw as soon as the Sweets resumed occupancy. Instead, the NAACP helped Dr. Sweet with monthly payments on the empty home while he joined Gladys and Iva in a small apartment a mile away in another neighborhood. Dr. Sweet worried about the two of them coughing so much all winter, but mostly he reveled in his new celebrity status, feeling immensely self-important.

Not unexpectedly, Prosecutor Toms announced his intention to retry the eleven defendants for murder. The defense had the right to demand separate trials. This time, they did so. Darrow had concluded that the jury had too many options for assigning guilt with everyone tied together—he wanted to confront them with making a decision on one man's freedom or imprisonment, thumbs up or thumbs down. Darrow exuded confidence, as did Ossian Sweet. But Prosecutor Toms surprisingly decided to start with his younger brother Henry, the only one to admit that he fired a rifle in Breiner's general direction. If Henry was convicted then the others would be tried in turn. If acquitted, no further prosecutions would take place.

By spring the political climate had shifted. The national KKK leadership had terminated the head of its Detroit branch in a messy exchange of accusations plastered all over the newspapers. Mayor Smith made amends for backing off support for the Sweets in the fall by naming a Blue Ribbon Commission to make concrete recommendations to improve race relations in the city. The retrial of Henry Sweet was scheduled for April 1,

1926. Darrow returned to Detroit, but learned in mid-March that Arthur Hays would not rejoin him. Instead, Darrow asked Thomas Chawke to serve as co-counsel, a sharply dressed Irish mob lawyer, reputed to be the best in Detroit. Chawke had no strong interest in the NAACP cause, but would sign on if the price was right. He bargained with the NAACP for higher compensation than Darrow and equal say in handling the case. The NAACP worried about his gangland affiliations, but agreed to his terms. They also kept one of the three original lawyers hired by its local branch, Julian Perry, on the defense team. Though given no active role before the jury, Perry was well known in Detroit. He had run a quixotic campaign as a Republican candidate for the Michigan legislature.

The trial actually started on April 19, 1926, the day after Darrow's sixty-ninth birthday, delayed in part by the death of Judge Murphy's father. Spectators again packed the courtroom, including nationally known figures specially invited by the NAACP to add their dignity to the proceedings. The gallery of the sixty-by-fifty-foot courtroom seated about a hundred on benches. On many days it was standing room only for the mostly black observers. A hundred and sixty-five potential jurors were asked the same general questions about their family background, religion, and politics as in the first trial. But Darrow also had a new tack: "Well you've heard about this case, I suppose? Read about it? Talked about it? Formed an opinion? Got it yet? And it would take evidence to change it? Well I s'pose you're right. Challenge for cause." Both he and Chawke focused on ferreting out prejudice: "Ever had any association with any colored people? No? Understand Dr. Sweet's a colored man—bought a house in a neighborhood where there were no colored people. . . . He was in the house at the time of the shooting. One of eleven. Now you wouldn't want not to be fair. You just tell me yourself whether any views you have or surroundings you have would handicap my clients or the state."[14]

The two defense lawyers were using their preliminary questions to educate the panel in advance on the merits of their case. When Darrow asked the judge to dismiss a juror because he did not want a Negro to move near him, assistant prosecutor Moll jumped to object that "This is not a trial of race prejudice." Darrow responded, "I think we're trying the race question and nothing else." Judge Murphy continued to give the defense broad scope in their questions, agreeing that the jury should be free from prejudice.[15] It took a week to select the jury. The youngest was in his mid-twenties, the oldest over eighty. There were three others over sixty, three middle-aged, and the rest in their twenties. To a keen-eyed reporter, all seemed "straight forward, average men," none of clearly superior intelligence, none below normal.[16] Darrow found it much easier going with one trial already under his belt. The prosecution team did not worry about proof that Henry Sweet actually killed Breiner; its theory was that Henry either fired the fatal bullet or aided and abetted whoever did. The bullet itself had passed through Breiner and never been recovered, so there was no way to ascertain from which gun it had been shot.

Toms had learned lessons from the first trial. He piled onto the table in front of the jury all of the guns that police had confiscated from the Sweets' home, one of which was the likely source of the bullet that killed Breiner. Darrow did not flinch. He stood up and casually admitted to the jury that the bullet may well have come from the gun Henry Sweet used. But that did not make him a murderer; the culprits were those who created the dangerous situation—the people about to testify for the prosecution. Toms then presented seventy-one witnesses—policemen, neighbors, and others on the street that night—who all downplayed the crowd's size and threatening nature. Though subjected to fiercer cross-examination than in the first trial, none would admit seeing a single stone thrown. Yet the police confirmed that they brought in reinforcements because they anticipated violence. By the end of the second week, Darrow was fighting a heavy cold. Yet he finally got a witness to say that the principal speaker at the July 14 meeting had urged the crowd to drive the Sweets out by violence.

Then the defense put on its own witnesses to establish that several hundred people had gathered in an angry mob, some hurling stones. Ossian Sweet testified again, but the defense team wisely kept Henry off the stand. Darrow had already conceded that Henry came to the house to help his older brother defend his home with guns and his life, if need be. The twenty-two-year-old did his part by just sitting at the defense table in his suit, an appealing, very serious young man of average height, short curly hair, and a moustache, a younger version of his much-admired older brother.

Assistant Prosecutor Moll ridiculed the defense for its focus on all of Ossian Sweet's experiences leading up to September 9 rather than just the events of that night and the death of Leon Breiner. Chawke responded with an appeal to the jury's recollection of Detroit's history of tolerance and the risks that people like the jurors and their families also ran: "Have we come to a point in the history of our city when a majority can ride roughshod and ruthlessly over the rights of a minority?"[17] By day's end, the disappointed spectators still had not seen Darrow get up to speak. The next day, the gallery was crammed as tight as could be with onlookers, both white and black, while a huge crowd filled the hall, hoping to catch some glimpse of the proceedings or hear part of Darrow's argument. They were excited just to be part of history in the making.

Darrow talked for seven hours, directly challenging the jury to admit their own prejudice and set it aside. He dissected the prosecution's case and pointed out that it would never have been brought against a white man in similar circumstances: "Life is a hard game, anyhow. But, when the cards are stacked against you, it is terribly hard. And they are stacked against a race for no reason but that they are black." He seemed ready to stop more than once, but resumed out of fear he had not yet convinced his targets. "I would like to see a time when man loves his fellow man, and forgets his color or his creed. . . . I believe the life of a Negro has been a life full of tragedy, of injustice, of oppression. The law has made him equal—but man has not." Finally he apologized for taking so much time, explaining "this case is close to my heart. . . . I ask you, in the name of progress and of the human race, to return a verdict of not guilty in this case!"[18]

Toms had the last opportunity to speak the next morning, but it was anti-climactic. Judge Murphy gave the jury a special instruction that "Real justice does not draw any line of color, race, or creed or class. All charged with crime, rich or poor, humble or great, white or black, are entitled to the same right and the same full measure of justice."[19] The lawyers assumed that deliberations would take nearly as long as the first time, but it was only four hours later that they learned the jury had reached a verdict. A packed courtroom watched the jurors enter one at a time, looking solemn and inscrutable. When the clerk asked for their verdict, the foreman answered in a faltering voice, "Not guilty." Toms, in disbelief, asked for the verdict to be repeated. Ossian Sweet was overcome with emotion. Henry Sweet, Chawke, and Darrow could not help shedding tears of gratitude, nor could the judge. As he stepped off the bench, he told a friend, "This is the greatest experience of my life. That was Clarence Darrow at his best. I will never hear anything like it again. He is the most Christ-like man I have ever known."[20]

In his autobiography, Darrow called his closing argument one of the most satisfying he had ever given. He interpreted the jury's message as "simply that the doctrine that a man's house is his castle applied to the black man as well as to the white man. If not the first time that a white jury had vindicated this principle, it was the first that ever came to my notice." Both Robert Toms and Lester Moll later told Darrow they thought "the verdict was just and did a great deal of good in Detroit."[21]

Toms followed through on his promise that he would hold no further trials against the other defendants. Yet Ossian could take small comfort from the news. Both his wife and daughter had been diagnosed with tuberculosis, which they assumed stemmed from Gladys's three weeks in jail. Dr. Sweet sent them to Arizona for the summer, hoping the heat and dry climate would benefit their lungs. Iva died in August. Gladys brought her body home for burial by their infant son. At the cemetery, a white custodian tried to redirect the funeral procession to the rear entrance for colored folks. Ossian pulled his equalizer out and obtained access through the main gates.[22] Gladys returned to Tucson to try to recover while Ossian stayed in an apartment in Detroit. He moved back into his house in mid-1928, after it had stood vacant for almost three years. Gladys's health continued to decline. She came back to Detroit in early November of 1928 to die at home and be buried with her children. Noting this sad outcome, Darrow did not resent the people who "grievously wronged" his clients, but rather blamed "the bitterness bred through race prejudice . . . So long as this feeling lives, tragedies will result."[23]

Ossian's younger brother Henry earned a law degree and rose to prominence in the Michigan NAACP, but he, too, caught tuberculosis and died in 1940, only thirty-six years old. By then, the clout of the Ku Klux Klan had all but disappeared. From a height of five million members in the 1920s, by 1930 a host of scandals starting with Grand Dragon Stephenson's murder conviction reduced its numbers to 30,000, which dwindled further year by year to near extinction as a national political party. (In the '50s and '60s the name Ku Klux Klan would be used by many new local white supremacist groups in the Deep South and Midwest, often allied over the ensuing years with neo-Nazis. In 2010, the Southern Poverty Law Center counted Ku Klux Klan members as the largest single component of 1000 active hate groups across America. The Anti-Defamation League divides them into 100 chapters with about 5,000 members.)[24]

Supported by a coalition of minorities, Judge Murphy later became Mayor of Detroit and then Governor of Michigan and U.S. Attorney General before he ended his career as President Franklin Roosevelt's appointee to the United States Supreme Court. Justice Murphy joined the high court in 1940, just in time to participate in the landmark decision in *Hansberry v. Lee* that opened the door nationwide to constitutional challenges to discriminatory housing covenants. Four years later Justice Murphy introduced the word "racism" into the Supreme Court's vocabulary in his scathing dissent in *Korematsu v. United States,* the controversial six to three decision upholding the validity of war-time internment camps for Japanese-Americans. Justice Murphy saw no defensible distinction between the internment of Japanese-Americans and "the abhorrent and despicable treatment of minority groups" by Nazi Germany and its allies.[25] Sweet prosecutor Robert Toms became a judge as well, surprisingly devoted to civil rights. In 1947, Toms spent a year in Nuremberg presiding over Nazi war crime trials under the direction of Supreme Court Associate Justice Robert H. Jackson, on leave from the high court. Jackson had been one of Justice Murphy's two colleagues who also dissented in the *Korematsu* case.

Historian Kevin Boyle researched and retold the story of the Sweet trials in *Arc of Justice: A Saga of Race, Civil Rights, and Murder in the Jazz Age.* His prize-winning 2004 book inspired Arthur Beer's 2007 play *Malice Aforethought: The Sweet Trials.* From 1928 on, Ossian Sweet lived in his bungalow in his white neighborhood unmolested. He stayed there for twenty-five years while his practice in Black Bottom flourished. His patients called him "Big Doc." He bought more land and dabbled in politics, remarried and divorced twice. Yet in the end, his finances foundered. Ossian sold his home to another black family and moved to an apartment above his office in the slums. Overweight and in deteriorating health, he became bitter and disillusioned. Ever since Ossian and Gladys had decided to pursue their dream house, he had likely never been without his equalizer. On March 20, 1960, Ossian picked his gun up and held it to his head, firing one shot to end his misery. Soon afterward Black Bottom itself was condemned and replaced in a major urban renewal project. During the July 1967 Detroit riots, vandals destroyed his brother Otis Sweet's dental office, forcing Otis out of practice. Detroit remains highly segregated to this day, suffering from severe economic problems exacerbated by white flight and the collapse of the automobile industry that brought so many blacks to the city for the promise of a better life.

* * * * *

Darrow joined the NAACP board and stepped up his lobbying for civil rights as he wound down his practice. But after he closed his doors for good, the Depression nearly wiped out Darrow's assets. In 1931, the NAACP convinced him to represent nine black teenagers in a compelling Alabama death penalty case involving dubious charges of gang rape. A full quarter of a century since a blood-thirsty Chattanooga lynch mob kept the high court from deciding Ed Johnson's claimed denial of a fair trial, the Ku Klux Klan's political clout had plummeted. The time looked ripe to convince a reticent Supreme Court to tackle the mockery that often passed for justice in capital cases against black defendants. This time the NAACP had fierce competition from the Left as to whose voice would champion the rights of the Scottsboro Boys.

11. SOUTHERN JUSTICE REVISITED: The Railroading of the Scottsboro Boys

Southern trees bear strange fruit,
Blood on the leaves and blood at the root,
Black bodies swinging in the southern breeze,
Strange fruit hanging from the poplar trees.

Abel Meeropol

When Clarence Darrow wrote his autobiography, he considered his summation to the jurors in the Sweet case the highlight of his career. Nothing challenged Americans to reexamine their own souls the way that the cancer of racism repeatedly did throughout the century. In 1855, two years before Darrow's birth, French philosopher Alexis de Tocqueville had focused on the Achilles' heel of the United States: "An old and sincere friend of America, I am uneasy at seeing Slavery retard her progress, tarnish her glory, furnish arms to her detractors, compromise the future career of the Union which is the guaranty of her safety and greatness, and point out beforehand to her, to all her enemies, the spot where they are to strike."[1]

Not much had changed in Darrow's lifetime. In the 1920s, the NAACP reported an average of two lynchings in the Deep South each week. Only a federal law against lynching could be expected to be enforced. Yet not until the fall of 1921 did any sitting President ever dare endorse such a bill. Even then, Warren Harding's support won little respect. It had been whispered for years that one of his own great-great-grandfathers in the West Indies was black. Ignoring the President, Southern Democrats readily blocked passage of the proposed new federal anti-lynching law. Eagerly casting one of his first no votes was Tennessee's freshman Congressman Samuel McReynolds. The former judge still likely recalled with fondness his front-row seat at Ed Johnson's abduction from the Chattanooga jail, frustrating Supreme Court review of the travesty of a rape trial over which McReynolds had presided.

It took another decade before serious national attention turned to ending lynch mobs. One catalyst for action was a ghastly photograph of two black men, Thomas Shipp and Abram Smith, taken in August of 1930 in Marion, Indiana. The night after the two men were arrested for robbery and murder of a white factory worker and alleged rape of his girlfriend, local police collaborated with an angry crowd that broke the two men out of jail and strung them up. The haunting photograph prompted New York school teacher Abel Meeropol to write the poem "Strange Fruit," which he later set to music. (Two decades later Meeropol, a Communist friend of accused spies Julius and Ethel Rosenberg, would adopt their orphaned sons).

The Tuskegee Institute kept a grim tally: 1,837 documented lynchings in the United States from 1900 to 1930, of which 182 were white men and 1,655 blacks. Civil rights activists focused not only on eliminating vigilante justice, but on attacking the thornier problem of "legal lynching" by kangaroo court proceedings. In Cotton Belt states, white men convicted of raping white women were almost never executed, and white men who raped black women were seldom, if ever, prosecuted. At the same time, black men accused of raping white women customarily received the death penalty from all-white juries. The most famous of these cases arose in the spring of 1931 and became a continuing legal saga through the next decade.

The incident on March 25, 1931, started with racial taunts by a white teenager who stepped on the hand of a black nineteen-year-old clinging to the side of a rail car. Soon a race fight broke out among a score of unemployed youths riding hobo on the freight train. As the slow train crossed into Paint Rock, Alabama, from Tennessee, some black teenagers took over a gravel car occupied by white boys and forced all but one of them off the train. The dispossessed boys complained to the station master, who called the sheriff. He quickly deputized a posse to "capture every Negro on the train."[2] When the sheriff arrived at the next station with fifty armed men, they searched all forty-eight cars and hauled off nine black youths they found on board, threw them all on a flatbed truck, and took them to the local jail where the terrified teenagers were held for assault with intent to commit murder. In fact, several blacks involved in the fight had already left the train. To the posse's surprise, in the gravel car where they found six of the youths, they also found, dressed in overalls, twenty-one-year-old Victoria Price and seventeen-year-old Ruby Bates. Both tried to run away and were arrested and jailed, too.

Only after the sheriff asked Price and Bates if the colored boys had bothered them, did they make rape accusations. Price told an elaborate story in which she claimed six boys had attacked her. She identified three of the defendants. Bates could not decide whom to blame. Doctors confirmed that both Price and Bates had recently had intercourse, though all the sperm were dead and not likely the result of sex in the last half hour of the train ride as they both claimed. Bates later confessed that Price, a known prostitute in their home town of Huntsville, Alabama, made up the rape story to fend off prosecution under the Mann Act for transporting Bates across state lines for immoral purposes. All of the boys taken from the train were charged with rape. They were from out of state and broke. None was allowed to contact his family or a lawyer. Locals instantly spread false rumors that one girl had her breast bitten off. A lynch mob gathered at the jail and demanded the boys be turned over for hanging. Officials only dispersed the angry crowd by calling in the National Guard and promising a quick trial "to send them to the chair."[3] Five days after their arrest, armed reserve units transported the boys to the county seat of Scottsboro where they were promptly indicted by an all-white jury.

Barely a week later, the Scottsboro Boys faced trial—the same day as a county fair. The governor again sent armed guards to protect the prisoners with machine guns and bayonets. Permits to enter the gallery became the hottest ticket in town as a standing-room-only crowd of white men filled the garrisoned courthouse. Some 10,000 defenders of Southern womanhood gathered outside awaiting the results. A Tennessee real estate lawyer volunteered to ask for a change of venue on the boys' behalf in light of the lynch mob atmosphere. The trial judge denied the motion based on the sheriff's characterization of the swarming crowd as just friendly and curious. Under continuing armed guard, the prosecutor then conducted four separate trials back to back that, together, took all of five days.

Though the Tennessee lawyer told the judge he was unprepared and unfamiliar with Alabama law, the judge asked him to act as co-counsel for the boys along with a senile sixty-nine-year-old local Alabama lawyer who had not been to trial in many years. The two were given less than half an hour to consult with their clients before the first trial started. They made no objection to the defendants being tried in groups despite the grave risk of guilt by association rather than proof that each of them participated in the capital crime. The boys ranged in age from twelve to nineteen. They had not all been traveling together. A few had not even met each other on board or seen Price or Bates. One was nearly blind and crippled from syphilis. He had been sitting alone in a different car.

In the very first trial, one of the two defendants, Clarence Norris, caught his lawyers by surprise when he tried to save his life by testifying that he had witnessed the other eight rape Price and Bates. He later claimed that police had taken him from his cell the night before and beat him into making that false statement on the promise that he would be spared. Two other defendants later tried the same tactic. The dumbfounded lawyers should have moved to withdraw and request mistrials. They could not represent all of the defendants with such a basic conflict in their stories. Instead, the lawyers solved their dilemma by failing to make any closing argument at all, even to ask the jury to use its discretion to send one or more of the youths to prison instead of the electric chair. When the first two teenagers were sentenced to die, the elated gallery burst into applause. Outside, a band struck up, "There'll be a Hot Time in the Old Town Tonight."[4] Each of the next three trials lasted only a day. The trial of twelve-year-old Roy Wright was last. All but one juror voted for the death penalty against Wright even though, in view of his age, the prosecutor only asked for life imprisonment. The judge had no choice but to declare that one a mistrial.

As eight of the teenagers endured the miseries of death row, national newspapers reported the outrageous details of their prosecution. The

Scottsboro Boys immediately became a cause célèbre for civil rights advocates. The ACLU sent an investigator to gather facts. The Communist Party saw great recruiting potential in embarrassing the American system of justice as they had done through the martyrdom of Sacco and Vanzetti just four years before. Their International Labor Defense Committee ("ILD") immediately sent lawyers to sign the boys up as clients.

The NAACP was at first reticent to champion the controversial cause, but talked Clarence Darrow into coming out of retirement to argue the appeal and represent the defendants on retrial. By then, the ILD had already obtained the consent of the Scottsboro Boys and their parents to represent them. When Darrow arrived in Alabama, a telegram signed by all nine prisoners awaited him. The obviously ghost-written message informed Darrow that he could only join the defense team if he severed his connections with the NAACP and let the ILD control the litigation strategy. For the first time in his long career, the seventy-four-year-old warhorse quit a case in disgust. He felt the ILD lawyers "cared far less for the safety and well-being of those poor Negro boys than the exploitation of their own cause."[5]

On appeal to the Alabama Supreme Court, the convictions were affirmed over the lone dissent of the state's Chief Justice that the defendants had not received a fair trial.[6] On review in *Powell v. Alabama*, the United States Supreme Court found that there had been a clear denial of due process in the trial judge's failure to allow enough time for the defendants to obtain competent counsel. It cited as key factors "the ignorance and illiteracy of the defendants, their youth, the circumstances of public hostility, the imprisonment and the close surveillance of the defendants by the military forces, the fact that their friends and families were all in other states and communication with them necessarily difficult, and above all that they stood in deadly peril of their lives." For the first time ever the high court held that "the necessity of counsel was so vital and imperative" that if the defendants could not obtain their own lawyers the trial court had to make its own "effective appointment of counsel" to comply with the federal Constitution.[7]

On remand, the cases were moved from Scottsboro to Decatur, Alabama. To quell criticism following Darrow's ouster, the ILD recruited as head of the defense team another nationally known defense lawyer,

New Yorker Samuel Leibowitz. Leibowitz was a master of cross-examination reputed to nearly match Darrow in his prime. He agreed to work for free and, with the help of investigative work by the ACLU and ILD, amassed substantial evidence that the two women were lying. Bates admitted that none of the accused rapists had even so much as spoken to her on the train. She agreed to testify for the defense at trial.

The atmosphere in Decatur was again extremely hostile. One local diner owner quipped to a journalist: "There shouldn't be any trial for them damn niggers—thirty cents worth of rope would do the work and it wouldn't cost the county much."[8] In the first retrial, the lead defendant was Haywood Patterson. The chief prosecutor was the son of the Alabama Supreme Court justice who wrote the decision affirming their original convictions. His assistant aroused the jury's anger with anti-Semitic rhetoric like that used in Atlanta against Leo Frank: "Is justice going to be bought and sold in Alabama with Jew money from New York?"[9] Liebowitz immediately called for a mistrial, which was denied. The jurors quickly reached a guilty verdict and sentenced Patterson to death.

Yet in this case Judge James Horton had been troubled by the evidence. Himself the proud descendant of Confederate soldiers, Horton did not let that stand in the way of doing justice. He set aside the jury verdict and postponed the remaining trials, writing, "The testimony of the prosecutrix in this case is not only uncorroborated, but it also bears on its face indications of improbability and is contradicted by other evidence . . ."[10] The incensed prosecutor demanded that Horton be replaced. (Horton lost his seat at the next election for his courageous handling of these cases). The new assigned judge refused to request state troops to protect the defendants, and Alabama's governor declined to order any. Panicked, Liebowitz cabled President Roosevelt to urge federal intervention to prevent the "extremely grave" risk of a massacre.[11] The judge and prosecutor also received hate mail and threats which they attributed to Communists.

The next judge showed open hostility to the Northern lawyers. Each of the defendants was again convicted by an all-white jury and all except one sentenced to die. More protests followed in Washington, D.C. and cities in the North. In 1934, Liebowitz had a falling out with the ILD after Price accused three ILD attorneys of trying to bribe her to change her testimony. In 1935, the United States Supreme Court again reversed the convictions for denial of due process. In another landmark ruling, *Norton v. Alabama,* the high court for the first time found a violation of the Fourteenth Amendment based on a factual determination that qualified black citizens were systematically excluded from the jury panel even though state law supposedly permitted their service.

In the war of attrition the state had the upper hand. Determined Alabama prosecutors subjected the Scottsboro Boys to more retrials than in any other criminal proceeding in American history. Finally, in 1937 they agreed to drop charges against four of them. Four others received lengthy prison terms. Only Clarence Norris was sentenced to die. After the Supreme Court declined any further review, Alabama's governor commuted his sentence to life in prison. In 1948, Patterson was still serving a seventy-five-year sentence under his fourth conviction when he escaped to Michigan, where the governor refused to extradite him. In 1976, at the instigation of the NAACP, Alabama's Gov. George Wallace pardoned Clarence Norris, the last of the Scottsboro Boys over whom the state still had jurisdiction. That same year the story became a TV movie. It had earlier inspired folk singer Leadbelly and poet Langston Hughes. Two documentaries appeared at the century's end (1998 and 2001). The travesty of justice inspired the 2006 movie *Heavens Fall* and a short-lived Broadway musical in 2010.

Of all the cases promoted as trials of the century, those against the Scottsboro Boys likely had the greatest impact—not for their outcome, but for twin landmark rulings: that due process requires defendants in capital cases to receive competent counsel; and that black citizens cannot be systematically excluded from the jury pool. By 1963, in *Gideon v. Wainwright,* the Supreme Court unanimously extended the right to effective counsel to all indigent defendants facing charges that could result in a year or more in prison. That decision finally prompted the widespread creation of public defenders' offices, seven decades after they were first proposed.

Back in 1939, when lynching was still common and the fight for the lives of the Scottsboro Boys remained a relatively fresh memory, songstress Billie Holiday appeared at Café Society in Greenwich Village—the first integrated nightclub in New York. As the staff dimmed all but one spotlight, she closed each performance with an emotional rendition of "Strange Fruit." It became Holiday's signature song, often moving listeners to tears. Her Grammy Hall of Fame recording wound up prominently featured on the Recording Industry of America's list of 365 historically significant hits of the century. In 1999, *Time* magazine singled out "Strange Fruit" as "THE" best song of the century, surpassing in significance, in its estimation, the top three listed by the National Endowment of the Arts: Judy Garland's "Over The Rainbow," Bing Crosby's "White Christmas," and Woody Guthrie's "This Land is Your Land."[12] Despite the power of "Strange Fruit" in the rest of the country, in the South lynching remained a defiant tradition for decades. After World War II ended, peace representatives of fifty countries came to San Francisco to draw up the charter for the United Nations to promote human rights and fundamental freedoms. To the embarrassment of the United States, both the National Negro Congress and the NAACP immediately filed petitions with the U.N.'s Commission on Human Rights to protest America's history of barbaric treatment. In this effort, the NAACP and the ILD's William Patterson were temporary allies.

The United States used its clout to prevent the charges from gaining an official audience. Actor Paul Robeson and Patterson embarked on overseas lecture tours criticizing the genocidal policies of their homeland. The long history of racial atrocities belied the United States' carefully nurtured foreign image as the champion of democracy and greatly undermined America's claim of superiority to totalitarian governments like the Soviet Union and Communist China.[13] The government responded by taking away both men's passports for eight years.

In July of 1946, a Georgia mob hauled two black World War II veterans and their wives from their car, tied them to a tree, and riddled their bodies with bullets. No state investigation occurred. The incident followed on the heels of news that a black sergeant had returned from combat as a decorated hero only to be beaten blind by South Carolina police on his way home through the state by bus. President Truman ordered a federal investigation of both chilling incidents and vowed to make civil rights a priority. Public awareness of the need for national reforms had escalated after publication in 1944 of an in-depth study funded by the Carnegie Foundation, *An American Dilemma: The Negro Problem and Modern Democracy* by internationally acclaimed economist Gunnar Myrdal. By 1946, the Navy had already begun desegregating its units. Jackie Robinson had just broken the color barrier in modern baseball and made the cover on *Time* magazine as National League Rookie of the Year—after ten years of lobbying by a New York sports reporter for the American Communist press.[14]

Truman's newly appointed Commission on Civil Rights issued an historic report the following fall, criticizing the doctrine of separate but equal and recommending new laws and regulations "to end immediately all discrimination and segregation based on race, color, creed or national origin in . . . all branches of the Armed Services."[15] The panel recognized that continued state-sponsored racism was America's own worst enemy in the court of world opinion. In the 1948 presidential race, the Republican platform included a long-overdue federal anti-lynching law. When the Democrats met for their Convention in July of 1948, Minneapolis Mayor Hubert Humphrey made an historic speech urging the party to shift from states' rights to human rights and adopt a civil rights plank in its platform. Birmingham Police Chief "Bull" Connor was among the dyed-in-the-wool segregationists ready with their own agenda; he and thirty-four other Mississippi and Alabama delegates walked out.

After President Truman endorsed the civil rights plank, South Carolina Gov. Strom Thurmond joined the insurgent white supremacists in Birmingham, Alabama, where they organized the States' Rights Democratic Party, dedicated to maintaining Jim Crow laws. Their official motto was "Segregation Forever!" The splinter group of Dixiecrats nominated Thurmond for President and Gov. Fielding L. Wright of Mississippi as his running mate. Thurmond campaigned with a line-in-the-sand message, "All the laws of Washington and all the bayonets of the Army cannot force the Negro into our homes, our schools, our churches."[16] (At the time, the forty-six-year-old governor was secretly supporting an illegitimate bi-racial daughter, Essie May Washington, almost the same age as his twenty-one-year-old bride. Washington's mother, a Thurmond family maid, was just fifteen years old at the time she gave birth. The avowed segregationist never publicly acknowledged that relationship.)

The Dixiecrats were incensed when President Truman desegregated the United States military by executive order. In most states, Dixiecrats ran as a third party. But in Alabama, Louisiana, Mississippi, and South Carolina the Thurmond-Wright ticket replaced the official Democratic

Party ticket. As Dixiecrats tried to cost Truman the presidency on the right, on the left former Democratic Vice President Henry Wallace headed a new Progressive Party ticket for President, with Idaho Senator Glen Taylor as his running mate. When Taylor boldly accepted an invitation to speak in Birmingham, Alabama, at an integrated gathering sponsored by the Southern Negro Youth Congress, Police Chief "Bull" Connor gloated, "There's not enough room in town for Bull and the Commies."[17] Senator Taylor arrived at the church hosting the anti-establishment event only to be arrested for using an entrance that Connor's police force had just temporarily marked "Negroes." The liberal Idaho Senator was convicted of disorderly conduct for bypassing the door for "Whites."

While Dixiecrats branded Liberals as Communists for supporting African-Americans, Communists were using every opportunity to exploit on the world stage flagrant civil rights violations in the United States as evidence of the superiority of Communism. In 1948, Mississippi obliged with a mockery of a death penalty trial that lasted only one day. An all-white jury took less than three minutes to declare black truck driver Willie McGee guilty of raping a white woman. Like so many other blacks before him, McGee was slated for execution, though no white man had ever been executed in the state for that crime. Just as Communist lawyers raced to represent the Scottsboro Boys in the '30s, top Leftist constitutional lawyers volunteered to handle McGee's appeals.

Both the United States Supreme Court and President Truman faced intense pressure from prominent figures throughout the world urging clemency for McGee, though Truman had no constitutional authority to pardon a state convict. Despite the flagrant due process problems, in the height of the Cold War mainstream American commentators considered open Communist support for McGee "the kiss of death."[18] When the high court declined review, McGee was executed in 1951 for a crime he likely did not commit and for which no white man would have received such a Draconian sentence. On the eve of electrocution, McGee wrote to his wife: "Tell the people the real reason they are going to take my life is to keep the Negro down in the South. They can't do this if you and the children keep on fighting."[19]

Yet it was not just in the South that inter-racial rape charges drove the populace to a frenzy, nor only Negroes who excited irrational fears. Shortly after the Scottsboro Boys rejected the NAACP as their counsel, Clarence Darrow received an invitation to fight murder charges arising out of another sensationalized rape case. This time he was asked to represent four people in Honolulu indicted for a claimed "honor" murder. Practically everyone in America had heard of the lustful Hawaiian brute killed on January 8, 1932, in retaliation for a reported sexual attack on the wife of a white Navy officer. The perpetrators quickly became the darlings of a wide spectrum of high-powered politicians, the press, and the public. Many conservatives who had ridiculed Darrow as a radical in the past now welcomed him as an ally. Civil rights activists compared the kidnap/murder to lawless mainland lynchings. Darrow received stacks of outraged letters from friends and supporters who could not fathom how he could represent vengeful white racists.

Darrow had second thoughts. Trying to bow out gracefully, he forwarded a copy of his closing argument in the Sweet case to show his commitment to civil rights. Yet Darrow's astounding success in the face of the hostile political situation in Detroit only made his assistance that much more coveted. Darrow shocked the NAACP by accepting the challenge. Tired of bitter winters in Chicago, Darrow admitted he could not pass up the chance to visit the balmy island of Oahu and earn a $40,000 fee for defending the year's highest profile trial. Top movie stars commanded no more per film than he would get for his role in this wildly popular real life drama. Like his recent co-counsel in Detroit, Thomas Chawke, Darrow had represented scores of amoral clients. The thick-skinned Chicago lawyer endured both piles of hate mail and death threats when he represented Leopold and Loeb; why balk here?

Ruby dutifully packed their bags, unsure why her husband took this offer on the opposite side from the Scottsboro Boys case. Perhaps this platform would allow him to establish "a bridge between the white and brown folk, a new understanding, a better code of conduct" but she felt "dreadfully uncomfortable about it all."[20] The infamous "Massie Affair" would prove a most ironic end to Darrow's long career.

12. THE EXPLOSIVE MASSIE AFFAIR: Truth Battles Raw Power

"Life is a Mysterious and Exciting Affair, and Anything Can Be A Thrill if You Know How to Look For It and What To Do With Opportunity When It Comes"

FAKE SUMMONS USED TO LURE JOE KAHAHAWAI TO HIS DEATH

By December of 1931 when the "Massie Affair" ignited mainland fears of a Hawaiian civil war, the islands had officially been a United States territory for thirty-three years. That annexation simply acknowledged a coup years earlier, effectively rendering the islands an American colony. Starting in the late 18th century, native Hawaiians had been decimated by new maladies—measles, influenza, leprosy, whooping cough, venereal diseases, and diarrhea—introduced by British sailors accompanying explorer Captain Cook in his discovery of "The Sandwich Islands." Not until 1795, sixteen years after Cook died in a skirmish on the Island of Hawai'i, were all the islands forcibly unified under one monarch, Kamehameha I, with firearms obtained from British seafarers.

By 1819, Kamehameha II abolished the traditional worship of gods who demanded human sacrifices, leaving the populace receptive to New England missionaries bent on converting heathens to Christianity. By the 1840s, King Kamehameha III, himself a born-again Christian, was convinced to adopt a Constitution and to reverse his father's edict and permit foreign ownership of Hawaiian land. All too soon, a handful of Europeans and Americans would own more than seventy-five percent of island real estate in a parliamentary monarchy modeled after that of Great Britain. To work their sugar, rice, and pineapple plantations, the owners began to import Chinese labor. When Congress barred that practice by the Chinese Exclusion Act of 1882, first Portuguese men, then Japanese and other Asians were imported to work the fields. (Chinese immigrants would remain banned for six decades.)

The plantation owners grew wealthy when the price of sugar skyrocketed during the American Civil War, and, in 1875, the owners negotiated an even more lucrative exclusive trade agreement with the United States. Then, in 1887, to solidify their power, the businessmen threatened to depose King Kalakaua at gunpoint unless he adopted a new Constitution that disenfranchised all Asians; set literacy, property, and income thresholds that kept most native Hawaiians from voting; and limited the king himself to a largely ceremonial role in the parliamentary government. The move paralleled successful efforts on the mainland to disenfranchise blacks in the South. Over time, five companies—four owned by British and American investors and one German company—dominated the island's politics as their virtual fiefdom. In 1893, when Queen Liliuokalani sought to reform the much-despised "Bayonet Constitution," the sugar plantation oligarchy forced her from power, with naval support from the U.S.S. Boston. A hundred years later President Clinton would make history by formally apologizing for the illegal removal of Hawai'i's queen. The coup in 1893 installed the Big Five's leader, missionary descendant Sanford Dole, as President of Hawai'i's new government and paved the way for the United States to annex the territory in 1898. That same year the United States fought the Spanish-American War, acquiring further-flung Pacific islands, the former Spanish colonies of the Philippines and Guam.

At the time Hawai'i became a territory, Caucasians constituted barely five percent of the population. Native Hawaiians called them haole, "foreigners." Congress established a bicameral territorial government with the governor serving at the pleasure of America's President. All other officials were elected locally. Dole became the first governor of Hawai'i. The Hawaiian language was banned in favor of English. Uneducated workers remained largely segregated by ethnicity, with each group developing its own pidgin English dialect.

By the end of World War I, ownership of the "Big Five" was all Anglo-American, with cozy interlocking boards drawn from families that had long since intermarried. This Republican oligarchy controlled the banks, warehouses, major exports and imports, and the territorial senate. The plantation owners had always found it hard to find cheap, compliant labor. When congressional exclusionary acts curtailed Asian immigration, the owners turned to Portuguese, Spanish, Eastern Europeans, Puerto Ricans, and, on rare occasion, to African-Americans and poor non-Hispanic or Portuguese whites. While Hawai'i still recognized members of its prior monarchy as symbolic figures of authority, they were now closely aligned with the Republican elite; and propertied Hawaiians held many governmental and teaching positions.

Tension grew within the brutally suppressed majority Asian population. The United States Department of the Interior likened plantation workers to slaves. Most had no hope of leaving the land. Despite post-war inflation, in 1920, the men earned only 77 cents per ten-hour day for their grueling field labor, the women only 58 cents—substantially less than child laborers in Atlanta's mills seven years before. In early 1920, island-born Japanese and Filipinos banded together in Hawai'i's first major multicultural strike. Three-quarters of the labor force on sugar plantations refused to work for five months, demanding $1.25 per day. The owners instead paid $3 to $4 per day to Chinese, Portuguese, Hawaiian, and Korean scabs hired to quash this "anti-American" rebellion. In June of 1920, when the owners finally broke the costly strike, someone dynamited the home of a Japanese interpreter at a leading sugar plantation—the same tactic anarchists and labor militants had used for years on the mainland. The Japanese strike leaders were blamed for the bombing, tried, and found guilty. The territorial government then reported to Congress that the risk of Japanese laborers unionizing rendered them an ongoing menace. By 1924, Congress passed its most restrictive immigrant exclusion act, precluding further Japanese immigrants.

Since 1893, the United States had established both naval and army bases in Hawai'i in recognition of its strategic defensive location in the Pacific Ocean, two-fifths of the distance from California to Japan. The Russo-Japanese War impressed the American government with Japan's military strength. In the 1920s, the American Navy and Army greatly expanded their bases on Oahu and practiced war games, readying for an attack. The build-up resulted in a dramatic increase in the Caucasian population, consisting mostly of bachelor soldiers and sailors from farming and working class backgrounds—many from the South. The high proportion of diehard racists among the newcomers only increased the friction that had always existed between nonwhite islanders and heavy-drinking military personnel on shore leave in and around Honolulu. Unlike long-established haole, the navy men commonly referred to the dark-skinned native Hawaiians as "niggers." The Navy men were even more disdainful of Japanese islanders, who were considered potential enemies. Other minority islanders fared little better. Locals did their best to avoid any interaction with the dreaded Navy police.

Any crimes committed by whites received far less punishment, if any, than crimes by locals against haole. The disparity caused political turmoil in November of 1928 after the kidnap and murder of a ten-year-old white boy named George Gill Jamieson. All pretense at civility disappeared as tabloids egged on Oahu's white community to a "lynch mob" mentality against the Japanese community.[1] The police caught the perpetrator spending marked ransom money. Myles Fukunaga had wanted to save his parents from eviction. He modeled the crime after newspaper accounts of Leopold and Loeb's 1924 murder of Bobby Franks. Fukunaga had a history of serious mental problems. Yet he received only a two-day trial before being sentenced to death. In contrast, a haole who robbed and killed a Japanese cab driver received only a five-year sentence. In fact, out of seventy-five convicts executed in Hawai'i in more than a hundred years, only one had been white. But appeals of Fukunaga's death sentence proved fruitless, and Gov. Lawrence Judd refused to prevent the execution. The memory of that racist episode grated.

By 1930, there were 368,000 residents of Hawai'i, of which only about 15 percent were native Hawaiian. Fewer than 25 percent were Caucasian; almost sixty percent were non-Hawaiian Asian and Pacific Islanders or persons of mixed race; and just 563 were blacks. Within the broad category of Asian and Pacific Islanders, citizens were identified by country of origin. Japanese and Okinawans numbered nearly 140,000; 63,000 were

Filipinos; and 27,000 Chinese. The Caucasians included nearly 27,000 Portuguese, 6,700 Puerto Ricans, and 1,200 Spanish citizens, all considered of lesser status than Anglo-Saxons.

At the turn of the century, Honolulu businessmen began heavily promoting tourism. The first luxury hotels built along Waikiki Beach attracted rich Americans arriving by steamship from San Francisco. A spectacularly successful Hawaiian pavilion at the 1915 San Francisco exposition introduced millions more Americans to the exotic Hawaiian Islands. Through the 1920s, Hawaiian music and movies filmed in Hawai'i became hugely popular across the mainland, luring increased numbers of nouveau riche tourists to the land of hula dancers, bronzed surfboarders, coconut palms, luaus, and ukuleles. A major renovation project spearheaded by industrialist Walter Dillingham at Waikiki Beach spawned several new opulent hotels just a few years before the bubble burst in the stock market and Hawai'i suffered the effects of the Great Depression. In 1930, visitors declined 15.9 percent and continued to drop at a similar rate in 1931. Soon ugly news hit the headlines, giving the racial situation a frightening image that panicked Honolulu hoteliers even further about the prospects for future Hawai'i-bound pleasure cruises.

The marital deception that snowballed into an international uproar all started on the evening of Saturday, September 12, 1931, when a twenty-six-year-old lieutenant stationed at Pearl Harbor brought his twenty-year-old wife to the weekly "Navy Night" dance at the Ala Wai Inn in Honolulu. The four-year-old marriage of Tommie and Thalia Massie was already teetering on the brink of divorce. When they married, Thalia was an attractive brunette with stylish bobbed hair and a cupid's bow mouth. But she was no longer in good health and looked it, including weight gained in a recent failed pregnancy. Thalia suffered from Grave's Disease, which caused her eyes to protrude; she drank too much, walked with a list to compensate for a misaligned eye, and had for some time exhibited severe emotional problems. Thalia was also a total misfit as a dutiful Navy wife. She considered herself far superior to the other women stationed in Hawai'i with their husbands; others saw Thalia as an ill-mannered loner.

Thalia had come from a quasi-privileged background that placed high value on appearances. Her estranged father, Granville Roland

"Roly" Fortescue, was an adventurous, illegitimate younger cousin of President Teddy Roosevelt. Her mother, Grace Fortescue, was a socialite born to a wealthy banker cousin of Alexander Graham Bell. Roly dissipated all of his own inherited wealth. Yet the Fortescues had sent all three of their daughters to boarding school, likely funded through the generosity of their extended family. With little parental supervision, Thalia had developed a reputation for wildness as a teenager before she met Kentucky-born Tommie Massie in 1927. Rumor had it that Thalia began having flagrant affairs within a year after she married the diminutive Annapolis Naval cadet. Since Tommie joined the submarine corps in Hawai'i in 1930, Thalia had degenerated. Neighbors in the white district of Manoa gossiped about Thalia, often seen parading around half-dressed and drunk, and noticed that she entertained male friends overnight during her husband's absences at sea.

In the summer of 1931, the marriage hit bottom. Tommie threatened divorce but agreed to put Thalia on probation for three months. Thalia had no marketable skills and desperately wanted to stay married. Even so, she had been loath to attend the Waikiki dance with Tommie on the night of September 12, 1931. He had invited two other Navy couples to their home for drinks before they left for the dance. The three couples consumed a fair amount of bootleg whiskey and beer before they headed off in two cars to the Ala Wai Inn on the outskirts of Waikiki Beach, arriving after 9:30 p.m. Tommie joined other submarine buddies at the bar and abandoned Thalia largely to her own devices.

Around 11:30 p.m. Thalia got into an argument and slapped a drunk skipper. Other guests summoned Tommie to intercede in yet another embarrassing scene caused by his wife. Tommie went back to his friends, only realizing sometime later that Thalia had left without telling him, as she had done on a number of other occasions. He stayed until the dance ended at 1 a.m. and went to a friend's home to party some more. When Tommie called to check on Thalia, she told him "something awful has happened" and urged him to come home.[2] On Tommie's arrival around 1:30 a.m. he could see that Thalia's jaw was swollen and bruised. Thalia told him she had been walking alone when she was kidnapped, beaten, and raped. Over Thalia's objections, Tommie insisted on reporting the crime.

The police came right out. They knew the address; they had responded to calls from irate neighbors when the couple engaged in loud fights.

Initially, Thalia provided few details to the police except that she left the inn around midnight and had been picked up by several Hawaiian men in an old black Ford or Dodge, who drove her to the former animal quarantine station on Ala Moana Road, where they raped her repeatedly in the bushes. Thalia doubted that she could identify them again, but did not tell the police she had left her glasses at home on Saturday night. Without them, Thalia's vision was so poor that she had not even been able to tell the race of the people with whom she hitchhiked home. Against her wishes, Thalia was taken to a hospital for examination.

The allegation was powerful. No one could recall a Hawaiian ever being accused of raping a haole. Police drove to the site on Ala Moana Road that Thalia had described as the scene of the crime and found a soda bottle that smelled of alcohol and a few items from a woman's purse. They quickly linked the claimed rape with another crime report that night. Around a quarter-to-one, a heavy-set Hawaiian woman named Agnes Peeples had shown up at the police station. Peeples complained that just minutes earlier four locals in their twenties had almost collided with her husband's car. The incident ended in a shouting and shoving match. One of them took a poke at Peeples and bloodied her ear. She took down the license number and gave it to the officers, who sent it out over the police radio. Police soon traced the tan 1929 Model A Ford to a young Japanese woman living in one of the city's worst slums, a rundown neighborhood called "Hell's Half Acre." The car owner's brother, Horace Ida, at first denied using the car. Then he admitted that he drove it to a wedding luau and then to a dance party with four friends: boxer Joe Kahahawai, another well-known boxer and football player named Benny Ahakuelo, David Takai, and Henry Chang.

Within hours, police returned to interview Thalia again, now under sedation at the hospital. With their prompting Thalia changed her story. She now recalled that the Hawaiians had driven up behind her in a fairly new tan Ford and that she caught a glimpse of the license plate. When brought in for questioning early Sunday morning, Ida thought the police wanted to arrest his friend Kahahawai for taking a swipe at Peeples after she insulted Ida's driving skills. When Thalia was discharged from the hospital, police immediately brought her to the station to see if she could identify Ida. Ida, whose nickname was "Shorty," was a small Japanese man, not a large, dark Hawaiian as Thalia had described. Thalia was noncommittal about Ida, but impressed Chief Inspector McIntosh with her recollection of most of the numbers matching the license plate on his car.

McIntosh was now on a mission to prove Thalia had been gang raped by the same rowdy bunch of hooligans that gave Peeples a hard time. It was the first rape ever reported of a white woman by a gang of locals, and he already had the sensational case solved. The Irish police inspector had two decades of experience working on British colonial police forces before he arrived on Oahu. He had leapfrogged over officers with more experience on the force based on his ruthless work as a field overseer on an Oahu plantation. McIntosh flaunted his connections to Honolulu businessmen. Most of the police who worked under him were minorities whom he openly mistrusted. He preferred to work with his white subordinates. Handed this extraordinary case, McIntosh took the initial responders off the case. He had already made up his mind. Two of the arrested men already had prior criminal records. Mixed-race gangs posed the greatest threat to white supremacy on the islands. Unlike their parents, who often kept to their own kind, the next generation showed far less respect for the ruling oligarchy. McIntosh subscribed to the same philosophy as Los Angeles Detective Mark Fuhrman, the infamous star witness for the prosecution in the O. J. Simpson trial: "Even if you get the wrong guy, this guy's done something before, or he's thought about doing something."[3]

After Thalia and Tommie returned home, she was examined by her own doctor. Like the hospital staff, Dr. Porter found her claim of rape highly dubious. He knew that Thalia was almost blind without her glasses. He tried to convince Tommie to drop the prosecution and take Thalia off the islands. On Monday morning, McIntosh drove Ida's car to Thalia's home. She now claimed it looked similar to the one her abductors used. In fact, Thalia owned a Model A similar to Ida's and had driven a Model T in her teens. No one that familiar with both models would mix the two up even had they been of similar color. On the way back to the station, McIntosh and one of his underlings, Officer Sato, took Ida's Model A Ford and repeatedly drove it through the mud near the old animal quarantine station before they called in Officer Claude Benton, to analyze the car track "evidence."

Navy men passed around ugly rumors that Hawaiian thugs had violated Thalia Massie every way possible in all "three orifices . . . And they kicked her and broke her pelvis and they bit the nipple practically off one of her breasts. . . They broke her nose. Blackened both of her eyes . . . [and stomped on her face]."[4] The outspoken Naval Commandant, Rear Admiral Yates Stirling, Jr. was livid with rage. He proposed that the honor of his young lieutenant's wife be avenged by stringing the accused men up without a trial. Stirling's public comments escalated the reported crime to a power play, which was soon backed by Honolulu's Big Five and wealthy industrialist Walter Dillingham. Truth was secondary to symbolism. The nonwhite majority needed to be sent a strong message to keep them in their place. Stirling had another agenda. Maybe this crime would galvanize Congress to restructure the government into quasi-military rule, which he greatly preferred to the uncertainties of civil government. Stirling placed no faith in any democratic institutions when the majority were Asians or mixed race, and he much preferred court-martials to jury trials.

After police arrested Ida and his four friends and charged them with rape, Honolulu's Republican-owned dailies ran banner headlines about the gang of "thugs," "degenerates," and "fiends" who attacked "a white woman of refinement and culture."[5] The inflammatory language did its trick. Yet one Japanese-owned newspaper ran against the tide, pointing out major problems of proof, some of which had been leaked by the first policemen to interview Thalia Massie. Those who read its English-language edition or its Japanese version had a totally different take on the alleged crime, a divide that only increased over time. At Dillingham's instigation to solve the crime and help reassure skittish tourists, Honolulu's businessmen quietly offered police several thousand dollars for use in developing evidence against the five Pacific Islanders. The police then made an offer to David Takai, whom Thalia had never identified. Charges would be dropped and he would get the reward money if he testified against his friends. When that ploy did not work, they offered the same deal to the other defendants. None wanted to turn against his companions.

All five arrestees supplied detailed accounts of their whereabouts on the night of September 12 along with names of corroborating witnesses from the wedding luau and the dance, all of which checked out. The police could trace the travels of the defendants from 11:30 p.m. on September 12 through 12:40 a.m. on the 13th, when Benny had already walked home and the other four almost ran into Agnes Peeples and her husband at the corner of King and Lilia Streets, some six miles from the site of the alleged rape. By 12:45 a.m., Peeples had reported the near collision to the police. Thalia had hailed a ride home from Ala Moana Road shortly before 1 a.m. The five islanders simply could not have committed the crime in that time frame.

No evidence of semen had been found on Thalia's dress, which had not been torn or even wrinkled in the purported ordeal. Nor was any semen found in the five accused men's underwear. When the police fingerprint expert found no prints belonging to Thalia in Ida's car, Detective McIntosh insinuated that was because the expert was Japanese. Thalia had by now identified Kahahawai and Chang as two of her assailants, but remained unsure about Ida. Even Takai faced prosecution and the same lengthy prison term as the others, if convicted. At the request of Ahakuelo's mother, Hawai'i's Princess Kawananakoa arranged for the island's top lawyer to interview the defendants. The lone Democrat in the territorial senate, Chinese-Hawaiian attorney William Heen, first wanted to assure himself of their innocence. The princess then lent her name to fund-raising efforts. Native Hawaiians raised money for the defense of Kahahawai and Ahakuelo; the Japanese community dug deep for Ida and David Takai; and the Chinese community raised funds for Henry Chang, who was half-Chinese and half-Hawaiian.

Heen figured that, if he was to take on this highly politicized defense, he wanted a Caucasian co-counsel. He asked another political outsider, transplanted Mississippian William Pittman, who was then eyeing a seat on the county board of supervisors. They each grilled two of the defendants and compared notes. Heen and Pittman concluded the four were telling the truth. David Takai obtained his own lawyer, Robert Murakami, who had represented Myles Fukunaga on his unsuccessful appeal of the death penalty three years before.

Tension between whites and other racial groups escalated. Rumors circulated that Thalia had been seen walking unsteadily down the John Ena Road past midnight in the company of an unidentified white man. Whatever happened to Thalia in the next half hour—possibly just an argument that ended with a punch to her jaw—she wound up alone on Ala Moana Road before she flagged down a carload of five Caucasians to get a ride home between 12:50 a.m. and 1 a.m. If a sexual assault had actually occurred, the timeline developed in the course of the investigation should have alerted the police that they had jailed the wrong men.

The trial began on November 16, 1931, before Judge Alva Steadman, the very same judge who had overseen the rush to judgment in the Fukunaga murder trial. Of critical importance was the jury composition. To Rear Admiral Stirling's dismay, the case proceeded under controlling civil law. Since 1900, the Hawaiian territory had required jury panels to be chosen from all literate male citizens, but expressly prohibited a jury comprised solely of one race. (Caucasians feared bias against a haole defendant.) Because of the skewed population base from which the panels were drawn, half the jurors usually wound up being haole, and the remaining jurors tended to be far more conservative than the non-Caucasian island population as a whole. The defense had twice as many challenges allotted as did the prosecutor. They peppered potential jurors with questions on their backgrounds and politics. Both sides together used all forty-five challenges, but still managed to complete the selection of the jury in two days. Only one juror was an Anglo-Saxon white. Four others had Caucasian surnames, but were among six jurors who were half-Hawaiian. Two were Chinese; two were Japanese. The last one was Portuguese. All of them worked for the city of Honolulu or a major company. Three had jobs with the Big Five.

The courtroom was packed, though Tommie Massie was conspicuously absent. He had requested active duty and put out to sea for the duration of the trial. So much for lending his wife moral support. Exhibiting far more interest were some of Honolulu's top businessmen.

They took prominent seats to stare at the jury. The defendants thought the message was clear—jurors working for companies in the Big Five likely had their jobs on the line. Others might also expect retaliation against themselves or family members if they did not vote to convict. Prosecutor Griffith Wight put on his case in just over three days, including a trip to the alleged scene of the crime. The jury was not sequestered, though warned against reading newspapers. The attorneys wrangled in court over the prosecutorial bias in most of the coverage. It was hard to imagine that news reports did not reach the jurors when they returned home every night. Judge Steadman assumed his instructions to ignore such influences sufficed.

Deputy City Attorney Wight was in his early forties, but had only practiced law for a short time. The business community provided him behind the scenes help from a private firm used by the Big Five. Wight started off strong. Thalia Massie gave a tearful account of the rapes and her broken jaw. With information since obtained, Thalia described the clothing worn by two of her assailants, their Model A car, the partial license number she had memorized, and the nicknames she heard them call each other. She was now sure it was defendant Kahahawai who punched her in the face. She claimed she had become pregnant and had to undergo an abortion. (Thalia's doctor did perform a precautionary dilation and curettage procedure, but determined she was not pregnant.)

Under Hawaiian law, to prove rape, Wight needed to show corroboration for Thalia's account. The hospital physician who had examined Thalia took the stand and left it ambiguous whether she could have been gang raped without any sperm being found. The skeptical defense attorneys feared that questioning whether any rape occurred might backfire. Instead, they focused on proving Thalia was confused as to the identity of her assailants. Thalia's original statement to police that she left the Ala Wai Inn at about midnight contradicted the notes Inspector McIntosh took at the station that she left the party at 12:30 or 1 a.m. At trial, Thalia claimed she left the party at "about 11:35" and that she had walked "five or ten minutes" along John Ena Road when two of the defendants jumped her from their car. That now placed the start of the crime at 11:45 p.m. when defense witnesses saw the quintet at the Honolulu dance party on the other side of the city.[6]

Thalia had originally claimed it was too dark to see her assailants, but identified the car as old and black. At trial, she insisted it was the tan 1929 Model A driven by Ida, still in nearly pristine condition. Thalia's belated recall also had Ida wearing a suede jacket during the rape. Actually, he wore it only when arrested on Sunday, a fact noted in one of the police reports. Thalia said she was raped several times for "perhaps twenty minutes."[7] Her time table had the crime ending just after midnight when many people saw the defendants in the dance hall parking lot across town.

A detective testified that Ida made a key admission at the police station—he already knew of an assault on a white woman before police ever told him about the crime. Yet Ida denied making the statement, which the policeman admitted was never recorded in any of several detailed police reports. The defense was even more effective in destroying the testimony of Officer Claude Benton, the designated expert on tire tracks. Prodded by Wight on direct examination, Benton described how he had identified the make of the tires from markings in the mud at the crime scene early on Sunday morning before any suspects had been apprehended. On cross-examination, however, Benton admitted that he did not investigate the tracks until Monday morning after police already had possession of Ida's car. Benton had no expertise on tires of recent vintage like Ida's. Benton also admitted that his original report of the crime scene—written on Sunday morning—made no mention of any tire tracks at all. Later in the trial, the defense produced Officer Sato, who admitted manufacturing the track marks with Inspector McIntosh early Monday morning before Benton's second visit to the site.

The defense produced a total of fifty-two witnesses, including a parade of credible alibi witnesses, of different ages, race, and ethnicity. They not only established the defendants' whereabouts during all critical times from 11:45 p.m. to 12:40 a.m.—miles from the alleged rape scene—they testified that they had also given the police similar sworn statements. Most telling were three witnesses who had seen someone dressed in a long green evening gown on the John Ena Road just after midnight on September 13. One was a Japanese hair salon worker. The other two were a couple, Mr. and Mrs. Goeases, who were headed toward a food stand. All three testified that the young woman resembled Thalia and had stumbled along drunk talking to herself, with a white man trailing after her.

One of O. J. Simpson's lawyers called "the Fuhrman tapes," in which Los Angeles Detective Mark Fuhrman infamously revealed his own blatant racism, "the most devastating evidence ever presented in an American court of law to completely destroy the credibility of a police officer."[8] The unmasking of Honolulu's Chief Inspector McIntosh more than rivals Furman's courtroom demolition. Much of the undoing of McIntosh came from his staff's own grudgingly produced police reports. Departmental witnesses also testified that they had suppressed evidence at his direction. In rebuttal, Wight tried to salvage his case with surprise testimony of a man who said he and three friends had actually witnessed the abduction. But on cross-examination, the four companions admitted that the people they saw did not look at all sinister and may have just been a group of guests leaving the Navy party together.

The whole trial took just two weeks to reach closing arguments. Prosecutor Griffith Wight still lacked any cohesive theory as to when the crime occurred or any evidence at all implicating David Takai. He raced through his argument in little over half an hour, happy to let the jury choose any version of the story Thalia told that suited them. He reminded them grimly of her injuries and intoned, "Death is preferable" to what Mrs. Massie had gone through. Murakami and Pittman took the rest of the morning dissecting the flaws in the prosecutor's case. Murakami was low key, Pittman emotional: "If you convict [these men] you have got to have no conscience, you have got to have no soul, you have got to be cowardly. I know these men are innocent . . ."[9]

After the luncheon recess, Heen spoke for nearly two hours ridiculing the prosecution's impossible alternate theories of the crime's timeline. As he started to sum up, the city attorney received a message from a bailiff and went out into the hall. Spectators became distracted as Wight's boss returned to huddle with Wight, who then scribbled a note he gave to another bailiff to hand to the judge. Judge Steadman then surprisingly declared a break in the proceedings and invited the lawyers into his chambers. For two hours the packed courtroom sat in puzzlement as the lawyers argued over a request to reopen the trial to present important new evidence. The defense team must have been livid. A well-known civilian Navy contractor and his wife now offered to testify that they were on the John Ena Road just after midnight on September 13. The McClellans had been at the Navy party, and Mrs. McClellan had worn a long green dress. The prosecutor wanted to show that the eyewitnesses had seen Mrs. McClellan, not Thalia, that night.

Judge Steadman had already demonstrated prosecutorial bias in his prior rulings, but granting this motion over the objections of defense counsel was simply outrageous. Once the prosecutor rested his case, he should have been precluded from reopening it absent a compelling showing. Wight had no good reason for the delay in locating the pair. They were regulars at the weekly Navy dance. Yet Judge Steadman reopened the trial the next morning. By the time defense counsel put on its rebuttal, the ploy had backfired. A friend at the dance recalled seeing Mrs. McClellan wearing a white gown that night, not a green one. All three people who had seen the drunk woman after midnight on the John Ena Road testified there was no way they could have mistaken Mrs. McClellan for Thalia Massie. The Goeases were well-acquainted with the McClellans and would have recognized them instantly.

When finally allowed to complete his closing argument, Heen minced no words. He told the jury that the police were "caught red-handed in framing the tire evidence to send innocent men to jail." He urged the jurors to "be courageous" and "return a verdict of not guilty on your first ballot." Wight had a final opportunity in rebuttal again, asking the jury to vindicate Thalia by convicting these "lust-sodden beasts." He regretted that the death penalty was not available. He blamed turncoat police who were traitors to their own department and asked the jury to find that the rape happened well before midnight. Under his latest theory, the young men raced back from their crime to establish alibis at the dance. Blustering along to the finish, Wight implored the panel to "justify your manhood" and "protect our women." The jury asked to review portions of Thalia's testimony while an impatient crowd waited outside. As deliberations entered a second day, Honolulu tabloids tried their best to whip the white community to a lynch mob frenzy as they had done after the murder of the Jamieson boy three years earlier. One paper highlighted a recent lynching of a Negro in Maryland by a mob of 4,000. Under the tense circumstances, reporters were surprised at the calm demeanor of the defendants, who were out on bail and resting on the lawn. The islanders said they were innocent and had faith the jury would acquit them.[10]

The jurors cast a number of ballots before they reported to Judge Steadman that they were hopelessly deadlocked. Rumor had it that the vote was ten to two for conviction. Judge Steadman, as jurists commonly would do at that early stage, sent the panel back to continue deliberating to avoid a hung jury if at all possible. On Friday, new rumors spread that a verdict was near, with only one hold-out preventing conviction. Then two jurors engaged in a heated argument, only stopping short of fisticuffs when a bailiff intervened. The defense lawyers moved for a mistrial, to no avail.

On Saturday night the jurors reported they were at an impasse that no further rereading of the law or review of any evidence would resolve. The judge still advised them to keep meeting one more day. He later admitted he was trying to force a conviction despite qualms about the defendants' guilt. Like other haole of his class, Judge Steadman viewed them as dispensable, second-class citizens worth sacrificing to resolve the ugly political situation. After a record-setting 97 hours of deliberation, the worn-out jurors reported to the judge on Sunday evening they simply could not agree. Judge Steadman then declared a hung jury. They ended in a six-six tie, never having had a ballot that was more lopsided than seven-to-five either way. Contrary to rumor that the voting split on racial lines, the lone haole had voted for acquittal on every ballot. Commandant Stirling still refused to believe the result reflected anything other than race bias.

Honolulu's leading tabloids displayed similar views. One paper called the result "The Shame of Honolulu." Taking his cue from *New York Post* muckraker Lincoln Steffens, the reporter recharacterized a number of minor Honolulu crimes over the past year as a wave of violence and predicted the jury verdict would just encourage more rapes of white women "by gangs of lust-mad youths."[11] No white-owned papers discussed the evidence of a frame-up. Prominent white women in Honolulu reacted to the unexpected verdict by vowing to replace the mixed-race police force with white men whom they could trust to protect their safety.

The women lobbied the governor, who immediately appointed a citizens' "Advisory Committee on Crime." That body then recommended stripping the sheriff's office of almost all investigative authority and creating a new Honolulu Police Department with a police commission appointed by the mayor and board of supervisors. Gov. Judd then convened a special session of the legislature. By the end of January 1932, the new law was in place, and the commission appointed Dillingham's personal secretary and chief lobbyist as the first chief of police—his total lack of law enforcement experience proved no impediment. At the same time, the Legislature followed recommendations to revise the rape law to make the crime punishable by death, with no corroborating evidence required. Having a politically connected chief of police in place, they could assume no minority woman victim would be allowed to invoke that law against a white man. The prospect that claims against islanders might be false did not bother them.

Following the hung jury, Navy men ran riot in the streets. Emotions were running so high that Commandant Stirling once again had to cancel all shore leave. The Pacific fleet avoided Hawaiian ports for the time being as Stirling sought authority to impose martial law to maintain order.[12] Of course, under martial law, as would be enforced in Hawai'i during World War II, citizens' right to habeas corpus would be suspended, as well as the right to jury trial.[13] The Navy could then rearrest and detain the alleged rapists and conduct its own proceedings with impunity, including summary execution. But try as he might, Stirling could not get enough support for that Draconian suggestion.

Under the laws of the territory—as on the mainland United States—after a hung jury, the prosecutor was free to retry defendants. The Chamber of Commerce raised $5,000, which it now openly offered as a reward for anyone who came forward with evidence implicating the defendants. To ensure conviction, several sailor friends of Tommie Massie kidnapped Ida at gunpoint and severely beat him to obtain a confession. Ida was rescued by a passerby and taken to the hospital "lucky to be alive."[14] The welts on Ida's back were photographed as proof of his ordeal.

Tommie Massie quickly learned from a lawyer that the confession the men had beaten out of Ida would be useless in establishing his guilt.

Back in October, Thalia Massie's mother, forty-eight-year-old Grace Fortescue, had arrived from the states. Unlike Tommie, she sat through the rape trial. Afterward, the socialite found all the ugly innuendoes about her daughter intolerable. Fortescue instigated a plan by which she and Massie could vindicate the family honor. They decided to kidnap Joe Kahahawai and get him to confess at gunpoint, leaving no telltale marks to ruin his confession. They recruited two sailors to help them, Deacon Jones and Edward Lord.

Kahahawai reported regularly to a probation officer. Early in the morning of January 7, 1932, Tommie put on a chauffeur's outfit and, in a rented Buick sedan, took Jones to the courthouse where Grace Fortescue was waiting to point out Kahahawai as he came for his appointment accompanied by his cousin Edward Ulii. Jones jumped out and showed the islander a crudely faked summons, purportedly from the sheriff. Jones waved his gun and forced Kahahawai into the car. Grace followed the kidnappers in her own automobile, accompanied by Lord. Ulii witnessed the abduction and reported it immediately to the police.

A couple of hours later, a detective spotted Fortescue speeding in the blue Buick sedan on Oahu's south shore. She was headed out to a remote cliff overlooking the Halona Blowhole. The detective gave chase. When he forced the sedan off the road, he arrested Fortescue and two passengers: Tommie Massie and Lord. In the back was Kahahawai's naked body wrapped in a bloody sheet. They had been on their way to dump the corpse over the cliff into the sea. Other police arrived at Fortescue's rental home where they found Jones, who had just wiped the room of blood. Jones had handed off the gun to Thalia and her younger sister to hide. He still had a .32 cartridge in his pocket. Nearby was a rope used in the abduction, Massie's chauffeur costume, and a bloody towel. Jones later commented, "We were in a peck of trouble and we knew it."[15]

Thousands of islanders flocked to Kahahawai's funeral, treating the slain boxer like the most revered royalty, while whites painted his shameful death as an honor killing. Rear Admiral Yates Stirling received permission to house the defendants in plush accommodations onboard a ship at Pearl Harbor rather than have them spend time in jail. There the co-conspirators received baskets upon baskets of flowers and thousands of letters of support. Commandant Stirling wasted no time writing up an inflammatory report that became a principal source of mainland newspaper accounts of the crime. Tabloids in New York carried explosive headlines: "Honor Killing in Honolulu Threatens Race War"; "Bayonets Rule Honolulu as Races Boil In Killing." *The New York Times* ran front-page stories highlighting the urgency of congressional action to safeguard the Navy. All this alarm was prompted by Stirling's reports.

Newspapers from coast to coast focused on the sensational story. Nearly a quarter of all newspaper readers subscribed to one of William Randolph Hearst's thirty-five papers which, on national issues, spoke with only one voice, that of their owner. Hearst echoed Rear Admiral Stirling's call to arms:

> The situation in Hawaii is deplorable. It is becoming or has become an unsafe place for white women. Outside the cities or small towns the roads go through jungles and in these remote places bands of degenerate natives or half-castes lie in wait for white women driving by. At least forty cases of such outrages have occurred and nobody has been punished . . . . The whole island should be promptly put under martial law and the perpetrators of outrages upon women promptly tried by court martial and executed. Until such drastic measures are taken, Hawai'i is not a safe place for decent white women and not a very good place for self-respecting civilized men.[16]

On January 21, 1932, prosecutor Griffith Wight convened the twenty-one member grand jury. Most seemed eager to whitewash the boxer's kidnapping and death with no indictment. But conservative Republican Judge Albert Cristy kept the panel deliberating for four days, emphasizing the critical role of the rule of law in all civilized societies. The panelists needed "to lay aside all race prejudice" in doing their duty or resign.[17] Judge Cristy managed to convince a dozen members of the grand jury to indict the four on charges of second degree murder.

The editor of *The Honolulu Times* then printed up 3500 copies of his next incendiary column and sent it to Navy personnel, asking them to forward the news to family and politicians in the States. The story included a long list of minor crimes that falsely painted the Honolulu situation as an epidemic of native violence. Picked up by papers nationwide, the barrage of shocking reports outraged the public at the supposed hideous treatment of American women by savage Hawaiian islanders. *Time* magazine wrote that the islands were not a safe destination due to the territorial government's inability to restrain "the yellow men's lust for white women."[18]

Rear Admiral Stirling continued to inflame the American public with speculation that an officer under his command and his gray-haired mother-in-law might spend the rest of their lives in "a disgusting and revolting Hawaiian prison" for avenging their family's honor.[19] Congress made it a priority to look into the indictment as Stirling lobbied to suspend all privileges of nonwhites in the territory and intimated that Hawai'i was edging closer to civil war. Yet a few Congressmen were appalled at the race-based hysteria and skeptical of its factual basis. Among the harsh critics of the fear-mongering was the lone black in the House of Representatives. Oscar DePriest's parents had fled Alabama when he was seven, after his father saved one friend from a lynch mob only to see another die at his door. The Illinois Congressman noted that the Scottsboro Boys still faced death for false accusations of rape while a white Navy man remained at liberty, his rank in the Navy unaffected. "Murdering a Hawaiian did not even rise to the level of 'conduct unbecoming an officer and a gentleman.'"[20]

Despite the defendants' widespread political support, the murder trial was going forward. With such open and shut evidence of her complicity, Grace Fortescue wanted the best criminal defense lawyer in America. Arguably, that was still Clarence Darrow, though he had retired for good back in 1928. Broke again, Darrow was tempted, but not eager to travel that far and afraid his brain would not "click with its old-time vigor."[21] He insisted on a $40,000 fee and assuaged his conscience with the assumption that he might help calm the extraordinarily volatile situation more than any other defense attorney could do. The defendants had become such a cause célèbre that contributions to their defense poured in from Grace Fortescue's wealthy society friends and from Navy families. For assistance, Darrow recruited a young New York lawyer, George Leisure, who had tried a case in Honolulu and was so excited about working with Darrow that he offered his services for free.

Grace Fortescue proved a difficult client. She proudly gave out interviews, including one to *New York Times* reporter Russell Owen. Fortescue said she only wished they had done a better job of getting rid of Kahahawai's corpse. Owen left out of his printed interview Grace's candid rationale for the murder: "She said that she came from the South and that in the South they had their own ways of dealing with 'niggers.'"[24] Tommie no doubt had similar memories of regular lynchings, as he grew up in Kentucky.

Darrow arrived with much fanfare on March 24, ten days before trial. He quickly learned that local defense lawyers from the same firm that had helped with the rape prosecution had already prepared much of the case. Judge Cristy was now off the case, challenged by the defense for bias. His replacement was another conservative, Judge Charles Davis. The upcoming trial was the talk of Honolulu, rivaled only by guesses on the contents of a pending report from Justice Department investigators charged with making recommendations to Washington on the future government of the island. The Richardson Report was issued on the first day of trial, on April 4, 1932. As locals were afraid, it suggested shifting to greater federal control of the territory to meet military defensive concerns. Yet the report fell far short of accepting Stirling's call for martial law. Appended to the report was his letter describing the urgency of the islands' current situation with its potentially "traitorous Orientals" and morally degenerate and otherwise inferior mixed-races.[23] Walter Dillingham then wrote to top Pentagon officials challenging the need for the report's governmental changes, revealing an even more pronounced rift between the island's powerful families and Rear Admiral Stirling on the issue of the continued rights of Asian citizens. When the full Richardson Report became public, Stirling's racist comments to the federal investigators incensed islanders.

The most remarkable accomplishment of the Richardson Report was its professionalism in shedding light on the hysterical atmosphere surrounding the Massie Affair. Conducted in just two months of exhaustive research, the investigation's results included fifteen volumes of interviews with hundreds of knowledgeable island professionals and another volume of compiled statistics. The federal team concluded that Hawaiians showed no propensity for sexual crime and that Hawai'i had "no organized crime, no important criminal class" and no crime wave of any substance. "Serious crimes . . . seem few in number and wholly sporadic." They found no evidence "of the supposed racial turmoil that has filled countless mainland newspaper headlines for the past three months." The report also questioned the wisdom of making rape a capital offense solely on the word of an alleged victim.[24]

The Richardson Report did little to change entrenched public opinion supporting the four defendants accused of murdering Joe Kahahawai. Journalists flocked to the islands to cover the story. New underwater cables allowed direct radio transmissions to the mainland for the first time. Seats were at a premium. The judge refused to grant privileges. Among the many people denied admission to the packed courthouse the first day was Hearst's society reporter. Honolulu matrons soon realized they could secure seats by having servants wait all night to hold their place in line. The prosecutor, John Kelley, was considered among the island's best lawyers, when he wasn't on a bender. In this case, he faced mountains of hate mail for doing his job. Kelley intended to try the case on the theory of felony murder. That meant the four defendants who kidnapped Kahahawai were equally guilty of his murder no matter which one pulled the trigger. Judge Davis took the death threats against Kelley seriously and had everyone, including the lawyers, searched daily for weapons before they entered the courtroom. It took a week to select seven whites, three Chinese, and two Hawaiians for the jury after a number of potential panelists showed eagerness to be dismissed, much as those not chosen for the Huey Newton jury panel would later be seen practically skipping out of the courtroom with undisguised relief. Six jurors were college graduates, four worked for the Big Five, including the foreman, while three others worked for Dillingham or affiliates.

Prosecutor Kelley went first, putting on evidence of the abduction, the arrest of three of the co-conspirators attempting to dispose of Kahahawai's body, and the incriminating evidence at Grace Fortescue's rental home, where the fourth defendant was arrested. Analysis of the bullet wound in the corpse showed that Kahahawai had been sitting at the time he was shot. The jury heard that police found buttons from his shirt in Fortescue's bathroom. A gun vendor matched the fatal bullet to the cartridge found in Jones' pocket and identified Jones as the man to whom he had sold the .32 Colt that was the likely murder weapon. Joe's mother identified her son's bloody clothing. Clarence Darrow wasted no time calling Thomas Massie to the stand to change the focus. Darrow then launched into the events of September 12, 1932—the night of the alleged rape of Thalia Massie. Over the prosecutor's objection, the judge allowed that line of questioning to establish Darrow's defense of temporary insanity. Darrow argued that what Massie had learned from his wife about the gang rape affected his mental state, and that Massie shot Kahahawai without being aware of what he was doing. Darrow claimed that, if so, the defense of temporary insanity would also exonerate his fellow kidnappers. Though Kelley strongly suspected Jones had actually pulled the trigger, he had no proof. Darrow was allowed to proceed.

Massie then described to the jury how distraught he and his wife had become after the gang rape. Thalia was suicidal. She greatly feared that she might be pregnant, which he claimed proved true and that she then underwent an abortion. Court ended that day with women brushing back tears. The next day, proceedings were unexpectedly cancelled due to Darrow's ill health. He claimed an attack of gastritis; according to others, he was suffering from a hangover. Perhaps Darrow needed liquid courage to complete his key role in this rewrite of history. Many years later, Jones would reveal that it was Darrow's idea to claim Massie did the shooting so the quartet could all hide behind the defense of temporary insanity. Jones told an interviewer that Darrow had never asked which of them pulled the trigger, but Jones told him anyway before the end of the trial. Massie never held the gun. It was Jones who shot the "black bastard."[25]

After one day's delay of the trial, Darrow led Massie to say that Massie picked up Jones' gun and got a confession from Kahahawai: "Yeah, we done it."[26] With those words (which were not phrased the way locals spoke), Massie said his mind had been overcome with the image of his wife when this brute broke her jaw. Massie claimed he did not recall what he did next. Two defense psychiatrists testified that Massie was temporarily insane at the time of the shooting. (In Jones' version, unlike the one Massie told in court, Kahahawai never confessed. Jones impatiently pulled the trigger when the Hawaiian leaned forward in his chair as Massie questioned him.)[27] Darrow was quite pleased with Tommie's performance and even more so with Thalia's when she took the stand to elaborate on the alleged rape. This time she claimed Kahahawai both hit her and swore at her. On cross-examination, Kelley confronted Thalia with a questionnaire she had filled out when she sought marital counseling in the summer of 1931 detailing her ongoing troubles with her husband. Thalia tore it to pieces and refused to answer any questions challenging her devotion to Tommie. She ran over and hugged her husband. Her courtroom histrionics even impressed Darrow, himself a past master.

In rebuttal, two psychiatrists testified that Massie acted like an angry spouse, but not someone who could not control his actions. Kelley also put on compelling evidence that undermined the entire theory that temporary insanity absolved the quartet of Kahahawai's murder. The autopsy revealed that Kahahawai was not killed instantly. He died of internal bleeding that may have taken twenty painful minutes. None of the defendants had made any effort to call a doctor to attempt to save Kahahawai's life after he was shot; they had dragged him bleeding to the bathroom, where he died. Both sides then rested.

For the entire month of trial, American newspapers printed detailed reports from Honolulu that had readers on the mainland totally invested in its outcome. Darrow's emotional four-hour summation was then broadcasted nationally on radio. Darrow pleaded to the jury to put an end to racial strife by acquitting the defendants. He argued that to act otherwise would only increase civil unrest and compound the suffering of the devoted mother and husband who stood accused before them. Prosecutor Kelley derided the "serpent of lynch law" that the defense would sanctify and reminded the jurors: "We must abide by the law or descend into chaos."[28] Fans of Darrow's performance in the Sweet trial could only cringe at his turnabout.

Judge Davis instructed the jury that their duty was to apply the law as written, emphasizing that no one had the right to take it into his own hands. The vast majority of Americans following the case disagreed—if the law called for conviction, the victim's presumed participation in the gang rape of Thalia Massie cried out for the law to be ignored. Navy personnel stationed at Pearl Harbor were adamant that Massie should go free or they might seek their own revenge upon the populace. Shore leave remained suspended. Islanders seethed at the injustice of Kahahawai's murder, but they still showed no propensity for revolt—it would only have given the Navy excuse for mass reprisals and possibly bring on martial law.

The jury deliberated for almost forty-eight hours without reaching a result. Then, after returning briefly to the courtroom, they only took another half hour before announcing they had reached a verdict. When they returned to the packed courtroom, Darrow anticipated acquittal. That proved too optimistic—the jury compromised on a manslaughter verdict with a recommendation of leniency. Top officials in the Navy and powerful Hawaiian business leaders immediately demanded full pardons for all four. The judge sentenced each defendant to ten years' hard labor. In Washington, D.C., Congressmen immediately denounced the result, the jury, Judge Davis, and Judge Cristy, and demanded that all four defendants be pardoned. A House Committee voted to investigate the territorial government with the threat of removing local control altogether. Stirling now requested that Hawai'i be run by a quasi-military commission headed both by civilians and representatives of the Army and Navy. The plan still contemplated taking away voting rights and other privileges like jury service from almost all non-whites.

The twelve jurors seemed eager to repudiate their verdict. They told the defense team that they had been forced to vote guilty under the judge's instructions. Darrow vowed to appeal the case to the Supreme Court. Then, the attorney general surprised Darrow with a visit to his hotel room. The chief prosecutor confided that he now faced a major dilemma. If he tried to jail the defendants, he might well cause a furor that could topple the government. Instead, defense counsel were summoned to the office of Republican Gov. Lawrence Judd, where the sheriff had just brought their four clients. According to the lawyers, the governor then received an urgent call from President Herbert Hoover pressing for the defendants' release.

Gov. Judd risked subjecting the territory to a quasi-military government if he allowed Massie and his mother-in-law to spend time in a Honolulu jail. In the alternative, he faced islanders' wrath if he granted a full pardon for the murder. Instead, the governor commuted the sentence of the four defendants to one hour in the Old Palace. When Darrow and his wife Ruby boarded a luxury liner to leave the islands a few days later, the Massies, their mother-in-law, and the two sailors departed with them. Tommie and Thalia would divorce within two years.

Princess Kawananakoa reacted with controlled outrage to the slap on the wrist for cold-blooded murder that the commutation represented: "Are we to infer from the Governor's act that there are two sets of laws in Hawai'i—one for the favored few and one for the people generally?" The answer to her question was an emphatic yes—Hawai'i was a U.S. Territory where the minority of whites intended to remain supreme. Back in Washington, D.C., Congress was incensed that the judgment of the defendants' guilt remained intact, depriving them of the right to vote. Congress reduced the eligibility of nonwhites in the territory's public service jobs and made it more difficult for them to hold local political office on the islands.[29]

Gov. Judd knew whom he blamed for exacerbating tensions on Oahu to the boiling point. He wrote to the Secretary of the Interior, excoriating Rear Admiral Stirling for his bigotry and racial insensitivity. At Judd's request, Stirling was reassigned elsewhere. Gov. Judd also requested the Pinkerton Detective Agency to thoroughly reinvestigate the gang rape allegations. Six months after the Massies emigrated from Oahu, the agency issued a nearly 280-page report exonerating the accused rapists and finding no evidence Thalia had been raped. The double negative conclusion exposed the strong prosecutorial bias with which the agency had undertaken its charge: "It is impossible to escape the conclusion that the kidnapping and assault was *not* caused by those accused."[30] Based on the report, Kelley asked the court to dismiss all charges against the remaining four defendants.

At Dillingham's instigation, the governor suppressed publication of the complete Pinkerton report to forestall political upheaval. Yet Princess Kawananakoa had already galvanized a few prominent white Hawaiians to chip away at the old order with a vision of how they might achieve even greater success. Leaders of the Chinese and Japanese communities and Native Hawaiians recognized how much more influence they had when they teamed up to address issues affecting them all. It offered a model for future concerted action in pushing for statehood, which would receive a further boost from the demonstrated heroism of Japanese-American soldiers from Hawai'i in World War II.

Two decades later, when the detailed Pinkerton findings were finally publicized they still had the powerful effect Dillingham had originally feared. Dissemination of the truth about the baseless 1931 rape prosecution swept so many Republicans out of office, the Democratic landslide was dubbed "The Revolution of 1954." In the summer of 2006, the American Bar Association used the information contained in the Pinkerton report to reenact the rape trial at the Hawai'i Convention Center, where the Ala Wai Inn once stood. This time, a jury of volunteer lawyers voted unanimously for acquittal.

* * * * *

In *Honor Killing: How the Infamous "Massie Affair" Transformed Hawai'i,* author David Stannard analyzes how the case prompted ethnic groups in the territory to identify themselves all as local islanders rather than by their country of origin and to recognize how that sense of unity magnified their political clout. Ironically, the man who organized the Japanese and Filipino grassroots campaign to establish the modern Democratic Party in Hawai'i was a white police officer born in Montana, who bonded with the people on his beat oppressed by the Republican territorial government. With the overwhelming support of nonwhite Hawaiian citizens, John Burns was elected the territory's congressional delegate in 1956 and convinced Senate Majority Leader Lyndon Johnson to engineer Hawai'i's acceptance as America's fiftieth state in 1959. Burns then became its second governor. Progressive Democrats would dominate the state for the next forty years.

Other historical accounts of the Massie Affair include Cobey Black's *Hawai'i Scandal* and Peter Van Slingerland's *Something Terrible Has Happened.* Fictionalized versions of the two sensational cases include the 1986 miniseries "Blood & Orchids" and the novel *Damned In Paradise.* In 2005, the true story aired as a dramatic PBS movie.

* * * * *

In his autobiography, Clarence Darrow gave himself credit for helping resolve the Massie Affair peacefully. Darrow did play a major role in deescalating the extraordinarily polarized situation. He kept his bigoted clients under a tight leash during the trial and helped minimize race-baiting. Most importantly, he convinced the Massies to leave the territory, which forced the prosecutor to drop plans for a retrial of the baseless rape charges. That compromise resolution, coupled with the governor's success in getting Rear Admiral Stirling reassigned, defused the situation enough for political processes to begin to address the underlying racial tension. But none of that justified Darrow's unethical conduct at trial or explained why he still publicly defended Thalia Massey's veracity after the summary of the Pinkerton Report came out. Darrow had befriended Dr. Porter during the Honolulu trial and likely knew Thalia was lying when he put her on the stand.

* * * * *

By the time the Massies fled the islands, the public had a new drama to replace their fascination with the alleged honor killing. Despite the thousands of stories written about the two Hawaiian trials, by mid-May of 1932, the saga had already been eclipsed by news of a shocking kidnapping and murder in New Jersey, the third decade's "crime of the century."

13. NATIONAL FRENZY: The Lindbergh Baby Killing

I am glad that my life in a world which has not understood me has ended. . . . I am dying an innocent man. Should, however, my death serve the purpose of abolishing capital punishment—such a punishment being arrived at only by circumstantial evidence—I feel that my death has not been in vain. . . [translated from the German]

Bruno Richard Hauptmann's last statement, April 3, 1936

In the depths of the Depression, *The New York Times* ran feature stories on a lucrative wave of kidnappings—averaging more than two a day nationwide since 1929. Worried Hollywood stars signed up for ransom insurance from Lloyd's of London. Then came startling radio announcements late on the evening of March 1, 1932, that Charles Lindbergh, Jr.—the toddler son of America's most revered hero—had just been snatched. The public was stunned. It seemed that no child in America was safe. The astounded global reaction was like the one that would occur at the century's end to news of Princess Diana's sudden death.

Charles Lindbergh had burst into international public consciousness with an historic solo transatlantic flight in May of 1927, heralding a new geopolitical era. His achievement—flying for more than thirty-three hours from New York to Paris nonstop in a monoplane—was a remarkable feat of endurance. Far more renowned competitors had died attempting the journey, but as planes improved it was just a question of time before some daring aviator was bound to succeed. Winning that lottery transformed the former barnstorming stunt man into the most celebrated individual on the planet. Congress gave the lanky Minnesotan its first civilian medal of honor. He inspired an outpouring of poems, songs, and even a new dance craze—the Lindy Hop.

The American public was not alone in eating up details about this teetotaling, sandy-haired mama's boy with a passion for flying, all things mechanical, and crude practical jokes. He was *Time* magazine's first man of the year, acing out homerun phenomenon Babe Ruth. Tall and handsome, the socially awkward Minnesotan received a flood of endorsement offers. Every city he visited honored their blue-eyed Scandinavian hero with a parade. He drew record-breaking crowds. Roads and lakes were named in his honor; his face adorned new air-mail envelopes. Real and imagined accounts of his exploits filled books, magazines, and newspapers until he was sick to death of reporters.

Most importantly, Lindbergh became the spokesperson for new airlines. He promoted government subsidies of much-needed airports at a critical time in the fledgling industry's development. Embracing Lindbergh as a national hero allowed top brass in the military to save face after their hugely embarrassing confrontation with Colonel Billy Mitchell in 1925. Just two years before Lindbergh's historic intercontinental flight, turf-defending Neanderthals in the military had stubbornly ignored Mitchell's plea to develop an independent air force. After they ignored his dire warning, the World War I hero bluntly accused the Navy and War Departments of "almost treasonable" negligent administration of our national defense.[1]

President Coolidge instigated a military "trial of the century" in October of 1925 charging Mitchell with insubordination. Mitchell was then drummed out of the service and ridiculed for his predictions: the need for a unified department of defense (presaging the future Pentagon); protection of Pearl Harbor's fleet from a Japanese air attack (which caught Americans by surprise 16 years later); and preparation for future wars in which unmanned missiles and planes would unleash bombs and chemical weapons on civilian populations.

Ironically, Colonel Mitchell's proposals played a pivotal role in bringing Charles Lindbergh together with his future wife, Anne Morrow.

Mitchell had enough political support for his ideas to convince a congressional committee to propose an umbrella department of defense and an independent air force. To stymie that movement, in 1925 President Coolidge appointed his own special board, headed by his college friend Dwight Morrow—then one of the top movers and shakers in the Republican Party. The general counsel for J. P. Morgan's bank had served as the top American civilian aide to General Pershing in France in World War I. The Morrow Board's far more conservative proposal for military airplane usage left the Secretaries of both the Army and Navy with their powers undiminished, but elevated the status of the air service to an Army Air Corps.

In June 1927 Morrow remained a key player in American aviation policy; not surprisingly, he was one of the first dignitaries to greet Lindbergh on his triumphant return from Paris with an extravagant military escort to Washington, D.C. The uncouth Minnesota barnstormer was thrilled when the fabulously wealthy and influential power broker took him under his wing. That same month President Coolidge appointed Morrow ambassador to the first relatively stable Mexican government since its 1910–20 revolution. Morrow instantly realized Lindbergh's value as a one-man ambassador of good will to the nation's southern neighbor. By the 1920s, Mexico was the world's leading exporter of oil products, mostly through fields developed and exploited by American companies. At the time Morrow arrived in Mexico in October of 1927, the relationship between the two countries was extremely tense: persecuted Catholics were in armed revolt against President Plutarco Calles, and American oil companies were demanding federal action to protect their pre-existing rights to oil fields that had been nationalized along with American land-holdings in Mexico by the radical changes adopted in the 1917 Mexican Constitution.

While involved in treaty negotiations with President Calles, Morrow engineered a public relations coup that December: Morrow convinced Lindbergh to accept an invitation from the Mexican President to fly to Mexico City. Lindbergh added to the drama by flying through the night to make the first nonstop flight from Washington, D.C., to Mexico's capital. On his arrival Lindbergh once again received an elaborate hero's welcome. It was while staying with the Morrow family in the ambassador's residence in Mexico City over Christmas that the rough-hewn mid-Westerner—now America's most eligible bachelor—first met Morrow's three daughters. He seemed taken by Elisabeth, the beautiful but fragile eldest daughter, and paid far less attention to her shyer younger sister Anne. Constance was still a young teen. Like Lindbergh's myriad other female admirers, all three Morrow daughters found the invitation to fly in the celebrity's modern magic carpet thrilling beyond belief.

Amid speculation that a romance had begun between Lindbergh and the delicate Elisabeth Morrow, paparazzi pursued the Flying Eagle relentlessly as he spent more time with the Morrow family and their four children in the United States. At the time, many believed that Dwight Morrow might become the Republican Party's next presidential nominee. Meanwhile, Lindbergh delighted in hiding from the press his courtship of Morrow's middle daughter Anne, circumventing press coverage of their unannounced wedding at her parents' home, and—with less success—their honeymoon destination. Meanwhile, Lindbergh trained Anne to be his co-pilot and radio operator, intoxicating the Smith graduate with the opportunity to take to the skies on daring expeditions by his side. Together, they set new flight records and were featured regularly in theater newsreels and the tabloids. In a welcome change for Americans from the enormous negative publicity generated by the Sacco and Vanzetti case, record crowds all over the globe had greeted Lindbergh as a hero from the day he landed outside Paris. Heads of state welcomed first Lindbergh and then Lindbergh and his bride as American royalty and showered them with gifts—enough to fill a museum in St. Louis soon built to house most of them.

By the summer of 1930 Lindbergh had fathered a son and namesake. A strong proponent of eugenics, Lindbergh later claimed that he chose his wife in part for the superior offspring he expected that the two would produce. (Certainly Anne was far sturdier a prospective life partner than her sister Elisabeth, who would die in her early thirties from heart failure.) The papers called the blond, blue-eyed boy the "Eaglet" and vied for stories and pictures to feed the public's insatiable appetite. But photo opportunities remained few and far between as the Lindberghs shielded Little Charlie from cameras while living with Anne's parents at the Morrows' lavish estate in Englewood, New Jersey. So few pictures emerged that rumors circulated something was wrong with the boy—perhaps birth defects from his mother being deprived of oxygen on a harrowing cross-country flight when she was seven-months pregnant.

By the morning of March 2, 1932, the whole nation was feasting on mysterious details surrounding the snatching of the "Eaglet" the night before. The Lindberghs had just completed building a much-publicized new home near Princeton, New Jersey, on the sparsely populated "Sourland Mountain" ridge that was the highest promontory in rugged territory known as "The Sourlands." The famous couple still spent most of their time at the Morrows' Englewood estate and had only begun to spend every weekend at Highfields in January. Though the ridge jutted up less than 570 feet from sea level, there was no highway access to the Lindbergh's new home. Visitors could only reach it on back roads, some of them unpaved. In the daytime, celebrity seekers got lost in The Sourlands trying to find the estate for a glimpse of its reclusive owners. At night, the narrow unlit roads were far trickier to negotiate.

Normally by Monday morning the couple and their young son would have been back at Englewood with Anne's recently widowed mother. But both Anne and Little Charlie had a cold. Since the weather remained windy and rainy, the Lindberghs decided at the last minute to stay at Highfields through Tuesday night. By Tuesday morning, Anne was exhausted from three long nights with her sick child and summoned the boy's Scottish nurse, Betty Gow from Englewood. That evening both Gow and Anne put Little Charlie to bed at 7:30 p.m. Following strict rules laid down by Lindbergh against coddling his son, no one was to check on the toddler again until 10 p.m.

Lindbergh himself arrived at Highfields around 8:30 p.m. for a late dinner with his wife. At ten o'clock, Gow went to check on the twenty-month-old baby. By then, Anne was getting ready to retire in the couple's bedroom, separated only by a short passageway from the nursery. Lindbergh sat reading in his downstairs study. When Gow went to the crib, the toddler was gone. Gow first asked Anne if she had her son. Both women then accused Lindbergh of taking the toddler. He was notorious for pranks and had once panicked the Morrow household by hiding his eight-month-old son in a closet for almost half an hour before the baby was found. But Lindbergh swore otherwise. He bolted upstairs, peeked at the empty crib, and ran for his rifle, announcing that it must be a gang of kidnappers. He then dashed outside. His butler joined him. When the two came back, Lindbergh called his lawyer. At Lindbergh's direction, the butler called the police and then drove off in the dark toward Hopewell to buy some flashlights so they could explore the property.

The women fruitlessly searched the nursery for clues to Little Charlie's disappearance and then explored the rest of the house as well, to no avail. Lindbergh came back, went to the nursery, and summoned Gow to show her a plain envelope sitting unopened near the center of the foot-wide inner sill of the closed window to the right of the second-story-fireplace. He instructed her that it should remain sealed and untouched until the police arrived. The local Hopewell police chief arrived soon afterward. The chief later told a journalist how unlike a crime scene the room looked. All the windows were closed and all but the one with the sealed envelope in the center of its sill remained locked. On one end of that same sill rested an antique beer stein, which managed not to have been dislodged. Most surprisingly, on the floor up against the wall under the unlatched window sat a wooden chest with a suitcase on it. On top of that lay undisturbed a roof piece of Little Charlie's toy Noah's Ark. It was hard to see how a gang of kidnappers could have climbed in and out of the one unlocked second-story window, snatched Lindbergh's son, and hurriedly departed the same way, while leaving the stack under that window unmoved. It was equally difficult to envision a brutal kidnapping when the toddler's crib sheets and blanket remained pinned in place the way they were fastened when he was put to bed.

Police carefully opened the envelope with a knife. It contained a misspelled ransom note demanding $50,000. Outside, with the aid of flashlights supplied by the police, Lindbergh showed them marks in the sod under the nursery window and, some twenty-five yards from the house, a crudely fashioned sectional ladder lying on the grass in two pieces. When checked against the impressions by the house, the foot of the sectional ladder fit precisely. Lindbergh immediately insisted on taking charge of the official investigation himself, joined by his attorney, Henry Breckinridge, who had just arrived from New York. Together, they directed the efforts of Colonel Norman Schwarzkopf (the father of the Gulf War General), who headed the New Jersey State Police. The Coast Guard and all airports were alerted, police stopped all drivers headed into New York. Gov. Harry Moore of New Jersey immediately sent telegrams to his counterparts in every state in the region seeking their help. President Hoover offered full support from the federal government.

Within hours, police set up a temporary headquarters in the Highfields garage with a bank of telephones installed to receive tips. Yet they did not prevent hundreds of newsmen from swarming the estate, destroying valuable clues underfoot. When Lindbergh announced his theory that the kidnapping was the work of organized crime, the first police responders were nonplussed. If professional kidnappers had executed such an audacious home invasion, why wouldn't they have cut the telephone wires? None of the five adults at home from 8:30 p.m. to 10 p.m. had reported seeing anyone else near the premises that night. Anne said she heard a noise around 8:15 p.m. Lindbergh reported that he heard a cracking sound shortly after 9 p.m. that he thought came from the direction of the kitchen on the far side of the house from the nursery.

The State Police fingerprint expert arrived at midnight. He found no usable prints in the nursery and remarked that it looked like someone had wiped all fingerprints from the walls and furniture, including the crib. Lights were on in rooms near the nursery most of the evening in a house that still lacked curtains and shades. It seemed extraordinarily bold for a stranger to climb in the nursery window and risk discovery while the adults were all still up. Police assumed the kidnappers had to know in advance about the household rule that the baby was not to be disturbed between 8 p.m. and 10 p.m. Gow told the police that the toddler hated to be touched by anyone but her and his mother. Yet the police noted that he had not cried out and no one smelled any odor of chloroform. The skittish family dog uncharacteristically never barked that night to warn of strangers approaching the home. Most baffling was the question why the kidnappers chose to enter the estate at all on a Tuesday night when the family routinely left by Monday morning at the latest.

Police also found the ladder odd. Instead of standard spacing for the rungs, it looked specially built for a very tall man. Yet its rungs could barely hold an average man's weight. The police openly wondered if the ladder might be a decoy from an inside job with a member of the household staff handing the baby out the front door to an accomplice. The police focused first on Betty Gow, who had not reported seeing the envelope when she first searched the room. They grilled Gow's illegal immigrant boyfriend and issued a warrant for his deportation (later rescinded without explanation); they questioned other household staff to no avail. Colonel Schwarzkopf suggested subjecting the staff to lie detector tests, but Lindbergh refused; it would "humiliate and insult innocent people."[2]

J. Edgar Hoover, head of the FBI since 1924, chafed at his inability to control the investigation or even pry information from the resistant New Jersey State Police. The FBI found particularly interesting the report taken from a neighbor's teenage son, Ben Lupica, who came forward the day after the kidnapping. Lupica described a man wearing an overcoat and fedora, driving a 1929 Dodge with a local county license plate near the Highfields driveway at around 6 p.m. on March 1. He told investigators the man had a sectional ladder in the back seat. The FBI listed the unknown Dodge driver as suspect "number one." Yet the New Jersey police inexplicably dropped that lead among others the FBI considered promising, including reinvestigation of an anonymous threat the Morrow family had received in 1929 that Constance Morrow would be kidnapped if $50,000 ransom were not paid. In private, FBI Director Hoover also heaped criticism on the ineptitude of the local police in failing to preserve the crime scene, including footprints found outside the nursery window and tire prints in a nearby abandoned lane.

New Jersey's Gov. Moore wanted to see the matter solved as expeditiously as possible. The cost of the investigation was running $15,000 per day. That did not count federal and other states' expenditures for a nationwide manhunt for the kidnappers and the baby. Even the notorious gangster Al "Scarface" Capone, serving time for tax evasion, publicly offered to use his gangland connections to assist in bringing the culprits to justice. A follow-up ransom note was soon posted in Brooklyn, followed by a third. Over the course of a little more than a month a total of fifteen communications were received, including the one found in the nursery. One expert opined that the unusual number of notes with repeated assurances of the baby's health had all the earmarks of an elaborate wild goose chase for a child that was already dead.

A week after his son's disappearance, Lindbergh opened negotiations with the alleged kidnappers through a volunteer named John Condon, a retired teacher from the Bronx. Condon met a mysterious contact twice in local graveyards. The press dubbed the man "Cemetery John." Cemetery John reportedly told Condon that the kidnappers were a gang of six, four men and two women. To prove they had the toddler, they sent Condon a pair of freshly washed gray Dr. Denton pajamas, which Lindbergh quickly identified as the ones his son wore the night he disappeared, though Schwarzkopf remained unsure that was so. Lindbergh then accompanied Condon to St. Raymond's Cemetery in the Bronx, where Lindbergh sat in his parked car while Condon delivered $50,000 in small bills to Cemetery John. In exchange, Condon received a note that said the boy was on a boat called "The Nelly" off the Massachusetts coast.

By Lindbergh's specific request, the New Jersey Police did not tell the New York Police about the cemetery rendezvous, and the New Jersey Police undertook no surveillance either. Cemetery John disappeared with the ransom money after his conversation with Condon. The offshore location he had designated was where the Lindberghs had honeymooned four years earlier. Lindbergh quickly followed that lead, but found nothing. He then took off to pursue other suggested aerial and sea searches for his kidnapped son, while police continued to stop any cars or pedestrians with small children who resembled the missing child, even little girls. Parents of toddlers became paranoid about leaving home. The editor of a crime magazine criticized the investigation as a "monumental fizzle . . . Miserably bungled from every angle."[3]

Meanwhile, the family started receiving huge stacks of mail, all screened by the police. Some letters expressed sympathy; others were the work of cranks and hucksters. A number even accused the Lindberghs themselves of the crime, based on rumors that the child had serious health problems that the perfectionist father could not abide. The police rejected such accusations out of hand. They did not even consider it appropriate to check Lindbergh's alibi before he arrived home at 8:30 p.m., late for dinner, having uncharacteristically failed to show up as a featured guest at a Manhattan fund-raiser.

All efforts nationwide ended abruptly on May 12, 1932, when an African-American trucker accidentally found the toddler's badly decomposed body. William Allen had been traveling with a co-worker on a road a few miles south of Highfields, when they stopped so Allen could walk a short way into the woods to relieve himself. That was when Allen spotted a toddler's head poking out of a pile of leaves. The body was so mutilated that it was hard to tell if this really was Little Charlie. Most of his internal organs were missing; even the child's sex could not be determined. Yet he still wore his diaper and hand-made tee shirt. A burlap bag was found close to the nearby road. Police summoned Dr. Phillip Van Ingen, the Lindbergh's pediatrician. Dr. Van Ingen had seen the toddler in mid-February when he diagnosed the boy with rickets. Dr. Van Ingen brought his medical records with him, but told the coroner that he could not identify the remains "if someone were to come here and offer me ten million dollars."[4] Betty Gow was brought to the morgue where she recognized the shirt she had sewn for Charlie the night he disappeared. It was still stained with Vapo-Rub. She also recognized Charlie's overlapping small toes. The coroner and county physician preliminarily concluded that death had occurred by a severe blow to the head at least two months' before, but took no photographs. The next day, Lindbergh hastily identified the corpse and then ordered the baby's remains cremated without any further tests.

The police thought they were about to break the case open on June 10, a month after finding the child's remains. They drove out to the Englewood estate to question one of the maids again. They had already spoken at least once to all twenty-nine household employees at the Morrow mansion and were concerned about discrepancies in Violet Sharp's prior interviews. The morning of March 1, Sharp had taken Anne Lindbergh's telephone call asking for Betty Gow to go to Hopewell. Police thought Sharp might have tipped off the kidnappers. Before they could talk to Sharp again, the butler told them Sharp had just fallen violently ill. Within minutes, Sharp was dead. A can of cyanide, normally used for cleaning household silver, was found in her room. Schwarzkopf announced that Sharp's apparent suicide "strongly tends to confirm the suspicions of the investigating authorities concerning her guilty knowledge of the crime" and identified a companion named Ernest Brinkert as "her associate on the night of the kidnapping." Condon thought Brinkert's picture looked like Cemetery John, but later decided he was too short.[5] Anne Morrow publicly criticized the investigators for their heavy-handedness, refusing to believe Sharp had anything to do with her son's murder. Sharp's role, if any, would remain forever unknown.

Within a week after Sharp died, Congress passed a new "Lindbergh Law" making kidnapping across state lines a federal crime. J. Edgar Hoover's men could now legally pursue suspects with or without local cooperation. Police alerted tellers nationwide to the serial numbers of the ransom money and turned up several gold certificates in circulation the year after the kidnapping. The police also uncovered several scams and beat many kidnapping suspects only to release them later when their alibis proved ironclad. Despite an unprecedented dragnet, enormous publicity, a $25,000 reward, and many false leads, no real progress in the murder case was made for two-and-a-half years.

After President Roosevelt withdrew gold certificates from official currency in 1933, it became easier to trace gold certificates that had been included in the ransom money. In the fall of 1934, a German immigrant by the name of Bruno Richard Hauptmann used a few of the small denomination gold certificates in New York. By then the police and FBI were desperate to solve the infamous case. Hauptmann, who still only spoke broken English, turned out to have entered the country illegally a decade before. When arrested, he lied about having no criminal record as a youth in Germany. Americans still remembered Germans as their hated enemy in World War I. Hauptmann had served as a machine gunner and had older brothers who died fighting against the Allies. Police believed they finally had their man. The press thought so, too.

Hauptmann professed his innocence of the kidnapping from the day he was arrested. Yet he had originally lied about how many gold certificates he possessed and how he obtained them. Only after police found nearly $14,000 in certificates still hidden in his garage, did Hauptmann explain that he had recently found the stash in a shoebox left behind by a friend named Isidor Fisch who owed him money. Hauptmann claimed to know nothing of the origin of the certificates or about the kidnapped Lindbergh baby. Attempts to beat a confession out of Hauptmann got nowhere. He denied even knowing where the Lindberghs lived.

Initially after his arrest, police isolated Hauptmann in a small, brightly lit cell and deprived him of reading materials and mail, or even conversation with his guards. Fighting insanity, he still refused to confess. Soon, his wife Anna was allowed to visit twice a day, two or three times a week so the police could secretly monitor their German conversations in hopes of obtaining some type of admission. Instead, the couple blamed his friend Fisch for getting them into this predicament and joked that the police were using Hauptmann as a fall guy for their own ineptitude. Fisch was in fact a known scam artist who had bilked a number of people. He had returned to Germany in December of 1933 and died a few months later of tuberculosis. The police undertook no serious effort to determine if Fisch might have been the mysterious Cemetery John, even though Condon had originally described the unknown man to whom he gave the ransom money as having a persistent cough.

Hauptmann reconstructed his whereabouts two-and-a-half years earlier. He insisted that he was employed on a job in New York the day of the March 1 kidnapping and used his car to pick his wife up at the bakery where she worked that night, as he always did on Tuesdays. He and his wife produced witnesses to prove it. Hauptmann's first lawyer was James Fawcett, a hard worker who believed in Hauptmann's innocence and began marshaling corroborating evidence. But Hauptmann's funds were confiscated by the police and the couple could little afford the high cost of a murder defense. New Jersey would not fund a public defender's office until the late 1960s, but it spent lavishly on getting this conviction.

Hearst reporter Adela Rogers St. John cultivated Anna Hauptmann's trust and persuaded the distraught woman that the Hearst papers would support her and her son during the trial if she just switched lawyers. The offer should have seemed too good to be true. William Randolph Hearst had befriended Lindbergh back in 1927 when he first became a media star. The wealthy publisher would foot the bill only for a flamboyant Irish criminal defense attorney from Brooklyn named Edward Reilly. What neither Anna nor her husband knew was that Hearst wanted to make sure Hauptmann was convicted, and cynically expected "the Bull of Brooklyn" to help inflame the public against his own client.[6] The Hauptmanns were impressed with misleading news of Reilly's success in a difficult case. It never occurred to them that the pompous, flashy dresser would alienate a rural New Jersey jury. Nor did they realize Reilly was an alcoholic on a downhill trajectory whose recent failures had earned him the nickname "Death House."

Reilly accepted a flat fee of $7500 from Hearst, for which he and his client agreed to provide the Hearst newspapers exclusive defense stories through trial. Today it would be highly unethical for an attorney to make such an agreement, compromising a lawyer's loyalty to his client with a promise to feed a newspaper sensational stories. But Reilly had worse conflicts of interest. He was an unabashed fan of Lindbergh and proudly displayed a photo of his hero on his desk. During the proceedings, Reilly told an FBI agent that he "knew Hauptmann was guilty, didn't like him, and was anxious to see him get the chair."[7]

Hauptmann quickly became demoralized when Reilly only met briefly with his client four times before trial. The consultations totaled less than forty minutes and each time Reilly reeked of alcohol. Hauptmann placed far more faith in the local attorney who sat as second chair, C. Lloyd Fisher. Fisher came to the jail often and believed in Hauptmann's innocence. The case went to trial in the Hunterdon County Courthouse in the small town of Flemington on January 2, 1935, less than four months after Hauptmann's arrest. The atmosphere in the New Jersey town was little different from the carnival-like celebration in Southern towns eager for a lynching, which Northerners had long since ridiculed as barbaric. Reporters booked every hotel and motel room for miles around. Prostitutes flocked there, too. (For two decades, from 1990 to 2010, an annual reenactment of "Lindbergh & Hauptmann: The Trial of the Century" again highlighted the small town's claim to fame.)

The actual trial was full of larger than life characters. Reilly, who suffered from syphilis, would often party at night with a prostitute and show up in court with a hangover. A number of reporters did the same.

Scalpers hawked trial tickets. Bettors gambled on the trial's length, not its outcome. When potential jurors were questioned, practically the entire pool had been tainted by prejudicial pretrial publicity. One said he had not made up his mind about the case, "not more than anybody else."[8] He became the foreman. Though Hauptmann spoke English only haltingly, no translator was provided.

In the thirties, prosecutors could still play their case close to the vest with impunity. Although the New Jersey State Police had compiled 90,000 pages of documents during their investigation, Hauptmann's lawyers never saw any of it. Fisher requested access to the crime scene and Hauptmann's apartment. Both requests were denied. In 1963, in *Brady v. Maryland*,[9] the Supreme Court rejected the historic practice of prosecutors to conceal information that might lead to acquittal. It found that such a strategy of winning at all costs was incompatible with the prosecutor's role to seek justice and violated due process guarantees. From then on, the Constitution was interpreted to require prosecutors to turn over evidence important to the defense of the case. But Richard Bruno Hauptmann was among countless accused criminal defendants prior to *Brady* to whom the high court had shown no empathy.

With all of the conflicting witness accounts and suspects in the New Jersey police file, ample ammunition existed to raise reasonable doubts of Hauptmann's guilt that never surfaced before the jury. Despite the long-held police view that Cemetery John headed a gang of six, the prosecutor went to trial on the theory that Hauptmann acted alone. Ninety witnesses were called for the state. None were subjected to pretrial depositions by the defense team or even interviews. The defense had little clue how to proceed at trial and feared alienating the jury by cross-examining either Lindbergh or his wife. When Reilly conceded that the mutilated corpse was that of Charles Lindbergh, Jr., his co-counsel Fisher left the courtroom in disgust, convinced that their one hope for saving Hauptmann from execution had just been thrown away. Throughout the trial, Lindbergh dominated the proceedings. He sat glaring at the defense from a prominent seat directly behind the prosecution table, wearing a gun in a shoulder holster. Lindbergh only took it off when he took the stand briefly to testify. The jury got the message how much the conviction meant to their hero.

An accountant gave elaborate testimony demonstrating how Hauptmann could have spent the missing bulk of the $50,000 ransom. J. Edgar Hoover monitored the trial from afar. He considered the reconstruction totally unconvincing, but stayed silent. The prosecutor then set out to prove that Hauptmann was Cemetery John through three witnesses: John Condon, a cab driver, and Lindbergh himself. But police thought Condon mentally unstable. He and the cab driver had already misidentified a number of other men as Cemetery John. The jury paid rapt attention when Lindbergh claimed to recognize Hauptmann's voice from hearing the defendant repeatedly recite in court on command the words "Hey Doctor, Here Doctor! Over here!" Lindbergh said he heard the mystery man shout more than two-and-a-half years before. The jury did not learn that there was a dispute over whether Lindbergh had previously told the police the phrase he heard while sitting in his parked car a block away from the rendezvous was "Hey Doc, over here," and that Lindbergh doubted he could ever identify who said it.[10]

Prosecutor Wilentz also put on evidence that Hauptmann's closet had Dr. Condon's telephone number and address inscribed in it. Hauptmann denied writing it, though at some point during his earlier grilling, he had told police interrogators that he must have written what they found there. The coerced confession made little sense. Why would Hauptmann write Condon's number in his closet when Hauptmann did not even have a telephone in his home? A reporter later claimed the note in the closet was his own prank written after Hauptmann's arrest when free access had been afforded the press to Hauptmann's apartment.

Wilentz presented two neighbors of the Lindberghs, Millard Whited, who identified Hauptmann as the stranger he saw near the property twice during the month before the 1932 kidnapping, and Amandus Hochmuth, who placed Hauptmann in the area of Hopewell, New Jersey, on the day of the kidnapping. Whited had originally told police he saw no one unusual that day, and Hochmuth had not come forward until two-and-a-half years after the crime. Neighbor Ben Lupica was never called by the prosecutor. He testified for the defense that he saw a dark blue or black 1929 Dodge with ladders in the back by the Highfields driveway on the evening of March 1. Lupica recognized the New Jersey plates and noted they had an "L," signifying the same county where he lived. He was sure that the car was not green like Hauptmann's New York sedan. Yet, on cross-examination, Wilentz confronted Lupica with a newspaper article that claimed Lupica had previously identified Hauptmann. It was false. Flustered, Lupica testified that Hauptmann resembled the driver.

Two types of expert testimony provided further damning evidence. Trial lawyers all know that, if both sides have money, they can almost always find experts to support their client. The state hired eight handwriting experts to say they were sure Hauptmann wrote all of the ransom notes. At least two had privately told police they were convinced at one point that Hauptmann did not author the ransom notes. In fact, their original report concluded that the first note found in the nursery had been written in a disguised hand; the rest appeared to be copycat notes by a forger. Only after police told the experts they had found gold certificates in Hauptmann's home did the men shift gears and identify Hauptmann as the author of all the notes.[11] Hauptmann could only afford one handwriting expert to dispute the state's eight witnesses. Yet doubts should have been raised. Hauptmann's handwriting samples resulted from police instructions to rewrite notes many times in different styles. As evidence of his authorship, the experts relied in part on similar misspellings which should have had no weight. Hauptmann testified "I was told to write exactly as it was dictated to me and this included writing words spelled as I was told to spell them."[12] Even Schwarzkopf would later concede that Hauptmann—without any attorney to object—had been given spelling "help" by one or more officers.[13]

Lastly, the prosecutor produced Arthur Koehler, a wood expert, who testified that he traced some of the wood used for the ladder to a Bronx lumber yard. Koehler also identified a missing floor board in Hauptmann's attic as the source of one small piece of the ladder. Hauptmann thought the ladder evidence was the most bizarre. The workmanship of the ladder was not that of a master carpenter like himself. He weighed one hundred eighty pounds and was of only average height. He would not have built a makeshift ladder with rungs spaced for a tall, light man that might collapse under his own weight. Nor would he have bypassed the pile of spare wood in his garage to remove a plank from his landlord's attic and cut it to size to use in making a ladder. In fact, no one had noticed any missing plank in Hauptmann's attic until a week after his arrest—even though fifteen police had searched the house high and low before then.

At trial, Hauptmann had his own volunteer fingerprint expert who had assisted the prosecutor early on in the investigation. When no suspect had yet been identified, Erastus Mead Hudson had carefully taken the ladder apart and used a new technique employing silver nitrate to reveal hundreds of usable prints, not visible through standard procedures. Some of the prints were on the ends of the rungs that Hudson had just disassembled. No one could have touched them to make those prints but the person who handled the pieces of wood before they were put in place to construct the ladder. Dr. Hudson testified that he had been quite surprised not to be contacted when Hauptmann was arrested. It prompted him to call a New Jersey police officer, who said, "We got our man." When asked if Hauptmann's prints were found anywhere on the ladder, the officer said, "No." Hudson responded "Then you'll have to look further." The officer said "Good God, don't tell us that, doctor!" Shortly afterward, an extraordinary order issued from State Police headquarters to wash off *all the fingerprints*—no evidence of any fingerprints on the ladder remained by the time of trial.[14]

Wilentz originally argued that Hauptmann took the toddler from the house as a kidnap for ransom and then the boy died accidentally falling from the ladder. But when the defense lawyers focused on the infant's failure to cry out, Wilentz switched theories in his closing argument and argued that the child had his life brutally snuffed out inside the nursery before Hauptmann ever descended. This presented a quite different scenario—with no corpse or autopsy to back it up. Nor was any blood found in the nursery or on the ground outside. Hauptmann was seriously prejudiced in trying to address the shifting charge. His lawyers would not have emphasized that the toddler never cried out as an argument that no stranger kidnapped him had the prosecutor claimed from the outset that the child had been murdered in the nursery. The new theory horrified the jury with the charge that the ransom note planted in the room—and the fourteen more that followed—evidenced a cruel hoax from the outset perpetrated by the heartless fiend at the defense table.

Despite huge inconsistencies in the prosecutor's case, Judge Thomas Trenchard left little doubt what he thought the jury should do. Spectators commented on the judge's sarcasm when he summarized defense claims and asked the jury, "Now, do you believe *that?*" [15] Such obvious bias paralleled that of Judge Webster Thayer in the Sacco and Vanzetti case. A crowd of ten thousand outside the courthouse kept yelling, "Kill Hauptmann," while the jury deliberated.[16] When the guilty verdict was announced eleven hours later, they erupted in celebration. It turned out that the jurors had immediately voted to convict, but had taken time to consider whether to recommend leniency. After sixteen hours on the stand, despite his bristly nature, some jurors found Hauptmann sympathetic.

Hauptmann's appeals proved fruitless. Clarence Darrow counted himself among the skeptics. From the accounts he had read, the nation's most famous criminal defense lawyer called the evidence flimsy and urged New Jersey Gov. Harold Hoffman to delay Hauptmann's execution and allow him a new trial.[17] Gov. Hoffman was greatly troubled by the evidence and the manner in which the case had been investigated. Like Gov. Jack Slaton of Georgia in the Leo Frank case twenty years before, Hoffman gambled with his political future and delayed the execution for thirty days. Hoffman forced Colonel Schwarzkopf to retire and started reinvestigating the case in an attempt to determine what really happened. The governor originally assumed Hauptmann might have been part of a gang. Yet, after visiting the Hauptmann's former home himself, Hoffman became convinced of the Hauptmanns' claim that the police had manufactured the evidence of the attic plank after the force took control of their apartment.

The governor also revisited the damning testimony of neighbors Millard Whited and Amandus Hochmuth. The two had provided no useful information at all to police when the case was first investigated in 1932. They only came forward in 1934 after Hauptmann's picture circulated in the newspapers and the huge reward was offered. Whited told Gov. Hoffman he was paid for his testimony. Hochmuth was 87, had cataracts in both eyes, and was legally blind. The disgusted governor tested Hochmuth's vision and found that the old man could not tell a vase from a woman's hat at ten feet. Many years later, Ben Lupica recalled the trial as a sham. He knew the other neighbors received money for fingering Hauptmann. He had been offered money, too, if he changed his testimony. Lupica had refused. He told investigators that the only similarity between Hauptmann and the driver was that Hauptmann was also white.[18]

Before Lindbergh and his family could be questioned further about the many unresolved aspects of the kidnapping/murder, they were gone. In late December of 1935, immediately after newspapers announced that Gov. Hoffman was reopening the case for further investigation, Lindbergh abruptly told his wife to pack up to leave the country. With their second son Jon, they secretly boarded a ship to England. Lindbergh gave a *New York Times* reporter an exclusive interview on his promise not to publish the fact they had departed until after their ship sailed. Lindbergh told the reporter that they were fleeing out of fear for his son Jon's continued safety. They would not come back for three years. The public blamed Gov. Hoffman for prolonging their hero's ordeal.

Despite his own misgivings, the governor could not convince the New Jersey Court of Errors to commute Hauptmann's death sentence. Yet Hauptmann did gain more supporters when he turned down a $90,000 offer from a Hearst newspaper for his confession. The condemned man obtained even more converts to his cause when he refused the prosecutor's last-minute offer of a life sentence in exchange for revealing the names of the co-conspirators with whom he was assumed to have worked. A confirmed Christian, the death-row prisoner told the governor that he believed in salvation and could not offer a false confession even to obtain much-needed support for his loyal wife and baby. The state of New Jersey executed Hauptmann on April 3, 1936. He professed his innocence to the end. All the evidence was circumstantial. As author James Fisher states, "No one saw Hauptmann snatch the baby from his crib and no one, save the killer, witnessed the child's death."[19] To this one could add no reliable witness ever placed Hauptmann anywhere near central New Jersey on the day or evening of the toddler's disappearance. No cause of death or even date or place of death was reliably established. No murder weapon was ever found; no one ever saw Hauptmann with the Lindbergh baby; and no fingerprint evidence ever placed him at the Lindbergh home.

The O. J. Simpson Dream team would have made much of the inconsistencies in the evidence used in court and the extensive evidence withheld from the Hauptmann trial. Once the police caught Hauptmann in a lie and found that he had hidden thousands of dollars of the ransom money in his home, they settled on him as the culprit. When they learned he was an illegal alien with a prior criminal record in Germany, nothing could convince them otherwise. Even with all the problems that surfaced, they assumed he was at least complicit. At that point, the police did whatever it took to prove their case to a jury. In *Actual Innocence* co-founders of the Innocence Project Barry Scheck and Peter Neufeld detail serious flaws in 135 death penalty trials where juries convicted men who were later exonerated on death row. Many other inmates have proclaimed their innocence right up to their executions. A *Stanford Law Review* article, "Miscarriages of Justice in Potentially Capital Cases" counts the much-discussed Hauptmann conviction as a "classic case" among hundreds of documented examples of wrongly convicted defendants with their life on the line.[20]

* * * * *

Experts estimate that wrongful convictions—due to mistaken eyewitness identifications, false confessions, ineffective assistance of counsel, police or prosecutorial misconduct, and other causes—occur each year in one to three percent of felony cases nationwide. Criminologist C. Ronald Huff argues we must do better: "In societies that value the freedom of their citizens . . . it is arguable that being convicted of a crime that one did not commit, and being incarcerated with criminals or even put to death, represents one of the worst nightmares imaginable."[21] As Barry Scheck points out, for each wrongfully convicted felon, the true perpetrator likely stayed on the streets.

Periodically over the following decades, someone would surface claiming to be the real Lindbergh baby and that the corpse belonged to another child. Continued fascination with the kidnapping has spawned movies, novels, and various conspiracy theories implicating various members of the Lindbergh and Morrow family. Convinced that the execution of the German immigrant was a travesty of justice, British muckraker Ludovic Kennedy aired a documentary on the Hauptmann trial in 1982. In 1985, with the full cooperation of Anne Lindbergh, Kennedy published *The Airman and The Carpenter: The Lindbergh Kidnapping and the Framing of Richard Hauptmann.* Kennedy claimed that the aviator's widow assured him "that if in fact a miscarriage of justice did take place, and notwithstanding any difficulties this might create for her and her family, it should not be glossed over."[22]

In 1993, New Hampshire legislator and criminal defense attorney Gregory Ahlgren collaborated with his sometime adversary, local police chief Stephen Monier, in authoring *Crime of the Century: The Lindbergh Kidnapping Hoax.* The book hypothesized that Charles Lindbergh accidentally killed his son in a failed prank and sought to cover it up with a false report of a kidnapping. Other authors argue that a sibling of Anne Morrow—her jealous older sister Elisabeth or her schizophrenic younger brother Dwight—killed the baby. Under each of these theories, Lindbergh was accused of covering up the crime and misdirecting the investigation that led to Hauptmann's conviction. A website has been devoted to exploring the "Lindbergh kidnapping hoax."[23] There is certainly ample evidence that Lindbergh obstructed the investigation, intentionally or otherwise.

In 2004, in *The Case That Does Not Die: The Lindbergh Kidnapping,* historian Lloyd Gardner also reached the conclusion that Hauptmann was wrongly executed. Gardner did not rule out the possibility Hauptmann played some lesser role, such as constructing the ladder used in the crime or laundering the ransom money. In 2005, the true-crime documentary program "Forensic Files" aired a review of key Hauptmann trial evidence. Experts used advanced technology to reexamine the ladder and reanalyze the ransom notes. They reaffirmed that a ladder piece came from Hauptmann's attic, but that did not solve the question of whether the police planted that evidence. The results on the ransom note were mixed, as they had been previously. The 2005 documentary did not address claims that Hauptmann never got a fair trial with all the prejudicial publicity, circuslike proceedings, compromised physical evidence, and perjured testimony.

Most of all the Hauptmann trial, like the Leo Frank and Massie cases, suffered from an atmosphere electric with the desire for revenge, and a setting where the prosecutor had similar latitude in suppressing facts that did not fit his theory. There is no doubt that a modern investigation and trial of Hauptmann would proceed quite differently.[24] Among other things, the crime scene would be cordoned off; the corpse would undergo a proper autopsy to determine exactly how and when the baby died; and key evidence like the fingerprints on the ladder would likely be far less susceptible to charges of tampering. Prosecutors would be required to provide the defense with potentially exculpatory evidence; the judge would be required to take far more precautions against prejudicial publicity tainting the trial; the jury panel would not exclude those with general reservations about the death penalty; and that issue would be addressed in a separate sentencing hearing, only if guilt was first determined.

Yet some criminologists still defend the prosecution and conviction of Bruno Richard Hauptmann. Chief among them is former FBI agent Jim Fisher, who reinvestigated the case at the behest of the New Jersey State Police. In *The Lindbergh Case* first published in 1987, Fisher set out to refute accusations of Ludovic Kennedy and other vocal critics of how the case was handled. In the introduction to his book, Fisher lists his assumptions in concluding that Hauptmann was guilty as charged, all of which are questionable. First, Fisher states as a given that the New Jersey State Police conducted a thorough investigation—failing to address the FBI's own serious criticisms. As J. Edgar Hoover realized at the time, while the New Jersey state investigation was extraordinarily extensive, it had major gaps stemming largely from the fact it was controlled from the outset by a parent. By April of 1932, the FBI suspected Lindbergh of holding back on information. Under Lindbergh's watch, key evidence was lost and crucial leads never pursued thoroughly, including determining who owned the 1929 Dodge Sedan with local plates seen at the Highfields driveway that night with a ladder in the back.

The FBI has since documented that a parent is ultimately found to blame for more than half of all reported infanticides; of those committed at home, nine out of ten are perpetrated by a family member.[25]

Nowadays, even millionaire parents reporting a child's abduction and death at the hands of mysterious strangers remain prime suspects. That was what happened in the still unsolved kidnap-murder of JonBenet Ramsey, which generated a similar media circus in 1996 as the Lindbergh baby kidnapping.

Second, Fisher assumes that no evidence was fabricated or materially altered to implicate Hauptmann, discrediting the claim that police pulled up the plank from Hauptmann's attic. Yet there was no question that hundreds of fingerprints on the ladder were eradicated while that crucial piece of evidence was in police custody before trial. The timing also appears highly suspect: the ladder was not wiped clean until after their own expert told police the prints might prove Hauptmann's innocence.[26]

Third, Fisher defends the trial as being "as fair as could be expected under the circumstances," while others cite shocking deficiencies. (See, e.g., Robert R. Bryan, "The Execution of the Innocent: The Tragedy of the Hauptmann-Lindbergh and Bigelow Cases" ["Surrounded by a hostile atmosphere, the proceeding featured mistakes, fraud, concealment of evidence, witness intimidation, and false testimony"])[27] and Gilbert Geis (Past Pres. of the American Society of Criminology) and Leigh B. Beinen ["whatever else, the untainted evidence did not support a verdict of guilt beyond a reasonable doubt of the charge against him"]).[28]

Fisher also reports confidence that "the small, mutilated corpse discovered a few miles from the Lindbergh estate more than two months after the crime," was that of the missing Lindbergh toddler without acknowledging that the police fostered doubt by their inexcusable negligence. Even before identification, the body was immediately recognized as that of a crime victim. A full autopsy could have provided key information. The police should never have allowed Lindbergh to prevent full tests from being conducted and to cremate the remains, precluding definitive identification and analysis of exactly how and when the baby died.

Even reasonable doubt about Hauptmann's guilt of the kidnap/murder would have been enough to save the carpenter's life. All that was really proved beyond a reasonable doubt was that he hoarded and spent some of the gold certificates whose source as ransom he may not have known. It should not have taken a Clarence Darrow to defend

Hauptmann from execution had the illegal immigrant been afforded a fair opportunity before an impartial tribunal.

*****

In 1936, many Americans rejoiced as twenty-two-year-old Jesse Owens and twenty-six-year-old speedster Ralph Metcalfe punctured the myth of Aryan supremacy with their spectacular track and field performances in the tense 1936 Summer Olympics hosted by Adolf Hitler in Berlin. Charles and Anne Lindbergh had a different vantage point—front row seats as honored guests of the Führer, whom Lindbergh in exile now openly admired, much to the shock of the ace pilot's fan club in the United States. In 1939, when Charles Lindbergh returned from England, he quickly became President Roosevelt's most vitriolic foreign policy critic. The following year, as spokesman for the new isolationist movement America First, Lindbergh continued to argue vociferously against the United States joining the Allies' war against the Axis. Lindbergh had already shocked Americans by accepting a medal of honor from Hitler. While making the case for neutrality, Lindbergh horrified many more fellow countrymen with his anti-Semitic speeches. For most Americans, their hero transformed into an anti-hero.

Later in the war, Lindbergh volunteered to train pilots on dangerous missions against the Japanese. He succeeded in substantially redeeming his image. In the early '50s, President Eisenhower named Lindbergh a reserve brigadier general in the new Air Force. Eisenhower's successor, President Kennedy, made Lindbergh a senior adviser to the Apollo space mission. For the remainder of his life, Lindbergh insisted that the right man had been executed for the kidnap and murder of his first-born and actively discouraged any mention of his son Charlie. In the lengthy *Autobiography of Values* he worked on until his death, Lindbergh barely touched on the unprecedented three-year investigation and "trial of the century." When he died, Lindbergh was eulogized as the last American hero. Many years afterward, it became public that, in addition to his five known surviving children with his wife Anne, the aviator also fathered seven illegitimate children by three secret mistresses in Germany. His posthumous reputation became so tarnished that few eyebrows were raised when the 2009

Oscar-winning animated Pixar movie *Up* modeled its villain, adventurer Charles Muntz, in large part on the former national hero.

* * * * *

Back in 1939, while President Roosevelt and Charles Lindbergh publicly debated America's entry into World War II, the President authorized an enormous, super-secret military project. Alarmed American scientists had reported that the Nazis were already purifying uranium to use in developing nuclear weapons, and the Russians might be as well. Roosevelt committed the United States to work with the British and Canadians to win that deadly race. After Roosevelt died, President Truman dropped the world's first nuclear bombs in Japan, ending World War II. Six years later, with the Cold War at its height, the government sensationally accused an obscure Army Signal Corps civilian engineer of masterminding delivery of America's nuclear secrets to the Soviet Union. The latest "crime of the century" dwarfed public memory of the infamous Lindbergh baby kidnapping.

14. SHAMELESS HASTE: The Rosenberg Espionage Trial

"She called our bluff."

U.S. Deputy Attorney General William P. Rogers
commenting on Ethel Rosenberg's execution

On January 20, 1945, when President Franklin Roosevelt took his oath of office for an unprecedented fourth term, scientists assigned to the top secret Manhattan Project were in their sixth year of work on atomic weapons. New Vice President Harry Truman had just stepped down from heading the Senate Special Committee to Investigate the National Defense Program. Yet the Missouri Senator had never been briefed on the Manhattan Project—a two-billion-dollar joint project with the British and Canadians (over $24 billion in today's dollars) that employed more than 130,000 people in thirty locations. Even after Truman became Roosevelt's Vice President, Truman had no idea the project existed. In fact, in Truman's first two-and-a-half months in national office, Truman seldom even met with the ailing Commander-in-Chief, who was using his limited energy to oversee the endgame of World War II.

By early February, the Allies could see that they were on the verge of winning in Europe. In a conference at Yalta, Roosevelt met with British Prime Minister Winston Churchill and Soviet Premier Joseph Stalin to plan for the post-war occupation of Europe and to conclude the war in the Pacific. The three leaders agreed their countries would divide control over Europe and convert the joint efforts of their numerous war-time

Allies into a permanent United Nations, the concept President Wilson had first proposed as a League of Nations more than twenty-five years before. The Soviets already dominated Eastern Europe, but Roosevelt counted on Stalin limiting his sphere of influence to what he already controlled and hoped that, with such concessions, Stalin would work toward world peace. At Roosevelt's request, Stalin also committed to join the Allies in the war against Japan. Roosevelt died on April, 12, 1945, instantly elevating his unprepared Vice President to the Oval Office. It was only then that Truman obtained his first briefing on Stalin's rampant violations of promises to Roosevelt and Churchill by ruthless acts of aggression in Poland and other parts of Eastern Europe. Then, too, Truman first learned of the Manhattan Project and its near completion of the world's first nuclear weapons.

By early May of 1945, World War II officially ended in victory for the Allies in Europe with Hitler's suicide, the complete surrender of German troops, and the capture and killing of Mussolini in Italy. By then, President Truman feared yielding too much power to Stalin in the Far East as the war against Japan headed to a close. By late May, Japan was withdrawing from China; by the fifth of July, the Philippines were freed; and, on July 10, the United States began more concentrated bombing missions over the islands of Japan to induce its surrender. The following week, American physicists tested their secret weapon in rural New Mexico, releasing a mushroom cloud seen for two hundred miles. In July of 1945, Russia was known to be readying its own plans for invasion of Japan while the Japanese were trying to get the Soviets to broker a peace in which the Japanese Empire would still be recognized. President Truman decided that a quick, decisive victory was needed to keep Stalin from claiming joint authority when a peace treaty was reached with Japan. At a conference in Potsdam, Truman forewarned Stalin that the United States had "a new weapon of unusual destructive force."[1] The United States gave an ultimatum to Japan to surrender unconditionally or promptly face utter devastation, which the Japanese rejected, vowing to defend their homeland to the death.

Meanwhile, Manhattan Project scientist Leo Szilard drafted a petition signed by 155 anxious scientists. In an urgent plea to President

Truman, they asked the Commander-in-Chief to witness a demonstration of the bomb's power before authorizing its use and to give a detailed warning to the Japanese beforehand to promote chances of unconditional surrender without its deployment. The Secretary of War did not communicate the scientists' moral reservations to President Truman; nor was the Szilard Petition made public for another sixteen years.[2] Truman followed up his Potsdam ultimatum on August 6, 1945, by giving the order to drop a uranium bomb on the densely populated port city of Hiroshima, where the Japanese army and marines were headquartered. The rationale was that the bomb would prevent massive casualties from a secret plan called Operation Downfall, a two-pronged attack scheduled to begin in October of 1945 to invade Japan with American soldiers prepared to take the island nation in bloody hand-to-hand combat. Estimates prepared for Operation Downfall ranged from one million to four million American casualties, including several hundred thousand deaths. At least ten times as many Japanese people were expected to die defending their homeland.[3]

In authorizing the bombing of Hiroshima, Truman wrote in his diary that he instructed Secretary of War Henry Stimson to target the military and not women and children, but no such limitation was transmitted to those who carried out the order.[4] The first use of a nuclear weapon of mass destruction killed close to 140,000 people, mostly civilians—more than half by the direct hit and the rest over several months of agony from burn and radiation injuries. Two days later, the Russians declared war on Japan and invaded Japanese colonies in Manchuria and Korea. The following day, Truman ordered a plutonium bomb dropped on Nagasaki, which killed another 80,000 people. This executive action completed the one, two punch that ushered in the atomic era. Strong consideration had been given to bombing Kyoto as well, but it was spared by seventy-seven-year-old Stimson for sentimental reasons—he had honeymooned there in 1893.

Truman then made a public address to the American people:

> The atomic bomb is too dangerous to be let loose in a lawless world until means have been found to control the bomb so as to protect ourselves and the rest of the world from the danger of total

> destruction. I shall ask the Congress to co-operate to the end that its production and use be controlled, and that its power be made an overwhelming influence towards world peace. We must constitute ourselves trustees of this new force, to prevent its misuse, and to turn it into the channels of service to mankind. It is an awful responsibility which has come to us. We thank God that it has come to us instead of to our enemies, and we pray that He may guide us to use it in His ways and for His purposes.[5]

The Japanese immediately surrendered and the island nation was occupied primarily by American troops, joined by allies, including the Australians and British, but not the Russians. Instead, Stalin agreed to split Korea at the 38th parallel, with North Korea under Communist control and South Korea controlled by the Americans. Truman believed he had just faced down the Soviets "with an iron fist" and that America emerged as the preeminent global power.[6] World War II had become a Cold War that historians would date back to the historic conference at Yalta. But the Allies had commenced World War II with the assumption that targeting civilians was an act of barbarism. The instant obliteration of major cities as an act of war by the United States sent a chilling message to people everywhere on the planet. After hostilities ended, Albert Einstein was among many scientists gravely concerned about the future: "Our world faces a crisis as yet unperceived by those possessing the power to make great decisions for good and evil. The unleashed power of the atom has changed everything save our modes of thinking, and thus we drift toward unparalleled catastrophe."[7]

Pacifists throughout the world hoped the fledgling United Nations might become a true global government capable of ensuring the security of all nations by overseeing nuclear power. Einstein was among those who strongly believed that world peace could only be assured if the United States and Great Britain agreed to share nuclear science with other superpowers to eliminate the "mutual fear and distrust" of the emerging Cold War.[8] In 1946, Winston Churchill blasted Stalin's empire for holding hostage satellite European states behind "The Iron Curtain." In Congress, the House Un-American Activities Committee ("HUAC") responded zealously to the renewed Red Scare. In 1947, a black list of entertainment professionals developed after many Hollywood celebrities and screenwriters were called to testify before HUAC and refused to name Communists within the movie industry. HUAC made headline after headline.

In 1948, in a highly publicized trial, Australian-born labor leader Harry Bridges was finally convicted of perjury for lying about his Communist Party membership. Conservatives in Congress and the FBI had been trying to deport the spokesman for California's longshoremen as an "undesirable alien" for more than a decade. This try would fail, too, after the decision was reversed by the Supreme Court in 1953. Republicans' anger at Bridges dated back to the "Big Strike" of 1934. That spring, 32,000 dock workers earning an average $10 per week shut down all the ports on the Pacific Coast for two months, demanding better working conditions and pay increases. In the '30s, strong public sentiment favored the underpaid workers. On "Bloody Thursday," July 5, 1934, in a pitched battle in San Francisco between a thousand armed policemen and thousands of strikers throwing stones and bricks, the police killed two men as scores of others were wounded, including bystanders. Eight hundred demonstrators were arrested. Peace was restored by 2,000 National Guardsmen sent by new Republican Gov. Frank Merriam, who had thousands more in reserve. When the funeral procession drew 40,000 San Franciscans sympathetic to the union's demands, Merriam was preparing to declare martial law. Negotiations were instead undertaken to end the general strike peacefully with federal assistance. The end result was a major victory for organized labor through a new labor-management arbitration process set up by President Roosevelt.

After World War II, with the Depression now long behind everyone, the transition from a global shooting war to the Cold War changed the political climate decidedly against both radicals and Roosevelt Liberals. In 1946, for the first time in 18 years, the Republicans won control of both houses of Congress, while President Truman faced strong internal opposition from Democrats on both his left and right. Meanwhile, California's Republican Congressman Richard Nixon rocketed to fame by accusing a very high-level State Department employee, Alger Hiss, of being a Communist spy. Nixon had been fed secret information for this purpose from FBI Director J. Edgar Hoover. The source was former Communist Whittaker Chambers, who asserted that he and Hiss had both lied to HUAC about spying for the Soviets while Hiss worked for the federal government. President Truman and other leading Democrats found the charges outrageous and assumed they were a political ploy. It was too difficult to believe. Hiss was the lawyer who had presided over the chartering of the United Nations in 1946. Hiss sued Chambers for libel, but substantial evidence would later support Chambers' dramatic charges.

In 1948, J. Edgar Hoover convinced President Truman to use the 1940 Smith Act to prosecute Communists and their followers for the ideas they promoted. The law did not require proof of any overt acts—just revolutionary speech. In a major trial in New York, eleven defendants were tried for conspiring "to organize as the Communist Party and willfully to advocate and teach the principles of Marxism-Leninism," which would lead to "overthrowing and destroying the government of the United States by force and violence."[9]

In another high-profile prosecution, Justice Department political analyst Judith Coplon was accused of handing over classified data to her Soviet lover. Hoover's men were caught employing illegal wiretaps and suborning perjury, which resulted in reversal of her two convictions. In a continuation of the ongoing attempt to out Alger Hiss, in yet another much-watched trial in 1949, Hiss was criminally prosecuted for allegedly lying under oath to HUAC. The Hiss perjury trial would later be dubbed "the first morality play of the red-baiting era."[10] Whittaker Chambers was the star witness against the patrician Democrat. By then, Hiss could no longer be prosecuted for espionage, because too much time had elapsed. Hiss was defended by Leftist lawyers in the National Lawyers Guild. Guild members were supporters of Roosevelt's New Deal legislation, who formed the new organization in 1937 as the only nationwide bar dedicated to promoting civil rights. At the time, the conservative American Bar Association officially banned black lawyers from its ranks. Guild members launched test cases against key Jim Crow laws, meeting with their first major success against housing discrimination in *Hansbury v. Lee.* (The plaintiff was playwright Lorraine Hansbury's father.) After World War II, Guild members helped prosecute Nazis at Nuremberg. But the Cold War brought a backlash against Communists and Communist sympathizers, with Guild members among those increasingly under suspicion for representing accused Communists.

Though the Guild succeeded in ending the first Hiss trial with a hung jury, when it continued to champion controversial causes, its membership began to shrink. By 1950, fewer than half of the original thirty-five chapters of the Guild still functioned. The ABA urged states to disbar lawyers who advocated Marxism and to discipline those who took the Fifth Amendment in HUAC hearings. In 1952, Attorney General Herbert Brownell would officially add the Guild to his list of subversive organizations for failure to require its members to sign a loyalty oath.

The retrial of Alger Hiss in January of 1950 ended in the Ivy League lawyer's conviction of two counts of perjury after only one day of jury deliberation. He was sentenced to one to five years in prison. (Hiss would defend his innocence to his dying day: his autobiography *Recollections of a Life* accuses J. Edgar Hoover of a politically motivated frame-up. Yet most historians now consider the question settled by recent release of KGB files implicating Hiss as a Soviet spy.) That same month, British prosecutors convicted Klaus Fuchs, a German-born physicist, of passing key information to the Soviet Union during World War II about British and American research on the atomic bomb. Fuchs had worked at the Manhattan Project headquarters in Los Alamos National Laboratory, where he had made significant contributions to the development of the hydrogen bomb. By 1949, Soviet scientists had progressed enough to test their own bomb. Fuchs received a fourteen-year sentence—the maximum then available for passing secrets to a friendly nation, Russia's then classification as Britain's former World War II ally. Fuchs also implicated people with whom he worked, including an American named David Greenglass, who had been a machinist at Los Alamos.

In June of 1950, Julius and Ethel Rosenberg lived quietly in a three bedroom apartment in Manhattan's lower East Side with their two small sons, aged seven and three, when Ethel's brother, David Greenglass, confessed to the FBI that Greenglass had been a member of a Soviet spy ring masterminded by his brother-in-law. The Rosenbergs had both joined the Young Communist League in the Great Depression, when Communist attacks on capitalist exploitation of workers struck a chord with so many impoverished laborers. Communists could also point to their leadership role in promoting racial equality in contrast to the world view of white supremacists who dominated American politics. By the last week of June of 1950—the same month in which Greenglass implicated the Rosenbergs as spies—Communist North Korea invaded South Korea, plunging the United States into the Korean War. It was the next round in the Cold War chess game with Stalin. In July, Julius Rosenberg was arrested for violating the 1917 Espionage Act. Ethel was arrested the following month. A third named co-conspirator, engineer Martin Sobell, fled with his family to Mexico in late June. The FBI tracked Sobell down and arranged for Sobell and his family to be kidnapped at gunpoint and brought to the border where FBI agents arrested Sobell.

The man in charge of the Rosenbergs' prosecution was United States Attorney for the Southern District of New York Irving Saypol, born Ike Sapolsky. Saypol already had proved himself a ruthless crusader against the evils of Communism, just as FBI Director J. Edgar Hoover had been since World War I. It was the square-jawed Saypol who sensationally convicted Alger Hiss in January of 1950 for lying under oath to HUAC. As 1950 drew to a close, Saypol prosecuted William Remington for perjury. Remington was a government economist who had, like Whittaker Chambers, become an avowed enemy of Communists, but lied about his own prior Communist connections. Remington's conviction would be reversed on appeal in part based on Saypol's relentless insinuations that one of the defense witnesses legally changed his name because that is what Communists do. Saypol was apparently undaunted by the hypocrisy of such an accusation given his own name change. The grand jury indictment against Remington had itself been tainted; the defense discovered that the grand jury foreman had a deal to co-author a book with the former Soviet spy who turned FBI informer and became Remington's chief accuser.

While Remington's and Hiss's convictions were on appeal, Saypol decided to make an even more dramatic statement. Both Alger Hiss and William Remington had only faced a maximum of five years in prison. Saypol went all in against the Rosenbergs, seeking the death penalty. His plan was to use capital punishment as a bargaining chip and to offer the couple leniency if they would plead guilty and cooperate with the FBI in naming their collaborators. Both refused, maintaining their innocence of the treasonous charges. By the time of the Rosenbergs' and Sobell's trial in the spring of 1951, the McCarthy Era was fully launched and the Korean War was at its bloodiest. (Before the war's end, the FBI would expand to more than six thousand agents monitoring suspected subversives). In what was already an atmosphere of hysteria, simply being a Communist was enough to alienate any jury. Critics charged that the Rosenberg trial judge, Irving Kaufman, himself showed serious bias in favor of Saypol. Some would later claim that the Rosenberg prosecution was also anti-Semitic—a tricky charge to lodge when the chief prosecutor and judge were both Jewish.

Neither of the Rosenbergs presented a sympathetic figure to the general public or the mainstream press. The key testimony against them was that of Ethel's younger brother David Greenglass and his wife Ruth, who was given immunity in exchange for her husband's confession. Leftist attorney Emanuel Bloch passionately defended the Rosenbergs to no avail, as Saypol and his assistant Roy Cohn accused the couple of "the most serious crime which can be committed against the people of this country" by helping the Soviets develop their own nuclear bomb.[12] A lone woman juror expressed qualms that, if Ethel Rosenberg were executed, it would leave her two small sons orphans. But she was persuaded to go along with the others, and the panel returned guilty verdicts against both Rosenbergs and against Sobell. The judge described the Rosenbergs' crime as "worse than murder" and sentenced the Rosenbergs to death—the only civilians to be executed by the United States in the Cold War.[13] Though the usefulness to the Soviets of the information the Rosenbergs allegedly conveyed was disputed, Judge Kaufman blamed the Rosenbergs for altering the course of history to the disadvantage of the United States, leading directly to the Korean War. He held the Rosenbergs personally responsible for all 50,000 American casualties in that war and perhaps millions more innocent lives in the future. Judge Kaufman ordered Sobell to serve a thirty-year sentence for his lesser role in the espionage.

As with Sacco and Vanzetti and the Scottsboro Boys, strong support for the Rosenbergs did not emerge until after the trial was over. A weekly leftist newspaper, *The National Guardian,* ran a series of articles asserting that the Rosenbergs were "the first victims of American fascism."[14] The weekly Leftist paper quoted Ethel Rosenberg's death row letters to her husband in his own isolation cell expressing her "horror at the shameless haste with which the government appears to be pressing for our liquidation."[15] Claims of due process violations fell mostly on deaf ears. Members of the National Lawyers Guild themselves were derided by Attorney General Brownell as "the legal mouthpiece of the Communist Party."[16] The new McCarran-Walter Act authorized rounding up alleged subversives under loyalty clearance programs. During the early stages of the Rosenbergs' appeal, a broad spectrum of humanitarians and civil libertarians rallied to their cause, concerned that the Rosenbergs had not received a fair trial and their sentence was disproportionately harsh. Post-trial motions addressed to Judge Kaufman proved fruitless as did two appeals for stays of execution. Sitting on the Supreme Court, Justice Felix Frankfurter—who had written so passionately about the Sacco and Vanzetti case thirty years earlier—blamed Judge Kaufman for creating a record that ensured the high court's unwillingness to review the Rosenbergs' conviction for error. Frankfurter later told Judge Learned Hand, "I despise a judge who feels God told him to impose a death sentence."[17]

In 1952, an influx of Communists shifted control of the Rosenberg defense committee. The committee then changed its focus from winning a new trial to convincing the public of the couple's innocence—a tactic later criticized as a cynical ploy to guarantee their execution and turn them into martyrs.[18] The question remained why the Rosenbergs were singled out for execution when others equally or more to blame for sharing state secrets received lesser sentences. President Eisenhower twice denied executive clemency, despite receiving petitions from hundreds of thousands of people across the globe, including Albert Einstein and Pope Pius XII. Many protests were staged to no avail. It later became known that ACLU veteran Morris Ernst had offered his services on the Rosenbergs' appellate team for the sole benefit of the FBI, a betrayal of loyalty that ought to have been a disbarrable offense. Without meeting with either client, Ernst then offered the FBI his unscientific analysis that the Rosenbergs had a master-slave relationship in which Julius only did Ethel's bidding. The FBI in turn secretly passed on Ernst's patently unreliable conclusion to President Eisenhower.

While their appeals pended, Julius and Ethel Rosenberg spent two years in separate cells in the Death House at Sing Sing on the Hudson River sixteen miles north of Yonkers, New York. The maximum security prison in the town of Ossining had been the state's only location for executions since 1914. Justice William Douglas granted the Rosenbergs a temporary reprieve, only to have it immediately reversed by a special session of the Supreme Court. The couple were electrocuted on June 19, 1953. The time was moved to just before sunset out of deference to the Jewish Sabbath. Eyewitnesses reported that Julius died quickly, but Ethel Rosenberg remained alive when the straps were removed following her electrocution. The straps were rebuckled and oficials zapped her body three more times with electrical charges until eyewitnesses saw smoke coming out of her head and she was pronounced dead. Ironically, the electric chair had replaced hanging in New York in 1891 as a humane method for executing prisoners on the assumption that the first jolt would render the subject unconscious before the body registered any pain.

Women in the Death Row House were relatively rare; of 614 executions at Sing Sing, Ethel was the ninth and last woman electrocuted. The first, in 1899, was a deranged housewife named Martha Place, who murdered her stepdaughter and chased after her husband with an axe. In 1928, Ruth Snyder (the husband-killer who inspired the book and classic film noir *Double Indemnity*, starring Barbara Stanwyck) was infamously photographed strapped blindfolded to the chair in her final moments. Two years before Ethel Rosenberg died, "Lonely Hearts" serial killer Martha Beck met her death in Sing Sing's chair, as did her common law husband Raymond Fernandez. The chair was retired for good in 1963. New York has conducted no executions since then.

By the time of the Rosenbergs' electrocution, Irving Saypol was sitting on the New York trial court bench, to which he had been appointed in 1952. He would serve as a jurist for sixteen years. Meanwhile, Alger Hiss served forty-four months in prison and eventually regained his law license at age seventy, the year after his nemesis Richard Nixon resigned from the presidency in disgrace. William Remington, on retrial, received a three-year sentence. He was murdered in prison in 1954 for being a detested "Commie."[19] In March of 1954 CBS television's hard-hitting commentator Edward R. Murrow, host of the television program, "See It Now," aired a program comprised mostly of news clips of McCarthy's own vitriol, topped by the proclamation that the presidencies of FDR and Truman had constituted "twenty years of treason."[20] Joe Welch, chief counsel for the United States Army, accused McCarthy of "reckless cruelty." Welch famously added: "You've done enough. Have you no sense of decency, sir; at long last? Have you left no sense of decency?"[21] The Senate censured Joseph McCarthy for his irresponsible accusations. The FBI had more recently begun reporting to Congress a major decline in "known" Communists.[22] The American Communist Party lost much of its remaining support after February of 1956, when Nikita Khrushchev published details of the bloody purges during Stalin's reign.

* * * * *

David Greenglass served ten years of his fifteen-year sentence. In 1976, Saypol and another judge, S. Samuel DiFalco, were indicted for alleged bribery and perjury in a scheme to benefit Saypol's son. The charges were dismissed shortly before Saypol died of cancer in 1977. Martin Sobell spent nearly nineteen years in prison. He was released in 1969. In 2008, Martin Sobell confessed his guilt—nearly four decades after his release from prison and almost a quarter of a century after writing a book, *On Doing Time,* adamantly maintaining his innocence. By then, other evidence from a variety of sources corroborated that Julius Rosenberg had, in fact, headed a spy ring to funnel information to Russia. Rosenberg's Soviet contact claimed that Julius did not provide him with anything useful about the atomic bomb. However, in memoirs published after his death, Russian Premier Nikita Khrushchev asserted otherwise, based on secondhand reports he had heard from Stalin.

In an interview in 1989, the former director of the Soviet agency that developed the Russian bomb flatly rejected the utility of the intelligence Julius Rosenberg had conveyed, telling *New York Times* reporter

Robert McFadden, "You sat the Rosenbergs in the electric chair for nothing."[23] But that assumed the FBI and prosecutor were only focused on the actual damage done by the Rosenbergs themselves. As pointed out by historians Ronald Radosh and Joyce Milton: "At the very least, [by making an example of unpopular defendants] the Justice Department was sending a message to other Party members who might be tempted to spy for the Soviets."[24]

Proof also emerged that Ethel Rosenberg was convicted with perjured testimony by Ruth and David Greenglass. The prosecutor knew he had no evidence to convict Ethel of the capital crime. He had deliberately elicited Ruth and David's lies about Ethel typing key notes to force Julius Rosenberg to confess and name names. Ruth Greenglass had earlier testified secretly before the grand jury to a completely inconsistent account that was suppressed for half a century. David Greenglass ultimately confessed that he felt compelled to sacrifice Ethel to save his own wife from prison. The sensational revelation appeared in *The Brother: The Untold Story of Atomic Spy David Greenglass and How He Sent His Sister, Ethel Rosenberg, to the Electric Chair.* It was Ethel's refusal to succumb to this improper pressure to name names in exchange for her own life to which Assistant Attorney General William Rogers alluded when he said, "She called our bluff."[25] The FBI did not even know when they decided to prosecute both of the Rosenbergs whether Ethel was "aware of Julius' espionage activities."[26] In 1954, the FBI became even bolder. In defiance of an adverse Supreme Court ruling, the FBI installed hundreds of electronic bugs in traditional criminal investigations on the false premise that they were related to national security.[27]

* * * * *

The Rosenberg saga has reverberated for close to sixty years. It gave rise to a number of historical accounts (two by the Rosenbergs' sons) and novels, including E. L. Doctorow's *The Book of Daniel,* later made into a movie. *The Rosenberg File,* by historians Ronald Radosh and Joyce Milton, sets forth a detailed and balanced analysis of the evidence implicating the Rosenbergs. It also lays bare the unethical tactics of the government lawyers and FBI to get a chilling victory in that highly volatile political era. The Rosenbergs' granddaughter made her own movie, *Heir to an Execution*, featured at the 2003 Sundance Festival, the same year actress Meryl Streep memorably portrayed Ethel Rosenberg's ghost, haunting prosecutor Roy Cohn in the award-winning mini-series "Angels in America." (Cohn had been disbarred for fraud shortly before his death in 1986.)

* * * * *

When Russia joined the United States and Great Britain as an ally during the war years, much to the dismay of American Communists, Stalin ordered the suspension of civil rights work by Communists in the United States. In the late forties and fifties, as part of the Cold War propaganda campaign, American Communists resumed a leading role in challenging racism. FBI Chief J. Edgar Hoover seized on this renewed Communist effort to discredit the growing civil rights movement. Any proven ties to Communists branded civil rights advocates as unpatriotic Reds. Bugging became an agency specialty as activists gained momentum in targeting entrenched segregation.

15. THE DEATH OF INNOCENCE: Hate Crimes and the Civil Rights Movement

"The civil rights movement owes Bull Connor as much as it owes Abraham Lincoln."

PRESIDENT JOHN FITZGERALD KENNEDY

In June of 1954 the Supreme Court issued its unanimous decision in *Brown v. Board of Education,* a Kansas class action for injunctive relief consolidated on appeal with four other NAACP cases filed in three other states and the District of Columbia raising similar arguments. *Brown* started as a two-day judge trial in 1950. The plaintiffs were denied relief based on the ruling in *Plessy v. Ferguson.* On appeal, the high court overturned more than a half-century of decisions under its 1896 "separate but equal" doctrine. Aside from the inherent stigma of enforced separation, the notion that equality was intended or achieved under segregation had always been a cruel joke. Per pupil expenditures for white students in the South might total forty times the amount spent for blacks.[1] The controversial *Brown* ruling met with anger and disdain throughout the South. With calls for Chief Justice Warren's impeachment, Dixiecrats aggressively defended their white supremacist values. A shocking example was the kidnap/murder of Emmett Till.

On August 21, 1954, the fourteen-year-old Chicago boy took the train with his cousin to visit his great uncle in the rural Mississippi delta outside Greenwood. At a grocery store in the town of Money that catered to sharecroppers, Till showed off his daring by whistling at the attractive white proprietress. After word of the incident spread, Till was brazenly kidnapped at gunpoint from his relatives' home where he shared a bed with his cousin. Till's mutilated body was found days later in a nearby river. Till's mother, a Chicago school teacher, only recognized Emmett's decomposing remains from the ring she had given him that bore his late father's initials. She had then mustered the fortitude to have Emmett's corpse displayed in an open casket at an African-American church where thousands of outraged people filed by night and day until his burial. (Mamie Till-Mobley would later co-author *The Death of Innocence: The Story of the Hate Crime That Changed America.*) Chicago rabbis were prominent among the civil rights activists demanding redress for Till's death.

The NAACP and other groups asked President Eisenhower to intervene in the Mississippi investigation and lobbied for a still-elusive federal anti-lynching law to take such cases out of the hands of biased state officials. Chicago-based *Jet* magazine featured gruesome photos of the corpse, outraging blacks across the country at the barbarity of Till's death. The governor of Mississippi tried to cut off further criticism by promising that the perpetrators would be found and prosecuted. Soon Roy Bryant, the husband of the woman who had been whistled at, and his half-brother J. W. Milam were arrested. No one in the county was surprised. When the case went to trial in late September in Sumner, Mississippi, Emmett's great uncle pointed the two men out in court as the kidnappers and his mother identified Emmett's corpse. It made no difference. The all-white male jury deliberated for only an hour, counting a soda break, before exonerating Bryant and Milam. The jurors claimed there was no proof that the mutilated body was really that of Emmett Till. A few months later, *Look Magazine* paid the two exonerated defendants for their story. Since double jeopardy prevented their retrial, Bryant and Milam freely confessed to mutilating and killing Till for his perceived uppity behavior.

The Till murder shamed America and has been credited as the spark that ignited the Civil Rights Movement. It came on the heels of the killing earlier the same year of two prominent civil rights activists—Rev. George W. Lee of the NAACP and World War II veteran Lamar Smith—who had been trying to encourage black voter registration. Their deaths remained uninvestigated, although suspects could be found in the White Citizens Council, newly formed to deter desegregation and expanded ballot rights.

People around the globe reacted even more to the 1957 crisis in Little Rock, Arkansas, in which Gov. Orval Faubus called out the National Guard to block nine black teens from enrolling in all-white Central High School. Like other Dixiecrats, Faubus vigorously resisted integrating public schools as mandated in *Brown v. Board of Education.* President Eisenhower's alarmed advisors warned him of anguished pleas from American diplomats overseas that the Little Rock crisis was having a profound impact on the two-thirds of the world that was non-white. Finally, the unwilling President felt he had no choice but to call in federal troops to ensure the black students were admitted. Eisenhower then addressed the nation via television and radio in late September of 1957 to explain how the Little Rock situation had severely damaged the image of the United States as the leader of the free world:

> At a time when we face grave situations abroad because of the hatred that Communism bears toward a system of government based on human rights, it would be difficult to exaggerate the harm that is being done to the prestige and influence, and indeed to the safety, of our nation and the world. Our enemies are gloating over this incident and using it everywhere to misrepresent our whole nation. We are portrayed as a violator of those standards of conduct which the peoples of the world united to proclaim in the Charter of the United Nations.[2]

That same year, Rev. Martin Luther King, Jr. and his mentor, Pennsylvanian Bayard Rustin, helped co-found the Southern Christian Leadership Conference ("SCLC"). Rustin had been a Communist in the 1930s in Harlem when he worked to free the Scottsboro Boys, but then quit the Party in disgust in 1941 when Stalin ordered American Communists to stop focusing on civil rights. In 1959, both King and Rustin went to India to study Mahatma Gandhi's successful tactics in nonviolent resistance to British colonial rule. In the spring of 1960, at King's instigation, a new organization, the Student Nonviolent Coordinating Committee ("SNCC") was formed in Atlanta. Under the leadership of James Forman, an Air Force veteran in his early thirties, SNCC soon evolved into an effective grassroots organization, chaired from 1963 to 1966 by Freedom Rider and future Congressman John Lewis. Attorney General Robert Kennedy urged SNCC to direct its energy to voter registration and away from more sit-ins that routinely resulted in arrests, or Freedom Rides, which ended with integrated buses being bombed in Birmingham.

The ballot appeared to be an easy target—Mississippi had the most overtly racist electoral laws in the country. Less than five percent of blacks were registered to vote. In the fall of 1963, SNCC mobilized volunteers from the North for the Mississippi Summer Project. The goals of "Freedom Summer" were to register voters, organize the Mississippi Freedom Democratic Party, and conduct Freedom Schools. The Freedom Summer project attracted the support of many national civil rights organizations. Bringing in Northern white students and lawyers to assist was a deliberate gamble to entice the federal government into action in the event of threatened violence (on the premise that society deemed white lives far more valuable). SNCC also expected arrests of civil rights activists for picketing or violating selectively enforced local laws. The strategy was to remove such cases from biased state judges to federal court. For the past several years, in the wake of *Brown v. Board of Education,* the Fifth Circuit, which oversaw cases from most of the Deep South, had issued some landmark civil rights decisions, largely by four judges, including Republican Chief Judge Tuttle.[3] The champions of constitutional rights on that court became known as "The Fifth Circuit Four." In 1963, an irate dissenting judge made headlines with sensational charges against the Chief Judge of "panel packing"—assigning judges to hear civil rights appeals who were predisposed to favor desegregation or, as one of the "Fifth Circuit Four" put it, "follow the law honestly and . . . without prejudice."[4] By late 1963, appellate panels were assigned randomly, resulting in fewer victories in the Fifth Circuit for civil rights advocates.

Testing of the judiciary through civil disobedience continued unabated. Rustin orchestrated many successful sit-ins and freedom marches, including the powerful August 1963 March on Washington in which Dr. King gave his famous "I Have a Dream" speech. But the FBI found Rustin a vulnerable target as a former Communist and admitted homosexual convicted of violating California laws. FBI Chief J. Edgar Hoover then became fixated on destroying Dr. King, much as he had been bent on taking down popular entertainer Paul Robeson. Hoover kept his own confidential files focused in large part on both men's sex lives.

Hoover meanwhile kept his own private life and back-ground closely guarded. In *Secrets Uncovered: J. Edgar Hoover, Passing For White?* African-American author Millie McGhee asserts that she hired a genealogist to trace her own and Hoover's ancestry because of a whispered family story that they were related. She believes that Hoover's biological father was a bi-racial Mississippian in her family tree named Ivery Hoover and that J. Edgar Hoover was raised by other relatives in Washington, D.C., so he could pass for white.[5] The results were inconclusive without unavailable DNA testing, but her investigation led her to extensive research into four generations of census and other data compiled by Ohio State University sociologist Robert Stuckert. Prof. Stuckert concluded that more than three-fourths of all Americans classified as black actually had one or more white ancestors and almost one-quarter of those classified as white had one or more black ancestors: "As many as 155,500 fair-skinned African-Americans slipped across the color line during the 1940s alone."[6] Historian Kenneth Ackerman considers it "not unlikely" that Hoover had an African-American ancestor, as McGhee believes. Also plausible, but not proved, are persistent rumors since the 1940s that the lifelong bachelor, who subjected gay political opponents like Rustin to ridicule, was himself homosexual. However, like other Hoover biographers, Ackerman rejects a widely disseminated story that Hoover engaged in cross-dressing.[7]

Armed with Hoover's leaks, editorials in the Cotton Belt openly ridiculed "the Rev. Dr. Extremist Agitator Martin Luther King junior" and "the miserable 'non-violent' street rabble" led by the "unspeakable Martin Luther King and his ilk."[8] On Good Friday, April 12, 1963, Bull Connor's men arrested King, Rev. Ralph Abernathy, and six other ministers for violating a court order prohibiting a protest march without a permit. As the nation watched in shock, Connor then instructed his officers to use fire hoses and attack dogs against the assembled marchers, including children. A report issued by the Federal Commission on Civil Rights four days later minced no words, warning that the flagrant situation in Mississippi and Alabama appeared headed for a complete breakdown of law and order, affronting "the conscience of the nation."[9]

At the time, King was serving a five-day sentence imposed by a local judge. In "Letter from a Birmingham Jail," King compared Alabama's brutal treatment of civil rights marchers to the Soviet Union's ruthless suppression of Hungarian freedom fighters and the Nazis' implementation of the horrors of the Holocaust. King reminded people on the fence about his tactics of civil disobedience that "everything Hitler did in Germany was 'legal'."[10] Professor Alan Dershowitz lists King's conviction and appeal as one of the pivotal legal battles of the 20th century that transformed our nation, though it involved almost no courtroom time. Long before the Supreme Court addressed King's defiance of the Birmingham judge's injunction, King had already won the 1964 Nobel Peace Prize. In 1967, a sharply divided Supreme Court affirmed King's conviction for defying the law. Two years later in *Shuttlesworth v. City of Birmingham* the high court held the Alabama city's parade ordinance unconstitutional—the very rationale King used to justify his civil disobedience.

By the spring of 1964, both King and the NAACP had distanced themselves from Communists. But the Lawyers Guild had not, nor had SNCC. Feisty Detroit labor lawyer George Crockett had just become the new vice president of the Guild—the first black to hold that office. Crockett credited jail time for contempt after he represented Communist leaders in the 1949 New York Smith Act trial as a life-changing epiphany: "After prison, I learned not to fear."[11] He proposed that the Guild document official misconduct disenfranchising would-be black voters in the Magnolia State and volunteered to head up a new Guild outpost in Jackson, Mississippi—"the belly of the beast."[12]

By June of 1964, the State of Mississippi had established compounds for imprisoning the many blacks and civil rights workers it expected to arrest for engaging in the SNCC voter-registration drive. State officials anticipated the need for armored vehicles in Jackson as part of their battle plans. Two teenage black civil rights workers, Charles Moore and Henry Dee, went missing in May. At the end of the third week of June, three other civil rights workers were declared missing, two white students and one black—Andrew Goodman, Michael Schwerner, and James Chaney. At George Crockett's request, the trio were investigating the burning of a church in Philadelphia, Mississippi. Ironically, when the three civil rights workers arrived in the "city of brotherly love," local police immediately arrested and then released them at night without an opportunity to telephone anyone. They were never seen alive again.

The Justice Department was immediately alerted. The mutilated bodies of Moore and Dee, along with two unknown other bodies, were found in the Mississippi River while search teams looked for Schwerner, Goodman, and Chaney. Because of the public outcry, the FBI was forced to invest three million dollars in an intensive, two-month federal search to locate civil rights workers for whom its Chief had zero sympathy. In fact, Andrew Goodman's parents, Robert and Carolyn Goodman, were well-known Manhattan labor activists, who had often hosted prominent targets of the McCarthy Era in their upper West Side apartment. Robert Goodman was also President of Pacifica Foundation, a New York-based radio station suspected by the FBI of Communist affiliation, which had antagonized J. Edgar Hoover and the Bureau by airing a former FBI agent's exposé in 1962.

Civil rights activists were arrested on creative charges: parading without a permit in violation of a newly enacted ordinance; contributing to the delinquency of a minor; the use of vulgar and profane language; disturbing the peace; assault and battery; inciting to riot; operating a motor vehicle with improper tags; interfering with a police officer; and reckless driving. Congress responded to the persecution of civil rights workers in Cotton Belt states by passing the 1964 Civil Rights Act. With a stroke of the pen, Johnson abolished all remaining Jim Crow laws and prohibited mandatory racial segregation in schools, housing, or hiring by the government or private sector. Within days of each arrest, attorneys filed removal petitions to get the cases into federal court.

In August 1964, searchers found the bodies of the three missing civil rights workers buried in a red clay dam in Neshoba County, north of Meridian. There was no hope the state would follow up on a proper murder investigation and prosecution. The FBI had already turned the Moore and Dee murders over to state authorities, who promptly dismissed all charges against the arrested suspects. Federal prosecutors would not reopen the Moore and Dee case until 2000. In 1964, the FBI itself was instead preoccupied with proving that Martin Luther King, Jr. was "the most dangerous Negro" threatening the nation's future with Communism and "taking steps to remove King from the national picture."[13] Meanwhile the federal government took three years to complete the high profile investigation of the Schwerner, Chaney, and Goodman deaths. Ultimately, it arrested twenty white men, including the county sheriff and one of his deputies and obtained a conviction for conspiracy to deprive the three young men of their civil rights. The longest sentence meted out was six years.

Angry white locals felt all of the civil rights workers were just "unkempt agitators" and "race mixing invaders"[14] and that the trio who disappeared had brought their fate onto themselves for meddling where they did not belong. It would take decades before state officials in Mississippi prosecuted murder charges against the man who orchestrated the ambush of the three civil rights workers, Ku Klux Klansman Edgar Ray Killen. Not until 2011, on the fiftieth anniversary of the 1961 Freedom Rides to desegregate interstate bus travel, would a Republican governor officially extend an olive branch to thank the civil rights activists his predecessors had jailed for "your courage, commitment, your sufferings and your sacrifices." Gov. Haley Barbour added pointedly, "It is good we are rid of segregation, and we are right grateful for the role you played in helping us get there."[15]

* * * * *

When SNCC decided to accept the National Lawyers Guild's offer of help in launching Freedom Summer, the NAACP Legal Defense Fund threatened to cancel its own participation. SCLC held a similar view. FBI Director J. Edgar Hoover opened an investigation into SNCC's Communist ties and soon assembled thousands of pages on SNCC's organization, leaders and activities, as the FBI was still doing with the Lawyers Guild. Throughout his career, Hoover was privy to highly sensitive information on an extraordinary number of public figures. He learned early on that nearly everyone has secrets that they would do almost anything to prevent being made public. It was often just a question of who wielded power as to which secrets came out and destroyed careers, reputations or lives, which rumors were disbelieved and never acted upon, and which ones could be manipulated to advantage through blackmail. Hoover clearly abused the immense power of his office. After the FBI Chief died in 1972, rampant speculation about his own hypocrisy severely compromised his legacy, and he was the frequent butt of jokes about his own personal life. The supposition he was a closet gay gained credence from Hoover's close relationship with his aide and longtime inseparable companion Clyde Tolson. (Tolson inherited the bulk of Hoover's estate and secret files on public figures from Presidents to movie stars, dissidents, and civil rights leaders. Reportedly, the day Tolson died in mid-April of 1975, FBI agents raced to his house to retrieve the explosive cache.) Ironically, despite the FBI's best efforts, it is Rev. King whose reputation has grown astronomically since his death, culminating in a federal holiday and monument on the National Mall in his honor.

When President Lyndon Johnson applied his signature to the historic 1964 Civil Rights Act, he famously told an aide, "We have lost the South for a generation."[16] In August of 1980, presidential candidate Ronald Reagan took advantage of continuing resentment among former Dixiecrats when he launched his presidential campaign at fairgrounds outside Philadelphia, Mississippi, the town where the murders had occurred. His speech included a strong endorsement of states' rights as yet another signal to segregationists that they were welcome into the Republican fold. The Southern strategy worked. The Cotton Belt is still a Republican stronghold forty-seven years later, after welcoming Dixiecrats outraged by the Democrats' embrace of newly enfranchised blacks. At a televised 100th birthday celebration for Senator Thurmond in 2002, Senate Majority Leader Trent Lott of Mississippi told a gathering on Capitol Hill: "I want to say this about my state: When Strom Thurmond ran for president, we voted for him. We're proud of it. And if the rest of the country had followed our lead, we wouldn't have had all these problems over all these years, either."[17] Lott misgauged the impact of his comments on the national stage. Those remarks forced him out of his leadership role in the Senate.

Despite the enormous hurdles and physical dangers faced by civil rights lawyers, the '50s and '60s resulted in significant legal victories in which Thurgood Marshall and Constance Baker Motley of the NAACP Legal Defense Fund often led the charge: to integrate schools, restaurants and other public facilities and to prohibit states from outlawing inter-racial marriage. But urban blacks, already impatient with the pace of progress and Rev. King's pacifism, started listening more to the fiery Malcolm X. The emerging Black Power movement and frequent urban riots increasingly polarized Americans over both racial and socio-political disputes.

16. BEYOND CIVIL RIGHTS: Other Movement Cases

There's a battle
Outside and it is ragin'
. . . .
[T]he present now
Will later be past
The order is
Rapidly fadin'

Bob Dylan, "The Times They Are A'Changin'"

By the late '40s, key Leftists in the San Francisco Bay Area had joined Chicago and New York advocates in the forefront of the national Civil Rights Movement. During the early part of the Cold War, the Lawyers Guild was still among activist organizations bringing civil rights cases, though its ranks were greatly diminished. As the '50s drew to a close, "New Left" activists in their twenties began to join the Old Guard. Some were excited by the recent Cuban revolution and developments in third world countries seeking to overthrow European colonial governments; others were greatly disturbed by nuclear proliferation or eager to help bring new civil rights cases after the Warren Court rejected "separate but equal" facilities and began holding more Jim Crow laws unconstitutional. With the influx of young blood, the San Francisco Lawyers Guild and Northern California ACLU collaborated with other Progressive groups, using Civil Rights tactics employed mostly in the South to give birth to the expansive '60s protest movement. The new era first erupted on the national scene with "Black Friday" and a highly publicized criminal trial brought against a Cal undergraduate English major named Robert Meisenbach.

By 1959, American Communist Party membership had long since dwindled due both to years of intense targeting and public exposure of Stalin's bloody purges. Yet that year the House Un-American Activities Committee subpoenaed more than a hundred California teachers to testify at hearings in San Francisco. The Cold War was far from over. That same fall Soviet Premier Nikita Khrushchev warned Americans their grandchildren would live under Communism. Russia still led in the space race it began by launching Sputnik in 1957. Washington had its eye on Communist East Germany where escalating tension would lead to the erection of the Berlin Wall in 1961; Castro's Cuba ninety miles from America's south coast, where the Soviets now had access to install a military outpost that would lead to the October missile crisis of 1962; and South Vietnam where the potential for a Communist takeover fueled escalating American involvement into all-out war with North Vietnam in 1964 pursuant to the Gulf of Tonkin Resolution.

HUAC still went on the road periodically, employing the same blunt methods to intimidate witnesses and blacklist targets as had been its modus operandi for the past two decades. Ruined careers and a dozen or more suicides lay in its wake. By 1959, former President Harry Truman reflected the views of a growing number of outraged citizens when he characterized HUAC itself as "the most Unamerican thing in America."[1] The 1959 San Francisco hearings were ultimately cancelled, but HUAC notified California education officials of their charges and, as a result, some teachers were fired. The following spring HUAC issued a new set of subpoenas for almost fifty presumed Communists or their sympathizers, enraging the ACLU and National Lawyers Guild and a coalition of the American Federation of Teachers, California labor organizations, the Quakers, the Episcopal Diocese, and hundreds of faculty members and students in Bay Area colleges. In the Spring of 1960, HUAC scheduled new hearings in San Francisco, subpoenaing both new targets and usual suspects like longtime International Longshore and Warehouse Union leader Harry Bridges, who had been an FBI target for over a quarter of a century. Local Liberals and Leftists regarded this highly publicized road show as simply a witch hunt. A rally was planned by members of Students for Civil Liberties, which had recently begun lobbying against restriction of free speech on the Berkeley campus. The protest was set for May 12, 1960, the first day of the scheduled hearings.

Many of the Cal student activists were members of SLATE, a Progressive student organization founded in 1958 principally to oppose the nuclear bomb, racism, and the death penalty. SLATE forced the university to address illegal discrimination in the Greek system and ended domination of campus politics by conservative fraternities. When HUAC subpoenaed a Cal undergraduate among witnesses to be grilled in San Francisco, SLATE quickly mobilized many of its hundreds of student members.[2] Progressive students from Stanford University and other local colleges planned to gather at San Francisco's City Hall as well. To prevent a largely hostile audience at the hearing set for Thursday May 12, 1960, HUAC issued special passes to its own supporters, who used a side entrance. Officials then cited the room's capacity as the basis for turning away many students and union supporters who had lined up earlier at the front door.

When the hearing started, the chairman denied requests to relocate to a larger venue, prompting audience members sympathetic to those left outside to start singing the Star Spangled Banner and reciting the Pledge of Allegiance. While witnesses and their counsel proceeded to spar with their interrogators and invoke First and Fifth Amendment rights inside the hearing room, the people gathered outside peacefully picketed or attended a political rally several blocks away. The next day, Friday, May 13, a crowd of neatly dressed protesters returned en masse to City Hall and sat by the entrance to the HUAC hearing room chanting for access. Many began singing the spiritual "We Shall Not Be Moved." Their approach mimicked the civil rights sit-ins that had spread throughout the South that spring. City police responded to the sit-in by spraying fire hoses full force on the surprised demonstrators. To the shock of onlookers, officers then dragged or pushed many screaming protesters down the long marble staircase that served as the principal entryway to City Hall. Some fled the flooding building; others grappled with the police. Several were seriously injured or knocked unconscious. A few officers were hurt as well. Sixty-four protesters were arrested. The press dubbed the incident "Black Friday."

All but one of those arrested were charged with minor offenses such as disorderly conduct, resisting arrest or being a public nuisance. The remaining individual was Robert Meisenbach, a junior at Cal charged with felony assault. According to the police report, Meisenbach started all the violence by jumping a barrier, picking up an officer's club, and using it repeatedly to beat the lawman. Only then did police respond with hoses. A young lawyer named Mal Burnstein, who worked nearby at the California Supreme Court, grew alarmed when a friend employed at the Judicial Council was arrested. Burnstein immediately contacted criminal defense attorney Charles Garry. Garry spontaneously decided to post bail for all of the arrestees. On Saturday, a crowd of five thousand formed a picket line around City Hall, condemning the hearings. Black Friday made headlines across country as an alleged student uprising.

The FBI considered Garry's move to post everyone's bail as key evidence of a pre-existing Communist conspiracy to foment student unrest. The FBI had started a file on Garry years earlier for his representation of accused Communists. He and two of his partners had themselves been subpoenaed in 1957 to appear before a HUAC committee in San Francisco focused on exposing Communist professionals in the Bay Area. The primary target at the time was Garry's partner Barney Dreyfus, who had taken the lead in opposing Smith Act loyalty oaths and recruiting California State Bar leaders to come to the defense of HUAC targets. The 1957 hearings had turned into a circus as a crowd of sympathetic onlookers cheered the uncooperative lawyers.

J. Edgar Hoover issued a report blaming the student "riots" on a handful of manipulative Communists. The HUAC Committee then produced a widely distributed documentary called *Operation Abolition.* Its chair, Pennsylvania Democrat Francis Walter, narrated the forty-two minute film spliced together from subpoenaed local television and newsreel footage. He described the picketers and sit-in participants as "toying with treason."[3] Like Hoover, Walter blamed Communist agitators for using students as dupes to do its dirty work by instigating violence in the name of free speech. Fifteen million people viewed that propaganda film, which was so heavy-handed that it wound up being used by both sides. Progressive activists on college campuses viewed it as a recruiting tool. The Northern California ACLU produced its own documentary *Operation Correction*, which exposed the HUAC film's serious distortions. Using the same footage, ACLU Director Ernest Besig explained how *Operation Abolition* rearranged the sequence of events, suppressed contradictory evidence, and relied on guilt by association to link everyone present with accused Communist witnesses they had never met.[4] Meanwhile, a local judge dismissed the charges against all the arrestees but Meisenbach. Fifty-eight of the released students joined in a statement: "Nobody incited us, nobody misguided us. We were led only by our own convictions, and we still stand firmly by them."[5]

The San Francisco legal contest played out in a three-week trial in April 1961. Meisenbach was represented by both Charles Garry and former assistant district attorney Jack Berman, the veteran of a World War II War Crimes Commission in Manila. At the time of the Meisenbach trial, Berman had recently divorced his colleague in the District Attorney's office, Dianne Feinstein (later to become California's first woman Senator in 1992). The defense team had sources inside the police department willing to cooperate for cash. Garry secretly bought copies of suppressed police reports which helped the lawyers skewer the official account of Black Friday attested to by prosecution witnesses. Several eyewitnesses for the defense and a *Life* magazine photo placed Meisenbach standing completely dry against a wall on the sidelines as the police began hosing demonstrators. One after another of these credible bystanders attested that Meisenbach never jumped a barrier, never hit an officer with his own club, or initiated any violence at all. When Meisenbach himself took the stand, he tearfully described to the jury how he had been dragged and beaten black and blue by officers, had his glasses broken, and, to his acute embarrassment, became so frightened that he fouled his pants in the process. The jury came back in less than three hours with an acquittal.

The evening after the verdict was announced, the defense committee held a noisy celebration at a local Italian restaurant. Even two of the jurors attended. The successful trial was all over the front pages and the talk of the Leftist community. After that humiliation, HUAC never held hearings outside Washington, D.C., again. The results greatly energized Progressives in the Bay Area. Many soon became the chief fund-raisers for the Student Nonviolent Coordinating Committee and responded to calls for legal support for 1964 and 1965 Freedom Summers in Mississippi and Alabama. Bay Area lawyers also donated their services to bring local civil rights suits challenging housing and employment discrimination. They volunteered at little or no cost to defend hundreds of protesters arrested for picketing against racist hiring practices at San Francisco's elite Sheraton Plaza Hotel and the city's Auto Row. In one marathon defense, two Guild members set a record for the longest misdemeanor trial in the history of the San Francisco courts.

The results at these numerous jury trials were mixed, but the underlying discriminatory practices embarrassed San Francisco officials sufficiently to prompt the creation in 1964 of a Human Rights Commission with a mandate from the city that included investigating and resolving problems of prejudice and discrimination and advocating for human and civil rights. The San Francisco Human Rights Commission set aside May 13 of each year as a day of remembrance of Black Friday. On its thirtieth anniversary in 1990, the activists arrested on Black Friday received an official apology from San Francisco's Mayor Art Agnos. On its fiftieth anniversary, many former student activists—now all senior citizens—gathered at San Francisco City Hall for a reunion. Among them was Bob Meisenbach, then in his seventies, sporting white hair and a beard. When a reporter interviewed Meisenbach, he commented,"My kids sometimes ask me what I did during the '60s. I tell them I started the '60s."[6]

* * * * *

By the mid-'60s, Cal Berkeley had become a center of protest against both political censorship and the Vietnam War, spawning what soon became known as The Free Speech Movement ("FSM"). Some of the leaders had been among Northern volunteers who participated in Freedom Summer in the Deep South. Curly-haired junior Mario Savio was among them. Returning to Berkeley in September of 1964, the gangly youth became incensed that his own university banned solicitation of SNCC volunteers and funds for other civil rights organizations. The ban on political activity was total, outraging Students for Goldwater—supporters of the Republican 1964 nominee for President—as well as Leftist groups on campus. They banded together, united (however briefly) in opposition to political censorship.

On September 14, 1964, the dean of students announced that the university's prohibitions would extend outside the main entrance gate on the south side of the campus. A sit-in and demonstrations followed, led in part by Savio and former graduate student Jack Weinberg, who had organized the Sheraton Plaza Hotel demonstration earlier that year. Six students were ordered suspended for leading the Cal sit-in, including Savio. This spawned more demonstrations with hundreds of students participating. On the first of October, Weinberg was arrested in another rally when he openly defied the solicitation ban by setting up a table for the Congress of Racial Equality on the steps of Sproul Hall. (CORE had employed Michael Schwerner, one of the three civil rights workers murdered four months before in Mississippi.) Throngs of nearby student protesters spontaneously surrounded a police car, preventing it from leaving. A thousand more students arrived and barricaded the police car for thirty-six hours, with Savio and another activist taking turns addressing the crowd from atop the vehicle.

Student mimeographers distributed leaflets with daily updates on the ongoing campus dispute. One of these, future celebrated lithographer David Lance Goines, had been among the protest leaders suspended in September with Savio. The handouts portrayed a far different version of events than did the traditional campus paper. *The Daily Cal* derided the Free Speech Movement, as did U.C.'s President Clark Kerr, the visionary who had championed universal access to college regardless of ability to pay. Though Kerr had earlier backed expansive opportunities for students to exercise First Amendment rights, he had no sympathy with demonstrators whom he called "rabble-rousers . . . dominated by Communists."[7] Kerr greatly underestimated the scope of the unrest and the determination of the participants. Meanwhile, the local ACLU office threatened to take the university to court over the constitutionality of regulations that foreclosed student political activity on campus. At the end of November, the Regents of the University sought to suspend indefinitely several student leaders, including Savio, who was accused of biting a police officer. In response, on December 2, 1964, thousands of students amassed on the plaza between Sproul Hall and the Student Union. Folk singer Joan Baez sang for the gathering, and Savio gave his famous call to action: "There is a time when the operation of the machine becomes so odious, makes you so sick at heart, that you can't take part; and you've got to put your bodies upon the gears and upon the wheels, upon the levers, upon all the apparatus and you've got to make it stop. And you've got to indicate to the people who run it, to the people who own it, that unless you're free, the machine will be prevented from working at all."[8]

The size of the demonstration prompted the University Police Department and Berkeley Police Department to call for several hundred reinforcements from the Alameda County Sheriff's Department, the Oakland Police Department, and California Highway Patrol. Together they implemented Democratic Gov. Pat Brown's order of the largest mass arrest in California history. On site to supervise the nearly eight hundred early morning arrests were two high-level lawyers from the office of the Alameda County District Attorney's office—Chief Assistant District Attorney Lowell Jensen and Assistant District Attorney Ed Meese. These two representatives of law-and-order would repeatedly clash with radicals for the better part of the next two decades. Meese became Republican Gov. Reagan's Chief of Staff and then joined President Reagan as his Attorney General. Jensen stayed in Alameda County where, in 1967, he would be assigned to prosecute Huey Newton. He was later elected District Attorney, then left to serve in the Reagan administration and return as a federal judge in California's Northern District, where he still sits.

A week after the December 1964 demonstrations, negotiators reached an agreement with the administration by which the university backed down. Political speech would be permitted on campus starting January 4, 1965. With almost eight hundred arrestees facing charges, the forty defense lawyers who had volunteered their services themselves proposed one mass trial instead of depleting their meager resources in numerous small trials. Prosecutors refused to hold a jury trial; one with so many defendants was practically guaranteed to turn into a circus. Instead, they proposed a representative judge trial of 155 defendants with the understanding that the remaining defendants would be bound by the outcome. The defense team assumed they had a good chance of drawing a local judge sympathetic to the underlying free speech issue and calculated that forfeiture of a jury trial was worth the savings of time and expense.

The Free Speech Movement arrests in December 1964 became a landmark in American history, but the single-judge trial the following summer of nearly eight score representative defendants garnered hardly any attention at all. The arrestees were unceremoniously convicted and sentenced. Their chagrined lawyers vowed never to waive a jury again in a political case. Throughout this time, the FBI fostered a climate of fear by planting stories in the newspapers characterizing the Free Speech Movement as a Communist plot. In November 1966, California voters elected Ronald Reagan the state's next governor, based in large part on a campaign "to clean up the mess in Berkeley."[9] Once in office, Reagan made it a priority to oust Clark Kerr as president of the University. Kerr noted that he left the University the same way he had started there, "fired with enthusiasm."[10]

Looking back some forty years later, former activist Goines viewed the Free Speech Movement with mixed feelings because of its role in jumpstarting the career of Ronald Reagan as a two-term California governor. "And that was, of course, his stepping-stone to the White House. I'm not sure that he would have been elected without the FSM to use as his punching bag."[11] But the Free Speech Movement had another impact as well. Ultimately, students advocating any political, religious, or social cause were permitted to set up informational tables in Sproul Plaza—the center of student activity on campus—and to distribute handouts there as well as gather at Sproul Plaza to protest or march. The steps adjacent to Sproul Hall were later renamed the "Mario Savio Steps," and permitted to be reserved for speech-making. The Mario Savio Free Speech Movement Café opened nearby as a new campus fixture.

* * * * *

In the late spring of 1965, the first of several "Vietnam Day" teach-ins, co-led by a Marxist Cal sociology graduate student by the name of Jerry Rubin, permanently secured Berkeley's preeminence "on the war-protest map."[12] As the Vietnam War became increasingly unpopular, an amateurish ally of anti-war activists surfaced in the form of a new underground Berkeley newspaper, *The Berkeley Barb*. Over the next few years, it would achieve the highest national circulation for an anti-establishment newspaper. (Its founder Max Scherr later claimed the distinction of being the first to report on the political activities of two then unknown black radicals, Huey Newton and Bobby Seale, arrested in 1966 for disturbing the peace on a Berkeley street corner. At the time, both were students at Merritt College in Oakland and active in student protests against the drafting of black soldiers for the war effort).

In the mid-'60s, civil rights advocacy and anti-war activities both came within the umbrella of what was now a broad-based anti-establishment "Movement," which already had its own nationally circulated monthly paper of the same name published by activists in San Francisco. SLATE co-founder turned ACLU lawyer Peter Franck and Lawyers Guild members Marvin and Fay Stender collaborated with other local Guild lawyers to start a "Council for Justice" to represent protesters and draft evaders against the Vietnam War. They quickly added another Movement cause, representing union organizer Cesar Chavez in immigrant farm worker strikes against vineyard owners. Both causes gave rise to numerous lawsuits with non-traditional, political defenses that the attorney volunteers could ill afford. Operating on a shoestring budget, the Council for Justice would fold within a little over a year for lack of resources.

From 1965 through the summer of 1967, Berkeley and Oakland anti-war advocates were among the most active in the nation. They staged multiple sit-ins, marches and teach-ins, held vigils at a weapons depot, and several times tried to prevent the arrival of troop trains at the Oakland Army Terminal. But it was a speech in New York by Rev. Martin Luther King, Jr. in early April 1967 that was credited with first publicly linking the Civil Rights Movement and the Vietnam War in the eyes of the general public.[13] SNCC leader Stokely Carmichael quickly echoed Dr. King in earthier language as both observed that white males disproportionately avoided the draft through student deferments, while draft-aged blacks often became unwilling cannon fodder.

In coordination with a planned march on the Pentagon in October of 1967, Bay Area anti-war activists implemented a major protest called "Stop the Draft Week" which involved several days of massive demonstrations October 16–20, 1967, designed to shut down the Oakland, California Induction Center—known to be one of the largest such facilities on the Pacific Coast. On the first day of "Stop the Draft Week," some three thousand protesters blocked the entrance to the center, with folk singer Joan Baez in the lead just as she had been at the Free Speech sit-ins at Cal. More than a hundred were arrested. The following day twice as many demonstrators blocked the doorway and the surrounding streets. An estimated 250 Oakland police sheriff's deputies and highway patrolmen broke through and dispersed the crowd, spraying mace and swinging batons in a bloody confrontation in which a number of people were injured. Many arrests ensued as Oakland city officials reacted with outrage at the disruption and high cost of "Stop the Draft Week."

Conspiracy charges were then brought against the planners of the demonstration—veteran anti-war organizers from Students for a Democratic Society ("SDS"), the Vietnam Day Committee, the Free Speech Movement, and the Peace and Freedom Party, as well as the editor of *The Movement* news monthly. All would eventually be tried together by prosecutor Lowell Jensen as "The Oakland Seven." A team of three defense lawyers was quickly assembled, headed by Lawyers Guild veteran Charles Garry. They audaciously planned to invoke the Nuremberg Principles as a key part of their defense—the right to refuse to participate in crimes against humanity. Their aim was to put the legitimacy of the Vietnam War itself on trial. At the time, the FBI, with help from the local District Attorney, investigated for subversive activity lawyers who openly protested the war. Had any of the Oakland Seven instead turned to the Public Defender's office for legal representation, they probably would not have gotten such an aggressive defense.

The Alameda County Public Defender at the time was John Nunes, a brusque, pipe-smoking conservative in his second career after many years of dedicated service in the Probation Department. Nunes recently learned that three of his deputies had lent their names to a full-page newspaper ad listing professionals against the war; others in Nunes' office were planning to join a protest march on a day off. Nunes warned all six that their jobs were in jeopardy for disloyal conduct. It was hard to imagine that coverage of the highly controversial "Oakland Seven" pretrial proceedings would begin to be dwarfed within a fortnight by another Oakland arrest. It would pit the same lead counsel against each other with even greater repercussions in the community and the world at large.

Part Two

Cartoon from MY FELLOW AMERICANS by Ron Cobb.

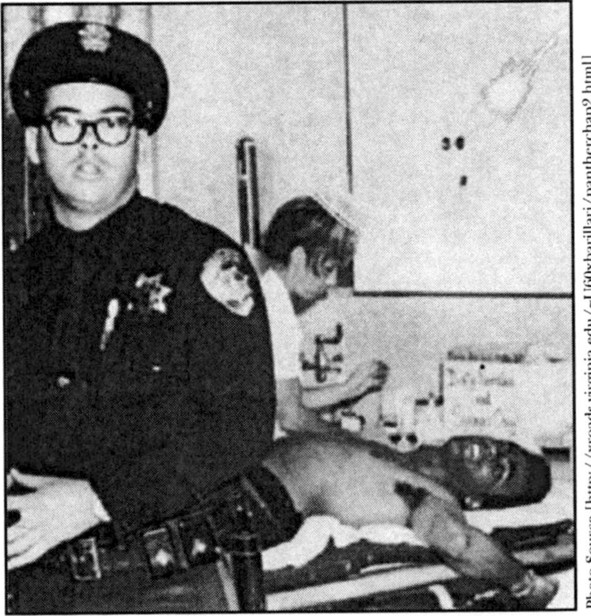

Photo Source [http://xroads.virginia.edu/~UG0xbarillari/pantherchap2.html]

Widely distributed photo of Huey Newton, arrested and shackled to a gurney at Kaiser Hospital, before surgery on his stomach wound on the morning of Oct. 28, 1967.

1. FREE HUEY NOW!

Pushed into the corner
Of the hobnailed boot,
Pushed into the corner of the
"I-don't-want-to-die" cry,
Pushed into the corner of
"I don't want to study war no more,"
Changed into "Eye for eye,"
The Panther in his desperate boldness
Wears no disguise,
Motivated by the truest
Of the oldest
Lies.

LANGSTON HUGHES, "BLACK PANTHER"

A newspaper photographer wormed his way past police guards into the Kaiser Hospital emergency room and snapped a quick photo before being evicted. That afternoon's front page displayed black militant Huey Newton lying bare-chested, a bullet wound in his abdomen, his hands shackled to a hospital gurney. In front of him stood one of the Oakland police guards, wearing an expression like that of a deer caught in the headlights. On the morning of October 28, 1967, Oakland police had put out an all-points bulletin for Huey Newton following a pre-dawn shootout in West Oakland's red light district. As co-founder of the Black Panther Party, Newton was already well known to local law enforcement, infuriating them with his official title, Minister of Defense. Police immediately suspected Newton of killing Officer John Frey and wounding Officer Herbert Heanes, who now lay hospitalized in critical condition with a gunshot wound in the chest, knee, and one arm. Police headquarters immediately released pictures of the young policemen to the press and mentioned that both were fathers of young children.

The Panther leader was arrested just an hour afterward at Oakland's Kaiser Hospital. Shortly before dawn, Newton had staggered into the emergency room with a bloody rag clutched to his stomach. The middle-aged blond nurse on duty, Corinne Leonard, heard a car door slam and the car drive off, but did not see who deposited Newton outside. The police later thought that it might have been Newton's girlfriend. They knew that a young black woman later stopped by the hospital, but left before she could be questioned. The police confiscated the tawny 1958 Volkswagen sedan registered to LaVerne Williams that Newton was driving early that morning on Seventh Street when he was pulled over by Officer Frey. At first, the police assumed LaVerne was male and must have been the passenger who had accompanied Huey in the car and fled the scene soon after the shooting. The next day, Oakland attorney John George told the police that he represented aspiring singer LaVerne Williams, Newton's twenty-two-year old girlfriend, who worked in a local office of the Job Corps. LaVerne acknowledged she was the young woman who had visited Newton in the hospital, but had only learned of his whereabouts from an anonymous phone call.

Newton's passenger still remained a mystery. At the hospital, Newton created an immediate stir by shouting for prompt medical care while refusing to sign hospital forms. Though in agony, he withdrew notes from his wallet, tore them up, and threw them in the trash. It had not been his idea to go to the hospital. He had wanted to die among his close friends in the neighborhood. Though the bullet in his abdomen had not hit any large blood vessels, it had punctured his intestine. Nurse Leonard did not realize that peritonitis would kill Newton if he were not quickly operated upon, underestimating the seriousness of his condition because of the wound's small size. Frightened by Newton's belligerence, she called the police before she summoned a doctor.

The police arrived at the hospital emergency room in less than half an hour, shortly after the doctor arrived and had Newton placed on a gurney. A patrolman immediately arrested Newton. Newton screamed in pain and spat blood as the officer slapped handcuffs on his wrists, shackled him to the gurney, and recited his Miranda rights. Newton was still shouting obscenities at the police as the doctor wheeled him off to surgery, barking at Newton to shut up. Listed in fair condition following surgery, Newton was transferred to Highland Hospital and placed under twenty-four-hour guard by six policemen armed with shotguns. That was how Charles Garry and his co-counsel, fellow Guild lawyer Beverly Axelrod, first saw Newton when the two arrived to meet their new client.

The impetus to hire Garry came from now legendary black civil rights activist William Patterson, whom Garry's friend, publisher Dr. Carlton Goodlett, happened to be hosting in San Francisco that same week. Patterson, as head of the American Communist Party, also had close ties to East Bay civil rights lawyer Bob Treuhaft and his wife Decca Mitford, both of whom were stalwarts of the "Old Left," which included Garry and his scholarly law partner Barney Dreyfus. They had all met through Bay Area Communist Party educational programs in the '40s. Since then, the Oakland firm of Treuhaft & Edises and the San Francisco firm of Garry, Dreyfus & McTernan had numbered among the few white law firms representing black working class clientele.

When Patterson heard of the shooting incident, he immediately asked to meet Huey Newton's older brother Melvin, to offer help from the American Communist Party. Patterson had relished political drama since he first worked on the Sacco and Vanzetti appeals in the mid-1920s and followed up with the Scottsboro Boys' appeals and retrials in the '30s and Willie McGee's fruitless appeals in the late '40s. Back in 1951, Bob Treuhaft's work on McGee's appeals helped earn him a place on Senator Joseph McCarthy's short list of the most subversive lawyers in America, a distinction Treuhaft and his wife considered a badge of honor. The two were then active members of the Communist Party and had joined Patterson and Paul Robeson in formally protesting racial discrimination before the new United Nations. Patterson immediately sensed that Newton's trial presented a similar political opportunity to embarrass the United States for abusive police practices against members of the black community. He suggested that a Huey Newton defense fund be immediately established, to which the Communist Party would contribute heavily. Melvin Newton and Eldridge Cleaver readily agreed. They had just been told to expect the cost of the trial to reach $100,000, a staggering amount at the time.

Eldridge Cleaver had secretly joined the Black Panthers in the spring of 1967 as its Minister of Information, while pretending to cover the group solely as a reporter for *Ramparts.* At the time, Cleaver could not publicly admit to his membership because he was still on parole and prohibited from associating with "undesirables" like the Panthers. In the early predawn after the October 28, 1967, shootout, Cleaver took the risk of declaring himself acting head of the Black Panther Party, since Bobby Seale, co-founder of the Party, was then serving a short jail sentence, as were several other Panthers arrested in the spring of 1967. In fact, unbeknownst to the police, by October's end when Newton was arrested, the fledgling group was in near total disarray, without even a headquarters.

San Francisco Lawyers Guild member Beverly Axelrod, a former CORE attorney, was then Cleaver's fiancée and the first person he called for legal help. Axelrod had been the lead defense attorney in the longest of the 1964–65 Auto Row and Sheraton Palace protest trials. A longtime proponent of civil rights, Axelrod had corresponded with Cleaver when he was still at Folsom Prison. By then Cleaver had taught himself to read political books critically and write on social issues. Influenced by the writings of Malcolm X, Cleaver got the idea of marketing his own autobiographical essays from the best-sellers published from death row by convicted "Red Light Bandit" Caryl Chessman. Cleaver had systematically written to lawyers listed in a professional directory offering his own manuscript as legal fees for anyone who helped him to gain his freedom. Axelrod responded enthusiastically. She arranged to have parts of Cleaver's manuscript and letters to her critiqued by Pulitzer Prize–winning author Norman Mailer and then published in *Ramparts* magazine.

Axelrod also engineered Cleaver's release from Folsom in December of 1966. By then, the confessed serial rapist had served nine years for attempted murder. Cleaver's political essays gained him a national following and a job offer as a full-time staff writer for *Ramparts.* In the spring of 1967, *Ramparts* republished the essays as the book *Soul On Ice,* dedicated to Beverly "with whom I share the ultimate of love." Because of her relationship with Cleaver, Newton had come to trust Axelrod as a close friend. She hosted many Panther gatherings at her San Francisco home. It was in Axelrod's living room that Newton had posed in her wicker chair for a photo to adorn the new, ten-cent newsletter the Black Panthers began publishing in the spring of 1967. When Cleaver contacted Axelrod with news of Newton's arrest early on the morning of October 28, Axelrod knew there was no time to waste. She had the highest respect for Garry and had previously collaborated with him on Lawyers Guild cases. But despite her recommendation, and Cleaver's blessing and that of Melvin Newton, the jailed Panthers and their supporters on the outside were outraged. They lobbied for Huey Newton to retain a black attorney.

As Melvin Newton's decision was being second-guessed among the few Party members recruited by then, Garry and Axelrod rushed to Newton's bedside. On their first visit on November 1, 1967, the two lawyers encountered a platoon of heavily armed police in the hospital corridors, and had to convince a hierarchy of belligerent officials to obtain permission to see Newton. When they arrived at their client's room, he was still being fed intravenously and had a tube in his nose. Newton had been under sedation since his arrival, had lost a lot of blood, and appeared to be in great pain. Newton painted a grim picture of his ordeal, recounting different police guards' taunts: "Nigger you are going to pay for this." One officer threatened to cut off the tube "so you will choke to death, so that the state won't have to bother trying you or gassing you."[1] Newton said he awoke once to see a shotgun pointed at his face and heard a policeman joke that they should get a razor to kill him with and say it was suicide. Axelrod was alarmed. She called her Lawyers Guild friend Alex Hoffmann, who had recently opened his own solo practice in Berkeley after he had returned from coordinating legal assistance to Cesar Chavez's farm workers union through the now defunct Council For Justice. With Hoffmann in tow, Axelrod immediately set off to find Police Chief Gain and demand that nursing aides be permitted to attend to Newton round-the-clock at his defense team's expense. She and Garry had no doubt that the threats had occurred—the hatred the Oakland police felt for Newton was palpable. For the better part of a year, armed Panthers had been tailing officers around black neighborhoods, calling them "pigs" and challenging their authority.

Back in early May, the Panthers had dramatically set foot on the world stage when over twenty armed emissaries (including several friends along for the ride) marched into the State Assembly in Sacramento to oppose pending gun control legislation and read a confrontational prepared statement from Newton. Shocked by the gun-toting visitors, the Assembly members passed a new "Panther Rider," which specifically prohibited the carrying of loaded weapons in any public place or street. During the last six months, Oakland police often invoked this new law when stopping Black Panthers with or without cause. The early morning shootout marked the first exchange of gunfire. Now they had Newton in their custody facing potential execution for killing one of their own.

The police not only wanted revenge, they wanted to put an end to the Panthers' growing popularity in the black community for offering protection against racist brutality from the police, whom they called a "white army of occupation."[2] Unbeknownst to the police, at the time Frey confronted Newton, the Panthers only numbered a dozen members in and out of jail. Shortly after Newton's arrest, a white hippie commune loaned Hilliard a psychedelic double-decker bus so the Panthers could drum up support in local neighborhoods to "Free Huey!" With a bullhorn he repeatedly blasted the question: "Can a black man get a fair trial in America . . . defending his life against a white policeman?"[3]

Within a few months' time, a new Panther chapter opened in Los Angeles. Even then, the two branches totaled about 75 people who identified themselves as Party members. The Oakland police would have been far more incensed had they gazed into a crystal ball: galvanized by the campaign challenging Newton's imprisonment over the next year and a half, the Panther Party would burgeon to over forty chapters, nearly 5,000 members, numerous community programs, and a nationwide newspaper with a six-figure circulation. The paper featured a lot of photos and the social realism drawings and graphic cartoons of Minister of Culture Emory Douglas. From its spectacular Sacramento debut in the spring of 1967, the Party would rise in less than eighteen months to be listed as the highest internal national security threat of all Black Nationalist "hate groups."

* * * * *

The Black Panther Party for Self-Defense sprang to life in the fall of 1966 when Newton, aged twenty-four, and Seale, aged thirty, were part-time students at Oakland's Merritt College. They got together with a radical former G.I., Richard Aoki, who had been sent to a Japanese internment camp as a child during World War II and became a street friend of Newton's back in his high school days. In 1966, Newton and Seale both worked at the North Oakland Anti-Poverty Center where Seale, with Newton's help, supervised eighty at-risk high school students in work programs. Together, the three radicals hammered out a ten point platform for a new militant group. The new organization's name was inspired by a January 1966 front-page story in the monthly paper, *The Movement,* put out by the Friends of SNCC. The story described the Lowndes County Freedom Organization run by SNCC's Stokely Carmichael, a voting-rights effort in Alabama that used a Black Panther logo and embraced armed self defense. By that time, both Newton and Seale had grown frustrated with the Leftist political organizations to which they had previously belonged. Seale wrote for information and received a brochure, which he shared with Newton. The Alabama group had adopted the panther as its symbol because the law required an animal mascot for every political party, and the panther was said to defend itself vigorously, but not to engage in unprovoked attack. Newton decided to use the same logo. Others in large cities were starting to do so, too. When leaders of SNCC first heard of an Oakland group using the symbol and the Black Panther name, they did not think much would come of it.

Over the next several months, Newton and Seale refined the Black Panther Party platform at Seale's home near the Merritt campus and at work, using the Nation of Islam's "What We Believe" as a model. Newton's older brother Melvin helped polish its language. The platform addressed racial exploitation in fighting wars, in housing, education, and employment, but emphasized police conduct in the black community and racism in the criminal justice system:

> WHAT WE WANT NOW! . . .
>
> 7. WE WANT AN IMMEDIATE END TO POLICE BRUTALITY AND MURDER OF BLACK PEOPLE.
>
> 8. WE WANT FREEDOM FOR ALL BLACK MEN HELD IN FEDERAL, STATE, COUNTY, AND CITY PRISONS AND JAILS.
>
> 9. WE WANT ALL BLACK PEOPLE WHEN BROUGHT TO TRIAL TO BE TRIED IN COURT BY A JURY OF THEIR PEER GROUP OF PEOPLE FROM THEIR BLACK COMMUNITIES. . . .
>
> WHAT WE BELIEVE . . .
> 7. WE BELIEVE WE CAN END POLICE BRUTALITY IN OUR BLACK COMMUNITY BY ORGANIZING BLACK SELF DEFENSE GROUPS THAT ARE DEDICATED TO DEFENDING OUR BLACK COMMUNITY FROM RACIST POLICE OPPRESSION AND BRUTALITY. . . .[4]

Seale's wife Artie typed the platform, and they surreptitiously made copies late at night on the Anti-Poverty Center's mimeograph machine. By the time the Black Panther Party formed in the fall of 1966, Newton and Seale had developed a strong friendship and shared politics. African-American Studies Professor Ekwueme Michael Thelwell would later describe the two as combining the spiritual values of their hard-working, rural Southern parents in "uneasy tension with another incompatible current: the in-yo-face, up-against-the-wall-motherfuckah, quasi-criminality and macho violence of the urban street-gang culture."[5] The deliberately calculated "in-yo-face" strategy of young blacks looking "boldly into the eyes of white authority" took the breath away from observers on both sides of the racial divide. Newton and Seale were determined to lead by example "above ground," ostentatiously waging "ideological and material battle in plain view."[6] They quickly became known as "the baddest niggas on the scene,"[7] a reputation that new recruits found irresistible.

2. THE PANTHERS' ROOTS

We're hip to the fact that
Superman never saved no black people.

BOBBY SEALE

Until 1940, the black populations in Berkeley and Oakland were relatively small; even fewer lived in San Francisco—small wonder given the historic dearth of good jobs. The official 1940 United States census for Oakland listed a total of 8,462 blacks, up less than a thousand from 1930. In 1940, they still lived in basically the same areas they had occupied since the turn of the century, alongside white working class and poor families. There were no identifiable racial ghettos. Many African-American men worked for the Southern Pacific and Western Pacific Railroads as porters, all called "George" after the founder of the Pullman Company, as if their own given names were of no consequence. The porters were part of the emerging black middle class—members of the Brotherhood of Sleeping Car Porters, America's first black-led union. Oakland contained the biggest concentration of blacks in the Bay Area in 1940 and the second largest in the state. One segregated firehouse served the black community, and just one black plainclothes detective and a few black deputy sheriffs. Locals only saw black city policemen in uniform as temporary additions during the Pacific Coast Big Strike of 1934, and again when World War II decimated the supply of white recruits.

Back before World War II, Oakland's Seventh Street saw a lot more activity than it did in the '60s. Before the Bay Bridge was built, an electric Key Train connected commuters to a ferry to San Francisco. Black professionals located their offices in the bustling area. At night, vice predominated. Near the railroad yards were pawn shops, houses of prostitution, blues clubs, bars, barbeque joints, and gambling establishments (the Pullmen porters called theirs "The Shasta"). One wealthy West Oakland entrepreneur stood out: Charles "Raincoat" Jones, a veteran of both the Spanish-American War (as an infantryman) and World War I (as a cook) who made most of his fortune moneylending and running gambling rooms. By the late '20s, Jones (who always wore a macintosh) reputedly owned the entire block of buildings abutting Seventh and Willow, the corner where the October 1967 shooting would occur. Jones and a small group of successful business friends made it a point to support enterprises that the black community needed, such as providing start-up money for a pharmacy or a timely loan in the late '40s to help save *San Francisco Sun* publisher Dr. Carlton Goodlett from having to close his newspaper's doors.

Before World War II, vice peddlers like Raincoat could maintain a "live and let live" relationship with the police. Raincoat was happy to pay protection money, which his attorney, Leonard Richardson, then the most prominent African-American lawyer around, hand-delivered by messenger directly to a police captain in City Hall each Friday.[1] Whenever Raincoat's gambling room was raided, he pulled out his wad of bills and bailed out whoever got arrested. But that peaceful co-existence rested on a relatively stable minority population that did not threaten the status quo. As Bay Area industries geared up for the war effort in 1941, black-white relations began to change for the worse in a hurry.

Job discrimination remained so pervasive that local black labor leaders joined with white civil rights leaders to organize a proposed march on Washington to compel equal job opportunities. Roosevelt had wooed African-Americans from their traditional home in the Republican Party with his New Deal programs. He avoided the embarrassment of a major civil rights protest by issuing Executive Order 8802, an unprecedented presidential decree forbidding discrimination on grounds of race, color, or national origin in hiring workers for the national defense program. Kaiser Shipyards then recruited heavily in the South, encouraging mass migration of blacks to fill 10,000 jobs. Some hailed Roosevelt's order as "the breakthrough of the century in the Negro's battle for civil rights"; others recognized it as but one of many hard-fought for milestones over the prior several decades.[2]

In the first three years of the war, over 320,000 blacks had migrated to the Bay Area. Berkeley created an Emergency Housing Committee to help address the problem. Civil rights advocates like African-American pharmacist William Byron Rumford went further. They formed an interracial welcoming committee to help new families from the South adjust to their new environment.

By 1945, there would be more than four times as many blacks counted in the official Oakland census as in 1940. Shortly after the war's end, a professor at the University of California's School of Social Work observed that "Negroes are rapidly becoming the most significant minority group in California."[3] Many came from the rural south by the trainload and, for the most part, only found housing in the most undesirable locations. In Berkeley, that meant the flatlands below Shattuck Avenue. In Oakland, they poured into similarly neglected neighborhoods, mostly in West Oakland.

Low-rent housing complexes first opened in West Oakland in 1941 as a wartime redevelopment project, but they were woefully inadequate. West Oakland "began to overflow." One Oakland resident remembered: "We'd go down to the 16th street station after school to watch the people get off the trains, and it was like a parade. You just couldn't believe that that many people would come in, and some didn't even have luggage; they would come with boxes, with 3 or 4 children with no place to stay . . . and they would ask everyone if they had any place to stay or could they make some space into rooms."[4] A riot started on a Key System Train in downtown Oakland. It involved both black and white servicemen and civilians and grew to a mob of 2,000. A local newspaper, *The Observer*, commented:

> That riot on Twelfth Street the other day may be the forerunner of more and larger riots because we now have (a) a semi-mining camp civilization and (b) a new race problem, brought about by the influx of what might be called socially-liberated or uninhibited Negroes who are not bound by the old and peaceful understanding

> between the Negro and the white in Oakland, which has lasted for so many decades, but who insist upon barging into the white man and becoming an integral part of the white man's society.[5]

In 1968, a Blue Ribbon Commission convened by President Johnson would instead place most of the blame on "[w]hite racism . . . for the explosive mixture which has been accumulating in our cities since the end of World War II."[6]

In 1943, George and Thelma Seale quit Bobby's birthplace of Dallas, Texas, and resettled in the Berkeley flatlands with their three surviving children. Bobby Seale's first major influence was his hard-working mother, a star athlete and history buff with indelible memories from age eleven in Jasper, Texas, when she witnessed some of the outrages of the Red Summer of 1919. The Seales arrived in California just a year before the worst disaster of World War II on continental United States soil took place in nearby Port Chicago, less than twenty-five miles northeast of where the family resettled. Munitions improperly loaded by overhead nets onto cargo ships had suddenly ignited on July 17, 1944, destroying two ships and adjacent docks. The explosion of 5,000 tons of ammunition rattled windows fifty miles in every direction.

The devastating accident annihilated 320 men, almost two-thirds of whom were African-American, and wounded over 400 others. It accounted for fifteen percent of all African-American casualties suffered on Naval duty during the war. Considered a dirty and risky job, munitions loading had been left largely to untrained sailors in segregated units that some likened to a slave labor camp. In another infamous trial, fifty black sailors who refused to return to active duty in Port Chicago were tried for mutiny in the fall of 1944, for which they risked the death penalty. Future Supreme Court Justice Thurgood Marshall headed their NAACP legal team. All were found guilty and sentenced to lengthy jail terms. Though it would be fifty years before the mutineers received a presidential pardon, behind the scenes the appalling incident became a political catalyst for change. As one historian put it, "U.S. government officials realized their ability to promote democracy among people of color around the world was seriously hampered by racial injustice at home."[7] The Navy began desegregating its units in 1946.

Seale's family moved from Berkeley to Oakland in the 1950s. Having inherited his mother's athleticism, Seale tried out for two sports teams at Oakland High. He blamed his exclusion on racism. In disgust, he quit school and joined the Air Force, ending three years of service with a bad conduct discharge, court-martialed for insubordination. Seale obtained a high school degree after he left the service. An extrovert with occasional success as a stand-up comic and musician, Seale also had worked at various times as a carpenter, sheet metal mechanic, and mechanical draftsman. His mother always said, "Whatever job you hold, be the best at it."[8] His original ambition was to become an engineer, but he had abandoned that goal by the time he met Newton.

* * * * *

Newton's father, Walter Newton, emigrated from Louisiana in 1944 when he became fed up with being called a "crazy nigger" for not accepting Jim Crow laws as the way society should operate.[9] The rest of the family joined him by the following year when Huey was three. After the war, Walter Newton left his first job as a longshoreman and worked as a handyman and truck driver and volunteered as an assistant minister at a local Baptist church. The Newtons moved several times to different parts of the Oakland community and ultimately settled in a mixed, working-class neighborhood in North Oakland. Armelia Newton stayed at home to raise their children. The couple doted on Huey—their youngest son—whom his older sisters also favored. A very bright but shy child, Huey had a phenomenal memory. When he displayed musical talent, his parents arranged three years of classical piano training.

A quick study with obvious potential, Huey memorized epic poetry in junior high to impress the girls. His parents hoped he would follow their son Melvin's dogged pursuit of higher education and a steady job. Melvin, four years Huey's senior, was the only sibling of Huey's to finish college; only one other finished high school. Growing up, Huey felt severely handicapped by his light complexion and medium build, with a Caucasian nose inherited from a white grandfather who had forced himself on Walter Newton's mother. Newton's handsome bi-racial features, coupled with a high, squeaky voice and a funny name, proved an albatross on the streets of Oakland. Kids on the block may not have heard of Louisiana's demagogue Gov. Huey P. Long for whom he was named, but they teased Huey "Pee" Newton unmercifully.[10]

Among a minority of black students at his junior high school, Huey quickly developed a thin skin. Despite the best efforts of his devout parents and brother Melvin, Huey became an indifferent high school student, often skipping school in Oakland to spend hour upon hour in the pool halls. The rougher elements of Oakland acted as a magnet to Huey, as they had with his oldest brother, Leander "Lee" Edward, a generation older than Huey, who had already served a jail sentence. Another older brother Walter, Jr., nicknamed "Sonny Man," was an accomplished street hustler, often found at the race track. He taught Huey how to aggressively defend himself against local hoodlums. An admirer of professional boxers, since the age of five Huey had been encouraged by his father to defend himself against bullies with his fists. Ever since, he had engaged in numerous fights with neighborhood toughs, establishing a reputation on the street as someone not to tangle with.

Constantly worrying his parents, Huey disguised his reading and learning disabilities by acting out. Many years later, doctors would diagnose him as bipolar. He was suspended from Oakland Tech his sophomore year for classroom misbehavior and truancy. In his junior year, his parents enrolled him in Berkeley High. Not long afterward, the school suspended Newton and referred him to juvenile court for retaliating against a classmate with a hammer. Placed on probation, Newton returned to Oakland Tech where he managed to obtain a degree, graduating in the bottom third of his class. Newton escaped the 1963 Vietnam War draft with a 1-Y psychiatric exemption,which he dismissed as a response to his outspoken criticism of racism in the military. Still, with a military exemption, high school degree, and family support, Huey was better off than many. One-third of young black males in Oakland were then unemployed high school dropouts, six times the national average.

Much to his parents' dismay, Newton grew a scruffy beard and quit the family home to share a flat near the Merritt campus with William

Brumfield, aka Richard Thorne, a co-founder of the Sexual Freedom League and later the cult of Om Lovers. Though Newton enjoyed sharing the favors of the young women Brumfield attracted, Newton had his own ambitions. In high school, Newton was told he was not "college material." Under the tutelage of his brother Melvin, Huey began reading Plato's *Republic.* For the first time in his life, he felt engaged by the written word. (He later would claim that he was completely illiterate until then and had faked the ability to read and write in high school). As he pursued a social science degree at Merritt College, Newton focused on the study of philosophy and militant politics, particularly the recent Cuban revolution and guerrilla leader Che Guevara. Newton had liked alcohol since he was a young teen; in a show of solidarity, he made "Cuba Libra" his drink of choice.

At age twenty, Newton was a well-known figure on Oakland's Merritt College campus. In the spring of 1962, his roommate Brumfield introduced him to Seale at an Afro-American Association rally. Newton was already a member. Seale was new to the organization. At first, Newton enjoyed its focus on the works of Leftist political writers like W. E. B. DuBois, James Baldwin, and Jean-Paul Sartre. It promoted the wearing of dashikis and the teaching of Swahili and arranged for prominent speakers, including Malcolm X and the newly-converted Black Muslim, heavyweight boxer Cassius Clay, both of whom Newton heard in 1962 at Oakland's McClymonds High School. Newton attended Black Muslim meetings to learn more about the teachings of Elijah Muhammad. Malcolm X, an ex-felon, electrified Newton by melding street smarts and scholarship in the explosive rhetoric of "the ballot or the bullet" and change "by any means necessary." Newton began to see himself as a revolutionary, inspired as well by a new book, *Negroes With Guns.* Its author, Southern activist Robert Williams, had sought asylum in Cuba and Communist China, but inspired in his absence the formation of the Revolutionary Action Movement ("RAM"), a secretive East Coast organization that advocated guerrilla warfare.

Newton learned that Seale was involved locally almost from its inception in a new West Coast branch of RAM. When Newton applied for membership too, he was rejected because he then resided with his parents in a "bourgeois" Oakland neighborhood. His home was outside the *lumpenproletariat* flatlands—the poorest area of the city where one could find in abundance pimps, hustlers, prostitutes, and thieves.[11] Ironically, at the same time RAM turned down Newton as unfit, RAM had unknowingly accepted undercover agents as members. By the fall of 1962, Newton was holding forth on street corners, criticizing President Kennedy's Cuban blockade. He impressed Seale with his rhetorical skills and phenomenal memory. Seale in turn impressed Newton by revealing he owned a gun and was an expert marksman—Seale had been trained in the military to take apart and reassemble an M-I carbine blindfolded. Between 1962 and 1965, Newton and Seale saw each other only occasionally. During this time, Newton often took seasonal jobs at the Del Monte cannery in nearby Emeryville, where two of his sisters were employed. Occasionally, Newton was hired on as a construction worker or longshoreman or street cleaner for the city of Oakland, though he never held any job for long. Meanwhile, Newton secretly supplemented his legitimate income with petty burglaries from unlocked cars, parking lot robberies, selling stolen property, and, for several months, pimping.

Newton's reckless streak was patent. He liked to scare friends by racing his car across the railroad tracks to barely beat an oncoming train. At five-foot-ten, he did not intimidate anyone by sheer size, but he still cultivated a fierce reputation on the street. Shortly after his twenty-first birthday, Newton was arrested for stealing a book. He managed to talk his way into an acquittal. Arrested again in Berkeley for burglary a year later, he again persuaded the police to let him go. Arrested once more on five counts of burglary in early May of 1964, he got the charge reduced to petty theft.

Newton had his first serious brush with the law in the late spring of 1964, when he attended a birthday dinner party and got into an argument with a scar-faced bully named Odell Lee he had never met before. Lee was so hostile and aggressive, Newton acted first. He picked up a steak knife and stabbed Lee, which got Newton arrested for assault with a deadly weapon. He cockily decided to represent himself once again. This time, after a two-day jury trial, Newton was convicted. (Tom Broome, who years later became Huey's probation officer, was coincidentally also present at the birthday party. Broome thought "there was so much provocation that a third grade attorney could have beaten the case or at least had it reduced. Huey didn't know how to go about it, made a fool of himself and wound up with a felony conviction to boot.")[12] This conviction would play a key role in Newton's prosecution for the death of Officer Frey. Newton served six months in jail at Santa Rita before being released on three years' probation. En route to Santa Rita, the 22-year-old spent one month in an isolation cell in the Alameda County jail, infamously known as "the soul breaker."[13] At Santa Rita, Newton received similar punishment in the "cooler." In December of 1964, he watched from the Santa Rita prison yard as busloads of arrested Free Speech Movement demonstrators from Cal Berkeley arrived for a brief stay. The magnitude of their political statement impressed him.

Upon his release from Santa Rita, Newton returned to Merritt to take a few courses, including one in criminal law. He mostly wanted to use the college as a political base. From his perspective, its location in a run-down flatland neighborhood was ideal. In 1965, Newton and Seale joined disaffected blacks who had just founded the Soul Students Advisory Council. The Council opposed the drafting of black soldiers for the Vietnam War and organized hundreds of people to attend a rally—one of the largest such protests on the Merritt campus up to that time. The Council also increased awareness among blacks of their heritage and indicia of colonial status, lobbied for courses in black history and pushed for the hiring of African-American faculty. Yet Newton and Seale soon left the group when other members objected to the use of Council funds to bail the two out of jail for an unrelated Berkeley arrest.

Like Newton, Seale's political consciousness had been awakened by the fiery rhetoric of Malcolm X, who had himself been strongly influenced by Algerian revolutionary Dr. Frantz Fanon. Seale read and reread Fanon's *The Wretched of the Earth* and recommended it enthusiastically to Newton. Seale later pointed to the moment in 1965 when the two focused on the impact of Dr. Fanon's writings as the true genesis of the Black Panther Party. Both viewed blacks in America as colonial subjects, just as Dr. Fanon and Malcolm X had done, but they differed from traditional Marxists who considered it unwise to try to build a party with *lumpenproletariat.* The two budding revolutionaries disdained most white students at the college, but, unlike SNCC and cultural nationalist groups, they recognized the benefits of strong alliances with white radicals. They readily accepted money from Bob Scheer, a Peace and Freedom anti-war candidate for Congress in 1966, to help them organize support on the Merritt campus. Other black student organizations on the Oakland City College campus in 1966 rejected outright Newton's insistence that the time had come for defending the black community with guns. They considered it suicidal. So did Newton.

Newton expected not to live more than a year, taunting police to join him in a life-or-death game, but found the prospect exhilarating. He often likened the sensation to the "deep flow of play" Buddhists characterized as the essence of life.[14] The Eastern philosophical term struck a chord; it matched the sense of peace Newton felt after coming to terms with his own mortality. His older brother Melvin still hoped to persuade Huey to behave with caution; he warned his little brother the police were already digging his grave.

3. TAKIN' CARE OF BUSINESS

Some people say we've got a lot of malice
Some say it's a lot of nerve
But I say we won't quit moving until we get what we deserve
We have been bucked and we have been scorned
We have been treated bad, talked about as just bones
But just as it takes two eyes to make a pair, ha
Brother we can't quit until we get our share

JAMES BROWN, "SAY IT LOUD"

Newton and Seale's new endeavor started out slowly. At the invitation of their friend Richard Aoki, who had transferred to Cal, the two fund-raised in the fall of 1966 by hawking copies of the quotations of Chairman Mao for $1 apiece at anti-war demonstrations on the Berkeley campus. They figured, correctly, that inner city blacks would do brisk business with white radicals when they offered them Mao Tse-tung's *Little Red Book,* with sayings like "Political power grows out of the barrel of a gun." At seventy cents profit per copy, the proceeds mounted quickly and were used to purchase guns as an inducement to enroll new Panther Party members.

Newton then went off campus to recruit street-wise acquaintances. The promise of guns lured neighborhood toughs and high school truants to Newton's lectures on his new party's philosophy. Their first recruit, sixteen-year-old Bobby Hutton, had been one of Seale's charges at the Anti-Poverty Program in Oakland. Newton routinely carried a pump-action shotgun, Hutton an M3 carbine, and Seale a .45 automatic in a holster. As they gained off-campus supporters, they became a force to be reckoned with. By 1966, the whole atmosphere at Merritt College had already become racially polarized. Unofficial taboos kept most whites from using a particular water fountain or congregating with black students in the hallway outside of classrooms or the snack room as they waited for their next class to begin. White students who made eye contact with black males often generated icy stares. They were now commonly derided as "Honkies." Graffiti on campus included death threats. When members of the new Black Panther Party brought rifles on campus, the open display of weapons intimidated and frightened many. At the same time, it inspired and empowered others. Seale and Newton had begun to tap into simmering black community outrage at chronic police abuse.

* * * * *

Back in 1949, the local branch of the leftwing Civil Rights Congress had investigated charges of Oakland officers regularly beating up black residents. Oakland-based civil rights lawyer Bob Treuhaft and his wife, Decca Mitford, had searing memories of that eye-opening experience: "[Our investigation disclosed] monstrous beastliness, authority cloaked in nightmare garb . . . On Fridays . . . police would regularly lie in wait outside the West Oakland bars that served as banks for the cashing of pay checks, arrest those emerging on charges of drunkenness, and in the privacy of the prowl cars beat them and rob them of their week's pay en route to the West Oakland police station."[1] The scathing report led to a legislative inquiry into police brutality in Oakland, one of the first official inquiries ever undertaken of a major police department for alleged abusive treatment of minorities. But the report drew little media coverage and no meaningful state action.

The continuing racial divide between the black community and the Oakland police department greatly exacerbated the situation. The first noticeable progress occurred in 1951 when Treuhaft and his law partner Edises amazingly obtained the reversal of a death penalty conviction in a highly publicized murder case involving a local black shoeshine boy, Jerry Newson. Newson had been accused of murdering a white pharmacist and his assistant. In his defense, Newson testified that the police induced him to make a false confession under threat of facing "the hard boys" of the department who would coerce a confession through brute force.[2] On remand from the Supreme Court, the case was tried twice more, both trials ending in hung juries. Newson eventually went to jail for an unrelated robbery. As a small boy growing up in Oakland, Newton had heard all about the Newson case. Newton considered Bob Treuhaft and Bert Edises two of his childhood heroes; they offered the black community a glimmer of hope that police misconduct might sometimes be redressed.

By 1966, Oakland's population was over one-fourth black and thirty percent minority. African-Americans mostly occupied West Oakland; East Oakland remained dominated by people of Portuguese descent as it had been for several decades. Of 658 sworn police personnel, only 27 were nonwhites—four percent. With the exception of one of 95 sergeants and one of 11 captains, the leadership was entirely white. After the war, many new white police officers were hired from the South. Two decades later, the Oakland Police Department was still recruiting with ads placed in Southern newspapers,[3] and local reporters maintained their longstanding color code for news stories, leaving ghetto murders and beatings largely unexamined. Looking back a decade later, one black elected official in the East Bay likened local law enforcement at the time to "the most rabid, cracker police force in a small Mississippi town."[4]

Starting in January 1967, a few members of the newly formed Black Panther Party for Self-Defense began tailing Oakland police, pulling their cars over to observe firsthand when the police stopped to arrest someone in the neighborhood. The basic idea of keeping tabs on police behavior toward ghetto blacks was not new—a Community Alert Patrol had been established with federal funding in Watts following the historic 1965 riots in that largely black Los Angeles district. But in Watts they just used tape recorders and notebooks. A clandestine, armed group of black war veterans had formed in Louisiana in 1964 to defend their neighborhoods from the Ku Klux Klan—but brandishing loaded weapons in public gave the Black Panthers a distinctive, threatening aspect.

On January 1, 1967, using paychecks Seale, Newton, and Hutton received from the anti-poverty program, the Panthers opened their first office in North Oakland near the Berkeley border. A large sign in their window at the corner of Fifty-sixth and Grove streets proclaimed, "Black Panther Party for Self-Defense." (Grove since has been renamed Martin Luther King, Jr. Way.) Newton began holding weekly meetings for walk-ins who learned they would get weapons training if they could sit still long enough through lectures in political theory. Armed Panthers continued to monitor black neighborhoods in Oakland, following testy police around on their patrols. Newton commuted to San Francisco Law School to take another course in criminal law and spent many hours studying in the law library above the Poverty Center. He kept a copy of *California Criminal Laws* in his car, ready to read chapter and verse about the constitutional right to bear arms, as well as the rights of arrested citizens. But when Newton and Seale brought guns with them to work, they were fired by the Chairman of the Oakland Economic Development Council, Superior Court Judge Lionel Wilson. (A political protegé of Assemblyman William Rumford, Wilson had been appointed in 1960 by Gov. Pat Brown as the first black judge in the county.)

In early April 1967 in nearby Richmond, California, the Panthers attracted hundreds of angry residents to a rally protesting the recent killing of an unarmed 22-year-old, Denzil Dowell, by a sheriff's deputy who insisted he had reasonable cause to shoot Dowell for fleeing arrest for attempted car theft. The family disbelieved the deputy, but got nowhere challenging the department's shoot-to-kill policy. Before forming the Panthers, Seale had already been working for a few years at community-building in North Richmond, which even more dramatically than Oakland, had become a breeding ground for deep resentment toward local police. At the beginning of World War II, fewer than 300 blacks lived in the city. Richmond's black population increased over 5,000 percent in seven years as Southern transplants were lured into overcrowded neighborhoods to work on defense contracts and in shipyards.

At the time of the Richmond killing, Newton and Seale had only recently met Cleaver. They saw him speak at a San Francisco anti-war rally where they were hawking Little Red Books and tracked him down to introduce themselves after Cleaver gave a radio interview. Cleaver suggested they start a newsletter with the Richmond killing as the lead story of its first issue. Beverly Axelrod helped them craft two mimeographed pages in her living room while "The Times They Are A-Changin'" blared on the phonograph. By the second issue in mid-May, they launched a more professional-looking *Black Panther* newspaper published biweekly by a printer. At a quarter each, sales soon regularly exceeded 100,000 per issue and became the Panthers' primary source of income.

To establish a unique identity, besides carrying weapons, the Panthers adopted uniforms for themselves: black pants, a powder blue shirt, a black leather jacket (which most of them already owned), and a black beret (like that worn by Che Guevara and the French Resistance). Jean Genet later proclaimed that the Panthers "attacked first by sight."[5] They soon realized that their macho organization would spin out of control if they did not establish strict rules of behavior. Some new Panthers had undermined the Party's mission by getting drunk or high on drugs while wielding guns or by committing crimes against people in the community. It was not surprising, given Newton's aggressive recruitment efforts in pool halls and taverns.

The rules, inspired by those of Black Muslims, were enforceable by expulsion. They included exclusive allegiance to the Party as a military force; following orders; and learning the Ten Point Program and rules by heart. Members were not to possess any drugs while on Party business or engage in unnecessary use of a firearm. That must have relieved Axelrod, whose teen-aged sons had often witnessed Panthers waving guns in their living room as points of emphasis. Commission of crimes against blacks was banned as well as possession of a weapon while under the influence of narcotics, "weed," or alcohol. Members were officially urged to speak politely, "not to take liberties with women and not to hit or swear at people."[6]

Apart from Axelrod, whose role in the Party was unofficial, women recruits became Pantherettes, adapted from the Raiderette cheerleaders at Oakland professional football games. Pantherettes often endured harassment by male recruits. Eldridge Cleaver would soon alienate many potential female supporters by urging them to exercise their "Pussy Power." A number of Pantherettes quit the Party rather than be treated as sex objects.[7] To discourage such conduct, the Party started calling members who repeatedly indulged in unrestrained, boorish behavior "renegade Jackanapes" whose "antics" involved attempts to "bogart down the brothers" or "gorilla a sister" for sex.[8] Maintaining Party discipline would always be an issue.

In April of 1967, a local radio station invited Newton to speak on a call-in talk show. When he read the Ten Point Program on the air an irate assemblyman phoned in to announce to the radio audience his sponsorship of a new bill in Sacramento to ban carrying loaded guns in public. At Newton's suggestion, Seale took Panther recruits and friends and members of the Dowell family to the State Capitol in early May to oppose the bill. Newton wisely accepted the recommendation that he stay home—he remained on probation, and they anticipated trouble. Newton had prepared for Seale to read an Executive Mandate that accused the California Legislature of seeking to keep the black community "disarmed and powerless" while police repression increased throughout the country. The statement echoed the new bellicose direction of SNCC since the spring of 1966 in asserting the American black power movement as part of an international struggle against imperialism, linking U.S. domestic policy to the "racist war of genocide in Viet Nam."[9]

All together, thirty activists emerged from six cars driven in a caravan to Sacramento on May 2, 1967. Twenty of them wielded rifles, shotguns, and Magnum .357s. Seale also sported a .45 pistol on his hip. Following Newton's strict instructions, they kept the unholstered weapons pointed straight up or down at the ground as they walked toward the Capitol building. Like Newton, those on parole could not carry hand guns, nor could Hutton, who was still under age. At the time, carrying loaded weapons in plain sight and not directed at anyone was legal. Still, Newton counseled Seale that, if fired upon, he should shoot back. Cleaver went along with no gun, on official assignment to cover the event for *Ramparts* magazine. As the attention-getting entourage approached their destination, Gov. Ronald Reagan happened to be standing on the lawn with a group of visiting school children. At the startling sight of an armed squadron of black militants, he broke into a trot in the opposite direction.

The day the Panthers arrived at the Capitol, the police had been caught off guard. They stopped a few in the building and temporarily relieved them of their guns, but then gave the weapons back and let them go. NRA supporters had brought guns before and some traditional gun lobbyists were present to oppose this new bill, too. On both the way in and out of the Capitol building, Seale read to the media Newton's "Executive Mandate No. One," which attracted immediate television coverage. Newton watched with glee at his parents' home in Oakland at the success of what he called "shock-a-buku"—sudden moves that keep the enemy off balance."[10] As the Panthers drove out of Sacramento, they were arrested on a variety of charges and taken to the city jail. During the next few days, the Panthers were deluged with media inquiries as *The London Times* and other international papers featured their spectacular political confrontation. The widespread publicity garnered Newton his first paid speaking engagement, at San Francisco State College. With the $500 fee, Newton and his childhood friend David Hilliard, a newly-recruited Panther, then bought a pound of marijuana, which they broke up for sale on the street to raise bail money for those arrested in Sacramento. As they drove through Oakland, Hilliard spotted policemen on patrol and asked: "Hey, Huey, what are we supposed to do if the police stop us?" Newton laughed. "We shoot them. You know, we fight."[11] Fortunately, the police car drove on by.

In May, a few weeks after the Sacramento arrests, Seale and Newton had words with policemen on a street corner outside Panther headquarters, which resulted in several minor charges against Newton: brandishing a weapon, possessing an illegal knife, and disturbing the peace, including using profanity in public. (In 1967, just wearing a "Fuck the Draft" jacket on the street was considered an arrestable offense.) A much more serious encounter had only been narrowly avoided three months earlier when Seale and Newton showed up at *Ramparts* headquarters in San Francisco with other Party members to escort Malcolm X's widow, Betty Shabazz, to a local speaking engagement. On the streets of San Francisco, several policemen confronted Newton and his companions as well as a competing group of black militants, who had adopted a similar name—the Black Panther Party of Northern California. Huey accused one of the policemen of having an itchy finger and dared him to draw.

Seale immediately realized how close Newton had come to a shootout on that occasion: "If just one of them had gone for his gun, he would blast him, because Huey had his gun at a 45 degree angle to the ground and he was ready. He had the barrel of the gun in his left hand. His finger was on the trigger, he had knocked the safety off, and had jacked a round into the chamber."[12] The police had then backed off, but they recognized that armed confrontations were occurring with greater frequency across the country. In June, a group of whites in Prattville, Alabama, emptied their rifles into homes in a black neighborhood, prompting SNCC leader, H. Rap Brown, to call for "full retaliation." He characterized Alabama as the "starting battleground for America's race war."[13] Brown also encouraged violent confrontations elsewhere, repeating before various audiences his strong support for armed self-defense: "If America chooses to play Nazis, black folks ain't going to play Jews."[14]

Maddeningly to the police, over the summer of 1967 the Panthers' aggressive, watchdog behavior quickly turned Newton and Seale into neighborhood celebrities. Local Leftists started to take notice, too. Muckraker Decca Mitford counted herself among their earliest white fans. She later observed, "I admired the idea of the BPP since its origin. I felt such an organization was badly needed in Oakland, based upon my experiences and observations . . . during the 1950's and 1960's.[15] The Panthers built upon their growing community support by using issues like lobbying for traffic signals at dangerous intersections. By August, the Panthers became sufficiently mainstream in the local black community to be asked to patrol a Juneteenth Day celebration in West Oakland's DeFremery Park commemorating freedom from slavery. Oakland police were officially asked not to monitor the festival. Entertainers and speakers were all African-American, including San Francisco Assemblyman Willie Brown (later Speaker of the State Assembly and then Mayor of San Francisco) and State Senator Mervin Dymally (later Lieutenant Governor of California) as well as Berkeley's new anti-war Council Member, Ron Dellums (the nephew of pioneer sleeping car union organizer C. L. Dellums would go on to serve in Congress for over 25 years and later became Mayor of Oakland). The police were affronted, but acquiesced. It turned a new page in local police-community relations.

4. THE DEFENSE TEAM

THE ONLY CLIENTS OF MINE THAT GO TO SAN QUENTIN ARE THE ONES WHO LIE TO ME.

SIGN ON CHARLES GARRY'S DESK

By the fall of 1967, though the police still viewed the Panthers as thugs, they were beginning to appreciate that the Party was unlike any street gang they had previously encountered. Soon the department furnished patrol cars with a list of known Panther vehicles to stop on any pretext. Garry learned all this later. When he and Beverly Axelrod headed to Newton's hospital room on November 1, 1967, Garry knew virtually nothing about the Panther Party. Newton remained heavily guarded while municipal court judge Stafford Buckley conducted a bedside hearing by which Newton was formally transferred to county custody on charges of murder, assault with a deadly weapon, and kidnapping.

Following the arraignment, sheriff's deputies took over guard duty from the Oakland police because Newton was now a county prisoner. Still fearing for Newton's life, Garry asked Judge Buckley to order that Newton not be moved, which the judge took under submission. Meanwhile, at a Catholic Church not far away, the slain young policeman, John Frey, only a year and a half on the force, received the special treatment reserved for fallen heroes. His funeral included a twelve-man honor guard, a long procession of private cars, and a squad of motorcycles, with over 150 colleagues participating. Officers' wives showed up for the funeral service as well, each acutely aware of how easily it could have been her own spouse's funeral they were attending. The pallbearers included Police Chief Charles Gain, County Sheriff Frank Madigan, the City Manager, a Superior Court judge, a Municipal Court judge, and the local Assemblyman. *The Oakland Tribune* gave the funeral extensive coverage.

The situation looked grim for Newton. He expected the death penalty if convicted for the capital offense of killing a police officer. Garry later described the case as "the most complex, emotional, fascinating case, I've ever tried."[1] Without asking Newton any questions, Garry "felt right away that this man was totally and completely innocent. Huey was the kind of a person I immediately felt a warmth and friendship with; his charisma and his openness and frankness just came right through, even while he was lying in a hospital bed with a tube through his nose."[2] The fifty-eight-year-old Armenian-American was married, with a wife and a mistress, but no children. This self-described streetfighter in the courtroom related to Huey as the son he never had.

Garry's first advice to Newton was what Garry told all of his clients, "Make no statements to anyone." Garry knew that even a good friend or relative or cellmate might be forced to reveal anything Newton said about the case. Garry himself never asked Newton for any information about the shootout until a few days before he took the witness stand in the middle of the trial. When asked why not, Garry later explained, "I wasn't particularly interested."[3] Many criminal defense lawyers don't want their client's story. The defendant has a right not to testify on his own behalf and knowing what he has to say could limit the array of defenses. Here, Garry's primary aim matched that of Newton—to conduct a political defense, painting a picture of an entrenched racist establishment that itself should be on trial. The Panthers reminded him of some of his most militant union clients decades before, who had been even more vilified by society. He saw in the Panthers "a kind of cohesion of all the things that the labor movement originally started out in the '30s fighting for."[4]

The timing of the breaking story was excellent for gaining Leftist political support. Legendary guerrilla leader Che Guevara had been captured and executed in Bolivia early in October 1967, just a few weeks before Newton's arrest. Only a few months before, a daring live interview with Che in South America had been broadcasted on Berkeley's community-supported station KPFA. Radicals rushed to champion the cause of Huey Newton as a revolutionary like their martyred hero Che. Garry instantly realized that any chance of winning the case required him to orchestrate two high-powered defense strategies: one, a first-rate, aggressive defense on the facts of the case and existing law, relying heavily on research and writing assistance; two, and more importantly, a spirited political defense of the Panthers as a peacekeeping organization devoted to protecting their community from police oppression. As Garry planned his public relations campaign, he knew the audience he really needed to convince was an as-yet unpicked panel of jurors, likely unfamiliar with life in black ghettos. In the crucial selection process, he would need help from expert witnesses and top-notch support staff.

Now thirty-five years old, Guild lawyer Fay Stender had been a part-time associate at the firm since shortly after the Meisenbach "Black Friday" trial in 1961. The opportunity to work for clients she believed in put Stender in an enviable position; few established local firms then hired any women lawyers, or Jews for that matter. Stender was the only woman lawyer ever hired by the firm and had, after six years, become Garry's right hand for legal research and briefing. The son of immigrant Armenians fleeing Turkish massacres had never fully mastered English syntax. Unlike his far more genteel partners, it was not unusual for Garry to instruct his secretary to "get that motherfucker in here to pay his child support." Uniquely structured phrases became "Garryisms" fondly repeated in the office. Recently, in light of landmark Supreme Court rulings on procedural rights of criminal defendants, court practice had evolved from the old-fashioned shoot-from-the-hip style with which Garry was comfortable to incorporate more strategic pretrial motions to challenge court procedures or potential evidence that might severely prejudice their clients. If Stender's sexist mentor had his way, the five-foot-eight, dark-haired Jew would have stayed his assistant for her entire career.

With her two children now both in elementary school, Stender had just begun working full time. When she started at the Garry firm in 1961, the former California Supreme Court clerk had much preferred library research and writing that she could do on a flexible schedule. At the time, Stender was recently separated from her husband Marvin, racing back from San Francisco each work day to relieve the patchwork of babysitters she had cobbled together for her toddler daughter and three-year-old son. By the late fall of 1967, the Stenders had been reunited for the better part of three years. Fay Stender was eager to take on new challenges at work to prove she was partnership material.

Though she had little criminal trial experience, Stender had honed her knowledge of the controlling precedents by assisting Garry's highly demanding partner Barney Dreyfus on several death penalty appeals. Garry expected Stender's analytical and writing skills to be essential to this difficult defense. He popped his head into her tiny cubicle as the dowdily dressed lawyer pounded away on her typewriter—Stender typed faster than any secretary in the office and saved the firm from offering her much technical support. Garry then asked Stender to join him when he made his next visit to Newton. Stender's eyes lit up immediately. This might be the break she was looking for in her career. Stender had some background handling civil rights cases, but by 1967 had made a niche for herself by representing draft dodgers. It had not taken her long to become extremely dissatisfied with her clientele. "I knew for every one I handled [for a white, middle-class male], there were many Third World People who really needed a lawyer and couldn't get one."[5]

Though Garry would immediately proclaim his client's innocence to the press, the prospects of Newton's acquittal at that point looked slim to non-existent. When Newton's arrest for murder hit the front pages of local papers, two other, totally unrelated, police shootout cases were scheduled for trial the following week. The attorneys in both cases successfully invoked mounting hostility in the community at large from Officer Frey's death to obtain continuances to avoid juror prejudice against these unrelated defendants. Newton's arrest had polarized the community. As much as the charges against him inflamed many whites, officials became concerned about increased unrest in black neighborhoods precipitated by the arrest of a local hero.

As he had done so often in the past for other high-profile clients, Garry immediately sought to generate public sympathy for Newton. He decided to put the hospital and the police on the defensive for their handling of the arrest. A local physician who had seen the newspaper photo of Newton handcuffed to the gurney before surgery had been flabbergasted that doctors at Kaiser Hospital would allow police to stretch out the arms of a man with an abdominal wound. She contacted Garry to tell him how unprofessional the treatment was. Garry asked Stender to quickly draft a complaint charging Kaiser with medical malpractice. Meanwhile, the inflammatory photo was reproduced on the cover of a widely circulated pamphlet with the caption, "Can a black man get a fair trial?" As soon as the police could arrange it, Newton was transferred to San Quentin for cost-savings and greater security while he needed additional medical attention. Similar transfers had occurred with a half-dozen or more other prisoners charged with serious felonies earlier that year. The defense objected because the municipal court judge had not yet ruled on Garry's request that Newton not be moved from Highland Hospital. Newton was returned to Oakland. A few weeks later, when sufficiently recuperated, Newton was transferred to the Alameda County jail in the courthouse on the shores of Lake Merritt.

To bring Newton to trial on the charges stemming from the October shooting, the prosecutor had alternative paths he could pursue: convening a grand jury or conducting a preliminary hearing in municipal court. A preliminary hearing would entitle Newton's counsel to cross-examine the prosecutor's witnesses in open court. In contrast, appearances before the grand jury were confidential and counsel for the defense was not permitted to be present, much less participate. Grand juries were (and are) notorious for doing the prosecutor's bidding—they only hear one version of events. Not surprisingly, the district attorney took the case to the grand jury. It had the added benefit of avoiding a media circus. (Ten years later, the California Supreme Court ruled that choosing a grand jury provided the prosecutor with such a tactical advantage that defendants should have the right to ask for a preliminary hearing after an indictment is issued; in 1990, prosecutors went to the voters and won a change in the Constitution, taking that right away). The grand jury convened on November 13; it issued its indictment against Newton by mid-afternoon of the same day on charges of murder, assault, and kidnapping and, for purposes of sentence enhancement, included the allegation that Newton already had a prior felony conviction on his record.

One ray of hope emerged the next day when the California Supreme Court stayed two executions scheduled later that month at San Quentin and ordered the fate of all sixty men on Death Row placed on hold while the high court considered a challenge to the state's death penalty. Fay Stender immediately went to work day and night under the direction of Garry's partner Barney Dreyfus. Their first task was to prepare a constitutional challenge to the grand jury on the grounds it did not reflect a cross-section of the community as the law required. The product of an Irish-Jewish marriage, Dreyfus was a gentleman of the old school who routinely opened doors for women, called Stender "little girl," and notoriously had his own mistress on the premises, the firm's office manager. Dreyfus, a past president of the National Lawyers Guild, shared with Garry a reputation as "a humanist who battles for the disadvantaged and the despised."[6] Unlike Garry, Dreyfus was a constitutional scholar, thorough and meticulous in his research, under whose critical tutelage Stender had learned over the past several years to hone her own painstaking research. Stender methodically gathered information on how the grand jury system operated. Each of twenty county judges submitted three names from county residents "personally known to them" to be good citizens. Not surprisingly, those selected were largely middle class, mostly white, contemporaries of the judges.

The defense aimed to demonstrate that, in practice, grand jury panels systematically left out young people, blacks, poor, and low-income wage earners. This resulted not only from the way the grand jurors were chosen, but also from the hardship service imposed. Grand jurors were paid only $5 per day plus expenses. Service was for one year, a financial sacrifice wage earners could not afford. Exemptions were also given to mothers with preteen children. Stender obtained the current list of grand jurors to determine its racial composition. The Alameda County grand jury serving in 1967 had only one black member, who was not present the day Newton was indicted.

The date set for accepting Newton's plea was November 16, only three days after the grand jury had convened. Before the hearing, the defense made a motion for discovery of twenty-seven categories of information they believed the prosecutor was required by law to reveal. Five years before, in *Brady v. Maryland,* the United States Supreme Court had ruled that the state violated criminal defendants' constitutional rights if it withheld evidence important to the defense of the case, even unintentionally. The District Attorney's office would have to honor most, if not all, of these defense requests or risk reversal on appeal. The list Stender and Alex Hoffmann prepared included the guns allegedly used, ballistics reports, the clothes worn by Officers Frey and Heanes, files in the custody of the prosecutor that contained data on the Black Panthers, and police memoranda on their general strategy toward the militant group.

Newton made his appearance at the November 16 hearing neatly dressed in slacks, a blue shirt, and a green jacket. He appeared recovered from his gunshot wound, though he still complained to his attorneys of lingering numbness in his hands from the tight handcuffs used to shackle him in the hospital. Upon entering the courtroom, he raised a clenched fist salute to the gallery of mixed race supporters, who sat quietly throughout the short proceedings. Garry immediately requested a continuance for entry of Newton's plea, telling the court he had not had sufficient opportunity to meet with his client or to obtain the transcript of the four-count grand jury indictment.

Heightened security was already evident as three uniformed court bailiffs and three police in plainclothes patrolled the hallways directly outside the courtroom. Outside, demonstrators chanted "Free Huey, Jail the Pigs," while teenage Panther supporters passed out leaflets, announcing one of several press conferences that Garry had arranged. Garry had immediately sought to counter negative pretrial publicity about the Black Panthers by publicizing their Ten Point Program and their focus on self-defense and not aggression. The publicity also explained why the Panthers carried guns and tape recorders while patrolling black neighborhoods: to protect the residents from police harassment. Axelrod joined Garry in portraying Newton to the press as a selfless example of a courageous man deliberately hounded by the police for safeguarding his community.

The mainstream press that covered criminal trials was quite familiar with Garry's remarkable record of never losing a murder client to the death penalty. Many could also recall a decade earlier when the flamboyant Leftist and his partners first opened the doors of their new office in San Francisco: three of its four principals were immediately subpoenaed to appear before a House Un-American Activities Committee hearing in San Francisco focused on exposing Communist professionals. Barney Dreyfus had specially been targeted because he had taken the lead in opposing the Smith Act loyalty oaths and recruiting State Bar leaders to come to the defense of HUAC targets. Both Garry and Dreyfus were identified by a witness who had attended clandestine Communist educational programs in San Francisco with them in the '40s. The Bay Area hearings turned into a circus as a crowd of sympathetic onlookers cheered the uncooperative lawyers, who invoked the Fifth Amendment right not to incriminate themselves in response to every question asked of them. The FBI still kept a file on the Garry and Dreyfus firm.

In contrast, Democrat Lowell Jensen had risen through the ranks of the Alameda County District Attorney as a reliable straight arrow. The tall, lanky graduate of Boalt Hall School of Law in Berkeley had thirteen years of experience in the D.A.'s office, starting just before the county's infamous trial of Berkeleyite Burton Abbott for the rape and murder of fourteen-year-old Stephanie Bryan. Abbott was executed in 1957 based solely on circumstantial evidence of his guilt. Jensen had recently been promoted to oversee all criminal trials in the county. His recent cases included the mass Free Speech Movement prosecution of anti-war activists who occupied the University of California's Sproul Hall in December of 1964. Relatively apolitical, Jensen made an odd sparring partner for Garry. Jensen liked to play by the rules and not request anything he considered unfair. He quickly noticed that Garry routinely made outrageous demands, recognizing that judges have a tendency to split the difference between the parties' positions. That gave Garry a decided advantage by moving the midway point much further in his direction than it would have otherwise been.

In addition to Garry and Fay Stender, the basic defense team included Viennese-born Yale Law School graduate Alex Hoffmann, two paralegals and a volunteer from outside the mainstream black legal community, Carlton Innis. Most local black lawyers were still angry about the choice of Garry as lead counsel. They assumed the trial would inevitably result in Newton's conviction and wanted Garry to bear all the blame. Thc inclusion of Carlton Innis on the defense team did little to assuage them. Innis had only been admitted to the Bar five years earlier, was not highly skilled, and performed functions similar to those of the paralegals. In fact, Garry soon discovered that at the time he joined the defense, Innis was under temporary suspension from law practice for failure to pay his bar fees, an administrative requirement that was soon remedied. (Years later, Innis would get in repeated trouble with the State Bar on more serious infractions; ultimately, he resigned.)

The legal team had already gone on the political offensive in filing the malpractice claim against Kaiser Hospital. That lawsuit helped counter adverse publicity, but it was a diversion from the criminal trial. The quartet of lawyers was inundated with ideas on how the defense could best challenge the constitutionality of the proceedings. Everywhere they looked, progressive attorneys and law professors wanted to volunteer their assistance. The first step for the team was to read the grand jury transcript: it outlined the prosecutor's basic case. The testimony before the grand jury included a police dispatcher who spoke early on the morning of October 28 with Officer Frey. Frey was then alone in his patrol car in the middle of his rounds on "the dog watch" in West Oakland's red light district. Spotting a Volkswagen sedan with two black men inside, he radioed in a request for a "rolling check" from police headquarters. The dispatcher told Frey the license number was on a list of twenty "known Black Panther vehicles." Officer Frey told the dispatcher he was going to stop the car and ask the driver for identification. Frey asked for a report on any unpaid traffic fines and for a back-up patrol car, common practice when there were two people being stopped. The dispatcher told Frey the car was registered to LaVerne Williams and had outstanding tickets.

Officer Heanes, just released from the hospital, made a dramatic witness. He told the grand jury he was Frey's back up. When he arrived, Newton was still in the driver's seat of the Volkswagen and identified himself by name. Frey was then standing behind the police car, writing Newton a ticket. After Heanes got out of his police car, Newton got out, too, and walked toward Frey. At that point, neither policeman had a gun drawn. Heanes had not seen one in Newton's hand either, but gunfire suddenly erupted from Newton's "general vicinity." Heanes then saw Frey and Newton wrestling. He recalled hearing a shot, being struck in the arm and then firing at Newton. Heanes heard other shots, was hit twice more, and "blacked out."

Dell Ross was parked in his Ford convertible around the corner from the shooting. He testified that two black men kidnapped him and forced him to drive them away. One of the men was wounded and said, "I'd 'a kept shooting if the gun hadn't jammed, I'm too mean to die" and the other had replied, "You shot two dudes. You still got two dudes." Ross said the wounded man had a gun in his hand. After asking to be driven to 32nd and Chestnut Street, in Oakland, the two men instead left the car on Adeline Street, where the wounded man limped into a dark alley, aided by his companion. Ross later identified the wounded man as Newton.

Other police arrived at the scene following the shooting to find Frey dying and Heanes seriously wounded. By then, the two men whom Frey had pulled over were gone, leaving their parked Volkswagen behind. A half-written ticket for driving without a license was found near Frey's body. Also found on the street near Frey was a blood-soaked copy of a law book with Huey Newton's name written in it. In less than fifteen minutes following the shootout, police were circulating Newton's photo as the prime suspect, describing him as "armed and dangerous" and "last seen on foot . . . on Seventh Street in Oakland, wearing a light brown jacket and a dark hat." They were also looking for Newton's companion. Within forty-five minutes, an all-points bulletin went out to stop any male Negroes. Then police heard Newton was at Kaiser Hospital, where they sent officers to arrest him.[7]

Police technicians concluded three guns had been fired, though only Heanes' was found. A search of the Volkswagen turned up two small, penny match boxes of marijuana in a paper bag on the floor by the front seats and a live 9-mm bullet. The autopsy on Officer Frey showed he was shot five times, twice in the back at close range. It was unclear who started the shooting and the order in which the guns were fired, but both the bullet removed from Frey and the slug removed from Heanes came from the same weapon, which was not Heanes' revolver. The police still did not know the name or whereabouts of Newton's passenger. They interviewed Newton's twenty-two-year-old girlfriend, LaVerne Williams, who confirmed that it was her car Newton was driving when he was stopped, but she had not been with him that evening and knew nothing about the shooting.

While Garry's associates reviewed the grand jury transcript for holes in the prosecutor's case, a handful of Panthers and a growing number of other activists built community support to "Free Huey." They ambitiously announced plans to picket the courthouse four hours per day, seven days a week, until Huey was free. Newly elected Berkeley City Council Member Ron Dellums was persuaded to bring before his colleagues a resolution condemning Newton's indictment by an unrepresentative grand jury. Circulation of *The Black Panther* increased a thousand percent. Sympathy and rage were easily generated by Newton's picture chained to a gurney and the filing of malpractice and civil rights lawsuits. The "Free Huey" chant intentionally avoided any call for a traditional fair trial—most of Newton's militant associates assumed he had done what he was accused of. They considered him amply justified in killing an oppressor and wanted their leader out of jail by any means available.

Many Radicals thought Newton had just started the revolution. As Cleaver later wrote: "We all knew that it was coming. When, where, how—all had now been answered. The Black Panther Party had at last drawn blood, spilled its own and shed that of the pigs! We counted history from Huey's night of truth."[8] A front page editorial in *The Black Panther* newspaper with a half-page headline "HUEY MUST BE SET FREE!" placed the shooting squarely in the context of historic race relations, emphasizing that it occurred in a black ghetto between a black resident and white cops who lived in the white suburbs:

> On the night that the shooting occurred, there were 400 years of oppression of black people by white people focused and manifested in the incident. We are at the cross roads in history where black people are determined to bring down the final curtain on the drama of their struggle to free themselves from the boot of the white man that is on their collective neck. . . . Through murder, brutality, and the terror of their image, the police of America have kept black

> people intimidated, locked in a mortal fear, and paralyzed their bid for freedom. [Newton] knew that the power of the police over black people has to be broken if we are to be liberated from our bondage. These Gestapo dogs are not holy, they are not angels, and there is no more mystery surrounding them. They are brutal beasts who have been gunning down black people and getting away with it. . . . Black people all over America and around the world . . . are glad for once to have a dead cop and a live Huey . . . we want Huey to stay alive . . . we want Huey set free.[9]

Garry agreed with the Panthers that Newton stood for historically oppressed individuals pitted against a repressive society. He viewed Newton's rap sheet as that of a scrappy warrior. The only clients Garry could never imagine defending were Nazis or fascists. Garry believed that the job of the "Movement" lawyer was to expose the system as rotten and "tie it up."[10] His empathy for Newton was reinforced by reading the black revolutionary literature Newton assigned him as homework: if one viewed the black community as a colony oppressed by its mother country, then crimes like those Newton was charged with were either self-defense or self-liberation.

The Panthers' efforts to galvanize support for Newton paid off. At his second court appearance on November 28, over sixty followers filled the public gallery. *The Sun-Reporter* newspaper, run by Dr. Goodlett in San Francisco, actively drummed up funds for Newton's defense, as did *The Berkeley Barb*, the Panther newspaper, and other underground publications. This time when Newton arrived in the courtroom in his new gray sharkskin suit, emboldened supporters stood up and greeted him with a Panther clenched fist salute. Newton returned the salute and invited the attendees to be seated. His usurpation of authority caused them to break into laughter. Superior Court Judge Staats called for order in the courtroom, warning the crowd against any more demonstrations, but his remarks only generated more derisive laughter. The judge quickly took control. He ordered Newton returned to his cell and used the recess to lecture Newton's supporters: "This is a courtroom and we require that people remain quiet and seated except for the counsel and principals involved. If you are not prepared to do that, we will ask to clear the courtroom. Is there anyone who will not comply?"[11] Only after the crowd grew silent did the judge order Newton brought back. When the judge addressed him, Newton insisted that he be called "Minister of Defense" Huey Newton rather than simply by his given name. In an informal discussion in chambers in December, the judge asked Garry if he would seek a change of venue due to the bad publicity *The Oakland Tribune* had already generated. Such a strategy would have presumed there was another county with a better possibility of achieving a fair trial, but the Black Panthers had their base among Oakland's now almost 40 percent black population. Across the bay, San Francisco was at the time only 13.5 percent black and had only 3.3 percent blacks in its jury pool.

Garry already had a useful proxy to measure a community's entrenched racist attitudes—the vote on Proposition 14 in the 1964 general election. That ballot initiative proposed a state constitutional amendment to void the mandate of California's highly controversial Fair Housing Act of 1963, also called the Rumford Act for its sponsor, East Bay Assembly member William Byron Rumford of Berkeley, who in 1948 had become the first Northern California black to achieve elected office. The Rumford Act prohibited discrimination by sellers and landlords on the basis of race, religion, sex, national origin, ancestry or marital status. Proposition 14 sought to override that law with a state constitutional amendment granting landlords and sellers the unfettered right to accept or reject prospective tenants or buyers without risk of being sued. Among other discriminatory consequences, Proposition 14 was designed to enshrine the right to prevent black families from purchasing a home in an all-white neighborhood. In1966, the California Supreme Court struck down Proposition 14 as unconstitutional; a bare majority of the U.S. Supreme Court affirmed that ruling in May of 1967. While Garry publicly charged that no militant black could get a fair trial anywhere in the state, he recognized Alameda County had rejected Proposition 14 by 54 percent of the vote, a better result than any other county. Garry responded to the judge with his own question: where in California did the judge think Newton could get a fair trial? The judge joked "Orange County", a notoriously conservative white enclave in Southern California. Garry laughed and said he was thinking about some place in Cuba.

During this early phase of the Newton case, Bobby Seale had been serving a short sentence arising out of his arrest in May in Sacramento, at first in a local jail and then at Santa Rita. Represented by the Treuhaft firm, he and several other Panther demonstrators who had no prior police record had pled guilty in August to disturbing the peace so the others who were then on parole or probation would not have to serve any jail time. Seale was in the maximum security wing of Santa Rita when he heard about the shootout in Oakland. As soon as Seale saw the front-page photo of Newton manacled to a gurney, he became consumed with getting his Party co-founder out. He knew from past conversations that Newton could not abide the idea of sitting on death row, enduring the mental torture of an unknown execution date, waiting years while stays and appeals took their course.

During November, while Seale was finishing his sentence, other Panthers visited him, urging him to countermand Cleaver and get rid of Garry. Their first choice was forty-seven-year-old Clinton White, General Counsel for the NAACP's local office. Tall and athletic with a booming voice and aggressive style, White was universally acknowledged as one of the most formidable criminal defense attorneys around. His colleague Willie Brown claimed, "if you wanted to learn how to cross-examine someone, no matter who you were, you had to watch Clinton White."[12] The unhappy Panthers' distant second choice was John George. He had once worked out a favorable compromise for Newton on an assault charge, but had no known history of trying death penalty cases and did not inspire many of them with confidence he was up to this challenge. Seale already had serious reservations of his own. As soon as he walked free on December 8, 1967, he would personally check Garry out. It was not just Newton's life that hung in the balance, but the future of the Black Panther Party. If Newton were found guilty, how would they justify having asked a white lawyer to represent the leader of the vanguard? What would they tell new recruits from the black community shouting, "Free Huey or Else"?

5. WHO DO YOU TRUST?

The first lesson a revolutionary must learn is that he is a doomed man.

Huey Newton

Given his precarious position, Garry knew how important it was to keep Newton's morale buoyed and his lines of communication open to Panther leaders on the outside. But hand-holding was not Garry's forte, and his law practice in San Francisco kept him from scheduling non-essential visits at the Alameda County jail in November and early December of 1967. Instead, Axelrod regularly crossed the Bay Bridge to visit Newton and bring messages back to Cleaver from the jailed Party leader. Her participation soon became too awkward. Axelrod was still head-over-heels in love with Cleaver. Less than a month after Newton was jailed, Cleaver rejected her.

* * * * *

When Axelrod first met Cleaver in the mid-1960s, she was already in her early forties. She had recently left her husband to marry her lover, Reggie Majors, a San Francisco neighbor of her brother's and a well-known African-American journalist and author of books on black liberation. But Majors had surprised Axelrod by then declining to divorce his wife, contrary to his promise in advance of Axelrod's own divorce. Greatly hurt, Axelrod had found solace in correspondence and jail visits with her new client, Eldridge Cleaver, who resembled Majors in height and build.

Cleaver seemed to embody everything she had been searching for nearly all her adult life—a soul mate with the same radical, egalitarian goals.

When Cleaver left prison in 1966, he used Beverly's brother's San Francisco house as his official residence to meet with his parole officer, though he actually often lived with Beverly. The couple bought a Volvo together, and Cleaver told his mother he and Beverly planned to marry. Already a celebrated author, Cleaver became a popular speaker after his release, addressing political rallies and promoting his book, while traveling to conduct high profile interviews for *Ramparts.* On Easter weekend at the end of March, 1967, SNCC scheduled a student conference at Fisk University, in Nashville, Tennessee. The small, highly prestigious black college counted civil rights leader W. E. B. DuBois, co-founder of the NAACP, among its early alumni. Eldridge was honored to be invited to serve on a panel with playwright Leroi Jones (later known as Imamu Amir Baraka).

SNCC also scheduled a higher profile conference early the following month at nearby Vanderbilt University, featuring the Rev. Martin Luther King, Jr., beat poet Allen Ginsberg, and Stokely Carmichael. Carmichael had sent shock waves throughout the country ten months earlier with his historic "Black Power" speech repudiating King's pacifist marches for civil rights. Instead, Carmichael urged his followers to "fight back" against white supremacists.[1] As soon as word leaked out that Carmichael had been asked to speak, Vanderbilt's administration cancelled the invitation for fear of riots. Cleaver agreed violence was likely: "We were dancing with death, and we knew it. But we did not call for the music to stop. Instead, we called for the band to play louder, stronger, and longer."[2]

Fisk immediately cancelled its own SNCC conference. A local minister offered his church social hall as a last minute substitute, which SNCC organizers gratefully accepted. Once Cleaver learned his conference was back on schedule, he flew to Nashville only to discover that a huge East Coast blizzard prevented all other speakers from attending. But then he learned that Carmichael had also defiantly headed for Nashville. Earlier that winter, Eldridge had interviewed Carmichael in Chicago and Atlanta for *Ramparts.* The two men met again and decided to crash the April conference at Vanderbilt together. After Carmichael addressed an angry crowd, police, students, and activists clashed in the worst violence in Nashville's history. The battleground over the next few days engulfed Fisk and nearby Tennessee Agriculture and Industry University, with students barricaded inside their dorms while police stormed the campuses. The violence quickly spread to include armed confrontations with the police in the black community at large.

Even after the violence had subsided, Cleaver remained in Nashville. Among the staff that had come from SNCC headquarters in Atlanta to oversee the two conferences was Kathleen Neal, a beautiful young recruit from New York. Cleaver became so infatuated with Neal that, when he learned she did not drive, he chauffeured her around Nashville on SNCC errands in his rental car. Axelrod grew so concerned by Cleaver's extended absence that she flew to Nashville to find him. Showing up on the Fisk campus wearing a California sun dress, sandals, and long, dangly earrings, Axelrod might not have been conspicuous if she had been twenty years younger and black. She caught up with Cleaver as he was about to transport several new young SNCC friends, including Neal, back to Atlanta. Cleaver introduced Axelrod to his new friends in Nashville simply as "my lawyer," leaving them quite curious and her palpably angry.

Axelrod's suspicions were confirmed after she returned to San Francisco. Cleaver had recently moved into his own apartment. Though he still spent a lot of time with Axelrod, as both helped launch *The Black Panther* newspaper, he kept up with Neal in a long distance romance. In April, Cleaver made a fiery speech at an anti-war rally in San Francisco, which he followed with his high-profile trip to Sacramento with the Panthers in early May. Not surprisingly, Cleaver was told that his speeches now needed to be vetted in advance by his parole officer and he could no longer travel out-of-state. Anxious to see Neal again, he invited her to visit him in San Francisco. Neal flew to San Francisco in early July and stayed with Cleaver for over a month. Still unable to drive, she depended totally on Cleaver to take her places. Once he disappeared for a couple of days and then called her to come by taxi to pick him up at Axelrod's house. It had been an awkward scene. During the several weeks that Neal stayed at Cleaver's apartment, Axelrod often parked her Volvo outside the apartment, spying on them. Axelrod was greatly relieved when Neal left in early August, unaware Cleaver had proposed to Neal the second day of her stay.

Shortly after Cleaver assumed the role of spokesperson for the Black Panther Party following Newton's arrest on murder charges, Cleaver called Neal in Atlanta and asked her to help fund-raise for the incipient "Free Huey" campaign. He also invited Neal to fly to California to help organize demonstrations on Newton's behalf. Neal had already met Newton when she was in California the prior summer: he often visited Cleaver at his San Francisco apartment. Neal immediately started soliciting contributions while still at SNCC headquarters in Atlanta. She then moved to the Bay Area in mid-November, as David Hilliard was gathering supporters for Newton's next hearing. Neal settled for good in Cleaver's apartment, and the two made wedding plans for late December. Cleaver soon had an ugly falling out with Axelrod. He told her he could no longer associate with white women. He then named his newly disclosed fiancée the Party's Communications Secretary, the only woman with a title.

Axelrod was deeply wounded. Newton empathized and offered to decree her an honorary black woman, but the rift between Axelrod and Cleaver made it impossible for her to continue to serve as a go-between. Newton's childhood friend, David Hilliard, began recruiting supporters in Berkeley and Oakland, with pointers from Kathleen Neal on what to say to get their attention.[3] When Eldridge Cleaver visited Newton in jail in late November, Newton told him he was convinced that if he went to trial, he would die in the gas chamber. In Cleaver's words, "His preference was to be broken out, to have a red-light trial, with the red lights flashing." Newton agreed to let Cleaver try to address the situation.[4]

Meanwhile, local black lawyers still lobbied hard for an experienced black criminal lawyer to replace Garry as lead counsel for the Panther Party founder. John George and Clinton White remained under consideration. The discontented group also considered Donald Warden, Newton's former mentor at the Afro-American Association, but were leery of Warden's track record—too many convictions. Seale had started out as an ally in seeking to replace Garry, but Seale also heard rumors that some unhappy former clients felt Warden had sold them short. Though unsubstantiated, the gossip from disgruntled inmates Warden had represented made Seale uneasy. Seale knew of Clinton White's stellar reputation as a trial lawyer and could not fathom how Garry had been selected instead. When Seale met Garry at his law offices in December of 1967, Seale immediately asked how much money it was going to cost. Garry responded, "Let's not worry about that."[5] Garry explained how he handled political trials and tried to reassure Seale of his Leftist credentials and philosophy.

Seale remained dissatisfied and went to see White, who asked for $10,000 to $12,000 in advance, which the Panthers did not have. Given White's reputation for taking many cases without pay, one colleague later guessed that White asked for the large advance fee to dissuade the Panthers from hiring him. White was more skilled than Garry, but definitely more traditional in his approach. He would not have promised or delivered a political defense as Garry was planning and likely felt quite relieved that this polarizing, high-profile trial was in someone else's hands. But it was also possible that the savvy trial lawyer simply realized that the Newton defense would be all-consuming and that he might risk bankruptcy, taking on such a huge case without a substantial advance fee.

Seale confirmed Garry's personal record of winning some two dozen murder trials. Garry had in fact first gained fame in the early '50s representing an African-American named Bob Wells, the street-fighting Armenian's first death-penalty case. Garry painted Wells—who was originally caught stealing a $26 suit as a teenager in the late 1920s—as a reincarnated Jean Valjean. A series of increased penalties for altercations put Wells on death row. Looking back three decades later, Garry called Bob Wells "the first Black Panther"[6] because of his feisty attitude toward his jailers. Psychiatric evidence of Wells' unbalanced mental state caused by beatings, hosings, and repeated isolation in the "hole", helped Garry win delays in Wells' scheduled execution. One writ was issued when Wells was only thirteen hours away from death. A successful public-relations campaign eventually convinced Gov. Knight to change Wells' sentence to life without possibility of parole.

In 1959, the California Supreme Court had reaffirmed the admissibility of psychiatric evidence of diminished capacity to commit murder in *People v. Gorshen.* In representing Gorshen, Garry and Dreyfus had relied on the admissibility of similar evidence in the prior *Wells* case. From then on, the diminished-capacity partial defense became known in California as the *Wells-Gorshen* rule. Proof of impairment would not result in acquittal, but conviction only of a lesser-level crime. A defendant who acted with diminished capacity would not have the mental state needed to prove first-degree murder: proof beyond a reasonable doubt of premeditation, deliberation, and specific intent to kill. When Seale met Garry, the determined lawyer was still working periodically to secure Wells' release, a long term project finally realized in 1974. With funding offered from the Communist Party and Garry's impressive record as a radical defense lawyer, Seale decided that the best course was to accept Garry even though other Panthers remained vehemently opposed to any white lawyer. Garry himself later admitted: "I thought I knew something about Negro America because some of my intimate friends are Negro professionals who have been accepted partially in our great white society . . . It wasn't a week or two weeks after I got into this case, I came to the conclusion I knew absolutely nothing about black America." [7]

Seale and Cleaver had to repeatedly argue to other Panthers against judging Garry "by the color of his skin."[8] White was too expensive, Warden and George too risky. George was also too cautious for their taste. When representing the rival, Black Panthers of Northern California (founded by SNCC), George had advised these "paper Panthers" to walk around sporting unloaded weapons. Newton would never do that. Seale, Cleaver, and his bride Kathleen remained unable to convince all doubters. Some quit the defense committee, while local black lawyers took their grievance to the press, arguing the legal work should have gone to a black brother. And so it was that America's black Che Guevara came to be represented by a white radical lawyer the Panthers did not completely trust.

Ironically, the law firm paid a high price for taking on Newton's representation. As the firm's principle rainmaker, Garry had been bringing in $20,000 to $30,000 per month in personal injury fees before he took on the Newton case. The firm's support for the Black Panthers also did not sit well with some of its other clients. A large labor union that new partner Al Brotsky had just brought to the firm took all of its legal work elsewhere. As the Panthers' debt to the partnership grew, Seale realized that many of the black lawyers who wanted a piece of the action would not have held on anywhere near as long without getting paid. He did not regret his decision to endorse Garry or the equally controversial decision he and Cleaver made to keep strong ties with the Peace and Freedom Party. As Seale saw it, the road to success required allying themselves with like-minded whites.

6. HONKIES FOR HUEY

They took away Sacco, Vanzetti,
Connelly and Pearse in their time
They came for Newton and Seale

From "No Time for Love" by the Irish political folk-rock group "The Moving Hearts"

At the next pretrial hearing in the Newton case in December of 1967, among the prominent picketers were Free Speech Movement Leaders Mario Savio and Jack Weinberg as well as Bob Avakian, the radical son of Judge Spurgeon Avakian of the Alameda County Superior Court. All three were then leaders of the Peace and Freedom Party, which still consisted mostly of white anti-war radicals. The Peace and Freedom Party viewed the Newton trial as a great opportunity to cement an alliance with radical blacks. It formally passed a resolution calling for Newton's freedom and offered $3,000 towards defense costs. This overture coincided with its support of members of "The Oakland Seven."

Guild members Beverly Axelrod and Alex Hoffmann were among the first attorneys to represent demonstrators arrested during "Stop the Draft Week." It was during a jail visit to a defendant in "The Oakland Seven" that Axelrod introduced Hoffmann to Huey Newton, then held in a nearby cell. Hoffmann had been curious to meet Newton since the day he had helped Axelrod confront Police Chief Gain to obtain permission for twenty-four-hour nursing care for Newton to protect him against the police. Arrangements were also made for Hilliard and Seale to attend a meeting of the Stop the Draft steering committee and ask them for their support. One of their members, Karen Wald, had valid press credentials and was deputized to visit Newton at the Alameda County jail. Hoffmann then joined the Newton defense team in Axelrod's stead as she abandoned her California practice and fled the state for New Mexico, unable to remain any longer in the same community following her emotionally devastating rejection by Cleaver and his followers among the Black Panther Party she had helped launch. Before Axelrod left, she exacted a measure of payback by drafting an agreement for Cleaver to sign, granting her twenty-five percent of the net proceeds of his book *Soul On Ice* "in perpetuity."[1] Axelrod showed up at Cleaver's apartment to obtain his signature while Kathleen looked on from the bedroom as a silent observer. The two women would not formally be introduced to each other until Eldridge Cleaver's memorial service thirty years later.

For the December hearing in the *Newton* case, demonstrators first conducted a rally on the Berkeley campus and then moved to the Alameda courthouse, shouting "Free Huey" and "Support the Oakland Seven." The first-floor corridor and entrances of the courthouse were blocked by about 400 Black Panthers, Peace and Freedom Party members, and other demonstrators, including a large turnout of a new white radical support group, "Honkys for Huey," who hauled down the American flag at the courthouse and reraised it upside down as a distress signal. Inside the courtroom at the December hearing, Judge Staats had to silence the audience as they cheered Garry's remarks. Garry argued that the evidence before the grand jury was not enough to hold Newton on the murder charges. The witnesses had not seen Newton holding any weapon in his hand, nor had the prosecutor even identified the murder weapon. Garry posited that officer Herbert Heanes might have killed Frey accidentally. The judge was not persuaded.

At this early stage of the proceedings, Newton was kept in the same cell block within earshot of defendants in the Oakland Seven case. Concerned officials moved Huey to an isolation cell on the tenth floor. To keep his spirits up, he kept a dog-eared copy of *The Wretched of the Earth* in his cell, which he reread in between visits from friends, family, reporters, and lawyers. He had to enjoy the alarmed account in a local paper of Seale firing up supporters in the streets of Richmond by calling the prosecution "trumped up charges by the white racist, Gestapo pig cops. That was no murder in Oakland. That was the execution of a pig cop."[2] The small cell often grew so unbearably warm that Huey peeled off his flannel jail uniform and paced naked. He could sometimes hear cries of "Free Huey" raised by followers on the sidewalk below.

At the next hearing in January of 1968, Garry arrived with a briefcase overflowing with the more than two dozen motions Stender and other members of his team had feverishly assembled over the past few weeks. The motions sought disclosure of police reports and the names of all witnesses whom the D.A.'s office might call to testify against Newton. They included a request that the prosecutor identify all other evidence he intended to rely on. Garry also asked the judge to permit him to order the appearance of former grand jurors who had recently testified before an Assembly committee in Sacramento on major flaws in the grand jury system. As soon as he took the bench, Judge Staats revealed that he had received a gold-embossed invitation to a fund-raising cocktail party for Newton. As he started to say he did not consider it appropriate to attend, Newton interrupted, telling the judge it was too bad, because he would have enjoyed himself. The circus atmosphere had begun. Outside were many young black picketers mostly recruited by David Hilliard. At Kathleen Cleaver's urging, they chanted loudly enough to be heard inside the room: "Huey will be set free! Free Huey now! Down with Gestapo pigs! Black power!"[3]

Garry only won permission to subpoena the superior court judge who had presided over the 1967 grand jury selection. He would be allowed to question the jurist regarding the method used. Judge Staats set January 26, 1968, for argument of the constitutional challenge to the grand jury. He also took under submission all the other motions Garry had made, intending to rule on them later. The judge then requested Newton's plea to the murder and related charges. On Newton's behalf, Garry pled not guilty to all three counts. He asserted that the 1964 assault conviction was invalid because Newton had never received any legal counsel in defending against that charge. The validity of this prior conviction would be a key issue; unless it was voided, the jury would hear about it if he testified, and it could easily prejudice the jury against Newton. Outside, after the hearing, Seale urged the boisterous crowd to return to the next hearing in late January and asked each to bring two additional picketers.

Ironically, the very same day, *The Oakland Tribune* featured the passing of eighty-nine-year-old "Raincoat" Jones, the city's most flamboyant black resident of the past half century. Due to his declining health and fortunes, "Raincoat" Jones had not been seen for years on the blocks of Seventh Street he once owned. Yet the overflow bi-racial crowd of mourners ranged from high-level city officials and West Oakland businessmen to hustlers and regular patrons, all of whose lives had been touched by the unforgettable old-timer. As reporters noted the casket generously strewn with flowers, it is unlikely any realized their papers were already covering the first stages of the next, far more transformative era of community-police relations.

Back in his cell, Newton continued to receive visitors, who strained to hear him through a three-by-twelve-inch window in his isolated cell. The first week of January, a Kaiser Hospital lawyer sought to take Newton's deposition under oath about his pending claim for malpractice. In mid-January, Newton gave an exclusive interview to white radicals from *The Berkeley Barb.* In it, he talked about how he and Garry thought the Kaiser lawyers were acting at the bidding of the D.A. to induce him to make incriminating statements. Instead of focusing on the manacles that held the wounded Newton to the gurney, the Kaiser lawyer had sought information about the shooting that had occurred before Newton reached Kaiser, a line of inquiry both Garry and Newton considered highly suspect. A representative of the prosecutor's office had recently appeared at a hearing on the Kaiser suit, pressing for similar details. Rather than risk having Newton explain his version of the shooting, which could be used against Newton in the murder case, Garry dismissed the malpractice action. By then, the civil suit had served its true purpose of generating positive publicity for Newton and rallying supporters to his cause.

Garry realized a bit late that he should not allow any press unfettered access to Newton, even if it was a friendly underground paper, because anything Newton said could be used against him. Shortly after *The Berkeley Barb* interview, Garry issued ground rules that no interviews with Newton would take place without an attorney present. This not only brought any future statements Newton made to the press under his attorneys' control, but provided a more civilized setting for all future interviews—an attorney-client meeting room with table and chairs.

Another large crowd of supporters attended the January 26, 1968, hearing. By then vocal opposition was also mounting. Late that night the defense team got a crank anonymous call describing Garry as a "Nigger lover." Upon learning that Garry had gone home to bed, the caller left a chilling message: "Hope you keep on sleeping forever and soundly."[4] Staff simply chronicled this and later threats in the same manner as other office messages and kept them in the case file for presentation to the court. The prosecutor also collected threats received by witnesses and the police: an anonymous male caller had dialed the home number in San Francisco of Dr. Thomas Finch, the first physician to treat Huey Newton at Kaiser Hospital, and threatened the doctor's life if he returned to Oakland.

7. THE SMELL OF REVOLUTION

We counted history from Huey's night of truth.

ELDRIDGE CLEAVER

With money from Cleaver's advance for *Soul On Ice*, the Panthers decided to open a new storefront office in North Oakland. Back in late June of 1967, the Panthers had built on the momentum from their theatrical moment in Sacramento by another dramatic announcement. As their Second Executive Mandate, Newton and Cleaver sought to link the Panthers to SNCC by calling a press conference to proclaim Stokely Carmichael as their new "Field Marshal . . . [with authority to] establish revolutionary laws, order, and justice . . . [East of the Continental Divide]."[1] Although Carmichael was honored by the unsought proclamation, that effort to form a tie with SNCC fizzled. H. Rap Brown had just replaced Carmichael as head of SNCC and Carmichael was headed off on his own personal extended speaking tour of Cuba, China, North Vietnam, and Africa.

After Carmichael returned to the United States, Cleaver and Seale talked the Peace and Freedom Party into paying their expenses to go to Washington, D.C., to convince Carmichael to come to the Black Panthers' aid. They were planning a major fund-raiser to be held at the Oakland Arena on Newton's twenty-sixth birthday, February 17, 1968. The city had initially refused to rent the facility to discourage the possibility of riots, but the Panthers had brought an attorney with them, who obtained the venue by threateningto go to court to enforce their First Amendment right to peaceable assembly.

When they met with SNCC officials in Washington, D.C., Cleaver and Seale ran into further opposition for hiring a white attorney to defend Newton and for forming a coalition with the mostly white Peace and Freedom Party. The two Panthers assured SNCC leaders that the alliance was tentative and limited in scope. They succeeded in bringing back a skeptical Carmichael for his first major public address since his return to the country and also lured H. Rap Brown and James Forman of SNCC to Oakland as well. Forman was now living with Decca Mitford's daughter, Friends of SNCC organizer Dinky Romilly. Forman objected to the Black Panthers' plan to name Carmichael its Honorary Prime Minister. He suggested H. Rap Brown, revealing a rift between Carmichael and other SNCC leaders that the Panthers had not previously appreciated. The Panthers decided instead to give all SNCC leaders positions of importance in the Party. Titles were cheap, even if their scope was ill-defined. The Panthers thought this would cement a SNCC-Panther alliance with access to SNCC's national infrastructure, not realizing it was then crumbling.

Just before the rally, Carmichael made a quick visit to Newton in the Alameda County jail, telling him that the only way he would get out was "armed rebellion culminating in race war." Huey disagreed. Carmichael then told Newton he had no faith in the Black Panther alliance with the Peace and Freedom Party, warning Newton "that whites would destroy the movement, alienate Black people, and lessen our effectiveness in the community."[2] But Newton rejected Carmichael's argument as weak and misguided.

Police Chief Gain contacted Cleaver in advance of the rally to offer traffic supervision for the anticipated crowd. Cleaver turned him down. The event attracted three generations of people from the black community as well as radical white longshoremen, students, and professionals. Adults paid $3, students $2, and the unemployed half-price. Networks had inquired about coverage, but refused to pay $1000 each for the privilege. The Panthers raised $10,000 and would soon draw a similarly huge crowd in Los Angeles, featuring most of the same speakers. The defense funds were sorely needed; the entire Garry firm was then working "round-the-clock," with at least $30,000 of time billed on the case so far. To the surprise of the police, the Oakland fund-raiser turned out to be well-managed, disciplined, and peaceful—an unprecedented gathering, as Eldridge called it, of "the biggest line-up of revolutionary leaders that had ever come together under one roof in the history of America"[3] (colonial insurgents in the 18th century obviously being excluded). SNCC leaders had only reluctantly agreed to share the podium with Bob Avakian of the Peace and Freedom Party. The Panthers, in turn, let Forman include Maulana Ron Karenga, a former Oaklander named Ron Everett. Karenga founded the holiday of Kwanzaa in December 1966. He now headed the rival black militant group, US, in Los Angeles. Huey's mother, Amelia Newton, joined them on stage, as did Berkeley City Council member Ron Dellums.

An empty wicker chair sat center stage at the rally—the same one in the photograph featured in almost every issue of the Panther newspaper, depicting a seated Huey Newton holding a spear and a shotgun with African shields on either side of him and a zebra rug under his feet. Ironically, in recent months Newton had told everyone he hated that primitive image. He considered it cartoon-like. But Newton had used similar symbolism himself in speaking of the fear that the man who invented the spear had engendered in people, until the shield was invented to protect them from its use. He, the wicker chair, and accompanying props now symbolized for Party members and their supporters "a shield for black people against all the imperialism, the decadence, the aggression and the racism in the country."[4] Copies of the poster soon adorned the walls of all new Panther branches and in dorms on college campuses across America.

With the empty throne as backdrop, many speakers talked of Newton in the past tense as having given his life for the cause. Amelia refused to consider that possibility—the heartsick mother could not believe her youngest son would be found guilty and summoned the strength to make her own plea for help to the crowd. Rap Brown railed against his listeners as "chumps" for buying into a white society. He called recently appointed Supreme Court Justice Thurgood Marshall a "Tom of a high order" and condemned the status quo for blacks in America.

Garry was the only lawyer invited to speak. Despite his best efforts, the audience did not share Garry's faith in securing Newton's acquittal. Over the past year both Seale and Newton had repeatedly exhorted their followers to kill oppressive cops. In a *New York Times* magazine profile less than three months before the Oakland shooting, Newton had boldly repeated that "every time you execute a white racist Gestapo cop, you are defending yourselves."[5] Newton stated that, when the time came, he was both willing to kill a cop and willing to die as part of a coordinated national revolt. All the other speakers at the birthday rally gave the impression they believed that Huey had followed through on his boast. They expected him to be convicted and sentenced to death. If that occurred, Forman warned, "The sky is the limit."[6] Bobby Seale had severe misgivings about that threat, but went along with the overwhelming sentiment of the others.

Carmichael followed with his own incendiary speech. He changed into an African robe for emphasis before taking the podium to urge blacks to reject Communism and Socialism in favor of an ideology solely for blacks. Carmichael ended by proclaiming, "Brother Huey belongs to *us*." His exclusion of anyone not black alienated many of the radical whites in attendance. Carmichael continued, "He is flesh of our flesh, he is blood of our blood . . . Brother Huey will be set free—or else."[7]

8. CLIENT OR COMRADE?

He is a truly great man. Huey is a loving, gentle, kind person. . . . He has a righteous force, a fierce combination of moral outrage and anger.

FAY STENDER

Since Garry was planning a political defense, Newton had given his attorneys background on the origin and purpose of the Black Panther Party, as well as a reading list. At his suggestion, Garry and Stender were now studying the writings of Malcolm X and the revolutionary Frantz Fanon, among other authors. Unlike SNCC, Newton and Seale still welcomed white support for their revolutionary efforts. In the new year, Stender began visiting Newton more regularly in jail. Nowadays she was dressing chicly and making sure her fingernails were painted and her lipstick was on when she met with her charismatic client. Captivated by Newton's courage and intelligence, she was but one of a growing number of smitten women devotees of the handsome icon. Garry charged Stender with putting together a motion to have Newton released on bail, which they expected Jensen to vigorously oppose. She needed to gather personal information she could use to show Newton posed little risk of flight prior to trial. With gentle persistence, the deceptively soft-spoken lawyer learned from Newton that he was taught to play classical music from a tutor and had developed a fondness for Tchaikovsky's Nutcracker Suite. It immediately deepened the attraction she had felt at her first sight of him, bare-chested under armed police guard in a hospital room.

Stender was born Fay Ethel Abrahams in San Francisco in March of 1932, the older of two daughters of an ambitious middle-class Jewish couple. She had been a child prodigy at the piano; the family spent much of its time and discretionary funds from her father's career as an asbestos expert to focus on developing Fay's talent. At age fourteen, after ten years of private lessons, she had been offered a solo performance at the San Francisco Symphony. Shortly afterward, she rebelled against her parents and the rigors of concert training. By the time she graduated college, she was radicalized by a Marxist professor she had fallen recklessly in love with and abandoned any thought of music as her career. Fay aspired instead to become a lawyer to challenge the inequities in the world. She wanted desperately to wield the power to change things.

Fay met her husband, fellow Guild lawyer Marvin Stender, in law school at the University of Chicago where he graduated two years ahead of her. Their rocky marriage of more than two decades had involved more than one separation, but both remained devoted to Movement causes. Even when apart, they socialized as well as worked in the same Leftist circle of activists. The spring before, Fay had toasted Beverly Axelrod and Eldridge Cleaver at a party in the Berkeley hills celebrating the publication of *Soul On Ice* as well as Axelrod and Cleaver's engagement. The idea of a similar opportunity for her own close relationship with the Panther Party's chief strategist was intoxicating. Newton further impressed Stender by telling her that he learned to read for the first time after high school, by repeatedly tackling his brother Melvin's copy of Plato's *Republic.* She was amazed to learn that Huey also had taken a course in criminal law for a semester. Ironically, one of his professors had been Ed Meese, moonlighting from his job as assistant district attorney in Alameda. By 1968, Meese had moved on to head Gov. Reagan's staff.

With so many second-guessers and political followers of the Panthers counting on them to keep Newton from the gas chamber, Stender felt enormous pressure to deliver first-rate legal assistance to Garry. Although there was no realistic chance that the local superior court would free Newton on bail while he faced charges of murdering a policeman, anything that could be attempted would be done. Garry encouraged such constant legal activity because it also helped keep Newton's supporters motivated and guaranteed sustained news coverage. The California Constitution allowed an arrestee's release prior to trial on payment of a bond "unless for capital offenses when the proof is evident or the presumption great."[1] Since Newton was charged with a capital offense, Stender set out to convince the court that proof was *not* "evident" *nor* "the presumption great." There was no evidence of premeditation; no competent evidence Newton had a gun; and no evidence he planned a crime. The bail motion was denied, just after the Newton birthday rally. The judge also rejected their attack on the grand jury.

Meanwhile, on January 16, the police had raided Cleaver's San Francisco apartment before dawn, kicking in his front door. On February 28, 1968, the Berkeley police invaded Seale's home, also without a warrant. The police charged the five people they found there, including Seale and his wife, David Hilliard and Bunchy Carter (an ex-felon friend of Cleaver's recruited from Southern California) with conspiracy to commit murder and criminal violations for unlawful possession of weapons whose identifying marks had been obliterated. Judge Lionel Wilson would dismiss the sensational conspiracy charge; the minor weapons charges would be prosecuted. The same day, three other Panthers were stopped for a minor traffic offense, searched and charged with violating laws prohibiting concealed firearms and carrying loaded firearms in public. The Panthers and their lawyers saw a pattern in these arrests evidencing a purpose to harass and crush the Party. Newton quickly issued Executive Mandate No. 3 ordering all Panthers to defend their homes with weapons against illegal searches or be permanently expelled from the Party.[2]

Garry considered it vital to delay the trial. He desperately needed breathing room while his office investigated the circumstances of the October shooting. It was Stender's job to exhaust all avenues for appellate review of Judge Staats' ruling denying the challenge to the all-white grand jury. She prepared a detailed petition to the First District Court of Appeal, denied the very next day without opinion. The next step was a petition for hearing before the California Supreme Court. Barney Dreyfus oversaw her efforts as constitutional law specialists outside the firm provided the pair a continuous stream of advice.

Stender and Dreyfus knew they had an uphill fight, but proceeded aggressively on several fronts. One was an attack on the institution of the grand jury itself as an anachronism lacking constitutional safeguards because of its secrecy, failure to permit cross-examination of witnesses, and denial of any advance warning to the defendant of the evidence to be used against him. Other angles included an attack on the statutes by which the grand jury was selected and the method by which judges picked the panel—not from a cross-section of the community, but from a short list of middle-class contemporaries, excluding blacks, the working class, and the young. The defense team also argued that the grand jury acted too fast to have truly made any decision on the evidence in front of them. These were like arguments Stender had used to no avail against deferments denied her former clients by draft boards. Reconstructing the grand jury's actions, Stender and Dreyfus concluded the grand jury had heard the evidence, gone to lunch, and issued its indictment just under half an hour afterward, including roll call, the prosecutor's explanation of the law, and the court's instructions. Where was there any time spent on deliberations? Lastly, the two lawyers argued that the grand jury was not presented any reasonable basis to believe Newton murdered Officer Frey or assaulted Heanes because no one testified Newton had a gun in his possession and no such weapon was ever found.

Irregularities in selecting grand jurors, even if shown, historically did not prevent a criminal case from going to trial. The Attorney General's office answered each argument in turn. The grand jury system is centuries old and recognized in the Constitution. The limited record on the selection process did not demonstrate systematic discrimination by age, race, or economic class; and, most importantly, there was ample evidence to support a determination of Newton's guilt. At this preliminary stage, the prosecutor needed only to demonstrate probable cause to believe Newton committed the offense. "Probable cause" meant reasonable grounds to arrest Newton for the offense, a far lower threshold than the high standard of proof beyond a reasonable doubt which the prosecutor would have to meet at trial. Here, they had an undisputed exchange of gunfire, one officer dead and Newton and another officer wounded. In addition, the grand jurors heard the damning testimony of Dell Ross identifying Newton as one of two men who kidnapped him minutes later. Ross testified that the wounded kidnapper had a gun and that he heard the pair discussing the man had just shot "two dudes."[3]

While the Garry firm awaited word from the Supreme Court, trial preparation proceeded. The law firm subscribed to a news-clipping service to make sure the attorneys did not miss any negative press about the case to bring to the trial judge's attention. Volunteers also reported biased radio and television coverage. Pretrial publicity in sensationalized murder cases had just become a hot legal topic. The American Bar Association asked a special commission to address the problem. Its report came out in February of 1968 with a startling statistic: adverse newspaper publicity often resulted in the disqualification of 99 out of every 100 potential jurors in a high profile murder case.

The commission suggested that media be prohibited from publishing a defendant's prior criminal record, whether he had confessed, the identity of proposed witnesses, and most other material relating to the merits of the case. None of the ABA's recommendations would be in force for the Newton trial. Instead, it would be up to the trial judge to make his own orders, and no one had yet been assigned. In the meantime, police, other public officials, and the defense attorneys waged a publicity war, though Lowell Jensen's office steered clear of the media fireworks.

During this time, more calls and letters poured in to the defense team with suggestions or information that they might want to follow up on, some of which proved quite useful. Cleaver left a message for Garry supposedly received from a source inside the Oakland Police Department to the effect that when the police learned Newton was at Kaiser, they were given an order to work him over. Treuhaft forwarded an inflammatory clipping from *Newsweek* describing Newton as a man with a "rage so blinding he can look on white America comfortably only through the cross hairs of a gun." The article quoted Newton as saying, "Guns are very, very political. A gun makes me immediately equal to anyone in the world."[4] The defense team also learned that a San Francisco radio station had started one March broadcast with the preface "Cop Killer Huey Newton." A local paper quoted an unnamed state legislator prejudging Newton's guilt.

A tip came in for Garry of a witness who lived over a record shop near the Willow Street intersection where the shooting had occurred. The witness was said to have observed a very tall man do the shooting, not a man of five-foot-ten as Newton was. The firm employed investigators to assist Garry in tracking down this man and other witnesses, including interviewing a number of prostitutes who lived and worked in the area. They were desperate to find someone, anyone, who could help them deliver on their mission to set Newton free.

As the trial date loomed menacingly, Garry took to walking at night in the run-down West Oakland neighborhood where the shooting took place, hoping to meet someone who could provide useful evidence for the defense. He could not bear to think of Newton becoming the first client he lost to the death penalty. Garry had once dug up the trial record of the Rosenberg espionage case and convinced himself that he could have won their acquittal had he been their trial attorney. Freeing Huey seemed a far more formidable challenge.

9. POWER TO THE PEOPLE

Free black panthers
Free humanism
Free black men
Free goodness & honor
Free Huey, now,
And Free us all.
SARAH WEBSTER FABIO

A death penalty case then pending before the United States Supreme Court offered a ray of hope. The defense attorneys in *Witherspoon v. Illinois* challenged the prosecutor's right to disqualify prospective jurors simply because they generally opposed capital punishment. The result of this practice was death-oriented juries. This was an issue on which Garry's firm had already undertaken extensive research in *People v. Ketchel*, then en route to its third death penalty appeal. *Witherspoon* was of huge importance to the Newton defense team, which would do everything possible to keep jurors opposed to the death penalty on the panel. Oral argument before the United States Supreme Court was scheduled for late April of 1968. At best, its ruling could be expected sometime toward the end of spring—another reason to push for as late a trial date as possible for Huey Newton.

The defense still wondered who would take the bench as the trial judge. Local rules provided that the judge would be chosen by forty-five days before the trial. Odds were that they would draw a white male since almost all of the twenty local judges fit that description. Lionel Wilson was the only African-American superior court judge in the county, and the only woman on that bench was former prosecutor Cecil Mosbacher. Garry considered Mosbacher, a conservative hardliner on crime, a worse draw than most of her male counterparts. On March 10, they found out that the judge they drew was liberal, seventy-two-year-old Monroe Friedman. He had a reputation for being very organized and strictly controlling his courtroom. They knew the draw could have been much, much worse. Judge Friedman was a Democrat appointed to the superior court by Gov. Pat Brown in 1959, after a failed nomination to the federal bench by lame-duck President Truman. By the spring of 1968, Judge Friedman was one of the most senior judges in the county, and as such, the bespectacled 1920 graduate of U.C. Berkeley's Boalt Hall could have easily declined the controversial and thankless assignment. Instead, the former presiding judge figured it would be his last major case and would be as good a way as any to end his career. He set the trial for May 10.

Judge Friedman was not considered one of the sharpest judges on the local bench, but thorough, with a low reversal rate. Garry, the self-proclaimed streetfighter in the courtroom, did not relish the idea of being kept on a short leash, but he did not believe the defense had a realistic choice. Though he had the right to refuse Judge Friedman and get someone else assigned, he did not want to gamble and draw someone far worse whom he could not remove. If a particularly difficult judge were assigned—of which there were several Garry could name—he would have to risk contempt citations at every turn, hoping to lure the judge into committing mistakes that the court of appeal would feel compelled to reverse. To Garry's knowledge, only about one percent of criminal convictions were ever reversed on appeal. No. This case would have to be won at trial.

The defense doggedly pursued a strategy to convince Judge Friedman to delay the trial date for at least two months. To win more favorable public opinion, the Newton team published a declaration signed by forty-five members of the local black community describing Officer Frey's reputation as an aggressive and obstinate officer, a discredit to the Oakland Police Department. Meanwhile Garry granted as many interviews with Newton as possible with Left-leaning media. Substantial interest had already been generated by an early political interview of Newton in *The*

Movement by two Free Speech Movement arrestees whom Newton had first seen at Santa Rita in December of 1964. One of them, Joe Blum, knew Newton from Merritt College. Newton considered Blum a trusted friend. He shared with Blum his philosophy and view that "The Black Panther Party is the beacon of light to show Black People the way to liberation."[1]

Now requests for additional interviews came in fast and furiously: Ray Rogers of *The Los Angeles Times*; freelance reporter Karen Wald; Eldridge Cleaver for *Ramparts* magazine; Kennedy assassination conspiracy theorist Mark Lane; Joan Didion from *The Saturday Evening Post*; Collin Edwards and Elsa Knight Thompson from local public radio station KPFA; and even a reporter from the decidedly unfriendly *Oakland Tribune*. As armed deputies looked on through a thick glass partition, Huey enjoyed puffing on cigarettes offered by some of his visitors and educating the press about the party platform and its goals. Each interview required a separate permission slip to be prepared for Garry's signature and submitted in advance to the County Sheriff. Once approved, every reporter would be accompanied by a member of the legal staff, often Alex Hoffmann, sometimes Fay Stender, and, rarely, Charles Garry.

Meanwhile, the California Supreme Court declined to review their grand jury challenge. Notice of the ruling had simply arrived at the law office by postcard, signed on March 28 by Chief Justice Traynor. Her quest for pretrial review temporarily exhausted, Stender lost no time moving onto her next challenge: finding sociologists to testify at trial. She already was acquainted with activist David Wellman, who had co-authored the favorable article about Newton in *The Movement*. They had met at a joint gathering of Friends of SNCC and staff of *The Movement* in August of 1964 when they were planning ahead for Freedom Summer 1965. Wellman had reacted to meeting Fay Stender as did the students at "Legal Central" who had coordinated lawyer assistance for their friends arrested in the Free Speech Movement in December of 1964: Stender simply left him in awe. Wellman noticed how she drew people in with her soft voice, but then could bowl them over with her insights. He recalled her at the Friends of SNCC meeting quietly raising excellent points. That impression was reaffirmed whenever their paths crossed.

Stender knew that Wellman was working on a Ph.D. in race relations at Cal Berkeley. She asked him to bring a couple of his professors with him to her home in Berkeley to have them help her strategize for trial—then a novel concept. Wellman still recalled four decades later how thrilled he was. Here she was both a confirmed Leftist and an articulate, well-dressed woman lawyer. Wellman still knew of few women lawyers of any political persuasion. Fay Stender seemed to have it all. She was married, had two children, was physically attractive, intense, and smart. Now she was his access to a front seat at the Huey Newton trial. He would do whatever she asked. The first meeting at Stender's home included Wellman, Sociology Prof. Jan Dizard, and Assistant Sociology Prof. Robert Blauner. In the last few years, Blauner had made race issues his primary focus. After a productive evening session exchanging ideas, Stender provided the experts with the intelligence test then given Alameda County prospective jurors. She accompanied the document with a short lesson on the law and explained the grounds for challenging jurors for bias in criminal cases. Her aim was to use the professors' help to get as diverse a jury as possible and, if need be, to create a record for appeal.

The defense was buoyed by a brand new trial court ruling which held unconstitutional the IQ tests used to screen local jurors. The timing could not have been better. The victory was the brainchild of two deputy public defenders, Bob Boags, then the first and only African-American in the Alameda County Public Defender's Office, and one of his two women colleagues, Penny Cooper. Female deputies would remain scarce. The Public Defender considered himself on a mission to protect women from embarking on such a seamy practice, telling interviewees in the mid-'60s that the job was "like going down a sewer in a glass bottom boat." The pair of young criminal defense lawyers had secretly strategized for over a year when to bring a test case challenging the IQ tests as racially biased. During that time, Boags gathered expert opinions and crafted motion papers to hold in readiness. Ultimately, Cooper spotted on the master calendar a low-stakes criminal case with a black defendant that the Presiding Judge assigned for trial to Judge Spurgeon Avakian. He was the only local judge they perceived to be liberal enough to give serious consideration to their proposed constitutional attack on the fairness of the standard IQ test.

When Boags brought the motion in *People v. Craig*, the prosecutor was taken completely by surprise. Confronted with undisputed evidence that only 14.5 percent of residents of white middle class neighborhoods flunked the intelligence test, while 81.5 percent of those in the ghetto of West Oakland failed it, the judge focused on questions like:

23. If a person asks you for something you do not have, you should:
    1) Tell him to mind his own business;
    2) Say you don't have it;
    3) Walk away.
25. If it rains when you are starting to go for the doctor, should you:
    1) Stay at home;
    2) Take an umbrella;
    3) Wait until it stops raining.

The judge could not see how a person's choice of one of these answers over another bore on their intelligence. Rather, they produced unrepresentative jury pools by focusing on vocabulary and presumed conventional wisdom not often shared by ethnic minorities. Judge Avakian concluded the test was both biased and of questionable use. Prominent East Bay attorney Tom Berkley, the publisher and editor-in-chief of *The Oakland Post,* California's largest black and Latino newspaper, applauded the ruling. Berkley noted that black lawyers considered the out-moded IQ test "absurd, misleading and wicked," measuring "moral and social attitudes and level of education rather than mental capacity" with an intrinsic cultural, education, and environmental bias.[2]

Though Judge Avakian's rejection of the IQ test was a good sign, Stender realized they would still be hard-pressed to use the ruling to their advantage. The Presiding Judge had just announced that the county was now dropping the IQ tests, and the old policy would not have any effect on the jury pool for the upcoming Newton trial, still set for early May. Stender asked the experts to review the analysis in *People v. Craig* and promised to let them know when their testimony might be needed. In the month of April, the professors heard nothing at all from Stender because the Garry firm's frantic trial preparations received a shocking last minute reprieve. On April 4, Martin Luther King, Jr. was assassinated by a lone rifleman when the civil rights giant stood on the balcony of his motel room in Memphis, Tennessee. The murder of this unwavering pacifist generated an immediate visceral response throughout the country, halting presidential candidates in their tracks as they absorbed the enormous impact of this tragedy just days after embattled President Johnson—demoralized by his dismal polls and the quagmire of the Vietnam War—had startled the nation by announcing his decision not to seek reelection, leaving the Democratic field wide open.

Facing violent unrest against whites in nearly a hundred cities, President Johnson declared a national day of mourning and ordered flags flown at half mast—the first time ever for the death of a black man in America, and only the third ever noted for any private citizen.[3] Gathering African-American leaders to the White House, the President vowed that King's dream had not died with him, but would become a blueprint for united action to assure young blacks that the "fullness of life" would not be denied them "because of the color of their skin."[4] A sea change was occurring in national race consciousness. Many white leaders were overcome with shame, blaming pervasive white racism for Dr. King's death and vowing to work together with black communities to address "the white problem."[5] As President Johnson convened a special joint session of Congress to address new proposed legislation, coverage of the assassination of Dr. King trumped regularly televised shows.

All three African-American megastars slated to perform at the Academy Awards on April 9—Louis Armstrong, Sammy Davis, Jr., and Diahann Carroll—withdrew. So did Sidney Poitier, the country's very first black matinee idol. To avoid appearing insensitive, the network then postponed the annual event for two days out of respect for Dr. King. Then Katherine Hepburn won an unexpected Oscar for best actress in *Guess Who's Coming to Dinner?*[6] The comedy drama, in which Hepburn played her last role opposite Spencer Tracy, revolved around Liberal parents surprised by their daughter's proposed inter-racial marriage to a doctor, portrayed by Poitier. The stilted, groundbreaking film proved exceedingly popular at the box office, hitting the theaters the same year that the Supreme Court had finally ruled anti-miscegenation laws unconstitutional.

Meanwhile, newspapers counted over twenty deaths from violence following King's assassination by an unknown sniper. Despite thousands of arrests for curfew violations, widespread looting and firebombing broke out in Chicago, Baltimore, Detroit, Kansas City, and Washington, D.C. More than sixty thousand National and State Guardsmen were mobilized to keep the peace. Outbreaks of vandalism prompted Oakland and several other Bay Area communities with large black populations to close their schools.

Coincidentally, the day before the assassination a dozen Oakland police wielding shotguns arrived at the church of Huey Newton's pastor, Rev. Earl Neil. The police were accompanied by two local clergymen, one of whom was black, apparently both asked along to lend legitimacy to the intrusion. The police claimed they were searching for a fugitive, but Eldridge Cleaver later assumed they were after him and Bobby Seale. The Panthers had recently switched to using St. Augustine's as a regular meeting place, having guessed correctly that their own headquarters were bugged. Cleaver had just left a meeting run by David Hilliard. The young black pastor was already alarmed by a letter from a sympathetic black Berkeley policeman warning that Seale and Cleaver's lives were in grave danger. Hilliard blocked access to the sanctuary, while the normally soft-spoken, bespectacled Rev. Neil insisted that the police leave. Rev. Neil was so outraged that he immediately called a press conference to denounce the armed intrusion as a Nazi storm trooper-tactic.

News of the Oakland church invasion was quickly dwarfed by coverage of King's death. Memorial tributes came from all sectors of the community, including one from Oakland's Republican Mayor John Reading, who had just been designated by Gov. Reagan to represent the state of California at the televised service for Dr. King in Atlanta, Georgia. But anger simmered in the black community. The media reported that Stokely Carmichael was inciting all blacks to pick up guns and seek revenge in the streets against white America for killing "all reasonable hope" with the death of the Nobel Peace Prize winner.[7] Yet, after a few minor incidents, local streets were surprisingly quiet. Seale publicly appealed to Black Panthers and their followers to refrain from any violent reaction that would bring the police out in force. He feared that all the work he had done in the Richmond community over the years would come to naught from senseless rioting. So Seale gathered two vanloads of Panthers, and the ten vigilantes put an end to any rioting they saw on block after block of North Richmond.

Like Stokely Carmichael, Cleaver vehemently disagreed with Seale's keep-it-cool strategy, particularly after Father Neil shared with him the warning letter. Ever since Huey Newton's "night of truth" at the end of October 1967, Cleaver had been eager for an opportunity to prove himself as a member of the vanguard by offing his own pig. Cleaver considered that goal to exemplify "theory and practice rolled up into one."[8] On Saturday evening, April 6, Cleaver sprang into action and took three carloads of armed Black Panthers on a cruise of Oakland's streets looking for a confrontation. They parked in a black neighborhood and attempted to ambush a patrol car. Four of the Panthers who participated were immediately arrested, including David Hilliard, but others fled the scene. Seventeen-year-old Bobby Hutton and Cleaver barricaded themselves in a nearby home. The police tear-gassed the home, forcing the two Panthers to emerge as a small crowd of neighbors looked on. Cleaver had been hit by a canister. He knew the drill from prison searches and wanted to prevent police from claiming he was reaching for a gun as an excuse to shoot him. He stripped and came out naked and limping from a leg wound: his arms were raised to show he held no weapon. Cleaver had warned Bobby Hutton to do the same, but the teenager was too shy. Hutton had come out clothed, wearing a coat. Someone yelled that Hutton had a gun. Officers on the scene said Hutton ignored a command to halt. They hit him with a barrage of gunfire. The teenager died on the street, unarmed.

In the ninety-minute siege, one other Black Panther besides Cleaver had been injured and two police officers were wounded. The police seized an arsenal of military-type weapons from the Panther vehicles. Eight Black Panthers were immediately arrested on felony charges, including Cleaver, who remained on parole for the 1958 conviction that had originally brought him to Beverly Axelrod's attention as a prisoner three years earlier. That same night Cleaver's parole was revoked by the Adult Authority for having a gun in his possession, associating with persons of bad repute, and failing to cooperate with his parole officer. No hearing had been conducted; none was believed to be required.

Cleaver was sent immediately from Highland Hospital to San Quentin and then to the State Medical Facility at Vacaville, just long enough to recover from his wounds before being returned to prison. As word spread of the killing, either Melvin Newton or Father Neil contacted Alex Hoffmann around midnight to let him know that Cleaver was under arrest at Highland Hospital. Hoffmann had been with his housemate KPFA Program Manager Elsa Knight Thompson, celebrating her sixty-second birthday, but rushed downtown when he got the call. Hoffman told the police he represented the arrestees without even knowing exactly who had been arrested. The police appeared to be playing games, and prevented him from learning useful details. Hoffmann briefly saw Cleaver before he was whisked away. Cleaver urged Hoffmann to contact his wife Kathleen immediately to let her know what happened to him.

Cleaver had spoken at a gathering in Berkeley earlier that afternoon and then left Kathleen at a friend's house near campus, telling her only that he was headed to Panther headquarters and would come back for her. Hoffmann used a hospital pay phone, but could not reach Kathleen. He called his clients to tell them the news and tried but failed to reach Elsa Knight Thompson. Her home phone was suspiciously rendered inoperative, only to be quickly cleared the next morning. It was already obvious that Cleaver's home phone was wire-tapped. It made a clicking sound before anyone on the receiving end picked up. Hoffmann ultimately reached Kathleen early in the morning. She had fallen asleep on the sofa at her friends' house awaiting Eldridge's call. In the meantime, Hoffmann tracked Cleaver to San Quentin and then to Vacaville. There, the official in charge told Hoffmann how shocked he had been to receive Cleaver with no accompanying paperwork. In his experience, that was not how the system had ever operated before. All prisoners were supposed to be duly accounted for with appropriately signed orders, not simply dropped off in the middle of the night.

On Sunday afternoon there was a pre-planned "Free Huey" rally at DeFremery Park on Adeline Street. Hoffmann had gotten no sleep. He arrived escorting a shell-shocked Kathleen Cleaver, who spoke in her husband's stead. The biggest Panther gathering so far became an impromptu memorial celebration for Bobby Hutton, with members of the Party eulogizing the young Panther as a martyr. Over 2500 members of the community would attend the teenager's funeral the following week — joined by actor Marlon Brando, who later accompanied some Panthers on a neighborhood patrol and offered $10,000 in bail for Hilliard's release. It was then that Hilliard first realized the Panthers had gained Leftist celebrity status. In the Alameda County jail, Newton was permitted to conduct his own memorial service with the recently arrested Panthers. Upset by Cleaver's recklessness and the death of Li'l Bobby Hutton, Newton took Hilliard aside and named him Chief of Staff, in charge of the Party's programs.[9] Hoffmann had already contacted Barney Dreyfus and secured the firm's commitment to take on the defense of Cleaver and seven other Black Panthers arrested following the April 6 shootout. At this point, Garry assumed he would have little trouble convincing Judge Friedman to postpone Newton's trial. No one could question the extremely negative racial climate in Oakland amid so much front-page coverage of the recent bloody confrontation.

Garry immediately assigned Stender to set a motion before Judge Friedman, asking for at least two months' more preparation time. A great deal of pretrial investigative work remained to be done. Garry also had in mind that they needed to free Cleaver from prison so they could send him on a speaking tour. Cleaver's celebrity as a best-selling author and his proven oratorical talents were critical to their efforts at fund-raising and rallying widespread support for the Free Huey campaign. Kathleen played a key role, meeting with Garry and Hoffmann frequently to strategize. The young activist had already proven her strong organizational skills at SNCC and in helping Hilliard form the "Free Huey" Committee. She quickly put her talents to work with even greater zeal on her husband's behalf, working with a new "International Committee to Release Eldridge Cleaver." Co-chaired by Sandra Levinson of *Ramparts* in New York and Nathan Schwerner, father of the martyred civil rights worker Michael Schwerner, the committee set to work raising money and inviting celebrity supporters to attend Cleaver's upcoming hearing.

Though Kathleen had met Garry before, she had not noticed Fay Stender until the spring, when Kathleen came frequently to his office. Stender entered her consciousness as a very striking woman, her black hair set off by a black dress with a square cut neckline, her smile highlighted in red lipstick. Stender seemed much younger and more vibrant than the other lawyers in the office. Collaboration with Kathleen to free her husband diverted Garry from necessary preparations for Huey's defense without providing any justification for postponing the Newton trial. To win further delay, Stender needed to call Judge Friedman's attention to issues anticipated to arise in the Newton case. The defense had already been put on notice that the prosecutor intended to rely on key witnesses not presented to the grand jury. Garry wanted their names, to investigate and possibly interview them. Jensen told the court that his witnesses' lives had been threatened, causing the prosecutor's office to place at least one of them in a safe location unknown to the defense. Judge Friedman pushed back the trial date one month, until June 10 at 10 a.m. He granted Lowell Jensen's motion to keep his remaining witnesses undisclosed until two days before they testified at trial. Stender put her long-planned family vacation to Europe and Israel on hold. The trial would likely go through June into early July.

In the meantime, the defense team felt that police propaganda had poisoned the local atmosphere. To offset its impact, they gathered signatures from prominent citizens and then volunteers wearing "Free Huey Newton" buttons distributed the flyers door-to-door throughout Oakland. Calling itself the "Oakland Tribunal," the flyer described how the Black Panther Party arose in response to police harassment. It accused the local police force of attempting to eradicate the Black Panther Party and urged that the charges against Newton be placed in the context of historic crimes against the black community. A "Racism in the Law" conference in early May featured both Charles Garry and Clinton White reporting back from the front lines. Meanwhile, the Peace and Freedom Party formally named Newton its candidate for Congress, and urged write-in votes for the imprisoned Black Panther leader in the upcoming June 4 primary.

Both the political and legal fronts of the defense were going full bore. Stender assisted Dreyfus with an ambitious federal class action filed on behalf of all black residents of the Bay Area living within the boundaries of the federal jurisdiction of the Northern District Court of California. They named as defendants the City of Oakland, the Mayor, the Chief of Police, the District Attorney, and the Superior Court. Filed in mid-April, the complaint alleged that the state prosecutions of Newton and other Black Panthers violated the new federal Civil Rights Act. The attorneys sought a preliminary injunction against both Newton's trial in June and the as yet unscheduled trials of Black Panthers involved in the April shootout.

The defense team had asked in their filing for a three-judge court to hear the case, hoping that would slow the process down, but the federal panel responded quickly, scheduling the first hearing for May 21. Dreyfus argued the case for the defense. The panel issued its decision with uncharacteristic speed on May 28, a week after the hearing. It refused to delay any of the contemplated state trials and dismissed the Superior Court and the City of Oakland as defendants to the case. However, in a small victory for the defense, it held that a potential claim was stated against the Mayor, the District Attorney, and the Chief of Police.

Delay of the June 10 date set by Judge Friedman for Newton's trial was still deemed critical. Stender immediately began work on a very long shot—a new legal brief addressed to the United States Supreme Court, which directly reviewed three-judge court rulings of this type. Stender then turned back to gathering information on the jury pool to discuss with her expert witnesses. They held an extensive pretrial planning meeting on May 1. Prof. Dizard at Cal provided the defense with his national and local research on race discrimination by white Americans. He concluded more than half of whites had feelings of prejudice against blacks. Dizard had also gathered local statistical evidence on the skewed source of the jury pool: 85 percent of all eligible adults were registered to vote in Alameda County, but only 60 percent of eligible blacks, and only 52 percent of blacks in West Oakland.

On May 27, Fay contacted Dizard again to alert him that, despite their best efforts, the trial would likely proceed on June 10. The defense intended to file a motion to disqualify the entire jury panel the week before. She had quickly redrafted his report as a legal memorandum arguing for the unusual step of having each juror examined individually for prejudice while all other jury panel members were excluded from the courtroom. Stender prepared a list of questions for Garry to ask Dizard and a memo on what Garry should include in an offer of proof to the court if Dizard were not permitted to testify. Her argument was that by using the voter registration list as the sole source of trial jurors the county disproportionately excluded racial minorities and lower-income citizens. Bob Treuhaft, with nearly twenty years of experience in handling East Bay race discrimination cases, again offered help, calling attention to the requirement that jurors be available for sixty to ninety days, which effectively excluded workers not reimbursed by their employers for jury duty.

Stender prepared declarations supporting the motion from several sociology professors, including Prof. Blauner from Cal and Dr. Bernard Diamond, Garry's favorite forensic psychiatrist since the '50s, when Garry and Dreyfus had successfully established the *Wells-Gorshen* diminished capacity defense. Stender had already begun working closely with Prof. Blauner, who was helping prepare the analysis of the skewed juror pool. Like her husband Marvin, Blauner had gone to the University of Chicago as an undergraduate. He had obtained his Ph.D. in Sociology at Cal, focusing on problems of the working class. In 1964–65, as a young professor, he participated in the Free Speech Movement, which had impelled the confirmed Marxist to switch his focus to race relations. Though he was excited to be involved in Newton's defense, he did not share David Wellman's infatuation with Stender.

After a Memorial Day weekend camping trip with her children, Stender returned to file two quick motions, seeking more pretrial discovery and another continuance of the trial for sixty days. Garry argued that the defense needed time to depose Officer Heanes, District Attorney Coakley, and Police Chief Gain in the pending federal suit. Not surprisingly the motion was denied, but they did win a key ruling—the District Attorney had to make the personnel records of Frey and Heanes available. Also, Judge Friedman modified his May 8 order on disclosure of proposed prosecution witnesses. Their names would have to be revealed immediately after the jurors and alternates were picked, instead of 48 hours before the witnesses were to testify. This would give the defense more time to investigate the witnesses for cross-examination. Still, Garry pressed Stender to come up with reasons for further delay. He felt it was urgent to get Eldridge Cleaver released from the State Medical Facility at Vacaville to travel on an international book tour and fund-raise for the Panthers. Kathleen and Garry also worried about

Cleaver's state of mind. He had taken to saying that he "died with Bobby Hutton" at the April 6 shootout and only a ghost remained to haunt "racists of America."[10] (Mental health issues actually ran in Cleaver's family.)

With guidance from experts in the field, Hoffmann prepared a writ petition challenging the arbitrariness of the Adult Authority's revocation of Cleaver's parole. The hearing was set to take place on June 3 in the town of Fairfield, an hour northeast of Oakland, in the same county as the Vacaville Medical Facility. To underscore its importance, Garry asked Kathleen to cram the courtroom with supporters. Kathleen delivered in style, bringing in, as part of the crowd, best-selling author Norman Mailer, Stokely Carmichael, and black comedian and actor Godfrey Cambridge. Kathleen sat up front, strangely calm after two frenzied months of activity. She had been so distraught and worn out from the intensity of hearing preparations and from lack of sleep that she took tranquilizers for the first time in her life. She later reflected it was very lucky she was not asked to testify.

The defense felt fortunate to draw a Liberal Democrat, Judge Raymond Sherwin, who permitted an unusual three-hour hearing for the high profile case. Garry argued forcefully that the state based the revocation in part on Cleaver's exercise of free speech. The police had targeted the Panthers as a political threat; the parole revocation was payback for Cleaver's inflammatory publications and prominent association with the Black Panther Party. Garry also challenged the entire premise of automatic parole revocation, where there was no presumption of innocence. He pointed to Cleaver's prior unblemished parole record and his parole officer's earlier recommendation that Cleaver be taken off parole for good behavior by the end of the year. Garry also touted Cleaver's success as an author, his job at *Ramparts,* and recent marriage. Alex Hoffmann added charges of interference with the defense, citing instances in which Cleaver's communications with his attorneys had been censored and delayed.

The state lawyer for the Adult Authority was ill-prepared to counter this barrage of arguments. Exercise of the discretion of the Adult Authority had seldom, if ever, been successfully challenged in the past. There was little question that, if the Adult Authority had not drawn a line in the sand and instead had held a hearing to revoke Cleaver's parole, the judge would have had ample evidence to support the decision to send him back to prison. The Oakland officers involved in the April melée had already testified before the local grand jury, resulting in Cleaver's indictment for attempted murder. Since then, the police had obtained confessions from all of the arrested Panthers, except for David Hilliard, that implicated Cleaver as the instigator of the shootout. But in the Fairfield proceeding in June, Cleaver was sworn as the only witness to the April 6 shootout. He denied all of the allegations against him and swore that the Panthers were ambushed by the police, not the other way round. All he had done was defend himself and surrender as his teenage companion Bobby Hutton was cold-bloodedly murdered on the street. Judge Sherwin took the case under submission.

Though she would have loved to be present, Stender could not attend the Cleaver hearing. She was too busy filing the notice of appeal from the three-judge ruling that same day in San Francisco. That very afternoon the Supreme Court issued its landmark ruling in *Witherspoon v. Illinois.* The highly significant case had drawn "friend of the court" amicus briefs on both sides: state attorneys general supporting the State of Illinois and various organizations on behalf of the appellant, including the ACLU and the NAACP. Banner headlines in Monday's afternoon papers proclaimed "Hanging Jury Declared Illegal." A majority of six justices found that the state of Illinois had violated neutrality by categorically excluding potential jurors in a capital case for philosophical opposition to the death penalty. The high court cited studies showing that more than half of Americans and roughly half of the potential local jury panel opposed the death penalty. By culling out the majority of people "harbor[ing] doubts about the wisdom of capital punishment" the state of Illinois had denied the defendant a jury drawn from a cross-section of his peers, producing instead "a jury uncommonly willing to condemn a man to die."[11]

The Supreme Court indicated that the impact of *Witherspoon* on other capital cases would have to be determined on a case-by-case basis. Its decision was met with immediate jubilation by prisoners on death row throughout the country and resounding anger and ridicule from district attorneys. Both groups anticipated that the new ruling would dismantle "Death Row, U.S.A." by sparing the lives of most of the nearly 500 prisoners then awaiting execution, seventy-seven of them at California's San Quentin.[12] Under the mandate of *Witherspoon,* the penalty phase of all capital cases would have to be retried if jurors expressing only general opposition to capital punishment had been automatically excluded from their original trial.[13] Fay Stender wasted no time getting a copy of the opinion. Its wording would be critical to their upcoming jury selection. A footnote in the Supreme Court decision had included Professor Hans Zeisel's preliminary unpublished summary of the results of a long-term University of Chicago study that her husband Marvin Stender had worked on after law school. Zeisel had reached the firm conclusion that: "A jury consisting only of jurors who have no scruples against the death penalty is likely to be more prosecution prone than a jury on which objectors to the death penalty sit." The study had also drawn a corollary: "The defendant's chances of acquittal are somewhat reduced if the objectors are excluded from the jury."[14]

Fay Stender contacted Prof. Zeisel immediately, realizing he could prove crucial to the Newton team. After all, the Supreme Court of the United States had just expressly relied on Zeisel's findings. Who better to convince Judge Friedman that he would need to delve further into the mindset of jurors who opposed the death penalty? Under the new mandate, Judge Friedman could now only dismiss for cause potential jurors who: "made unmistakably clear . . . that they would automatically vote against the imposition of capital punishment without regard to any evidence that might be developed at the trial of the case before them."[15] This was extraordinarily promising news, but still, the defense team needed more time to investigate potential witnesses to the charged crimes. They were nowhere close to ready to begin trial the following week. On June 4, they filed another of Stender's motions for continuance; it repeated the argument that white racism in the community and prejudicial statements continually disseminated by the media prevented a fair trial.

The moving papers challenged the entire jury panel of 1900 citizens as unconstitutional on the grounds that blacks, low-income, and culturally different persons were systematically excluded and underrepresented by the use of unsupplemented voter registration lists. As a member of a militant subgroup of blacks, Huey Newton was "virtually a stranger to most of the white American voters who will make up the jury under prevailing practice. They are not his peers. . . ."[16] The papers relied heavily on the declarations of the experts Stender had met with and on analogies drawn to the intelligence test rejected by Judge Avakian in April in *People v. Craig*, which she attached to the motion. Jensen characterized the motion for continuance as frivolous. He saw no evidence demonstrating white racism in the selection process.

On the morning of June 5, before Judge Friedman ruled on the pending motions, came the startling news that Democratic presidential primary candidate Bobby Kennedy had been shot in Los Angeles. Early that morning, Kennedy had made an upbeat speech to supporters after they had stayed up to celebrate his wins in two primaries the night before: California and South Dakota. The California victory had given Kennedy much-needed momentum following a setback the prior week in the Oregon primary that went to Eugene McCarthy. It put Kennedy in a strong position to challenge Vice President Hubert Humphrey for the Democratic nomination. The key to Kennedy's victory in the California primary had been a huge minority turnout on his behalf, enthused by his pledge to focus on education, housing, and jobs.[17] Kennedy was glad-handing staff in the kitchen of the Ambassador Hotel following his speech, when he and members of his entourage were shot at close range. Gravely wounded, he was removed from the hotel by ambulance and died the following day without ever regaining consciousness.

At the orders of a horrified President Johnson—who had himself been receiving over 1,000 death threats a month well before Senator Kennedy was shot—other presidential candidates began receiving Secret Service protection that same day. The boldly executed assassination of a Democratic presidential candidate would have stunned the nation once again without the added factor that he was President Kennedy's younger brother. But the intense media attention on his grieving widow Ethel, mother Rose Kennedy, widowed sister-in-law Jackie, and lone surviving brother Ted also brought renewed focus on the shocking death of his brother less than five years earlier. The Pope offered special prayers for Senator Kennedy's family and for his country. Condolences poured in to the family from world leaders on both sides of the Iron Curtain, while ordinary citizens in the U.S. and abroad grieved openly as another national day of mourning was proclaimed. People could not fathom that this had occurred while the country was still reeling from the assassination of Rev. Martin Luther King. Indeed, news of Senator Kennedy's death shared headlines with the capture by Scotland Yard of King's alleged assassin James Earl Ray in London, England, where he was traveling under a forged passport. Network radio and television coverage of these two stories was almost nonstop for the next few days, dwarfing all other news.

Kennedy's death had come as a huge blow to minorities. Mexican-Americans viewed his assassination as "La Muerte de una Esperanza"—the death of a great hope. Blacks throughout the nation also reacted with extreme bitterness and shock at this second assassination in the space of two months. In May, on the Mall between the Washington Monument and the Capitol building, Martin Luther King's followers had built a shantytown "Resurrection City" as the culmination of King's recently proclaimed "Poor People's Campaign." Resurrection City quickly drew a population of poor, mostly black activists from around the country, together with other minorities and a few supportive whites. Following news that Bobby Kennedy had been shot, civil rights leader Rev. Ralph Abernathy addressed a crowd gathered at Resurrection City. He had succeeded to the presidency of the Southern Christian Leadership Conference following Dr. King's assassination. Rev. Abernathy did not mince words, viewing Senator Kennedy's assassination as evidence of a racist conspiracy to eliminate leaders supportive of the poor. Another speaker captured the mood of the angry audience with a similar observation: "You noticed that every time we get somebody willing to speak out for the black man, they cut him down?" [18]

Local ramifications immediately surfaced. The Oakland City Council took up a proposal the next day to order an independent study of the turbulent race issues in Oakland, focusing on both the difficult relationship between the police and the black community and more general issues raised by the white community's control of local city administration. Local Democratic members of the State Assembly introduced a bill to implement tough gun-control laws as columnists and panelists contemplated whether violence and assassinations were "the American Way."[19]

On June 7, the day after Senator Kennedy died, Garry and Jensen appeared before Judge Friedman on the pending pretrial motions. In that highly charged political atmosphere, Garry argued there was no way that the murder trial of Huey Newton could be expected to proceed on Monday, June 10. Though Judge Friedman remained skeptical of Garry's arguments, he announced that he would move the trial date to July 8 to give himself time to analyze the impact of the *Witherspoon* death penalty case. At last, here was some breathing room for the defense.

The following Tuesday, Judge Sherwin issued his ruling on Cleaver's challenge to his parole revocation:

> The uncontradicted evidence presented to this court indicated that the petitioner had been a model parolee. The peril to his parole status stemmed from no failure of personal rehabilitation, but from his undue eloquence in pursuing political goals . . . . Not only was there absence of cause for the cancellation of parole, it was the product of a type of pressure unbecoming, to say the least, to the law enforcement paraphernalia of this State.[20]

Cleaver's bail on the attempted murder charge was already set at $50,000. Judge Sherwin ordered Cleaver's release on a token amount of additional bail. The Attorney General's office expressed total shock at the decision, calling it "unprecedented and amazing . . . far out of line and contrary to law."[21] Garry immediately posted the entire sum—$50,027.50—at the Solano County Courthouse so Cleaver could be released the next day. Garry and Kathleen drove out to retrieve him on the afternoon of June 13 for a triumphant press conference in Garry's San Francisco law office. That evening the defense team and friends celebrated their incredible victory with champagne. Cleaver was back on the streets! He could return to leading the Free Huey Movement and help fund-raise for the mounting costs of Huey's defense. The symbolism of Cleaver's release could not be overstated. A highly prepared and passionate plea by his lawyers in front of a courtroom full of supporters had won them that ruling—the first time they had *ever* heard of the Adult Authority losing a parole revocation case. The Attorney General's office filed an appeal the following morning. Upcoming hearings on Cleaver's and other Panthers' arrests still loomed large.[22] Hundreds of hours of work still needed to be done to prepare for Newton's murder trial. But for the moment, the defense team reveled in their success.

10. THE QUEST FOR A JURY OF HIS PEERS

If you kill this man, you are killing your wife kids and mother. We will kill all white dogs—stay in the open and be shot dog! A brother!

Anonymous letter sent to the Oakland police

Dear Nigger Lover: . . . I hope that race war they are always threatening would start right away. We outnumber the blacks ten to one so guess who will win, and a lot of damn nigger lovers will be lying there right beside them. I wish Hitler had won. Then we could have finished off the sheenies and started in on the coons. KKK

Anonymous letter sent to Charles Garry

Anyone who regularly read the newspapers or watched local news in June and early July of 1968 was inundated with pretrial publicity for the Huey Newton murder trial. The case always evoked an intense gut reaction, pro or con, since Newton had catapulted to international attention. To many in the United States, he was a homegrown terrorist; to many others, at home and worldwide, he was a political prisoner and a symbol of oppression of American blacks, in turn linked with charges of a racist war in Vietnam. By the summer of 1968, the Panthers' high visibility as a revolutionary party elevated it to public enemy number one in the eyes of FBI Director J. Edgar Hoover—a movement to be stopped at all costs.

Public awareness of the upcoming Newton trial extended well beyond the media. Treating the trial like a political campaign, Panthers and other volunteers posted signs on telephone poles and store windows throughout the community and distributed bumper stickers as well. Bus riders could expect to see fellow passengers sporting "Free Huey" buttons and hear responsive murmurs of "Right on."[1] California would soon be documented as one-third minority—the largest minority population in the nation. Yet judicial proceedings, like other governmental functions, were still almost universally controlled by whites. In his editorials, *Oakland Post* owner Tom Berkley expressed great skepticism about Newton's innocence and open disdain for the militancy of the Panthers. Yet the underlying issue raised by Newton's trial reverberated with him as well: "It is impossible for a minority to receive justice in a Court that 99 times out of 100 consists of a white judge, white clerks, white bailiffs, white opposing counsels and white jurors."[2]

Galvanized by the killing of Bobby Hutton in West Oakland in April of 1968, pressure escalated on city officials for community control of the police. A number of innocent victims of that shootout brought suits against the police for negligence, alleging that more than a thousand rounds of ammunition had needlessly been fired in the April confrontation with the Panthers, damaging many West Oakland residents' parked cars. The community pressure on public officials grew exponentially after the county grand jury exonerated the Oakland police of any wrongdoing simply on the testimony of members of the force who were present at the early April shooting. A group of law professors at U.C. Berkeley's Boalt Hall Law School petitioned the United States Department of Justice to conduct an independent inquiry. The county bar association also requested an impartial review since all of the Panthers at the bloody confrontation declined to testify before the grand jury, which could have easily skewed its findings.

On another front, a group calling itself "Blacks for Justice" picketed Oakland businesses to support community review of the police. Black ministers lobbied the Oakland City Council and the office of the mayor to the same end. Police Chief Gain responded to criticism of his almost entirely white police force by claiming it was difficult to find qualified black men, but he did impose a moratorium on the use of mace as a crowd control device and forbade shooting at fleeing car thieves and burglars. Mayor Reading sharply criticized the police chief for this move, charging that Gain had crippled public protection by yielding to intimidation. Reading himself owned a grocery—run largely by his wife—that was affected by the economic boycott. He became increasingly vocal as the Panthers and Peace and Freedom Party gathered signatures to put on the ballot the creation of separate police districts within the city, permitting blacks and whites to have officers of their own race patrolling their neighborhoods. Mayor Reading soon began openly talking of not seeking reelection; he gave an exclusive interview in the most widely read Sunday paper in which he cited the Panthers and the pending Newton trial as major factors. With blacks now 46 percent of the city's population and more than half of all students in its public schools, speculation grew rampant that should Reading retire, several prominent African-Americans might throw their hats into a wide open race.[3]

As the city grew increasingly polarized, Garry prepared for a preliminary hearing in late June representing several Black Panthers facing charges from the alleged April 6 ambush. Meanwhile, Stender flew out to Chicago to consult Dr. Zeisel, who offered to donate his time to testify at the trial. He even agreed to advance his own costs because money for the defense was so scarce. Stender tried to convince other experts from the East to come to California at their own expense. They declined, but offered to mail her sworn statements if the court would accept them.

Locally, Stender worked with the volunteer experts she had already recruited, Cal professors Blauner and Dizard and graduate student David Wellman, who helped draft hundreds of questions to ask potential jurors to smoke out evidence of racism. She learned from Penny Cooper in the Public Defender's office that the Alameda County D.A.'s office had the voter registration of every juror. Unlike Stender, Cooper had accumulated substantial trial experience by then, though Cooper was only thirty, six years Stender's junior. That was one of the benefits of going to work for the Public Defender. But in her three years in that office Cooper had experienced firsthand the downsides, too. She realized her days in that conservative office were numbered after the Public Defender pressured her unmercifully to recant her anti-war views and, not succeeding, had followed up with a series of undesirable assignments. A decade earlier, Stender herself had quit working as a law clerk for an ultra-conservative justice on the Supreme Court when she realized the extent of his bigotry. (Back in the 1920s when he was elevated to the high court, Justice Shenk had supported "Oriental exclusion." He still used the term "the yellow hordes" to describe Asian-Americans and had written a scathing dissent to *Perez v. Sharp*, the landmark 1948 ruling making California the first state in the nation to strike down anti-miscegenation laws. Shenk fervently believed there was scientific proof that: "The amalgamation of the races is not only unnatural, but is always productive of deplorable results."[4])

Identifying with a kindred spirit, Cooper eagerly informed Stender that the D.A. knew whether any potential jurors had ever been arrested, and, if so, he had a copy of the arrest sheet. District Attorney Coakley's office also had information on any juror who had served on a jury before, including how the juror voted. Cooper had just recently learned of the list and had promptly requested access to the D.A.'s jury file in a few of her own assigned criminal cases. But even liberal judge Sparky Avakian denied Cooper's requests. Judge Avakian reasoned that the same information the D.A. had accumulated would be available to the defense if they put investigators to work on digging it out. Cooper told Fay that this was not in fact the case—some of the information the District Attorney had accumulated on potential jurors was from a Sacramento Central Intelligence data bank, which was not accessible to defense investigators. Stender wanted Garry to make a motion for its discovery, putting the issue on the record even if Judge Friedman was likely to deny their request. Garry had other priorities. Garry interviewed a forensic medical expert in late June who analyzed Officer Frey's and Newton's bullet wounds. The expert had been puzzled by the multiple directions of the wounds to Officer Frey, but concluded that the fatal shot had been fired at close range through Frey's back. Immediate treatment would not likely have saved him. This was not going to be particularly helpful. Garry had been hoping to get the medical expert to say the fatal wound could have come from Heanes' gun, shot from thirty feet away. No such luck.

As the date for the Newton trial approached, the media covered both the Liberal response to racial violence following the twin assassinations — increased civil rights activism and new gun control efforts — and the even stronger backlash. Alabama's Gov. George Wallace entered the 1968 presidential campaign as a candidate on his own American Independent Party ticket. A proud white supremacist, Wallace threatened to take a majority of the Southern states as a base to build a larger coalition he hoped to use to direct the outcome of the presidential election. Some political analysts feared that Wallace's growing support among Northern blue collar whites could force the election to be decided by the House of Representatives. Republican candidate Richard Nixon responded by making subtle appeals to racism central to his own campaign, coupling images of violent urban protests with promises to restore "law and order."[5] Meanwhile, Senator Eugene McCarthy reached out to black youths, proclaiming that resolution of urban racial problems was of paramount national concern, trumping the Vietnam War.

As the Newton trial approached, *The Oakland Tribune* also gave front page coverage in early July to congressional hearings in Washington, D.C., on Associate Justice Abe Fortas's controversial nomination for Chief Justice. A lame-duck nominee of President Lyndon Johnson, the New Deal scholar from Yale would have replaced retiring Chief Justice Earl Warren. The local paper reported relentless questioning of the Jewish Democrat by Senator Strom Thurmond, one of many Republicans disgusted with the Supreme Court's liberal record of turning rapists and murderers loose on what critics dismissed as mere legal technicalities.

Of greatest impact locally was a hotly contested ruling on July 8 by Alameda County Superior Court Judge George Phillips. Judge Phillips declared a mistrial in an Oakland criminal prosecution against five black inmates of Santa Rita accused of attacking a white inmate. He based his ruling on arguments that the prosecutor had used his peremptory challenges improperly by removing every non-white from the jury panel. The prosecutor had also used a few of his peremptory challenges against prospective white jurors. Generally speaking, peremptory challenges could be used to strike anyone that a lawyer did not want on the jury, with no explanation necessary. An opposing attorney wishing to show that a peremptory challenge was used improperly had to meet an extremely high threshold of proof. But Judge Phillips ruled that the threshold was met in the case before him because the deputy district attorney had demonstrated a systematic, conscious intent to exclude non-whites as a class, depriving the defendants of a fair trial by an impartial jury of their peers drawn from a cross-section of the community. Not wanting the delighted defendants to read too much into his ruling, the judge added that he was simply delaying their day in court, intoning, "You will be tried for this alleged crime."[6]

The mistrial declaration made front page news as District Attorney Coakley sharply criticized Judge Phillips for holding that a member of Coakley's office had acted in a racially discriminatory manner. Coakley immediately announced he was exploring an appeal: the ruling gave his office a black eye in the community at a very sensitive time, with obvious implications for the imminent Newton trial. Coakley himself still smarted from charges of racism that Bob Treuhaft had levied when he ran for office against Coakley two years earlier.[7] As racial tension peaked in the community, Garry faced the added distraction of ongoing issues related to Cleaver's continued freedom. The Adult Authority had ignored Judge Sherwin's June 12 ruling in Cleaver's favor and set a hearing on the charge of parole violation for July 8, 1968, at San Quentin prison in Marin County—the same date Judge Friedman had reset the Newton trial. But then Judge Friedman moved the Newton trial one week later, to July 15.

Despite a new order from Judge Sherwin not to do so, the Adult Authority then proceeded with the July 8 hearing, ignoring the judge's threat to hold the state agency in contempt. The impasse was temporarily resolved when the court of appeal issued an order leaving in place Judge Sherwin's ruling. As a result, Cleaver remained free on bail pending an appellate decision in the matter. The review court set a date in late September for its own hearing. Meanwhile, Cleaver tried to generate international support by filing a complaint with the United Nations for human rights violations on the Panthers' behalf. He took advantage of his continued freedom to make a number of public appearances in support of Newton as well as to attack the police for persecuting the Panther organization. Now sporting a small beard and dark sunglasses, the leather-clad revolutionary told audiences he was convinced that on April 6 he had been marked for death along with Bobby Hutton, and the police only stopped short of double murder because there had been so many black people from the neighborhood crowded around as witnesses.

Cleaver's rhetoric and that of most Panthers had evolved in the past few months. Influenced by the Peace and Freedom Party, as SNCC leaders had predicted, Cleaver abandoned black nationalist positions and was now talking about the need for white and black unity in fighting capitalism. The Peace and Freedom Party then announced its plan to run Cleaver as their candidate for President of the United States, while Newton remained their candidate for Congress. They added Kathleen Cleaver as a candidate for State Assembly.

Thanks to the efforts of the Peace and Freedom Party, the door was now open for anti-war candidates to topple the incumbent Democrat in California's Seventh Congressional District. In 1966, *Ramparts* journalist Bob Scheer had paved the way by running as a Peace and Freedom candidate in a grassroots anti-war campaign that won him forty-five percent of the primary vote. But that opportunity was thrown away by running Huey Newton for that congressional office. Like Big Bill Haywood, Newton enjoyed the notoriety of running for office from his jail cell. But with no chance of success, the Peace and Freedom Party approach all but guaranteed another split among the Left-leaning voters of Berkeley and North Oakland.

Democrats like Ron Dellums on the Berkeley City Council and congressional candidate John George felt thwarted by the radical Left just as the East Bay finally seemed ready to vote for more politically mainstream African-American candidates. Cleaver did not care. He knew he was not going to get elected to anything. He told audiences, "I'm a Black Panther and a madman . . . a symbol of dissent, of rejection."[8] He despised the white power structure and wanted to build support for the Black Panther Party wherever he could find it. He suggested that women refrain from sex as an incentive to their men to take arms against oppression. He got crowds to yell that they would free Newton "by any means necessary." Cleaver declared, "I've been watching those pigs railroading Huey.

If they kill Huey P. Newton, they're going to have to kill us all first."[9] Cleaver met with representatives of The American Communist Party. For the first time since 1940, the Party openly supported a candidate for President of the United States. Its platform was twofold: freedom and justice for blacks and an end to the Vietnam War. The Party now estimated its membership at 14,000 to 15,000 people nationwide, of which twenty percent were black.

The FBI had, by now, not only assigned operatives to cover Panther leaders, but began to strategize on how to implode the Panther organization with a campaign of dirty tricks. In the spring of 1968, Alex Hoffmann had publicly documented the government's disabling of his home phone in connection with the April 6 arrest of Eldridge Cleaver. The FBI was listening in on other telephones of Panther officials as well, evidenced by a tell-tale click. They also planted false documentation, seeking to sow suspicion among the Panther rank and file that Stokely Carmichael, David Hilliard, and Newton himself were government agents.[10]

On the evening of July 3, Cleaver and Seale were invited to address an emergency session of the Berkeley City Council on which Dellums sat. It drew a crowd of over a thousand people to the 3,000-seat Berkeley High School auditorium. The specially called meeting capped several tumultuous days of violence and strict citywide curfews. Seale appeared haggard and unkempt. Cleaver looked in command of his audience. They used the podium to rail against racist "pig" cops as the council debated a controversial motion to close several blocks of Telegraph Avenue for a massive Fourth of July gathering, permitting rallies by hippies, Yippies, Black Panthers, Peace and Freedom Party members, and other anti-war activists. Though renewed violence was threatened, the holiday celebration on Telegraph Avenue turned out to be peaceful. Cleaver was again among the speakers addressing the Berkeley crowd. He urged them to rally for Newton's release from jail, but the audience was dominated by flower children more interested in enjoying a warm summer afternoon than in his political passion.

Cleaver's busy calendar of appearances at rallies was part of a concerted defense team strategy to draw a huge group of spectators to the Newton trial. Stender filed a motion the second week of July to have the trial moved to a different venue capable of seating a much larger audience, together with the more than one hundred media representatives expected to cover the trial. She could find no precedent for the unusual motion except that Newton was entitled to a public trial. Her moving papers argued that a larger space would more readily satisfy widespread interest in the case. Of course, the logistics of such a move would have also meant more delay in order to put necessary security precautions in place. The defense team would have welcomed any further postponement they could obtain. Tom Berkley of *The Oakland Post* assumed that no further delays would be seriously entertained by the court: "Barring something unforeseen up the sleeve of wily defense counsel Charles K. Garry, Huey Newton, baby-faced guru of the Black Panther Party . . . will go to trial Monday morning."[11]

At the end of that second week of July, spectators filled only about two-thirds of the seats in the small courtroom where the Newton pretrial hearing was set. Many other interested parties stayed away, not anticipating anything exciting to happen until the trial actually started the following week. Friday morning's spectators included court officials, lawyers, the press, and a dozen or so Black Panthers who stood to salute Huey Newton with *de rigueur* clenched fists as he strode into the courtroom. Garry told Judge Friedman of worldwide interest in the trial as he suggested it be moved to the Oakland Auditorium Theater, the Veterans Memorial Building, or, if available, the presiding judge's oversized courtroom. Reporters from the *Boston Globe* and *New York Times* were expected along with those from local dailies, a London reporter, network and local television and radio crews, and representatives from the wire services, *Time, Newsweek,* and *Life,* and from some underground papers.

Among the reporters already watching the proceedings that Friday was Gilbert Moore, one of two African-Americans on the staff of *Life* magazine. The seventy-two-year-old judge who held Newton's life in his hands impressed Moore as a man with "the demeanor, the gentle forbearance, the myopia of an aging beagle."[12] Unpersuaded by the hoopla, Judge Friedman denied Garry's motion to move the proceedings: "The court of justice is not a place for entertainment or amusement."[13] The media reacted in disbelief—only a fraction would receive passes from the sheriff's office, and they would need a different pass each day, first-come, first-served. Moore now urgently wanted to be among them. He had originally been assigned in late June to do a story "on Eldridge Cleaver, the Panthers in general or on Oakland: a tinderbox about to explode."[14] He had accepted the task reluctantly, not relishing the idea that he automatically was considered the best reporter suited to cover a story featuring people of his own race. Raised in Harlem and Jamaica, the thirty-three-year-old New Yorker had never set foot in Oakland. All that he knew at the time of his new assignment was that a man named Huey Newton headed a "bizarre bunch of California niggers, talking bad and occasionally shooting someone."[15]

On his arrival in California, Moore spent a couple of weeks learning the rudiments of the multi-step Black Panther handshake ritual (ending with a finger snap of African tribal origin), so he would be more welcome among the brothers. Moore wanted to nip speculation that he was a government spy. He interviewed Newton in jail, toured the cramped and disorganized Panther headquarters, visited Eldridge and Kathleen Cleaver at their San Francisco apartment, and tagged along after Cleaver and Seale at rallies and education sessions. By then, Moore had already accumulated more than enough information to write the story he had been assigned and had also concluded that none of the Panther leaders "gave a rat's ass whether *Life* magazine did a story on the movement or not."[16] His impatient editors demanded an explanation for his delayed return to New York. Moore overcame their skepticism with assurances that the Huey Newton trial would have "very wide political implications" which he felt compelled to cover firsthand.[17]

The Friday hearing addressed another, far more basic concern than spectator space in the courtroom. Before the trial began, the defense team wanted to seek review in both state and federal court on an issue Garry deemed critical to the defense—expunging Newton's prior felony conviction for assault. They fully expected to lose the issue before Judge Friedman. On that assumption, Stender had prepared a writ raising the very same issue later that morning before another Alameda County judge. If this petition was also denied, an appeal to the state appellate court was already planned, together with a request for an order postponing the trial date until the appellate court ruled.

The motion was deemed critical because the status of Newton's prior conviction greatly influenced Garry's trial strategy. He thought his handsome client would make a persuasive, articulate witness on his own behalf. If Newton explained the Panther platform, he might win the sympathy of at least some of the jurors. Garry definitely wanted to consider the option of putting Newton on the stand, though Newton had the constitutional right not to testify at all. But the prior conviction was a powerful disincentive, a sword of Damocles dangling over Newton's head. If it remained unchallenged, Jensen would focus the jury's attention on it, prejudicing the panel against Newton. The prosecutor would even be entitled to have the jury instructed that Newton's prior criminal conduct was reason enough to discredit his testimony on any subject. Unlike witnesses in general, felons could be presumed dishonest.

Garry was also concerned about the impact of Newton's no contest plea to the charges that had been filed against him for the incident in front of Panther headquarters the prior spring. In November, after Newton had been jailed on the murder charges, John George had entered a plea on Newton's behalf for the May 1967 incident and obtained a sentence of fifteen days' jail time, to be served simultaneously. It had seemed a reasonable deal at the time. George had since been persuaded to ask the court to reinstate the original charges against Newton and to set a hearing for late July on those minor charges. On Garry's advice, Newton now wished to plead innocent and have his day in court. George accommodated them by informing the court he had entered the original plea without Newton's approval.

After Judge Friedman denied the motion to expunge the conviction, Judge Lercara, the judge assigned to hear the other petition raising the same issue, took an unusual step to accommodate the parties and the press. Normally, he would have used his own courtroom several floors below. Instead, he simply took the still-warm bench as soon as it was vacated by Judge Friedman. Then he quickly told the parties he had read the petition and response and did not want to hear arguments. Within just minutes of his arrival, Judge Lercara denied the petition, giving the defense time the same day to seek review in the court of appeal. Part of the defense strategy had been to ask Judge Friedman for another continuance while awaiting review of his ruling on Newton's prior felony conviction. They had hoped the possibility of reversal would persuade him. Not so. Judge Friedman remained firm. Unless another court ordered otherwise before Monday morning, that was when trial would commence. Stender scrambled off to file the appeal as Garry announced, "We're prepared to go to the U.S. Supreme Court if necessary."[18]

When the media left the hearing on Friday, they realized they had obtained a preview of precautionary measures they could expect at trial on Monday. Cameras would be relegated to a makeshift press room on the sixth floor, temporarily converted from a jury room. Reporters figured that they had better plan to arrive early Monday morning to allow time for court personnel to process everyone entitled to enter. No one wanted to be left out. Judge Friedman might believe that a court of justice was not an entertainment venue, but show-time was about to begin.

The court of appeal quickly denied the defense request for review; that same afternoon Stender filed a similar petition with the California Supreme Court. She worked all weekend preparing other sets of legal briefs, including a federal petition in the event the California Supreme Court declined to act, and a renewed motion to present to Judge Friedman challenging the jury panel. Garry planned to call the expert witnesses Stender had prepared on this issue before starting the trial in earnest. While the legal work was being churned out, the "Free Huey" committee kicked into high gear. On Sunday, July 14, a huge crowd of Panther supporters gathered at DeFremery Park in Oakland for a four-hour picnic and rally. (By then many in the community called the site "Bobby Hutton Park," though no official name change could ever occur under the terms by which the wealthy financier's family had deeded the land and Victorian mansion to the city back in 1910.) Cleaver again stood out among the militant speakers, galvanizing throngs of followers to show up in force at the trial. Even as Cleaver rallied the troops, Garry hoped against hope that Stender could pull off a miracle and get another court to temporarily postpone the trial.

On Monday morning, July 15, 1968, *The Oakland Tribune* proclaimed that the city's main courthouse looked like a "besieged fortress."[19] Most steps leading to the building were covered with netting. Armed deputies, with walkie-talkies, mace, and batons, stood outside every entrance to the main courthouse augmented by the National Guard. A multi-racial mass of Panther supporters, many with children in tow, circled the building and overflowed onto the street, impeding traffic until they were dispersed by the police. All but one of the entrances to the building were locked. At the 12th Street doorway a guard required everyone who approached to show identification—couples applying for marriage licenses, attorneys and parties to other cases, as well as county employees. Such high security precautions had never before been implemented in the county. Equally strong security measures were evident inside the courthouse. Special passes obtained at the sheriff's office on the second floor allowed those authorized to attend the trial access to the seventh floor where Judge Friedman's sixty-two-seat courtroom was located. A few eager spectators had begun lining up at 5 a.m. Friends and family of Huey Newton complained they were singled out for photographing and fingerprinting before receiving passes.

Doors permitting seventh-floor access to the stairwells leading to the sixth and eighth floors were temporarily sealed. One elevator with its own armed guard was assigned exclusively for persons headed to the Newton trial. Veteran Judge Cecil Mosbacher could not hide her irritation when the long-time elevator operator on the basement floor turned down her request to let the judge board. She would have to take another elevator to her own courtroom on the seventh floor. No exceptions whatsoever were being made to the tight security arrangements. That morning, when members of the jury pool arrived at the courthouse they were promptly sequestered while more than 2,000 Newton supporters gathered outside. The Panthers had hoped to conduct a mass march through downtown Oakland that morning for the trial's start, but too few supporters had shown up at the designated assembly point. Instead, they all met at the courthouse where Black Panthers in full regalia—sweltering in leather jackets and berets—defiantly led the crowd in chanting, "Free Huey Now" and "Black is Beautiful."

Signs lofted above protesters' heads warned, "The Nation Shall Be Reduced to Ashes," "Free Huey or Else," and "If Anything Happens to Huey, the Sky's the Limit."[20] Though most unsympathetic onlookers held their tongue, reporter Moore heard a few from time to time saying things such as, "Jesus Christ, what is this country comin' to? Free Huey—my ass! They oughta burn the son of a bitch!" while others wondered exactly what was meant by "Free Huey": "Is it a command, a request or an exhortation—or perhaps all three? Does it mean, examine the evidence, go through the court rituals and then free Huey? Does it mean storming the Alameda County Jail and freeing him by force of arms? Or what?"[21]

Somehow, though most white males in the crowd wore long hair and beards, Judge Friedman circulated among them unobtrusively gauging the situation for himself. The din made it almost impossible for court staff on the first floor of the building to perform their work. Outside the courthouse, Peace and Freedom Party leader Bob Avakian ascended the flagpole and cut down the American flag as other demonstrators yelled, "Burn it." The sequestered jurors could hear the shouts through the windows of the courthouse high above the sidewalk. Avakian was immediately arrested and charged with petty theft, flag desecration, and malicious mischief.[22] Armed guards patrolled the courthouse corridors. Two stood guarding the door to Judge Friedman's locked courtroom. Inside, the bailiff inspected the underside of all chairs and tables. Once they exhibited identification and were allowed entry, spectators and media, on opposite sides of the central aisle, overflowed all available seats, spilling into the hallway. Plainclothes policemen spread out among them, attempting to blend inconspicuously into the crowd. To the discerning eyes of Panther supporters, they might as well have been wearing neon.

As expected, no photographers were permitted in the courtroom, but artists employed by the media busily sketched the high-ceilinged room with wood-paneled walls where the drama of the trial would be staged: the raised bench; the judge's empty leather chair with a huge American flag hanging on the wall behind it; the jury box on the right and the clerk's desk on the left; the Gettysburg Address framed on one of the courtroom walls. The two counsel tables were positioned in "the well" beyond a gate segregating the players from the spectators—the prosecutor's table sat nearer to the jury and the defense table to its left.

Unaware of all the last minute machinations, Blauner had obtained his trial pass as a designated defense expert witness on race bias in the jury pool. He showed up on Monday morning flushed with excitement at the unfolding drama. To his dismay, Stender and Garry arrived late, looking exhausted. By then Stender was routinely putting in twelve-hour days and had had no weekend break. She sat down in the front row, accompanied by Alex Hoffmann. Their seats were right behind Charles Garry at the defense table, where Ed Keating from *Ramparts* magazine also sat. After learning Keating wished to cover the trial for *Ramparts,* Garry had offered to designate Keating as his co-counsel. Unlike other reporters, Keating would have automatic access to the proceedings. Eager to have such a birds-eye-view of the historic event, Keating reactivated his little-used law degree, and offered help in the nature of a paralegal. He had no expertise in criminal law and had not practiced in years.

It quickly became evident to all present that the trial would not begin right away. Garry had persuaded Judge Friedman to agree to a late morning start in case the California Supreme Court or the federal district court granted a temporary stay. When no stay order materialized, the tension in the room was palpable. Twenty-eight credentialed reporters sat in the courtroom ready to chronicle the current trial of the century, leaving another seventy reporters outside due to insufficient space. Gilbert Moore and his new friend Rush Greenlee, a black reporter covering the story from a human interest angle for *The San Francisco Examiner,* had both obtained coveted seats. Greenlee often collaborated with a more senior white colleague assigned daily responsibility for reporting on the high profile case. The Panthers castigated Greenlee as part of the "spineless black bourgeoisie."[23]

The Oakland Post characterized the stakes for the American system of justice to be as high as those involved in the 1920s' Sacco and Vanzetti trial. Its reporter Almea Lomax expressed amazement that a "self-confessed small-time hood" like Newton could transform himself into a hero with "new-found socialist convictions."[24] *The Post* was not Huey Newton's only local black media critic. Early in the trial, the Berkeley campus student newspaper, *The Daily Californian,* featured a caustic editorial column entitled "The Paper Panthers" by an African-American graduate student. He derided the paramilitary organization's "vacant generalities and absurd manifestoes," its lack of "plausible short term goals," and reliance on pistols as "sex symbols." The author lambasted Newton's organization as the source of much wasted newsprint in the liberal and radical press as well as wasted time and energy of people in the ghetto.[25]

In contrast, the alternative press viewed the trial as a pivotal point in the nation's history of racism that was on the eve of engulfing the nation in flames, "Oppression. Revolt. Suppression. Revolution. Determined black and brown and white men are watching what happens to Huey Newton. What they do depends on what the white man's courts do to Huey."[26] As the trial officially began, Garry asked Judge Friedman to have the court reporter prepare a daily transcript of proceedings for both the prosecutor and the defense. It would be costly, but essential to have the ability to review each day's testimony for use in cross-examination and for summing up the evidence in closing arguments. Garry also requested that the judge list his entire firm as Newton's counsel of record so any of its attorneys could act on Newton's behalf, if need be, for particular aspects of the case. Everyone in the Garry partnership had by now been mobilized as reinforcements. With Fay Stender in the courtroom, Garry's partner Frank McTernan was back in the office readying appeals to the Ninth Circuit and the United States Supreme Court if the pending petitions were denied.

Jensen asked Judge Friedman to exclude from the courtroom any persons expected to be called as witnesses, a common order designed to prevent anyone who might be taking the stand from hearing what others had already attested to. Otherwise, the later-called witnesses might be tempted to tailor their testimony accordingly. Two exceptions to the order were requested and granted—an inspector from the District Attorney's office was allowed to stay and Huey's fiancée, LaVerne Williams, who was seated with Newton's siblings and his minister. Everyone else—reporters and interested observers—remained seated. Jensen also asked the court to prohibit any display of support for Newton in the courtroom, including leaflets, buttons, and signs. Garry, in turn, objected to the unaccustomed security measures. He charged that they created an atmosphere of fear and intimidation which gave members of the jury panel the impression Newton was a dangerous killer before the trial even began. Following his cautious custom, the judge took both motions under submission, though the likelihood that he would abandon the extraordinary security precautions was virtually nil.

It was close to 11:15 a.m. when the clerk called the names of forty-five prospective jurors for "The People versus Huey P. Newton." All but two acknowledged their presence in the packed courtroom, some seated on folding chairs that had been brought in, some allowed to sit temporarily in the jury box. Many shivered in the sixty-degree courtroom. Out of that group only six were non-white. Newton then entered from a side door, accompanied by a bailiff. Looking cheerful and relaxed, he created a remarkable first impression, with a new haircut, a sharp gray suit, and black turtleneck chosen for him by his brother Walter. As he made his way to the defense table next to Garry, Newton raised his fist to greet supporters.

Out of sight of the spectators, Newton had just been escorted in handcuffs down a stairwell from the tenth floor into a hallway leading to the courtroom. At the side entrance, his cuffs were removed to avoid prejudicing potential jurors against him. For a similar reason, he had been allowed to dress in a turtleneck, slacks, and jacket for the court proceedings. Once he returned to his tenth floor cell, he had to change immediately to his loose, county-issued jail clothes. The same ritual was repeated each court day. Sometimes spectators could get a glimpse of the officers recuffing Newton's wrists behind his back as they headed into the stairwell.

The court clerk called the names of all the potential jurors in the first group and immediately told them they could leave and report back the next morning. As soon as they departed, thirty more spectators streamed into the courtroom. Judge Friedman had dismissed the panel of potential jurors for the rest of the day because he needed the time to address several preliminary issues Garry had raised. These included a motion Stender had just prepared based on Judge Phillips' recent ruling. She anticipated that Jensen might use his jury challenges improperly, both to eliminate all black jurors and to exclude anyone with scruples against the death penalty. Garry told the judge he intended to call several witnesses in support of these motions, which the judge would need to rule upon before any jurors were selected.

Judge Friedman called both sides into his chambers. Jensen got up from his chair and started to enter the chambers by himself. When Garry rose to join him so did Ed Keating, Fay Stender, Alex Hoffmann, and Carleton Innis. The judge looked askance and promptly advised Garry that he had a rule that only two attorneys could represent one side in chambers. Jensen thought the judge made the rule up on the spot. Without hesitation, Garry summoned Stender to join him, leaving the others in the courtroom. In Jensen's view, that decision was a ringing endorsement of her vital role in the case. Garry was among the vast majority of trial lawyers who considered their practice an exclusive men's club, but he was also extremely practical—the decision who would accompany him into chambers was not even close. He could not handle this case without Fay Stender; everyone else was dispensable.

By the end of the first day, Garry's feisty attitude already irked Judge Friedman. Among all the other issues he had dumped on the judge's plate, Garry raised a complaint from Newton's family that they had been discriminated against in being photographed and fingerprinted to obtain trial passes. The judge shouted in reply that Garry needed to file proper papers if he wanted the issue considered. He then emphatically announced, "This court is in recess" and left the bench.[27] When the court session ended, Garry and Stender quickly learned from their office mates that the Ninth Circuit had acted that afternoon to deny review of the federal district court's ruling on a technicality—in their hurry, they had not provided proof they had given notice of appeal to the Alameda County District Attorney. Their last hope was the United States Supreme Court. Frank McTernan filed that petition for review Monday night.

On Tuesday, hot weather reduced the crowd around the courthouse to a few hundred, about one-fifth of the crowd that had gathered on Monday. The flagpole on the ground remained bare on Tuesday, but another on the courthouse roof still waved its state and national flags. Standing outside all day, marching and shouting, took its toll. One of the Panthers fainted from the heat. But the remaining crowd still demonstrated noisily. Inside the courtroom, Newton wore the same black turtleneck and gray suit on Tuesday as he wore on Monday. He complained to his counsel that he was chilly, but they were unable to convince the judge to adjust the air-conditioning. Newton often turned to smile at the spectators in the courtroom, particularly SNCC's leader James Forman, who was seated prominently in the audience. Forman, then in his late thirties, could be easily spotted, dressed in an African tunic with his graying hair uncombed, looking somewhat like a modern-day version of fiery abolitionist Frederick Douglass. Forman made himself even more conspicuous as the only person in the courtroom who remained seated when the judge entered, rising only after Judge Friedman glared at him.

Back in 1964, Forman had gained a reputation for his in-your-face attitude toward authority with an angry challenge: "If we can't sit at the table of democracy, we'll knock the fucking legs off."[28] Ironically, Forman was not deemed militant enough for SNCC's new leadership and that of the Black Panthers, who considered him paranoid and unstable. He and Dinky Romilly now had a one-year-old son. His ongoing relationship with her may have contributed to his impending political ostracism from SNCC. Other whites formerly integral to the organization had already been ousted from its power structure. This trial appearance was Forman's last show of public affiliation with the Party. They had a major falling out the following month. But on the second day of trial in mid-July, Forman appeared to offer his full support to Newton.

The first witness Garry called was the County Jury Commissioner to explain how the master jury panel was selected solely from registered voters. Every six months, the county drew the names of 7,000 prospective jurors. From that number, the county used a "working panel" of 1,600 potential jurors selected at random from nearly 1,200 precincts in the county. The master panel for the Newton case had instead been a 900-member emergency panel created after the springtime ruling in *People v. Craig*. The new panel avoided the constitutional problem that Judge Avakian had addressed; none of the 900 panelists had been required to pass a juror intelligence test.

Next came Prof. Vizard, who analyzed the voter registration of various county districts. He noted that Oakland's highest ratio of voter registration, 83.6 percent, was in the hilly Montclair District, which had only a minute percentage of blacks. Vizard also testified that low-income blacks were often apathetic about voting. It presented no meaningful opportunity to them, since they had little, if any, political power. On cross-examination, Jensen got the professor to admit that in South Berkeley most blacks did vote. The professor attributed this phenomenon to much higher education and income per capita compared to other black neighborhoods.

On Tuesday afternoon, Garry called his co-counsel Ed Keating to the stand. Keating had overseen a review Monday night of the jury commissioner's office records to analyze the number of potential jurors who had been excused and the reasons why. On cross-examination by Jensen, Keating conceded that almost twice as many juror forms were returned from West Oakland as undeliverable than in the county as a whole. On Wednesday, as a record heat wave continued, Panthers outside the building wisely left their leather jackets home, showing up in matching blue tee shirts instead. Inside the courtroom, Garry called Alex Hoffmann to the stand to report on his examination of juror records on Monday night. Seventy percent of potential jurors from West Oakland had been excused, while sixty percent were excused from Montclair. Reporters began to yawn—the showing of disparate treatment was hardly dramatic.

Garry continued a parade of experts, including Prof. Blauner. The bearded academic answered questions for half an hour describing the results of his research, including his work as an adviser to the California commission that investigated the 1965 Watts riot that left in its wake 34 dead, over 1,000 injured, and $40 million in damages. Blauner addressed the problems of racism in the country and how the jury might prejudge a black man accused of killing a white police officer. Blauner found that he enjoyed sparring with Jensen on cross-examination. He fully supported Garry's position that only poor residents of the Oakland ghettos would constitute a true jury of Newton's peers and freely admitted that he himself held residual racist attitudes.

Garry also called Dr. Nevitt Sanford, one of the principal authors of *The Authoritarian Personality*. The book focused on the type of personality predisposed to convict defendants, the phenomenon the Supreme Court had been troubled by in the *Witherspoon* case. As with the other experts, Stender had prepared the outline for Garry to use. One of the key points she wanted Dr. Sanford to mention on the stand was how few people would admit to prejudice when directly questioned. This was a major reason why the defense deemed it critical to question potential jurors individually, out of the presence of the other panelists. Reticence to admit prejudice was mentioned again by Dr. Diamond. Reporters might have noticed that he bore a strong resemblance to the then-prominent Hollywood actor, Canadian-American Raymond Massey. Dr. Diamond startled Judge Friedman by saying it was impossible to select a totally impartial jury, even with extensive questioning designed to expose latent racism. He told the judge he would need close to fifty hours alone in his clinic with each prospective juror to attempt such a task. The judge had been planning at most fifteen minutes per prospective juror. Dr. Diamond, like Prof. Blauner, admitted that he himself held residual racist attitudes, prompting Judge Friedman to ask if Dr. Diamond considered himself to be a good potential juror. Dr. Diamond said "No," leaving the judge to wonder who would.[29]

From the point of view of the press, the star witness on Wednesday was Dr. Hans Zeisel from the University of Chicago. Many were already aware that Dr. Zeisel's seminal work on *The American Jury* had influenced the United States Supreme Court in issuing the landmark *Witherspoon* opinion. Short and balding, with a heavy Austrian accent, the expert exuded an air of authority as he lectured the judge from the witness chair when prompted by Stender's questions. Dr. Zeisel testified that white males were most likely to favor the death penalty, about fifty-five percent in his studies, followed by less than half of white women, while the percentages of black men and black women who supported it declined to the mid to low thirties. He went into other statistics his researchers had derived. Judge Friedman tried to get to the essence of Dr. Zeisel's testimony, "Are you trying to say it is your opinion a white jury is more likely to wrongfully convict a Negro?" Dr. Zeisel spread his hands to underscore his response: "It's rumored it has happened."[30]

As he concluded his testimony, Dr. Zeisel was taken aback when the judge asked him his own personal views. Zeisel wondered if his objectivity was undercut when he honestly responded that he opposed the death penalty. Newton was pleased with Zeisel's testimony and asked Stender to thank the professor for him. Zeisel, in turn, told Stender he had been impressed with how remarkably attractive a person her client appeared.

"Not only attractive . . . courageous and intelligent," responded Stender as she promised Zeisel reimbursement for his $250 in travel costs.[31] She took great pride in how Newton impressed both experts and activists with the righteousness of his cause, his apparent inner strength, and extraordinarily handsome demeanor. She likely was unsurprised when one Oakland woman who saw Newton in jail in early July compared his charisma to that of Jesus Christ or Lenin.

Rev. Jesse Jackson, the highly touted, new heir-apparent to Dr. King, wired Newton a supportive message: whether found innocent or guilty, he represented "the disenchanted and degraded" against whom "unjust men" could not "render justice."[32] The same theme had pervaded the testimony of the expert defense witnesses who had come forward to defend their conclusions that overt and subtle racism was pervasive among white jurors. The timing for seeking court permission to ask jurors an extensive list of introspective questions could not have been better. Whether from perceived heightened national interest or out of a sense of guilt, or both, national television was for the first time showcasing programs like "The History of the Negro People," "Black Journal," and "Of Black America," narrated by comedian Bill Cosby. Suddenly, other prominent African-Americans were also featured commentators. Locally, since the late spring, *The San Francisco Examiner* had been running a series of articles on "Negro History in California."

Poet Maya Angelou hosted a ten-week television program, "Black, Blues, Black," seeking to educate white viewers on contemporary black culture and the current unrest among fellow African-Americans: "The hostility that some blacks are expressing now is just a stage we have to go through. The black person has always been pictured as either subhuman or superhuman . . . . We have to arrive at the stage where we're just human."[33] The distance to that goal was exemplified by a popular new show on Broadway in San Francisco's North Beach District. Already famous for its topless go-go dancers, the neon-dominated street now featured a marquee drawing patrons to a "nude inter-racial love dance" until the police arrested the manager and a naked performer.

The point made by all of the experts Garry called to the stand was that the community as a whole was exceedingly far from treating its black members as just "fellow humans." In the late 1960s there even remained strong disagreement on the subject of self-identification. Almost forty percent still preferred the term "Negro." Twenty percent favored "Colored People," though thirty percent despised that term. Close to twenty percent had warmed to the term "Black," but twenty-five percent considered that terminology the most distasteful. Ten percent preferred African-American and a roughly equal number found that nomenclature least appealing. Very few, however, did not care.[34] Garry himself had just undertaken a crash course on the subject of racism from the sociologists Stender had gathered. The professors were surprised at Garry's own lack of sensitivity on the subject and his arrogant assumption he had little to learn. Among his long-established black clientele was an African-American doctor then serving as a member of the San Francisco Police Commission. Much to the irritation of the Oakland Police Officers Association, Garry liked to flaunt the gold star the doctor had just bestowed on him, designating his longtime friend as an honorary member of the San Francisco Police Department.

Garry was persuaded by Stender and the experts to spend more effort educating the judge on this issue since his role in the upcoming jury selection phase of the trial would be crucial. To this end, the defense team wanted to offer the affidavits Stender had obtained from additional experts back East to bolster the expert testimony Judge Friedman had just heard. Garry then took a gamble. He had not decided yet whether to call Newton as a witness at trial, but summoned Newton to the stand at this stage to testify that he was penniless. Some of the press in the audience misinterpreted the reason for Newton's being called to testify about his lack of funds. They thought it was another ploy for delay, assuming he would seek to have court-appointed counsel, instead of Garry. But Garry had no such thought in mind. He wanted to impress on Judge Friedman that Newton could not afford to bring experts from the East Coast to the trial, hoping that the judge would then accept the declarations of the additional experts instead of requiring their live testimony.

Judge Friedman, taken by surprise, warned Newton that anything he said on the stand could be used against him at the trial and that the prosecutor might ask him questions unrelated to his financial status.

But Jensen accepted the limited purpose for which Newton had been called and focused his questions solely on Newton's finances and not on the charged crime. Secretly, Garry admired Jensen as a worthy adversary with strong notions of fair play. Jensen could be counted upon to follow "Marquis of Queensberry" rules in court—like the traditional good sportsmanship rules that governed boxing. An unapologetic streetfighter, Garry came from a different mold. He did not respect rules that interfered with his overall objective.

Newton then testified he had no savings, property, or money held in trust. The defense fund in his name was not under his control, and he did not know how much was in the fund or how it was being used. Newton elicited titters from the packed courtroom when he turned to the judge and said, "I probably could get the names if the court would permit me to be free for a couple of days."[35] Actually, Newton had made sure that his brother Melvin was in charge of the Newton Defense Fund, as Garry well knew. All that Garry acknowledged in court was that some $12,000 of the defense funds had been paid to his firm to date, primarily for cost reimbursements. Jensen still objected to the admission of the expert affidavits since the authors were not available for cross-examination. Judge Friedman agreed with the prosecutor and declined to consider them.

Outside of court, much of Stender's recent work on the case had been dedicated to preparing the expert witnesses and drafting the trial motions back in the office on weekends and evenings. In court, Stender alternated between sitting next to Garry at the counsel table or just behind him in a row of seats inside the barrier separating the audience from "the well" where counsel tables were located. She could usually be seen intensely scribbling notes and sometimes passing them forward to Garry or reviewing them with him at a break. When Keating came, he took his place next to Garry at the defense table, despite his far lesser role in Newton's defense. Reporter Gilbert Moore, attending regularly, saw how Stender's dedication equaled Garry's. He described her as the streetfighter's "nervous, hard-working assistant, like her boss passionately in love with lost causes."[36] Moore had to have numbered among the sympathetic reporters joining Stender for lunch at the Court Lounge restaurant. She had little opportunity to express her zeal as an advocate in court.

Whenever David Wellman attended the trial, Garry impressed the Cal graduate student as an overbearing egotist who seemed largely unappreciative of Fay Stender's remarkable talents. Cooper thought so, too. Stopping by occasionally to observe the trial as she pondered her own future career path, she found the Newton case fascinating. Watching Garry's brilliant *voir dire* of the jury had opened her eyes. She thought he had probably won over the black foreman on day one. Cooper could not help but notice Stender's relegation to an insignificant public role, despite the vital motion work she performed. Stender gave Cooper the clear impression that she would like to have much more responsibility in the courtroom if she could make it happen. Had his chief collaborator been a male, it is doubtful Garry would have bounced him back and forth from the counsel table in such fashion. As it was, Garry remained oblivious to Stender's ever-increasing dissatisfaction. After the lunch recess on Wednesday, July 17, Stender addressed the court briefly on a procedural matter. She reported to Judge Friedman that the United States Attorney's office had communicated an objection to one of their experts, Dr. Hunter, being called to testify before they completed a review of a government report he had prepared. There could be privileged information, which it might wish to protect from disclosure. But since the government had not obtained a restraining order, Judge Friedman let Garry proceed with his questioning of Dr. Hunter. Stender sat back down in her role as note-taker.

When the parade of experts concluded, Judge Friedman, like Garry, felt he had just taken an advanced crash course in sociology. The defense topped off their successful day of race-bias sensitivity training by granting interviews with Newton on the tenth floor of the courthouse to all the reporters who could squeeze into the small, green interview room with Newton and his attorneys. Amazingly, sandwiched like students in a telephone booth, sixteen had done so. Newton thrived on the attention. Asked to assess Judge Friedman, Newton was blunt: he did not believe the man presiding over his capital case was "very well versed in the law." He told the gathering that Garry sought to accomplish a "revolution in the courtroom" by obtaining a nontraditional jury, ideally from his same socio-economic background and race. Newton also welcomed younger white jurors who understood black culture in ghetto communities like West Oakland.[37] (Actually, Newton's lawyers likely had heard that in the relatively rare instances when two or three African-Americans had sat together on a jury in a criminal case in Alameda County, the case predictably ended in a hung jury split along racial lines.)

At every recess on the first three days, reporters rushed past the rail dividing the attorneys from onlookers to be the first to obtain quotes from the calm prosecutor and cocky defense counsel. By Thursday, Judge Friedman halted this practice. No reporters would again be allowed into "the well" where the attorneys sat during the trial breaks. On Thursday morning, Judge Friedman denied the pending defense motions. A jury of Newton's peers did not mean a jury of blacks from his neighborhood. Otherwise, a white truck driver defendant could argue that he was entitled to exclude all blacks from his jury and other ethnic defendants could make similar demands. Judge Friedman did rule, based on the United States Supreme Court decision in *Witherspoon*, that challenges for cause based on potential jurors' objections to the death penalty would be limited to those who could not set aside their personal views and consider imposing the death penalty in appropriate circumstances.

The rulings were all that the defense could realistically have hoped for. Stender's long hours preparing all the expert witnesses and briefing the issues of racism and prejudice had rendered Judge Friedman far more aware of the centrality of these issues to the defense's case. The judge would wind up allowing a substantially longer jury questioning process to weed out racists than he had originally intended. He would also bend over backwards to keep jurors opposed to capital punishment in the case who said they would consider imposing the death penalty if the specific facts warranted it. The time had come to see who would have Huey Newton's life in their hands.

11. A MINORITY OF ONE

I who am left here as . . . passive eye
in the center of a terrible storm.
ANNE CHRISTINE D'ADESKY

When proceedings continued after the pretrial motions were denied, Prof. Blauner surprisingly abandoned the role of disinterested expert and became a front row spectator and defense consultant for the duration of the trial. Like the other experts, Blauner had not charged for his testimony. He provided his continued consultation free as well. For a specialist in race relations with an open summer schedule, it was far too exciting an opportunity to pass up. Sitting next to Fay Stender and Alex Hoffmann, Blauner got into the habit of taking copious notes, thinking he might write a book about the racially charged case when the trial was over. The three enjoyed long lunches every day at the Court Lounge restaurant across the street from the court house. They were often joined by friendly reporters and Newton's radical Episcopalian minister, Father Earl Neil, who was sitting in on the trial with Newton's fiancée and family. Sometimes Ed Keating, who also planned to write a book about the trial, sat in, and occasionally Garry would join them for lunch as well, if he wasn't too busy working over the noontime break.

Prof. Blauner's expertise came in handy during the jury *voir dire.* Close to 160 prospective jurors would be examined under oath during that question-and-answer selection process over the next two-and-a-half weeks as the lawyers picked twelve jurors and four alternates. From the master panel of jurors, a group of up to fifty were sent to the courtroom at one time. There, the clerk would spin a wheel to select random people from that group to sit in the jury box for *voir dire.* The very first person questioned was a Hayward dental technician named Orville Miller, who announced that he had read accounts of the killing in *The Oakland Tribune* that made Newton's guilt appear an open-and-shut case. Yet Miller believed he had since "sort of become unbiased."[1] Garry would soon get Judge Friedman to dismiss Miller for cause. The first black of the six in the first batch of potential jurors was Leroy Steveson, a retired waiter who had worked for the Southern Pacific Railroad. But the seventy-year-old was dismissed for cause after he insisted he could not consider imposing the death penalty. Garry had done his best to save Steveson from automatic elimination by asking if his views might change if someone brutally murdered his own child, to no avail.

As the days wore on, many potential jurors, including a high percentage of minorities, insisted that they could not render the death penalty under any circumstance and were then excused for cause. Stender felt that minorities who took an absolute anti-death-penalty position confirmed how racism worked. These jurors clearly believed capital punishment was so skewed in its use, they could never support it. She hoped they would not have to wind up arguing on appeal that Newton's life should be spared because skittish minorities had voluntarily removed themselves from the jury pool, thus making his conviction more likely.

When she was preparing for trial, Stender had learned that the jury commissioner questioned members of the jury panel about their views on capital punishment. She added that to her list for Garry to ask about when he spoke with potential jurors. She was very proud to have collaborated with the sociologists on nearly 300 questions designed to elicit bias, such as the panelists' views of the Black Panther Party, "fair housing," and "Black Power." The list even included the panelists' views on the final report of President Johnson's blue ribbon commission on violence: what reaction did they have to the "Kerner Report," attributing urban blight to white racism? Predictably, Jensen objected to most of the questions as irrelevant. Judge Friedman would not let Garry ask how the jurors voted on Proposition 14 (rejecting the fair housing law) and how they perceived race issues generally. The judge restricted questioning to each juror's own state of mind or conduct on race issues. Yet, when reworded, most of the questions designed to elicit bias could still be asked. The reporters settled in for a long, slow, and tedious selection process.

After all the effort they had put into preparing the probing set of jury questions, Stender, Blauner, and Wellman (who attended the trial only sporadically) quickly grew disappointed. Garry had no intention of reading the entire list of questions to each potential juror. As an old-fashioned trial lawyer, he trusted his gut and had no patience for their scientific approach. In his experience, questioning potential jurors in *voir dire* was not just to elicit disqualifying bias. A major objective was to obtain a feel for the jurors' personalities. Garry did not want to bore the friendly jurors to death or spend more time than he felt he needed to smoke out an unwanted juror.

Dapperly dressed, Garry proceeded to woo middle-aged women jurors, and joked and tried to develop a rapport with many of the others. He could be warm and sympathetic one minute with a friendly juror and openly hostile and intimidating to the next panelist, hoping to force disqualifying responses. He put on quite a show, sometimes taking his glasses off for emphasis of a particular point. Quickly, he discovered that almost everyone had heard of the case and that some insisted they could put any preconceptions aside; that most of the white panelists had little interaction with blacks in their lives; had never heard of the blue ribbon "Kerner Report" commissioned by President Johnson; had heard of Black Power, but did not know what it meant; and had never heard the term white racism. His ego often got in the way, sacrificing the opportunity for a candid response to his desire to flaunt his skills.

Jensen, more rough-hewn in appearance and not a showman by nature, wore a suit that appeared to come off the rack too short for his long arms. The lanky prosecutor steered clear of most political questions, focusing on the specifics of the case. His approach was far more earnest and respectful of all jurors and relatively devoid of emotion. To some observers, he appeared unfeeling, but sitting at the defense counsel table every day, Keating sized Jensen up as a top-notch trial lawyer, who took his role as a champion of law and order very seriously. Jensen tried a little humor himself, but looked uncomfortable competing with

Garry in that fashion and the attempts largely fell flat. Jensen's aim in examining the jurors for bias appeared obvious—to probe anyone with anti-establishment views and anyone opposed to the death penalty in an attempt to get them dismissed for cause. Garry's strategy in selecting jurors was diametrically opposed and guided principally by intuition. Garry generally wanted to keep anyone who disfavored the death penalty, and all members of minority groups.

The first person seated as a potential juror was a black man employed as an Alameda Naval Air Station aircraft cleaner. He denied ever hearing of the Panthers or Huey Newton and vowed that he could apply the death penalty, if need be. By light questioning, Garry took a calculated risk. He wanted to create the impression that every member of a minority group would understand his client's perspective better than whites, but he knew better. Even most blacks in the Bay Area had varied reactions to the Panthers, viewing them with "a mixture of fear, embarrassment and admiration."[2] Other minorities often shared the fear and not the admiration. When conservative whites took the stand, Garry might probe them on any affiliation with the right-wing John Birch Society or their views on the Warren Court, as well as asking direct questions designed to elicit race bias. A registered Republican surprised Garry by anticipating a question Garry had asked many others: whether he would relocate his family if black families moved into his neighborhood. The year before, the retired Air Force supply sergeant had moved his wife and six children *into* a mostly black neighborhood in Oakland's flatlands. Garry still did not trust him.

Lowell Jensen reacted similarly to strike most potential jurors the defense favored. The Peace and Freedom Party member from Berkeley with a "Free Huey" bumper sticker on his car—who made pottery and got his news from *The Berkeley Barb*—did not stand a chance of remaining, despite his solemn promise to be impartial. Jensen also rejected the ex-wife of a Berkeley police inspector who, perhaps out of bitter personal experience, seemed too eager to point out that police were no better than anybody else. When the prosecutor used a peremptory challenge to excuse the African-American aircraft cleaner, Garry stood up and pointedly noted his race for the record. Garry would repeat that announcement each time Jensen challenged a black person, though Garry eventually drew an admonition from Judge Friedman that both the prosecutor and defense had the same right to dismiss jurors of their choice. Everyone could see that Garry had used his own peremptory challenges primarily for jurors from the white suburbs, which Jensen had not commented upon.

Yet Garry did get a rise out of Jensen when a supermarket clerk from the unincorporated Castro Valley took the stand. In answering Jensen's questions, Wesley Kissinger had mentioned his past experience as a reserve deputy sheriff who still knew several high-ranking members of the police force. Given his turn, Garry immediately went on the attack: "We plan to show that the police instigated and plotted the incident that brought Huey Newton here." Jensen's heated objection forced Garry to rephrase the statement as a question: "Would you find it hard to believe that police would plot and instigate an incident against a defendant?" As reporters scribbled notes of the day's highlight, the clerk answered in the affirmative. Try as he might Garry could not get Kissinger disqualified by the judge for cause and had to use his thirteenth peremptory challenge.[3]

Despite all his efforts to eliminate jurors predisposed to reject his theory of a police conspiracy to get Newton, Garry felt strongly that the entire panel was less than satisfactory because of a pro-prosecution tilt. He had been forced to use his very last peremptory challenge after prolonged questioning of a man from the predominantly white city of Alameda, who belonged to a health club that barred Negro members. The assistant bank manager said he thought the club's "whites only" policy was wrong and that he would not be influenced in evaluating the evidence by the fact one of his handball partners was an Oakland police officer.[4] Judge Friedman saw no reason not to take him at his word. Garry assumed that Hitler himself would lie about his racist beliefs if asked about them in a polite and respectful manner, the way judges were wont to do with jurors—"Do you have an open mind? Can you be fair?"[5] *Life* reporter Gilbert Moore empathized with Garry's unusual burden in defending a revolutionary: "[I]f Lowell Jensen had had only twenty and Charles Garry had had *two hundred* peremptory challenges at his disposal, it still would not have been enough."[6]

If jurors seemed unsympathetic, Garry tried to force a reaction with questions such as "If the charge were made in this courtroom that white racism was responsible for most of the problems of black people, would that make you mad?" Though Garry might not elicit a knee-jerk response from the juror being addressed, other panelists would sometimes react visibly. Hearing this question, three potential jurors in the back row hissed loudly; the defense team noted their identities and made sure that none of them were selected.[7] Some of the challenges had been easy, like the prospective juror who published a newspaper that criticized the Black Panthers, the one who was a close family friend of the District Attorney, or the man who was a local auto mechanic for the FBI. Every successful challenge for cause meant one less peremptory challenge that had to be used. Garry viewed each of his twenty challenges as if Huey's life depended on it. It may well have.

Judge Friedman performed as hoped, applying his discretion to use great latitude to keep jurors who said that, under some circumstances, they might apply the death penalty, even though they opposed it in principle. Stender also realized that, because of the new restrictions on juror disqualification, Jensen was required to use up more than one of his valuable peremptory challenges on jurors whom he did not trust to apply the death penalty. Under prior standards the same jurors would likely have been excused by the judge for cause as persons too biased toward the defense. Moreover, by persuading the judge to permit juror questioning in far greater depth than was customary, the defense team was able to glean more information about the jurors than was ordinarily exposed.

Garry had another reason for lengthy, repetitive questioning of some jurors he perceived as potentially hostile. He was using the opportunity of *voir dire* to put all of the white panelists on the defensive about their possible latent racism and to educate all of the panelists about key, negative facts before the prosecutor had the opportunity to do so. Garry figured that if he mentioned the prosecutor's best arguments first, they might lose their punch. So he asked potential jurors if the fact that there would be evidence of Huey Newton having a felony conviction would affect their view of his credibility. Or whether they would assume that if Huey Newton testified he would be motivated to lie because his life was on the line. He also asked whether they would be resentful of Newton and the Panthers for referring to police officers as "pigs."

One prospective juror, June Reed, a married secretary with three children, took offense at the derogatory Panther term for policemen—the same reaction she had to hearing "white people call colored people niggers."[8] She was uncomfortable that anyone carried guns for self-protection. Reed admitted that she might harbor some residual racist attitudes and that she disapproved of inter-racial marriage. Another prospective juror, Jenevie Gibbons, who was married to a fireman and was herself a factory worker, expressed no problem with the term "pigs." She volunteered, "People used to call them 'the fuzz' and that didn't bother me either."[9] Both eventually made it onto the jury.

As was customary, though Garry had requested otherwise, all of the potential jurors were present as the rest of the panel was interviewed. Each could absorb what the others said. The judge dismissed one man who was frightened by a rumor that the Black Panthers would seek revenge on any person who convicted Huey Newton. The man said, quite frankly, that he assumed a juror who rendered a guilty verdict would have to plan to leave town. In contrast, a white Hawaiian refused to participate because he had an inter-racial son who was unfairly blamed for neighborhood pranks. He emphatically stated, "I have seen with my own eyes how colored people are treated in California . . . So I don't want no part of this."[10] Two blacks who were dismissed said they were friends of the Newton family or their kids went to school together, one of them pointing out how nice a kid Huey had always been.

The judge dismissed a woman who admitted that she moved out of her Oakland neighborhood after her other white neighbors left because too many black people had moved in. They had resettled in the white suburb of San Leandro. Another woman prompted Newton to laugh when she said she could not be sure of her impartiality because she sympathized with both the police and the Black Panthers. Jensen issued a peremptory challenge to excuse her from the jury. Most of those who were discharged demonstrated immense relief, jumping at the proffered dismissal slip from the court clerk and scurrying from the courtroom with a perceptible lilt in their steps.

Prof. Blauner did not always agree with Garry's approach. He shared his views frequently with Fay Stender and Alex Hoffmann and sometimes with Garry during breaks, and made suggestions for alternative wording of questions. He thought Garry asked too many directed questions that led to uninformative responses. Blauner favored open-ended questions that might reveal honest, prejudiced answers. He would have asked a juror, "Tell me what feeling Black Power brings to your mind" rather than "Black Power, does that create a revulsion in your mind?"[11] Anyone would be expected to say no to Garry's formulation. His critical team members soon realized that, where grounds for excusing someone for cause were not readily apparent, Garry was less interested in the actual answers to bias questions than in trying to read the body language with which the answers were delivered. Garry never expected to achieve an impartial jury. He hoped for one in which he had a few favorably disposed jurors and others intimidated from acting on their pro-prosecution bias.

Prof. Blauner thought the least racist person would not deny race prejudice, would be knowledgeable about Afro-American culture, would interact with blacks daily, and actively seek to combat discrimination. Newton had found his testimony "out of sight" and invited the highly flattered Blauner to meet him in his cell.[12] But *voir dire* was not designed to find and keep the people Bob Blauner would have considered most receptive to Huey Newton's defense. He would have kept the middle-aged woman who was the last to leave her neighborhood in Oakland for an all-white enclave in San Leandro. Her honesty had impressed him as she was excused by the judge for cause.

On Thursday of the first week, the defense filed a renewed motion to exclude Newton's prior conviction from the jury's consideration. They had just obtained the transcript from the prior assault trial in which Newton had acted as his own attorney. They pointed out to Judge Friedman that Newton had asked the court at the beginning of the prior proceeding, "If possible, I would like to have a legal adviser, but I would like to speak for myself."[13] They argued that the judge in that case had been too quick to deny Newton legal assistance. On Friday at noon, the trial adjourned for the week. Judge Friedman said he wanted to use the afternoon to research the renewed defense motion to expunge Newton's prior felony conviction. By then, he had issued a new ruling for the media—from now on twenty-five seats would be reserved for the local dailies, the two wire services, television and radio, with only three seats guaranteed for all other reporters, first-come, first-served. Dismayed reporters also realized that the focus of the second week promised to be more repetitive questioning of the remaining members of the jury panel. Despite Garry's feisty approach, they would be in for a fairly boring couple of weeks until jury selection was over. Seventeen jurors had been eliminated for cause out of the twenty-four questioned, leaving seven jurors tentatively chosen—subject to later rejection by either attorney using their remaining peremptory challenges.

The Oakland Post reported that the Alameda County Courthouse was not "where it was at" on Monday and Tuesday, July 22 and July 23.[14] Kathleen Cleaver thought otherwise. Using a bullhorn on Monday morning, she had orchestrated the handful of Panthers and twenty or so children chanting and shouting in Swahili and English until her voice went hoarse. The small crowd on Monday dispersed by noon and no one except Kathleen showed up on Tuesday, amid rumors of a planned rally elsewhere. Kathleen was livid when her husband then told her to go to their new apartment to unpack boxes instead of attending the trial.

Complaints were registered with Judge Friedman about his decision to skew access in favor of mainstream press, leaving representatives of underground papers and other sympathetic media outside the locked courtroom. Yet, by the second week, there were more specially prepared badges for media representatives than reporters seeking access to the trial. Empty seats could be found inside the courtroom as the jury selection process wore on. By then, *Life*'s Gilbert Moore was taking no chances, rising as early as 2 a.m. to become a daily fixture. He was obsessed with the absurd theatricality of the event. Moore realized the potential jurors felt otherwise: among the hundreds of mostly white, middle-class voters called to serve, "almost none of the 'talent' wanted to be in the show."[15] All in all, through methodical questioning by Jensen and alternately hard-hitting or playful questioning by Garry, forty-one people of the more than 150 panelists called were successfully challenged for cause because the judge agreed they demonstrated prejudice. Of those, most admitted that they had some preconception of Newton's guilt, low regard for the Black Panthers, or high regard for police that they could not set aside. Throughout Newton remained cheerful, looking just as dapper when he wore his brown suit accompanied by a mustard-colored turtleneck as he had on day one in sharkskin gray.

One juror, a Hayward technician named Strauss, said that for the last ten months he had assumed that Newton was guilty, but believed he could set that aside and be impartial as instructed by the judge. Jensen argued that the juror should be allowed to stay since "virtually every resident of the county" had some exposure to the sensational murder.[16] Garry was then permitted to probe further. The particularly impressive interchange later made its way into legal textbooks. It began when Mr. Strauss indicated that "to a certain extent" he had already formed an opinion about the case from the pretrial publicity and the fact that the officer was dead. Under further questioning, he professed to be willing to decide the case solely on the evidence presented. Garry's intuition told him otherwise. Ruling in Jensen's favor, the judge denied Garry's challenge for cause, but acceded to Garry's request to ask Mr. Strauss just a few more questions.

> Q: As you sit there right now do you believe that
> Huey Newton shot and killed . . . Officer Frey?
> A: I don't know whether he shot him or not.
> That I cannot say.

The court then instructed Mr. Strauss on the presumption of innocence.

> THE COURT: So, therefore, as it stands right now, do
> you believe he is guilty before you hear any evidence?
> A: No.

Garry then questioned Mr. Strauss again, only to hear him repeat that he would apply the presumption of innocence and look solely to the evidence presented at trial. Garry remained unsatisfied that he was getting a straight answer, so he pushed it one step further:

Q: As Huey Newton sits here next to me now, in your opinion, is he absolutely innocent?
A: Yes.
Q: But you don't believe it, do you?
A: No.
THE COURT: Challenge is allowed.[17]

On the issue of race prejudice, Garry still felt dissatisfied with most of those in the remaining pool whom he could not get to make disqualifying statements. He then had to consider how best to use the remainder of his twenty peremptory challenges after eliminating those with obvious ties to law enforcement, racially exclusive clubs, or conservative political causes. He followed his gut in using some of them on liberal whites who seemed to think too deeply about race issues, attributing some of the civil rights problems to black racists as well as white racists. After two weeks of questioning, Fay Stender and Bob Blauner would have accepted the jurors then impaneled. although the defense still had three of its original twenty peremptory challenges left. David Wellman could not help but notice Garry's conceit as he dismissed Stender's input and that of the sociologists. It made Wellman angry. But Garry trusted no one's instinct but his own and was still not satisfied. Moore described Garry's jury selection efforts as a man "stuck in the apple orchard with a taste only for oranges."[18] Garry had continued to exhaust all of the remaining peremptories and to challenge other potential jurors for cause until he "finally accepted a jury with a few people on it I would not want to have lunch with let alone let them decide Huey's fate."[19] The veteran defense lawyer later insisted that he would have eliminated "at least six of the jurors if I had had any peremptory challenges left."[20]

Fourteen jurors, presumably favorable to the defense, had been removed by Judge Friedman for cause on Jensen's objection because they stated they rigidly opposed the death penalty and could not apply it if requested to do so. Observers doubted that all of them in fact were so opposed. Anyone listening to prior answers knew that taking such a fixed position was a sure way off the jury panel. In the entire three-week jury selection process, Garry had not objected to a single minority, implying that race and class affiliation were at the center of the case. Garry had also used the time to remind the jury panel that reality was not like the popular "Perry Mason" television show. It was not Huey Newton's burden to prove who killed Officer Frey and have the killer confess on the stand.

Of the twelve jurors who were finally selected on Monday July 29, there were seven women and five men. At the time, it did not fit most observers' image of a felony jury panel, let alone one charged with considering the death penalty. Across the country, juries still looked much more like the *Twelve Angry Men* in the classic 1957 Henry Fonda movie. Though American women officially became eligible to serve on juries when they won the right to vote in 1920, state legislators had immediately responded with protective legislation, primarily by exempting women from jury duty who checked a box on the form indicating they were needed at home with their children.[21] As a result, until the women's movement in the 1960s women were rarely seen on juries.[22] In fact, not until 1975 did the still all-male United States Supreme Court hold that women constituted such a "distinctive group" from men that laws categorically excluding women from serving on criminal juries violated the Sixth Amendment right to be tried by a jury of one's peers.[23] Garry generally favored women jurors, but the candor of two of the women during *voir dire* had given Garry particular pause. One was June Reed, the loquacious Safeway secretary who bristled at the term "pigs." The second was Mrs. Marian Butler, who worked in a pharmacy and was married to a stockbroker. Mrs. Butler had mentioned that her Presbyterian church in Berkeley invited representatives of the Black Panthers to speak to its parishioners only to be insulted by (expletive-laced) accusations that all white Protestants were racists. But Garry had felt obligated to use up all his peremptories on other jurors he trusted even less.

Five of the twelve jurors were minorities: one, Harvey Kokka, an always smiling Japanese-American, was a Shell laboratory technician. He generally disfavored the death penalty, but promised to apply it in an extreme case. Two were Latino women, both employed full-time. The fourth was Joseph Quintana, a well-traveled Cuban immigrant machinist with two children, who admitted to having limited English skills, but felt he could understand the testimony. This quartet represented all but one of the non-black minorities in the entire set of prospective jurors called to the courtroom. The last nonwhite on the jury was David Harper, a middle-class married black man with six children who was the only one among twenty-two black voters called for service to make it onto the panel. The defense team assumed that Jensen would have excluded all blacks as his colleague had done the week before in Judge Phillips' courtroom, if Jensen had not been concerned about its legality. Unlike Garry, Jensen had left five challenges unused. The panel was completed by five Caucasian women and two Caucasian men. The women were all middle-aged, three were married, and two—landlady Mrs. Eda Prelli and airline caterer Helen Hart—were widowed mothers. The two remaining males were Ronald Andrews, a middle-aged, married engineer with three grown children, and Thomas Hofmann, an unmarried bank-trust officer, who lived with his parents in Berkeley and professed to have no familiarity with the Panthers.

The alternate selection took a few days more before the lawyers selected one woman bank secretary from Oakland, who was married and the mother of two children, and three men, all of them white, including one who had been a student at Merritt College. Among those dismissed for cause the chief reason was again opposition to the death penalty—one woman from Berkeley announced her view that capital punishment was "legalized premeditated murder."[24] When the last one had been picked, all of the jurors and alternates were sent home until the following Monday morning. Garry immediately renewed his motion that the entire panel be dismissed since it did not consist of Newton's peers. He also made a motion for mistrial on the basis that Jensen had systematically excluded blacks as alternates. Judge Friedman denied both motions.

David Harper, the only black man seated on the jury, quickly became the subject of great speculation as to whom he might favor. He had handsome features, somewhat resembling an older, more heavy-set version of Huey Newton. Harper was a veteran of the Air Force and worked at the Bank of America as a lending officer. At night, he also taught a college accounting course. Harper wore his hair long enough to look like a modified statement—halfway between an Afro and the conservative, short cut one would expect at the time of a man in his line of work. Questioning revealed that the Bank of America also employed his wife as head of security.

During *voir dire*, Harper admitted "some reservations" about the death penalty. He said he had heard of the Panthers, but that he had not discussed the case much with anyone. He explained that his colleagues largely steered clear of the subject, just as they had pointedly refrained from talking to him following the Martin Luther King assassination a few months earlier. When asked if he harbored any feelings against the Black Panthers, he said, "Not at all." He had never formed an opinion from media coverage that Huey Newton killed Officer Frey.[25] The defense team thought Jensen made a mistake in keeping Harper on the jury. But the prosecutor was privy to the bank executive's prior service on three other jury panels, including most recently in an armed robbery prosecution. Penny Cooper had warned Fay Stender that the D.A.'s office knew how jurors who served before had voted. One could assume the armed robbery case resulted in conviction and that Harper had not participated in any hung juries. Otherwise, Harper would have posed far too great a risk to impanel on the biggest case of Jensen's career, when the veteran prosecutor still had several unused challenges at his disposal.

Harper, on occasion upon entering the courtroom, appeared to nod slightly as a greeting to Newton's minister, Father Neil. But when Harper passed Newton at the defense table, he invariably kept his face expressionless. Harper was also sometimes observed looking fleetingly at the reporters. As he bore their intense gaze, he maintained an enigmatic expression while they searched for clues to the lone black juror's thinking.

12. ON TRIAL—NEWTON OR AMERICAN SOCIETY?

I'll be judge, I'll be jury, said cunning old Fury.
I'll try the whole cause and condemn you to death.

LEWIS CARROLL

On his way into the courthouse during July and August, prosecutor Lowell Jensen often endured ironic shouts of "Power to the People." As a career public servant, Jensen officially represented "the People" in *The People of the State of California vs. Huey Newton.* Yet which people? Newton's defense team pointed to serious flaws in a governmental system that ostensibly derived its authority from the democratic process, but had historically excluded large segments of the population from meaningful participation. Though Jensen was as straight an arrow as you could find in the district attorney's office, he knew that the defense team's message of endemic prosecutorial bias resonated with some local citizens. Jensen had reason to feel confident that none of the impaneled jurors were predisposed to be anti-establishment—he had weeded out the few who turned up in their jury pool. That was why, unlike Garry, he had left several peremptory challenges unused. Jensen expected that his customarily careful presentation, coupled with a reminder of the jury's role in preserving law and order, would win the Newton jury over just as that strategy had prevailed with so many other panels in his career.

By nature methodical and thorough, Jensen put on as simple a case as possible: a policeman had been killed in the line of duty at the hands of a felon fearing imminent arrest for violating the terms of his probation. The shooting was intentional, and thus "The People's" protection necessitated the death penalty. Behind the scenes, law enforcement pressure on Jensen for a conviction was intense. The Oakland Police Department expected the conviction to send an unqualified message that no one—particularly the head of a militant organization that vilified police as "pigs"—would go unpunished for murdering a cop. Statewide law enforcement and the FBI wanted the Panther organization dismantled before it gained national traction. As Gov. Reagan's Legal Affairs Secretary, Jensen's former superior Ed Meese could naturally be expected to keep an eye on the case for the governor. Reagan was highly interested in the outcome. Jensen believed that he possessed strong evidence of Newton's guilt, but he also knew Garry to be a formidable, no-holds-barred opponent. Garry would try his best to paint the prosecutor as a vengeful old Fury and his witnesses as biased and untruthful. Jensen prepared as thoroughly as possible; Garry's defense team did the same.

As the first day of trial testimony approached, tensions ran high. Eldridge Cleaver, covering the trial for *Ramparts* magazine, had made news a week earlier by publicly warning that if Newton were found guilty of murder, the state could only execute him "over our dead bodies."[1] The media could not see how, given the pool of county voters from which the jury would be selected, Newton had any prayer of acquittal. They were primed for fireworks. Radical media representatives reiterated their complaints of favoritism in the allocation of seats. The mainstream press received up to three badges per agency, including a courtroom artist. Though there was a 9:30 a.m. cut-off for picking up reserved badges, it seemed that the local dailies obtained entry no matter when they arrived, while many reporters from underground papers steamed indignantly in the hallway as the testimony continued behind locked doors. Some members of the alternative press lobbied Garry to petition the court again to move the proceedings to a larger venue to accommodate all of the media, but Judge Friedman remained firm.

By Monday, August 5, Stender had worked hard to ensure that all eyes of the Movement were upon them. Among those carrying press passes in the packed courtroom was award-winning author Kay Boyle, blacklisted in the '50s and now a prominent anti-war activist. Boyle had sent Stender a draft of the article she was writing for *The Progressive* magazine on the jury selection phase of the trial and asked Stender to point out any glaring factual errors. Though she was already burning the candle at both ends, Stender had been eager to accommodate Boyle. She considered such assistance an essential part of her job.

Judge Friedman began the August 5 session with the jury still sequestered while he announced rulings from the bench that could have a significant effect on the course of the trial. He had previously decided not to exclude reference to Newton's 1964 conviction, rejecting the argument that it was obtained in violation of Newton's constitutional right to counsel. In a last-ditch effort the prior Thursday afternoon, Stender had acted on the advice of other criminal defense lawyers in submitting a brief arguing that Newton's prior assault conviction should be reclassified as a misdemeanor instead of a felony. If so, the defense could achieve the same result they had sought in attempting to strike the felony conviction—a misdemeanor could not be mentioned to the jury as a basis for discrediting his testimony and would not be relevant to the trial. Newton had in fact only gone to county jail for six months, a typical misdemeanor sentence, not a year or more in state prison, as felony convictions permitted. But on Monday morning Judge Friedman rejected this latest argument. Case law cited by Jensen in response made it clear that the crime was defined by the longer suspended prison sentence imposed on Newton. Regardless of the much shorter time he actually served in county jail, Newton was a convicted felon. Thus, despite the valiant efforts of the defense, the jury would get to hear about his prior felony conviction if Newton took the stand. His status as an ex-felon could serve as a basis for discrediting all of his testimony.

Judge Friedman also announced that rumors of potential harm to the defendant or witnesses reported by both attorneys indicated that tighter security was called for. Over the objection of the defense that searches would harass Newton's supporters, Judge Friedman declared he was now ordering that everyone but counsel and the jury—whether they were "black, white, brown or yellow"—be searched for weapons daily before being permitted entry into the courtroom.[2] The order would take effect after lunch that same day. After this series of disheartening rulings against the defense, the jurors were seated in the jury box and the trial itself finally commenced, three weeks after the July 15 official start date and almost three months after the first trial date of May 10.

As prosecutor, Lowell Jensen went first because he had the burden of proof. In his much-awaited opening statement, Jensen informed the jury it was their duty to decide the facts for themselves from the courtroom reconstruction of key events alleged to have occurred. The veteran prosecutor proceeded to convey his certitude of the outcome as he gravely summarized the incriminating evidence he intended to present. He limited himself to a brief account of the events of the early morning on October 28, 1967, the day of the shooting, but described Newton ominously as a man with a history of violence and known animosity toward the police. Jensen told the jury that the fatal incident had happened very quickly after Officer Frey made a routine stop of Newton in a car with outstanding traffic violations. Marijuana found in two matchboxes in the car Newton drove provided a specific motive for the shooting—Newton feared being caught with contraband. Garry jumped up and objected that Jensen's remarks were highly prejudicial. Garry demanded a mistrial. He pointed out heatedly that Newton had not been charged with marijuana possession and asserted that Newton had no knowledge whatsoever about the contents of the matchboxes. The judge let Jensen continue, but instructed the jury that opening statements were not themselves evidence. The jury needed to wait to determine what proof was offered at trial.

Jensen plowed ahead with confidence. He asserted that Newton knew he was still subject to parole restrictions for a prior felony when Office Frey stopped his car. Conviction for "knowing possession of marijuana" would have constituted an automatic parole violation, forcing Newton back to prison to serve the rest of his suspended 1964 felony sentence for assault. Jensen continued his chilling narrative: shortly after Officer Heanes arrived, Newton decided on a bold surprise move, pulling a gun on Officer Frey, who grappled with him as it went off. Newton had then wrested Frey's own gun from Frey, killing him with his own weapon and wounding Officer Heanes with that same weapon in the resulting exchange of gunfire. The jury then heard how Jensen expected to prove that Newton and his passenger had escaped on foot with both his own and Officer Frey's weapons, commandeered a nearby car at gun point and were driven away. Only a short time later, wounded in the stomach, Newton would turn up for treatment at Kaiser Hospital, where he was arrested for murder. Jensen dramatically promised the jury that, in addition to the kidnap victim, he would produce an eyewitness to the shooting, a bus driver who would identify Newton as the killer. The media reacted with surprise as Jensen made this revelation. Newton and Garry immediately huddled together in whispered conversation, though they already knew about this bombshell.

Before they had adjourned on Thursday, August 1—the day jury selection was completed—Jensen had provided the defense team his list of thirty anticipated prosecution witnesses. That was when the defense finally learned the identity of Jensen's key surprise witness for the trial, an African-American municipal bus driver named Henry Grier. Grier was now safely sequestered in an unidentified location under police protection, which Jensen had arranged the day Grier's name first surfaced. At the same time he disclosed Grier's identity, Jensen had provided the defense with a transcript of Grier's tape-recorded statement to the police. Grier's statement identified Newton as the civilian he saw with a police officer when driving his bus route early that morning. The statement said that Grier observed the civilian pull a gun from inside his jacket or coat, spin around, and struggle with the officer. The gun went off, hitting another officer, who fired his own gun. The civilian then fired several shots at the first officer, who fell forward.

After summarizing Grier's expected testimony, Jensen concluded there was proof beyond a reasonable doubt that defendant Huey Newton was the civilian Grier saw shooting the fatal bullet into Officer Frey's back and was guilty of first degree murder. One local reporter expressed surprise that Jensen did not then ask for the death penalty, forgetting that the jury would only face that issue in a separate hearing if Newton were first found guilty of premeditated murder. From the extensive questions on capital punishment at *voir dire* the jury already knew that they might be asked to vote for Newton's execution. Spectators knowledgeable in criminal trial procedure wondered whether Garry would respond immediately with his own opening statement or wait until Jensen completed his case-in-chief and give the defense opening statement at that time, probably two weeks down the road. But those who knew Garry well could harbor no doubt that he would ever seriously contemplate the option of waiting a fortnight to educate the jury on his view of a death penalty case.

Given his turn, the streetfighter stood up and jabbed back with the exact opposite approach to Jensen. The prosecutor had zeroed in on the morning of the shootout. Garry gave it the back of his hand. Spectators noted his confident demeanor as he claimed Newton was not guilty of any of the charged crimes. He dwelt upon Huey Newton's life history, his decision to join the Black Liberation Movement and then form the Black Panther Party with Bobby Seale. Reporters observed Seale in the courtroom for the first time that day, seated among several other Panthers. Garry read the jury the Black Panther Party's Ten Point platform and asserted that because of their stand against police brutality, the Panthers had been singled out for persecution. Jensen repeatedly objected to Garry's charges of police harassment, but Garry was allowed to continue. Garry told the jury that Officer Frey was a known racist with no justification for stopping Newton that October morning. Frey had done so only to abuse the Panther leader yet again with anticipated impunity. Frey then mistreated Newton and precipitated the shootout in which he died.

Garry reiterated the death threats Newton received from police officers while in the hospital, strung with obscenities such as "nigger" and "Black bastard." The veteran trial lawyer then emphatically summed up what he intended to show in defense of the murder and assault charges: Newton did not fire a gun at any time on that date. He did not kill Officer Frey. He did not shoot Officer Heanes, and he had no knowledge of any marijuana in the car. The jurors had listened intently to both opening statements—the two lawyers had just advised them they would present starkly contrasting versions of that October day for them to consider, and Huey Newton's life hung in the balance.

As one of the few blacks among the reporters present, Gilbert Moore was torn by conflicting reactions: Newton was too smart to have shot Officer Frey in cold blood when he knew the police watched his every move. But then Moore pictured the early morning scene with Newton facing an oppressive enemy spewing hatred. Where did all the bullets come from that resulted in one dead and two wounded participants? Given the context, Moore could not believe the Panther leader had not fired a shot. He thought to himself, "You can bullshit the judge and the jury and the press all you want to, but I'll bet a million dollars you shot John Frey." Raw emotion then bubbled to the surface as he pondered the huge flag behind the judge: "Do I really give a damn? I hope to God he did shoot him. Shoot him, Huey! Shoot him dead! Kill him for me, Huey, kill him for us. Revenge is ours, saith the Blacks."[3]

When court adjourned, Rush Greenlee singled out Huey's graying father for a reluctant interview. Huey's mother had been too upset to attend as Rev. Walter Newton made his very first appearance in the courtroom seated in the front row with his six other children, Huey's fiancée LaVerne Williams, and Rev. Earl Neil. Greenlee noted that Rev. Newton greeted Greenlee's request with suspicion and disgust, claiming that newspapers always printed lies. When asked to express his view of the charges his son faced, Walter Newton exclaimed: "Now that's a damn fool question. Of course I don't think he's guilty. When I raised my boys I never even let them get a near a gun, much less learn how to shoot one."[4]

The enormous problem facing Newton's lawyers was that two key prosecution witnesses were African-American men. Despite Garry's air of confidence, the defense team agonized over what they could do to attack Henry Grier's anticipated testimony. How in a trial that was predicated on racism did you refute a black, presumably neutral, eyewitness to the shooting? They had a three-day weekend to get a head start. Stender and Keating immediately prepared a subpoena for the bus driver's employment records at AC Transit and the company's daily log for the morning in question. Stender obtained another lead from Garry's veteran expert witness Dr. Diamond, who suggested that she check out a rumor that Grier's sons were involved in a bicycle-thief ring. If so, perhaps, some deal had been cut with the D.A. for leniency that would call into question Grier's motivation. There was so much ongoing leg work for the defense to do behind the scenes during the trial that the firm could not handle it all even with the help fo volunteer experts. Various tasks were allocated to members of the Black Panthers, to private investigators, law students, and other, largely unpaid, trial assistants.

Jensen was required to present his evidence first. Late on the afternoon of August 5, he had Oakland police dispatcher Clarence Lord play a tape-recording of Officer John Frey made less than half an hour before his death, talking over the radio with another dispatcher. The jurors and courtroom audience strained to hear Frey ask the dispatcher for a "rolling 36" auto license check and back-up support for stopping a car on Seventh and Willow Street. The dispatcher's voice confirmed, "It's a known Black Panther vehicle." A few minutes later, the dispatcher's office identified the car's owner as a "man" named LaVerne Williams, on whom they had no further information available. Frey told the dispatcher he thought the driver gave him something "phony." Jensen then had Lord fast forward to play the tape of Officer Heanes shouting the "940B" code for an officer needing immediate assistance. The dispatcher sent all units to Seventh and Willow. Next, the tape skipped to the radio transmission from the officers who arrived at the scene to find Officer Frey dying on the street and Officer Heanes wounded, slumped inside a parked police car. On cross-examination, Garry replayed the entire tape and focused the jury's attention on Frey's identification of the car he stopped as a Black Panther vehicle. Garry pointed to time lags in the tape to indicate the stop was far from routine and that Frey was deliberately harassing Newton. The dispatcher conceded the Oakland Police kept a list of Black Panther vehicles in their radio room.[5]

Jensen next called pathologist Dr. George Loquvam, who had performed the autopsy on Officer Frey. Dr. Loquvam demonstrated on a model torso the path of five bullets that he concluded had struck Frey, one of which Dr. Loquvam found still in Frey's body and gave to the coroner's office to turn over to the police. Dr. Loquvam attested that Frey bled to death within five to ten minutes of the shooting. Garry realized that lengthy cross-examination of this witness would gain nothing and quickly guided Dr. Loquvam to admit that it was possible that there had only been four bullets that hit the officer, leaving those in attendance to wonder what difference that would make. Jensen then introduced into evidence an envelope containing the bullet removed from Frey's body.

The next morning, Tuesday, August 6, Jensen called Officer Gilbert De Hoyos to the witness stand, the first officer to respond to Heanes' call for assistance after the shooting. The Oakland policeman described how he had just returned from the jail where he had transported a drunk arrested earlier that morning by Officer Frey when De Hoyos' police radio announced a "940B" emergency call for help at Seventh and Willow. Already back cruising the neighborhood on Eighth, he came upon the scene of the shooting in less than thirty seconds. There, he spied the three parked cars, hit his brakes, and rushed to the side of Officer Frey lying in the street, still alive, pleading for help. De Hoyos covered him with a blanket. De Hoyos saw another officer, Thomas Fitzmaurice, arrive behind him. Fitzmaurice heard moans coming from the first police car and went to the aid of Officer Heanes, collapsed in its front seat.

The audience stirred in anticipation as Jensen called Officer Heanes as his next witness. But before Heanes testified, the jury was temporarily excused while Judge Friedman listened to arguments over whether Heanes' acute depression following the shooting would be fair game for Garry to pursue on cross-examination. Garry argued that hospital records of Heanes' emotional state following the shooting could shed light on his mental state prior to the shooting. Judge Friedman denied Garry that latitude. The jury returned and Heanes, dressed in his uniform, testified that he arrived as back-up for Officer Frey's traffic stop and was told by Frey that the driver identified himself as LaVerne Williams. Heanes then said he walked to the Volkswagen, and the driver himself told Heanes that he was Huey Newton. Newton was, in fact, well known to many cops on that beat. Heanes continued his testimony, explaining that Officer Frey then joined Heanes by the driver's side of Newton's car. The two officers asked Newton to get out of the car where Frey planned to arrest him for falsely identifying himself to a police officer and failing to carry his license. Heanes added that they both suspected Newton "might have something in the car he didn't want us to see."[6]

Heanes recalled that Newton had not appeared belligerent. Newton emerged from the Volkswagen and walked "rather briskly," followed by Officer Frey, back to the second of the two parked police cars. But when they reached the rear of Officer Heanes' car, Heanes told the jury that

Newton "turned around and started shooting." Heanes identified Newton in court as "the gentleman in the gray coat," pointing to the defense table. When Garry objected, Judge Friedman asked Officer Heanes to step down from the stand and touch the man he saw that day. Jensen had never seen defense counsel use such an intimidating tactic before. Fearful as he was, Heanes dramatically walked over and placed his hand on Huey Newton's shoulder as Newton remained motionless.[7] On cross-examination at the end of the day on Tuesday, Garry startled Heanes by his first question: "Did you shoot and kill Officer Frey?" Heanes froze in shock, suggesting that he did not know the answer. He then said, "No sir, I did not." He recalled only firing one shot and didn't see anybody fall. Garry continued, "There were two shots expended, were there not, sir?" Heanes replied, "I have been told this, yes." Garry then asked him, "What happened to the other shot?" Heanes answered, "I have no idea, sir." He then admitted he never saw a gun in Newton's hand, but had heard gunfire from Newton's direction.[8]

On Wednesday morning August 7, testimony was delayed as Garry requested that the judge reconsider the scope of cross-examination. This time, Judge Friedman relented and decided to allow questioning of Heanes regarding his depressed emotional state following the shoot-out. Heanes retook the stand. On further cross-examination, he testified that during the incident, out of the corner of his eye, he spotted the former passenger in Newton's car, standing on the curb. Stender quickly scribbled a note for Garry, pointing out that there were no street lights on then and a nearby fence was so close to the Volkswagen that Officer Heanes should not have been able to see the passenger standing there. Responding to further questions from Garry, Officer Heanes described how he turned and aimed his gun at the man on the curb, who raised his arms in surrender and declared that he was not armed. Heanes described to the jury that he shifted his glance from the surrendering passenger to see Officer Frey and Huey Newton wrestling with each other on the trunk of Heanes' police car. After being shot in the right arm, Heanes switched his gun to his left hand, firing one shot at Newton's mid-section. Both Frey and Newton were still standing after he fired. Heanes was later told that the gun found in his hand at the scene had fired two cartridges.

Garry had earlier obtained from the prosecutor a pile of clothing; Heanes said the items appeared to be what Newton wore that morning. Garry made sure the courtroom saw the ripped shirt, its front covered with an enormous bloodstain. Garry also showed the witness a blood-stained law-book. Heanes could not recall that Newton had the book under his arm when he ordered him out of the car for questioning.

Garry then stunned everyone present by asking Heanes and Newton to reenact where they had stood in relation to each other and Officer Frey at the scene of the shooting. Garry portrayed Officer Frey. Reporters could not believe their ears as Garry's questions to Heanes suggested yet another surprise person at the shooting, a gentleman about five feet tall. Heanes had not seen such a person. He concluded his testimony by revealing that he now constantly feared attack by the Black Panthers. Though he had never received any death threats, since the shooting, even in the hospital, he slept with a gun under his pillow. The cross-examination of Heanes had been remarkable in its boldness and its ability to diminish the persuasiveness of a star prosecution witness. Garry had masterfully begun to create doubt that Huey Newton had shot Officer Frey. Was there another man on the scene that the police had ignored in their zeal to "get" Huey Newton? Had Heanes, in the confusion, killed Frey by mistake?

Heanes' testimony was followed by that of Officer Fitzmaurice, who had arrived at the scene shortly after De Hoyos. Fitzmaurice testified that he had found Heanes sprawled on the front seat of the car, with his head down, the gun still in his hand. Fitzmaurice asked him if he was hurt and by whom. Heanes weakly responded, "My leg, my leg . . . Huey Newton did it."[9] Just before he fainted, Heanes added that he had shot back at Newton, but did not know if he had hit him. Fitzmaurice took Heanes' gun, put it in his own belt, and used his police radio to call in Heanes' description of Newton as the perpetrator. An ambulance had already been summoned; they now needed two, which were quickly demanded by the beat patrol supervisor, Sergeant Ream. Ream had just emerged from another police car, after rounding the corner at full speed with siren blaring and red light flashing—announcing to the world a "Code 3" situation.

At 2:30 on Wednesday afternoon the drama heightened as Jensen called his surprise witness, forty-year-old AC Transit bus driver Henry

Grier. The six-foot-one, two-hundred-pound Navy veteran had closely cropped hair and a trim moustache. Calm and straightforward, Grier testified that he had started at the transit company two years before the incident. Early on the morning of October 28, 1967, he drove his No. 82 express bus on his accustomed route between Hayward and Oakland and arrived at the stop at Seventh and Willow about 5 a.m. Though the early morning was overcast, he testified that he had a clear view of two policemen and a male civilian in a light shirt and dark coat. One of the policemen was facing him, apparently tugging the man under the arm as they walked toward the rear of a parked police car with its light on about thirty feet away. The other police officer followed "about ten paces behind."[10]

As had occurred with Officer Heanes, Grier's examination was interrupted to have him get up from the stand and place his hand on the shoulder of the man whom he saw in the shootout with the policeman the morning of the crime. Grier then rose from the witness stand, walked over to the defense table, and touched Newton's shoulder. Newton remained expressionless. Before a rapt courtroom, Grier returned to the stand and answered further questions from Jensen. The bus driver said the scene was illuminated by the headlights of his bus. Grier saw the civilian whirl and pull a gun from inside his shirt while the officer grabbed the civilian's arm. The gun fired and another policeman, several yards away, fell. Grier radioed his dispatcher for help and saw the civilian crouched over the first officer, firing "at least three or four shots" into his back. The man then fled across Seventh Street.[11]

As Garry rose to cross-examine Grier, he planned to be thorough and aggressive. In part, he wanted to stall for time so that Stender and Keating would have time to rifle through all available papers, looking for anything contradictory that could impeach the credibility of Jensen's star witness. If Garry proceeded slowly enough, they could have the evening to search for more ammunition to paint Grier as a liar. After court closed for the day, Stender obtained the daily transcript and spent hours on a detailed comparison of Grier's prior statement—given to the police an hour-and-a-half after the shooting—to his direct testimony, highlighting discrepancies for Garry to use in cross-examination. She headed her outline boldly: "GUTTING OF HENRY GRIER."

On Thursday morning, Garry again started the day with motions before the judge, outside the jury's presence. He asked the judge to strike Grier's testimony and for a mistrial on the grounds that the defense did not have access to Grier before he testified. Lowell Jensen pointed out that he had offered to allow Grier to be interviewed in the District Attorney's office, which Garry had rejected as inadequate. Garry made a second motion for mistrial on different grounds, arguing that the unusually heavy security around the courthouse could not help but prejudice the jury against his client. Both motions were denied.

When the jury was brought in and Garry resumed his cross-examination of Grier, he noted that Grier originally had only tentatively identified Newton's photo for the police as resembling the civilian he saw. In court he was positive. Using Stender's comparison chart of Grier's inconsistent statements, Garry pointed out that Grier had also told the police the man he saw was a light-complexioned pygmy, no more than five feet tall and about 125 pounds. In the statement, Grier said he first saw the incident from thirty to forty yards away. In court, Grier said he saw it first from just fifteen to twenty feet. In his original statement, Grier said the civilian wore a light tan jacket, dark shirt, and dark hat. Now he was unsure about any hat. Grier had also changed his mind on the stand to say the jacket he saw on the civilian was dark, not light, and that the civilian reached into his shirt for the gun, not the jacket as he had first told the police. Grier's description now matched the bloody shirt and jacket in the pile of clothing Officer Heanes had earlier identified. Garry assumed that Police Inspector McConnell had influenced Grier's changed description of the civilian.[12] When on the stand, Grier further denied that he had seen the gunman run off through a nearby post office construction site, as he had originally told the police.

Garry dramatically asked to have Grier step down from the stand to reenact the position of the gunman he saw. This time, Garry asked a surprised Alex Hoffmann to play the fatally wounded Officer Frey, summoning Alex from his seat in the front row of spectators without any prior warning. Instead of landing on his back as Grier had told the police, Grier now demonstrated the officer falling on his stomach. In an aggravated tone, Garry inquired if Grier knew what an Uncle Tom was. Jensen rose with a quick objection, but Garry had finally succeeded in rattling the bus driver's composure. How could Grier be sure the five-foot-ten-inch, 155-pound defendant was the same man he saw wrestling with the officer? At this point, to some observers, Grier seemed overconfident and a bit too self-righteous.

Grier was dismissed, and Jensen called Sergeant Ream to the stand to attest to the evidence he found at the site of the shooting, including the bloodstained uniforms of the two officers, Frey's gun holster, and both officers' bullet pouches. On cross-examination, Ream revealed that the officers in his command had seen pictures of Black Panther Party members and had been briefed on the Panthers after their armed appearance at the State Assembly chamber in May of 1967. Ream denied that orders had been given to pull over Panther-owned vehicles on sight or that his office singled out the Panthers for persecution. Rather, the Panthers were only one of several organizations that the police considered possibly armed and dangerous. Sergeant Ream's testimony was followed on Thursday afternoon by a police technician detailing other evidence found at the site; two fired 9-mm shells; a brown leather button and a small black button that may have come from Newton's clothing; a police citation book on the front fender of Frey's car with a partly written ticket; and, near the pool of blood surrounding Officer Frey, a bloodstained California criminal law book with Newton's name inscribed in it. Garry stipulated that the book belonged to his client.

Because used 9-mm shells were found at the site and similar live bullets were found on the floor of the Volkswagen, the police concluded that Newton had a 9-mm Luger concealed in his shirt or jacket when he was arrested by Frey and that after Newton fled the scene, the weapon had been discarded. They had questioned Bobby Seale about the 9-mm pistol they had previously seen him with, hoping to get Seale to confess he had supplied the presumed murder weapon to Newton, but got nowhere. Proof of a concealed gun on his person would automatically make Newton guilty of felony murder either in the first or second degree—a long prison sentence or death. For Charles Garry, it was critical to sow doubt that Newton was packing a weapon when stopped. Garry focused on the 9-mm shells. Though a Luger was not a standard-issue hand gun that Officer Frey would have normally carried, the police witness could not say whether Frey might have carried more than one gun or bought his own non-standard ammunition, such as the 9-mm bullets.

On Friday, August 9 came a much-needed day with no court proceedings. By Saturday, August 10, the defense team had used the prosecutor's witness list to locate a passenger on the bus, Tommy Miller. Alex Hoffmann was dispatched to interview him and made a key discovery—Miller disputed the driver's vantage point and ability to see what transpired on the early morning of October 28. On Monday August 12, Jensen called his second star eye-witness, the alleged kidnap victim, Dell Ross—the man whom Jensen told the jury had been sitting in his parked convertible near the corner of Seventh and Willow when Newton and his companion leaped in and ordered him to drive them away at gunpoint. The media representatives' antennae perked up again. They were well aware of Ross's devastating grand jury testimony identifying Newton as the shooter and assumed Ross would clinch the prosecutor's case. Ross, in his mid-thirties, came to court colorfully attired in dark pants, a red sweater, and an azure sports jacket. He sported dark sun glasses. When Jensen asked Ross his first question, "Where were you on the morning of October 28, 1967?" Ross shocked the judge, onlookers, and Jensen by refusing to testify on Fifth Amendment grounds of potential self-incrimination.[13]

Ross, a migrant laborer with a low IQ, had somehow developed a sophisticated new strategy of non-cooperation sometime after appearing before the grand jury. He had been accompanied in court that morning with his own counsel, Doug Hill, a radical Berkeley lawyer in partnership with Peter Franck, a close friend of Stender's from the Lawyers Guild. Hill then sat down unannounced at Garry's counsel table. When Hill rose to address the court, Judge Friedman, surprised by Hill's presence, harshly informed Hill that he had no authority to speak since he was not an attorney representing any party in the case. Actually, the judge was wrong; however rarely it comes up, a witness is entitled to have the services of his own counsel. Disconcerted, the judge then temporarily halted the proceedings, sequestered the jury, and heard arguments from the lawyers on the novel issue. Jensen was uncharacteristically irate. He could not fathom how a kidnap victim could claim he would expose himself to prosecution if he testified. Hill argued that Ross might be subject to prosecution for being an accessory after-the-fact to murder. Jensen suggested he could resolve the issue by offering Ross immunity from prosecution. The judge took the issue under submission and dismissed proceedings for the day before noon as news representatives ran from the courtroom to report the stunning trial development.

On Tuesday morning, August 13, Judge Friedman granted Ross immunity from prosecution, and Ross retook the stand before the jury. He again refused to give any details of the morning in question on Fifth Amendment grounds. With growing exasperation, Judge Friedman explained to Ross that he no longer faced any possible criminal jeopardy for his testimony because immunity had been granted. What Ross now risked was a citation for contempt of court. While he could not go to jail for any crime that his testimony revealed, Ross could be sent to jail for refusing to testify. Hill objected that his client would be entitled to a separate hearing on ten days' notice, but the judge had his dander up. In his entire career, Judge Friedman had never sent anyone to jail for contempt, but he had no problem making Ross his first. Ross said, "Send me to jail then."[14]

Jensen appeared to have another way out of the impasse. He asked Ross if he remembered the events of the October morning of the shooting. Ross said that he could not remember. Jensen showed Ross the grand jury transcript and asked him to read it. Ross replied, "I can't read." Jensen then started reading aloud Ross's damaging grand jury testimony as a means of attempting to refresh Ross's recollection. The prosecutor started with Ross's earlier testimony that he was sitting in his black and white Ford convertible at the intersection of Seventh and Willow with a friend around 5 a.m. when they heard gunshots and his buddy fled, leaving the car door wide open. According to his prior testimony, two men had then jumped into the car. The one in the back carried a gun and threatened to kill him if Ross did not do as he was told, stating, "I just shot two dudes. I'm shot." Jensen read to the jury how Ross had earlier identified a police photograph of Newton as that backseat passenger.[15]

Garry repeatedly objected that this reading was improper because defense counsel had been precluded from participating in the grand jury proceeding and had no means of cross-examining Ross at the time. These were valid points, but Judge Friedman, like Jensen, assumed that Ross would have his memory refreshed by this reading and could then be cross-examined by Garry on all of these prior statements. It would have been far wiser for the judge to have sequestered the jury after Ross said he could not read. Jensen could have attempted to refresh Ross's memory by reciting the challenged testimony to Ross outside of the jury's presence. Then, if Ross still professed no memory of the events, the jury would not have heard inadmissible grand jury testimony. But Judge Friedman overruled Garry's objections, allowing the jury to hear Jensen read Ross's entire damning grand jury testimony. On the stand, Ross claimed that he still could not recall any of the events of that morning. Garry asked that the jury be instructed to ignore the grand jury testimony and moved for a mistrial on the ground that the jury was prejudiced by hearing Ross's prior statements. Judge Friedman denied the motions. Despite having been sandbagged by Ross's sudden lack of cooperation, it looked to the press like Jensen had won a key battle. The prosecutor had backed Ross into a corner, the *Oakland Post* reported, "like a rat in a trap."[16]

When it was time for cross-examination of Ross, Garry rose and asked Ross if he recalled being in Garry's law office in San Francisco in late July. Ross also professed to having no memory of that very recent interview. Garry then announced to a flabbergasted courtroom that he had tape-recorded Ross at his office on the evening of July 28. He obtained the judge's permission to play the tape to refresh Ross's recollection, as Jensen had just been permitted to do with Ross' grand jury testimony. Garry also produced a written transcript of the recently taped interview for the jury.

The jury, press and other spectators, listened intently and heard a man's voice on the tape, which Garry identified as Ross. The man explained that he had been a witness before the grand jury and had also given a statement to the police and that both were "not true." Ross stared at the ceiling while the recording played. The voice on the tape said he had been frightened by the police and had gone along with suggested testimony implicating Newton because the police had a warrant outstanding against him for a parking violation. He specifically recanted seeing Newton holding a gun and that Newton had spoken at all on the morning of the shooting. "He was kinda out" in the back seat of his car. Garry could also be heard on the tape advising Ross that when he came to court he would be entitled to be represented by his own attorney.[17]

When asked about these taped statements on the stand, Ross repeated, "I don't know nothing," including whether he recognized his own voice or that of Charles Garry. Jensen barely contained his fury, convinced that Garry had tampered with the witness. When Garry concluded his cross-examination, Jensen questioned Ross on redirect. How had he gotten to Garry's office? Ross responded that he did not even know where Garry's office was. Jensen pointed to Doug Hill and asked if he was Ross's attorney. Ross identified Hill as his lawyer, but when Jensen asked whether Ross obtained Hill as his lawyer before or after he visited Garry's office, Ross replied, "I just can't remember." When asked to identify his signature on the police statement, Ross said: "I see some writing here, but I don't know what it is." Stymied, Jensen excused Ross as his witness.[18]

The next day, Wednesday August 14, Jensen shifted gears and produced Oakland Police Crime Laboratory Director John Davis, a ballistics expert, who testified matter-of-factly that unburnt gunpowder deposits on Frey's clothing revealed that he had been shot in the back from a distance between six inches and one-and-a-half-feet. Illustrating his testimony with color slides, the soft-spoken expert explained to the jury that the slug removed from Officer Frey's body appeared to come from the same gun as the bullet that wounded Heanes. It was his opinion, however, that neither one of the slugs could have been fired from Heanes' gun, the only one recovered at the site of the shooting. The ball powder around Frey's wounds indicated that the fatal wounds most likely came from Officer Frey's gun, matching live bullets remaining in his holster. So much for Garry's theory that Heanes might have accidentally shot Frey.

Davis identified two buttons found near Frey's body as similar to those on Newton's jacket. On the other hand, he admitted on cross-examination that his office had not run any tests on Newton's hands to determine whether he had recently fired a gun. The criminologist explained that his office had not subjected Newton to tests it had previously conducted in other cases because the test results would likely have been inconclusive.

Jensen also put on the stand Officer Robert Fredericks, the police officer who arrested Newton at Kaiser Hospital. After Jensen elicited a matter-of-fact account from Fredericks on direct examination, Garry jumped up and went for the jugular on police bias, accusing Fredericks of manacling the wounded Newton to the gurney "because you hated him and wanted to see him die." Fredericks responded that an officer had the right to protect himself if he felt his life was in danger, to which Garry countered that Fredericks had been armed. "So was Officer Frey" came the icy reply.[19]

Next came Dr. Finch, the emergency room doctor whose life had since been threatened. Dr. Finch admitted having told Newton to "shut up" as he was hysterically spewing invective at the police from the hospital gurney. Dr. Finch explained that he was trying to shock Newton into silence. Garry asked him to identify Newton's scars, and Newton stood up, lifting his shirt and turning to allow the jury to see both the entrance and exit wounds. The hole in his abdomen and in his back dramatically underscored to the jury Garry's focus on Newton as a victim. Nurse Corinne Leonard, the person in charge of the hospital emergency room when Newton arrived, was next on the stand and made a very poor impression with her bleach-blonde hair, excessive make-up, and brand-new, spiked heels. Garry treated her with hostility as he questioned her delayed treatment of a gunshot victim while they had argued over whether he was a patient of the medical plan. Visibly upset by his questions, she snapped that Newton's wound had appeared slight with no hemorrhaging and that he had called her a white bitch, "I'm not there to have people swear at me and call me names."[20]

Jensen objected that Garry was yelling at the witness, but Judge Friedman announced, "Counsel can ask questions in any tone of voice he wishes."[21]

On August 15, Garry made one more effort to keep Newton's felony conviction from the jury, but committed one of his famous Garryisms by telling the court that the conviction "far outweighs the prejudicial harm it can do." Jensen called the mangled phraseology a Freudian slip. The motion was denied.[22] By the end of the day that marked exactly one month into the trial, Jensen completed his case. His last two witnesses were brief, but powerful in impact. Huey's probation officer set off loud whispers among the spectators when he said the probation officially ended three years from October 29, 1964, on October 28, 1967, the day of the shooting, not the day before as the defense contended. On cross-examination of the probation officer, Garry had gotten him to admit he didn't know what date he had told Newton his probation ended.

Then a chemist for the Police Department identified the contents of the two matchboxes found in the car as marijuana and also attested to having found tiny amounts of marijuana in the right front pocket of Newton's pants. In total, Jensen had called 26 of the 30 witnesses he had originally listed. When Jensen announced in a flat tone that "the People rest," he seemed deflated. The defense team read Jensen's body language—so different from the confidence he exuded on the first day of trial—as recognition his presentation had fallen well short of its goal.[23] Garry then jumped up and asked the court for acquittal on all three pending charges. The routine motion asked the court to evaluate the prosecutor's case. If Jensen had not put on enough evidence on a particular charge, no defense to that charge would be necessary. The jury would be directed accordingly.

Garry had no serious expectation that the judge would grant the motion in its entirety. But Jensen knew the motion had merit with respect to the kidnapping charge. He told the judge he would not object to dismissal of that charge since the sole witness, Dell Ross, refused to testify and denied remembering anything. Judge Friedman indicated he would hear argument and rule on the motions for acquittal on all three charges before Garry was scheduled to begin his defense on Monday morning. Garry was in a good mood when he reached the elevator at the same time as Jensen. Knowing he would be overheard by others in the hall, he playfully told Jensen, "I'm going to call you for my first witness."

Jensen replied, "Can I take the Fifth?"

Garry said, "You better get yourself a lawyer."

Jensen retorted, "I'll be up to your office Sunday night to give you a statement."

At the press conference that followed, a reporter asked Garry who his first witness would be, and he answered "Lowell Jensen."[24] Though he was obviously being facetious, the implication was clear: if Jensen were put under oath, Garry could elicit facts that would destroy the prosecutor's whole case.

13. THE DAY OF RECKONING ARRIVES

This is not a threat. We are four retired Marines USA. We . . . do not see why any attorney would see fit for a fee to defend Huey P. Newton. We all knew Policeman John Frey. So, to make this short and to the point, you or Newton will not be alive ten days after this trial is over. Makes no difference which way the jury disides [sic].

ANONYMOUS LETTER TO CHARLES GARRY, TURNED OVER TO THE FBI

Once Jensen rested his case on Thursday August 15, the defense team faced a daunting litany of tasks and needed almost every moment of the three-day recess before they returned to court. Stender had completed one hundred twenty-five hours of work on the case in the last two weeks, but eagerly started her latest to-do list:

- Talk to the hospitalized prisoner who could describe officers beating Huey when he was a wounded patient at Kaiser.
- Check whether a friend of Huey's could corroborate that Huey was celebrating the end of his probation on the evening of October 27, 1967; that would refute the prosecutor's claim Huey knew he was still on parole when stopped by Officer Frey.
- Follow up on another alleged witness in Sacramento.

Stender also needed to research cases for Garry to rely on during Monday's arguments; he would seek Newton's acquittal on first-degree murder charges on the ground that Jensen had failed to produce evidence of premeditation or malice. This was the only charge that carried the death penalty. If she could find persuasive cases, the judge might direct the jury to acquit Newton on that murder charge, just as he was planning to dismiss the kidnapping charge. Stender planned to outline the examination of two witnesses for Garry and to contact a third witness and tell him what time his appearance would be necessary. She reminded herself to have the Panthers conduct a background check on Tommy Miller, the passenger on Grier's AC Transit bus. Lastly, she wanted to follow up on the suggestion that Grier's children were involved in a bike stealing gang.

The court day on Monday, August 19, started with the jury sequestered as the defense moved for acquittal. Garry cited Stender's federal case research, arguing there was no basis in the record for the jury to convict Newton on the murder charge because Heanes did not see a gun in Newton's hands and the bus driver Grier had not identified Newton positively in his original police statement. Judge Friedman agreed with Jensen that the jury had ample evidence to consider both the murder and assault charges. As expected, Judge Friedman granted the motion to dismiss the kidnapping charge. Everyone agreed that Ross had never admitted to having his memory refreshed and had not testified to anything incriminatory against Newton. Reporters were impressed that Garry managed to make the kidnapping charge evaporate and were eager to see who Garry planned to call as defense witnesses. Many wondered out loud about the still unidentified "mystery man" who had accompanied Newton in the car. Would he show up as a defense witness? Would Newton take the stand on his own behalf?

As his first witness, Garry called AC Transit passenger Tommy Miller to the stand. Miller, a young black employee of the Alameda Naval Station, testified that he had boarded the bus at the corner of Seventh and Willow at about 5 a.m. on October 28 after waiting ten or more minutes at the bus stop. While waiting for the bus, he saw some activity about a block away that he had trouble making out since it was very dark at the time. Miller said bus driver Henry Grier was making change for him from a five-dollar bill as they pulled out into the street. Grier then received payment from a passenger who boarded behind Miller as Miller took his seat. The bus immediately slowed to a stop, and Miller heard shooting. He looked out the window, but could not see what was happening. He was sure the bus had passed the police cars before the shooting took place. You could see an officer tussling with a man, but it was impossible to see their faces. Court recessed for the noon break with Miller still on the stand.

After the jury left for lunch, Garry apologized to Judge Friedman for bringing the subject up again, but felt compelled to read two racist death threats into the record. He asked again for a mistrial, arguing that community hysteria made it impossible for Newton to receive a fair trial. One menacing note came from four unnamed retired Marines, the other purportedly from a member of the KKK. The second one, addressed "Dear Nigger Lover," assumed that Garry would get "that murdering coon off because the judge, jury and witnesses have all been intimidated . . . It's too bad we ever stopped lynching."[1] Garry reported that the Panthers were temporarily providing him with a 24-hour bodyguard, and he had turned the threat over to the FBI. Lowell Jensen reported to Judge Friedman that he, too, had received death threats. They came with the territory. He would still vainly attempt to try the case as if it were not politically sensitive.

Makeshift screening rooms had already been set up the week before in a small room across the hall from Judge Friedman's courtroom. Everyone emptied their pockets. Male trial attendees were patted down by armed male deputies, searching for concealed weapons. On one occasion, narcotics were found on a spectator, who was released after he explained that he had borrowed his jacket from someone else. Women attendees were carefully searched by female deputies, who also reviewed the contents of their purses and confiscated any sharp objects, such as nail files. A reporter for the London-based *Daily Telegraph* told others that the tight security matched that of the Israelis when they tried Nazi Adolf Eichmann in Jerusalem.

Though he obtained some press coverage of the death threats, Garry was not surprised his oft-repeated motion for mistrial had been denied. After Jensen concluded his cross-examination of Miller, Garry called to the stand as his next two witnesses a woman friend of Newton's and a male friend, a Ph.D. candidate from Cal, who had seen Newton relaxed and celebrating the end of his parole earlier on the evening of October 27 at Bos'n's Locker, Newton's favorite Oakland bar. Both witnesses were called to refute the prosecution theory that Newton still believed himself to be under parole restrictions as his motive for shooting Officer Frey early the next morning. Garry also called ACLU attorney Marshall Krause, who had been approached three years earlier by Newton to appeal his 1964 assault conviction. At the time, Newton had been concerned that he would lose his voting rights, and Krause had told him that would not be the case. Krause informed Newton that the crime would be treated as a misdemeanor due to the short county jail sentence. Apparently Krause's advice was admitted to show what Newton mistakenly thought at the time; Judge Friedman had already ruled earlier on a pretrial motion that this characterization of the conviction as a misdemeanor was mistaken.

Jensen did successfully object to Garry putting on the stand an inmate who had been a patient at Kaiser after the shootout. The man was an alleged witness to retaliatory police threats to Newton's life when he was in the hospital recuperating from his wounds. Judge Friedman agreed that evidence of police misconduct after October 28, 1967, was irrelevant. Tempers flared as Jensen also won a heated dispute with Garry over excluding three other black male witnesses regarding a conversation they had with an investigator for the D.A.'s office. Judge Friedman had reacted angrily, shouting, "I will run this court in my own way."[2]

But Judge Friedman overruled Jensen's objections to a parade of witnesses Stender and other members of the defense team had located, who attested to Officer Frey's history of racist and abusive conduct toward black arrestees prior to the confrontation with Newton in late October. This offer of evidence had been difficult to find, since many had moved, and tricky to get admitted in the face of Jensen's vehement objection. It was relevant only to show that, if Frey had acted the same way toward Newton, Frey might have provoked the shooting. At the same time, Garry contended that Newton's primary defense was that he had no gun and was innocent of the shooting charges. The judge concluded that the theory of Frey's aggressive racism on the beat could affect the degree of murder if the jury convicted Newton on that charge, i.e., whether he acted with premeditation or was goaded into a lethal response. Stender had carefully reviewed both Frey's and Heanes' employment files and their own investigative reports looking for evidence on provocation as well as possible impeachment of Heanes' testimony. She told Garry that some of the information they had turned up on Officer Frey was not useful. Frey lived in a mixed-race neighborhood and maintained a cordial relationship with a few of his black neighbors. But he did collect guns, had engaged in aggressive racist conduct on the beat, and had specifically requested assignment to West Oakland's red light district.

The defense then put on the stand Daniel King, a teenager arrested the night before the early morning shootout. King testified that Frey had called him a "nigger" and a pimp and then left him to be beaten up by a white man dressed only in a shirt, who claimed that King had stolen his pants. Another man, Calvin Hudson, whom Frey had stopped for speeding, testified that Frey had called him a "black motherfucker." Belford Dunning, a black insurance agent, received a ticket a couple of days before the shootout and came forward to say that Officer Frey, assisting at the scene, had proudly told Dunning, "I am the Gestapo."[3] (Jensen would later put on the stand one of Oakland's few black police officers to contradict Dunning's account of abuse from Officer Frey.)

Stender also tracked down a high school student, Tom Parson, who had heard Frey address his class on police work as a career choice and told her that Frey used the word "nigger" at least once in his talk. But when called at trial, the teenage witness got cold feet and denied hearing Frey use the word "nigger." Garry felt he had no choice but to call Stender next to the stand to impeach the credibility of Parson—his own witness—by having her repeat to the jury Parson's out-of-court statement. Garry also called the teacher to the stand to say that he had heard Frey start to use the word "nigger" and then correct himself. While various witnesses testified, Newton often appeared disengaged to the press, perhaps daydreaming about some fantasy world instead of following the court proceedings.

After portraying Officer Frey as a racist who should be condemned for his abusive language, the defense team considered it absolutely essential to educate the jury on the Panthers' own use of explosive terms. They offered two experts, including Dr. Herman Blake, a black professor of sociology, to explain that rhetoric like "off the pigs" had a different, non-literal meaning in the black community than whites might interpret it. The judge was skeptical of this novel argument and denied the request, but allowed Garry to reargue the issue in a lengthy hearing outside the presence of the jury.

As Dr. Blake testified before Judge Friedman on the true import of Panther terminology, Prof. Blauner was distracted by news the night before of global consequences. On August 20, 1968, tanks rolled into Prague, reigniting the dormant Cold War. Shocked observers saw the Soviets kill a hundred people and arrest local Communist Party leaders to crush their "Prague Spring" experimental reforms of free speech and freedom of assembly. The developing Czech crisis had been front-page news for a month. Deeply upset by the Soviet massacre of the Czech reformers, Prof. Blauner turned to Stender as he sat next to her at the trial on the morning of August 21 and said "The Russians are pigs, too." She did not respond. He found her lack of reaction disquieting. Blauner had himself joined the Communist Party as a student in the '50s, but quit when Stalin's bloody purges came to light. Blauner believed whole-heartedly that summer of 1968 in the Black Panthers, but decades later when interviewed, he questioned how easily he and others had rationalized the Panthers' own guns and violent rhetoric, down-playing their dangerousness.

When the jury returned, Garry called to the stand another African-American, Gene McKinney, who, like Hilliard, had been a friend of Huey Newton's since boyhood. The press then learned to its amazement that McKinney was the mysterious, previously unidentified passenger who had accompanied Newton in his car when Officer Frey pulled up behind it that fateful October morning. McKinney had fled the scene with Newton, his name had never before surfaced. Shortly after the shootout, the police had advertised their desire to speak with Newton's passenger, letting the community know he was not considered a suspect. Garry had kept McKinney's identity so close to the vest that even some members of his own legal team were taken by surprise.

Like Ross, McKinney also came to court in the unusual posture of bringing his own lawyer, a black man named Harold Perry. Garry had wanted the symbolism of McKinney being represented by a black lawyer, but had been forced to look long and hard to find one to represent McKinney. None except inexperienced Carleton Innis had wanted to associate in any way with the case after Garry had become Newton's lead counsel. After McKinney responded to a few preliminary questions, Garry dramatically asked McKinney the same question he asked Officer Heanes—whether he had shot the deceased officer "by chance or otherwise."[4]

On Perry's advice, McKinney refused to testify further about the incident on the grounds that it might incriminate him. Jensen argued that the witness could not start to testify and then invoke the Fifth Amendment. When Garry abruptly concluded his questions, Jensen offered immunity to McKinney as he had done to Ross. McKinney still invoked the right not to incriminate himself. He refused even to elaborate on his testimony that he was in Newton's car when it was stopped. This time Judge Friedman made good on his threat of holding in contempt the first witness of his long judicial career. McKinney was hauled off to a tenth floor jail cell; he would be incarcerated for six weeks before an appellate court ordered his release. Garry's office assisted Perry in his work on the appeal.

The jury had at this point seen two different black men—other than the defendant—who were on or near the scene of the shootout. Both claimed they could be incriminated if they answered questions about the events of the morning of October 28 that led to Officer Frey's death and Huey Newton's arrest for murder. Following the spectacle of McKinney's brief and extraordinary appearance, Garry escalated the drama by calling Huey Newton as his next witness—intended as a signal to the jury that the defense had nothing to hide. The following day, Jensen's efforts to keep the trial focused narrowly on the shootout rather than on politics and race would face its biggest challenge.

Garry considered it crucial for Huey to tell his life story and political philosophy to place the shooting incident in context. Allowing Newton to testify, of course, was part of what Garry alluded to when he said the case was one of the most complex and fascinating cases he had ever tried. Garry's claim puzzled his partner Al Brotsky. He had visited Newton with Garry in jail early on and thought, like Jensen, that the case would be a rather straightforward one. But Garry considered that approach too dangerous. He was willing to gamble on having Newton testify only within a strategy to shift the jury's focus to the broader picture of police brutality and Panther persecution.

For Newton's day of testimony, Stokely Carmichael (now completely disassociated from SNCC), Eldridge and Kathleen Cleaver, and Bobby Seale were all prominently in attendance. Cleaver now garnered more publicity than ever since the California Peace and Freedom Party had just ratified him as its candidate for President of the United States.[5] In a recent report, an FBI agent had noted both the rivalry between Cleaver and Seale for leadership of the Panthers and Kathleen Cleaver's devotion to furthering Cleaver's more aggressive, openly threatening agenda. He suggested in his next report that Kathleen might split from Cleaver if the agency gave her reason to believe Cleaver was having an affair. (Eldridge's sexual exploits were common knowledge among Party leadership; the Central Committee had already called him on the carpet on a mother's irate complaint that he had raped her fourteen-year-old daughter. Hilliard later wrote that Cleaver admitted having consensual sex with the girl. Cleaver's only response was that he wished she were 12-years old.[6])

By 6 a.m. on August 22, crowds again surged outside the courthouse, which had more than the usual complement of security guards stationed outside. Gilbert Moore of *Life* reported that anger erupted as a few blacks wanted to know "what the fuck" white boys were doing in the front of the line just because they had arrived earliest that morning. The latecomers asserted their own priority, proclaiming, "We been standing on line for four hundred years."[7] The weight of the crowd pushed against the double glass doors and broke one of them as everyone pressed to be among those chosen to see Huey Newton take the stand.

Gazing upon a full courtroom from the witness chair, Newton looked to be in his element, buoyed by the strong show of supporters counterbalancing increased numbers of plainclothes policemen. He appeared slightly nervous, perhaps shivering from the cold courtroom, but spoke in a conversational tone with no quaver in his voice. His focus was on winning over David Harper. Every day so far, Newton had carefully observed the one black man on the jury, but could not take Harper's measure—was he an Uncle Tom "blinded by the crumbs the system offered him"[8] or a brother who, like the Panthers, seethed at the unfairness of a racist society? Newton considered his testimony an opportunity to address Harper one-on-one, hoping he could develop a bond.

As Garry began the questioning, Huey flatly denied shooting either officer. He knew the police kept a list of Black Panther vehicles and that he risked being stopped at any time. He had in fact, by his count, been accosted by police forty to fifty times before, which was one of the reasons he kept his law book handy, as he did that day. Newton told the jury that, when he got out of his car that morning at the officers' direction, the book was all he held; he never carried a handgun because that would be in automatic violation of his parole, as would the use of marijuana. The pants he wore had been purchased secondhand from Good Will and he had not checked the pockets to make sure they were empty when he bought them. He was unaware of any marijuana in the car or in his pants pocket. He insisted that the only gun he ever carried was a permissible shotgun and only when he was on police patrol. Newton added that it was also a basis for expulsion from the Black Panther Party to carry a gun when not patrolling police or to have narcotics in his possession at any time.

The defense team was well aware that if the jury believed Newton knowingly transported marijuana, Jensen had his motive. If Newton carried a concealed handgun when stopped by the police, that would in and of itself constitute a felony violation of his parole. Under California law, that felony would automatically have rendered Newton guilty of second degree murder of Officer Frey under the felony-murder rule: *any* death, even an accidental one, occurring during the commission of an inherently dangerous felony rendered the felon guilty of second degree murder. All the prosecutor needed to prove was that Newton had a hidden gun in his possession when he was frisked. Only four minutes of Newton's direct testimony concerned the early morning shooting. The defense theory was tricky, given that despite Newton's denials, they still hoped to convince the jury that it was possible Newton acted in self-defense or with diminished capacity. By putting Newton on the stand, Garry gave the highly experienced assistant district attorney the opportunity to cross-examine him at length on the events of that fatal morning. If they had exercised Newton's right to remain silent, Jensen could never have called him as a witness.

Newton relished his familiar role as lecturer and talked at length on direct examination. Unperturbed by frequent relevancy objections from Lowell Jensen, Newton managed to describe hundreds of years of oppression, telling the jury that blacks were the most brutalized people in the country. The jury appeared rapt as they marveled at his dignified and scholarly account. In contrast, the jet-lagged Stokely Carmichael, seated near the front of the spectators, had fallen asleep. Newton explained that when he and others sought to organize members of the black community, they realized they needed to unite with all people who were oppressed. He said that the Black Panther Party was not a racist group and had formed an alliance with many cultural minorities, as well as disillusioned youths in the white majority.

Newton further informed the jury that the Black Panther Party had adopted rules against drinking or drug use among its members and advocated only peaceful methods of achieving their goals. While Newton gave this testimony, outside the courthouse beyond the jury's hearing newly returned demonstrators shouted, "Revolution Has Come—Time to Pick Up Your Gun" and "Off the Pigs."[9] In addition to Panthers, demonstrators with "Free Huey" and "Off the Pigs" signs included a contingent of more than three dozen whites from the Citizens Committee Mobilized for Huey Newton, headed by an Oakland housewife.[10] Jensen was fighting a losing battle to treat the shootout in a vacuum. Refreshed by his nap, Carmichael conducted a press conference during the noon break characterizing the proceedings as a political "trial of a black man . . . trying to liberate his people."[11] Overseas press loved this angle. *The Sunday Telegraph* had just published an in-depth article for the consumption of its two million readers analyzing the case in political terms.

By dwelling on Newton's political philosophy, Garry opened the door wide for Jensen to cross-examine Newton on the virulent anti-police rhetoric in his writings, urging followers to "off the pigs." Garry actually had no choice—Jensen could have introduced those writings anyway. If Newton's hate-filled essays were not placed in political context, Garry considered them inflammatory enough to convict Newton of murder. Garry could best explain the purpose and background of these writings with Newton on the stand, testifying on his own behalf. Garry still desperately wanted to convince Judge Friedman to let the jury hear Dr. Blake's more benign interpretation of the Panthers' frequent exhortation to followers to "off the pigs."

Jensen had all weekend to finish preparing his proposed cross-examination on Monday, August 26. He planned to take Newton through all of his movements on October 27, starting from his speaking engagement on the future of the black liberation movement at San Francisco State College that afternoon. Jensen started off with softball questions designed to put Newton at ease. He was then hoping to draw Newton's ire with tougher tactics so the jury could see Newton's explosive temper, but Huey had been forewarned and kept his irritation largely in check. He testified he had earned $75 for two hours of his time as a speaker. He then described going to his fiancée LaVerne's home because they had a date to celebrate the end of his probation, but she felt ill and instead loaned him her car.

Newton went to his favorite bar, Bos'n's Locker, where he had one rum Coke and then left to attend a party at a church social hall where he linked up with his friend Gene McKinney. When they left the party, they went to Seventh Street, intending to stop at an all-night restaurant. They were looking for a parking space when they were pulled over by Officer Frey. Newton described for the jury how Frey had frisked him abusively, feeling his genitals. He held out his law book and told Frey there had been no reasonable cause for stopping him, but Frey called him a "nigger" and told him "to take the law book and stick it." Frey then "straight-armed" Newton, who stumbled. The audience perked up when Newton asked Jensen's permission to demonstrate what he meant by getting off the stand and pretending he was Frey. Newton then pushed Jensen back with his hand extended to Jensen's chin, using obvious restraint to avoid causing the prosecutor to lose his balance. Newton then said, "This is the way it happened. Excuse me," and resumed his seat on the witness stand.[12] Newton then testified that Frey drew his revolver and Newton felt a sensation "like hot soup." He heard explosions, and the next thing he remembered was crawling onto the platform at Kaiser Hospital.[13]

Shifting to the Black Panther newspaper and Newton's prior writings, Jensen sought to repulse the jurors by the Panthers' philosophy, pointing out that the late Dr. Martin Luther King was listed in the Panthers' "Bootlicker's Gallery." Newton said that characterization changed when Dr. King came out against the Vietnam War. Jensen then called specific attention to an article Huey had published in the Black Panther newspaper the summer before, called "The Correct Handling of Revolution." Written as a critique of the Watts Riot and other urban riots that had recently taken place, Newton's article included a potentially very damning passage:

> The Vanguard Party must provide leadership for the people. It must teach the correct strategic methods of prolonged resistance through literature and activities. If the activities of the party are respected by the people, the people will follow the example. . . When the people learn that it is no longer advantageous for them to resist by going into the streets in large numbers, and when they see the advantage in the activities of the guerrilla warfare method, they will quickly follow this example. But first, they must respect the party which is transmitting the message. When the Vanguard group destroys the machinery of the oppressor by dealing with him in small groups of threes and fours and then escapes the might of the oppressor, the masses will be overjoyed and will adhere to this correct strategy. When the masses hear that a Gestapo policeman has been executed while sipping coffee at a counter, and the revolutionary executors fled without being traced, the masses will see the validity of this type of approach to resistance.[14]

Newton's supporters all considered him a hero for such fiery rhetoric against oppressive police. How would Newton convince the jury that he had not acted on his own words? Newton explained to the jury that the article was referring to an unspecified revolutionary time in the future and that conditions had not yet risen to the level of impasse where peaceful struggle was fruitless and revolutionary tactics were appropriate. Jensen also confronted Newton with a poem he had published in the Black Panther newspaper the summer before. It was called "Guns Baby Guns!" and elaborated on the same theme as his essay:

> Army .45 will stop all jive
> Buckshots will down the cops
> P-38 will open prison gates

The carbine will stop the war machine
A .357 will win us heaven.
And if you don't believe in playing
You are already dead.[15]

Jensen had Newton read the poem aloud to the jury along with the list of weapons on the same page of the newsletter that the Panthers advocated as necessary for self-defense: an Army .45 pistol, a 12-gauge shotgun, an M-1 carbine, a .357 Magnum pistol, and a .38-caliber police revolver. The jury already knew that Frey had apparently been killed with his own .38 caliber revolver after struggling with Newton. Newton repeatedly stated the Panther Party was an organization for self-defense working to combat violence. When he gave speeches on black liberation in which he advocated "taking care of business" through guerrilla bands on the streets, it did not include executing policemen. He claimed he had been misquoted in a *Ramparts* magazine article that portrayed him as unequivocally advocating bloodshed.

As Garry had dreaded, Jensen then examined Newton regarding his prior assault conviction, inquiring whether racism was involved. Jensen knew that Odell Lee, the victim of the assault, had been black. But Newton surprised Jensen by claiming that ethnicity may have been a factor, describing how Lee had used a Chinese greeting at a party and Newton replied with a Swahili salutation he had learned from cultural nationalists. The two had then gotten into an argument. Newton had seen a scar on Lee's face that indicated he was a streetfighter. He considered their conversation over and went back to his dinner. When Lee tugged insistently on Newton's arm to continue their argument and reached into his pocket, Newton knifed him in what he believed to be self-defense. However, without a lawyer, the jury had not seen it that way.

Jensen then asked about Newton's arrest in Berkeley in March of 1966, when two policemen sought to arrest his companion, Bobby Seale. Jensen began most of his questions, "Isn't it a fact." Newton sparred with Jensen, recalling that Seale was reading poetry from a chair on a street corner when the police harassed him. Newton denied he had tried to grab the policeman's gun as the arrest record indicated and then turned to ask Jensen, "Isn't it a fact" the plainclothes officer accompanying the uniformed policeman had been drunk at the time? His sarcastic attempt at role reversal brought angry intervention from the judge, causing spectators to laugh out loud. Garry quickly asked for a mistrial. Much subdued, Judge Friedman responded, "Your objection is noted."[16]

One sympathetic lawyer observer told Eldridge Cleaver during a break that he thought Newton was being crucified on the stand like Jesus Christ. Cleaver had responded instinctively, "Yes, Huey is our Jesus, but we want him down from the cross."[17] The Panthers and the defense team had engineered the enormous turnout that day of some eight hundred Newton supporters—a crowd second only to that on the first day of trial. About a fifth of them wore Panther uniforms and circled the courthouse with the women shouting, "Revolution Has Come—Time to Pick Up Your Gun" and the men yelling, "Off the Pigs." Of the remaining crowd waving "Free Huey" signs and related slogans, more than half were white. A noticeable contingent were Asian. One banner read, "Yellow Peril Supports Black Panthers."[18] Jurors could hear them chant as the panelists entered the courthouse.

At the day's end Garry was relatively upbeat, convinced that Newton had handled himself very well. Dr. Blake, sitting in the audience, had almost been moved to tears watching Newton on the stand, carrying the banner of the black revolutionary. The professor wrote Newton shortly afterward, "You were absolutely beautiful. Your manner and presentation on the witness stand were the highest manifestation of the integrity of the black experience. I shall never forget what I saw and heard, regardless of the outcome."[19] After two days of watching Newton being cross-examined on the stand, trial observers all appeared in agreement that he had handled himself impressively. In chambers, Judge Friedman confided to the lawyers, "He could have been a fine young man, It's really too bad. . . ."[20]

Journalist Rush Greenlee recognized that Garry and Newton had achieved a remarkable feat:

> [T]he political nature of the Black Panthers seemed to have transcended the stark events of 5 a.m. last Oct. 28. The jury must

> still decide the fate of Newton—whether he lives or dies, remains imprisoned or is set free—not the question of his politics. And yet in the back of the minds of the jurors, what he stands for may loom large, perhaps larger than the murky evidence pointing to his guilt or innocence. . . He wishes to stand or fall on the validity of his cause.

Greenlee noted that the extraordinary political overtones lent the courtroom battle over what exactly happened in the morning shootout an atmosphere of unreality: "The testimony inside the courtroom and the evidence outside show all too plainly that the case is at least in part one of people who feel they have been discriminated against and who are not willing to take it any longer."[21]

Garry brought in a forensic chemist to testify that the police failed to perform tests that could have determined if Newton had fired a gun that morning. Garry sought to plant in the jurors' minds the idea that the omission was not an oversight, but a deliberate decision because tests would have proved his client's innocence. Introducing this idea after bringing in strong evidence that Frey's aggressive, racist behavior might have provoked Newton to shoot him did not bother Garry in the slightest. Consistency was not his problem; it was Jensen's.

Throughout the trial Garry counted on juror confusion. As long as there was no proof beyond a reasonable doubt that Newton committed any of the charged crimes, he should go free. Garry had originally raised the issue of self-defense: that if Newton had fired the gun that killed Frey, it was only after Officer Frey had put Newton's life at risk. But Garry dropped this theory at trial as inconsistent with Newton's unambiguous testimony that he had not shot the second officer and had not killed Frey. Deprived of the self-defense theory, Garry had raised the question whether Heanes had shot both Frey and Newton, though the ballistics expert established convincingly that Heanes was too far away to have fired the fatal shot. The defense also raised the possibility that an unapprehended, pygmy stranger or maybe Newton's friend Gene McKinney, had shot Frey. Garry had himself spent many nights in the months before the trial following up leads to potential eye witnesses developed by Black Panthers and volunteer law students from Boalt Hall in Berkeley. Garry interviewed numerous prostitutes in the whorehouses and cheap hotels on Seventh Street, one of whom tried to convince him she had seen the whole thing, including the mysterious killer who got away. Garry had found her version of events so inconsistent that he reluctantly concluded she would not be worth calling as a witness at trial.

On Tuesday, August 27, Garry called as his last witness Dr. Bernard Diamond, the veteran forensic psychiatrist he had hired before on the issue of diminished capacity. Dr. Diamond testified for the defense as to the reflex shock reaction and state of unconsciousness commonly caused in combat by bullet wounds to the abdomen. At the time, Dr. Diamond served on the faculty of U.C. Berkeley as a criminologist; his impressive resumé included more than a decade of experience in the Army Medical Corps and publication of more than two dozen articles in medical journals. Over Jensen's objection, Judge Friedman let Dr. Diamond answer a hypothetical question posed by Garry based on a summary of Newton's testimony. In Dr. Diamond's view, the facts he was asked to assume about Newton reacting in shock with little or no recall of what transpired after he felt a hot flash from the bullet he took in the stomach were "fully compatible with a penetrating gunshot wound of the abdomen."[22] Garry also asked Dr. Diamond whether most people were more credible in their first recollections of an event than when they reconstructed it later, trying to discredit Grier's trial testimony in favor of his earlier statement to the police. Judge Friedman upheld Jensen's objection, instructing the jury that credibility determinations were solely their job.[23]

After Garry rested the defense, Jensen had the opportunity to present four rebuttal witnesses from local law enforcement. These included two Berkeley officers who testified about Newton's high school arrest after hitting a fellow student with a hammer in 1958, and his arrest for punching an officer in the process of arresting Seale in 1966 and for trying to grab the officer's gun from its holster. When it came Garry's turn, Judge Friedman announced some welcome news: the defense would be allowed to present novel expert testimony on ghetto slang. At last, Dr. Blake could explain to the jury that the violent language used by Newton and the Panthers in their newspaper signified something different to the black community than the white community. Stender worked closely with Dr. Blake in preparing his testimony. He explained that a phrase like "takin' care of business" had multiple meanings depending on the context. It could refer to politics, sex, or a variety of other subjects. "Off the pigs" was not intended literally, but figuratively, as an exhortation to free the community from police oppression. Graphic phrases like "buckshot will down the cops" and "carbine will stop the war machine" were similarly figurative expressions of the desire for an end to police brutality and for peace.[24] Though some observers remained quite skeptical, Dr. Blake considerably softened the impact of the Panther rhetoric. The jury would likely give some deference to an African-American professor's benign interpretation of Newton's writings, undermining Jensen's argument that the hate speech provided strong evidence of Huey's motivation to kill Officer Frey.

Melvin Newton also came forward as one of Garry's rebuttal witnesses, explaining away his kid brother's juvenile record. After describing his own education leading to a master's degree in social work, Melvin corroborated Huey's testimony that the Panther co-founder had been functionally illiterate in high school. (Huey had been at his least credible when he told the judge he graduated from high school unable to read or write even simple words like "cat.") Melvin also described how badly beaten Huey had been his junior year the day before his rash use of a hammer against one of his assailants from Berkeley High. After Melvin Newton finished his testimony on August 28, the jury was dismissed for the day while the judge heard defense motions and invited the lawyers to his chambers to decide what jury instructions he would give. The informality of the judge in chambers contrasted with his manner on the bench. He liked to quickly doff his robes and relax in his shirt sleeves, smoking a cigar. He offered his couch to visitors as they chatted off the record. Judge Friedman would have cause to regret this particular instance of informality.

In chambers, Garry raised the defenses of unconsciousness and diminished capacity, i.e., that the jury should be instructed that Newton had not deliberately shot Officer Frey, but maybe he did somehow shoot him unknowingly. He argued that if Newton did shoot Frey, it was when he had been hit first. Newton was not conscious of his acts when he then picked up and fired a gun or, if conscious of his acts, had diminished capacity to appreciate their quality due to his own wound. Officer Heanes had similarly testified as to his own lack of memory after he was wounded. The trial judge agreed to give the diminished capacity instruction, but not the instruction on unconsciousness. It was decided that the trial would resume the following week.

In his final arguments on Tuesday morning, the day after Labor Day, Jensen appeared confident and used no notes. He talked with restrained indignation of John Frey as "a forgotten man" who had been precluded from telling his story on the witness stand, murdered in the line of duty and then subjected to character assassination in court.[25] Jensen sensed the jury's rapt attention as he stayed clinical in his approach, reviewing the forensic evidence in detail to convince the jury that only Newton was in a position close enough to inflict the fatal gunshot wound to Officer Frey. Jensen pointed to the torso of a mannequin propped up next to him, marked by the pathologist who testified that Frey was shot multiple times from a distance of about a foot and that the fatal bullets did not match those from Heanes' gun. Jensen then explained to the jury that premeditation and malice were required for a verdict of first degree murder. Even a moment's reflection where Newton had a choice and made a decision to kill Frey would constitute premeditated murder. Jensen pointed out that the partially written traffic ticket at the scene of the shooting showed that Newton had given Frey a false name and had not produced his driver's license. When Officer Heanes arrived, Newton had belatedly identified himself because he knew that they would shortly figure out who he was.

At times, Jensen spoke softly as he paced in front of the jury. At other times, he invoked sarcasm in describing Newton's political posturing as a protector of the black community and alleged victim of police abuse. Jensen vigorously denied any police conspiracy to "get Huey Newton" and Garry's insinuations that prosecution witnesses had been coached and evidence altered to frame Newton. Jensen intoned: "Actions speak louder than words."[26] A convicted felon, Newton was "no stranger" to violence. Caught with marijuana in his car and in his pants pocket, he had motive in not wanting to be caught in possession of drugs in violation of parole.

On a number of prior occasions, Newton had demonstrated patent hostility toward the police, looked for an excuse to kill one, and had been caught once before trying to take a policeman's gun from him. Jensen pointedly relied on Grier's testimony as an eye witness. Brushing aside as minor all the discrepancies that Garry had shown between Grier's testimony and his prior statement, Jensen called the jury's attention to Grier's original statement to the police—"I did get a clear view of his face."[27]

After lunch, the veteran prosecutor explained the law the jurors would be instructed to apply. First, he described the various degrees of murder and manslaughter that pertained to the charged killing of Officer Frey and the separate crime of assault upon Officer Heanes. Jensen reminded the jurors that not every killing was a crime, but that it depended on the circumstances. To make the degrees of murder as understandable as possible, he suggested that they compare the situation to a pedestrian killed by a driver. If the pedestrian stepped out suddenly in front of a car that could not stop in time, it would not be the driver's fault. If the driver were speeding or drunk, he or she could be held criminally responsible for manslaughter. If the driver deliberately ran the pedestrian down, it would be first degree murder. Second degree murder was a death caused by reckless disregard for human life. He told the jurors to assume the same driver had raced wildly through a busy intersection and crashed and killed a bystander. Jensen then told the jurors the trial had reached "its moment of truth."[28] He ended with a request that they find Newton guilty of assault upon Officer Heanes and first degree murder of Officer Frey—premeditated murder with malice. His presentation had been methodical and extremely persuasive. Taking no apparent pleasure in his task, he had called it "a sad and melancholy truth that Huey Newton . . . is a murderer."[29] Most of the reporters assumed the prosecutor had the jury convinced. Gilbert Moore wrote that when Jensen concluded, "you could feel the noose tightening around Huey Newton's neck; you could well-nigh sniff the gas chamber fumes seeping up through the floorboards."[30]

When Jensen sat down, all eyes turned to Garry, who stood and opened his final argument with a quote from *Alice in Wonderland*: "The King said, 'The evidence first, and then the sentence.' The Queen said, 'No. The sentence first and then the evidence.'"[31] Garry quickly became animated and emotional, focusing primarily on the numerous discrepancies in Henry Grier's testimony and the contrasting testimony of the bus passenger, Tommy Miller. Garry noted that the police who arrived within minutes of the incident did not mention seeing a bus stopped nearby. He quoted Heanes' testimony that he never saw a gun in Newton's hand and reminded the jury that no paraffin test was done. The small traces of marijuana found in Newton's pants pocket could have been placed there by police after the fact or have already been in the pants' pocket when he bought them from Good Will: "You have seen exposed his entire past. Frankly, I wish my own past was as clean as his was. Did you see in any one of the things, the difficulties that he had ever gotten into, where he had stolen so much as a loaf of bread, a pencil? [Huey had never been convicted for any of his parking-lot robberies or petty burglaries, so none of those arrests had been referred to at the trial.] Did you see anything about his past, his juvenile record was even brought in, which is supposed to be sacred."[32]

Referring to Newton's high school hammer-wielding incident, Garry suggested to the jury:

> This youngster sought some way of defending himself. Every one of you would have done the same thing. . . . Huey Newton doesn't ask very much for himself. Huey Newton in my opinion, is a selfless man. I am sure that came out in his testimony. A man who is not interested in himself as a person; he is a devoted man; he is a rare man. Mr. Jensen tried to make this man a liar. He says he (Newton) talks about love and he preaches violence or words to that effect.[33]

Garry then compared Huey Newton to Christ in the *Gospel according to Luke* telling his disciples to defend themselves. He reminded the jurors of the findings of the Kerner Report on white racism, of Malcolm X, of the prevalence in the English language of words denoting white supremacy, like a white lie versus a black one, of the pejorative "blackball" and "blacklist" as opposed to the benign term "whitewash." He spoke of Frantz Fanon and Dr. W. E. B. DuBois. Garry wove in reference to the massacre of his Armenian relatives and the genocide of six million Jews in World War II as he defended the black ghetto fighting for its right of survival. He then exclaimed, "This case is a diabolical attempt to put an innocent man into jail or into the gas chamber."[34]

To make his case, Garry had to take bus driver Henry Grier on directly, but it still shocked the courtroom when he castigated Henry Grier as "either deliberately lying or . . . a psychopath."[35] Highlighted among the discrepancies was Grier's shifting description of the clothing he thought he saw the perpetrator pull a gun from—a tan jacket on the morning of the shootout and a dark one at trial. Garry demonstrated to the jury that the dark jacket police had confiscated from Newton at the hospital had pockets far too shallow to hold a gun.

Garry then focused on key features of Newton's testimony: that he had been subjected to a degrading, complete frisk and had a law book, but no gun in his hand when he was shot. He spoke generally about discrimination, racism, and ghetto life, and even referred to the actions of Mayor Daley and the Chicago police in the riots that had dominated the news that past week in the coverage of the Democratic Presidential Convention in Chicago. Garry had the courtroom spellbound, the jurors in rapt attention, as he ended almost three-and-a-half hours of final argument, brushing back tears. Emotionally exhausted, Garry embraced Newton's shoulders with one arm and haltingly urged the jury to find his client innocent of all charges. Newton looked equally teary-eyed. Judge Friedman appeared moved and offered Garry time to compose himself. Garry thanked him and told the judge he had "said all I have to say."[36] Jensen jumped up in rebuttal, livid at Garry's accusations of perjured testimony and a police frame-up. Garry had impugned his own integrity as well as the state's chief witness. Any discrepancies in Grier's testimony were the product of honest mistakes. With those last words from the prosecutor, the trial itself was over. The jury would be instructed the following day.

Onlookers marveled at Garry's legerdemain—reporters, lawyers with cases on the same floor who dropped by for a glimpse of the trial of the century, and even the most skeptical Black Panther supporters who had lobbied for a black lawyer for their leader. They had just witnessed a master magician in the courtroom. Newton was both a tough and articulate revolutionary hero and a hapless target of police brutality. Kidnapping victim? I'll make him disappear before your very eyes.

Mysterious passenger? Now you see McKinney, now you don't. Eyewitness story, impossible to penetrate? Shot full of holes. Like Houdini, Garry made his showmanship appear relatively effortless as Stender and others labored mightily behind him, often out of sight.

Outside, under constant surveillance by a deputy sheriff, Black Panthers stood in military formation waving black and blue Party flags. Some Panthers remained behind at the courthouse, continuing their vigil, as others left for their headquarters on Grove Street or headed for a planned 5 p.m. rally at DeFremery Park. The Peace and Freedom Party had planned its own courthouse vigil, but they cancelled those plans when fewer than two dozen people showed up.

After forty minutes of instruction on the morning of Thursday, September 5, the jury began its deliberations in a locked jury room on the eighth floor of the courthouse. The room was not large: it contained two small tables, chairs, and a blackboard and had its own private bathroom. The window of the room was too high up for anyone from the street to see into. An old cigar carton sat on one of the tables, presumably for paper ballots. The alternate jurors were sent to a separate room accompanied by a bailiff and frustratingly told not to discuss the case. The alternates would only play a role if one or more of the jurors took ill or otherwise could not participate in continued deliberations. If that were to occur, the alternate or alternates chosen to join in deliberations would be disqualified if they had discussed any of the evidence with any of the alternates who were not selected.

Meanwhile, the reporters, defense lawyers, and Newton's family moved to the sixth-floor press room and hallway, where the media representatives engaged in a free-flowing analysis of the trial, and a few placed wagers on the anticipated verdicts. That same day in San Francisco, Eldridge Cleaver addressed a press conference before he gave a luncheon speech to the Barristers Club as the Peace and Freedom candidate for President. When asked by one of the young lawyers about the Newton case, Cleaver declared ominously that "consequences" would be "inflicted" on whites if Newton were "railroaded," adding, "then all the strings will be cut . . ." Bobby Seale held a short conference on the steps of the Alameda County Courthouse, reiterating that the "sky's the limit around the world" if Newton were not freed.[37] Later that day, Newton told skeptical reporters that "the sky is the limit" was merely a symbolic statement meaning the Panthers would "exhaust all judicial and political resources throughout the world."[38]

Shortly after 6 p.m. Thursday evening, everyone piled into court again, alerted that the jury was returning. Hearts sank among some of Newton's supporters. A quick verdict usually meant conviction. But once in session, the judge revealed a signed request from David Harper, as the newly selected foreman of the jury. Harper asked for a copy of Grier's statement to the police as well as a rereading of Grier's testimony and that of Officer De Hoyos, the officer who had first responded to the scene of the shooting. The jury also requested to see Newton's wounds again. With the judge's permission, Newton walked to the jury box, removed his coat, and pulled out his shirt. Garry helped Newton once again display the scars of the entrance and exit wounds.

The Panthers took no pleasure in learning of Harper's selection as foreman; they assumed from his successful career and suburban lifestyle that he must be a bootlicker. But the defense team was greatly buoyed by the jury's questions and the opportunity for this second demonstration of Newton's wounds. The jurors continued deliberating all day Friday and through the weekend, accompanied by armed bailiffs or sheriff's deputies every time they left for lunch or dinner or to retire for the night. As a safety precaution, the jurors slept at a different, undisclosed hotel each night. Most of the reporters remained holed up at the courthouse, afraid they would miss a scoop if they left. Many crammed into the sixth floor press room, sleeping, eating, and playing cards. They occasionally left to check out rumors, which often proved unsubstantiated.

Gilbert Moore, Fay Stender, and Bob Blauner were among those who passed some of the time playing chess on the floor while they awaited the verdict. Tension mounted as the jury deliberation continued. By Friday, all of the reporters had taken sides on the outcome and began trading speculation on suspected government or rightwing plants at the trial. The local police had begun preparing for rioting when the expected murder verdict was announced. In London, the week before, an angry demonstration had broken out after an erroneous announcement that Newton had been convicted and sentenced to die. A much larger, violent reaction was expected locally if a guilty verdict issued. A group of white radicals, the Berkeley Socialist League, announced that it would hold a vigil and retaliatory action within two days of an adverse verdict. The county had already paid tens of thousands of dollars in overtime for extra deputies. In anticipation of rioting, several hundred police officers were immediately placed on extended duty, augmented by members of the California Highway Patrol. There were eighty-two extra units of law enforcement, primarily from the CHP, arranged to work from Thursday to Tuesday on the assumption the verdict would occur during that time period. Thousands of National Guardsmen remained on alert surrounding the city of Oakland, equipped with helicopters. A large contingent of the police were hidden from public view in the basement parking lot of the new Oakland Museum across the street, half a block from the court house.

That same day the Panthers had gotten out the latest edition of their newspaper. At the top was the usual head shot of Huey in a beret wearing a grim expression on his face. But this time underneath the photo was the caption "Huey Must Be Set Free" underscored with the image of a rifle. Covering the entire front page below the logo was a photo of three militant Panther Party members on the steps of the Alameda County Courthouse. The trio stood at attention in full dress uniform waving "Free Huey" banners emblazoned with the panther emblem. In bold print above the building were the words "WORLD AWAITS VERDICT" and, ominously below the photo, "FREE HUEY . . . OR THE SKY'S THE LIMIT!"

After the jury requested a copy of bus driver Grier's original statement to the police, the defense realized that they had never received the original police tape of the bus driver's interview, but only a transcript. When Jensen produced the tape itself along with the transcript in court on Friday morning, the defense team obtained Judge Friedman's permission to double check its accuracy. Marvin Stender was quickly pressed into service and left with Ed Keating to find an expert to retranscribe the tape for the defense. The new transcription they hurriedly obtained had a small, but significant wording difference from the transcript provided at trial. On the tape, the driver had said he "*didn't*" get a good look at the civilian. The transcript said he "*did*" get a good look.

The defense team quickly contacted the judge and Jensen to schedule immediate argument on this newly disclosed issue. On Saturday afternoon, the jury remained sequestered while the judge heard highly charged arguments on both sides. Judge Friedman then himself listened to the tape and heard the word "*didn't*." Yet he refused to reopen the trial as Garry angrily demanded. Jensen persuaded the judge that to call the jury back for the sole purpose of reading the corrected version of Grier's statement—"*didn't* get a good look"—would overemphasize the significance of the change. Newton never denied being at the scene—he had in fact identified himself to Officer Heanes, testified to being shot in the stomach, and identified the law book he left behind.[39]

Judge Friedman's solution was to allow the correction of Grier's prior statement to be transmitted without comment to the jury as it continued its deliberations. At quarter to eight in the evening of that same day, the jury created a stir by asking to return to court. They had already been back in the morning for a lengthy rereading of testimony. Reporters again wondered if there was a verdict, but the jury only wanted to have the instructions on the degrees of homicide recited to them again along with the definition of assault. Two of the women jurors looked like they might have been crying. Interpreting the tea leaves, it appeared that a decision was imminent. But the jurors ended Saturday, September 7 at 9:45 p.m. with a request that they be taken to their hotel for the night with no indication a decision had been reached.

On Sunday, the jury started deliberations again at 10 a.m. and returned to court immediately, asking the judge to reread the definitions of murder and manslaughter slowly. After he obliged to their apparent satisfaction, the jurors retired once more to the jury room. After having all but ruled out first degree murder on Saturday, the reporters in attendance sensed an overpowering feeling of gloom and concluded that the debate had actually come down to a choice between first and second degree murder—their original assumption when the trial began. Newton's surprisingly effective testimony had temporarily lured some into thinking otherwise, but none now held the view he would be acquitted. In his office, Lowell Jensen noted the eerie calm in the city, like the prelude to a major storm. He and his staff remained unavailable to the press. Mayor Reading expected violence, too. All of Oakland seemed almost ground to a halt awaiting the verdict. Though he still hoped to vindicate Frey's killing with a conviction for first degree murder, Jensen really did not know exactly what to expect at this point. It amazed him to hear from the police that crime in the city was at an ebb as even would-be burglars awaited the jury's verdict.

As the nerve-racking weekend wore to a close, Garry, KPFA program director Elsa Knight Thompson and Alex Hoffmann spent Sunday afternoon and evening closeted with Newton at the jail, with Fay Stender, Blauner, and others coming in and out during their extended vigil. Thompson had the surreal experience of flying back to await the verdict in the Newton case after covering the chaotic Democratic Convention and demonstrations in Lincoln Park in Chicago, where television network crews and newspaper photographers had been targeted with billy clubs. As the confrontations escalated, police and National Guardsmen had responded to sporadic rock and bottle throwers by indiscriminately spraying everyone on the streets with mace or tear gas before they dragged them into paddy wagons off to jail. Elsa Knight Thompson, herself a veteran World War II BBC radio announcer, had relished witnessing firsthand the brutal tactics of American police captured on camera with ninety million Americans watching. The overreaction exceeded the Yippies' expectations of provoking Gestapo-like repression to galvanize revolutionary fervor among their most militant followers.[40]

Thompson stopped off on her way back to Berkeley from Chicago to visit Beverly Axelrod in New Mexico and brought Axelrod's well wishes to Newton. As he knew, Axelrod was now working on major land rights issues for Reies Lopez Tijerina, a militant New Mexico counterpart to Cesar Chavez's farm workers' organization in California. Newton enjoyed the distraction of Thompson's travel tales and likely envisioned how much more turmoil his murder conviction could create. Thompson was amazed at the calm in the small, tenth-floor visiting room at the Oakland jail. Newton acted as if he were entertaining guests in his living room rather than awaiting a life or death verdict from jurors sequestered two floors below. Newton even joked that: "If they come in with an acquittal, I'm going to ask to poll them individually."[41]

Thompson had a sixth sense that the jury had just reached a verdict shortly before a knock on the door summoned them back to the courtroom late Sunday evening. Foreman Harper had sent a note out to the judge that the jury had completed the verdict forms. Their adrenaline flowing, only a couple of dozen rumpled and unshowered members of the press still waited on the sixth floor of the courthouse. They answered the call to the courtroom along with a few spectators, the cheerless, exhausted lawyers, and Newton's nervous family, leaving a large number of empty seats. Newton arrived dressed in olive drab slacks and a green shirt, looking dour but determined. He told reporter Rush Greenlee, "No matter how it goes it's not the end of the road. I've prepared myself."[42]

When everyone was inside, Judge Friedman took the bench and announced that the doors to the courtroom would be locked and stay locked until the verdicts had all been read and the jury dismissed, a precaution that had not been taken before. Sheriff's deputies remained on guard at the building's entrances and in its abandoned hallways. The atmosphere was eerie, the audience in suspense. Moore felt the room seem to shrink "as though we had all been stuffed into some malodorous bottle. The stench of death was everywhere."[43] When the jurors entered a side door and sat down, they, too, looked bedraggled and exhausted. None looked at Newton as they walked past him, which veteran reporters considered a sure sign of conviction.

Judge Friedman then asked for the verdicts. Harper handed the verdict to the bailiff, who brought it to the judge. The judge reviewed the form silently and passed it to the clerk, who read it aloud as Newton stood at the counsel table waiting. First degree murder—not guilty. Second degree murder—not guilty. Sighs of relief escaped from the defense team and Newton's family. Voluntary manslaughter—guilty. Newton swallowed hard, but remained impassive as the reading of the verdicts was completed. Assault upon Officer Heanes—not guilty. The jury had also followed instructions to determine for themselves if Newton had been convicted of a prior felony. Their affirmative vote on that issue automatically increased the penalty. Jensen tried not to show his disappointment. Newton's family looked stunned. His sister Doris Godfrey collapsed in shock. Stender squeezed Newton's hand. The jury verdicts surprised nearly everyone. The jury found that Newton had shot Frey, but it must have decided Newton did not possess his own gun. By now, all of the press knew that possession of a concealed firearm, a felony itself, would have automatically rendered Newton guilty of second degree murder. The jury must have concluded that Officer Frey had pulled out his gun, that Newton had wrestled it away from him and shot Frey after Heanes had shot Newton in the stomach.

Each juror was polled individually on all three counts and affirmed that he or she agreed with the verdict. Judge Friedman, dabbing his brow with a handkerchief, thanked and dismissed the jury for their hard work and expressed his appreciation to the alternates for standing-by in readiness. The bailiff then led them out by the side door. Garry immediately made three motions: for a new trial, for Newton's release on bail, and for the sentencing to be delayed. The defense team would have their work cut out for them to accomplish all of these in short order. Judge Friedman set a date for that Thursday, September 12, to take testimony on the bail request, set the hearing itself for September 27, and then adjourned the proceedings. As Newton was taken from the courtroom, his minister raised a fist up high with an emphatic "Power to the People," and Newton responded in kind.

When the brief Sunday evening court session concluded, bailiffs opened the locks on the seventh-floor stairwell for the first time since the trial had begun almost two months earlier. As soon as the judge left the bench, the reporters rushed for the telephones in the building and for quotes from the lawyers, Newton, and Newton's family—trying to get a read on which side felt it had won. They also sought out the jurors before they left the building, but they all refused to discuss their decision with the press. After Garry spent half an hour with him in his cell, Garry reported that Newton believed he had been "sold down the river by a white racist society."[44] But the legal team had also buoyed Newton's hopes that the low-level verdict could make him a likely condidate for release on bail pending appeal. Newton instructed Garry to tell Seale to get word out immediately on the street "to keep it cool"—Newton wanted no uprising in response to the verdict that would spoil his chances for release.[45]

Seale felt the same way—there was no point to giving the police an excuse to bash heads and make mass arrests. He got on the phone and then jumped in his car to spread Newton's message. Field Marshall Don Cox was livid. Based on prior instructions from Party leaders, Cox had been all set to assault the jail with his men and liberate Newton. The change of plans rankled long afterwards, causing Cox to side with Cleaver when the Panthers later split.[46] Yet even Cleaver saw merit in holding off revolution in the streets—at least, for the time being. Everywhere Seale went, he passed caravans of police and highway patrolmen in riot gear.

Upon hearing the verdict, most of the members of the defense team were in a celebratory mood. They all knew that the result was far better than it could have been, though Alex Hoffmann, who had spent the most time keeping Newton company in jail, still found the voluntary manslaughter conviction traumatic. The sensitive lawyer may have secretly been in love with Huey, though it would be many years before Hoffmann acknowledged his homosexuality. Fay Stender—another hopelessly passionate devotee of Huey and his cause—also remained unsatisfied. In her view it would have been unthinkable for the jury to find Newton guilty of first degree murder and subject to execution.

True to form, Lowell Jensen refused to publicly second-guess the jurors, recognizing they had been very conscientious in their efforts. Privately, he assumed the verdict was likely a compromise. Even diminished capacity usually reduced premeditated murder to second degree "reckless" murder, not voluntary manslaughter. (Eleven years later in San Francisco, a jury instructed on what became known as "the Twinkie defense"—impaired judgment from too much junk food—would come back with a similarly surprising verdict of voluntary manslaughter against former supervisor Dan White on charges he assassinated San Francisco Mayor George Moscone and the city's first openly gay supervisor, Harvey Milk.)

While Jensen deliberately kept his thoughts to himself, Garry postured to the press that the verdict was a disappointing, "chicken shit" compromise. After he met with his attorneys, Newton told reporters the same thing—that the jury had reached a compromise unsupported by the evidence. Most other observers subscribed to that view as well. But on his way out of the courthouse, Garry poked reporter Gilbert Moore in the ribs and whispered, "We got 'em. We got 'em."[47] He shouted to another supporter, "It is a victory, buddy, it's a victory!"[48]

14. AFTERMATH

*"I just hope we did the right thing.
We certainly tried."*

NEWTON JUROR EDA PRELLI

The day after the ordeal ended, an *Oakland Tribune* reporter interviewed Mrs. Gibbons, the factory worker who was the only person chosen the very first day of jury selection. She described how the jurors had all been anxious to reach agreement and had decided that conviction of Newton for assault of Officer Heanes would only follow if they concluded that Officer Frey's death had been premeditated, first degree murder. During deliberations, one of the jurors had brought up the threats made by demonstrators, "Huey must be free or else." They decided it was not their problem to address and focused instead on reaching the result they considered the evidence to support. They believed that Officer Frey had stopped Newton for no reason, that he had called Newton a "nigger" and frisked him abusively. They found no malice in Newton's swift reaction, but did find him culpable of manslaughter. Mrs. Gibbons said no ballot was ever taken on first or second degree murder, and no one took a hard line position on finding him guilty of first degree murder.[1]

Mrs. Eda Prelli, the widowed landlady on the jury, gave a somewhat different version to Rush Greenlee of *The San Francisco Examiner*. She revealed her own strong belief that there had been a fifth person at the shootout and that Huey's passenger Gene McKinney might have known more than the jury heard. Two of the women had strongly favored second degree murder, but Mrs. Prelli had started out for acquittal. She later joined with David Harper and Tom Hofmann, the bachelor bank officer who lived with his parents, when they switched from acquittal to manslaughter.

Examiner reporters interviewed many Oaklanders for their reactions and found them divided on racial lines. Most blacks believed that Newton "got a raw deal"; most whites thought he had no basis for complaining about the fairness of the trial and a result many considered better than he deserved. Clinton White, whom Bobby Seale had interviewed for chief defense counsel, was more evenhanded. He had anticipated acquittal, but thought the jury had conscientiously applied the law and "may have believed part of Newton's story and part of bus driver Grier's testimony." It was not inconsistent to acquit Newton of shooting Heanes if they thought Heanes was hit accidentally by errant gunfire during a struggle between Frey and Newton.[2]

* * * * *

Observing the Newton trial was a career-altering experience for reporter Gilbert Moore, who could not force himself to write a story short and neutral enough for publication by *Life* magazine. He left his job to write a cathartic book about the rage and raw nerves he had witnessed in the Panther leaders, "cursing them for raising ten thousand questions and answering none of them."[3] In tying up loose ends, Moore tracked down the jury foreman, David Harper, who had since been lured to Detroit to become president of an African-American owned bank. Harper was immensely proud of his accomplishment in the Newton trial and puffed on a cigar as he recounted the details. He had observed Oakland's political tensions rising to the bursting point before the trial and had been quite happy to receive notice he was in the Newton jury pool. He thought that resort to the law was the best answer. During voir dire, Harper had concealed how much he coveted the opportunity to serve in this extraordinarily high profile challenge to the establishment. (Harper had originally studied in a seminary for the priesthood, so his concerns about the death penalty were likely more pronounced than he had stated.) He wanted to prove enough progress was being made so that "a black guy could be part of the legal system and come out with something fair."[4]

During the trial Harper had been offered police protection for his home after threats were received against his wife's life. They had declined because she had been just as afraid of the police. Once selected for the jury, Harper had deliberately set out to become the other jurors' choice for foreman, though he let them think it was their own idea. Then, drawing on his prior jury experience, he refused to conduct a formal vote right away, telling the group they first needed to review all of the evidence together and see how much they could agree about what they thought had happened. As the defense had guessed, Harper was strongly for acquittal at the time. He kept his opinions close to the chest, concerned that if he revealed his position too early, he would no longer be persuasive.

The jurors quickly concluded that they had all been impressed by Newton and thought Davis, the ballistics expert, had been highly credible. All but Harper admired the bus driver Grier's courage; Harper had considered him an Uncle Tom, though he never told the others that for fear of losing his own credibility. When they began deliberations on Thursday several had doubted that Newton was telling the truth about being shot first. Harper got them to focus on Newton's wound. He suggested that if Newton were already on his knees when he was shot—as Newton claimed—the bullet would have entered Newton's abdomen at a higher point than it exited through his back. That was why they had asked to see the wound again on Thursday and had verified that the exit wound was lower than the entrance wound, supporting Newton's version of the shootout.

Not until Saturday did they take their first formal vote, using scratch paper brought in by the bailiff and the cigar box already at hand. When Harper anxiously tallied up the votes, he determined they were split three ways: three for acquittal, four for voluntary manslaughter and five for first degree murder. To his dismay, three-quarters of the panel believed Newton was criminally responsible for the death of Officer Frey, disagreeing only on whether the killing was provoked or premeditated. After two days of painstaking efforts to reconstruct the shootout, five of them were prepared to consider sending Newton to his death and just two thought like Harper did that Newton should walk free. How was he to bridge that extraordinary gulf? Harper had to wonder what direction the deliberations would have taken if no black served on the jury. He needed to persuade the five hardliners to join the other seven jurors who believed that the police had instigated the shootout by their own abusive conduct. He led the panel back through their analysis. They agreed that Newton had been frisked for weapons before the shooting started. They then discussed the conflict between Grier's version of the shootout and Heanes' version. The majority concluded that Heanes was not telling the truth—that Heanes shot first, and that only after he was shot, did Newton wrestle with Frey and obtain his gun, which Newton then fired at close range, killing Frey. But still positions did not budge.

As the third day of deliberations wore on, the jurors' tempers started to fray from the tension of their prolonged confinement. The most difficult person to confer with civilly was the factory worker, Mrs. Gibbons, who always cut off any argument by saying Huey "did the dirty deed."[5] The fiery Cuban, Joseph Quintana, favored acquittal, but could not persuade anyone of his reasoning. Mrs. Reed, the vocal opponent of the term "pigs," had been the strongest supporter of a murder conviction. As deliberations dragged on, Ron Andrews appealed to them all to consider their decision as if they were in Newton's shoes, which demoralized Harper who thought that had been their charge from the outset. When reasoned discourse seemed to have totally evaporated, Harper threatened to send a note to Judge Friedman asking for a reminder that they were required to be dispassionate in their deliberations. Some of the other jurors took offense, and no note was sent. They rededicated themselves to their assigned task. Ultimately, at a quarter past nine that Sunday evening, another vote was taken with ten for manslaughter and two for murder. Harper had changed his own vote from acquittal to avoid a hung jury and convinced others to do the same.

Harper recalled that Tom Hofmann, the bachelor who lived with his parents, had favored murder, not acquittal as the landlady Mrs. Prelli had thought. Hofmann then switched to make it eleven to one for voluntary manslaughter. At that point only Mrs. Reid voted for conviction on the murder charge. She had gone to the bathroom while the final tally was taken and, upon hearing the new results, called her change of heart out from behind the closed door. Greatly relieved that their ordeal was over, the men all shook Harper's hand and the women kissed him. Everyone recognized that Harper's extraordinary efforts had produced the consensus, one which he fervently hoped would avoid a bloodbath and restore faith in the justice system. Just before turning in their verdicts, the jurors made a pact to keep their deliberations shrouded in secrecy, to let them go on with their lives unmolested by curious media. Two of the women changed their minds the next day and spoke to the press.

* * * * *

In preparation for a murder verdict, Police Chief Charles Gain had put twice as many officers on patrol as normal, intent on such a strong show of force, combined with state highway patrolmen and National Guardsmen, they would together deter any violence. He was well aware that the devastating six-day Watts riots of 1965 had escalated from a single incident: a policeman pulling over an African-American drunk driver and impounding his car in front of hositle neighborhood spectators. After the polarizing reactions to two bloody skirmishes with the Panthers in the last year, Oakland was so on edge over the Newton trial that the slightest new confrontation could trigger horrendous consequences.

Yet in the aftermath of the surprising verdicts, most of the 650 Oakland colleagues of the slain policeman were more incensed at the perceived failure of the justice system than Newton's defense team professed to be. A *Los Angeles Times* reporter observed: "[F]rustration fear and anger are straining the nerves of big city policemen close to the breaking point."[6] After the Panther ambush in April 1968, police on patrol in the flatlands all kept alert for similar attacks. Panther newspapers urging followers to "kill the pigs" and "Sky's the Limit" placards and speeches left patrolmen in West Oakland increasingly jittery, especially after they heard that the Panthers were stockpiling ammunition.

On Sunday night after the verdict was issued, calm had prevailed. When Monday evening turned out similarly, Gain must have gone to bed breathing a sigh of relief. Then the telephone woke him before 2 a.m. with most unwelcome news. Around 1:30 a.m., two members of his force had driven past Panther headquarters at 4451 Grove Street in Oakland

and fired a shotgun and a carbine repeatedly from their squad car at the portrait of Newton in the front window. Luckily, no one was present in the building, but the barrage of bullets struck office furniture and shattered an interior room divider. They also damaged posters of Eldridge Cleaver and Bobby Hutton that hung on the wall. Three shots struck an adjoining café, and one errant shot went through the roof of their own patrol car.

The first shots woke up neighbors, who saw the second barrage of gunfire after the officers made a U-turn, wrote down the number of the patrol car, and called the police dispatcher. Gain wasted no time calling for an investigation into the potential crisis. The patrol car was assigned to Officers Richard Williams and Robert Ferrell, who were on duty at the time of the shooting spree. When stopped for questioning, breath and blood tests showed their blood alcohol at .19, well over the generous definition then in place of .15 for a person "under the influence of alcohol." Unlike the radicals, the police could not afford any appearance that they condoned lawlessness as a response to a disappointing trial outcome. Less than thirty hours after the jury's verdicts were announced, the pair were arrested on felony charges of firing into an occupied dwelling. On Police Chief Gain's recommendation, they were immediately fired for gross misconduct.

Panther spokesmen took the episode as proof of what they had repeatedly argued: "That the Oakland Police Department is racist and determined to wipe out the Panthers."[7] However, Newton again sent out word for Party supporters to lay low and not give the police an excuse to come down hard on the community. That same day, Mayor Reading issued a press release calling the policemen's behavior "most regrettable and deplorable." Meanwhile, Police Chief Gain urged citizens not to impugn the department as a whole for the shooting spree.[8] The Oakland Police Officers' Association refused to cover the fired men's legal fees. Most members were anxious to distance themselves from the two miscreants to avoid putting the rest of the department at risk of retribution. The organization's president lamented, "I can't think of anything worse they could have done. Policemen long after they're gone are going to have to live with this."[9] Gain's prompt action was credited with playing a major role in averting riots. The National Guardsmen were sent home as radical militant supporters of Newton retreated to contemplate their next move.

Despite all of the preparation for mob violence following the anticipated death penalty verdict, the only serious misconduct had been that of two rogue policemen unhappy with Newton's conviction of a lesser crime. Harper was right. He had defused the situation by convincing the jury to reach a result in which there were no unqualified victims, but apportionment of blame on both sides—a day of reckoning that few, if any, had reckoned on.

Shot up Panther headquarters in Oakland — Tuesday, September 10, 1968.

102-160 2M 7/61 (Rev.)

SUPERIOR COURT OF THE STATE OF CALIFORNIA IN AND FOR THE COUNTY OF ALAMEDA

ABSTRACT OF JUDGMENT
(Commitment to State Prison)

The People of the State of California, Present:

vs.

HUEY P. NEWTON
Defendant

Present:
Hon. MONROE FRIEDMAN
Judge of the Superior Court
D. Lowell Jensen
Asst. District Attorney
Charles R. Garry
Counsel for Defendant

This certifies that on Sept. 8, 1968 judgment of conviction of the above-named defendant was entered as follows:
(1) Case No. 41266 Count No. One of the Indictment.
On his plea of not guilty
he was convicted by verdict of jury of a felony, to wit: voluntary manslaughter, a violation of Section 192, Subdivision 1 of the Penal Code of the State of California, a lesser and included offense within the offense charged in Count One of the Indictment.

with prior felony convictions charged and proved ~~or admitted~~ as follows:

Date County and State Crime Disposition

On October 29, 1964, in the Superior Court of the State of California in and for the County of Alameda, defendant was convicted of a felony, to wit: assault with a deadly weapon, a violation of Section 245 of the Penal Code of the State of California under the name of Huey Percy Newton, and pursuant to said conviction, sentence was suspended for three years, during which time he was placed on probation.

[illegible struck-out lines]

(3) IT IS THEREFORE ORDERED, ADJUDGED AND DECREED that the said defendant be punished by imprisonment in state prison of the State of California for the term provided by law and that he be remanded to the Sheriff of the County of Alameda, and by him delivered to the Director of Corrections of the State of California at California Medical Facility, Vacaville, California.

[illegible struck-out lines]

FILED
SEP 27 1968
JACK G. BLUE, County Clerk
By K. I. FAGRE

(4) To the Sheriff of the County of Alameda and to the Director of Corrections at the California Medical Facility, Vacaville, California

Pursuant to the aforesaid judgment, this is to command you, the said Sheriff, to deliver the above named defendant into the custody of the Director of Corrections at the California Medical Facility, Vacaville, California, at your earliest convenience.

Witness my hand and seal of said court September 27, 1968.

JACK G. BLUE, Clerk

(SEAL) By K. I. Fagre Deputy

RECEIVED CALIF MEDICAL FACILITY GUIDANCE CENTER 27 10 43 AM '68

State of California, County of Alameda, } SS.

I do hereby certify the foregoing to be a true and correct abstract of the judgment duly made and entered on the minutes of the Superior Court in the above entitled action as provided by Penal Code Section 1213.

Attest my hand and seal of the said Superior Court this

(SEAL) 27th day of September, 1968

JACK G. BLUE,
County Clerk and ex officio Clerk of the Superior Court of the State of California in and for the County of Alameda.

By K. I. Fagre, Deputy.

Monroe Friedman
Judge of the Superior Court of the State of California in and for the County of Alameda

The foregoing instrument is a correct copy of the original on file in this office
ATTEST: SEP 27 1968
JACK G. BLUE, County Clerk and ex officio Clerk of the Superior Court of the State of California in and for the County of Alameda
DEPUTY

EXHIBIT A

Courtesy of Department of Special Collections and University Archives, Stanford University Libraries.

Part Three

1. THE "FREE HUEY" CAMPAIGN EXPANDS TO BURSTING

If he had been outside, he would never have belonged to us in the same way, but locked away, he was ours.

RANDOM HOUSE EDITOR GREGORY ARMSTRONG

In just three weeks, Fay Stender coordinated community volunteers to obtain 20,000 signatures in support of Newton's release on bail pending appeal from his voluntary manslaughter conviction. Yet few besides his family and most devoted advocates were surprised that Judge Friedman found far more persuasive the combination of Newton's negative probation report detailing a decade of serious run-ins with the law, and the District Attorney's argument that Newton demonstrated "nothing but contempt for the rules that govern civilized men."[1] Newton was ordered to begin his two-to-fifteen-year sentence even though he might easily wind up serving the minimum time before an appellate decision issued. Reversal seemed most unlikely.

Newton remained stoic; his mother, who had spent most of the past eleven months since her son's arrest in seclusion, screamed hysterically. Following Garry's orders, Cleaver had not attended the hearing and remained silent. Police returned Newton to his cell on the tenth floor only to remove him moments later to transport him for evaluation at the Vacaville Medical Facility. The suddenness of his client's departure shocked Charles Garry; he had no opportunity to discuss some important matters with Newton. Local papers took notice that no "Sky's the Limit" reprisals occurred. Garry insisted to skeptical reporters that the "The sky is the limit" meant only that they intended to exhaust all the Panther leader's legal rights. A reporter for the *People's World* commented, "No doubt there are those in the black community for whom the slogan means more; a warning of the pent up frustrations and anger in an oppressed and exploited people, which might easily explode into violence if provoked by the power structure."[2] One reporter assumed that, for some of the Panthers, Huey would have made "a much finer martyr" if he were instead headed for execution.[3] The day after Newton's sentencing, San Francisco narrowly avoided sparking a riot. An itchy-fingered white policeman shot a black truck driver, who died. Newspapers noted the officer sported a homemade tie pin—"Gas Huey." He was quickly suspended and arrested on a charge of using excessive force.

At the beginning of October, Newton was transferred to the Men's Colony in San Luis Obispo, a medium-security facility four hours' drive south, which housed mostly white, nonviolent (and gay) convicts. Officials obviously wanted to isolate Newton from his supporters. Coincidentally—or not—on October 3, two bombs went off in the Alameda County courthouse where he had been tried, breaking one hundred windows. The administration called in a Navy bomb squad. Elsewhere, Kathleen Cleaver made headlines, rallying supporters with her own twist on H. Rap Brown's call to action: "We have to civilize America . . . or let it burn."[4] She posed for *Ramparts* with a rifle at her side, illustrating that she was prepared for armed self-defense against another warrantless invasion of her home, as Newton had commanded in Executive Mandate No. 3.

To the warden's dismay, Newton was an instant celebrity among his fellow inmates at the Men's Colony. The administration considered Newton a headache. News agencies all over the United States inundated the prison with requests for interviews. In mid-October, Newton was thrilled to learn of the defiant gesture made by San Jose State's star athlete, Tommie Smith, upon winning a track gold medal at the 1968 Olympics. After other black teammates had last-minute second thoughts, Smith and bronze medalist John Carlos earned boos for mounting the podium shoeless in black socks to honor those of their race living in poverty, whom they offered power-to-the-people salutes. The image became etched in people's minds, underscored by the pair's immediate lifetime banishment. By the end of the month, Newton launched his own protest. He demanded the minimum wage instead of working in the prison kitchen for three cents per hour, which he called "slave wages." The warden isolated Newton in lock-up for rule violations, and announced that his celebrity prisoner had just forfeited all privileges. As in the Alameda jail, Newton often paced naked in his poorly ventilated cell, roughly four-and-a-half feet by six feet. When the press again demanded access, exasperated prison officials permitted limited numbers of dailies to set up further interviews.

* * * * *

By late September 1968, Charles Garry had resumed preparations for the upcoming Oakland Seven conspiracy trial over the blockading of the local army induction center the year before. Stender took over the slow process of reviewing the 4,000-page trial record and researching and writing the brief on Newton's appeal. She eagerly accepted the challenge, which included orchestrating the "Free Huey" campaign to build on Movement demands for his release. The FBI started keeping closer tabs on her. One covert agent was assigned to mingle with the crowd at a keynote address Stender gave to a thousand students at a teach-in in San Diego. He noted in her file that he found the soft-spoken lawyer surprisingly persuasive when she proclaimed that the Black Panther Party was the best thing ever to happen to African-Americans.

Stender squeezed in as many fund-raising and speaking events as she could, recruiting celebrities to lend their names and trumpeting the need to "Free Huey" with flyers invoking left-wing martyrs of the past—Sacco and Vanzetti, the Scottsboro Boys, the Rosenbergs, and Malcolm X. Meanwhile she drew on more volunteer help from professors and students, often working late into the night over the next year, researching and writing a nearly 200-page opening "brief" and another lengthy reply "brief." She visited Newton frequently to update him on her progress, buoy his spirits and serve as a go-between for those denied visitation privileges. Hilliard sought to oversee the growing Party, with Newton's advice from behind bars, while Eldridge Cleaver remained a loose cannon.

A congressional hearing on violence in late October generated more headlines about Newton's revolutionary agenda. During Prof. Herman Blake's testimony, sparks flew as the bearded assistant professor argued with a Congressman over Newton's pronouncement that blacks should go to war if necessary to overcome racism.[5] Alarm bells had gone off when a staff member from the Kerner Commission told the congressional panel the results of his August 12th interview with Newton in the Alameda County jail. Newton predicted "future bloodshed" and opined that the outcome of his trial was less important than its role as a "springboard that mobilizes the community."[6] He expected the Movement to mushroom to two million members in two years. Newton also shared his view that, by forming a coalition with the Peace and Freedom Party, the Panthers could gain political control of black ghettos throughout the country.

Back in August, Stender had arranged for Newton to be featured in a film whose crew came to visit Newton at the Alameda County jail. By early November, *Prelude to Revolution* drew crowds at a black film festival in Pasadena and elsewhere across country. With the whirlwind of activity she generated, friends saw Stender as an irrepressible force on a mission for which she refused to consider failure a possibility, despite exceedingly long odds. Luckily, Newton was in no hurry to get released. Though subject to depression and mood swings in isolation, he felt safe in prison. It gave him time to strategize while all hell was breaking loose on the outside between militants and anti-war protesters and the establishment, particularly on college campuses.

The Panthers figured prominently in the first and longest campus strike in American history that began in November 1968 at San Francisco State College. The protest started in response to the suspension that fall of Black Panther Minister of Education George Mason Murray from the adjunct faculty of the English Department. The highly controversial suspension of Murray, without a hearing, came at the instigation of the State College Board of Trustees. Tensions had been building since the year before with sit-ins, picketing, and sporadic vandalism. The target of student protests was twofold: the university's cooperation with the draft and its refusal to accede to demands for ethnic studies programs. The Black Student Union had derived their demand for educational reform from the Panther Ten Point Program. The Third World Liberation Front made similar demands for their own programs.

Students for a Democratic Society ("SDS") played a central role in orchestrating anti-war rallies at San Francisco State, with considerable support from liberal faculty and staff. SDS leader Tom Hayden had been famed since his undergraduate days at the University of Michigan as the principal author of the 1962 "Port Huron Statement" of New Left principles. At the time his wife was a SNCC volunteer. In 1968, Hayden moved his headquarters from a community project in the slums of Newark, New Jersey, to San Francisco. By September of 1968, Hayden was recognized as "the most influential leader . . . of the New Left and the most effective young radical in the country."[7] Hayden, in turn, labeled the Black Panthers "America's Vietcong,"[8] whom SDS hailed as freedom fighters. The FBI kept a close eye on SDS as well as the Panthers.

Aggressive lobbying for an African-American Studies Department at San Francisco State and for the hiring of more black staff had taken a violent turn in November 1967. Several black students assaulted the editor of the school newspaper, who had voiced strong opposition to a grant for new ethnic studies programs. Amid protests by sympathetic classmates, six students were suspended and faced felony prosecution when Bobby Seale was invited to speak on campus in March 1968. Seale alarmed the administration with a speech to a mostly white audience claiming that blacks only achieved power by carrying guns. George Mason Murray, a part-time instructor, reportedly endorsed black students arming themselves. Word got back that he then told a black student group at a Fresno State College rally: "We are slaves and the only way to become free is to kill all the slave masters."[9] Murray infuriated state officials even more in August 1968 when he, Chief of Staff David Hilliard, and another prominent Panther were intercepted in Mexico City, headed to Communist Cuba at Castro's invitation in defiance of the United States travel ban.

Then came the explosive confrontations at the Democratic Convention, which emboldened activists to plan further disruptions. Hayden said he hoped to instigate "two, three, many Chicagos."[10] Shortly afterward, Gov. Reagan was shocked by the Newton jury verdict.

Reagan became apoplectic when he discovered later that month that Eldridge Cleaver received invitations at U.C. Davis, U.C. Berkeley, and Stanford to lecture that fall on the topic of urban unrest. More than ten thousand infuriated citizens lodged letters of protests with the governor. An equally irate State Superintendent of Public Instruction told reporters: "Mr. Cleaver certainly would be as well-qualified to lecture on urban unrest as Attila the Hun . . . on international mass murder and as Benedict Arnold to lecture on treason."[11] The enormous controversy only induced more students to rush to enroll for the guest lecture series featuring the Peace and Freedom candidate for President. Prompted by Gov. Reagan, the U.C. Regents intervened to deny course credit for more than one lecture.[12] Cleaver then surprised everyone with his first lecture, a surprisingly serious talk about racism devoid of his trademark obscenities. Some students found it boring.

Across the bay at the same time, the San Francisco State student body then invited the ex-felon to their campus to accept an honorary lifetime membership in their association, and to read to the assembled crowd from his book *Soul On Ice.* But Cleaver had other ideas. Itching to provoke the administration even more, he told the audience that "we have to throw this capitalist system into the garbage can of history." He urged listeners to harness "red, yellow, brown and even white power" and warned, "If Huey isn't freed, we're going to free him, and we're going to do it with guns." He then invited the students to listen to a poem he had just dedicated to the governor. To great applause, he recited a three-line chant, pausing for the audience to echo his words. "Fuck Reagan . . . Fuck Reagan . . . Fuck Reagan. . . ." The students enthusiastically joined in a loud chorus. As an afterthought, Cleaver added, "Fuck the Regents—ten lectures to one."[13] Maligning the governor with obscenities and threatening armed revolt guaranteed more outraged headlines. Where would it lead?

In late October 1968—just a month before his scheduled return to prison for parole violation—Cleaver gave *Playboy* magazine an interview at his lawyer Charles Garry's office. Relishing the limelight, Cleaver hinted darkly that the day of reckoning was coming soon: "We don't work on a timetable, but . . . the situation is deteriorating rapidly. . . This isn't the 1930s. We're not going to play Jews,"[14] echoing H. Rap Brown's earlier oft-repeated warning. Three weeks later San Francisco police stopped a bakery and Black Panther newspaper delivery truck bearing the Party logo as the occupants fled from a local service station robbery. Another gun fight ensued in broad daylight near police headquarters at the San Francisco Hall of Justice. Three officers were shot and eight Panthers arrested.

Newton learned from visitors to the Men's Colony in San Luis Obispo that Cleaver was making plans to barricade himself and supporters inside an Oakland building to precipitate a final bloody confrontation with local police just before Thanksgiving. The Panther Minister of Defense still blamed Cleaver for the foolhardy confrontation with Oakland police that had gotten young Bobby Hutton killed back in April of that year. Though Newton had previously given the green light to violent reprisals in the event he wound up on death row, the manslaughter verdict had changed his mind. With Gov. Reagan and the FBI hell-bent on eradicating the Party, Newton ordered Cleaver to flee the country, head for Cuba, and recruit international Panthers. Cleaver failed to show up for his last lecture at U.C. Berkeley, eluded the FBI agents on his tail, and did just that, vanishing into thin air just before Thanksgiving as an all-points bulletin was issued for his arrest.

Meanwhile, the tension at San Francisco State escalated. Murray was a popular instructor and the manner of his suspension highly irregular. Supporters not only demanded his reinstatement, but reasserted other unmet demands for ethnic studies and renewed their calls for American disengagement from the Vietnam War. When the college's new President S. I. Hayakawa literally pulled the plug on speakers at an outdoor rally, he became an overnight Conservative celebrity. Gov. Reagan weighed in, sending police from various jurisdictions to occupy the campus and arrest seven hundred demonstrators. Over the next several months, while San Francisco State remained in turmoil, similar strikes and sit-ins erupted at 300 college campuses across the country. The escalating student unrest occurred at the same time as unprecedented attempts by militants to stop the nation's business as usual. A record-breaking forty planes would be hijacked in 1969, triggering new laws requiring metal detectors at airports. Acts of arson, explosions, and violence were reported almost daily in the media. The Justice Department noted an extraordinary rise in threats and actual attacks on public buildings, predicting that 1969 would be dubbed the "year of the bombings."[15]

Preaching to the choir of fellow Lawyers Guild members, Charles Garry noted that in such a charged political climate it was "impossible to get a fair trial for a serious political case which involves a militant and a revolutionary spokesman who speaks about destruction of America—and is also black."[16] Recognizing a guaranteed draw, the prestigious De Young Museum in San Francisco mounted a photographic essay on the Panthers, featuring iconic pictures of Huey Newton, Eldridge and Kathleen Cleaver, Bobby Seale, David Hilliard, and George Murray. Students at Merritt College in Oakland hosted a national conference aimed at converting Merritt College into an all-black college renamed for Huey Newton. Meanwhile, a local paper reported that over the last few years the beleaguered campus had suffered increased incidents of windows shot out, arson, mugging, rapes, and theft, while its book store sold out copies of *Soul On Ice* and the *Quotations of Chairman Mao.*

Exasperation of government leaders reached a new pinnacle in the Bay Area in April 1969 when U.C. veterans of the Free Speech Movement took possession of dilapidated university property near Telegraph Avenue on the south side of the U.C. Berkeley campus. The lot was awaiting an administrative decision as to its future use. Over the next month about a thousand students and locals cleared the debris from the 2.8 acre parcel and planted donated trees and shrubbery for "People's Park." Meanwhile, U.C.'s Vice Chancellor proposed that the land be devoted to a sports field, but promised not to take any action without notice.

Already smarting from having eggs thrown at his car when he attended a February Regents' meeting, the governor refused to wait for the university to resolve the current impasse. In early April he spoke unguardedly at a gathering of the Council of California Growers about his tough opposition to militant U.C. activists: "If there has to be a bloodbath, then let's get it over with. No more appeasement." When advised how bad that sounded, the governor shortly afterward withdrew any suggestion that he wanted a literal bloodbath "on the Berkeley campus or anywhere else."[17] Yet on the morning of May 15, 1969, he sent 250 highway patrol and police officers without notice to uproot "People's

Park," install a chain-link fence around the property, and defend it with live ammunition. Three thousand students, gathered at Sproul Plaza for an unrelated rally that day, became incensed at the precipitous police action. ASUC president Dan Siegel urged them to "Take the park."

A melée ensued, thirty people were shot, one was killed, and one bystander blinded. Gov. Reagan then declared martial law in Berkeley. For the next few weeks helicopters circled the city, prepared to spray tear gas on any Berkeley residents who assembled. Serendipitously, Penny Cooper had quit the Public Defender's Office two weeks before the People's Park confrontation to go into private practice with her colleague Jim Newhouse in Berkeley. By precipitating so many arrests, Gov. Reagan handed the duo a superabundance of clients. (Siegel was charged with inciting a riot and acquitted. On his behalf a Lawyers Guild team led by the Treuhaft and Garry firms later successfully challenged a State Bar recommendation to the California Supreme Court that Siegel's conduct at the rally made him morally unfit to become a lawyer.)

Historians started describing the situation in 1969 as the worst violence since the Red Summer of 1919. In late June, *Time* magazine predicted "Guerrilla Summer." The administration feared the role Panthers could continue to play in that tense environment. President Nixon's new Attorney General, John Mitchell, created a special unit just for Panther prosecutions. Meanwhile, Newton reassessed the Party's priorities. That same summer, Stokely Carmichael officially broke his ties with the Panthers, denouncing them in print for their alliances with white radicals instead of embracing Pan-Africanism. Yet Cleaver still was intent on growing international support for the Panthers from his new outpost in Algeria, publishing another book in which he called Newton "the ideological descendant, heir and successor of Malcolm X."[19]

Newton rejected black nationalism, but he also saw that his *lumpenproletariat* were not ready for the revolution he espoused. To forestall arrests while he built up a strong enough base, he needed to dispel the Panthers' image as "trigger-happy, gun-toting thugs,"[20] and directed David Hilliard to focus instead on expanding community programs. In Oakland and Los Angeles the Panthers were feeding thousands of children daily. Assembly Speaker Jesse Unruh (famed for authoring the state's pioneering 1959 Civil Rights Act) soon credited the Panthers with serving more meals to needy youngsters than the government was doing. In the process, the Panthers were building mainstream political alliances and luring large numbers of new recruits.

J. Edgar Hoover reacted to this new Panther strategy with alarm. Back in August 1967, when the FBI Chief had given COINTELPRO the directive to "neutralize" Black Nationalists, what worried him most was the rise of a black "messiah who could unify and electrify the militant nationalist movement." Hoover originally focused on Dr. Martin Luther King as the biggest threat. He then added Stokely Carmichael, H. Rap Brown, and the Nation of Islam's leader Elijah Muhammad.[21] By 1967, Dr. King was seeking to build a peaceful coalition of poor and working class people of all colors in a revolutionary human rights movement, of immense potential. Only after Dr. King's assassination in 1968 did Hoover begin to worry about the Panthers. By 1970, a poll indicated that a quarter of blacks held the Black Panthers in high regard, including an eye-popping 43 percent of those under twenty-one.[22] Hoover realized how the Panther paper served as a potent tool for attracting support for its revolutionary agenda and the great momentum the Panthers had already achieved by focusing on much-needed community programs.

The FBI Chief had already warned his staff that the breakfast program "represents the best and most influential activity going for the BPP," which made feeding hungry children "potentially the greatest threat to efforts by authorities to neutralize the BPP and destroy what it stands for."[23] He invited local FBI offices to use a variety of dirty tricks to isolate the Panthers from moderate blacks and whites, humanitarians, churches, and suppliers like Safeway and fast food chains. Panthers in cities across the country were arrested, prosecuted, and thrown in jail on charges that were often later dismissed. An appalled Leftist commentator for *The Nation*, the country's oldest weekly news journal, wrote, "Panther arrests with charges later dropped, and bail in the millions, constitute an unprecedented national scandal which beggars the fifties." He quoted author and educator Donald Freed, who was then working on a play about the Rosenbergs: "If what is being perpetrated against the Black Panther Party was being done to any white group, including the

Nazi Party, the liberal establishment—from the ACLU to *The New York Times*—would absolutely refuse to tolerate it further."[24] Indeed, Hoover's aggressive campaign resembled the much-criticized Palmer Raids on the IWW offices Hoover had participated in a half century before. When the head of the San Francisco office balked at some of the tactics, the FBI Chief scolded him: these Panther breakfast programs were not undertaken for humanitarian reasons, but represented a cynical ploy "to fill adolescent children with . . . insidious poison."[25] Several years later, a Senate investigation of "The FBI's Covert Action Program to Destroy the Black Panther Party" would document such lawless undertakings as disrupting delivery of Panther newspapers, trashing the Party's branch offices, spreading malicious false rumors, and sending forged letters and anonymous threats to instigate retaliatory killings by rival organizations.[26]

In the fall of 1969, trial proceedings began in Chicago against eight men charged with inciting riots in Chicago during the 1968 Democratic Convention, including SDS leader Tom Hayden and Panther Chairman Bobby Seale. The radical Weathermen had just spun off from SDS and planned "Four Days of Rage" in early October to protest the upcoming trial. They started with the symbolic bombing of a statue dedicated to police victims of the 1886 Haymarket Riot. The vandals were quickly overwhelmed by the police. Yet, urged on by activists, opposition to the war grew exponentially among college students. In November, a million protesters gathered in Washington, D.C., to demand that America pull out of the Vietnam War.

David Hilliard, as the Panther Party Chief of Staff, was invited to speak at a similar demonstration of some 250,000 people in Golden Gate Park in San Francisco on November 15, 1969. Looking out at the sea of mostly white faces as he waited his turn at the podium, Hilliard realized that most were pacifists. What did they really have in common with the Panthers, whose offices were being systematically ransacked to prevent them from achieving support for their Ten Point Program? Hilliard had recently caused a scene at a local fundraiser with Jean Genet at the Treuhafts' home by accusing Tom Hayden of making the Panthers' cause take a back seat to the anti-war Movement. Incensed that Bobby Seale remained jailed in Chicago while Hayden and the other white defendants were free to come and go, Hilliard abandoned his prepared remarks for media consumption at Golden Gate Park. He announced to the surprised gathering the Panther Party's proposal that Eldridge Cleaver be authorized to negotiate with the Viet Cong for the exchange of POWs for Bobby Seale, Huey Newton and other Panthers. Then Hilliard lambasted American society as fascist and cursed President Nixon as an evil "motherfucker" who sent his "vicious murderous dogs" out to destroy the Black Panther Party children's breakfast programs. Fueled by boos, Hilliard shouted, "We will kill Richard Nixon. . . . We will kill any motherfucker that stands in the way of our freedom." Someone started the appalled crowd yelling "Peace! Peace!" to cut off Hilliard's vitriol. Hilliard at first echoed their refrain, but then felt his anger rise all over again. "Well, we ain't here for no goddamned peace. Because we know that we can't have no peace because this country is built on war. And if you want peace you got to fight for it."[27] Charles Garry soon advised Hilliard what to expect from his public outburst, so Hilliard was not at all surprised two weeks later when federal agents surrounded his car and arrested him for threatening the President's life.

In early December 1969, COINTELPRO dramatically escalated its campaign against the Panther Party. In a predawn raid, plainclothes officers invaded the home of Chicago Panther leader Fred Hampton, killing him and twenty-two-year-old Mark Clark, and wounding four other Panthers. Four days later, the Los Angeles Special Weapons Tactics Team conducted another predawn raid, this time on the Panthers' local headquarters, and seriously wounded three members. Charles Garry forestalled a similar raid in Oakland by immediately calling a press conference and charging that the Panthers were being targeted for annihilation. Many civil rights leaders and mainstream press echoed Garry's concerns. Fay Stender talked San Francisco Lawyers Guild members into spending a couple of nights at Party headquarters in Oakland. One of the volunteers later admitted that the gun-wielding Panthers frightened him more than the police did. Indeed, from his safe haven in Algeria, Cleaver urged retaliation.

At the beginning of 1970, Hilliard was out on $50,000 bail, while Newton remained at the Men's Colony. *Newsweek* talked Hilliard and Panthers' Elbert "Big Man" Howard and Donald Cox to pose for its cover in front of a poster of Bobby Seale. To make them look more sinister magazine staff insisted that the Panther's wear leather jackets though they had already abandoned that look as inviting police harassment. By then, Bobby Seale's prosecution in the Chicago conspiracy case had been severed from that of the other seven defendants. He instead sat in a San Francisco jail facing extradition to Connecticut on charges of ordering the torture death of suspected informant Alex Rackley. During his prolonged incarceration, Seale had dictated *Seize the Time: The History of the Black Panther Party and Huey Newton.* By then, the Party had been in the headlines for two years. One freelance reporter noted that the Panthers were "deeply revered in colonial and liberated, formerly colonial countries; Eldridge Cleaver is a household word, and the names Huey Newton and Bobby Seale are familiar in homes from coast to coast."[28]

Meanwhile they faced one legal crisis after another. Charles Garry, now the unquestioned lawyer of choice for all the Panthers, planned to gear up to head Seale's Connecticut defense team right after Garry and Stender argued Newton's appeal in San Francisco. The oral argument took place in mid-February 1970, accompanied by a three-hour "Free Huey" rally at the adjacent Civic Center. The spectacle now required a lot more effort to put together. Two jaded regulars joked that "Free Huey or else" simply meant "or don't free Huey." For some, the gatherings had grown old. Nearly a hundred observers accompanied Newton's counsel into the appellate courthouse for the much-anticipated oral argument. As Stender knew from her clerkship days, the sheer size as well as the composition of the crowd was most unusual for the staid setting.

A skeptical Panther reporter noted that the elevated bench seemed designed to make attendees feel as if they were "going before the throne of the Lord." He left the building convinced that "the pigs had no intention of allowing Huey to receive anything close to another trial."[29] Yet from the questions asked by the three-judge panel, Newton's lawyers emerged cautiously optimistic. A heavily promoted birthday benefit for Newton the following week in Berkeley brought stunning disappointment. The year before celebrations of his birthday in major cities brought crowds of 3,000 to hear a taped messaged smuggled out of prison from the Party leader. This event was expected to generate similar funds to defray the costs of appeal. The speakers instead faced an echo chamber.

On April 30, President Nixon stunned the nation with the announcement that he had ordered bombing in Cambodia five days earlier. The news touched off student strikes and flag-burnings across the country in protest of the war's escalation. At Kent State in Ohio National Guardsmen killed four unarmed student demonstrators and wounded nine others. Nixon blamed the students for the tragedy, but that use of excessive force prompted even more campus strikes, estimated to involve eight million students. At Jackson State in Mississippi, another lethal police response resulted in the deaths of two students and the wounding of twelve more. Such unprecedented confrontations following a year of extraordinary violence may have had an impact on the care with which the California Court of Appeal reviewed alleged errors in the conviction of Movement icon Huey Newton. By late May word leaked out that the court's opinion would be released shortly and that it was lengthy. Newton's lawyers sent word to their client and debated amongst themselves what to expect. Stender panicked and feared the worst—a detailed explanation rejecting every argument she had made.

On May 29, 1970, the appellate court issued its unanimous fifty-one page decision *reversing* Newton's conviction. The amazing news spread immediately. Reporters looking for an inside angle tried to contact Newton by telephone for his reaction, but prison officials refused to bring him out of his cell for an interview. The Men's Colony prison yard erupted in glee while most of the country reacted with astonishment. Of Stender's many claims of error at trial, three gained traction. One was Judge Friedman's failure to instruct the jury about the correction of the taped statement of eye witness Grier that he "didn't" get a good look at the perpetrator. A second assigned error was that the judge allowed prosecutor Lowell Jensen to read kidnap victim Dell Ross's damaging grand jury testimony in the presence of the jury. Since that testimony was then struck from evidence, the court of appeal ruled that it was prejudicial for the jury to have heard it in the first place. The panel could have improperly taken the disallowed hearsay into account in assessing Newton's guilt on the remaining manslaughter charge.

Third, the court of appeal blamed the judge for not giving one of the jury instructions Garry had offered. The rejected instruction would have let the panel consider if Newton killed Frey while not being conscious of his actions. The key instruction on unconsciousness could have exonerated Newton completely from responsibility for the shootings. Instead, Judge Friedman had given only the requested instruction on diminished capacity. It appeared likely from the manslaughter verdict the jury found that Newton's mental capacity was temporarily diminished by his wound. Would they have instead acquitted Newton if given an unconsciousness instruction?

Normally both sides note their objections for the record if the judge rejects one or more jury instructions that the lawyers believe are warranted by the evidence. Yet, in this extraordinarily high profile case, the entire discussion of which jury instructions would be given and why others were rejected had taken place off the record in the judge's chambers. The appellate court had no idea whether Garry objected to the judge's refusal to give the unconsciousness instruction in addition to one on diminished capacity. (Actually, Fay's private notes on her copy of the proposed jury instructions indicated "agree one or the other" next to the unconsciousness instruction and marked that instruction "out.")[30]

Noting its irritation, the higher court held that Judge Friedman should have given the unconsciousness instruction on his own initiative even if Garry did not insist upon it. "Although the evidence of the fatal affray is both conflicting and confused as to who shot whom and when, some of it supported the inference that the defendant had been shot in the abdomen before he fired any shots himself."[31] Newton had testified about his mental state similarly to Officer Heanes: neither recalled what happened after being wounded, which Dr. Diamond had testified often happened as a shock response to abdominal wounds suffered in combat. The facts before the jury thus permitted the conclusion that Newton was so traumatized by his stomach wound that he may have grabbed Frey's gun and shot Frey without realizing he was doing so. As a result, Newton was granted a new trial limited to manslaughter. Already acquitted of murder, he could not be tried again for that offense.

By the time of that stunning victory, Stender had left her dead end role at Garry's firm. The prior fall she became a name partner and, at 37, the oldest member of a new Leftist law collective in Berkeley representing Movement clients. The venture was co-founded by Peter Franck, with whom she had collaborated in the short-lived Council for Justice a few years before. Franck now specialized in personal injury and entertainment law, having launched the latter practice with the popular band Country Joe and the Fish. Franck's co-founder was criminal defense lawyer Doug Hill, who had assisted in the 1965 Free Speech Movement trial, and made a surprise cameo appearance in August 1968 representing kidnap victim Dell Ross in the Newton murder trial. Stender amazed many celebrants at the new collective's catered opening when she wore a tight-fitting black sheath. Nearly forty years later one of her former partners recalled in amazement, "The lady was hot!"

* * * * *

At Newton's behest, a few months after she joined her new firm, Stender met a black militant inmate at Soledad prison, whom she would soon turn into another Movement cause célèbre. Shortly after Newton arrived at the Men's Colony back in the fall of 1968, a radical white inmate named Michael McCarthy had gotten into instant trouble for passing Newton a lengthy note informing Newton of clandestine meetings of a Marxist study group in the prison. McCarthy was immediately shipped off to an unknown destination. Newton feared the worst and asked Stender to come to McCarthy's aid. Stender immediately got on the phone, calling prison official after official for two days' straight. She tracked McCarthy to San Quentin. From there, he was sent to Soledad. (McCarthy later credited Stender's persistent inquiries with likely saving his life). At Soledad, as elsewhere, McCarthy stood out for his animosity toward white racists. He got involved in another Marxist study group with militant African-Americans that was ultimately joined by George Jackson. Jackson was then serving his tenth year on a sentence of one to life.

Newton was aware that Stender abhorred indeterminate sentences, which were instituted as a reform to let some offenders out early for good behavior. Instead, she viewed them as a license for arbitrarily jailing some prisoners for longer periods than others, often based on the color of the prisoner's skin or his anti-establishment politics. Stender had already obtained local counsel for McCarthy to seek his release on parole. Likely through his new lawyers, McCarthy got word to Stender to ask Newton to help George Jackson win parole, too.

Jackson had been convicted of a $71 gas station robbery at age eighteen, during which his companion had brandished a cap pistol (the toy belonged to Jackson's younger brother). On the advice of a public defender, Jackson had pled guilty in the expectation he would likely be convicted anyway and that the plea would encourage leniency. But Jackson already had an extensive juvenile record. The judge sent Jackson to prison where he could face life behind bars. Though most inmates only served three years of an indeterminate sentence for robbery, correctional personnel had since written the uncooperative youth up for jailhouse infractions that kept him from returning to his family. Jackson had been denied parole several times, but some prison staff noted that he was smart and had a lot of potential. He had once been promised release if he behaved himself well until the next hearing. Jackson then studiously avoided being seen talking with militant prisoners, in order to enhance his chances to go home. His father duly arranged for a job to be waiting for George, only to learn that new members of the parole board felt differently. By late 1969, Jackson refused to abase himself again in front of the parole board and expected to die behind prison walls, probably before he turned thirty.

Newton had checked George Jackson out with Newton's own unofficial bodyguard at the Men's Colony, Jimmy "Jackal Dog" Carr. The Panther leader had been told by Carr that Jackson was an old friend. Carr bragged that when both were at San Quentin, they had organized a ruthless extortion gang they called the Wolf Pack. Through McCarthy, Jackson now sought Newton's support because Jackson thought a Panther alliance might prove useful. Among the state's African-American prison population, Jackson had already become a legendary figure: a karate expert with a tough, unbroken spirit. Sight unseen, Newton named Jackson a field marshal of the Black Panther Party and asked Stender to see what she could do to get his new recruit released on parole. (In 1971 Stender would win a major victory challenging San Quentin's disciplinary hearings. The ground-breaking federal decision in *Clutchette v. Procunier* held that due process required the prison to provide inmates with lawyers and give them written notice of all charges. Inmates also had the right to confront accusers and to cross-examine witnesses, to produce evidence on their own behalf, and to appear before an impartial hearing officer.)

On Friday evening, January 16, 1970, three weeks before Stender's appointment to meet Jackson, a twenty-five-year-old unarmed guard was found with his skull fractured near a prison stairwell. John Mills was the first guard ever killed in Soledad's long history. Local papers linked Mill's murder to the killing of three black inmates earlier that week, though the public did not get the full story until years later in a successful wrongful-death suit brought by the families of the three dead men.

Soledad held over 3,000 inmates in minimum to maximum security wings on a site that covered almost a thousand acres. It had originally been intended as a midlevel prison for likely candidates for rehabilitation—but that became for many a cruel fiction. Like similar prisons across America, Soledad provided a setting where prison rape was an everyday occurrence, and murder and extortion were facts of life often condoned by administrators because they kept the inmates in line. Soledad's notorious "O" and "X" wings held the most violent offenders in isolation from the main inmate population. By the 1960s, these two wings had earned an unofficial nickname, "the Gladiator School." These were "the specially segregated areas where . . . the race wars become the most irrational; where the atmosphere of paranoia and loneliness congeal to create a day-to-day existence composed of terror."[32]

Back in April 1968, several Chicano inmates had killed a black prisoner named Clarence Causey. Two were charged and acquitted of his murder. In December 1968, another black prisoner, William Powell, died in a reported accident at the hands of guards, but a hospital orderly noticed severe trauma to Powell's head. Black inmates later swore they saw the guards shouting "Fuckin' nigger" as they dragged the unconscious man from his cell and clubbed him to death with a billy club and flashlight.[33] For the entire year of 1969, the prison kept white, black, and Chicano prisoners in "O" Wing segregated. Causey and Powell's names were on everyone's lips, either as "no-good niggers who got what they deserved" or "black martyrs" to be avenged with "honky blood."[34] Everyone knew whose side the prison administration favored; blacks and Latinos made up less than half of the prison population, but a substantial majority of felons held in lock-up.

In 1966 Federal District Court Chief Judge George Harris had personally inspected strip cells in "O" Wing. The jurist then made history by issuing an injunction ordering the prison to fix shockingly unsanitary conditions, poor ventilation, insufficient heat and light, and inadequate healthcare. By 1969, the mandates of Judge Harris's order had not been met. Five black prisoners filed another civil suit, charging that prison officials purposely created intolerable living conditions. The suit accused guards of letting white and Mexican trustees serve black inmates meals adulterated with cleanser, crushed glass, feces, spit, and urine—charges later repeated in a complaint to the United Nations for human rights violations. The daring litigants were led by W. L. Nolen, who was a former boxing champion as well as George Jackson's Marxist mentor.

In July 1969, a group of black prisoners attacked white prisoners seated on a bench in a TV room, sending several victims to the prison hospital with serious wounds, including McCarthy, who upon his recovery, would wind up released on parole before the end of the year, still committed to Marxist revolution. Meanwhile, prison staff made plans to end recurring race-fights in "O" Wing by releasing all the men into the yard with a sharpshooter prepared "to kill a couple of those black bastards" if any trouble erupted.[35] On January 13, 1970, fifteen of the most violence-prone inmates in "O" Wing were released together in the exercise yard for the first time in almost two years. The only guard outside was Opie Miller, a sharpshooter stationed with a carbine rifle in a gun tower thirty feet above. When fist-fighting erupted, Miller killed one black inmate on the spot. He shot two others, who bled to death before prison officials let them be removed. Miller also wounded one white prisoner, with a bullet that first traveled through one of the black inmates. Among the dead was Nolen. The killings prompted black prisoners to go on a two-day hunger strike.

The official report blamed the dead men as the instigators and claimed they ignored a warning whistle before Miller opened fire. It included statements from eleven prison officials who had not been present in the yard at the time the fighting began. The cover-up offended even one white supremacist involved in the melée, Billie "Buzzard" Harris of the Aryan Brotherhood. Harris later told an investigative journalist that he thought the prison officials had committed cold-blooded murder.[36] On Friday, January 16, prisoners gathered in television rooms to watch the six o'clock news, all anxious to hear Monterey County's District Attorney Bertram Young announce whether sharpshooter Opie Miller would face criminal charges. Instead, Young proclaimed that Miller had acted justifiably. Just half an hour later another guard, John Mills, was found dead by a stairwell on the first floor of "Y" Wing. The local paper reported that near his corpse investigators seized a note reading "One Down, Two to Go."[37] Prison officials had in fact found no note of any kind.

Dozens of men had been outside their cells early Friday evening within the locked block where Mills' body was found. Staff interviewed all 146 inmates of that wing and quickly isolated five prime suspects, all black. Among them were George Jackson, John Clutchette (pronounced Cloo-chay), and Fleeta Drumgo. Clutchette, like Jackson, had a list of prior violations. Drumgo had drawn officials' attention because he taped political posters of Malcolm X and H. Rap Brown on his cell wall. For three days no further progress was announced. Then three inmates claimed they saw Jackson, Clutchette, and Drumgo attack the hapless guard. The accused men were stripped and examined for recent injuries to their hands. No new contusions or scratches were found. Indeed, Clutchette sported unbroken fingernails more than an inch long. Jackson mocked his interrogators, telling them blacks liked to sing and dance, not engage in violence.

Clutchette and Drumgo were both twenty-three and in their third year of six-month to fifteen-year sentences for burglary. Drumgo expected to be given a release date at his probation hearing later that spring. Clutchette had already won a parole date scheduled for late April, just before his twenty-fourth birthday. The three were whisked off in chains to separate grand jury appearances and then placed in solitary confinement. Clutchette managed to get a one word note, "Help," out to his family. On January 27, based on confidential testimony from the three inmates (two whites and a British-born black), the grand jury indicted the trio of blacks on two charges each: murder and assault. Since

Jackson was already under a life sentence, proof of assault alone carried a death penalty even if the guard's death was accidental. Clutchette and Drumgo, if convicted only of assault would be spared execution but get more prison time. All three faced arraignment the following Monday. Then the court would appoint them public defenders.

Stender arrived at the prison in early February 1970, following up on Jackson's prior request for help winning parole. The guards fetched the powerfully built, light-skinned prisoner from solitary confinement. They returned with Jackson shuffling along shackled at the ankles, his hands handcuffed to a chain that looped under his crotch. One of the guards entered the room, too, intending to stay at the lawyer's side for her protection while she conducted the interview—standard policy at Soledad for violent felons. Stender was shocked. Even Huey Newton had never been brought from his cell in chains or been denied private interviews with his attorneys.

Stender marched off to find someone in authority to demand removal of Jackson's chains, since he was just a suspect in the murder and entitled to a presumption of innocence. The captain to whom she was first directed stood firm. Undaunted, Stender barged into the office of the prison's superintendent, who also refused to budge on the policy. Stender likened Jackson's treatment to a Nazi concentration camp and threatened to sue to enforce Jackson's rights.[38] She returned to the interview room, convinced the guard to wait outside with the door open and then held a whispered conversation with her prospective client out of the guard's hearing. Jackson called her "Mrs. Stender" and told her he could not see that well without his glasses. Her heart melted. Jackson, in turn, basked in the unaccustomed warmth emanating from a white, middle-class professional woman—part of the establishment he had long since given up on.

By the day he met Stender, Jackson had spent almost six of his last seven-and-a-half years in isolation at San Quentin or Soledad in cells the inmates called "the hole." The fetid concrete boxes resembled zoo cages—nine or ten feet long by four feet wide with a mat in place of a bed and a raised platform in the floor with a hole in it in lieu of a toilet. A heavy screen covered the door opening. While "in the hole," Jackson was let out only half-an-hour per day for exercise. He got to shower once or twice a month. He relieved the overwhelming monotony with letters to and from his supportive parents and siblings, infrequent visitors, and his avid reading habit. Jackson's taste had evolved from Jack London to revolutionary authors with whom he held imaginary conversations in his cell. Wanting to impress Stender, Jackson quoted Che Guevera and told her how much he admired Huey Newton, as the American equivalent of Chairman Mao.

After she left, Stender immediately began corresponding with Jackson. She talked her partners into letting her take the case and quickly assembled a large defense team and fund-raising committee. Stender began widely publicizing the historic mistreatment of minorities at Soledad and her fear of a legal lynching of the Soledad Brothers. To Stender no cause was greater—even working to end the Vietnam War. Her zeal reminded some mutual friends of Beverly Axelrod's ill-fated devotion to Eldridge Cleaver. To rouse widespread Movement sympathy for Jackson and finance the defense, Stender arranged for publication of his correspondence to family and friends. *Soledad Brother: The Prison Letters of George Jackson* would hit the stands that fall with an introduction by French playwright Jean Genet, who was already an avid Panther supporter. It proved to be an international best seller. Impressed by her intense passion for his cause, Jackson dubbed Stender his "small but mighty mouthpiece."[39]

Prison officials saw a lot that spring of Stender and lead trial counsel John Thorne. When not suited up for court, the burly Leftist lawyer from San Jose wore blue jeans, a Chairman Mao cap with a red star, and a denim jacket with a gold, clenched-fist lapel pin. Stender likewise did not dress like a lawyer. She usually wore a leather mini-skirt with her hair in a ponytail, probably intentionally mirroring the look of Weathermen leader Bernardine Dohrn, the student coordinator for the 1968 Lawyers Guild Convention in California, who had recently fled underground. Stender had also found two young local lawyers to represent Drumgo and Clutchette. Drumgo's lawyer, Richard Silver, worked in Carmel with an attorney formerly associated with Stender's partner Peter Franck. Silver's friend Floyd Silliman, who represented Clutchette, came from a wealthy Republican family in Salinas but was himself a liberal Democrat with a burgeoning reputation as a criminal lawyer. Silver's recent service as an army captain gave the team additional credibility with the conservative local bench. Still, Stender and Thorne were far more seasoned and the undisputed core of the defense team.

As she gained Jackson's trust, Stender learned more of his background. Until he was kindergarten-aged, his mother had sheltered George and his older sister from their Chicago neighborhood's rough crowd. By the time George was five, he had little exposure to children outside his family and no experience at all of interacting with white kids. On the first day of kindergarten he went up to a white boy, felt his hair, and scratched him on the face. The boy retaliated after school by bashing George on the head with a baseball bat. George's mother immediately transferred him to a Catholic school. George's father pushed the mama's boy to fend for himself and punished him severely when he misbehaved. For several summers George's parents sent him to visit his mother's relatives in the Southern Illinois countryside, to remove George from bad influences. Yet, while visiting family in the country, George learned to use rifles, shotguns, and pistols. Back home, the Jackson family moved into the projects. George saw no future emulating his father, who often worked sixteen hours a day with little to show for it. The rebellious son became a frequent truant. If there was a fight, he was in it. The police frequently picked him up for muggings or just on suspicion of misconduct. His mortified father decided to uproot the family and accepted a transfer to a postal job in Los Angeles, California. George was seldom home. He later told his editor, "My family knew very little of my real life."[40]

George's major run-ins with the police included a burglary shootout in which he was wounded. It landed him in the California Youth Authority. His file detailed repeated escapes from detention. Upon his recapture from one such incident when he was sixteen, he was chained naked to a bed and beaten by guards for two days. After fifteen months' incarceration his counselors and the parole board considered him rehabilitated and released him. Not much later, George and his friend pulled the gas station robbery that had kept him incarcerated ever since.

Stender portrayed Jackson as a victim of the system, galvanizing Leftists with the same grim visions that haunted her. She realized that for any chance of success it was essential—as it had been in Newton's case—to produce a strong show of Movement support for the Soledad Brothers. She urged activists from Berkeley and Oakland to drive down to observe the hearings, wear pins, carry signs, and pass out defense literature. A typical leaflet began: "Three young black inmates of Soledad prison, may soon be murdered by the State of California. . . . They are innocent. Their right to a fair trial is being systematically and intentionally destroyed by the prison administration. . . . They will be railroaded to the gas chamber unless we move to stop this injustice and show the state that the lives of black men and prison inmates are not expendable."[41] Jackson bristled at the flyers portraying him as haplessly suffering cruel indignities, but he trusted his lawyers' judgment. Still, there was little hope of shifting public sentiment in Monterey County. On the Friday before the postponed arraignment, the guard's pretty young widow was invited to Soledad. There, white inmates presented her with a scroll of sympathy signed by hundreds of prisoners and a check for additional pledges to the Mills Memorial Fund for her infant son's education. *The Monterey Peninsula Herald* ran a large picture of the presentation and pointedly mentioned that Mills had cultivated friendships with both black and white inmates.

When the three prisoners arrived at court shackled together like animals for a pretrial hearing, their attorneys argued in vain to have the Presiding Judge order the manacles and chains removed. Over the lawyers' objection the grand jury transcript was unsealed. The damning statements of the three felons who claimed to be eyewitnesses made front page news. Anyone in the jury pool might make up their minds the Soledad Brothers were guilty before the star witnesses against them ever faced cross-examination. Yet the judge issued an order preventing both sides' lawyers from further pretrial publicity, blocking the defense team from passing out any more literature. Armed police officers mixed with the spectators as a local reporter noted "talk around the courthouse . . . that Monterey County may have another Huey P. Newton trial on its hands—a gigantic legal spectacle with a heavy emphasis on race."[42]

The case was being sped to trial faster than the defense lawyers could handle. As in Newton's case, Stender churned out motion after motion. But here she lost almost all of them, including a challenge to the mostly

Republican grand jury on the grounds that it did not fairly represent the county's diverse population. Monterey County admittedly had few African-American residents, but the question remained why no one of Mexican ancestry or even a Spanish surname had served on the grand jury in the past thirty years. Judge Campbell took umbrage. All the grand jurors were "pillars of the community" chosen for "fairness of mind." Thorne retorted, "We need understanding of soul as well as fairness of mind."[43] Gaining no headway, the lawyers criticized the proceedings as a "sham and farce."[44] George's family followed the proceedings with great concern. His mother Georgia had always doted on her namesake, but it was only late that spring that his father began to appreciate how other inmates and people outside prison looked up to his incarcerated son as a strong leader. Lester Jackson began to tap into his own long-buried anger at seeing so many other ex-cons emerge from prison broken men.

The prospects looked exceedingly grim if the case stayed in Salinas. The first glimmer of hope occurred when the defense team got Judge Campbell to take himself off the case for the appearance of bias. To the veteran jurist's chagrin, they based their argument on his own letter to the Salinas City Council seeking an emergency ordinance to prevent unruly crowds from disrupting the trial. The highly unusual request had just made front page news. The defense cheekily suggested that Judge Campbell had just violated his own pretrial gag order against publicity that might prejudice the jury pool. After they filed a federal court action raising their constitutional challenges, the embarrassed state judge withdrew from the case.

In mid-June, Stender and her new co-counsel brought their motion to change the venue of the murder trial from Salinas to San Francisco. They were buttressed again by busloads and cars full of mostly white activists from the Bay Area. If the case moved to San Francisco, the trial date would necessarily be delayed and the jury pool would likely be more sympathetic. If this motion did not succeed, the Soledad Brothers appeared doomed. Over the strenuous objections of the defense team, the fateful June 15 hearing started before the three defendants arrived from the prison. The newly assigned judge lost control of the hearing when Stender challenged a brand-new fire code restricting the number of spectators. To the applause of supporters, she proved that the premise of the restriction was wrong. It was based on there being only one exit. With the astonished judge's acquiescence, Stender marched from the courtroom through the private door to his chambers and returned from the main hall, proving a second way out to the street. After taking a short break, the frustrated judge suddenly retook the bench and granted the very first change of venue motion in the history of Monterey County.

Coming as it did less than a month after the opinion reversing Newton's conviction, the phenomenal success propelled Stender to instant stardom among Leftists. She credited all the Movement supporters who flocked to Salinas, creating pressure that traditional lawyering would never have generated. Stender then turned to arranging for the bail of her most famous client, whom she preferred to call a political comrade. Stender proudly stated that in the past two years, her identity had become almost "anti-professional" in order to build her revolutionary clients' trust and promote their shared goal.[45] Charles Garry proclaimed that Newton's release would give a great boost to the American liberation movement. As both lawyers knew, Huey Newton was not in a hurry to regain his freedom. Prison had been a haven, both from potential assassination attempts by Ron Karenga's rival US party and COINTELPRO, and from fear of disappointing the expectations of legions of new Panther recruits enamored of Newton's glorified image.

Four days after the victory in Salinas, at a Juneteenth celebration of freedom from slavery, Panther Chief of Staff David Hilliard announced brazen plans for all Panther branches nationwide to send representatives to a constitutional convention in Washington, D.C., in December. Eldridge Cleaver had lobbied for this move, which Newton had only reluctantly endorsed. A planning session was scheduled for September in Philadelphia—the site of the original Constitutional Convention in 1787. Meanwhile, Seale remained in jail awaiting trial for his life in New Haven and the "Panther 21" in New York City faced an array of felony charges for allegedly conspiring to bomb the Botanical Gardens, police stations, railroad crossings and department stores.

On July 24, Newton received an inoculation against being targeted on release by law enforcement via a lengthy article in the *Los Angeles Free Press* by best-selling author Mark Lane. The New York lawyer-politician, a past contributor to *Ramparts*, had gained international fame for questioning the investigation of President Kennedy's assassination in *Rush to Judgment* and *A Citizen's Dissent.* Over the Fourth of July weekend, Charles Garry had brought Lane with him to visit Newton at the Men's Colony, where prison officials presumably thought the two lawyers were preparing for Newton's retrial. Lane instead conducted three days of interviews for his exclusive article in which he publicized Newton as "America's authentic revolutionary" and vocalized Leftist fears for his life: "The administration considers Huey Newton to be the most dangerous man in America. . . . Huey's safety must be guaranteed. . . . For those who love peace and those who crave justice, Huey's leadership is crucial. He represents America's last, best hope for social change with a minimum of violence."[46]

Well before dawn on the morning of August 3, officials at the Men's Colony turned Huey over to two Alameda County Sheriff's deputies, who drove him shackled hand and foot in the back seat of an unmarked car to the Alameda County jail. His bail hearing was set for Wednesday, August 5, at 9 a.m. Hundreds of rabid Panther supporters, both black and white, gathered around the Alameda County courthouse early that morning yelling, "We want Huey! Where's Huey? Free Huey!" By 9:15 a.m. when the hearing before Judge Harold Hove began, a hundred people had crammed into the sixty-seat courtroom, with hundreds more in the corridors or waiting outside. The hearing lasted just half an hour.

Newton, dressed in a loose khaki shirt and matching trousers, spoke just once to waive his right to be retried within 60 days. Garry made a show of arguing for Newton's release on his own recognizance, but already knew from Fay Stender's negotiations with prosecutor Lowell Jensen, that Jensen would recommend $100,000. Jensen conceded that Newton had an obvious right to bail; Judge Hove considered $50,000 reasonable and ordered Newton returned to a 10th floor cell until the money arrived. It took a few hours. When the crowd spied their hero exiting the building, the throng exuberantly yelled, "Huey's Free! Huey's Free!"[47]

Newton's entourage kept them from mobbing him as he was escorted to Alex Hoffmann's VW, where Newton, Hilliard, and Panther branch leader Elmo "Geronimo" Pratt from Los Angeles climbed on top

Photo © 2012 Nacio Jan Brown

Huey Newton bares his chest celebrating his release from prison at the Alameda County Courthouse following the reversal of his 1968 manslaughter conviction.

Photo © 2012 Ilka Hartmann

Charles Garry, Huey Newton, and Fay Stender conducting a press conference in the defense firm's law library in San Francisco on the afternoon of Newton's August 5, 1970 release.

of the Beetle. As the roof of the makeshift platform dimpled under their weight, Newton shouted, "Right on! Right on! Power to the people!" He punctuated his chant with repeated Panther salutes toward the sky above.[48] Then, to avoid fainting in the heat, he famously stripped off his khaki shirt, celebrating his freedom by showing off his muscular body to photographers and frenzied supporters as he urged similar efforts to free the Soledad Brothers and Bobby Seale.

To avoid arrests for blocking traffic in downtown Oakland, at Hilliard's suggestion, Newton told the crowd to move its rally to Bobby Hutton Memorial Park (still officially DeFremery Park). Sheriff Frank Madigan was, in fact, itching for an opportunity to crack heads. Madigan had seen demonstrators arrive that morning in a bus labeled "Office of Economic Opportunity, Inc.," and it had made his blood boil to think that Panther supporters got federal jobs they redirected to their own purposes. When asked, "Just how do we handle these foxes in the chicken coop?" Madigan had a ready solution. "Shoot 'em. You can always raise more chickens."[49]

To the dismay of the crowd, Newton heeded his lawyers' advice not to make himself an easy target for a sniper by speaking at their rally. He headed off to change for a press conference in San Francisco with mostly sympathetic reporters from underground newspapers and magazines. Newton knew that he was not a crowd-pleasing orator like Bobby Seale or Eldridge Cleaver, but more persuasive talking with small groups or one-on-one. Eager journalists surrounded Newton in the cramped library of Charles Garry's office with Fay Stender beaming at her client's side. *The San Francisco Examiner* noted that Newton had become "something of a folk hero among militants and revolutionaries," but his appeal to political junkies, civil rights supporters and curiosity seekers was obviously far broader. His attorneys already had him booked to appear on "Face the Nation," where Hilliard had been featured back in December of 1969 following the raids on the Chicago and Los Angeles Panther branches. Ever ready to provoke controversy, at the press conference Newton threatened unspecified consequences if political prisoners, including the Soledad Brothers, were not freed. When asked for clarification, he did not rule out military action and warned that "the struggle is coming to a final climax."[50] Privately, Newton realized full well that neither he, nor his Party, were anywhere near ready for a revolution.

Newton then left to see the new Panther headquarters on Peralta Street in West Oakland and to walk his old neighborhood, exchanging salutes with the crowds who turned out to greet him. According to investigative journalist Jo Durden-Smith, that same day, Huey issued his first directives to the contingent of Panthers from Los Angeles headed by Pratt. Much to the new SWAT team's dismay, ex–Green Beret Pratt had not been among the Panthers arrested in the COINTELPRO raid on the Party's Los Angeles headquarters in early December of 1969. But shortly afterward he was separately charged with a murder in Santa Monica. Pratt and the Panthers arrested in the raid were out on bail awaiting their respective trials, which would predictably land them in prison on long sentences. In Pratt's case, he faced the death penalty if his alibi for the murder was rejected by a hostile jury. The contingent of Los Angeles Panthers had other ideas. They were reportedly now armed with weapons stolen from Camp Pendleton and intended to join a select group of Oakland Panthers and a demolition expert from New York to undertake a daring kidnap plot two days later at the Marin Civic Center before hijacking a plane to escape.

Most of the plot's description came from a former undercover agent for the Los Angeles Criminal Conspiracy Section ("CCS") Red Squad named Louis Tackwood, who was the brother-in-law of George Jackson's confidante Jimmy Carr. But key parts of that story were later confirmed by other sources. Earlier that summer, the Soledad Brothers had been transferred to maximum security in San Quentin prison in Marin County, awaiting their upcoming murder trial in San Francisco. Tackwood reported that George Jackson and his cohorts sought to escape by forcing an exchange of himself and several other San Quentin inmates for hostages. Huey himself had heard that Pratt and his men were intending to meet up with Jackson's younger brother Jonathan at the Marin Civic Center and seize the hostages at a pending criminal trial. An inmate acquaintance of the Soledad Brothers named James McClain was then representing himself against charges that he stabbed a San Quentin guard. McClain subpoenaed several other inmates to the courthouse for Friday, August 7, ostensibly to call them as defense witnesses.

As described by Tackwood, the plan included a second group of Panthers, who would head to San Francisco airport and commandeer a plane to fly the hostages to Algiers so Eldridge Cleaver could barter their lives for the release of Jackson and several of his militant San Quentin comrades. The plan made Newton uneasy and he cancelled all Panther support for the courthouse invasion.[51] Suspecting a possible set-up, Newton instead ordered Pratt and his cohorts to lie low. At Hilliard's suggestion, they took off for Alabama to set up a Southern underground military camp. (Within a few months it would self-destruct for lack of funding and discipline.) Newton then holed up in his new temporary home, the two-bedroom rental in Berkeley his lawyer Alex Hoffmann shared with KPFA radio's Elsa Knight Thompson. With Hoffmann acting as his scheduler and trusted confidante, Newton immediately began entertaining a parade of visitors from his fiancée to family, associates, friendly reporters, and his lawyer Fay Stender. Everyone came and went under the watchful eyes of plainclothes officers and obviously phony telephone repairmen perched for four days straight on a pole across the street from the Berkeley apartment.

In desperation, Jonathan Jackson decided to go ahead with the kidnap plot anyway. Tackwood said that the CCS Red Squad still anticipated that the Panthers would be coming to the Civic Center, too, where the Red Squad could catch them all in the act[52]—just as Newton suspected. Late Friday morning, August 7, Jonathan smuggled guns into the building under his raincoat and in the flight bag he carried. Inmate William Christmas stood in chains under the watchful eye of a San Quentin guard outside a second floor courtroom, awaiting his turn to testify. Thirty-one-year-old San Quentin inmate Ruchell Magee, also in chains, sat on the witness stand being examined by McClain.

Jonathan surprised the courtroom when he announced from the spectator gallery, "This is it. I've got an automatic weapon. Everybody freeze." He handed McClain a weapon and said, "We don't intend to hurt anybody."[53] Then they ordered a prison guard to free Magee and Christmas from their chains. McClain asked Jonathan if he had brought the tape and then taped a sawed-off shotgun to the torso of sixty-five-year-old Judge Harold Haley, pointed at his chin. McClain directed Christmas to tie three women jurors and Deputy District Attorney Gary Thomas together with piano wire. The kidnappers opted to leave a young couple behind with their baby. The group, including Magee and Christmas, then emerged into the hallway. After disarming more deputies and guards on their way out, they exited the courthouse while bystanders gaped in astonishment.[54]

Tackwood reported that George Jackson had not envisioned any bloodshed if everything went according to plan. He had assumed the government would place too high a value on the judge's and other hostages' lives to risk endangering them further. At McClain's direction, Judge Haley had called the sheriff and requested no interference as they emerged from the building. On the way out, the kidnappers paused to pose for pictures by a news photographer who had been driving on a nearby highway listening to the police monitor when an alert went out that there were gunmen at the Civic Center. The sheriff wanted to proceed cautiously to protect the hostages. He ordered his men not to shoot. But the San Quentin guards who had escorted the inmates to the courthouse had been trained to stop hostage-takers inside the prison at all costs without regard to the loss of innocent human lives. They did not believe different rules applied outside prison walls.

By then a hundred policemen and deputies had been summoned from nearby target practice to hide in the woods along the driveway. The San Quentin guards blocked the driveway as the armed kidnappers started to leave with their five hostages in the back. A guard named John Matthews stood in front of the van and said the driver and passenger were pointing guns at him when he fired his rifle at them. Tackwood later insisted that he saw internal reports showing that the opening shots were actually fired from alongside the van by a CCS sharpshooter named Daniel Mahoney hidden in the bushes on the driver's side, who killed both Jonathan Jackson and McClain with one bullet each.[55] Other officers started shooting as well. In the rear of the van, Judge Haley suffered two wounds, one in the chest and the other when the shotgun strapped to him partially blew off his head. Which came first was not then clear. Thomas said he saw Magee fire the shotgun (which Magee would later dispute) and then Thomas snatched Jackson's gun and shot three of his kidnappers. Thomas shouted for the police to stop shooting just before a bullet from outside penetrated his own spine, crippling him for life. The entire volley of shots lasted just nineteen seconds. The dead and wounded were all inside the van. Magee, who was unconscious, was rushed to the hospital for treatment along with Thomas and one of the jurors.

The following Monday, officials from all over Northern California joined hundreds of mourners attending the funeral services of the highly respected judge in San Rafael, accompanied by a phalanx of police. The Presiding Judge in San Francisco made headlines the same day with the extraordinary suggestion that the rescheduled Soledad Brothers' murder trial should be transferred for safety reasons to San Quentin prison. In Oakland, an elaborate Panther funeral attended by more than three thousand supporters was held for Jonathan Jackson, his casket covered by the Party's signature black and blue flag. Though Newton eulogized Jonathan as a fallen hero, whispers spread that Jackson's family blamed Newton for Jonathan's death. At a press conference Georgia Jackson tearfully announced that she probably would have helped Jonathan if she had known. She had by then reached the same conclusion as her sons: "A black man doesn't get justice in the courts. If you can't get justice one way, you take it another."[56]

Faced with pent-up demand, Newton gave a speech. Supporters expected a fiery call to action and instead received a lengthy, philosophical lecture on dialectical materialism and the steps needed to establish a revolutionary "intercommunal framework" for socialism to thrive, delivered in a high-pitched voice. Some left before Newton finished. By prearrangement, Newton then embarked for the East Coast with a full agenda: to visit Bobby Seale in New Haven and fund raise for his defense; have Hilliard introduce him to Panthers in several of the new branches opened while Newton was imprisoned and to promote his new ideas for the Party's future; to attend the Panthers' Revolutionary People's Constitutional Convention in Philadelphia; and to explore the possibility of relocating the Panther headquarters to Harlem in New York or Atlanta, Georgia, where SNCC had been based.

The boldest of his new proposals was an open invitation issued in August to the Women's Liberation and Gay Liberation Movements to join the Panthers in their revolutionary efforts — hailed as the first such overture from the black civil rights movement. The proclamation was prompted by Jean Genet's criticism of the Panthers' use of the term "faggot," Newton's favorable impression of Leftist gays at the Men's Colony, and a strong desire to broaden his base. But the invitation lacked support among the sexist and homophobic Panther rank and file. Though originally among the mixed raced thousands in attendance, Lesbian delegates reportedly found the Panthers so unwelcoming that they left the Philadelphia Convention in disgust. Male delegates from the Gay Liberation Movement attended both the September Convention and the one held in late November in Washington, D.C., only to end up frustrated at the disorganization that characterized both gatherings and the unreceptive audience for their own 16-point program.[57]

On his return to Oakland in September, Newton opted to keep his Party's base where it started. For safety's sake, Newton resettled into a penthouse apartment overlooking Oakland's Lake Merritt. His new digs were paid for by wealthy white donors. The spacious accommodations on the twenty-fifth floor of 1200 Lakeshore came with a doorman and a garage on the south edge of Lake Merritt. Under constant surveillance by COINTELPRO and wary of Cleaver as well as enemies in rival militant groups, Newton felt he needed the security the expensive surroundings provided, though Stender was among those advising him he was alienating many followers. Swearing off speech-making, Newton used the solitude to work on revolutionary writings, but quickly turned his gilded cage into a place of escape via drugs, alcohol, and hedonism.

Newton cultivated a coterie of Hollywood patrons enamored with the newly freed Leftist celebrity, including Donald Sutherland, co-star of the award-winning 1970 movie M*A*S*H; his wife, actress Shirley Douglas (the daughter of Tommy Douglas, the head of Canada's New Democratic Party); and actresses Vanessa Redgrave, Shirley Maclaine, Jean Seberg and Mia Farrow. Through Sutherland, Newton met M*A*S*H co-star Elliot Gould, then at the height of his career, and Gould's then wife, singer Barbra Streisand. Soon to become one of Newton's chief benefactors was "New Wave" Hollywood producer Bert Schneider. (Schneider first gained fame for bringing the Emmy award–winning "Monkees" to television in 1966 as a take-off on the phenomenally successful Beatles.

In 1969, Schneider had introduced Jack Nicholson to the public in the counterculture classic *Easy Rider* and in early September of 1970 had just released another ground-breaking film, *Five Easy Pieces,* with the anti-hero Nicholson in his first starring role.)

COINTELPRO agents took special note after author Mark Lane introduced Newton to top-billed actress Jane Fonda, who had become a new-age sex symbol when she starred in the 1968 science fiction fantasy *Barbarella.* Like the Sutherlands, Fonda was prominent in the anti-war movement and had fund-raised for bail and defense costs for Newton and other Panthers. By the time Fonda and Newton met in person, shortly after his release from the Men's Colony, she was making plans to embark on a national fund-raising tour of college campuses on behalf of Vietnam Veterans Against the War, who named her their Honorary National Coordinator.

Alarmed at Newton's heady new life style, Hilliard introduced Newton to a nineteen-year-old Party member Hilliard hoped would help Newton settle down. Gwen Fountaine did have some effect, but saving Newton from himself would prove too Herculean a task. By November, Hoover had Newton's penthouse broken into and bugged. The Panthers already knew that the FBI Chief was wire-tapping their headquarters and other Party members' and supporters' homes. Ironically, *Esquire* featured a several-page pictorial essay that month captioned "Is It Too Late for You to Be Pals with a Black Panther?" By then the FBI and state police also had many black informers besides Tackwood infiltrating the Party. Newton trusted few Panthers he had never met before. Invitees received instructions to take the elevator to the twenty-fourth floor, walk up one flight, and use a special knock to be admitted through the back door.

Someone had given Huey a high-powered, standing telescope he kept in his living room, focused north across Lake Merritt directly on the tenth floor of the Alameda County Courthouse. Back in July, Newton had told interviewer Mark Lane at the Men's Colony that people outside of jail were also prisoners, but under minimum instead of maximum security. Now Huey liked looking through his telescope across the lake at the window of the isolation cell where he had spent so many months before his 1968 trial. Alex Hoffmann asked if he was homesick. Newton admitted that he was having problems adjusting: life had been so much simpler when he was inside.

* * * * *

In early February of 1971 Newton was scheduled to participate in a three-day seminar at Yale University in New Haven arranged by one of his key supporters, author Donald Freed, to lend academic gravitas to the Panther's ideology as Bobby Seale prepared for trial. Freed closely followed Seale's case and would later publish a book on the trial (*Agony at New Haven: The Trial of Bobby Seale and Ericka Huggins*). The extraordinary event Freed set up for Newton featured conversations with world-renowned psychoanalyst Erik Erikson, arranged through the German-born professor's son Kai Erikson, a Master at Yale. Sociologist Kai Erikson counted himself among Huey's many fans. His father, nearly seventy, had just retired from the psychology department at Harvard. Newton prepared by reading Erik Erikson's writings, reassured by learning that Erikson was a high-school dropout who never got a college degree. Still Newton remained nervous about the possibility of being psychoanalyzed in public by the disciple of Freud who coined the term "identity crisis." As it turned out, Erik Erikson actually admired Newton's "superhuman will" that turned "a negative identity [of a people] into a positive one, in the sense in which a cornered animal turns on the attacker." The Eriksons later transcribed the dialogue into a book, *In Search of Common Ground.*[58]

To David Hilliard, who accompanied The Servant of the People on this East Coast excursion, the entire trip became a surreal nightmare as Newton's two worlds collided. Here was Newton aspiring to respectability as a post-Marxist theoretician while the ex-felon *lumpenproletariat* he counted on to lead his revolution were disheartened by too much talk and too little action. A select group of sixteen students and faculty members watched Newton and Erikson sip cognac between sessions in which they often talked past each other. Freed told David Hilliard that the Leftist intellectuals in attendance reacted to the two megastars "as if they were creatures in the zoo."[59] Meanwhile, members of the New York Panther 21 showed up to protect Newton from assassination. At the one session open to the public, 1400 students lined up outside hours earlier to get patted down for weapons before being seated to hear the two celebrity guests.

During this time, the FBI circulated rumors that the Panther 21, like treasonous palace guards, were themselves plotting Newton's death. David Hilliard thought that might be true. The FBI stirred the pot. Eldridge Cleaver received conspiratorial letters in Algiers that purportedly came from Connie Matthews, a Jamaican who had met Cleaver in Algiers at the Pan-African Conference in July 1969 and had since been named the International Coordinator of the Black Panther Party. Cleaver had sent Matthews to Newton several months earlier to coordinate activities between the two leaders, plan conferences, and maintain communications with European Black Panther support groups. On the last day of the Yale seminar, Matthews absconded with the two Panther 21 members, taking with her some of Newton's private papers. She later turned up back in Algiers collaborating with Cleaver. Newton immediately expelled the trio from the Party, which they had already quit. The Supreme Commander then addressed a broader insurrection. Following Hampton's death the year before, underground Weathermen had issued a "Declaration of a State of War" against the Nixon administration. The Weathermen then claimed responsibility for several bombing attacks on government buildings. When the Panther 21 openly aligned themselves with the Weathermen, Newton ordered the rest of them expelled, too. Both the Harlem and New Jersey Panthers then split off. Newton also gave orders "to wash everybody who's a Pratt man . . . right out of the Party."[60]

Still, Newton expected Kathleen Cleaver to return to the United States to be the keynote speaker at an Intercommunal Conference in Oakland advertised for early March 1971. It was a major fund-raiser for the Seale/Huggins trial in honor of Newton's birthday. As a draw, the event would feature a concert by the Grateful Dead. Another fake FBI letter warned Cleaver strongly against letting his wife show up. The growing rift between Newton and Cleaver erupted in public when Newton appeared on a San Francisco talk show on February 28, 1971. By prearrangement, the program included a telephone conversation with Cleaver hooked up live from overseas in Algiers. Angry at recent Party expulsions, Cleaver used this as an excuse to call for the resignation of

Panther Chief of Staff David Hilliard, who had been carrying out Newton's agenda. Furious, immediately after the show Newton expelled Cleaver from the Party. Kathleen Cleaver was a no-show at the conference. As the Panthers split into two factions, each accused the other of retaliatory killings, most notably the murder by Cleaver's followers of Sam Napier, the key distributor of Panther papers nationwide. Soon afterward, Stokely Carmichael proclaimed the Party was finished. The Panthers had indeed become all but invisible in most major cities where the Party had recently operated chapters.[61]

Meanwhile, Garry entered grueling pretrial proceedings for the New Haven trial. It took more than four months and interviews of over 1500 people to select the jury of seven women and five men; five of the women and none of the men were black. Though New Haven's Police Chief would not say so publicly until much later, he believed the police had "no solid evidence" to link Bobby Seale to Rackley's murder and was "astonished" when Seale was indicted by prosecutor Arnold Markle.[62] In May 1971, Garry obtained a hung jury that strongly favored acquittal of both Seale and his co-defendant Ericka Huggins. The judge surprised everyone by refusing to order a new trial. Instead, he dismissed the case, stating that it would have taken "superhuman efforts" to find another impartial jury."[63]

Both Garry and Seale then returned to the Bay Area, where Seale and Newton reunited as free men for the first time in nearly four years. Seale's success was largely a Pyrrhic victory because the gory details of the crime that the local office had committed alienated so many former Panther supporters. A similarly devastating high price-tag in diminished public opinion accompanied the acquittals that same month of "the Panther 21" in Manhattan after the longest political trial in New York history. As J. Edgar Hoover had hoped, the Panther Party was broke from defending so many prosecutions, and in great disarray.

A major public relations blow had been struck back on the first of March when Charles Garry accepted an invitation to debate journalist Edward Jay Epstein on "The David Frost Show." Only a little over two weeks before the debate, Epstein had published in *The New Yorker* a widely read article: "The Black Panthers and the Police: A Pattern of

Genocide?" challenging the eyebrow-raising charge made by Garry at his press conference after Fred Hampton's death that, by Garry's count, the government had murdered twenty-eight Panthers across the country. Example after example was disputed as a shootout or unproved. Epstein was equally persuasive on "The David Frost Show." Garry seemed oblivious to how poorly he came across defending the accusation of nearly thirty murders. Huey would himself be invited on the show in mid-May, making a similar claim. An outraged Senate Investigation Committee would later find substantial merit to the basic claim of persecution, but not Garry's estimated numbers. (Six years later Garry might have drawn some comfort from Frost's similar skewering of former President Nixon in a series of penetrating interviews that eventually turned into a play and movie.)

In the Panthers' version of musical chairs, at the beginning of June 1971, it became Chief of Staff David Hilliard's turn to face prosecution for his role in the April 6, 1968, shootout that resulted in Bobby Hutton's death—one that Garry featured on his list of government murders. Panther supporters again filled the courtroom for the high profile trial. Hilliard knew that he had no realistic chance of avoiding conviction, though he wished he could have benefited from Garry's talents at trial. Just weeks before Hilliard's trial Garry remained in New Haven finishing up the Seale trial. For the sake of the Party, Hilliard agreed to substitute in his own defense another feisty Leftist giant in the San Francisco criminal defense bar, Vincent Hallinan. Hallinan, who had run for President on the Progressive Party ticket back in 1952, had gained international recognition representing accused Communist Harry Bridges on perjury charges in 1949, which landed Hallinan in jail for contempt. Though Bridges' conviction was ultimately overturned, the evidence against Hilliard presented too great a hurdle. Confessions had been obtained from several other Panther participants in the April 1968 ambush, and Hallinan had no convincing way of explaining the arsenal of weapons the police had found in the Panthers' van that evening. Still, Hilliard blamed the all-white jury for the verdict that sent him to prison for one to ten years, of which he would serve four. (The federal charge for threatening the President's life had by then been dismissed.)

Now it was Huey's turn again. In July, Garry defended Newton's retrial in Oakland without Stender by his side. Shortly after moving into the penthouse, Newton had ostracized and humiliated Stender, deliberately diminishing her status in the eyes of fellow Panthers. After her heady run as his principal liaison to the outside world, Newton said he found her too controlling. But owing his freedom to a woman had never squared with his macho self-image. Since 1968, Jensen had been elevated to District Attorney. He delegated the second prosecution of Newton to another lawyer in his office. With the death penalty no longer an option—and competition from the higher stakes Soledad Brothers' case, among other Movement causes—Newton's retrial was far less of a draw than his first prosecution in 1968, though it still attracted substantial attention.

Not long before the retrial, *Ramparts* publisher Ed Keating published *Free Huey!* The skewed account of the 1967 shootout and 1968 trial suggested that there was still an unidentified midget on the loose, who had fled the scene after murdering Officer Frey. That description derived from Grier's first account of the man he saw bent over, struggling with Frey. Regardless of discrepancies in bus driver Grier's description of the perpetrator, no one had ever placed more than one person close enough to Frey to cause the bullet wounds that killed him. Newton himself admitted at the first trial that he grappled with Frey after being abusively frisked and that it was his bloodied law book police later found on the street.

When the first trial started, Eldridge Cleaver had published an article claiming that Newton had set a bold example for others in defense of the black community by taking justifiable action against murderous police. Despite protests from Huey's family that Cleaver would help send Huey to the gas chamber, the jailed revolutionary fully supported Cleaver's efforts to credit him with offing his first pig. Newton saw the boast as a useful recruiting tool and relished playing the contradictions to the hilt, fully aware that Cleaver's claims on his behalf were not admissible in court against him.[64] Huey's friend Gene McKinney, who went to jail for contempt rather than testify, privately admitted that they did have "a little weed in the car," just as Lowell Jensen charged.[65] David Hilliard could have attested that Newton was not unconscious after being shot in the stomach. McKinney brought his wounded friend to the Oakland home of Hilliard's mother-in-law where Newton argued with his friends not to bring him to the hospital because he feared that he would end up in the gas chamber. They dropped him off at the emergency room anyway. But he arrived there with a different shirt and jacket. After Cleaver spoke with Beverly Axelrod on the day of the shooting, Cleaver had directed Hilliard to get rid of the clothes Newton had been wearing when he first showed up. In an oil barrel in the backyard, Hilliard incinerated the bloody shirt, jacket, and beret Newton had left behind.[66] It would be more than twenty years before Hilliard brought these new details to light. The gun Grier testified he saw in Newton's possession (and Ross reported to the grand jury) never materialized.

In the retrial Garry managed some more courtroom magic tricks, aiming to obtain a hung jury. The proceedings lasted until early August. The panel—ten women and two men, including one African-American woman—deliberated for six days in a heat wave before they announced they were deadlocked eleven-to-one for conviction. Garry and Newton assumed that they had persuaded the African-American woman that the prosecution was part of a genocidal crusade against all blacks. But she was actually among those who did not buy Newton's story. The hold out was a Latina. The disappointed police strongly urged a renewed prosecution.

By summer's end a congressional report would conclude that the relatively small violence-prone Party, while "insidious and virulent," did not constitute a clear and present danger to the government's security—and never had. Several Republican committee members strongly disagreed.[67] That fall, Newton—whose conditions of release on bail neglected to include travel restrictions—accepted an invitation to go to Red China as a guest of Chairman Mao's regime, intentionally upstaging President Nixon several months before his own historic visit to reestablish diplomatic relations. Newton brought two companions: a bodyguard and his protégé and lover since his release, Elaine Brown, the current editor of the Panther newspaper, whom Huey had named as Minister of Information following Eldridge Cleaver's defection. Plainclothes agents tailed Newton and his two companions the whole circuitous way through Canada to China and back. Newton assumed the Nixon administration hoped he would accept the Chinese government's offer of asylum, but Newton returned after ten days. Jensen authorized yet a third trial in December

1971, which also ended in a hung jury. The District Attorney then most reluctantly called it quits, subject to new evidence possibly being uncovered—there was no likelihood of that. Newton reportedly later bragged that he was "the baddest nigger that ever walked" because he got away with killing a white cop.[68]

* * * * *

In response to the nationwide COINTELPRO crackdown, even before leaving prison Newton had begun closing beleaguered Panther branches across country to retrench and reorganize. With the ranks of male Panthers thinned out, Newton had decided to elevate women to the official status of Panthers rather than Pantherettes. He recognized the key role Elaine Brown and other women had played in expanding programs like free breakfasts. But Panther women would still chafe at blatant double standards in the Party, often enforced with beatings. Modeled after the Mafia, Panthers who disobeyed orders or Party rules met with stiff discipline. The Panthers also forced local black business owners to contribute to Panther community programs or face boycotts and, rumor had it, sometimes more dire consequences, including torture, arson, and death. Much of the money the Panthers received at that time was reportedly diverted to weapons and ammunition stockpiled locally and at a revolutionary training camp in the Santa Cruz mountains. There, Panther instructors used bootleg police manuals to teach members the official two-handed "Weaver" shooting stance used by the police, and other professional techniques honed by members with military expertise acquired in Vietnam. In the spring of 1971, it was also where the charred bones of a missing Panther leader, East Bay Captain Fred Bennett, were found, amid reports he had been executed by Newton's bodyguard Jimmy Carr for presumed acts of disloyalty.

* * * * *

By November 1970, Jackson's book had gotten rave reviews. *Look* praised his writings as "the raw stuff, [the coming of age of a black man] ragged and bleeding, or proudly refusing to bleed"; *The New York Times* called it "one of the finest pieces of black writing ever to be printed . . . the most important single volume . . . since *The Autobiography of Malcolm X.*" *The Washington Monthly* claimed "Jackson picks up where Cleaver left off . . . ." London's *Manchester Guardian Weekly* noted with awe Jackson's "Self-discovery, self-education, and self-mastery in a prison cell 5 feet by 8 feet. . . .[From] the stumblingly articulate letters of a boy to his parents, [p]rison makes him a poet and a revolutionary. Miraculously he refuses to be brutalized by a system almost unbelievably brutal."[69]

Reporters deluged Jackson with requests for interviews, including *Life* and *Time* magazine, which Stender engineered in the hopes the publicity would help keep Jackson from the gas chamber. At first, he was elated at the media frenzy Stender had generated with the deft editing the gifted English literature major had accomplished. But when Jackson reflected on all the omissions from the published book and the proud but innocent victim that she portrayed him as, the revolutionary grew furious. He liked to boast of being "a brigand all my life."[70] He had always rankled at his mother's attempts to view him through rose-colored glasses, and Stender's whitewashing enraged him far more.

Reflecting on his brother's sacrifice, Jackson most resented Stender's removal of his calls for armed reprisal. He complained to prisoners' rights activist Eve Pell that "Fay cut so much material away . . . that it turned out more her than me."[71] Meanwhile some of Jackson's close associates on the outside, including Jimmy Carr, who had been paroled in July, were collaborating with Jackson on an escape plan. They called themselves the August 7th Movement, named for the day Jonathan Jackson gave his life for their revolutionary cause. Carr tried to get Stender to divert Jackson's book royalties for his use, but she refused. Though Jackson knew that his rough, unedited prose would win no prize, he was already at work on a second book, *Blood in My Eye,* using the stubby pencil the prison allowed him to put back descriptions of all his planned lethal remedies, with instructions on various tools of guerrilla warfare. In his view, "the power of the people lies in its greater potential violence" not "to outshout [an opponent] with logic [but] slay him, assassinate him . . . shooting from four hundred yards away and behind a rock. Suffocation, strangulation, crucifixion . . ."[72]

By early spring Jackson fired Stender for refusing to help him try to escape. He rejected her pleas that he continue to rely on the defense team to get him acquitted at trial. Jackson had no intention whatsoever of sitting silently before a jury while watching his attorneys argue he was being railroaded for a crime he did not commit. Unlike Newton, the volatile inmate had little capacity for game playing. At his next hearing, he jumped up and yelled, "Power to the People. Death to the pigs."[73] He knocked a bailiff unconscious with a powerful karate chop. His friend Jimmy Carr, stationed among the spectators, leaped over the railing and joined other Jackson supporters in a confrontation with a squadron of San Francisco police summoned into the courtroom by the judge's push of an emergency button. In the ensuing scuffle, both Jackson and Carr were subdued. Jackson was returned to San Quentin, and Carr was among three spectators arrested for assault.

By then Jackson had already bragged to friends what he blurted out in a tape-recorded interview the summer before with his editor Gregory Armstrong. The state's eyewitnesses were lying about what they saw. Neither of his co-defendants had anything to do with it. Jackson had not needed their help. He killed Mills all by himself. Armstrong had kept the startling disclosure secret, as enthralled by Jackson's charisma as Stender was, and as giddy with power in packaging Jackson's revolutionary voice for global consumption. It was George Jackson that Armstrong referred to when he wrote, "If he had been outside, he would never have belonged to us in the same way, but locked away, he was ours."[74] But for Stender the intoxication of being the gatekeeper for a revolutionary, and his ticket to freedom, had applied equally to her role as Huey Newton's lawyer.

Even after both rollercoaster rides were over in the spring of 1971, Stender was still on a mission to expose the racism and cruelty of the prison system. In their effort to put Soledad on the defensive, Stender and her associates had heard so many egregious stories from prisoners at Soledad and elsewhere, the anguish made her throat swell. She created a new nonprofit Prison Law Project to address these issues in collaboration with the ACLU, Lawyers Guild, and other advocates of prison reform. By the summer of 1971, Stender and her prison law colleagues were fully immersed in a whirlwind of activity: speaking and writing about the horrors they found (later published in the Project's book *Maximum Security: Letters from Prison* and Jessica Mitford's *Kind and Usual Punishment: the American Prison Business*); providing inmates a hotline to call; supporting hunger strikes to meet prisoner demands; publicizing prisoners' rights; signing up volunteer lawyers, from solos to big firms, for thousands of prisoners who raised constitutional claims; proposing legislative reforms; providing inmates with pen pals and visitors; and helping launch a prisoners' rights specialty bar.

Stender's Berkeley Prison Law Project won immediate recognition as the largest such project in the country. It became a key player in a growing national movement for prison reform until forced to shut its doors two years later after public interest waned and funders disappeared. In the fall of 1971, a faction had split off to form the Prison Law Collective, which did similar work with a more radical tilt. Both groups irked officials no end when lawyers and paralegals or investigators they employed flouted rules they considered overly strict by smuggling in contraband cigarettes, photos, and reading material or bringing messages to and from inmates and friends on the outside. On several occasions, officials had caught women in the collectives having furtive sexual encounters with their favorite inmate among the hordes starved for female companionship. Stender considered all of these tactics humanitarian outreach, including the tape-recorded message she had smuggled into George Jackson at Soledad in the spring of 1970 from Huey Newton. State corrections officials nicknamed her "the dragon lady."[75] The prison soon instituted a policy permitting officials to open any mail addressed to and from inmates—including correspondence with their attorneys—until the California Supreme Court ruled that censorship practice unconstitutional.

The issue of attorneys smuggling notes and messages in and out of prison would hit the headlines again in 2005 when Lynne Stewart, a New York radical six years Stender's junior, became a Lawyers Guild cause célèbre. Stewart challenged the constitutionality of the federal restrictions she had violated by using her status as lawyer for a convicted Egyptian-born terrorist to communicate with his Mid-East followers. Mike Tigar's legendary skills as one of the 20th century's top criminal defense lawyers could not prevent sixty-six-year-old Stewart from going to prison and suffering automatic disbarment. Tigar had known Stender since his undergraduate and law school days in Berkeley when he headed SLATE and worked on Movement causes. In retrospect, he saw no distinction in the conduct Stewart engaged in from that of Stender and her colleagues acting as go-betweens for Jackson and Newton back in the late '60s and early '70s. It was only the rules that had changed.

* * * * *

Marin Police had quickly learned that the registered owner of four of the guns Jonathan Jackson used in the August 1970 kidnapping attempt was his tutor and frequent companion Angela Davis. For the last year the Marxist Ph.D. candidate had become a household name as the most controversial black female activist in the nation. She gained both notoriety and an international fan club in 1969 when the U.C. Regents bypassed normal procedures to fire her from teaching at UCLA for being a Communist. Davis had purchased the weapons and ammunition openly at gun shops; police already knew that Jonathan Jackson acted as her part-time bodyguard after she became Co-Chair of the Los Angeles Soledad Brothers Committee. Louis Tackwood later claimed that the Los Angeles CCS Red Squad had been tracking Davis closely for several days. They assumed she was in on the daring kidnap plot.[76]

Though George Jackson by then had attracted a coterie of radical women passionately devoted to him, he had become enthralled with Davis immediately upon reading a newspaper clipping his mother sent him about the outspoken activist. Davis was active in the Che-Lumumba Black Communist Party Club in Los Angeles and affiliated with the Panthers and other black militants. A bitter critic of the establishment, she often addressed anti-war rallies and lent her voice to the growing coalition against the death penalty. In 1969 when Gov. Reagan first insisted that the U.C. Regents fire her, the unorthodox action provoked a student outcry far more widespread than when the governor precipitated the firing of George Mason Murray at San Francisco State the year before. The American Association of University Professors censured the Regents for failing to give

Davis notice and a hearing. The dismissal was later overturned in court. The Regents then set a hearing to terminate Davis once again—this time for stated reasons: her incendiary speeches at rallies against racist "pigs" and against the Regents, accusing them of murder at People's Park. While preparing to fight that second termination, Davis had nonetheless found the Soledad Brothers case so compelling she immediately volunteered to take a prominent role in fundraising for their defense.

The two radicals were introduced at a court hearing in Salinas in May 1970 where George Jackson arrived in chains, focused less on the proceedings than on convincing the twenty-six-year-old Leftist scholar to fall in love with him. As Angela spent more and more time with the Jackson family and the Soledad Defense Committee working to gain his freedom, the two corresponded. Jackson fantasized that after he escaped they would share a revolutionary life on the run. He wrote: "I think about *you all of the time.*" Davis responded with equal fervor that he had "smashed through the fortress erected around my soul" and that she, too, dreamed of being lovers in combat together.[77]

On the afternoon of the Marin County kidnap attempt, Davis was seen at the San Francisco airport hurriedly catching a flight back to Los Angeles. The next day, as newspapers featured photos of the crime, Davis went into hiding and was put on the nation's most wanted list, only to be dramatically captured two months later hiding out at a motel in New York in disguise under an assumed name. The FBI put out word that Newton had been the informant who disclosed Davis's location, but that seemed most unlikely. After a losing battle over extradition, Davis was brought back to California from New York handcuffed and headed for pretrial detainment in maximum security. The Marin County grand jury indicted her together with survivor Ruchell Magee for conspiracy, kidnap, and murder. Demonstrations on her behalf erupted overseas as well as in America—the press reported a crowd of 60,000 "Angèle Libre" protestors just in Paris. Like millions of Americans, people throughout Europe were fascinated by ubiquitous newspaper, magazine, television, and radio coverage of the ongoing juicy American political saga combining allegations of kidnapping and murder, racism, black militants, free speech for dissidents, and a love angle: Angela Davis and Soledad Brother George Jackson.

As the celebrated revolutionary couple each prepared for their separate death penalty trials, they were allowed to meet in the Marin County jail together with counsel, ostensibly to consult on their legal strategies. Jackson's attorney John Thorne felt that arranging a rendezvous was the least he could do for the two imprisoned soul mates. A guard described their reunion as a "lovers' petting party."[78] Jackson made no secret from visitors that he still wanted to break out. He even told a *New York Times* reporter in April 1971 that the only way he would leave prison alive was escape. Government agents had advance knowledge of the plot by the August 7th Movement, yet somehow weapons were smuggled in.

On August 21, 1971, two weeks after the anniversary of Jonathan Jackson's aborted kidnapping plot, radio and television stations interrupted their regularly scheduled programs with reports of another Marin County bloodbath in which six men died and a number were gravely injured. Associate Warden Jim Park grimly announced to the press that Jackson had been killed trying to break out. He had been strip searched as usual before he met his visitor that day, but as the guards began another strip search on his way back, he surprised them with a gun. Jackson then freed several other inmates, who managed to slit the throats of several guards before the uprising was over. Jackson himself had been shot down in the prison courtyard. When Park was asked whom he held responsible for the aborted escape effort, he retorted sharply, "You can lay some of the blame for these six deaths at the doorstep of some of these radical attorneys who come in here and encourage the men to do this sort of thing."[79]

Two visitors to San Quentin that day had just gone missing. One was attorney Stephen Bingham, who had been the only one to see Jackson; the other was an investigator from Black Panther headquarters named Vanita Anderson, who unsuccessfully sought admission to visit Jackson that morning. She handed her tape recorder to Bingham when he received clearance to visit Jackson. The security guard manually examined the inside of the tape recorder and handed it back to Bingham to take with him. Bingham left Jackson alone in the interview room at one point to show some papers to Anderson, who was still in the waiting room. That was when the warden theorized that Jackson removed a hidden gun in the tape recorder and slipped it under an Afro wig. Soon afterward, on his way back to the Adjustment Center, Jackson reportedly declared, "The dragon has come," invoking the memory of his hero North Vietnamese leader Ho Chi Minh, before overpowering his guards and freeing other prisoners.[80]

Two days after the bloody melée, all twenty-six other inmates in the Adjustment Center issued a joint declaration accusing San Quentin's personnel of murdering Jackson and conspiring to kill the remaining prisoners. They alleged they had been ordered out of their cells, but retreated when they heard gunshots. They were then forced by guards at gunpoint to strip naked and emerge from their cells, where they were beaten with blackjacks and clubs and left for six hours on the ground without medical care. The entire area was scrubbed before any outside persons were permitted to visit the crime scene, making it impossible to reconstruct exactly what happened that day. Several attorneys and at least two journalists later tried without success to duplicate the trick George Jackson was said to have played on his guards, hiding an eight-inch, two-and-a-half-pound 9-mm gun and bullet clip under an Afro wig and walking with the weapon unnoticed for a distance of several hundred yards—like the distance from the San Quentin visiting room back to the Adjustment Center. They could not imagine how the awkward balancing act could have been accomplished for even a few feet without the guards becoming immediately aware of it.[81]

In October 1971 the surviving Marin County inmates involved in the bloodbath would be charged with murder and prosecuted over the next several years as the San Quentin Six. Though Bingham would be charged in absentia with complicity in the alleged escape attempt, neither Bingham nor Anderson were the main focus of Park's wrath. In an official report issued in October 1971 by a commission specially convened at Gov. Reagan's request, the commissioners echoed the San Quentin warden's office. They blamed the killings on a chain of events starting with Stender's wide dissemination of inflammatory accounts of the deaths of three black prisoners at Soledad. They concluded that Stender and her associates had generated bad press through false charges of inmate mistreatment and baseless lawsuits that encouraged disruptive prisoner behavior. As a result, correctional authorities contended that the Leftist attorneys instigated two years of prison violence, egged on by other radicals like Angela Davis and actress Jane Fonda.

More than a thousand people attended George Jackson's funeral at St. Augustine's in Oakland, the same church where Jonathan Jackson's funeral took place the year before. Tension between George Jackson followers and Newton was once again high. There was already bitterness over the fact that the Panthers had obtained Jackson's literary rights shortly before his death, when Jackson reassigned the royalties from his books to the Panthers and rewrote his will to give the Panthers his estate in hopes that would help finance weapons for the revolution. By the time of Jackson's funeral, a rumor spread that Newton was socializing at Lake Tahoe with his patron Bert Schneider and the wealthy producer's girlfriend Candice Bergen when he learned that Jackson had been shot down in the yard at San Quentin.[82] Newton was perceived to be exploiting Jackson commercially by negotiating through his Hollywood connections for a movie on Jackson's life. Newton's film plans never materialized. In 2007 the film *Black August* would chronicle the last fourteen months of Jackson's life, attempting to recapture for younger generations the dramatic impact he had made in 1970–71.

Jackson's death reverberated internationally. His family called for a United Nations investigation. Folk singer Bob Dylan soon dedicated a new song to the slain revolutionary with the refrain, "Lord, Lord, they cut George Jackson down." The Weathermen retaliated against the government for Jackson's death with a bomb set off at the Department of Corrections. Immediately upon word of Jackson's death, prisoners rose up in protest in a number of correctional facilities across the country. A widely syndicated columnist noted with alarm that prisons had become "schools for revolution."[83] The largest uprising occurred less than three weeks later at Attica in upstate New York. One thousand mostly black and Puerto Rican prisoners—nearly half of the men incarcerated in the facility—rebelled against the all-white prison staff that so often disciplined them with "Nigger sticks." The militant inmates took more than thirty guards hostage while they presented a list of thirty demands on the prison administration, almost all of which addressed pre-existing mandates that they charged the administration with failing to honor. Panther Chairman Bobby Seale flew to New York to join the team of negotiators.

Gov. Nelson Rockefeller then stunned the nation by storming the facility. Eleven hostages and thirty-two inmates were killed, ten by state troopers. The dead included four guards who had their throats slit. One observer described the scene as looking like the aftermath of a Civil War battlefield. Over sixty inmates and one state trooper would face criminal charges for their conduct, while the state defended suits for civil rights violations. The surgeon who served as the senior medical officer for the National Guard later described his horror, watching guards shout racist epithets as they clubbed already subdued prisoners, hitting them in the crotch and knees.[84] It took more than twenty-five years before the State of New York settled the litigation brought by prisoners and their families for $12 million and paid an equal amount to the families of prison staff who died.

* * * * *

By December 1971, when Newton walked out of court a completely free man, the Panthers decided that their "Free Huey" buttons and signs would remain their battle cry as a proxy for "Free Angela," for the freedom of the two remaining Soledad Brothers and oppressed black people everywhere. Back in May of that year Newton had announced that the Party was planning to lay down its guns after realizing the Party had alienated black churches. To win their support, Newton proclaimed that the Panthers were committed for the immediate future to organizing within the system and to collaborating in the use of traditional civil rights techniques of picketing and voter registration drives.

The January 1972 disarmament announcement marked a major modification of the Panther's Ten Point Program. Though Newton emphasized that he still anticipated an eventual violent overthrow of the government, he eliminated the call for all black people to "arm themselves for self-defense" against police brutality and murder. Newton thereby hoped to make his followers less threatening to ordinary folk and draw a sharp contrast between himself and Eldridge Cleaver, who was then threatening to return from exile in North Africa to wage "guerrilla warfare." Newton had been warned that Cleaver had placed him on a hit list. "The Servant of the People" now openly scorned Cleaver as a "renegade scab traitor." Yet criticism had already surfaced that Newton's own local Panthers operated like a Mafia protection racket, shaking down businesses that did not support Party programs.[85] Newton himself was rearrested in April of 1972 on misdemeanor charges after an alleged altercation in an Oakland bar in which he brandished a weapon.

Since May 1967, when the Panthers' gun-toting debut in Sacramento startled Gov. Reagan as he welcomed a group of children to the Capitol, the Panthers had galvanized the state's leader to transform the prison industry into California's Pentagon. Though its budget would skyrocket over the next few decades, even by the early '70s its expansion was remarkable. The number of inmates in California prisons had declined steadily since the mid '60s, when Gov. Reagan first took office. Yet with increased guards and equipment, by 1973 at San Quentin the cost per inmate equaled that of sending a student to Harvard. At the same time that longer and harsher penalties were being implemented, activists like Stender had become totally disillusioned at the overwhelming scope of the problems of reentry into society these inmates faced if and when they were freed. All but one man held in maximum security whose release on parole the Prison Law Project obtained, later returned to prison for other offenses. One violently attacked a girlfriend. Stender belatedly realized that, regardless of how salvageable maximum security inmates' lives might have been before they went to prison, most were psychologically damaged beyond repair by their experience in the hole. The vast majority of these men seemed no longer capable of productive lives on the outside without extraordinary support that society did not provide.

A *San Francisco Chronicle* reporter likened the shuttering of the Prison Law Project to the closing of a heavy prison door on the hopes of those inside. While correctional officials reviled Stender as a "demon agitator" and "one of the greatest threats to security in prisons," the reporter noted that "hundreds, perhaps thousands of inmates" considered her a "heroic figure" and "almost a legend in places where women once were seldom seen."[86] (Today over 20,000 inmates are similary located in "supermax" American prisons, some for lengthy periods of time long since condemned by human rights' advocates as inhumane.[87])

2. ECLIPSED

"So your brother's bound and gagged, and they've chained him to a chair."

Opening to "Chicago," by Graham Nash

Today the Chicago Seven conspiracy trial is far better remembered than the Huey Newton trial. At the time it also received huge publicity, bolstered by the international coverage originally given to the five-day unofficial "Celebration of Life" held in Chicago in late August 1968, and advertised as a giant, anti-war, free love, pot party.[1] Denied permits, Yippies gathered anyway, to lobby against the war and to nominate a hog named "Pigasus" for President in ridicule of the field of human candidates.

Amid rumors that Yippies planned to drop LSD in the Chicago water supply, fears of bombing, and other sabotage. Mayor Daley oversaw unprecedented security precautions for the Democratic Convention. Largely at President Johnson's unseen direction, Daley amassed 12,000 uniformed policemen backed up by 6,000 armed National Guardsmen. That did not count the firemen deployed at the barbed-wire ringed Convention Hall in case of arson attempts. Nor did it tally the thousand federal undercover agents, who swelled the ranks of local plainclothes men: one of every seven people at the various protest rallies was actually a mole gathering evidence to be used against the organizers.[2] Outside the convention hall demonstrators shouted, "The Whole World Is Watching," which was not much of an exaggeration, like the similar claim today made by Occupy Wall Street protestors. Originally, the charges of criminal conspiracy and crossing a state line to incite a riot were brought against eight men: Yippie leaders Abbie Hoffman and Jerry Rubin, Black Panther

The eighth defendant.

Bobby Seale, SDS leader Tom Hayden, and anti-war activists David Dellinger, Rennie Davis, John Froines, and Lee Weiner. Charges included teaching followers how to use fire bombs and interfering with firemen and police—under conspiracy theory it did not matter who did what. In response to outraged media outrage, the grand jury also charged several policemen with civil rights violations for assaulting a photographer and journalists from big city dailies. One officer was charged with lying under oath to the grand jury. But most attention was focused on the federal government's effort to throw so many leaders of the New Left in prison for allegedly conspiring to instigate the debacle. Rubin welcomed his arrest as "The Academy Award of protest" and gave a cheeky acceptance speech: "It is with sincere humility that I accept this indictment. It is the fulfillment of childhood dreams, climaxing years of hard work and fun." Besides his family, his list of people to thank included the Boston Tea Party, Che Guevara and Fidel Castro, Huey Newton and Eldridge Cleaver, and "last but not least [Mayor] Richard J. Daley."[3]

The new federal law under which the eight activists were prosecuted had just been enacted as the "Rap Brown Amendment" to the 1968 Civil Rights Act, prompted by Brown's incitement of urban rioting in 1967. The penalty for its violation was ten years in prison. The court of appeal would later note obvious First Amendment problems with this statute.[4] Indeed, Seale's inclusion as a defendant rested on scant evidence. He had only spent a couple of days in Chicago during the convention, invited to speak at Lincoln Park as an eleventh hour replacement for Eldridge Cleaver. In his speech, Seale allegedly urged his listeners to "barbecue some pork."[5] Apart from questions whether this provocative metaphor came within protected First Amendment speech, the government had to prove Seale entered into an advance agreement with the other activists to incite riots. Noting that Seale played only a "marginal role in the clashes" that followed, a journalist asked a representative of the Department of Justice what prompted the government to name Seale in the conspiracy charges. The official responded frankly, "The Panthers are a bunch of hoodlums and we have to get this guy."[6]

The judge who presided over the 1969–70 federal trial was seventy-four-year-old Julius Hoffman, a former law partner of Mayor Daley, who had earned a poor reputation among members of the local bar. He was not the first judge assigned to the case; the first had recused himself for personal knowledge of some of the facts. The court's practice was to select judges at random to avoid accusations of deliberately assigning a judge predisposed to favor one side or the other;[7] yet word leaked out that Judge Hoffman had been hand-picked for the assignment. Prof. Alan Dershowitz, who ultimately worked on the Chicago Seven appeals, considered the choice of Hoffman a colossal mistake. Dershowitz described the diminutive judge as "an arrogant and pompous martinet who played right into the hands of the defendants and their antics."[8] Abbie Hoffman predicted in advance that the trial would become a circus: "[the] Scopes trial, revolution in the streets, the Woodstock Festival and People's Park all rolled into one."[9] The irascible judge would crack the whip as its infamous ringmaster.

The Chicago Seven Trial did indeed live up to its reputation as the "most incredible trial in American history"[10]—a symbolic battle between the political establishment and the entire anti-war Movement. The defendants had learned from the trial of Dr. Benjamin Spock, of the "Boston Five," convicted the year before. The well-dressed, sixty-five-year-old pediatrician had been famed for two decades as the author of a pioneering bestseller on child-rearing, *Baby and Child Care* (with sales of 50 million copies, it had become the new mother's bible, one of the most widely distributed books in the world). Co-defendant Rev. William Sloane Coffin, Jr. was also a widely respected anti-war and civil rights activist, who had served in World War II and afterward in the CIA. The indictments had received international attention. They came hot on the heels of the shocking revelation by *The New York Times* of "The Hershey Directive." The four-star general heading Selective Service had responded to escalating student demonstrations against the war with a letter to all draft offices urging immediate reversal of deferments of any identified protesters and their reclassification as 1-A, eligible for the front lines. Outraged college presidents joined student organizations in a lawsuit challenging the legality of that directive.[11] Meanwhile, media focused on the "Boston Five" trial. Dr. Coffin looked forward to his prosecution for aiding and abetting draft resisters: "I wanted a trial of stature, to test the legality of the war and the Constitutionality of the Selective Service Act."[12] But the defendants played by the rules and were precluded from introducing the morality of the Vietnam War into their criminal trial. In retrospect, Dr. Spock himself questioned his lawyers' strategy: "We sat like good little boys called into the principal's office. I'm afraid we didn't prove very much."[13] The defendants were sentenced to two years each and released on their own recognizance pending appeal, which resulted in reversal of their convictions. Investigative journalist Jessica Mitford had followed the trial closely and published a book on it at the beginning of 1969.[14]

There were also lessons to be learned from the highly publicized October 1968 trial of the "Catonsville Nine," led by religious anti-war activists who burned draft files removed from a Selective Service office in protest of the killing in Vietnam. That trial of Catholic priests Philip and Daniel Berrigan and seven other defendants spawned anti-war demonstrations nationwide. Increasing numbers of Americans had become disheartened following the unexpected North Vietnamese Tet Offensive in early 1968, especially after Walter Cronkite, the most trusted newsman in America, predicted that the war would end in a stalemate. (In his indictment "acceptance speech," Rubin thanked Cronkite, too.)

At the time of the acts of sabotage of the Catonsville Nine in May 1968, the Berrigan brothers were awaiting sentencing for staging a media event at the Baltimore Customs House in October 1967, in which they symbolically poured blood on draft records. The priests then passed out Bibles while they awaited arrest. William Kunstler, who later became one of the Chicago Seven lawyers, acted as lead counsel in defending the Catonsville Nine. Kunstler argued that the court should instruct the jury in the common law concept known as "jury nullification." It prevents a court from second-guessing an acquittal even if the jury sympathized so much with a guilty defendant that it rendered a verdict clearly contrary to the facts and law. Kunstler wanted the trial judge to instruct the Catonsville Nine jury that it had the power to acquit the defendants if the panel agreed the war was immoral. Instead, following the court's instructions, the jury took less than two hours to convict all nine defendants, who were then sentenced to prison for terms ranging from two to three-and-a-half years. The appeals of the Catonsville Nine were still pending at the time the Chicago Seven started their trial, and would be affirmed long before the Chicago Seven trial ended. Moral opposition to the war was deemed no defense to prosecution for deliberate violation of the law. The appellate court explained that any other result would invite anarchy.

More helpful to the strategy of the Chicago Seven defense lawyers was the Oakland Seven case completed in March 1969. By then President Johnson had left office, amid increased disillusionment of the electorate over the wisdom of the ongoing war. The political make-up of the jury pool was also closer to that of Chicago than Harrisburg had been. The prosecution for conspiracy to block access to the Oakland Induction Center during "Stop the Draft Week" elevated to a felony what would otherwise be several misdemeanor charges: blocking sidewalks, creating a public nuisance, trespass, and interfering with local police. The case was tried to a jury before Judge George Phillips. He was the same judge who had issued the landmark ruling barring discriminatory use of challenges to non-white jurors by the Alameda County District Attorney's office the summer before.

The issue came up again in the Oakland Seven case because the defense argued that they opposed not only the war but a racist draft. Lowell Jensen dismissed six potential black jurors for opposition to the war. Each time, Garry noted the juror's race for the record. He also told jurors he was Huey Newton's lawyer and asked them what they felt about the Black Panther Party, and whether they bore any ill will to Garry as the Party's lawyer—questions allowed even though none of the seven white defendants belonged to the Panther Party. But the judge refused Charles Garry's efforts to widen the scope of the trial to consider the Nuremberg defense that the Vietnam War was illegal. The defense nonetheless managed to bring that issue in through the back door via testimony of an anti-war minister. Garry and his co-counsel pulled another major surprise on prosecutor Lowell Jensen in their defense of that case. They called a Stanford University physicist to the stand who admitted to organizing rallies on his campus for Stop the Draft Week, circulating flyers and coordinating busloads of demonstrators headed for the induction center. The physicist had never been prosecuted or even, to his knowledge, investigated. After his testimony was completed, the defense team abruptly rested their case without calling any of their clients to the stand. Garry said Jensen's jaw dropped and "he looked as if someone had just poured ice water over his head."[15] On March 28, 1969, after three anxiety-producing days of deliberation, the jury returned with acquittals of all seven protest leaders. As a local reporter interviewed Garry, one of the jubilant defendants asked Garry if he considered himself as good as the fictional Perry Mason, who never lost a case. Garry quipped in reply, "I'm *better* than Perry Mason. *All* of his clients are innocent."[16]

From the start of the Chicago Eight trial, Black Panther Bobby Seale was treated far differently than the rest of the defendants. The other seven were all released on bail, but Seale was considered ineligible for bail because he had been arrested in August of 1969 on murder charges. Seale had been jailed in San Francisco awaiting extradition to Connecticut to face trial in New Haven on that capital charge when he was instead spirited away by federal marshals by ground transportation to Chicago. His counsel received no notice of Seale's whereabouts until after Seale was delivered to the Cook County jail. Seale protested that his lawyer, Charles Garry, was about to undergo gall bladder surgery. Garry himself, despite his serious condition, came to Chicago in early September to argue for a six-week continuance of the trial from the end of September to mid-November, after Garry recuperated from surgery. One would normally expect such a request for a six-week delay, supported by a doctor's affidavit, to be granted. Judge Hoffman denied it. In the interim, Kunstler volunteered to represent Seale, which Seale rejected. Mindful of how Huey Newton had argued in his own defense several times, Seale requested the same privilege. In the alternative, he demanded that Judge Hoffman reconsider Garry's request for a delay so Garry could represent Seale and co-defendants who also sought Garry's representation. Both of Seale's arguments had merit under the Sixth Amendment. When deprived of either option, Seale decided on the third day of trial to keep confronting the judge. Over the next several weeks, Seale repeatedly insisted on his rights, calling the judge a "fascist dog," a "pig," and a "blatant racist." [17]

Judge Hoffman had rushed to impanel a jury with little regard for their exposure to prejudicial pretrial publicity or concern for ferreting out bias against members of the counterculture. Early in the trial two jurors received mailed threats signed "The Panther," which caused one to quit. Seale argued that these letters were likely fake, intended to prejudice the jury against him. Judge Hoffman ignored that possibility and sequestered the jury panel for their safety for the remainder of the trial. Seale again objected. Separating the jurors from their families based on fear of Panther retaliation would only exacerbate any prejudice the panel already held against him with no proof any actual threat existed. Judge Hoffman was unpersuaded. After warning Seale he would be bound and gagged if he continued to engage in disruptive behavior and name-calling, the infuriated jurist soon made good on his threat. Judge Hoffman ordered Seale bound and gagged and shackled to a folding chair—measures that stunned the public worldwide.

When the gag was removed, Seale still refused to let Kunstler represent him. By then, Kunstler had made a written request to be relieved of that assignment, which Judge Hoffman denied. In early November, Hoffman finally declared a mistrial against Seale and severed his case for future retrial. At the same time, Judge Hoffman cited Seale for sixteen separate instances of contempt and sentenced Seale on the spot to three months for each instance to be served consecutively—an unprecedented four years in prison just on the contempt charges. (Months later in 1970, with Seale's appeal of the contempt conviction still pending, the government dismissed the underlying case against Seale on its own initiative.)

The judge's severance of Seale's prosecution caused the remaining defendants—all whites—to go down in history as the Chicago Seven. In contrast to the Catonsville Nine, Dr. Spock, and Oakland Seven trials, the defendants managed to parade a number of singers, writers, and other activists before the jury as an effort to score political points on the illegitimacy of the Vietnam War. Judge Hoffman's old partner Mayor Daley also testified. Any trial that featured Pulitzer Prize–winning author Norman Mailer, folk singer Arlo Guthrie, psychedelic advocate Timothy Leary, and Beat Poet Allen Ginsberg had to be quite entertaining. Abbie Hoffman and Jerry Rubin wore blue jeans and headbands to court, ate candy, bared their chests, and blew kisses to the mostly female jury. They also angered Judge Hoffman by unfurling a North Vietnamese National Liberation Front flag and mocking him with the present of a birthday cake. Defense attorneys Kunstler and Weinglass engaged in frequent wrangles with the testy judge. During the five-month-long proceedings, Judge Hoffman wound up issuing nearly 160 contempt citations against both the defendants and their attorneys.

As the trial continued through early February 1970, the prosecutor was accused of making use of illegal wire-taps of the defense. With that issue postponed for resolution until after the trial ended, the defense lawyers managed to convince an unsympathetic jury that the so-called conspirators had never met together and had differing strategies and objectives. Abbie Hoffman put their defense most succinctly: "Conspiracy? Hell, we couldn't agree on lunch."[18] The jurors ultimately acquitted all seven on conspiracy charges, while convicting five of them (all but Froines and Weiner) on charges of crossing a state line to incite a riot. Judge Hoffman sentenced those defendants each to five years in prison and a $5,000 fine. Still irrepressible, Jerry Rubin gave the jurist a copy of his book *Do It,* inscribed with the message, "Julius, you radicalized more young people than we ever could. You're the country's top Yippie."[19] Observer Herbert Ehrmann, who had been one of Sacco's lawyers more than forty years before, commented that, "The conduct of the judge and the actions of the defendants were all disgraceful. The whole episode was a disgrace to American justice."[20]

The deliberate effort to get Judge Hoffman to commit major errors paid off. In May of 1972, the appellate court dismissed several of the contempt citations against Seale and reversed the others to be retried in front of a different judge with no personal stake in the outcome. The government then dismissed those charges, too.[21] Six months later, in November 1972, the convictions in the Chicago Seven case were overturned based on judicial errors, including failure to ensure a jury untainted by prejudicial pretrial publicity. The court of appeal recognized that some of the defendants and their lawyers had behaved provocatively, but the panel also noted the prosecutor went overboard in his summation, calling the defendants "evil men," "liars and obscene haters," "profligate extremists," and "violent anarchists." In conducting further proceedings, the appellate tribunal reminded both the trial judge and prosecutor of the high standards of behavior they were required to adhere to in the American system of justice.[22]

Meanwhile, within months of the trial's end, students across America rejected the violent radicalism of the Yippies in favor of mass peaceful protests.[23] As colorful as it had been, it was not "THE" trial of the century, but an intentional mockery of the criminal justice system by some of the defendants and an unintentional one by the abrasive jurist with a hair-trigger temper.

* * * * *

By February of 1973, after the Paris Peace Accords brought an uneasy cease fire to the Vietnam War, activists focused instead on the seventy-one-day occupation of Wounded Knee by hundreds of members of the American Indian Movement ("AIM"). The shooting confrontation with the FBI resulted in 120 arrests for a variety of crimes. As in the Chicago Seven trial, the defense was political, focused on the history of injustices against the country's native tribes. Prosecutorial misconduct resulted in the dismissal of all the charges in September 1974. The following year the murder of two FBI agents resulted in the controversial trial and imprisonment of militant AIM leader Leonard Peltier. Peltier was later accused of ordering the killing of one of his own followers to cover up Peltier's confession to killing the FBI agents.[24]

* * * * *

The biggest stakes, of course, always lie in criminal trials that involve the death penalty. The same year as the Chicago Seven verdict was rendered, another touted "trial of the century" took place in Los Angeles. It involved ritual murders by a bizarre cult headed by Charles Manson, a redneck ex-felon whom prosecutor Vincent Bugliosi called a "Mephistophelean guru."[25] Manson's aim was to precipitate a race war in which he and his followers would emerge victorious.

3. VISIONS OF APOCALYPTIC RACE WAR

Look out helter skelter, helter skelter,
Helter skelter ooh
Look out, 'cos here she comes.

When I get to the bottom
I go back to the top of the slide
And I stop and I turn and I go for a ride
And I get to the bottom
and I see you again
Yeah yeah yeah.
FROM THE BEATLES, "HELTER SKELTER"

Thirty-four-year-old Charles Manson may have been psychic when he started planning for a race-based civil war in November 1968. That same fall Eldridge Cleaver had been thinking along the same lines before he took off for Cuba on Thanksgiving eve, following Huey Newton's orders to flee the country instead. Manson in fact knew almost nothing about the Black Panther leadership or its precise agenda. The white ex-felon often referred to the Panthers interchangeably with Black Muslims, although the Panthers were unlike Elijah Muhammad's Nation of Islam in several key respects. The Nation of Islam characterized all whites as devils to be overthrown—the Panthers had no religious base to their organization, disavowed separatism in favor of alliances with white radicals, and identified far more closely with Black Muslim apostate Malcolm X.

It was common knowledge that in 1964 Malcolm X had dramatically broken all ties with Black Muslim leader Elijah Muhammad and the Nation of Islam to form his own Muslim organization. The following year, after several near misses, Malcolm X was assassinated by a trio of Nation of Islam gunmen. Oblivious to this split, Manson only noticed that revolutionary rhetoric among black militants had increased greatly after the assassination of Dr. King in April of 1968. That realization was enough for Manson to begin making his own bizarre plans for the apocalyptic war he called "Helter Skelter."

The Ohio-born singer/songwriter had experienced a nightmarish early childhood. Manson was the illegitimate son of a teenage runaway who battled alcoholism and sometimes worked as a prostitute. Shuttled among family members, Manson started stealing by the time he was nine. At age twelve, his relatives sent the troubled youth back to his mother. She refused to take him. Manson branched out into burglary and wound up in a juvenile detention facility, where he later claimed to have been sodomized and beaten. Soon afterward he was caught committing the same type of crime against someone else at knife point. After transfer to another facility, Manson behaved like a model prisoner and earned parole in 1954. Over the next thirteen years he was in and out of jail. In what turned out to be a serious understatement, prison psychiatrists characterized him as having "deep-seated personality problems."[1]

While on the outside, Manson had twice married and divorced and even lived for a while with his mother. Already showing signs that he was obsessed with gaining recognition, Manson fathered a son named Charles with each wife. Though he found some legitimate part-time jobs, Manson supplemented them with auto theft, passing at least one bad check, and pimping. When serving his second adult prison sentence at McNeil Island Penitentiary in Washington, Manson met lifer Alvin "Creepy" Karpis, infamous as the last of the "Public Enemies" rounded up by J. Edgar Hoover in the 1930s. The veteran of Ma Barker's gang played steel guitar and agreed to teach Manson. An eager pupil, Manson spent nearly all his available time practicing, writing and singing songs, convinced he was headed for stardom upon release.

Still, Manson was reluctant to face life on the outside. His perception of the world was largely shaped in prison where, for protection, inmates split into fiercely opposed racial gangs. In 1967, Manson earned parole and headed for San Francisco. It was the "Summer of Love." As an inmate, Manson had become enamored of Scientology long enough to absorb some of its terminology into his vocabulary. Besides mastering the guitar, Manson had learned to spout with some semblance of credibility his thoughts on reincarnation, karma, and "coming to Now." These skills established Manson as a guru among the drugged-out hippies in Haight-Ashbury. A master at mind games, Manson sometimes compared himself to Christ. He also used sex and LSD as recruiting tools. Manson soon attracted a large following of mostly young female runaways, a number of whom joined him when he left San Francisco to roam about in a Volkswagen van, like so many flower children of that era.

The growing Manson Family wound up in the Los Angeles area. In the spring of 1968, recently divorced Beach Boy Dennis Wilson spotted two of the girls thumbing for a ride in Malibu. The next time he saw them hitchhiking, he invited them to his Sunset Boulevard home. That same night when Wilson returned late from a recording session, to his surprise, a stranger named Charles Manson had moved in with his whole following. Manson fawned over Wilson, and he let them all stay. For months, Wilson found Manson intriguing company as both talked about music, sang, and enjoyed the slavish housekeeping and sexual services of Manson's women followers.

Wilson thought Manson's work had a fresh, spontaneous quality and suggested that the Beach Boys might themselves record his song "Cease to Exist." As far as Manson's own potential for stardom was concerned, Wilson privately thought, "Charlie never had a musical bone in his body."[2] Still, Wilson fell under Manson's spell; he spent $100,000 paying for expenses of the Manson Family over the next several months, including what Wilson called "probably the largest gonorrhea bill in history."[3] Wilson also rented a studio where Manson made a demo of his music. Wilson then promoted Manson to friends in the entertainment industry. One of them owned the house later rented to director Roman Polanski and his ill-fated wife, actress Sharon Tate.

By the end of August 1968, Wilson had long since tired of the moochers who took his money, borrowed all his clothes, and wrecked his car. He had come to understand more why the other Beach Boys considered Manson an unappealing "scruffy little guru."[4] Wilson moved out of his own home and asked his manager to get rid of the Manson Family. The Family then set up a new base on a movie ranch near Topanga Canyon. Manson began focusing increasingly on expected uprisings by black militants.

In November 1968, Manson and his Family established a second home in the desert. He had read the Book of Revelation in the Bible and considered himself the fifth angel, who would be given a key to the pit of an abyss. Manson interpreted that to mean a cave somewhere in Death Valley. Manson was also fascinated by the Beatles. When they issued their White Album in December 1968—which contained two songs on revolution—Manson considered it a sign that the Beatles were making references to the apocalyptic race war he himself foresaw. He believed that the Beatles left special clues in the song "Helter Skelter." Manson planned to produce his own album that would surpass the powerful Beatles recording; it would contain subliminal messages impelling listeners to start the coming race war.

Manson possessed the simplistic perspective of a man who had spent the better part of his life behind bars with vicious racial gangs. He assumed that whites would divide into two factions—racists and non-racists—and black militants would stay united and prevail. Meanwhile, Manson and his followers would wait out the war, hiding in an underground city in their cave in Death Valley, from which the Family would eventually emerge to control the country when the victorious blacks proved incapable of governing. In reality, black militants were no more united than whites. On January 17, 1969, the Black Panthers hit the headlines as murder targets of US, the rivals the Panthers dubbed "United Slaves." Two leaders of the Los Angeles Black Panthers, John Huggins and "Bunchy" Carter, were gunned down by a pair of hitmen from US just as the two Panthers emerged from a meeting of the Black Student Union on the UCLA campus. Bunchy Carter had founded the Panthers' Southern California branch office. Several years later a Senate investigation committee uncovered damning internal FBI memos that the slayings had been instigated by the FBI's Los Angeles office of COINTELPRO at the specific behest of J. Edgar Hoover.[5]

That spring of 1969, Manson could see society in turmoil all around him with all the student strikes and anti-government violence perpetrated by militant activists. By June of 1969 Manson became impatient for a major racial uprising and told the Family they might have to show blacks how to start "Helter Skelter." Manson then began identifying celebrities they might viciously murder in wealthy areas around Los Angeles and leave clues in blood— like a clenched fist symbol or the word "PIG"—that pointed to the Black Panthers as the perpetrators. One of his followers would later brag to a fellow inmate that the named targets included pop singer Tom Jones, Elizabeth Taylor, Richard Burton, Steve McQueen, and Frank Sinatra. This hit list of superstars eventually leaked to the press and was published to an astonished public toward the end of the Manson trial.

Manson assumed that these hate crimes would induce mass paranoia and start whites on a rampage "shooting black people like crazy." These new victims would be assimilated blacks, while "the true black race" of Black Panthers or Black Muslims would conceal themselves and wait for their own opportunity to avenge the bloodshed. The black militants would, Manson believed, find allies among radical and liberal whites offended by the prior senseless slaughter of African-Americans. Manson and his followers planned to wait out this civil war in hiding and then take over, as he had first envisioned the prior fall.[6]

Lanky twenty-three-year-old Charles "Tex" Watson had joined the Manson Family at Dennis Wilson's home the year before. Manson deputized Watson to raise the money needed to wait out the war. When Watson tried to con funds out of an African-American drug dealer named Bernard "Lotsapoppa" Crowe, the effort backfired. Crowe threatened the lives of the entire Manson Family. Manson then took matters into his own hands and, on July 1, 1969, showed up at Crowe's Hollywood apartment, shot Crowe, and left him for dead. When the next day's news reported the death of an unidentified Los Angeles Black Panther, Manson figured that had to be Crowe. Crowe was neither a Black Panther nor was he dead, but hospitalized in critical condition with a bullet lodged next to his spine. When questioned by police, Crowe claimed he did not recognize his attacker.

Manson meanwhile prepared his ranch for a siege and awaited retaliation from the Panthers. His friend Watson believed, as Manson did, that they had just triggered the apocalypse: "If we'd needed any more proof that Helter Skelter was coming down very soon, this was it, blackie was trying to get at the chosen ones."[7] Three weeks later, Manson sent three other Family members to rob a music teacher acquaintance named Gary Hinman, who had just inherited some money. Hinman was taken hostage. Manson arrived, slashed Hinman's ear, and departed while one of his followers stabbed Hinman to death and left behind misleading clues, including "Political piggy" and a bloody clenched fist mark on the wall. A member of the motorcycle gang the Straight Satans later told police, "They had cut some fucking idiot's ear off and wrote on the wall and put the Panthers' hand or paw up there to blame the Panthers. Everything they did, they blamed on the niggers, see. They hate niggers because they had killed a nigger prior to that."[8] But that revelation came several months afterward. In the meantime, this crime remained unsolved in the domain of the Los Angeles County Sheriff's Office.

On August 8, 1969, Manson directed three women followers—later described by one veteran reporter as "a trio of freaked out acidheads"[9] —to make a bolder move to precipitate "Helter Skelter." Just after midnight they infiltrated the Bel Air home of director Roman Polanski and savagely murdered five people gathered at a party, including Polanski's wife Sharon Tate, who was then eight months pregnant. Her body was left hanging from the rafters. Two other victims were tied with cord. Four suffered more than a hundred stab wounds; the fifth was killed with a gun. The word "PIG" was spelled in Tate's blood on the front door. When the women arrived back at the cult's base, Manson berated them for the sloppy way the murders were handled.

Contrary to Manson's expectation, when the police responded the next morning to the call by the Polanskis' horrified housekeeper, the officers did not assume the bizarre killings were the product of race hatred. With little to go on but some drugs found on the premises, the LAPD developed five working hypotheses: a drug party in which one participant freaked out and killed the others; a drug delivery that erupted in violence over bad drugs or nonpayment; a drug dealer who murdered his buyers to keep both their money and the drugs; a violent burglary; or a hired killer who murdered all the witnesses as well as the intended victim.[10]

The first person the LAPD questioned was a houseboy still on the grounds, who had somehow survived the bloodbath unscathed. He was still being questioned the next night when Manson went with six of his followers to set up another home invasion to reinforce his message. After abandoning several other possible targets, Manson led the Family members to the Los Feliz home of forty-four-year-old supermarket chain owner Leno LaBianca and his thirty-eight-year old wife Rosemary. The LaBiancas had the misfortune of living next to a house where the Manson Family had attended a party the year before. Manson tied up the couple and left his followers to cover their heads with pillow cases and stab them to death. When police arrived, they saw "DEATH TO PIGS" and "RISE" printed in blood on the living room walls. On the refrigerator was printed "HEALTER SKELTER" [sic]. Police at first saw no connection between this ritual crime and the Tate murders. They were busy following up on leads that two of the five victims at the Tate house had been taking mescaline for several days at the time of their death and remained in the midst of that hallucinogenic drug trip when they died. The police were also trying to track down a pair of eyeglasses found at the Tate home, an approach that had famously solved the Leopold and Loeb case decades before.

An all-points bulletin went out for a friend of one of the Tate victims, who proved to have an alibi. Three other potential suspects were confirmed to have been outside the state of California the night of the killings. As the cases remained unsolved, Manson could take some comfort from the fact that word somehow leaked out to the media that "DEATH TO PIGS" and "PIG" had been written at both murder sites. Much as he hoped, the randomness of the murders and the gruesome details of each home invasion engendered a state of panic in Southern California. People in Beverly Hills bought record numbers of guns and new door locks. They raced to obtain more private security services and guard dogs. They speculated like crazy on the intended victims and the perpetrators. Even *The Los Angeles Times* pointed out coincidences drawn from fiction: Tate had been promoted by her Hollywood studio for playing a movie role of a girl seemingly "possessed of mysterious powers"; her husband had directed several spooky movies, including the 1968 chiller *Rosemary's Baby.*[11] Anyone who had seen the macabre film knew that the heroine gives birth to the devil's child.

The police considered all kinds of theories behind both crimes. One of the victims, hair stylist Jay Sebring, had been Tate's boyfriend before she married Polanski. The LAPD discovered that Sebring had a history of tying up women he dated before they had sex. Was the August 9 party a sadomasochistic orgy gone awry? Had the Mafia executed the La Bianca hit and disguised it with knifings that made the killings look unprofessional?

Meanwhile, Manson thought he could get more money out of Dennis Wilson. The Beach Boys had decided to use the basic melody from Manson's song "Cease to Exist" on their album *20/20.* It came out in late 1968 with slight variations in the music and the lyrics under the title "Never Learn Not to Love." The album cover credited only Dennis Wilson for the song. Word had it that Manson was most upset about the lyrics being altered, diffusing the power of his message. After the Tate and LaBianca murders, Manson showed up at Dennis Wilson's house and demanded $1500 he said that the cult needed for life in the desert. Manson threatened that Wilson might never see his seven-year-old son again if Wilson did not pay. Shortly after his chilling visit to Wilson, Manson handed Wilson's close friend, talent scout Gregg Jakobsen, a bullet to give Wilson with a message that "there are more where this came from." Jakobsen knew that Wilson was already upset and did not pass the message on, concerned himself about the disturbing change in Manson: "The electricity was almost pouring out of him. His hair was on end. His eyes were wild . . . he was just like an animal in a cage."[12]

From the dates of the ritual killings in early August through September of 1969, the LAPD exhausted numerous leads without any progress, interviewing over three hundred people. Yet they failed to follow up on what turned out to be the Tate murder gun, which a ten-year-old found on September 1, 1969, discarded in the bushes of his yard. Not until mid-October did it occur to someone on the LAPD investigative team to contact the local sheriff's office just a few blocks away to see if they had any unsolved crimes of a similar nature. That was when they first learned of the Hinman murder.

By October 15, Manson had actually been jailed for three days on charges of grand theft following an Inyo County raid of the Manson Family quarters in Death Valley. During the raid, two girls who had just run away from the cult sought police protection, telling officers they were afraid for their lives. The police had already been interested in talking to one of them, Kitty Lutesinger, because she was the girlfriend of the prime suspect in the Hinman murder. Though investigators at the sheriff's office assumed all three murder cases were linked, their rivals in the LAPD still saw little connection between the Hinman murder and the Tate and La Bianca cases. The LAPD waited another week and a half before interviewing Lutesinger. That interview and surprising revelations from an arrested biker acquainted with Manson led to several bizarre confessions implicating Manson not only in the sensational crimes under investigation, but in yet another murder, that of a Spahn Ranch hand named Donald "Shorty" Shea. Police heard that Manson had ordered Shea dismembered because he knew too much about the cult's criminal activities. In fact, Manson had bragged of committing thirty-five murders.

Police arrested Manson, Tex Watson, and two other Family members in December 1969 on seven counts of murder in the Tate and La Bianca cases and one joint count of conspiracy. While imprisoned, Manson continued to have a cult following. A Movement reporter interviewed Manson in jail prior to trial and asked if he considered himself a political prisoner like Huey Newton. Manson had no idea what the interviewer meant. He responded, "Who's he?"[13]

The trial began on July 24, 1970, amid extraordinary media attention. Security was high because of death threats. This latest "trial of the century" would prove exceedingly difficult for prosecutor Vincent Bugliosi, in large part because Manson had taken no direct role in the ritual killings. The prosecutor's star witness was Linda Kasabian, one of the trio involved in the Tate killings. In exchange for her testimony, she had received immunity. Her two companions went on trial for their lives along with Manson. Still obviously under his influence, the women admitted their role in the killings, but claimed they had acted on their own. On the first day of testimony, Manson showed up with an X cut into his forehead. His followers in the courtroom soon followed suit, including his women co-defendants. Manson later converted the X to a Swastika. From day one, the trial attracted so much attention, President Nixon took time at a press conference to deride its constant appearance on the front pages of newspapers and evening news as if Manson were some "glamorous figure." Though a lawyer who should have known better, Nixon described Manson as "a man who was guilty directly or indirectly, of eight murders." The jury had been sequestered and did not see the media uproar Nixon's remark generated. Determined to make an issue of it, Manson himself held a local paper with the headline "MANSON GUILTY, NIXON DECLARES" up to the jury. When polled all the jurors and alternates swore that the President's opinion made no difference to them; they would make their decision only on the evidence. The defense motion for mistrial was denied.[14]

The trial and sentencing of Manson dragged on for ten months, prolonged by witness intimidation and repeated disruptions, including an attempt by Manson to physically assault the judge. The judge then started carrying a revolver under his robes. On November 30, 1970, defense lawyer Ronald Hughes disappeared and was later found drowned. The case set a record as the longest and costliest trial to date in American history (though the record was soon surpassed). Manson and his three co-defendants were found guilty and sentenced to death, only to have their sentences converted to life in prison when the California Supreme Court overturned the state's death penalty in 1972.

Prosecutor Bugliosi co-authored the best seller *Helter Skelter: The True Story of the Manson Murders* which, in turn, spawned two movies about the bizarre cult. The killings also inspired several plays, an opera—*The Manson Family*—and a musical, *Assassins.* Manson's recorded songs with Family members were released in an album. Some were popularized by other recording artists, most notably Guns 'n Roses and Marilyn Manson, who adopted that last name to honor the songwriter.

In September 1975, Lynette "Squeaky" Fromme, as head of the Family in Manson's absence, made headlines when she attempted to assassinate President Gerald Ford on a visit to Sacramento, California. (Apparently Fromme's motive was to impress Manson, who was imprisoned close by). Fromme received a life sentence and won release on parole in August 2009. Meanwhile, Manson's cult following continued to increase while he remained in prison. In 1988 Geraldo Rivera interviewed Manson behind bars. The convicted murderer used the opportunity to issue more chilling threats: "I'm going to chop up more of you motherfuckers. I'm going to kill as many of you as I can. I'm going to pile you up to the sky."[15] Not surprisingly, every time he came up for parole, it was denied. Manson is scheduled for his twelfth opportunity when he turns 77. Through the Internet, Manson has fascinated an entire new generation of music groupies. Manson tee shirts in several styles—including one with Manson dressed as Che—remain popular today. Those interested can join his fan club and collect other memorabilia. Over the past three decades, Manson received more mail than any other inmate in the United States, averaging four letters per day. He got the recognition he always coveted.

4. TRIPLE JEOPARDY—BLACK, FEMALE, AND COMMUNIST

Angela Davis is a woman; she is black; she has espoused an unpopular cause. . . . Because of NOW's commitment to ***equal rights for all,*** *we call on the courts of this country to guarantee Angela Davis a fair and just trial as is her right under the Constitution of the United States.*

Statement of Support Unanimously Adopted by the Board of Directors, National Organization for Women, Jan. 16, 1971 (emphasis in original)[1]

It was obvious why San Quentin inmate Ruchell Magee faced the death penalty if convicted of killing Judge Haley at the Marin Civic Center. Even if he had only seized the chance for freedom on the spur of the moment, the armed escape attempt had occurred in broad daylight before many witnesses. At the time, the seventh-grade dropout had already been serving an indeterminate sentence of one year to life imposed as his second felony offense when he was 24 for a $10 marijuana buy that ended with guns drawn. (He first went to prison before he turned seventeen, to serve six years in the infamous Louisiana State Penitentiary at Angola ("the Alcatraz of the South") for attempted rape of a white woman, a crime he denied committing.) Whatever chance Magee had to leave prison alive would evaporate if the new charges were proved. For safety, Magee's arraignment hearing in September 1970 took place in a makeshift courtroom at San Quentin prison. The local papers reported that, when guards dragged the scrawny thirty-one-year-old inmate into court, he complained loudly of mistreatment and shouted, "Power to the People" and "Death to the Pigs."[2] Magee's repeated interruptions of the judge, echoed by fifty rowdy, mostly white, spectators, forced a postponement of the hearing. At the same time, the media speculated that Angela Davis was headed for Algiers, where Eldridge Cleaver had just opened the first Panther office overseas. But after the FBI tracked Davis down in New York and extradited her to California, Magee became "the other defendant," not the primary target. He claimed that the state tried to offer him a deal to save his life if he implicated Angela Davis, but he only proclaimed her innocence more loudly, together with his own.[3]

The charges against Magee's co-defendant Angela Davis presented a much more difficult case. The Communist activist was not present at the scene of the crime, but prosecuted as a co-conspirator whose guilt had to be proved by circumstantial evidence beyond a reasonable doubt. The prosecutor was expected to rely on the fact Davis fled the state as strong evidence of her guilt. President Nixon did not help matters any when, upon her capture, he used a nationally televised signing of a new federal Omnibus Crime Control Act to praise the FBI for apprehending a "dangerous terrorist." Having learned nothing from the uproar over his pretrial comments condemning Charles Manson, he added, "it should be a warning to those who engage in these acts that they eventually are going to be apprehended." Seventeen members of the British Parliament signed a joint letter of concern. Nixon not only had to apologize for his comment, he invited fourteen Russian dignitaries to attend the upcoming trial to ascertain its fairness for themselves.[4]

In the summer of 1970, California Attorney General Thomas Lynch (a Gov. Pat Brown hold-over) specially assigned Assistant Attorney General Albert Harris to the case along with one of the Department's top young legal scholars, Deputy Attorney General Clifford Thompson, and two other assistants. Then forty-one, Harris lived in Marin County with his wife and children. He had graduated second in his class at U.C. Berkeley's Boalt Hall Law School in 1954 and had an excellent track record. Solidly built with a ruddy complexion, the bespectacled Harris had a disarming, unsophisticated manner. Usually stoic, the graying

Democrat got used to being hissed by Davis supporters when he opposed her motions. After one instance, he turned and gave the audience a clenched fist black power salute in response. The gesture earned him a surprised smattering of applause.

Harris was both the head of the San Francisco Criminal Division and responsible for prosecuting organized crime statewide. He had extensive experience in high profile cases, including a number of arguments before the United States Supreme Court. Many reporters covering the Davis trial had watched Harris win another "trial of the century" in 1967: the headline-grabbing prosecution of a suspended Los Angeles deputy district attorney, Jack Kirschke, based on circumstantial evidence that Kirschke killed his wife and her lover. Kirschke was now serving life in prison, pursuing appeals proclaiming his innocence.

Harris believed the state also had sufficient evidence to prosecute Angela Davis, some of which was public and some not yet. No one could challenge Angela Davis's dedication to freeing the Soledad Brothers; that Davis had spent a lot of time recently with Jonathan Jackson and his family focused on George Jackson's plight; or that four of her guns and ammunition were used in the kidnap attempt. Nor could anyone dispute her exchange of passionate love letters with George Jackson or her presence at the San Francisco International Airport on the afternoon of the kidnapping, where the government was convinced that the plotters anticipated hijacking an airplane. Several prosecution witnesses were prepared to identify Davis as the woman with an Afro they saw with Jonathan Jackson earlier that week, either spotted at San Quentin prison when Jonathan visited his brother or in the now infamous yellow Hertz van at a gas station near the Marin Civic Center. Her flight from the state after the plot went awry appeared to be strong evidence of her guilt.

Angela Davis's defenders were even more adamant that the prosecution was unwarranted. They pointed to the first count of the indictment, which charged as evidence of criminal conspiracy Davis's appearance as a speaker at a rally for the Soledad Brothers. Wasn't this obvious persecution for simply exercising her First Amendment right to speak out against racism in the penal system? They asserted that the other acts alleged were equally innocent: Davis purchased the guns in her own name for self-protection following death threats; her love of George Jackson was no proof she had done anything illegal on his behalf; there was no evidence that she had given the weapons to Jonathan or knew of his plans to invade the Marin Civic Center; she took a routine commuter flight back to Los Angeles; and only fled the state after she learned of the bloodbath because she expected to be railroaded for a crime she knew nothing about.

After all the invective directed at the young Communist from the President, the governor, and the head of the FBI, many people recalled Yale President Kingman Brewster's comment as Bobby Seale faced murder charges in New Haven: Where in America could Angela Davis expect to be afforded a fair trial? Angela's younger sister Fania Davis Jordan traveled widely as co-chair of the National United Committee to Free Angela Davis and All Political Prisoners ("NUCFAD"). Jordan helped organize hundreds of volunteer committees in the United States and overseas to rally for her sister's cause. Many thousands of sympathizers sported "Free Angela" buttons or tee shirts and plastered posters on their walls voicing their outrage at the Marxist lecturer's expected execution. The extraordinary outpouring of support mirrored that for Ethel Rosenberg two decades before and for a similar reason—fear that she would be martyred for her Communist beliefs.

The American Communist Party made the defense of Angela Davis their highest priority. On its own letterhead, NUCFAD added to the famous names of civil rights leaders, folk singers, and Hollywood celebrities Fay Stender had rallied to the Soledad Brothers' cause from a list she had obtained from the Chicago Seven defense team, which in turn had gotten the basic list from Dr. Spock. Entertainers like Sammy Davis, Jr., Roberta Flack, and Aretha Franklin headlined fund-raisers. Shortly after Angela Davis was extradited to California from New York, the Rolling Stones released "Sweet Black Angel," later included in their acclaimed album *Exile on Main Street*:

> Got a pin up girl, Got a sweet black angel, Up upon my wall. Well, she ain't no singer, and she ain't no star, but she sure talk good, and she move so fast. But the gal in danger. Yeah de gal in chains, but she keep on pushin', would you take her place? She countin' up de

> minutes, she countin' up de days. . . She's a sweet black angel, not a gun toting teacher, not a Red lovin' school marm; ain't someone gonna free her, free de sweet black slave, free de sweet black slave.[5]

Soon modern jazz enthusiasts were listening to Todd "Bayete" Cochran's new release, "Free Angela (Thoughts . . . and all I've got to say)." NUCFAD took a page from organized labor's aggressive public relations campaign in 1911 on behalf of the McNamara Brothers and quickly arranged for wide release on campuses and select theaters of a film that had been completed by one of her UCLA students well before Davis fled underground: *Angela—Portrait of a Revolutionary*.

When Angela Davis was arrested, the women's rights movement was also in full swing. As part of its mission, the five-year-old National Organization for Women added its voice in early 1971 in support of a fair trial for Angela Davis. Also in the news was Representative Shirley Chisholm from New York. In January of 1972, the very first African-American woman elected to Congress would become the first of both her race and her gender to enter Democratic presidential primaries in a quixotic, grassroots anti-war campaign as a "candidate of the people."[6] By the spring of 1972, forty-nine years after the Equal Rights Amendment was first introduced, feminists would finally convince both houses of Congress to send the proposed amendment to the states for ratification (it would ultimately fall three states short of the three-quarters needed).

As women's rights were being championed all around her, Davis received an elaborate defense provided in large part through extensive fund-raising by the Communist Party. The United Presbyterian Church endured extraordinary criticism from members of its congregations and outsiders alike when its Council on Church and Race contributed $10,000 "to ensure [Miss Davis] receives a fair and just trial."[7] A *New York Times* reporter described her legal team as "the best-organized, most broad-based defense effort in the recent history of radical political trials—more potent than that afforded to any of the Panther leaders or the Chicago Seven."[8]

John Abt, General Counsel for the Communist Party USA, represented Angela in the first round of court battles fighting her extradition from New York. Her former colleague from UCLA, Mike Tigar, who had represented Angela in challenging her firing by the U.C. Regents, collaborated on an early motion in her California criminal proceedings. (Ironically, it pitted the brilliant young Leftist attorney against his Boalt Hall classmate and old moot court partner Cliff Thompson.) But Davis had decided to do things differently from Huey Newton and the Soledad Brothers. She wanted her lead counsel to be black. While still jailed in New York, she had decided upon Howard Moore, the Atlanta-born former General Counsel for SNCC. The veteran trial lawyer looked somewhat like a modern Frederick Douglass: he sported a goatee and counterbalanced his receding hairline with a bushy, modified Afro. Moore had clerked for a federal judge and, over his career, was associated as co-counsel on a number of successful death penalty appeals and civil rights cases before the United States Supreme Court. He moved to the Bay Area expressly to handle Angela's case. A nationwide group of black law professors headed by the Dean of Howard University Law School offered their collective talents for back-up research and analysis.

At Angela's instigation, assisting from day one was her long-time family friend, a young lawyer with the NAACP Legal Defense Fund, Margaret Burnham. Doris "Dobby" Brin Walker, a highly skilled veteran, soon joined the team to oversee review of the daunting warehouse of potential evidence amassed from the crime scene and by police and FBI searches of Angela's apartment, the Soledad Brothers Defense Committee San Francisco headquarters, the apartment where the Che-LuMumba Club met in Los Angeles, and other locations. Walker was Bob Treuhaft's partner and a proud Communist who had participated in high profile civil rights cases dating back to the internationally publicized appeal of Mississippi truck driver Willie McGee's rape conviction. In the 1940s, the Texas-born Boalt Hall law school graduate (the only woman in the Class of 1942) had been married to African-American lawyer George Walker. In 1970, when police arrested Davis, Dobby Walker was the spokesperson for the National Lawyers Guild as its first woman president. The Guild itself strongly supported Davis as the latest in a long line of vilified defendants on whose behalf it had lobbied for more than three decades.

Magee and Davis started out jointly prosecuted in the same landmark facility where the fatal kidnapping had occurred. The Frank Lloyd Wright–designed building had since been enhanced with half a million dollars worth of security per year. The county installed a bulletproof glass wall to separate spectators from participants and placed extra male and female police on duty outside the courtroom for controversial strip searches of all attendees. When the two heavily guarded maximum security prisoners appeared at their first joint hearing in the Marin County courthouse on January 5, 1971, the kidnap/murder case was already a media magnet. Over the objection of prosecutor Albert Harris, the presiding judge allowed Angela Davis to make a statement. Davis dramatically declared her innocence of all charges and accused the state of a frame-up. The judge had already issued a gag order preventing both sides' lawyers from talking to the press about the case in the hope that would avoid the media circus that had occurred in the Chicago Seven case.

Finding a trial judge was not easy. Magee acted up in court and rejected all court-appointed lawyers (including top-rated African-American criminal defense lawyers Clinton White and Boalt Hall law professor Henry Ramsey). Magee had trained himself over the years as a jailhouse lawyer (when the Supreme Court issued its 1966 landmark "duty to warn" decision in *Miranda v. Arizona*, Magee had his own petition pending at the high court on the same issue). Yet in the Marin proceeding, Magee was repeatedly declared incompetent to represent himself. Delays also occurred as Magee unsuccessfully sought to remove the case to federal court so he could challenge the constitutionality of his original conviction. The Davis team strongly preferred to stay in state court—albeit in a different county—and grew increasingly impatient over the time it took to schedule a bail hearing as one assigned state court judge after another bowed out voluntarily or was removed for cause. Each defendant was also allowed one judicial challenge without stating a reason, and Magee used his on the sixth judge, Republican Alan Lindsay from Oakland.

Ultimately, Democrat Richard Earl Arnason in Contra Costa County accepted Chief Justice Wright's appointment and survived Magee's latest challenge for cause. The new assignment brought the conscientious trial judge his longest and highest profile case to date (though he later presided over other headline murder cases in his lengthy career that he felt matched the intense media spotlight of the Davis trial). Judge Arnason told the Chief Justice he had a robbery trial he wanted to complete first and had just two other requests: that he be provided an allowance to offer donuts and croissants and coffee to the lawyers each morning to facilitate a collegial atmosphere over the lengthy trial; and that he be assigned a law clerk to sift through the voluminous filings. Justice Wright agreed to both, but never delivered a law clerk.

Raised as the eldest of nine on a North Dakota farm, the fifty-year-old Arnason had long been used to hard work, but not the grueling sixteen hour days he routinely put in his first few months on the Davis pretrial proceedings. The hellish task came with extraordinary scrutiny and ubiquitous second-guessing. One Contra Costa County acquaintance saw Judge Arnason on the street not long after his appointment and called out, "Be sure you kill her." He ignored that piece of advice and soon stopped reading all the threats he received on his own life, mostly from people who hated Communists. As a precaution, the local sheriff had a patrol car swing regularly by the rural area where Judge Arnason lived. Each court day, an unmarked sheriff's car would arrive to take the judge back and forth on his lengthy commute to court.

By the early fall of 1971, NUCFAD published an anthology of writings edited by Angela Davis condemning the prison system and her own political prosecution as well as that of other black radicals—*If They Come in the Morning: Voices of Resistance.* Angela dedicated the unabashed defense of black militants to "all who have fallen in the liberation struggle," linking Jonathan Jackson and the inmates who died with him to Fred Hampton and "lil' Bobby Hutton." She elevated her recently felled lover George Jackson above all others as a symbol of fierce resistance who "lives on, an example and inspiration for us all."[9] The book included her biography and articles by her attorneys and committee chairs on various aspects of the pretrial proceedings and defense campaign for both herself and Ruchell Magee, including why they wanted to represent themselves (in her case as co-counsel).

Other parts of the book were devoted to the Panthers, whom Davis praised for greatly reducing police brutality through their patrols of Oakland's black community. Davis prefaced an article written in prison by Huey Newton with a description of the Panther Minister of Defense as "a radiant leader, a bold fighter, a hero" who was jailed for nearly three years despite his "manifest innocence"[10] on charges of murdering an officer. She included prison messages from recently freed Ericka Huggins and Bobby Seale and an essay describing the relentless government campaign since 1967 to destroy the Panther Party nationwide. Hundreds of thousands of paperback copies quickly disappeared off the shelves. Prosecutor Harris argued that the movie and book violated the court's prior gag order. He angrily pointed to the chapter written by Howard Moore as her chief counsel, which started out "Angela Davis had nothing whatsoever to do with the Slave Insurrection of August 7, 1970, the so-called shootout at the Courthouse in Marin County, California."[11] The controversy only increased public interest in the prisoner who was defending her ideology at the risk of death. Becoming a government target elevated Davis to cult status as another Movement celebrity like Huey Newton and George Jackson—yet another example of the great divide then separating a high percentage of those under thirty from their parents' generation.

By the time the book was published, Davis's team of nearly a dozen attorneys had already convinced Judge Arnason to sever her case for trial from Magee's. Her request made excellent sense from a legal standpoint. Not being present at the crime scene, she had a far better chance of acquittal if tried separately from the volatile inmate accused of pulling the trigger that blew off half of Judge Haley's head. She now pushed for a change of venue from Marin County, where Gary Thomas, the prosecutor wounded in the August 1970 escape attempt, had just been named Peace Officer of the Year. Her love of George Jackson and closeness to Jonathan also militated against trial in Marin County. No one could realistically expect its residents to be unbiased by the enormous publicity surrounding the most recent bloodbath in which George Jackson was killed, just a year after his brother. But from a Leftist perspective it was tricky for Davis to reconcile distancing herself and her stellar legal team from Magee while at the same time touting her complete identification with his cause as a fellow political prisoner.

Unlike the Soledad Brothers, Davis did not get her first choice of

San Francisco as her new trial venue, or even her second and third choices. Either Oakland or Los Angeles was acceptable, but over her attorneys' repeated objections, Judge Arnason instead ordered her case to proceed in Santa Clara County. The legal team pointed out that the South Bay county's population was more than three-quarters white. It did include eighteen percent, mostly low-income Chicanos, but less than two percent each of Asians and blacks. For a six month trial, as this was then estimated to take, the few minority members of the jury pool were expected to be excused for economic hardship or dismissed for other reasons, thus depriving Davis of peers who, as a group, were less than half as likely to support the death penalty as whites. The prosecutor had previously noted that Marin County, where the crime occurred, had a similarly small percentage of black voters in its population.

The Davis defense team decided to invest in an innovative tool: professional jury consultants. Now relatively commonplace for wealthy litigants, these non-lawyer consultants use social science techniques—like those of the volunteer sociology professors Fay Stender had consulted in preparation for the *voir dire* in the Newton trial—to help strategize on profiles for the most sympathetic jurors and the best way to package and sell their client to those jurors. (Sometimes these days, in high stakes cases, they even help the lawyers stage mock trials with simulated juries to provide vital pretrial feedback.) Though Charles Garry had trusted more to his instincts than to the elaborate questionnaire developed by Fay Stender and her team of consultants, soon other defense teams embraced scientific jury selection, starting with the third highly politicized trial of anti-war activist Father Philip Berrigan and his co-defendants, known as "the Harrisburg Seven."[12]

While the priest was imprisoned for his "Catonsville Nine" conviction, he was accused of smuggling out correspondence furthering a conspiracy to bomb steam tunnels, destroy more draft records, and kidnap then National Security Advisor Henry Kissinger. Because the venue was a well-known conservative enclave, volunteer social scientists polled residents and conducted extensive interviews to produce a demographic profile of persons most likely to sympathize with the anti-war movement. The results helped the defendants' chief counsel, former Attorney General

Ramsey Clark, produce a hung jury—a major setback for the Nixon administration in prosecuting Vietnam War protesters. The use of similar techniques in the *Davis* pretrial preparation produced some surprising findings. Her team initially assumed that Angela Davis could only expect to be treated fairly by peer groups of blacks, Chicanos, and the poor. In Santa Clara County, the Communist educator was viewed much more favorably by upper income residents.

The highest profile lawyer on the Davis defense team was added just a couple of months before trial. The addition was deemed necessary even though Judge Arnason denied the team's request to have the state foot the bill for the costs of defense. Leo Branton, Jr., a former radio announcer, actor, and producer, had represented accused Communists during the McCarthy Era and more recently defended Black Panthers. The handsome fifty-year-old fit his description as the "personification of both Black Hollywood and Perry Mason."[13] Branton exhibited great respect for Harris as a worthy adversary, winning appreciation from Judge Arnason for diminishing the tension that had previously arisen at times between the two sides. Branton's only complaint about the use of closed circuit television arose from vanity: it made him realize how big his bald spot was.

Judge Arnason later said that he could tell right away that Branton was an experienced trial lawyer like Moore, not a paper filer like almost everyone else on Davis's team, and Cliff Thompson at the prosecution table. Judge Arnason was of the old school. In later years, he would greatly admire Archie Robinson, the state's most famous civil trial lawyer, with a thousand cases under his belt. Robinson never spent a lot of time on *voir dire.* He said the most important thing he could do for his client was to get the jury to feel comfortable with him as an honest advocate, then get on with trying the case. The judge was aware of studies backing up the notion that most jurors formed early impressions of which lawyers they liked, got impatient with long opening statements, and paid even less heed to closing statements. Branton evinced similar instincts. His charming courtroom manners made his occasional displays of righteous indignation on his client's behalf all the more effective. His empathy for victims of injustice was kindled by memories of being jailed as a teenager in the South on charges that were later dropped for defending himself when hit by a white man. More painful still was the recollection of putting his life at risk in a segregated unit in World War II and then being refused a seat at a Texas mess hall that had no problem serving white prisoners of war.

Besides partitioned courtrooms, another change had occurred since the 1968 Huey Newton trial and the 1970 George Jackson pretrial proceedings in Salinas. Within months after Judge Campbell first proposed an emergency ordinance to the Salinas City Council to keep unruly crowds from gathering at trial, California legislators enacted a new statewide prohibition on courthouse picketing. It was modeled after a Louisiana law the United States Supreme Court had upheld against constitutional challenge in 1965. Effective in time for the relocated Soledad Brothers trial in San Francisco in late 1971, the statute outlawed parading or picketing near a courthouse "with the intent to interfere with, obstruct, or impede the administration of justice or with the intent to influence any judge, juror, witness, or officer of the court in the discharge of his duty."[14] On two occasions during pretrial proceedings in San Jose, Davis demonstrators, including her sister Fania, would test that law by picketing around the courthouse. They were arrested and convicted of misdemeanors but released without any jail sentences. A compromise was later reached, with the sheriff permitting rallies at a nearby lot.

Davis stayed in a Palo Alto jail as its far and away most famous prisoner as San Jose built a new, temporary, highly secure courthouse just for this proceeding. Meanwhile, the United States Supreme Court and the California Supreme Court both had before them serious constitutional challenges to the way the death penalty was imposed in some cases and not others. National support for the death penalty had reached a low of 42 percent in 1966, but by the spring of 1972 it was favored by half of men and 41 percent of women. [15] In California, since World War II, repeated legislative proposals to abolish the death penalty had all been defeated. After years of international lobbying to save death-row author Caryl Chessman from execution, on March 2, 1960, Gov. Pat Brown sent an urgent message calling for a special session of the Legislature to abolish the death penalty. In the meantime, Brown granted a two-month delay of Chessman's execution date. The governor explained that he did not act out of sympathy, but fairness after realizing that the death penalty was "primarily inflicted upon the weak, the poor, the ignorant, and against racial minorities."[16] Statistics then demonstrated that more than half of all those executed from 1930 to 1960 were Negro, though critics claimed that no showing had been made that Negroes as a race had a more violent temperament.[17] In mid-February 1972 the California Supreme Court issued its ground-breaking ruling in *People v. Anderson.* The high court vacated Robert Page Anderson's third scheduled execution date for a 1965 robbery and gun battle in San Diego. With one lone dissent, the California tribunal declared the death penalty unconstitutional under state law as cruel or unusual. Writing for a nearly unanimous court, Republican Chief Justice Donald Wright noted that imposition of the death penalty had steadily declined since the mid-1930s, and no one at all had been executed nationwide in the past four years. He appended to his opinion a chart prepared by the defense showing that more than forty countries had already abolished the death penalty.[18]

Both harsh criticism and enthusiastic support for the decision were quick to surface. Gov. Reagan—who had just elevated Wright to Chief Justice two years earlier—called the decision a "mockery of the constitutional process."[19] Anderson's lawyers pointed out the ruling could save the state up to a $100 million dollars in costs associated with litigating the death penalty. (A recent law school study shows that since California reinstituted the death penalty in 1978, it has cost taxpayers more than $4 billion, at a *yearly* rate of $184 million.)[20] As Reagan's newly appointed Attorney General, Evelle Younger immediately sought to reverse the ruling. At the same time, in an extraordinary show of disrespect for their own high court, two conservative colleagues of Judge Arnason on the Contra Costa County bench sent a letter to newspaper editors calling the *Anderson* decision "an outrageous display of judicial arrogance" and "a Magna Carta for Murderers."[21]

In the summer of 1971, with the aid of constitutional scholar Anthony Amsterdam, Angela Davis's attorneys had vigorously pursued her release on bail. Prof. Amsterdam was the same lawyer who had successfully argued, as lead counsel, the *Anderson* death penalty appeal before the California Supreme Court. He had also furnished key constitutional arguments in pretrial proceedings in the Soledad Brothers case. NUCFAD accompanied that bail motion with hundreds of thousands of signatures in support, including among other prominent names the entire Congressional Black Caucus. The Marin County Probation Department recommended her release on $100,000 bond. Judge Arnason said that he considered Davis a good bail risk, but denied the motion because of the statute making bail unavailable in capital cases when "the proof or presumption of guilt is great."

The same day the *Anderson* ruling came down eliminating capital punishment under California law, Angela's defense team raced to set a new bail hearing before Judge Arnason in case the window of opportunity soon closed. Meanwhile, Judge Arnason himself had received stacks of letters urging him to free Angela Davis on bail. Prosecutor Harris objected on the ground that the decision was not yet final and she might be a flight risk. Judge Arnason doubted that, after deliberating so long before issuing the *Anderson* ruling, the California Supreme Court would suddenly do an about-face and reinstate the death penalty. With Davis having spent sixteen months in prison already, Judge Arnason saw no good reason for further delay. He agreed to free Davis on bail on strict conditions, including that she could not take any trips out of the Bay Area, that she could not appear at any rallies, and that she would report weekly to a probation officer.[22] On her way out of court, Davis grinned at supporters and offered a clenched fist salute. When newspapers publicized the name of a Communist sympathizer who pledged part of his Fresno ranch for Davis's $100,000 bail, he and his family immediately faced a barrage of death threats that forced them into hiding for a week.[23] As a symbolic gesture, the New York Assembly voted to urge that Judge Arnason be impeached. One of his own outspoken colleagues on the Contra Costa bench also criticized him harshly in print.

Four hundred reporters were assigned to cover the Angela Davis trial, including representatives from 133 American services, many of whom had recently covered the Manson trial. The Soviet TASS agency was the most prominent among more than thirty foreign news agencies who sent correspondents. East Germany had to make special arrangements through the White House for its reporter—at the time the Communist country had no diplomatic relations with the United States. As proceedings began, everyone seeking admission had to pass through a well-guarded gate in a specially installed cyclone fence to reach an elaborate, time-consuming security checkpoint. There they were required to provide identification, empty their pockets, pass through a metal detector, and stop to permit photographs. Anyone appearing suspicious might be subjected to far more intrusive inspection. NUCFAD activists and members of the public vied for the limited seats in the small courtroom behind several rows of reporters. Over a hundred other reporters watched the proceedings via closed circuit television hooked up in a large jury room in an adjacent building. Every detail would be reported down to the colorful shirts and bright ties favored by the judge and the stylish Italian suits worn by Branton. A *New York Times* correspondent—one of the handful of African-American journalists covering the trial—himself made news when caught with several joints' worth of marijuana stashed in a film canister.

It was widely known that Davis's jury consultants had recently conducted a poll of residents in the county. More than seventy percent said they viewed Angela Davis unfavorably.[24] At the request of the defense, based on the constitutional amendment granting eighteen-year-olds the right to vote, Judge Arnason invalidated all the jury pools in Santa Clara County that excluded anyone under twenty-one, leaving out college students almost entirely.[25] In early February, when a new Santa Clara County list of 150 potential jurors that included young voters was first released, Judge Arnason authorized a lengthy questionnaire to be sent out. Since it predated the *Anderson* decision, it included questions about the voters' views on the death penalty. In addition, NUCFAD marshaled hundreds of volunteers to comb the county for every piece of information they could gather about each person on the list. Did they live in mixed neighborhoods? Did they oppose the war? What was their party affiliation? Judge Arnason received complaints from people who felt their privacy was being invaded. The defense investigators even snapped photos of the cars they drove. The results had since been assembled into carefully guarded binders.

Two weeks into the proceedings, 71 prospective jurors had been eliminated. Though Judge Arnason required a strong showing to avoid fulfilling their civic duty, some had valid medical or other excuses; some were excused at the defense team's request for cause. To the dismay of the defense team, most young voters sought to be excused on the basis that sitting through months of trial would seriously disrupt their schooling, jeopardizing their scholarships. They could not survive that long on the $5 per day awarded for jury service. Economic hardship was the same problem long since observed with low income workers.

As the largely middle class voters were temporarily seated in the jury box, reporters focused keenly on each one being questioned as a possible decision-maker in the latest trial of the century. It was assumed that most jurors who wanted to serve would insist they could be fair. The aim of the defense was threefold: to get the judge to excuse for cause jurors they considered biased; to gauge jurors' reactions for possible peremptory challenges; and to question lightly those they hoped were biased in their favor so they might survive challenge by the other side. Prosecutor Harris elected not to ask Judge Arnason to excuse any juror for cause, but otherwise had similar goals—with an easier path to finding a panel he trusted. One factor that helped the defense, however, was the elimination of questions following up on the jurors' previously solicited views on the death penalty. Those unalterably opposed to capital punishment would not be ferreted out and excluded from serving because Judge Arnason deemed the question irrelevant after the ruling in *People v. Anderson.*

If the case had instead been tried in federal court (as Magee had sought), the judge would have done all the questioning, and it would have been far more limited in scope. Aside from basic questions about each juror's marital status, occupation, and knowledge of the case, Davis's counsel—like Charles Garry and other veteran criminal defense lawyers—brought up issues of particular vulnerability to see what kind of responses were generated and to sensitize the entire panel to their responsibility not to jump to conclusions based on preconceived biases. How did they feel about Communists? People who wore Afros? Would they hold it against Angela Davis that she loved inmate George Jackson, whom she believed was falsely accused of killing a prison guard? That she used the word "pigs" for police? Would they be upset if she exercised her right not to take the stand on her own behalf?

Prosecutor Harris also sought to educate the panel with his questions and explanations. Did they understand what reasonable doubt meant? That it was not beyond a shadow of a doubt? That a co-conspirator did not have to be present to be just as guilty of the crime as the perpetrator? Did they know that circumstantial evidence was entitled to the same weight as direct testimony? Would they have trouble finding conspiracy based on circumstantial evidence? Had they read *If They Come in the Morning* and formed any opinions about the case as a result? Harris also sought to gauge their attitude toward law enforcement. Did they own guns? Did they or a close family member serve in the armed forces?

The audience speculated on which of the jurors currently seated would be the first to be challenged by the defense. One had been asked about Davis's association with the Panthers. The juror said that he considered the Panthers to be prone to violence, but no longer a threat since they had been disarmed by the government. Another had a favorite nephew who was a deputy sheriff. Many gasped when Angela Davis's lawyers played Russian roulette by passing at their first opportunity to use *any* peremptory challenges. Harris appeared startled at the move. At the time there was one middle-aged black woman temporarily seated. Davis's defense team expected the prosecutor to get rid of Janie Hemphill, who had started her hard life as a cotton picker, and to excuse a few other impaneled jurors whose answers indicated a possible pro-defense bias. They wanted the advantage of saving an extra challenge for the end game. They also liked making the prosecution team look more dissatisfied with the panel's composition than they were. If Albert Harris had passed as well, the jury would have stayed as it was then constituted, with at least two people the Davis team desperately wanted to remove. The gamble paid off.

By March 13, Harris had used three peremptory challenges and the defense none. The first two were used against white women. One had criticized Davis's firing and thought the radical activist had fled the state out of fear. The other seemed too eager to get on the jury while implausibly denying she had ever heard of Angela Davis. Then Harris had handed Janie Hemphill documents proving the state had just yanked a beer license from the Hemphills after her husband pleaded guilty to hosting illegal gambling. Harris gingerly questioned Mrs. Hemphill about its impact on her ability to be fair to the state given that her husband was still on probation. She replied that the weekend moonlighting venture had been losing money anyway so the closure did not affect her. When Moore objected that a prospective white juror's criminal problems had been addressed discreetly in chambers, Harris offered to continue in chambers, but Branton then jumped up angrily, saying it was too late. He called Harris's actions an "example of white racism."[26] (Actually, one man already dismissed for cause had been questioned publicly about a drunk driving conviction.) Mrs. Hemphill indicated she was not offended by the questions. It was obvious that Harris wanted to bring out the issues he considered disqualifying in open court, where the world could judge for itself his basis for questioning her impartiality. When she vowed that she could put aside any hard feelings against the state for her husband's legal problems, Harris used his fourth peremptory challenge, drawing a barely muffled reaction from fuming spectators, who knew there were no other blacks left in the entire panel.

On behalf of the defense, Branton then exercised his first challenge against an anti-Communist IBM engineer who was unhappy with his church for contributing to Davis's costs of defense. A second challenge dismissed a middle-aged Democratic voter, a building contractor who felt that Davis had already attracted way too much publicity and wanted her to testify to explain herself. Barring surprises, reporters settled back in for a lengthy jury selection process. Thirty-five prospective jurors remained, waiting to be called in this first panel. A second panel (and more) could be summoned if necessary. The prosecutor still had 16 challenges left, the defense still held 18.

The next morning after a delay for a meeting in chambers, Angela Davis stood up to address the court. This captured everyone's attention. Over Harris's vigorous objection, she had been designated as her own co-counsel and had already participated briefly in the questioning of potential jurors. Davis then repeated the claim her attorneys had previously made in several motions to change venue: that it would be "virtually impossible" for her to receive a fair trial in Santa Clara County. She then shocked all the spectators and the eight women and four men in the jury box by commenting, "As I look at the present jury I see that the women and men do reflect the composition of this county . . .

Although I cannot say this is a jury of my peers, I can say that after much discussion, we have reached the conclusion that the women and men sitting on the jury will put forth their best efforts to give me a fair trial."[27] Taking the position that questioning further panelists was unlikely to make a difference, she and her attorneys then accepted the panel as it was. (Actually, they thought the remaining pool looked worse.)

Faced earlier that morning in chambers with this unexpected defense gambit, Harris had met privately for forty-five minutes with his team before reluctantly agreeing to accept the jury as well. He did not like ending with fingers pointing at him for having just removed the only black juror. Before saying yes, Harris sought Judge Arnason's assurance that the defense team would not sandbag him by then changing its mind. Judge Arnason trusted Branton, who had earlier that morning come in for coffee to report he had a "helluva night" reaching consensus on his gut instinct to accept the jury as presently constituted. Both sides then surprisingly spent another four days carefully choosing alternates from sixteen seated prospects: the court dismissed six for cause; the defense used five peremptory challenges and the prosecutor just one.

The jury all had some college education; eight had degrees. Two thirds were women, though at the time Judge Arnason's usual experience was that eight out of twelve jurors were men (almost the reverse now). Mostly, the jury consisted of non-practicing Catholics, Jews, and Episcopalians; a few others attended regular religious services. The jury's political views were wide-ranging, but largely passive except for those engaged in local politics. Not surprisingly, most of those questioned during the entire *voir dire* expressed negative views of Communists, but those who were seated said they could set those views aside and judge the case solely on the evidence. The jurors were mostly married with children, had moved to California from a different state, and held jobs with large private or public employers who could afford to let them serve for several months. The panel also included a retired librarian and a twenty-year-old secretary, Michelle Savage, who held the distinction of being the youngest person to date ever seated on a jury. (Among the alternates was one student, a male who was just nineteen.)

Initially, there were two housewives (one who had read parts of Angela's book and said she would have no trouble finding a babysitter to watch her young children throughout the trial, and one whose brother had been an inmate at San Quentin). The latter would be replaced midway through the trial by the first alternate, a seventy-year-old male retiree. On the panel was one minority, a soft spoken thirty-six-year-old married Mexican man with two children. Luis Franco had first moved to San Jose at age eighteen. After a stint in the Army and night school, he wound up working at IBM as a data processor. By accepting a few jurors they felt uneasy about, the Davis team kept Franco, one other man, and a couple of women on the panel that they had been afraid Harris would soon challenge.

One juror the defense particularly coveted was the wife of a lawyer whose son was a conscientious objector with a misdemeanor conviction for an arrest at an anti-war rally. Their intelligence was that fifty-one-year-old Mary Timothy and her husband had been very supportive of their son throughout his difficulties with the government. To their delight, she wound up elected foreperson. (In one note to the judge she signed it "fore-Ms." in honor of the new feminist magazine.) In shortening the jury selection process, the team ingratiated themselves with the judge and reporters in the audience. They also had one major advantage over prosecutor Harris. He needed all twelve jurors to convict Davis. They just needed one holdout for a hung jury; they were optimistic that a majority of those now seated might be persuaded to vote for acquittal.

While the Davis jury selection proceeded, the news also featured developments on the death penalty. The third week of March, the California Supreme Court reaffirmed its ruling in *Anderson*, but clarified that trial courts retained discretion to deny bail in murder cases where there was sufficient incriminating evidence.[28] The modified Supreme Court ruling made clear that the *Anderson* decision was no Magna Carta for murderers; accused killers facing capital charges still risked pretrial incarceration and life in prison. Though Harris could have then sought reconsideration of Angela Davis's release on bail, to the relief of her legal team, he decided not to pursue that course even though he had been irate when Davis was first ordered released. Harris simply told reporters that there was not enough time before trial to take the issue up on appeal. Davis supporters had a different theory. They speculated that the new Attorney General had ordered Harris not to seek to put Davis back in jail to maximize public outrage at the perceived leniency of the *Anderson* decision, which even let a self-proclaimed Communist revolutionary loose on the streets as she faced trial for murder.

There was already plenty of controversy over the fact that the *Anderson* decision spared every death row inmate in California and rendered them potentially eligible for eventual parole. (Soon there would be a national moratorium on the death penalty as the United States Supreme Court began closely examining whether capital punishment violated the Eighth Amendment.) Irate California hardliners, spearheaded by Attorney General Evelle Younger and State Senator and future Governor George Deukmejian—both with their eyes on the governor's mansion—immediately asked police officers throughout the state to spend their off-duty hours gathering 750,000 signatures to put an initiative on the November ballot restoring California's death penalty for future prosecutions.

Meanwhile, among those benefiting from the historic *Anderson* ruling were the two remaining Soledad Brothers, John Clutchette and Fleeta Drumgo. They were then being tried for guard John Mills' death in a newly reinforced courtroom in San Francisco with a $15,000 bullet-proof window between the spectators and the trial participants. The inmate witnesses claimed they saw Jackson accost Mills with assistance from Clutchette and Drumgo and that Jackson then threw the guard's body over the rail. The eyewitness testimony was hotly contested. Drumgo was among the first witnesses called to the stand by the defense. He denied he had any knowledge of the killing of Mills and had been in his cell listening to records when it occurred. Clutchette testified that he was watching television when he heard the commotion and produced another inmate witness who saw him in the television room. A pathologist testified that the blow that killed Mills resulted from the fall.

A public defender testified that a deal for leniency had been struck in exchange for implicating the trio of black militants. A defense investigator took the stand and told the jury that one of the three accusers admitted that he had lied to curry favor with a prison overseer, Capt. Moody. If the known "snitch" did not implicate the three Soledad Brothers, Capt.

Moody had threatened to return him to the main prison yard where they both knew exposed snitches were often killed. Richard Silver and Floyd Silliman had been quite satisfied that they had effectively discredited the prosecutor's star witnesses without taking Greg Armstrong up on his bombshell offer to testify and disclose Jackson's taped admission that he had acted alone.

Yet on the last day of trial, the two young lawyers had cause for concern. Tempers flared out of control after derisive laughter from Soledad supporters drew the irate judge's condemnation. The judge ejected one spectator and threatened Silver and Silliman with contempt. Soon after being instructed, the forewoman of the all-white jury of nine women and three men announced that the jury was hopelessly deadlocked on the array of charges from murder to assault to not guilty. The judge sent them back to deliberate further. A couple of days later a full courtroom anxiously gathered to hear the verdicts. When both inmates were acquitted, their mothers burst into tears. The prosecutor from Monterey County held his head in his hands in frustration as the judge told the audience, "Most of you have doubted the system, but you know now that it really works."[29] The judge dropped the contempt charges against the exhausted defense attorneys, who were elated with their hard-won victory. Outside the courtroom Soledad Brothers supporters hugged each other in celebration.

Public focus returned to the Davis trial. Prosecutor Albert Harris made his opening statement the same day that the Soledad Brothers were acquitted. Harris's style was sincere, plodding, and relentless. When he announced at the outset that Davis was not on trial for her political views and that none of her speeches would be introduced into evidence, observers quickly realized that Harris had jettisoned the first overt act alleged in the indictment. Harris charged that Davis's motive was not to free all prisoners, but only George Jackson. He asserted that proof would come from her own letters: "that beneath the cool academic veneer is a woman fully capable of being moved to violence by passion."[30] Though the Davis team would succeed in excluding key proposed evidence that Harris relied upon, they made no objection to any part of his opening statement. Unlike during the pretrial proceedings in Marin County, the court permitted no noise to emanate from the audience. Judge Arnason wanted no hint of undue influence on the jury from the gallery.

Word of the Soledad Brothers' acquittal came at the noon recess and quickly spread, buoying the defense. Yet Harris's portrayal of the anticipated evidence against Davis appeared damning. Juror Mary Timothy later reflected that, had the panel voted when Harris was through, Angela Davis would have been convicted. Yet Timothy grew uneasy about government overreaching. Soon her own phone sounded like it was tapped, and her son reported that he was visited by a team of FBI men who said they were looking for a long-gone draft dodger.

The morning after Harris outlined his offer of proof, proceedings in the Davis trial dramatically came to a temporary halt after three inmates in a nearby building captured two hostages at knife point. The stand-off only ended after the instigator was killed. The defense team was alarmed that a mistrial might have to be declared. When the Davis trial reconvened the next day, Judge Arnason polled the panel to make sure that the close proximity of a violent crime similar to the one Davis was accused of participating in had not affected them. He reassured them that the hostage-taking had nothing to do with their case. Then the Dream Team took a back seat as Davis herself gave the opening statement, telling her life story and defense to the charges in her own words.

The jury was told that nothing Davis said as part of her own legal team was evidence. Harris worried about juror confusion on this point. Davis could not be cross-examined unless she later took the stand. (At the time, defendants could represent themselves or ask to be permitted to serve as co-counsel with their lawyer. Nowadays, criminal defendants must choose between representing themselves or having appointed counsel.) Davis herself felt somewhat uncomfortable in her dual role. At the beginning of the trial, when Judge Arnason invited her to join the other counsel in his chambers for coffee and pastry before morning sessions, she had declined—it was too awkward. But facing the jury with life in prison on the line, Davis exuded plenty of confidence. With professorial disdain, she charged that the prosecution sought to turn perfectly legitimate activity dedicated to social change into criminal conduct with no proof, just conjecture. She talked about her years of commitment to many causes, including the rights of working people of all races and combatting a racist penal system. She highlighted her support of protest efforts on behalf of Huey Newton, Bobby Seale and Ericka Huggins, and the Panther 21—all later freed through the courts. The Ph.D. candidate accused Harris of male chauvinism in offering a theory that, as a female, she was so besotted by love of George Jackson she was willing to join an ill-fated kidnap scheme while leaving a direct trail to herself by purchasing the weapons and ammunition in her own name.

Davis went further and ridiculed the prosecutor for offering "no consistent, credible proof of what the precise purpose of August 7 was."[31] Her attorney, Margaret Burnham, had reportedly made detailed notes on that very subject at the meeting between Davis and George Jackson and his attorney John Thorne in July 1971 in the Marin County jail cafeteria. Burnham's notes were said to include a summary of the aborted plans for a group of Panthers to join in the invasion of the Marin County Civic Center to carry off the hostage-for-prisoner exchange. Burnham had accidentally left the notes behind, where they were picked up by prison staff and delivered to Judge Arnason. The trial judge ruled the notes were confidential and inadmissible, so neither the prosecutor nor the Angela Davis jury learned what was in them.[32]

Davis noted that her experience with guns dated back to her youth in Birmingham, Alabama, when her father armed himself to protect their family from the Ku Klux Klan. She mentioned a highly publicized tragedy nine years before—four African-American girls killed by a bomb while attending Sunday school. Two of the victims were close family friends. She told of how in 1969 and 1970 she needed to buy guns to arm herself and a bodyguard because of the daily death threats she had faced for her Marxist beliefs. Davis also informed the jury of Fleeta Drumgo and John Clutchette's acquittal two days earlier and asserted that, "If George Jackson had not been struck down by San Quentin guards in August of last year he too would have been freed from that unjust prosecution."[33] (In fact, though he could not be posthumously convicted of the murder, the jury that exonerated Drumgo and Clutchette had not necessarily concluded that Jackson was innocent, too. The panel could have concluded that Jackson killed Mills by himself, as Jackson had privately admitted to a number of people, including his editor Greg Armstrong.)

In her statement Davis also emphasized "the network of police spies" that the prosecutor would *not* be calling to the stand.[34] Harris objected twice to her reference to information outside the record. One of Davis's co-counsel pointed out that no one had interrupted Harris when he made *his* opening statement. That argument appealed to Judge Arnason's sense of fair play, and he let her continue with perhaps more latitude than he would have afforded had her team interposed similar objections during Harris's opening statement. Davis made the sympathetic impression on the jury that her lawyers had hoped for.

As witness after witness testified for the prosecution, Harris made the mistake of overemphasizing all the gory details of the crime. Mary Timothy felt manipulated when two of the kidnapped women jurors broke down in tears when asked to identify the picture of the kindly judge with a shotgun strapped to his body. Judge Arnason refused to let Harris pass the judge's picture among the jurors. Testimony about the purpose of the kidnapping was muddled. The juror who was injured had heard Jonathan say: "We want our Soledad Brothers set free," and repeated shouts among the kidnappers to the same effect as they left the Civic Center.[35] She also said Jonathan mentioned that they were headed to the San Francisco Airport. Yet, arriving to testify from his wheel chair, Gary Thomas was among several other witnesses who said they never heard *any* demand that the Soledad Brothers be freed. The photographer heard McClain make that statement in front of the elevator, but a deputy at the chaotic scene in the hallway thought it was just a shouted slogan, not a specific directive for a hostage exchange. Harris piled up all the weapons used and left them in front of the jury for weeks as they waited for the evidence connecting Angela Davis to the plot. Outside the presence of the jury, Branton later argued for dismissal, telling Judge Arnason that Harris had established "a hell of a case against Jonathan Jackson,"[36] but no case at all against Angela Davis.

Harris was originally rumored to be planning to call Jimmy Carr as a surprise star witness to connect the dots. Months earlier, George Jackson's best buddy and Newton's recent bodyguard had been unexpectedly released early from the San Francisco jail after reportedly being interviewed by members of the Attorney General's office. By the time the Davis trial began, Carr was estranged from the Panthers and living with his wife Betsy and baby daughter in San Jose at his wealthy mother-in-law Joan Hammer's home. In exchange for leniency, Carr supposedly had cut a deal admitting that he was the person who sawed off the shotgun for use in the Marin Civic Center kidnapping. Word spread that Carr had abetted the crime at the joint request of Angela Davis and Jonathan Jackson, who drove together to see him on the evening of Wednesday August 5 at the Panther hideaway in the Santa Cruz Mountains. But there were also rumors that Carr later reneged on his promise to testify against Davis. Angela Davis's lawyers reportedly interviewed Carr and he denied turning state's witness.[37]

On April 6, Carr was ambushed and killed gangland-style in the front yard of Hammer's home on his way to work. Police had a description of the get-away car, and the two men who fled were arrested within half an hour. Newspapers reported that the pair confessed they had been paid $540 to kill Carr, though who ordered his death remained unknown.[38] He had been the target of prior death threats. The accused Panther hitman reputedly had numerous enemies on the right as well as the left and was expected to be a key prosecution witness in the upcoming San Quentin Six trial.[39] Front-page coverage of Carr's murder featured alleged ties to the Davis case. NUCFAD held a press conference denying that Angela Davis had ever met Carr. Harris complained to Judge Arnason that her attorneys had used NUCFAD to circumvent his gag order, while Angela Davis's lawyers demanded a mistrial for the rampant speculation in the newspapers that could easily have reached the jury. Although they had been warned not to read or listen to any coverage of the trial itself, they were free to read edited newspapers and watch or listen to other news. Once again, the jury was carefully polled to see if their impartiality was affected by the homicide. Even though several had heard about Carr's death, they swore it would not affect their consideration of Davis's guilt or innocence of the charges against her.

The jurors had reason to perk up when the prosecutor put a fingerprint expert on the stand. One of Angela's books on Marxism in

Jonathan's possession bore her prints on an inside page. But she never denied the books were hers; she was his tutor. Evidence that she cashed checks shortly before Jonathan spent money was inconclusive. Harris made far more headway when he presented witnesses at a gas station near the Marin Civic Center the day before the kidnapping. The owner identified Davis as a woman passenger in the yellow Hertz Rent-A-Car van, which Jonathan Jackson asked for help restarting when it stalled in the parking lot. Yet no fingerprints of hers were found in the van or on any of the guns, ammunition cartridges or elsewhere the expert looked.

Harris called to the stand the pawn shop owner who had sold Angela a cheap shotgun on Wednesday, August 5, when she came into his store accompanied by Jonathan Jackson—the same gun that was sawed off and strapped to Judge Haley two days later. It was the most damning piece of evidence the prosecutor had against Davis. The defense claim that Angela purchased the gun for a different purpose—protection of the San Francisco Soledad Brothers Defense Committee—did not explain why Jonathan Jackson accompanied her; why he wound up with it instead of the local committee; or why they settled on a gun that had to be reloaded after each use when other options would seem far more practical for protecting the headquarters. Yet the shop owner testified that, when Davis had offered her identification as verification for the purchase, he excitedly asked for and received her autograph. Her attorneys were laying the groundwork for arguing that Davis's conduct at the gun shop was hard to reconcile with someone planning to use the weapon for a high profile crime two days later.

A San Quentin guard testified that, earlier in the week of the kidnapping, he saw a light-skinned black woman with an Afro accompanying Jonathan Jackson. Jackson signed her into the register as Diane Thompson. She remained in the waiting room while he visited his brother George. In court, the guard identified Davis as the young woman he had seen. A prison trustee also identified her as the woman with an Afro he saw with Jackson in a yellow van in the prison parking lot on August 5 and 6 (his credibility was undermined by the fact that the van had not yet been rented on the 5th).

Harris also provided as evidence of guilt that, shortly afterward,

Angela Davis disguised herself with a wig when she fled. The jury was left to ponder why the easily recognizable celebrity would not have also tried to hide her Afro when visiting San Quentin under an assumed name. Indeed, when arrested at a Howard Johnson's hotel in New York in October 1970, Davis had been fingerprinted to verify that she was really the fugitive police sought. During the FBI nationwide search, the agency had investigated so many claims from callers across country that they had just spotted Angela Davis that the officers needed extra assurance they had the right woman.

How sure were these eyewitnesses of the identity of the woman they glimpsed with Jonathan in Marin County earlier that week? (Investigative journalist Jo Durden-Smith later was told that on at least two of those occasions the woman in question was actually a white woman wearing an Afro wig). The defense team tested the gas station owner's memory for faces. They had a young black woman investigator in the courtroom, who also wore her hair in an Afro and dressed similarly to Angela Davis. Before he took the stand, the gas station owner, like all the others, had been excluded from the proceedings so he would not be tempted to tailor his testimony based on what other witnesses had said. Three weeks before he testified, the investigator had accompanied Moore to the service station when the owner was on duty. On the stand the owner remembered seeing Moore, but could not recall ever seeing the investigator before.

After sequestering the jury Judge Arnason heard testimony from a former FBI agent, James McCord, about his raid on Angela Davis's Los Angeles apartment in August 1970 that produced, among myriad papers and books, some correspondence with George Jackson in June 1970. Dobby Walker challenged whether the scope of the warrant McCord had obtained permitted him to confiscate those letters. An even more hotly contested hearing ensued over an eighteen-page diary typed on a typewriter in Davis's cell in July 1971 and found in George Jackson's cell after he died. Judge Arnason allowed into evidence three love letters written in June 1970, but, in a major setback to the prosecution, excluded the eighteen-page diary.

Harris refused to give up on getting that July 1971 diary admitted as crucial evidence of motive, particularly the passages in which Davis described herself as Jackson's wife and where she evoked the memory of their last meeting as he arrived in chains "surrounded by the small army of mindless but armed automatons." Davis wrote that the image made her rage once again. As she sat locked in her own cell, she envisioned herself "tearing down this steel door, fighting my way to you, ripping down your cell door and letting you go free . . . so terrible is this love. . . .[40] In chambers, Moore had reacted with outrage to Harris's argument: if introducing the letter Angela Davis wrote to George Jackson in July 1971 was critical to the prosecutor's success, didn't that mean Davis had been kept in prison for the prior year without sufficient evidence to support the conspiracy charges?

Judge Arnason considered many of the entries irrelevant. He also remained convinced that Angela's desperate mindset in July 1971 (after more than half a year in a maximum security cell) was too remote in time and context for Harris to argue to the jury as evidence of her motivation back in August 1970. But the trial judge yielded to Harris's arguments that the letter should not be excluded in its entirety. Instead, Judge Arnason ordered the letter redacted down to two-and-a-half pages that illustrated her abiding love for Jackson, the selection of which the judge mostly undertook himself. Judge Arnason drew the line there. He did not permit testimony by the guard who observed Angela Davis embraced on Jackson's lap at one of their trial preparation conferences in the summer of 1971.

Harris then subpoenaed attorney John Thorne. Thorne had been present when Angela Davis and George Jackson had their jailhouse conferences and had spoken with her on other occasions. Harris was most anxious to get Thorne to repeat a statement he had given the prosecutor during the investigative stage in which Thorne described a telephone conversation with Davis on August 5, 1970, in which she mentioned she was with Jonathan Jackson en route to Santa Cruz. That provided a missing link toward proving that the pair were then headed to the Santa Cruz mountains to get the shotgun altered. Thorne showed up represented by Charles Garry, who claimed the attorney-client privilege as a bar. Davis briefly took the stand with the jury absent. She asserted that she had confided in Thorne about her publishing rights. At the time, Thorne also had pending on appeal a petition he filed on Davis's behalf to allow her to visit George Jackson. The privilege was upheld. Harris persisted with questions that did not invade the privilege and still met resistance. The prosecutor did wind up getting Thorne to testify about his telephone conversation with Davis, but Thorne was now certain that the date was in July, not August, rendering his testimony of no apparent consequence.[41]

It took Harris eight weeks to put 84 witnesses on the stand and introduce 200 exhibits. Part of his case was an attempt to imply another sexual relationship—one between Davis and Jonathan Jackson—to convince the jury Jonathan was just slavishly doing her bidding when he embarked on the ill-fated plot. That effort fizzled. One witness was a downstairs neighbor in the Los Angeles four-plex where Davis had moved in July 1970. When asked whether Jonathan Jackson shared an apartment with Davis for several weeks that summer, the neighbor said she had only seen him visit once or twice. Harris also put a motel manager on the stand to relate that Jonathan rented a room for two in San Francisco on Thursday night August 6, 1970, but the manager had no idea who, if anyone, joined Jonathan there.

Harris then called Mabel "Mickey" Magers to the stand, an attractive blonde in her early thirties who arrived with her own attorney. Magers said she had first been introduced to Jonathan in the middle of July 1970. On July 28, Magers drove Jonathan and her friend Joan Hammer to San Quentin and waited while they visited George. Magers then took Jonathan to the San Francisco Airport and drove Hammer back to San Jose. (Hammer was a major financial supporter of the Soledad Brothers Defense Committee on which her daughter Betsy and son-in-law Jimmy Carr were highly active; Magers was their house guest.) On Tuesday August 4, Magers loaned Jonathan the use of her VW bug, which she did not see again until a month later when she was notified it had been parked at the San Francisco Airport since early Friday morning, August 7. It had the remnants of several small cigars in the ashtray like the kind Angela then smoked. Harris wanted the jury to believe the VW must have been driven there that morning by Angela Davis, who then stayed for hours by an airport pay phone waiting for a call from Jonathan. (His wallet had contained a telephone number that matched that of the pay phone in question, which was located in a different building than the terminal from which Angela Davis flew to Los Angeles).

On cross-examination Moore got Magers to admit that she had used the name Mickey Jackson at one point because of her close friendship with Jonathan. He then asked her whether she was the person who spent the night with Jonathan in the motel. The question prompted Magers' attorney to call for a brief recess. Magers then denied the allegation, but revealed that the prosecutor had promised her immunity for her testimony. (No one on either side asked Magers about her one-year-old bi-racial son whom she had named Jonathan Jackson, Jr.—born eight and a half months after his father's death.)

More violent headlines were to follow. The day after President Nixon resumed bombing in North Vietnam, juror Mary Timothy showed up in court wearing a peace pin. On May 16—the day Davis took the stand to keep Thorne from being forced to testify against her—the nation was aghast at an assassination attempt on George Wallace while he campaigned for President in Maryland. A lone white gunman had crippled the Alabama governor, who went on to win two primaries that day. With much less public awareness, African-American candidate Shirley Chisholm avoided three assassination attempts. Meanwhile, each day the jury saw an attractive, frail defendant diligently taking notes while shivering in one of her brightly colored shawls. They had trouble equating the young professional, who freely came and left the courtroom as they did, with her terrorist pretrial image.

For their own evidence, the Davis team debated whether to call a wide array of witnesses (including actress Jane Fonda) or just zero in on targeted issues. Branton thought that the prosecution had presented such a flimsy case, they did not need to mount any defense at all. In no event did it seem wise to put Angela Davis on the stand. Branton and Moore had grilled her in private and were worried that she would not hold up well when questioned about her relationship with George Jackson. The group ultimately opted for the minimalist approach and took only three days to present a dozen witnesses and several binders full of hate mail. Harris had little idea what to expect. At the time, defendants were entitled to obtain discovery from the prosecutor, but had no reciprocal duty. (That would change significantly in California in 1990.)

A UCLA staffer attested to stacks of hate mail and a barrage of obscene phone calls received at the philosophy department when Davis was still employed there in 1969 and 1970. Davis was referred to as a "wooly-headed Hottentot" and "Commie bitch" among the more printable names.[42] The threatening messages explained why Davis had bought guns for the protection of herself and her friends. Another witness testified that the phone number without an area code that had been found in Jonathan Jackson's pocket also worked for a Los Angeles residence near where he lived, casting into doubt whether Jonathan planned to call anyone at the San Francisco Airport. Most other witnesses were alibi witnesses who accounted for Davis's whereabouts at times the prosecutor alleged she was with Jonathan Jackson casing the Marin County Civic Center, or at San Quentin, or staying with him at the San Francisco motel.

Among the defense witnesses was Marvin Stender, Fay Stender's husband. Stender testified that he consulted with Davis on legal issues related to the Soledad Defense Committee on the late morning of August 6 in San Francisco. As a favor, Stender then drove Davis to Berkeley, where he was headed to the law school to do some library research. On cross-examination, Harris evinced complete disbelief and hostility. If true, Stender's testimony negated the sighting of Davis that morning in Marin County. But Stender remained firm in his testimony under Harris's grilling. Harris was similarly harsh in questioning the editor of *The People's World* newspaper in San Francisco, who said Davis worked at his office from 8:30 a.m. until 1 p.m. on August 7, when he drove her to the airport to catch an afternoon commuter plane to Los Angeles. A friend then took the stand to attest that Davis had stayed as a guest at her San Francisco home all that first week of August 1970, and they had breakfast together every morning, including Friday, August 7 (when the prosecutor contended Davis had just spent the night at a motel with Jonathan Jackson and then drove the borrowed VW early Friday morning to the airport where she waited until mid-afternoon before flying out).

A fourth friend testified that Davis was playing Scrabble at her house in Los Angeles on the evening of August 7, 1970, when someone telephoned with the tragic news of Jonathan's death. Angela appeared stunned. The next day Angela Davis saw photos of the kidnappers in the newspaper with the shotgun and Angela reacted with astonishment, saying she had just purchased that gun for the protection of the Soledad Defense Committee. Davis hurried with another friend to the apartment where the Che-Lumumba Club met to check whether other guns she kept in a gun rack in an unlocked closet were still there, only to discover them missing. The two were told that Jonathan had dropped by that apartment to do some copy work for the Soledad Defense Committee the week before and could have sneaked the guns out when no one was looking. Davis reportedly said, "Oh no!"[43]

All of this alibi evidence went in without having to put the defendant herself on the stand. To bolster the alibi defense, her lawyers also employed innovative expert testimony to challenge the eyewitnesses who placed Davis in Marin County with Jonathan Jackson on August 4, 5, and 6. Judge Arnason was already familiar with that type of expert testimony and had no problem authorizing its use. Prof. Robert H. Buckhout, an experimental social psychologist who taught at a local college, then presented a slide show that the jury appeared to find fascinating. He gave them a lecture explaining why people sometimes become convinced in retrospect they had witnessed things they had not seen, particularly if the viewing was of short duration and there was no reason to pay close attention at the time. Prof. Buckhout described other factors that affect the memory of eyewitnesses, including their expectations, their own physical condition, their desire to conform what they saw with what others claimed to see, and a desire to play an important role in a matter of historical importance. Moore was excited to read the jurors' body language. They seemed quite relieved at Prof. Buckhout's suggestion they could disregard the eyewitnesses without having to decide they were lying. (Some of the jurors had themselves been confused when the trial started and they saw a young black woman investigator with an Afro sitting near the defense lawyers.)

In preliminary questioning of jurors, her lawyers had planted the idea that Davis might never testify. As expected, the defense never called her, though Branton later said the team had remained undecided until after the prosecutor rested. As a surprise witness, Fleeta Drumgo took the stand. While the jury was absent from the room, he had arrived in chains and was seated in the witness chair with one arm free, minimizing the jury's view of his shackles. Drumgo was then awaiting prosecution for attempted escape and murder in the San Quentin Six case. His testimony was brief: Drumgo swore that he never heard of any kidnap plan to exchange hostages for the Soledad Brothers release even though his cell was next to James McClain's, who supposedly helped engineer the plot. Clutchette was waiting in another room, but was not called to testify. The defense also asked Drumgo to identify the verdict acquitting him and Clutchette of the murder of Soledad guard Mills. (Prosecutor Harris had earlier read the entire indictment of the Soledad Brothers to the jury as evidence of Davis's motive.)

After the Davis team dramatically rested, Harris rose in rebuttal. He put on several witnesses to bolster the eyewitness identifications of Davis, but did not help his cause when he then called Lester Jackson to the stand. The grieving father refused to cooperate even when told he would be held in contempt. Out of obvious sympathy, Judge Arnason did not order Jackson incarcerated, but fined him only $100, which reporters in the audience took up a collection to pay. In closing, Albert Harris reviewed all the evidence pointing to Angela Davis's guilt, reminding the jury that an absent co-conspirator was just as guilty of the kidnap/murder as the perpetrators. He gave no weight to the alibi witnesses. Since they were all friends of Davis, Harris argued that the jury should disregard their testimony when it contradicted so many eyewitnesses. As he described the proof of conspiracy he had offered—motive, object, agreement, knowledge, intent, and flight—the jurors all paid close attention. Several took detailed notes. Jonathan Jackson was obsessed with his brother's dire situation. He had no reason to liberate the inmates at the Marin Civic Center, but for whatever help they could offer in freeing George. It crossed Mary Timothy's mind that, if there really were a reckless scheme to exchange hostages at the Marin courthouse for the release of the Soledad Brothers, it sounded like the pipe dream of a seventeen-year-old and men suffering from arrested development after being locked up in prison since their teens. It was hard to imagine even a lovesick Ph.D. candidate dropping all work on her dissertation to join in such a risky venture.

The next day, Branton and Moore shared the defense closing argument. Branton went first. He invited the jury to think of themselves as black for the moment, then painted a picture of what it was like to endure a long history of racist abuse. Clarence Darrow had taken a similar approach to compelling effect in the 1925 Sweet trial; Charles Garry had done so in Newton's defense in 1968. Branton wanted the jury to understand Davis's decision to disappear after her guns were found at the Marin County shootout—why she might be in fear for her life even though innocent. He pointed out that whether they liked or disliked his client, everyone recognized her fine intellect. She would have to be a fool to buy a shotgun openly and sign an autograph if she intended that the same gun be used in a risky kidnapping plot in broad daylight two days later. Branton read an edited version of the love letters the jury had seen; an uncredited Hollywood screenwriter had turned Angela's passionate outpourings into a beautiful free verse poem. (That task would have been exceedingly hard working with the unedited version.) Most impressively, Branton concluded his two-hour presentation by unveiling a cartoon showing Angela Davis bound in six large chains labeled motive, object, agreement, knowledge, intent, and flight. He then replaced it with another cartoon with her standing inside a pile of broken chains bearing those same labels.

Moore followed with an attack on the credibility of all the prosecutor's eyewitnesses as mistaken or lying. There was no way to reconcile the two conflicting versions of her whereabouts at key times. He then unexpectedly cut short his prepared remarks by two hours to force Harris to conduct his rebuttal that same afternoon without any opportunity for reflection. The next day the judge finished his instructions to the jury and told the panel to go home to pack for their secluded deliberations. On their return, two joked privately about not bringing suitcases. Judge Arnason had packed his own suitcase. He intended to remain in San Jose for however long it took until the jury returned.

Ironically, while the jurors were under guard in a motel, yet another hijacking attempt made banner headlines. The hijackers reportedly demanded $500,000 and Angela Davis's release. While that crisis unfolded, the FBI demanded that Davis be tracked down and taken into custody. When she responded to a summons to Judge Arnason's chambers, she was innocently eating lunch at a local restaurant with members of her committee and her brother Ben, a professional football player for the Cleveland Browns. The jury would not hear about the startling caper until after they had rendered their verdict. (It turned out that the hijackers had made no demand for Angela Davis.) As their chaperone drove them to the court for their deliberations, the jurors passed a small crowd of Davis supporters in front of the courthouse with a large cardboard sign that read "VIGIL."

Because of the enormous burden facing the jury with the eyes of the world upon them, Mary Timothy had taken it upon herself on a day off to research jury deliberations. She found a book—*What You Need to Know for Jury Duty*—that included an outline of how to proceed, which she shared with the other jurors. It emphasized that voting by secret ballots on each count taken up in turn was the last step in the collaborative process. The author strongly advised not taking any vote at all until after all the jurors had the opportunity to suggest topics of concern for group discussion and not until after satisfying everyone that their issues were fully addressed. (Timothy later wrote a book about her perspective on the extraordinary trial, *Jury Woman.*)

Timothy carefully prepared a list of points she had distilled from Judge Arnason's instructions:

- Motive is not an element of the crime of conspiracy and need not be shown;
- Flight is not in and of itself a sign of guilt, but can be considered in light of other evidence;
- Reasonable doubt is no abiding conviction of moral certainty;
- Conspiracy is a union of two or more, of thought and act . . . with certain specific intent to commit a crime;
- Indirect evidence proves a fact that leads to an inference consistent with the theory for which it is presented. It cannot be reconciled with any other theory—if so it must be weighed toward the theory of innocence [i.e., indirect evidence that is susceptible of either an innocent or blameworthy interpretation must be construed to favor innocence];
- It must be proved there was an illegal plan or agreement—mere

association is not enough;

- Any statement made by one of the conspirators . . . is not relevant unless it is part of the knowledge of the other conspirators. So unless it is an *agreed* part of the conspiracy, it is not part of the conspiracy.[44]

Unable to sleep with the sheriff's deputy pacing in the corridor outside, Timothy had just risen from her bed to make a list of 27 facts that the prosecutor said he had proven to demonstrate Davis's complicity in the kidnapping plot. She methodically crossed off all of them that she felt only implicated Jonathan Jackson or were capable of a totally innocent explanation, like the gun purchases in 1968 and 1969 and Davis's attendance at the May 1970 Soledad Brothers pretrial hearing in Salinas. Timothy concluded that neither the love letters, nor Davis's presence at the airport where she took a commuter flight on August 7 from San Francisco to Los Angeles evidenced a conspiracy. She boiled her list down to just three key issues: the shotgun Davis purchased when she was with Jonathan Jackson just a couple of days before the kidnapping; and the witnesses who placed her with Jonathan Jackson at San Quentin and at the gas station near the Civic Center within days of the kidnap attempt.

At the nomination of one of the men, Timothy was chosen foreperson in part to make a statement in support of women's equality. By then, they had all gotten to know one another and were a relatively collegial group. The first order of business was to lodge a complaint about the motel's inadequate breakfast offering. When they got started on deliberations, other jurors added issues they believed the group needed to discuss, but none felt the prosecutor had proved beyond a reasonable doubt that the object of the conspiracy was to free the Soledad Brothers. On their first vote on the charged crime, nine voted to acquit and three were undecided. On prior occasions when they were left in the jury room for hours, several had played penny ante poker to pass the time. They decided to allow the unsure members to sit in separate corners of the room to reflect privately on the issues that bothered them while the rest played another quiet poker game.

After only a day and a half, the jury returned with their verdict.

Would-be spectators had lined up before 3 a.m. for access. Most of Angela Davis's family was present, including her parents. Albert Harris reserved a seat for his wife; Judge Arnason invited one of his sons. The jurors filed in leaden-footed, wearing impassive expressions. An eery quiet accompanied Judge Arnason's request for the signed verdict forms. No one could decipher his stone-faced expression as he read each one silently and then passed them to the clerk to read aloud. When the clerk announced verdicts of acquittal on the murder and kidnapping charges, the entire courtroom seemed to hold its breath for the conspiracy charge. When Davis was acquitted on that one too, the enormity of the accomplishment overwhelmed the audience. Collective sighs gave way to applause while Harris and Thompson appeared numbed by the result.

Judge Arnason pounded his gavel and admonished the crowd back to silence. He thanked the jury for its dedication to duty and read an excerpt from an essay on jury service by G. K. Chesterton. The British author noted the singular importance placed by society on determining the guilt or innocence of one's fellow citizens as a "thing too important to be trusted to trained men" such as judges. . . . Rather when [civilization] wishes anything done which is really serious, it collects twelve of the ordinary men standing round."[45] The women in the jury were too relieved to take any offense.

Judge Arnason congratulated all the attorneys on their professionalism. He had been impressed by the quality of representation on both sides. Branton, in turn, showered the judge with praise. As the assemblage started to disperse, Moore followed an exclamation of "Power to the People" with a two-fisted cheer, "All power to the jury!"[46] Outside, a crowd of three hundred went wild with applause, hugs, shouts of victory, singing, and tears. Davis invited the jury to celebrate with her. All but three joined the festivities and brought their families along as jubilant well-wishers toasted the defense victory with champagne. The news spread like wild fire on radio and television. A Giants announcer at Candlestick Park in San Francisco interrupted the afternoon doubleheader to report the verdicts to great applause. Though the Davis trial itself had only occasionally garnered above-the-fold status, newspapers covered her acquittal with several page spreads akin to the saturation coverage accorded to the assassination of Martin

Luther King and Bobby Kennedy. Within a week John Lennon and Yoko Ono would record "Angela" on their new album *Some Time in New York City.*

Gov. Reagan joined editors who praised the American judicial system. He called the result an unsurprising outcome because he always believed that "establishing a connection" between her weapons purchases and the Marin Civic Center shootings would be difficult. But then the governor added, "I just know that one of the great things in our system . . . if we err, more often than not the error is on the side of letting someone go free." The verdict represented "pretty good proof that this society leans over backward" to protect the rights of the accused.[47] Angela Davis strongly disagreed. She attributed her victory to the pressure of worldwide scrutiny her supporters brought to bear. In her view, "a fair trial would have been no trial at all."[48]

In sharp contrast, Marin County District Attorney Bruce Bales told a reporter he was "shocked beyond belief" at the outcome. Bales had sat through the closing arguments. He exclaimed: "She didn't even take the stand to deny her guilt."[49] Bales did not care that defendants had that unfettered right under the law. He wanted retribution for the death of a county judge and crippling of one of his prosecutors. Bales evinced no concern that the Marin Civic Center bloodbath might have been avoided altogether had the county sheriff's orders not to shoot been followed.

Despite the time and energy devoted by the prosecutor to proving the crime, many questions remained unanswered. Judge Arnason had granted Ruchell Magee's motion to exhume the bodies in August of 1971, after a declaration from a defense expert convinced Judge Arnason that Judge Haley had been killed by a .357 magnum bullet fired from outside the van before the shotgun blast. The highly experienced pathologist who had performed the four autopsies a year earlier suddenly changed his mind. He had earlier attributed the cause of death to the shotgun, but now could not rule out the possibility that Judge Haley had already died from a fatal chest wound. Dr. Manwaring also reversed the trajectory of the bullets that killed Jonathan Jackson, James McClain, and William Christmas. He declared that he had misidentified all of the exit and entrance wounds in his original report and was now of the opinion that both Jonathan Jackson and James McClain were killed with a single bullet each shot from the left side that exited near their right shoulders. The Davis team suspected that Dr. Manwaring's original report was deliberately falsified and that the prosecutors knew it. By getting the doctor to volunteer corrections, they minimized damage from cross-examination.[50] At trial, Davis's attorneys had raised questions about which bullets were fired by whom, which proved impossible to ascertain since ballistics tests were undertaken only of a few guns, leaving some unidentified bullets that could not be tested because law enforcement personnel had immediately commingled their weapons with others in the armory.

According to investigative journalist Jo Durden-Smith, several sources later confirmed Louis Tackwood's revelations about the Jackson brothers' plans for a hostage-exchange kidnap scheme. Months later, California's Organized Crime and Criminal Intelligence Department uncovered a similar alleged plot by the Black Liberation Army to kidnap Nancy Reagan. An informer claimed the scheme included plans to communicate a threat to decapitate the governor's wife and return her head to him if he did not release specified members of their gang from prison. The threat led to stakeouts and heightened security, but no kidnap attempt ever materialized. No word was leaked to the public until several years later.

If what Tackwood alleged was true, members of the Red Squad secretly gathered in the vicinity of the Marin Civic Center on the morning of August 7 expecting a kidnapping. Dr. Manwaring's belated revelations about the bullet wounds dovetailed with Tackwood's claim of an expert rifleman hidden in the shrubbery on the driver's side of the van having dispatched both Jonathan Jackson and James McClain. The jury never heard any testimony about the Red Squad. Yet, consistent with the Red Squad already tracking Davis before the kidnapping, Harris did put on evidence of Jonathan Jackson and Angela Davis being sighted together on different occasions in July 1970. Harris also asked one of the defense alibi witnesses about a telephone call the prosecutor assumed the witness received from Angela Davis using a code name "Jamala" when she was on the run in mid-August 1970. The accusation—which smacked of illegal wire-tapping—backfired. It turned out an African-American woman nicknamed "Jamala" was among the spectators in court that day. The defense team delightedly put the unexpected witness on the stand to explain that she was Jamala and had called her San Franciscan colleague from the Los Angeles Airport to arrange transportation to Jonathan Jackson's funeral.

If, as Harris's questions seemed to imply, government agents had already been tailing Angela Davis since sometime in July, what kept the prosecutor from producing someone to prove Davis was where the prosecution said she was at key times during the week of August 7, 1970? Or did the surveillance confirm instead that some or all of her alibi witnesses were telling the truth? When Angela Davis cryptically mentioned in her opening statement that government spies were sitting on evidence undermining the prosecutor's case, perhaps that was what she had in mind.

Indeed, overlapping with the Davis trial, former Black Panther Elmer "Geronimo" Pratt went on trial in Southern California for a December, 1968, Santa Monica murder, for which evidence later came to light that he was framed. Pratt was convicted in large part on eyewitness confusion and perjured testimony of another Panther who had become a government informant. The FBI had audiotapes from its surveillance team proving that Pratt was actually where he testified that he was at the time of that homicide—hundreds of miles north at a Panther central committee meeting in Oakland—but the agency suppressed that evidence. Both Bobby Seale and David Hilliard could also have corroborated Pratt's alibi, but were then under strict orders from Huey Newton not to come to Pratt's aid, because he was an ally of Eldridge Cleaver.[51] Pratt's trial counsel Johnnie Cochran collaborated on appeal with the ACLU and a team of experts, including Anthony Amsterdam. Pratt, who had changed his last name and was now known as Geronimo Ji Jaga, drew considerable international attention to his claim of political persecution. He finally won his release in 1999 after 27 years in jail when his lawyers—now including Kathleen Cleaver—established to the satisfaction of a California appellate court the likelihood of Pratt's acquittal had the jury considered the suppressed evidence.[52] After prosecutors declined to retry him, Pratt sued and obtained a $4.5 million settlement from the City of Los Angeles and the federal government for false imprisonment.

Unlike in the *Pratt* case where the government relied on a former Panther to convict Pratt with a manufactured confession, COINTELPRO agents no longer trusted Tackwood by the time of Davis's trial. Tackwood had switched sides and offered to testify that Angela Davis was being framed. But Tackwood's credibility as an ex-felon with a track record of lying to friends and family was easily open to attack. Even if the jury believed him, Tackwood could only attempt to exonerate Angela Davis by naming a host of other Panthers as co-conspirators, including Geronimo Pratt, in the ambitious hostage-exchange scheme originally planned by George Jackson, which Pratt's Panther contingent then abandoned. Davis's lawyers reportedly were too leery of going down that path,[53] which would have provided the jury evidence that the August 7 plot Davis ridiculed actually did exist. Thus, both sides had strategic reasons why they did not tell the jury everything they knew about the shooting at the Marin County Courthouse on August 7, 1970.

* * * * *

Ruchell Magee also won a change of venue. At his own trial later that year in San Francisco, unlike Davis, Magee appeared in chains and engaged in many more courtroom outbursts. He had by then assumed the name "Cinque," after the West African who led the famous 1839 slave ship Amistad rebellion and then won acquittal of mutiny, with former President John Quincy Adams championing his cause. Magee's trial took eight and a half months from start to finish in the same high-security courtroom where the Soledad Brothers had been tried. It included an unprecedented hiatus, ordered by the California Supreme Court to permit former Attorney General Ramsey Clark to join the defense team as a volunteer, soon after his victory in the Harrisburg Seven trial. (Clark had also just hit the best-seller list in 1971 with his controversial book, *Crime in America*, finding overcrowded, uninhabitable prisons to constitute crime factories.)

Clark and his co-counsel argued to the six men and six women of the jury that Magee's life story was "a true American tragedy" of a man swallowed up and forgotten by the prison system for "a Saturday night fight and a $10 robbery." Unlike Angela Davis, Magee managed to obtain three black members on his panel. Clark asserted that "Mr. Magee was consumed with the desire for freedom" and took the unexpected opportunity to escape when it was handed to him. "We don't know what happened in the van . . . [but] you can't convict him [just] because he was there."[54] Unable to sit still while the judge instructed the jury, Magee erupted once more to yell, "You're the kidnappers. You're holding me in slavery!"[55] Magee flashed the jury a view of the scar he bore from his near fatal misadventure and was unceremoniously escorted from the courtroom.

The key issue before the jury was the credibility of the account of Judge Haley's death testified to by former prosecutor Gary Thomas, the same testimony Thomas had given at the Angela Davis trial. By the time of Magee's trial, Thomas had been appointed a judge by Gov. Reagan. Magee swore he did not pull the trigger on the shotgun. His attorneys argued that in the terrifying nineteen seconds in which all the shooting occurred, Thomas had only glimpsed Judge Haley's horrific head wound, not who inflicted it. Time after time over the next eight days, the jury announced it was deadlocked, only to have the judge send them back to try once more to reach consensus. Finally, after nearly sixty hours of deliberation, the judge accepted that he had a hung jury. Most of them were convinced—as Judge Arnason had been—that Judge Haley was already dead from the chest wound when the shotgun went off. Eleven of them voted for Magee's acquittal of Judge Haley's murder and the same number for conviction only of the lesser charge of simple kidnapping. The lone holdout for conviction of the murder charge was white; the lone holdout for acquittal of the lesser kidnapping charge was black.

When the Magee trial ended, it won the distinction (for the time being) of the costliest criminal trial in the state's history. Frustrated once again, prosecutor Harris vowed to retry the case. Ultimately on retrial, Magee dismissed all his attorneys and was permitted to defend himself. To forestall retrial on the more serious charge that he had joined the Jackson brothers' plot to exchange hostages for prisoners, Magee pleaded guilty to the simple kidnapping charge. He then had second thoughts and tried to withdraw that plea, with no success. Despite a campaign on his behalf by Angela Davis and others, Magee drew a sentence of life in prison without possibility of parole, a sentence most prisoners considered worse than death. (Ironically, life without possibility of parole was permitted at the time for kidnapping, but not for murder.)[56] As a consequence, to this day Ruchell Cinque Magee remains incarcerated, convinced that he was wrongly imprisoned from day one of his first conviction as a teenager. His followers call Magee "the longest held political prisoner in the world."[57]

* * * * *

Communists had fully expected Angela Davis's trial to embarrass the United States for its history of racism. TASS described her surprising acquittal as largely the result of all the pressure the Communist press had brought to bear on "a frame-up too offensive to be accepted even by an all-white jury."[58] But Western nations had the opposite view: that the verdict proved that even militant black Communists could receive a fair trial in the world's leading democracy. A prominent Italian daily praised the trial's "reconfirmation of the democratic validity of the most sacred [American] institution."[59] Unlike the black eye to American jurisprudence that the Sacco and Vanzetti case represented, the Davis trial showed the world how the American constitutional system operates when the checks and balances it incorporates live up to expectations: an independent judiciary and an impartial jury trial drawn from a cross-section of the community to hold a prosecutor to proof beyond a reasonable doubt, even of someone viewed by the executive branch as an enemy of the state. Credit goes to the extraordinary efforts undertaken by the California judiciary to ensure fairness, including six judges who either declined to take the case or were removed by a reviewing judge under rules designed to promote judicial neutrality.

Judge Arnason ignored enormous pressure and won praise for providing a level playing field, which included first and foremost a change of venue from the traumatized community where the crime occurred. Credit also goes to the jury with diverse political viewpoints who all took their role quite seriously. Looking back forty years later—still sitting on the bench—Judge Arnason considers the result in the Davis case a product of a different era of jurisprudence. With today's more liberal rules on admitting hearsay and someone like Angela Davis having to choose between representing herself or relying on experienced trial counsel, he seriously doubts she would win an acquittal.

Within the next year the strength of America's democracy would be put to another test as corruption at the very top levels of federal government took headlines away from a bizarre new revolutionary scheme of far less threat to the nation. The unraveling all began on June 17, 1972, less than two weeks after the Angela Davis trial ended, when five men were arrested for burglarizing Democratic headquarters in Washington, D.C. Chief among those caught red-handed was former FBI (and CIA) agent James W. McCord, whom reporters worldwide had just become acquainted with in May as the federal agent who tore apart Angela Davis's Los Angeles apartment in August of 1971, gathering evidence to try to send her to the gas chamber. What was his purpose now?

5. WATERGATE OVERSHADOWS THE COBRA

My beloved Tania,
We carry your gun deep within our hearts
For no better reason than our lives have no meaning
And we want to be on television.

"Tania," Camper Van Beethoven

Since 1968, support for the ongoing Vietnam War had diminished greatly. Dismay had followed the North Vietnamese Tet offensive, exposure of the My Lai massacre of women and children by American GIs, and a steady stream of flag-draped coffins on the evening news with names of fallen American soldiers. By the end of 1969, anti-war protests drew crowds of up to a million demonstrators. In 1971, the leak of the Pentagon Papers to the press damaged beyond repair mainstream America's confidence in the government's Vietnam War strategy. Among the revelations from these top secret government files was that the White House, under Presidents of both parties, had covered up the role of the United States in repeatedly enlarging the scope of that war, including wide-scale bombing in Cambodia and Laos.

By January 1973, national attention focused on the trial of former military analyst Daniel Ellsberg, who faced life imprisonment under the Espionage Act of 1917 for having disclosed those secrets to *The New York Times.* Barely had that "trial of the century" in Los Angeles begun when President Nixon brought a cease fire to the Vietnam War and ended the draft. In May 1973, the public was astonished when the federal judge dismissed all charges against Ellsberg and his co-defendant because of gross governmental misconduct—including illegal wire-tapping of Ellsberg and burglary of his psychiatrist's office. The month before, startling revelations occurred in the emerging saga of Watergate. The misconduct directed at Ellsberg turned out to play only a small part in the drama. What had started as five men caught burglarizing Democratic National Headquarters in June 1972 had mushroomed into the biggest political scandal in American history. Back in July of 1970, Nixon's Chief of Staff had secretly forwarded the "Huston Plan" to the CIA, FBI, and national security personnel. The executive order purported to suspend constitutional guarantees to preserve national security by authorizing burglary, illegal electronic surveillance, and opening mail of specified radicals, including the Panthers and Angela Davis at the top of the list. It would later form the basis of an article of impeachment against President Nixon.

Slowly the public learned from investigators what Attorney General Mitchell dubbed the "White House horrors": that their "law and order" President and his aides, had authorized other break-ins, campaign dirty tricks, improper tax audits, and widespread illegal wiretapping. They had also created a secret slush fund for paying off the Watergate burglars, among other covert agents (including Tackwood by his admission). By April 1973, the unfolding Watergate scandal dominated the news with resignations of key White House aides. Over eighty-five percent of Americans would tune into some part of the Senate Watergate Committee hearings that were televised beginning in mid-May.[1]

Later that same month, President Nixon responded to intense political pressure by appointing former Solicitor General Archibald Cox as a special Watergate prosecutor to investigate the growing scandal. Everyone began speculating on the identity of "Deep Throat," the whistleblower source for reporters Bob Woodward and Carl Bernstein's Pulitzer Prize–winning investigative journalism, whose stunning revelations in *The Washington Post* played such a key role in exposing the Watergate scandal. The two journalists collaborated in 1974 on the acclaimed book *All the President's Men,* which was then turned into an Academy Award-winning movie. Not until May 2005 did their source, Mark Felt, former Associate Director of the FBI, come forward.

Back in the summer of 1973, as Cox pursued his responsibilities to trace the official corruption to its source, the United States Attorney in Baltimore undertook a separate investigation against Vice President Spiro Agnew for tax fraud, bribery, and extortion. Agnew was charged with receiving over $100,000 in bribes, not only as governor of Maryland, but also in Washington, D.C., while serving as Vice President. On October 10, 1973, Agnew negotiated a plea by which he resigned from office and pleaded guilty to only one lesser charge: failing to report $29,500 in income in 1967. He thus became the only Vice President to ever resign from office due to scandal.

Ten days later, on October 20, 1973, came the shocking termination of the careers of three top federal prosecutors in one night. The riveting evening news was covered live by all of the nation's major networks. Commentators quickly dubbed it the "Saturday Night Massacre." First came word of Nixon's demand that Attorney General Elliot Richardson fire Cox to prevent the highly respected Harvard Law School professor from seeking Nixon's tapes of Oval Office conversations related to the June 1972 Watergate break-ins. Richardson refused to carry out Nixon's order and instead resigned. Deputy Attorney General William Ruckelshaus followed suit, leaving Solicitor General Robert Bork to implement Nixon's order to fire Cox.

By November 6, 1973, articles of impeachment were already in the works against President Nixon, whose approval ratings had just plummeted to 27 per cent. The media's attention was then temporarily diverted to the assassination of a black superintendent of schools in Oakland, California. On the evening of November 6, 1973, Marcus Foster and an aide were ambushed by gunmen as they left a school board meeting. Immediately following Foster's murder, in letters to a local radio station and *The San Francisco Chronicle,* a previously unknown group called the "Symbionese Liberation Army" claimed credit for the unfathomable crime as a political statement.

The SLA wanted to become the new leaders of a black revolution, expecting to pick up the mantle from other black militant groups. The Panthers were then splintered and diminished in number. It turned out that all but one of the SLA founders were white. To prepare for their entry onto the American political stage, they had spent several months fine-tuning their ideology and logo, while stockpiling weapons and practicing at firing ranges. One of the SLA's founders, Willie Wolfe, was a prisoners' rights advocate associated with Venceremos—Marxist activists based in Northern California who were working with the Soledad Brothers Defense Committee to politicize black inmates at Soledad Prison. There Wolfe met and helped radicalize black prisoner Donald DeFreeze, who, like George Jackson, had been sent to Soledad to serve a term for armed robbery. DeFreeze succeeded in obtaining a transfer from Soledad to the medical prison facility at Vacaville, where DeFreeze took political classes sponsored by the facility's Black Cultural Association. In early March 1973 DeFreeze escaped from Vacaville simply by walking off a fencing project when no one was looking. He holed up in San Francisco with his political allies from Venceremos. DeFreeze was then introduced to Patricia "Mizmoon" Soltysik, a Berkeley student radicalized by Gov. Reagan's lethal response to People's Park in May 1969.

DeFreeze and Soltysik became lovers and comrades. He changed his name to "General Field Marshal Cinque" after the same 19th-century slave Ruchell Magee admired. Together DeFreeze and Soltysik developed literature for the Symbionese Liberation Army, ironically deriving "Symbionese" from "symbiosis" to embody the concept of different organisms living peacefully together. The SLA's far from reassuring symbol was a seven-headed cobra based on an ancient Hindu and Buddhist snake deity. Each head stood for a different principle: unity, self-determination, collective work and responsibility, cooperative economics, purpose, creativity, and faith.

The SLA's poorly timed debut as urban guerrillas in November 1973 gained as little apparent traction on the Left as cult leader Charles Manson had achieved in 1969 among white supremacists on the right. The choice for the SLA's first victim was both bizarre and misinformed. Marcus Foster was a widely popular administrator serving as Oakland's first African-American superintendent of schools. The SLA had targeted him with a cyanide-laced bullet because Foster had approved student identification cards—a decision the group construed as an intolerable act of fascism. Anybody else tempted to draw up a list of people then in power to condemn as fascists would have skipped right over Foster's name. The pioneering African-American, selected with support from both the Left and the black community, was not even the proponent of the new student IDs. He had, in fact, initially opposed the restriction, but later accepted a less stringent new rule for keeping unauthorized people off school campuses. In any event, within a week and a half after Foster's assassination, the nation was far more preoccupied with Nixon's next press conference at which he uttered the much-ridiculed line: "People have got to know whether or not their President is a crook. Well, I'm not a crook."[2]

On January 10, 1974, two members of the SLA, Joseph Remiro and Russell Little, were arrested for Foster's murder. The SLA then plotted its next step designed to grab the headlines, win the release of Remiro and Little, and attract radical support. Its members were apparently oblivious to the fact that police had already demonstrated in the bloody Marin County shootout precipitated by Jonathan Jackson in August 1970 their willingness to let hostages be killed—including a judge and jurors—rather than negotiate with kidnappers seeking to free prisoners. The SLA also was blind to overwhelming evidence that militant Leftists no longer attracted a wide following. The prior coalition of white and black radicals with peace activists, Liberals, and draft-age college students had dissolved when the government discontinued the draft in 1973.

On February 4, 1974, hoping for headlines, they kidnapped newspaper heiress Patti Hearst from her Berkeley apartment where she lived with her fiancé. Hearst was then a sophomore at U.C. Berkeley. Her wealthy father Randolph Hearst was a trustee of the Hearst Corporation, the company formed to own William Randolph Hearst's publishing and real estate empire after his death in 1951. Ownership of the multi-millionaire's palatial estate and art collection at San Simeon—immortalized as Xanadu in the movie *Citizen Kane*—had been donated to the State of California in 1957. When Patti Hearst was abducted, the Hearst Corporation still ran scores of newspapers and had expanded into monthly magazines, radio and television.

The SLA did get the media attention they were seeking. Their first demand of the Hearst family was the exchange of Remiro and Little for their daughter, which was not in the cards. The two arrestees would later face prosecution for Foster's assassination by Alameda County District Attorney Lowell Jensen—his second-most famous trial as lead prosecutor. The SLA then demanded that the Hearsts ransom their daughter by paying for food distribution. The demand became a moving target that soon totaled $70 for each and every needy Californian, whoppingly priced out at $400 million. Hearst responded with a $6 million donation of food to poor residents of the Bay Area that the SLA rejected as insufficient. In the meantime, Patti Hearst was held most of the time in a closet, with all her contact to the outside world controlled by her captors. Within two weeks, she was tape-recorded spouting SLA slogans and supporting their ideology, sounding brain-washed. Apparently, she then became the lover of captor Willie Wolfe. Hearst may have succumbed to the well-recognized phenomenon in psychology called the Stockholm Syndrome, which describes hostages who come to demonstrate loyalty to their kidnappers. But the public was amazed when Hearst soon rejected her former fiancé, her wealthy upbringing, and her parents. She was now Tania the revolutionary—named for a female companion of Che Guevara.

On April 15, 1974, with Tania wielding her own M-1 carbine, the SLA robbed a bank in San Francisco of $10,000, wounding two people in the process. Hearst was featured repeatedly on the news, caught on the bank's videotape shouting orders to frightened bank customers. The SLA then went underground in Los Angeles. On May 16, 1974, some of its members were confronted by a security guard for attempting to shoplift in a sporting goods store, while Hearst acted as lookout in their parked van. The group got away when Hearst fired her gun at the store's sign, but the police were able to trace most of the SLA the following day to their heavily armed headquarters, a house on the 1400 block of East 54th Street in Los Angeles.

As mobile television camera crews rushed to the scene, the SLA hideout was surrounded by several hundred members of the LAPD. They were joined by the FBI, the California Highway Patrol, and a contingent of firemen. A SWAT team with a bullhorn warned the occupants to surrender. When the SLA members refused to come out, tear gas canisters were lobbed into the house, eliciting poorly aimed repeat gunfire in return. More than 9,000 rounds would be fired in the marathon shootout, which may have set a record for a police siege. It ended with the death of six members of the SLA from gunshot wounds, burns, smoke inhalation, and—in the case of Donald DeFreeze—suicide. Mesmerized live-television audiences witnessed the house become consumed in flames. Hearst and two other SLA members were then holed up in an L.A. hotel, their television tuned to the grisly event. They fled to the Bay Area where radical friends hid them from discovery. The spectacular conflagration was soon supplanted in the headlines when Watergate resumed its place as the biggest national story of the era.

Archibald Cox had been replaced in the fall as Special Prosecutor by Leon Jaworski. President Nixon then produced some of the requested Oval Office audiotapes, including one with a suspicious eighteen-and-a-half minute gap. Jaworski pursued other taped conversations that Nixon withheld as privileged. On July 24, 1974, Jaworski obtained a unanimous ruling from the Supreme Court that Nixon had to produce the requested tapes. On July 25, 1974, in a televised meeting of the House Judiciary Committee to consider impeachment articles against President Nixon, pioneering Texas Congresswoman Barbara Jordan etched herself into the national consciousness. First, the humbly raised black representative from Houston reminded viewers that when the Constitution was first adopted in 1787, "I was not included in that 'We, the people.' I felt somehow for many years that George Washington and Alexander Hamilton just left me out by mistake. But through the process of amendment, interpretation, and court decision, I have finally been included in 'We, the people.'" Jordan then set the stage for the historical step Congress was about to undertake: "If the impeachment provision in the Constitution of the United States will not reach the offenses charged here, then perhaps that eighteenth-century Constitution should be abandoned to a twentieth-century paper shredder."[3] By a bipartisan vote of 27 to 11, including every Democrat and six Republicans, the committee adopted articles of impeachment for obstruction of justice, abuse of power, and contempt of Congress.

Then came the smoking gun. On August 5, 1974, newly produced audio tapes revealed President Nixon's complicity in the Watergate break-in cover-up dating back to June 23, 1972, when he ordered his chief aide to halt the FBI investigation of the Watergate burglars to prevent their exposure as secret employees of his re-election committee.[4] Until then Nixon's Republican supporters in Congress had focused on lack of proof that the President himself was involved. What little political support remained for Nixon instantly evaporated. Facing certain adoption of the impeachment allegations by the entire House of Representatives and conviction by the Senate, President Nixon resigned on August 9, 1974, elevating new Vice President Gerald Ford to the presidency. Ford pardoned Nixon the following month. In the course of the *Presidential Scandal that Shook America,*[5] forty government officials were indicted or jailed. So many were lawyers that the National Committee of Bar Examiners soon incorporated ethics questions into the standard examination for graduating law students administered in almost all jurisdictions.

Meanwhile, the remnants of the SLA managed to recruit a few more members. They resurfaced in late April 1975 to rob another bank, killing one of its customers. Patti Hearst accompanied them in the getaway car. It took another five months to find and arrest Hearst for her role in the SLA robberies. She was tried in federal court in San Francisco in 1976, amid great fanfare. To defend the heiress, her wealthy parents hired F. Lee Bailey, the acclaimed veteran of several other high profile trials. Bailey had rocketed to fame a decade earlier when, while still in his mid-thirties, he won Dr. Sam Sheppard's acquittal in his 1966 murder retrial. The Ohio osteopath was vilified in the press before his first trial twelve years before, after he claimed a burglar murdered his pregnant wife. Pretrial publicity accused him of killing her himself to continue a three-year affair with his nurse. The papers had Sheppard virtually convicted before the trial began. Reporters described Sheppard as having an explosive "Jekyll and Hyde" personality which "bombshell witnesses" for the prosecution would reveal; they also invited readers to presume Sheppard's guilt from his refusal to take a lie detector test.[6] A divided Ohio Supreme Court upheld his conviction despite the media circus:

> Murder and mystery, society, sex and suspense were combined in this case in such a manner as to intrigue and captivate the public fancy to a degree perhaps unparalleled in recent annals. Throughout the

> preindictment investigation, the subsequent legal skirmishes and the nine-week trial, circulation-conscious editors catered to the insatiable interest of the American public in the bizarre. Special seating facilities for reporters and columnists representing local papers and all major news services were installed in the courtroom. Special rooms in the Criminal Courts Building were equipped for broadcasters and telecasters. In this atmosphere of a 'Roman holiday' for the news media, Sam Sheppard stood trial for his life."[7]

Though the United States Supreme Court originally denied review,[8] after Dr. Sheppard spent a decade in prison a new majority on the court viewed the issue differently on review of post-trial federal proceedings. The high court noted its long history of respecting the right of the press to "have a free hand" in reporting trial proceedings as an exercise of its First Amendment rights. But the court also had recognized the right of criminal defendants "to a public tribunal free of prejudice, passion, excitement, and tyrannical power."[9] In two prior cases, the high court had reversed convictions where the jurors were exposed to newspaper accounts that included information not admitted at trial. But now it went much further to consider the probability of prejudice from the circus-like atmosphere that the media frenzy had produced.

Realizing that journalists chasing after sensational scoops would never police themselves, the high court finally gave teeth to ethics rules and trial court orders designed to assure trials free from undue outside influence. For the first time, the Supreme Court held that "massive, pervasive and prejudicial pretrial publicity" deprived a defendant of a fair trial under the Fourteenth Amendment. It faulted the Ohio trial judge for neither sequestering Sheppard's jury, nor granting a change of venue. Noting that "participants in the trial, including the jury, were forced to run a gantlet of reporters and photographers each time they entered or left the courtroom," the high court held that the trial judge should also have taken "strong measures" to ensure Sheppard's right to a fair trial by ordering the lawyers, parties, and court officials not to speak to the media on the merits of the case. He should have warned reporters of "the impropriety of publishing material not introduced in the proceedings."[10]

The Supreme Court now set a new standard: "where there is a

reasonable likelihood that prejudicial news prior to trial will prevent a fair trial, the judge should continue the case until the threat abates, or transfer it to another county not so permeated with publicity." It also held the judge should have raised the need to sequester the jury on his own initiative. "If publicity during the proceedings threatens the fairness of the trial, a new trial should be ordered."[11] The Supreme Court encouraged the use of the court's contempt power and other disciplinary measures to enforce criminal defendants' rights. This decision by nine white male jurists—the year before the nation's first African-American Solicitor General, Thurgood Marshall, joined the high court—represented a complete turnaround from the Supreme Court's hands-off approach back in 1915, when Leo Frank's attorneys made a similar claim; in 1927, when Sacco and Vanzetti's lawyers sought its review; in 1935, when Bruno Hauptmann faced execution; and in 1952, when the Rosenberg trial took place amid anti-Communist hysteria, among countless other cases. The right to a fair trial in all state and federal criminal proceedings had now taken on a new meaning—one paved in the blood of so many defendants sacrificed over decades of lucrative yellow journalism.

The *Sheppard* cases inspired the "Fugitive" television show and movie and launched Bailey as a top criminal defense attorney. In a famous court-martial in 1971, Bailey, who was himself a former Marine pilot, supervised the defense team that won the acquittal of Captain Ernest Medina for allegedly ordering the 1968 My Lai massacre of hundreds of unarmed civilians in Vietnam. By then, Medina's subordinate Lieutenant William Calley, Jr. had already been convicted of the heinous crime. At Hearst's trial, as expected, Bailey sought to prove the kidnapped college student had been brain-washed by the SLA into assisting with all the revolutionary acts in which she collaborated. She also claimed that she was raped at the outset by DeFreeze and Wolfe. But Hearst had trouble explaining why she had stayed with the outlaw band for over a year and a half, even continuing to hide out long after the SLA's leadership was killed. When the jury came back quickly, Bailey thought he had won, but the veteran defense lawyer had not been in top form, and Hearst proved an unsympathetic defendant. She was convicted and sentenced to thirty-five years in jail. President Jimmy Carter later commuted her term to seven years; she won a full pardon from President Clinton two decades after her release.

Two SLA members, Russell Little and Joseph Remiro, had already been convicted the year before of participating in the murder of Marcus Foster following a long trial in Sacramento prosecuted by Alameda County District Attorney Lowell Jensen. The case was transferred from Oakland because of the potential prejudice to the jury pool from pretrial publicity about the popular superintendent's execution. The conviction of Russell Little was overturned on appeal for a mistake in a jury instruction, and on retrial he was acquitted. Another SLA member, Kathleen Soliah, who had gone underground, was finally captured in 1999. Living under the assumed name Sara Jane Olson, she had married a Minnesota doctor with whom she had three daughters. Olson finally faced trial for a 1975 charge of attempting to kill policemen in Los Angeles with a car bomb. She was convicted and sentenced to fourteen years. In 2003, she and four other surviving SLA members pleaded guilty to the 1975 death of a bank customer during a robbery the SLA committed. All were sentenced to prison for the second-degree murder and other charges. The last SLA prisoner remaining in prison won release in 2009.

The Patti Hearst story spawned several books, including Hearst's autobiography and the novel *Trance*, as well as documentaries and docudramas. It also found its way into song lyrics and rap music. Not surprisingly, the short-lived urban guerrilla organization with its heiress convert also became the subject of several satires and even turned up as a computer game, "Liberal Crime Squad."

6. DOWNWARD SPIRAL

"Dr. Huey P. Newton" The frailty's and Flaws of a Man.
Genius of an Innovator. Heart of a Black Panther.
Spoken about on the News like a Criminal, mentioning Drug use. So much
blood, from his head, they said
covered almost 15 feet in diameter around his body,
as Huey lay [in] eternal sleep on Concrete . . .
Who killed Huey YO!?
The same people he set out to feed,
educate and free.

EXCERPT FROM THE POEM "WHO KILLED DR. HUEY P. NEWTON,"
BY CAROLYN BAXTER

In 1972, Newton published *To Die for the People: The Writings of Huey Newton,* a collection of essays, statements, speeches, and articles that had mostly been printed in pamphlets over the past five years and had long since been required reading for members of the Party. Random House threw a champagne and fried chicken celebration in his penthouse. By the time his book went to print, Newton had officially renounced the Panther call to arms. Yet he included in this collection without editorial comment a debate he had with American Communist Party head William Patterson over that very issue. In 1970, Patterson praised the unique and remarkable past political achievements of the Panther Party, but argued strongly that "under today's conditions in the U.S.A. [asserting that liberation comes from guns] is to commit a provocation for which one will pay dearly." Newton responded, "Should we stop defending ourselves? Is he saying that the gun is not a tool we will eventually have to use?"[1] The very title of his book hinted that Newton the revolutionary remained very close to the surface even as his many Liberal friends toasted the new author in his penthouse. From his elitist perch, Huey then launched a populist political campaign that could easily have come from the playbook of the Louisiana demagogue for whom he was named.

Bobby Seale and his then assistant Huey Newton had first become involved in gathering 5,000 signatures urging the City Council to create a community police review board when they were both employed by the North Oakland Service Center—before the Panthers came into existence. In the summer of 1968, the Panthers themselves registered as a political party and conducted a number of other major signature drives in the flatlands after running candidates for office on the Peace and Freedom Party ticket. Now they renewed promotion of community policing and expanded the Panthers' popular free children's breakfast programs and testing for sickle cell anemia. (By the time the blood-testing program ended, the Panthers would check more than a million and a half African-Americans for that inherited blood abnormality.)

In 1973, at Newton's direction, the Panthers completed ambitious plans for an alternative learning center for elementary school children. Meanwhile, Dr. Herman Blake joined Newton in his penthouse library writing his autobiography, *Revolutionary Suicide*. Newton, who still reportedly had trouble with cursive, dictated his recollections, and Blake turned them into marketable prose, edited to leave out the most damaging admissions. Newton bragged about getting away with many robberies and thefts, but appeared mindful that murder had no statute of limitations. The pair aimed to convince readers that the Servant of the People was exactly what Pulitzer Prize–winning journalist Murray Kempton called him in his *New York Times* book review: "one and the same time the baddest and the goodest." Kempton recalled Malcolm X and others who became majestic as martyrs, and asserted that Newton almost did, too, but "must live . . . with the crime of having survived . . . a hero to the alienated and a thug to the comfortable . . . we must hear him out because we suspect that he comes not as avenger but as healer."[2] Later editions would list Dr. Blake as a co-author of Newton's enigmatic life story.

No longer looking simply for protest votes, Newton orchestrated both Seale's spirited race for Mayor of Oakland against two-term incumbent Mayor John Reading, and Elaine Brown's parallel race for City

Council. The campaign put the Panthers directly up against the Republican machine that had held enormous sway in Oakland politics since 1915—what opponents dubbed "The Power in the Oakland Tribune Tower." Its publisher, former Senator William Knowland, had inherited the newspaper from his extraordinarily influential Congressman father Joseph Knowland, who had run the newspaper for the past half century. Brown, still under thirty and a relative newcomer to Oakland, later said she ran only at Newton's insistence, to keep an eye on Seale for him.

With the Panthers' proven popularity in the flatlands, they could count on several key African-American politicians in the East Bay to support their slate. Though accompanied by bodyguards, the pair toned down their rhetoric and donned suits to glad-hand supporters as they promoted the idea of turning Oakland into a convention city attracting major hotels and upscale restaurants. But Brown later boasted in her autobiography, *A Taste of Power: A Black Woman's Story*, that switching to the ballot from the bullet was just a façade while the Party's underground operations continued unabated and they stockpiled weapons for the revolution. That same year, Newton elevated ex-Marine Ray "Masai" Hewitt to the post of Minister of Education. Among other things, Hewitt taught all new recruits the official "Weaver" two-handed stance American police had perfected to become what the Panthers called "some of the best combat-handgun-shooting motherfuckers in the world."[3]

Brown was more at ease than Seale schmoozing with potential white supporters for political endorsements. Most of her friends in private school growing up were Jewish girls. Her resumé included attendance at the Philadelphia Conservatory of Music and Mills College. Yet Elaine's impoverished single mother had to overcome daunting obstacles to give her daughter that opportunity for advancement. Like Huey, Elaine developed a lust for power. She had long since learned how to survive in the 'hood and embraced Newton's secret underworld life as necessary to the Party's success—without guns and the threat of violence she felt they would get nowhere. By the time Brown ran, the accomplished singer-songwriter considered herself Newton's queen—more accurately his office wife, his trusted confidante helping him carry out his plan to seize control of Oakland as the Panthers' base of operations.

Newton found particularly enticing all the cargo ships coming in and out of the Port of Oakland. In 1962, Newton had witnessed Oakland becoming the first city on the Pacific Coast where container ships could dock. (The huge cranes put in place for loading and unloading on the West Oakland shore gave George Lukas the idea for animated mechanical creatures in his original epic film *Star Wars.*) By the time Newton and Seale founded the Panther Party, the Port handled the second highest tonnage of cargo shipments worldwide. It still remained among the top few when Newton orchestrated Seale's 1973 mayoral campaign, though two Southern California ports were in the process of bypassing its volume of trade. Secretly, Newton expected to put the Party Chairman in a position to make puppet appointments of Commissioners to the Oakland Port Authority so that it would turn a blind eye to drug and gun smuggling. Ex-Panther Flores Forbes remembers Seale telling a rapt audience of recruits that once he was in office the Panthers could loot the port at will to fund the revolution.[4] But under Oakland's then weak, part-time mayoral system, the Panthers would also have to take over most of the council seats. All of the mayor's recommendations of candidates for staggered terms on the Port Commission were subject to approval by a majority of the City Council. More significantly, federal immigration officials—not Port Commissioners—monitored (and still monitor) all of the port's shipments.

Newton and Brown first met shortly after his release from prison in the late summer of 1970. By then, she had carried out several key Party assignments and was just returning from joining Eldridge Cleaver on a Panther good will tour to Communist countries, traveling on her passport to France and then secretly to Russia, North Korea, North Vietnam, Red China, and Cleaver's headquarters in Algiers, before resurfacing in Paris to use her passport to head home. Already radicalized before she joined the Panthers' Los Angeles branch in the spring of 1968, Elaine had become enthralled by Eldridge Cleaver's aggressive style and bold message when the famed author of *Soul On Ice* first came to Los Angeles to fundraise for Newton's defense. On his next trip to L.A. in the early spring of 1968, Brown met Cleaver at a party and spent a night with him before he headed back to Oakland. It was just before Martin Luther King's assassination and the newlywed Cleaver's return to jail for parole violation.

Soon afterward, Brown joined the recently formed second chapter of the Panthers. She already knew its founder, ex-felon Alprentice "Bunchy" Carter, who belonged to a local gang called the Slauson Street Renegades, and had earned the nickname the "Mayor of the Ghetto." Brown soon moved into a commune of Black Panthers run by Carter and his co-leader John Huggins and Huggins' wife Ericka. While living with them, Brown also met ex-Green Beret Elmer "Geronimo" Pratt and Ray "Masai" Hewitt and learned how to make Molotov cocktails and to shoot guns at target practice in the Mojave Desert. Brown soon started attending UCLA where she and John Huggins worked closely together on Panther projects and became lovers. She claimed joint credit with him for establishing the hugely successful Panther breakfast program in Los Angeles that prompted the FBI to instigate Huggins' and Carter's murder by the members of US. Brown was just a few steps behind the pair of Panther leaders leaving a UCLA black student meeting in January of 1969 when they were ambushed. Deeply shaken by that experience, Brown soon afterward hooked up for a short while with Hewitt and had his baby, but left early years of mothering to others as she committed herself wholeheartedly to Party business. Elaine was smart and skillful, but alienated many local Panthers. Hilliard decided to get her out of Los Angeles for her own safety. He had heard Elaine sing at Carter's funeral and arranged for her to go to Motown to record her first album, *Seize the Time.* Hilliard then sent Elaine to Bridgeport, Connecticut, with Huggins' widow Ericka to open a Panther office in John Huggins' home town. After Ericka Huggins and Bobby Seale were arrested on charges of conspiracy to murder suspected informant Alex Rackley, Hilliard asked Brown to handle pretrial publicity for their New Haven trial.

Newton had first been mesmerized by Brown's voice at the Men's Colony in San Luis Obispo. To while away the hours in his cell, Newton often played a tape of *Seize the Time,* including a song for Eldridge Cleaver that the Party adopted as its national anthem. On his trip East with Hilliard shortly after his release, Newton—now dubbed by the Central Committee the Black Panther Party's "Supreme Commander"—first stayed with Jane Fonda in her penthouse apartment on the upper East Side. (Fonda was temporarily based in New York filming *Klute* with Donald Sutherland, for which she would win her first academy award.) Fonda hosted a press conference and threw a party for Newton to celebrate the signing of Newton's first publication contract, which would be released two years later as *To Die for the People: The Writings of Huey P. Newton.* As COINTELPRO agents kept close watch, Hilliard and Charles Garry accompanied the Party leader to the airport to greet Elaine Brown on her return from Paris. Hilliard had arranged the meeting and rooms for the three at a hotel so Newton could privately get a firsthand account of Cleaver's newly announced plans for international Panther offices with a more aggressive agenda than those in the states. As Newton had already heard, Cleaver still wanted to proceed rapidly toward rebellion in the streets. Brown reported that she had a falling out with Cleaver and felt lucky to return alive after she resisted his efforts to enlist her to assassinate Hilliard.

Newton wasted no time adding Brown to his female conquests. For her part, Brown became enthralled the moment she met the muscle-toned leader of the Party. On his return to the Bay Area, Newton was still camped out at Alex Hoffmann's and Elsa Knight Thompson's home in Berkeley under constant FBI surveillance. Brown later recalled that within weeks she found a way to address Hilliard's concern for Huey's continued safety. She pillow-talked $12,000 from Bert Schneider for a year's advance rent on an upscale Oakland penthouse on Lake Merritt. The Panthers had rented it under the name of a go-between, assuming that if the landlord knew the true identity of his new tenant before Huey moved in, he would want to evict the revolutionary as soon as possible. David Hilliard recalls that Newton had already moved into the penthouse through the efforts of realtor Arlene Slaughter with funds from other supporters like author Don Freed and Donald and Shirley Sutherland when Brown introduced Schneider to Newton as an additional benefactor. Elaine then moved from Los Angeles to Oakland, where she helped Seale edit the Panther paper and in 1971, collaborated with Newton to create the highly successful Oakland Community School. The school's planning team was headed by Newton's Marxist friend, David Horowitz, a former editor of the now-defunct *Ramparts* magazine. When Brown later focused on running for office, Horowitz remained on the Board and Ericka Huggins was promoted from being one of the teachers to the school's director.

The key to Seale's and Brown's election in the city's changing demographics was greatly increasing black voter turnout. To register residents in the flatlands, they enticed them with truckloads of free groceries and shoes, delivering the fast food equivalent of Herbert Hoover's 1928 campaign promise: "a chicken in every pot." Civil rights leaders endorsed their new Fourteen Point Program—even widow Coretta Scott King. Yet Decca Mitford was likely not alone in considering the idea of a convention city a decidedly non-Leftist agenda. Having managed her husband's own unsuccessful run for District Attorney several years before, Decca also wondered how the Panthers managed an expensive campaign with so many give-aways without holding any fund-raising parties.

Despite Mayor Reading's popularity as the man who built the Coliseum Sports Complex and brought the World Champion Oakland A's to town, Seale won 43,000 votes. Seale also laid the groundwork—with Panther support—for former judge Lionel Wilson to become the city's first black mayor four years later and to preside in his three terms over what *The New York Times* called "a racial, cultural, economic and political revolution."[5] J. Edgar Hoover never lived to see Seale's historic 1973 Oakland race. The founder of the modern FBI died in early May 1972, a month before worldwide supporters of Angela Davis celebrated her amazing acquittal. Hoover was then 77 and had served almost 55 controversial years with the Bureau and its predecessor. (Concerned by the extraordinary power Hoover wielded, in 1968, Congress had changed the law to limit all his successors to ten-year terms.) Since the law-and-order czar's death, late night comedians have had a field day ridiculing the dossier-gatherer's own reputed private life with material none dared use during his tenure. In 1973 the public learned much about Hoover's role in the Watergate scandal. The extensive illegal wiretaps were already known to the Panthers, though the specifics of Hoover's secret war against the Party would only be brought to light by the Senate Church Committee in 1976.

* * * * *

Increasingly in the early '70s, as Newton spent his time mostly holed up in his penthouse, his heavy cocaine and alcohol use caused him to erupt in delusional rages. He liked listening to tapes blaring the lyrics of his new favorite song, the 1973 Johnnie Taylor megahit "I Believe in You": "One thing I can say about the people in the world today, they see you with a good thing they want to take it away." In early 1974, Newton started expelling old friends from the Party, including Gene McKinney and David Hilliard's wife, Pat, whom Newton accused of stealing from the Party. Newton then expelled his new chief of staff June Hilliard and David Hilliard, too, though he was still doing time in prison. Word circulated that David Hilliard was suspected of planning a coup, which no one believed about the diehard loyalist.

Newton had often gone marauding at night with bodyguards in the early years of the Party, but had only recently created two clandestine teams of five or six highly trained armed men, whom he dubbed "the Squad." Former Panther enforcer Flores Forbes later wrote that one or the other team always accompanied Newton in his late night forays to nightclubs and bars where owners were pressured for money. Squad members were rewarded for their loyalty with cocaine and liquor, women, and the thrill of basking in the aura of the Supreme Servant of the People or more recently just "The Servant"—Newton now rejected the term "Commander." For the Party leader, the Squad would do practically anything, even die.[6]

In July 1974, according to a number of sources, including Elaine Brown, Newton precipitated an argument with his co-founder Bobby Seale in front of the now largely powerless Central Committee. By then Newton dictated all decisions. The two were discussing a film Newton wanted Bert Schneider to produce and expected Seale to play the lead in. Suddenly, Newton erupted in anger at a comment Seale made. The Squad drew their guns as Newton assaulted Seale and whipped him severely. Hugh Pearson, author of *Shadow of the Panther: Huey Newton and the Price of Black Power in America,* reported that Seale went to a sympathetic local doctor who patched him up and then Seale fled into exile, hiding out on the East Coast in fear for his life.[7] Seale later vehemently denied any such confrontation, but admitted that he left the Party abruptly that summer. Many years later, Seale told a reporter that the big issue dividing the two Party founders was that, in 1974, Newton was trying to "shake down pimps and drug dealers, and as a result, the ne'er-do-well population of Oakland had taken out a contract on Newton's life. "I was very, very pissed," Seale maintains. "If I stayed around, I probably would have killed Huey myself."[8]

Soon after Seale's departure, Newton was in trouble again with the law, first threatening two plainclothes policemen and then for two far more serious alleged eruptions. A seventeen-year-old black prostitute named Kathleen Smith was shot in the head by a man who accosted her while she was loitering on an Oakland street corner. Newton then suddenly left town, disappearing south for a few days with his old friend Bert Schneider. When Newton came back to Oakland he headed for the Lamp Post, which he co-owned and was fully staffed with Panther loyalists. There, his explosive temper reportedly again got the better of him. Members of its staff and a couple of customers suffered injuries; the two women customers filed charges, accusing Newton of assault and false imprisonment.

That same night, Newton invited a tailor named Preston Callins to his penthouse to measure Newton for a new suit. Newton had adopted *The Godfather* image after watching the Coppola gangster film multiple times and making it required viewing for Party members. Callins told police that Newton started an argument with him over the cost of the suit and, when Callins tried to calm him down, out of habit Callins addressed Newton by the term "baby" just as Callins addressed good friends and members of his family. Callins said that set Newton off; he repeatedly bashed Callins in the head with a pistol, shouting, "Nobody calls me baby."[10] The name had enraged him since kindergarten. Callins suffered multiple skull fractures for which he was hospitalized. A search warrant produced the gun from Newton's apartment, which gave rise to a separate charge since ex-felons forfeited the right to possess a gun. (It was not the one used on Kathleen Smith, which Newton reportedly tossed into the Bay.) Elaine Brown later wrote that, by the time the police arrived, she and Gwen Fountaine had made sure all of Callins' blood on the walls, ceiling, and in the bathroom of the penthouse had been cleaned up.

At the time, Smith lay hospitalized in a coma, with a bullet wound through her jaw and spinal cord. Doctors gave her little chance of survival. Three prostitutes had identified Newton in a photo lineup as the man whom they saw drive by in a chauffeured new Lincoln Continental the night Smith got shot. One of them called out, "Hey, baby." The oldest of the three, Raphaelle Gary, whose street name was Crystal Grey, said the car then returned shortly afterward. The chauffeur parked, while the irate passenger got out and approached them. The others scattered as he pulled out a small caliber revolver and began to argue with Smith. Grey told police that she turned back after she heard the shot and saw the car speed off. The Party put up nine houses as collateral for Newton's $80,000 bail. At the same time, Newton was also targeted by a prison gang for execution. The Black Guerrilla Family ("BGF"), headed by San Quentin Six defendant Hugo Pinell, traced its roots to George Jackson, whom the BGF believed Newton had betrayed. Police Chief Gain relayed yet another threat: word that Newton had been placed on a Mafia hit list with a $10,000 price on his head.

After forcing out Bobby Seale in July, Newton had elevated Elaine Brown to Party Chair. Women in the Party still had great trouble commanding respect from the men, but few members dared question his choice to their leader's face. As later revealed, disobedient Party members were often whipped, beaten, or "mud-holed" in a pit of cold water on the Panther school property.[11] Facing the likelihood of prison or death in California, Newton opted to flee for Cuba with his fiancée and secretary Gwen Fountaine. Newton had friends who had visited Cuba recently and assumed he would be warmly received there. Though the Party leader and Fay Stender seldom crossed paths anymore, he may have heard from Charles Garry about Stender's trip to Havana in 1973 as part of a delegation of lawyers arranged by the Center for Cuban Studies in New York.[12] Stender had been introduced at a cigar factory as George Jackson's lawyer and received a spontaneous standing ovation. When Newton left for Mexico en route to Cuba on August 17, 1974, he expected his absence to be temporary. Meanwhile, he instructed his loyal cadre of enforcers and his personal bodyguard to back Elaine Brown up in his stead. It was obvious there were no men left that Newton trusted enough to act as his proxy, or could be counted on to step aside on his return.

Newton's disappearance gave others in the Party ideas about unseating her. Brown struck a deal to consolidate her new power as "the Dragon Lady." She became lovers with the new chief enforcer, Larry Henson, showering him with high-priced suits, an expensive apartment, and an unlimited expense account. Together they inventoried the secret locations of the extensive Panther arsenal, properties, and cash. She then called a convention of Panthers from the cities across the country where they still remained, had them frisked for weapons before they gathered, and warned them point blank against insurrection. Facing the biggest challenge of her life, Brown strode across the stage in high-heeled boots, projecting the fiercest image she could with the squad right behind her. She informed her street-smart audience that she controlled all the Party's assets, and that they could either leave the Party if they could not follow her orders or expect Newton's enforcers to deal harshly with disloyalty just as they had before.

By the time of that meeting, Newton was two weeks gone, which left the Party to suffer the consequences of his bail forfeiture. Some did test the reorganized Party leadership, but, according to Brown, chief enforcer Hensen soon whipped into submission "the hardest of the men, aboveground and underground."[13] Hensen also skillfully quashed a rebellion of extortion victims. Brown was delighted with the results, however they were accomplished. Brown herself had been badly beaten once by a Panther boyfriend in L.A.; during her reign, she personally oversaw him get beaten to a pulp for insubordination. In her purse she carried a .38 for protection as she was chauffeured around by Newton's four-hundred-pound, six-foot-seven bodyguard. Brown admitted that she herself sometimes threatened or slapped people who got in her way. However messily, the transition from Newton to his designee did get accomplished.

Ironically, Newton almost lost his life when the rowboat used for the last leg of the trip capsized. Newton had never learned to swim; Gwen saved him. To Newton's dismay, Castro declined to meet with him, but the Cubans did offer the pair asylum despite lingering unhappiness over their experience with Eldridge Cleaver. When Cleaver arrived in exile in December of 1968, he had envisioned being taught how to conduct guerrilla warfare together with ex-patriot hijackers already in Cuba. Most Americans were then unaware that hijackers who flew to Havana faced immediate arrest as suspected spies. Only after the Cubans assured themselves otherwise were the hijackers released from jail. Cleaver was housed in a comfortable apartment, but told not to meet with other American ex-felons or to draw undue attention to himself. He thumbed his nose at such restrictions and gave a published interview. Castro's government ended up considering "El Hacha" (the Spanish word for cleaver) an unwelcome guest and in early June of 1969 gave him a one-way ticket to attend the first Pan-African Cultural Festival in Algiers.

Cleaver still lived in exile in North Africa when Newton left for Cuba, but returned to the United States the following year. Long since expelled from the Panther Party and disillusioned with the Left, Cleaver announced on his return that he had undergone a religious epiphany. To the amusement of detractors, he had just tried his hand at revolutionary clothing design, marketing "the Cleaver sleeve" pants with a 20th century codpiece, and finding few takers. The born-again Christian turned himself in for his outstanding parole violation. Cleaver then faced trial on an attempted murder charge for the ambush of Oakland police in April 1968; he, in turn, alleged that the FBI tried to assassinate him. Ultimately, his high-powered legal team, headed by San Franciscan John Keker, negotiated five-years' probation in exchange for Cleaver's guilty plea simply to assault upon the officers. The Panthers suspected that another part of the deal was turning informant. They heard that, upon his return, Cleaver testified under seal before a closed session of a Senate Committee investigating Leftist plots.[14]

* * * * *

The marathon trial of the San Quentin Six had not yet begun when Newton fled. With Charles Garry among the lawyers on the defense, the trial lasted nearly seventeen months, from March 23, 1975, to August 12, 1976. It included three months just for jury selection from two thousand prospects. This time, Louis Tackwood became a star witness for the defense, detailing his claimed knowledge of a CCS Red Squad plan to smuggle in an unusable gun and fake explosives to Jackson through false friends like Tackwood, so Jackson could be cut down attempting to escape. The defense implicated the late Jimmy Carr as well. (Reportedly, Tackwood later claimed that Charles Garry paid him to lie about a CCS plot to kill Jackson.)[15] When the trial ended, it set a new record for California's longest criminal trial. Soledad Brother Fleeta Drumgo and two other defendants were exonerated, two were found guilty of assault, and only one, Black Panther Johnnie Spain (whom Garry represented), was convicted of murder for joining in the attempted escape. That verdict was overturned in 1986 based on the prejudicial effect of the jury seeing Spain shackled in 25 pounds of chains throughout most of the trial. Lawyer Stephen Bingham did not resurface from overseas for thirteen years. Then the Yale law school graduate was tried for allegedly smuggling the gun to Jackson to help his client escape—yet another front-page prosecution associated with the Soledad Brothers. Bingham also won acquittal.[16]

Since government agents knew of Jackson's elaborate plan to escape with the help of the Black Panthers well ahead of time, questions remained unanswered about whom to blame for the bloodbath. Who smuggled in a gun to Jackson—an accomplice or a mole? Was he set up for slaughter by COINTELPRO, or did the prison simply respond to an uprising? What was Huey Newton's role? Leftwing British journalist Jo Durden-Smith endeavored to discover the truth. In *Who Killed George Jackson? Fantasies, Paranoia and Revolution,* Durden-Smith concluded that both sides were to blame. He also noted many similarities between Newton and Jackson's personalities and elevation to godlike status among Leftists. Prosecuted for murder, each had "stood at the crossroads where two fantasies meet"; each "had been both victim and assassin, too good to have done it and too bad not to have done it."[17] By the time Durden-Smith finished his research and interviews with participants, including Newton, the freelance journalist felt he had just emerged from a snake pit and fled the country, afraid for his own life.

* * * * *

Though there were no direct telephone connections, Elaine Brown said she was in frequent communication with Newton in Cuba. Over the next year she gained greater influence in Oakland, forming productive alliances with Republican businessmen keen on economic development. Meanwhile, Squad members were suspected of committing more crimes, but victims were too afraid to come forward. Four months after Newton fled the country, a Berkeley resident, Betty Louise Van Patter, was reported missing by her family. Van Patter had been a bookkeeper at *Ramparts* magazine whom David Horowitz later recommended to Brown when the nonprofit Oakland Community School faced an IRS audit. The police suspected the Squad engineered Van Patter's disappearance because she had asked too many questions about hundreds of thousands of dollars in federal grant money that could not all be traced. Brown reported that she had fired Van Patter without notice a week earlier, but the bookkeeper was last seen at the Lamp Post bar, which police knew was a Panther hangout. The following month Van Patter's bloated, battered body washed up from the San Francisco Bay—a murder never officially solved, which sent chills through the local Leftist community. The grim discovery traumatized Horowitz, galvanizing his decision to quit working with the Panthers and to rethink his entire political outlook. He eventually emerged as the prominent Neo-Conservative scholar and political strategist he remains today, forever disillusioned with the radical movement he helped launch and the failure of its leadership to condemn Panther atrocities.

Yet no evidence ever emerged to prosecute anyone for the murder. A few years later, Horowitz met with Newton and reported that Newton then pointed the finger at Elaine Brown. Brown continued to deny any knowledge of what happened, though she had no kind words for Van Patter, whose inquisitiveness could have resulted in the "arrests of our people and the destruction of our programs. . . [There was] no question that many of our money transactions could be ruled illegal."[18] At the time of Van Patter's murder, Brown was hard at work improving the Party's public image, not only with the highly successful Oakland Community School, but also by offering assistance for seniors and classes for teenagers in martial arts and dance.

Brown visited Newton later in 1975 in Cuba. Portraits of Che Guevara were everywhere. Though the Cubans had implemented universal health care and education, many aspects of Newton's new life under the revolutionary government depressed him. Unlike Eldridge Cleaver, Newton followed instructions to keep a low profile. The Cuban government strongly favored traditional families and the work ethic. Brown arrived extremely angry at Newton for marrying Gwen, whose two children joined them in exile. Yet Newton had just quit his job in a Santa Clara cement factory—his first real experience in the blue collar world. Gwen took full-time employment, so when Newton was idle, the couple met the Cubans' expectations of at least one productive worker in the family.

As presents, Brown smuggled in $10,000 in cash Newton had requested and brought him leather pants and silk shirts, a watch, and other luxuries he missed from his old life style, even issues of *Playboy*, which he found unobtainable in Cuba. He told Elaine he felt like a man without a country, his sense of isolation undoubtedly exacerbated by his not having learned much Spanish. Nor did radios play American or British popular music, bourgeois culture which the new government strongly frowned upon as it sought to reestablish appreciation for traditional Cuban tunes. When later interviewed, Newton described exile as the worst experience in his life, apparently even in comparison to "the soul-breaker" isolation cell. While Gwen juggled household duties and her job, Huey and Elaine strategized on a plan for changing the political climate back home to allow for his return. Soon Newton would have another job assignment in a factory motor pool, biding his time until he had an opportunity to resume control of the Panther Party.

That same year, Brown ran again for Oakland City Council. This time she garnered a long list of endorsements, including from labor and newly elected Gov. Jerry Brown. Brown's chief of staff Tony Kline (now a presiding justice on the Court of Appeal) was a former Panther lawyer. In 1974, the Panthers turned out record numbers of voters for the Democratic gubernatorial candidate in Oakland's flatlands. Despite the cloud created by Van Patter's unsolved death and Elaine's embarrassing arrest at the airport for possession of a small amount of cocaine, she obtained 44 percent of the vote in her own second race. In April of 1976, Senator Frank Church's Senate Select Committee issued a report on "The FBI's Covert Action Program to Destroy the Black Panther Party." It followed several other reports shocking the public with details of international assassination plots by the CIA and illegal domestic spying by the FBI. The Party soon brought suit alleging $100 million in damages against the FBI, CIA, and local police (it would end in dismissal). Elaine then got selected as a presidential delegate for Gov. Brown to the 1976 Democratic Convention in Madison Square Garden. Later that same year, Elaine orchestrated the Panthers' get-out-the-vote effort in the flatlands to propel Newton's old lawyer, Democrat John George, into office as the first African-American to serve on the Alameda County Board of Supervisors in its one-hundred-twenty-three-year history. Newton could tell the tide was turning.

With blacks now a major factor at the ballot box, Oakland appeared primed to elect its first African-American mayor. Newton had heard through the grapevine before Elaine Brown visited him in 1975 that his old boss at the poverty project, Judge Lionel Wilson, found life on the bench did not suit his temperament and wanted to step down and run. The sixty-two-year-old Democrat had an impressive resumé for a man with political ambitions. Wilson grew up on the streets of Oakland. He first drew attention as a star athlete in baseball, basketball, and tennis in high school in Oakland and college at U.C. Berkeley, while supporting himself much of the time as a dishwasher, porter, or on a factory assembly line. Wilson then played baseball on the short-lived Oakland Larks Negro League team. His career ended just a few years shy of the first steps toward integration of baseball. Wilson saw combat toward the end of World War II and, on his return, studied law and focused his practice on civil rights. In the '50s, he made two failed bids to serve on the Berkeley City Council before Gov. Pat Brown appointed him in 1960 as the first black judge in the county.

When it became clear that Mayor Reading would leave office after his third term and create an open seat, Newton believed that Wilson, as a popular Liberal Democrat, could be the Panthers' Dr. Sun Yat-sen—the revolutionary doctor venerated by both the Communist Chinese and Nationalists in Taiwan for establishing modern China as a republic. Wilson might similarly unify Democrats and end long-time Republican control of California's fourth largest city. Elaine Brown invited Wilson to join the board of the Oakland Community School. She then discussed with him the idea of running for mayor, offering to organize his campaign and to provide him with a campaign manager. In return, she said she made three requests: that, if elected, Wilson would replace the police chief with a black who understood he owed his job to the Panthers; that Wilson would also accept Elaine Brown as "a silent partner in his selection of a new city manager"; and that as mayor he would support her "recommendations for vacancies on the port board." Brown later boasted that Wilson readily agreed to these conditions, as "the least" he could do.[19] As grateful as he was for Panther support, it is hard to believe that Wilson offered to sign away such blanket authority. Indeed, one of the Mayor's closest advisors finds the idea preposterous: the Wilson he knew so well was a strong-willed, self-made man who never let anybody dictate what he did.[20] Although the mayor's race was officially non-partisan, Wilson also had strong backing from every local Democrat and from labor. Before leaving the bench to run for mayor, Wilson received a gift box of Cuban cigars from Huey in Havana. The judge readily divulged their source to court personnel.

Wilson also garnered the endorsement of Reggie Jackson, Mr. October from the now three-time World Series Champion Oakland A's. To add to the momentum, at the Panthers' instigation, actress Jane Fonda, married since 1973 to Tom Hayden, campaigned for Wilson, too. (This presented a mixed blessing for Wilson. The academy award–winner's ill-advised 1972 photo taken in North Vietnam atop an anti-aircraft gun had branded her to many Americans as a traitor.) In the primary only 30 percent of voters turned out from the flatlands, but Wilson still headed the field by eight percentage points. Support from Liberal white Democrats helped propel Wilson into a run-off with Republican Dave Tucker, then President of the Board of Education. In televised debates, Tucker focused on the need for more police and accused Wilson of leniency as a judge, which Wilson attacked as a racist falsehood.

In the final week, Gov. Jerry Brown endorsed Wilson. Helped by Panthers walking door-to-door to turn out flatland residents, Wilson won 53 percent of the vote to become the first African-American mayor of a major city on the West Coast. Elaine Brown boasted to a reporter that "there is not a black who can get elected to office in Oakland without us."[21] What thrilled Wilson most was becoming the first mayor elected without the endorsement of *The Oakland Tribune.* At the packed swearing-in ceremonies, he vowed to "have an open and honest administration."[22] In his next editorial, Senator Knowland referred to Wilson's comment that "no one segment elected him and that no one segment will get preferential treatment." Knowland promised to be "watching with great interest."[23]

Eight days after the election, Wilson announced his transition team chief, his young white campaign lawyer Zach Wasserman. The press release shared headlines with news that Newton was negotiating the terms of his return from Cuba. Newton arrived at the San Francisco Airport on July 3, two days after Wilson was sworn in. He and Charles Garry brazenly held a press conference there before Newton surrendered to police. As a welcome committee, the Panthers transported close to three hundred members and their children to the airport only to be overwhelmed by thousands of other groupies, plus numerous policemen and reporters. The now bearded thirty-five-year-old surprised everyone by announcing that the Panthers would undertake as their new goal ridding Oakland of the menace of drug dealers. Elaine Brown had alerted Newton that heroin kingpin Felix Mitchell had established operations of his multimillion dollar criminal enterprise right across the street from Newton's award-winning Community School. While he transported his boss to the Oakland jail, enforcer Flores Forbes wondered what on earth drove Newton to make such a crazy commitment. Crossing the Bay Bridge, Forbes traveled in a joint caravan with the police—a first for members of "The Squad." At the courthouse, Newton surrendered on the felony charges that were pending when he had fled: pistol-whipping his tailor, assaulting two patrons of the Lamp Post, shooting seventeen-year-old prostitute Kathleen Smith, and carrying an illegal weapon. Newton was well aware that Smith had died in November of 1974 without ever regaining consciousness, so he now faced another first degree murder trial. This time, the death penalty was not at issue.

Newton's new attorneys boldly sought to have him released without bail because he had voluntarily returned to the jurisdiction. A large crowd once again attended his arraignment. Deputy Dist. Atty. Tom Orloff asked for $100,000 bail in light of Newton's demonstrated history of flight. Newton's new attorney countered that Newton was a "man of integrity, honor and decency" who only left in 1974 due to "imminent threats to his life."[24] To support release on his own recognizance, Newton's counsel filed an impressive array of declarations, including ones from former Atty. General Ramsey Clark, Congressman Ron Dellums and Assemblyman Willie Brown, Rev. Cecil Williams of Glide Memorial Church, Jessica Mitford, and David Horowitz, who vouched for Newton during the time he worked with him as "a man of his word who carried through on commitments." Less likely to persuade the court was one from Panther school director Ericka Huggins describing Newton as a "very calm, gentle, sensitive and powerful human being."[25] But these character references notwithstanding, the judge set bail at $80,000. This time, it was not as easy to raise as before. When he hit town, Newton must have already known that many more Party members had quit while he was away. Among the several hundred who remained, it may have surprised him how many had issues with his renewed leadership, and resented depleting Party funds once more to put up a hefty bail. Yet most of the money was raised by selling "Justice for Huey" bumper stickers. Newton and his family then moved into a two-story home in the Oakland hills purchased by benefactors. Newton prominently displayed on the wall a black Buddha Samurai, the other name Newton had given "the Squad."

With Newton back, *The Oakland Tribune* reported increased incidents of extortion and violence, but crime victims did not file any complaints against him. Still, Newton may have felt the heat not only from the police, but drug lords. On the Board of the Community School was a teacher who had helped design its curriculum. William Henry Moore had received his Ph.D. from a new program at U.C. Santa Cruz in the History of Consciousness. In 1974, at Prof. Blake's invitation, Newton had obtained a bachelor's degree there despite his growing drug addiction and rumors his papers were not entirely his own work product. He and Prof. Blake had since fallen out, but after returning from Cuba, Newton showed up at Santa Cruz with his bodyguards and talked an astonished faculty committee into admitting the internationally known militant into the Ph.D. program while he awaited trial for murder. The department head let Newton's bodyguards accompany him around campus, but drew the line when Newton came to class apparently high on drugs or sought a pass for a project by simply showing a movie about the assassination of Fred Hampton and taking softball questions from the audience. He did better when submitting papers.

With Newton often in Santa Cruz, Elaine Brown felt a foreboding of doom. Shortly before Newton's return from exile in Cuba, she had caused a backlash among the men in the Party by appointing a number of women to key leadership positions. Elaine now had her daughter living with her and attending the Oakland Community School. The two had moved in with Ericka Huggins, amid rumors among disgruntled Panther men that Brown had become a lesbian. Brown began spending more and more time in seclusion, fearful that she was now considered expendable.

The weekend before Newton's October 24, 1977, preliminary hearing for the alleged murder of Kathleen Smith, Flores Forbes set out with two other armed hit men in his Squad, Rendell Jefferson and Louis "Tex" Johnson. All three wore dark jumpsuits, ski masks, and gloves as they headed for Richmond with guns and ammo and back-up support. They resembled a government SWAT team, the new special units put into operation a few years back to combat the Panthers and other new militant threats. Forbes later wrote that he had been planning for months on his own initiative to kill Crystal Grey, but did not know where she lived. Prosecutor Tom Orloff had only been ordered to reveal Grey's address to Newton's new defense team in mid-October to allow them to prepare to question the star witness at Newton's preliminary hearing.

Despite Forbes' elaborate precautions, everything went wrong that could go wrong. Forbes did not realize that Grey lived in an apartment in the back of a duplex. He and his cohorts tried to invade the quarters of her landlady. Frightened but gutsy, the fifty-five-year-old black woman fired through the door with her bedside revolver and called the police. Jefferson responded with the M-16 they had brought along. One bullet ricocheted and hit Johnson in the neck, killing him instantly. Another shot disabled Forbes' gun hand. He and Jefferson stripped off their camouflage, abandoned their weapons, and headed back to Oakland. They then fled underground with the help of Panther free clinic paramedic Nelson Malloy, who bandaged Forbes' badly wounded hand. Crystal Grey told police that she must have been their intended target, but Newton claimed no knowledge of what happened. Two weeks later, tourists spotted Nelson Malloy buried alive in the Nevada desert, almost completely paralyzed from gunshot wounds. Under pressure from the police, Malloy grudgingly revealed his identity. After Malloy had gotten Forbes to a hospital under an assumed name, two Panther hit men had tried to silence him about his knowledge of the bungled attempt to murder Grey.[26] Forbes had since disappeared, as had Jefferson.

Newton again denied any knowledge of the entire bizarre sequence—one that could have been scripted by Mario Puzo. Elaine Brown was reportedly furious at the havoc to the Party's reputation resulting from the ugly episode. She was already upset about the retaliatory beating of a woman teacher at the Panther school for a minor infraction, her increasing difficulties with insubordinate Party members, and complaints of pervasive mistreatment of women in the Party. Now afraid that Newton might turn on her, she fled with her daughter before he could act, glad to escape with her life, like so many other former members of the Party's inner circle.

The following summer, with substantial inside information supplied by David Horowitz, two freelance reporters wrote an in-depth article on the Black Panthers for the avant-garde magazine, *New Times.* The pair created shock waves in Leftist circles with "The Party's Over." The daring piece marked the first time members of the Movement had written an exposé of the Panthers' history of violence.[27] One of the reporters, Kate Coleman, said she received a death threat from Newton after he learned of the article. Coleman had heavy bars installed on the windows and doors of her Berkeley home and fled to Japan for two months, taking the risk of returning only after the hoopla created by her article had died down. Coleman had reason to fear retribution. An *Oakland Tribune* reporter who wrote about Panther financial irregularities had her car firebombed.

Soon afterward, Newton went to trial on the assault charge. The tailor now refused to testify against him amid rumors Newton paid him $6000 to drop the criminal prosecution. Like Dell Ross, Callins suddenly claimed he could no longer recall what happened even when faced with being jailed for contempt of court. Newton then won acquittal of the assault charge, but could not avoid being found guilty of the gun violation. On September 29, 1978, Newton returned to jail pending release on bail for that charge. Interviewed there in his jumpsuit, the Panther leader told a skeptical national reporter that Grey's attempted murder "might have been the result of overzealous party members. There's no way my interests could have been served by activities like that."[28] Newton posted another $50,000 bond and was back on the streets in early November.

The Ph.D. candidate faced imminent trial on the murder charge. Garry was not on Newton's defense team. The aging streetfighter had his own personal nightmare to deal with. He barely escaped with his life in November 1978 from the mass, cyanide-laced Kool-Aid murder-suicide in Jonestown, Guyana, orchestrated by another client, San Francisco People's Temple founder Rev. Jim Jones. (Likely arranged through Garry, Jones had visited Newton in Havana in early 1977, and Newton had once addressed members of the People's Temple in Jonestown by telephone hook-up.)

Newton's lead trial counsel was Michael Kennedy, who went all out attacking Grey's credibility at the preliminary hearing. Among other things, Grey suffered from night blindness and had drug problems. Kennedy also pointed out that Grey had not identified Newton's photo as that of the shooter until a month after the incident. The trial was scheduled to start in February of 1979 before Presiding Judge Carl Anderson, himself a veteran of the Alameda County District Attorney's office. For Orloff, it turned into a nightmare. Two weeks beforehand, Grey backed out of testifying; another prostitute listed as a witness had to be scratched because she had been in jail the night she said she witnessed the shooting. The mistaken assault on Grey's neighbor was ruled off limits. Orloff went forward with the testimony of a third prostitute, Michelle Jenkins, who identified Newton in no uncertain terms as the man who pulled the gun on Kathleen Smith that night four-and-a-half years earlier, only to recant her testimony a week and a half later as a surprise defense witness.

Orloff also relied on a newly emerged male witness, Charles Buie, a hustler with his own rap sheet. Buie had been offered witness protection. After Buie identified Newton as the shooter, Newton's bodyguard Larry Henson, testified for the defense that it was Buie who actually shot Smith. Newton took the stand for two and a half days and calmly asserted he was home in his penthouse working on a religious essay at the time of the shooting, an alibi confirmed by his wife and author Don Freed. Charles Garry was also called as a witness for the defense. In rebuttal, Orloff must have been desperate when he called an admitted dope addict named Joanne West. When asked to identify the perpetrator, she surprised Orloff by walking slowly past Newton. She then picked out a six-foot-five, bearded white man in the gallery, defense witness Klemons Kopen, as most resembling the perpetrator. As thirty bemused reporters joined the gathering of Newton's family and friends for closing arguments, Orloff opted to ask the jury to find Newton guilty of second degree, rather than first degree murder. In summing up, Orloff accused almost every key witness of lying—except Buie. In his turn, Kennedy accused Orloff of being out to get Newton and pointed the finger for the crime back at Buie. Not too surprisingly, most of the jurors remained unconvinced that Orloff had met his high burden of proof. The mostly middle-aged suburban jury (nine women and three men) deadlocked ten to two in favor of acquittal.

After consulting with District Attorney Lowell Jensen, Orloff decided to retry Newton, figuring that the prosecutor's office now knew ahead of time what the defense arguments would be and could better attack Newton's alibi. The second trial was before Judge Donald McCullum, a veteran of the NAACP and former civil rights attorney, appointed to the court two years earlier. This time, Newton was represented by renowned San Francisco criminal defense lawyer J. Tony Serra who did an excellent job attacking the credibility of both Grey and Buie as star witnesses for the prosecution. Serra then surprised Orloff by not calling Newton to the stand, arguing the prosecutor had simply failed to establish his case. The jury this time consisted of four men and eight women, most of whom were under thirty. They hung eleven to one for acquittal. Following the second mistrial, Orloff called it quits. As Newton rejoiced with his family, an *Oakland Tribune* reporter noted how few Panthers attended this last trial and that the Panthers no longer represented a political force as they had been under Elaine Brown's leadership.[29]

The Panthers were clearly in irreversible decline. After Elaine Brown left, Mayor Wilson distanced himself publicly from them. He handily won reelection twice as a consensus builder, while pursuing an affirmative action agenda, filling many city positions with black applicants, and steering contracts to black-owned businesses. Wilson worked closely with both the governor and Republican businessmen to rejuvenate downtown Oakland with a building boom in new high rises. As an integral part of the plan, Wilson oversaw creation of 10,000 new jobs and hundreds of low income housing units for West Oaklanders, whose neighborhood had been razed to make way for a new freeway interchange designed to facilitate trucks heading to and from the busy port. Though white chief of police George Hart remained in charge of a mostly white police force, before Wilson's first term ended, the new mayor also instituted in 1980 Oakland's Citizen Police Review Board with jurisdiction to address complaints of abusive conduct—a key tenet of the Panthers' Ten Point Program.

That same year, Forbes tired of hiding underground and prepared to turn himself in for the attempted murder of Crystal Grey. He met with Charles Garry, who, according to Forbes, then revealed that Newton had authorized the murder attempt on Nelson Malloy to "clean house" after the botched Richmond home invasion. Forbes noted that Garry still sported a gold Panther ring that Newton had given him when Garry wryly acknowledged that the hit on the dedicated and popular Panther paramedic "was the straw that broke the big cat's back."[30] Since then, Newton continued in a downward spiral of diminishing stature and political influence as he became increasingly drug dependent and drunk on Courvoisier. Still out on bail while appealing his conviction for unlawful weapon possession, he relocated to Santa Cruz. He continued in the Ph.D. program in the History of Consciousness. His orals turned into a public spectacle with thousands of attendees at the campus auditorium. The test had to be moved to a new, closed session.

The university endured national ridicule for conferring the degree on Newton, one seemingly for *The Guinness Book of Records*. The increasingly dysfunctional candidate received his Ph.D. after just three academic years interrupted by three felony trials in Oakland. But the chair of the Department defended the quality of Newton's thesis. "War Against the Panthers: A Study of Repression in America." It placed the history of covert FBI and COINTELPRO operations against the Party in the context of historical repression from the executions following the 1886 Haymarket Square riots; to persecution of boxer Jack Johnson under the Mann Act; to the Palmer Raids on the Wobblies; to Sacco and Vanzetti, the Rosenbergs, the McCarthy witch hunts, the United Farm Workers, and the American Indian Movement. Newton's dissertation recounted his own persecution by the FBI in the third person, which was not surprising to those who assumed that this final paper, like so many of his others, was ghost-written—"a cynical joke" played by Newton on academia. Eventually, Dr. Huey P. Newton returned to Oakland a caricature of his former self, addicted to drugs and alcohol and mentally unstable. He jested that those who treated him with racist derision would now have to call him "Dr. Nigger."[31]

In 1982, Newton almost killed himself and his adopted kids, driving off the road while intoxicated. His wife Gwen left him and took her children. Newton remained on a suicidal bent, consuming two quarts of Courvoisier a day, as well as cocaine, heroin, and Valium. He often withdrew to his house in the Oakland hills with his new wife Fredrika (daughter of Panther realtor Arlene Slaughter), chain-smoking and wondering if he was headed back behind bars as he awaited the results of the appeal of his 1978 conviction for weapons' possession. In the biography of her husband that she and David Hilliard later collaborated on, Fredrika wrote that it was only after Huey put a knife to her throat in the spring of 1984, that she finally got him admitted to a costly rehab program in Berkeley. Fredrika also reported that the sobriety did not last. Newton faced mounting debt and relapses of paranoia and cocaine delusions. His life deteriorated even more rapidly after he lost his house to an IRS foreclosure, and pleaded guilty to embezzling $15,000 from the Community School—concerns that had prompted the hiring of the late Betty Van Patter. Newton once again resorted to stealing. Still, he retained valuable Panther memorabilia and hopes for a movie biography. The movie deal fell through. The couple placed a newspaper ad announcing a garage sale of Panther artifacts set for Saturday, August 25, 1989.

On the early morning of Tuesday, August 21, Newton went to a West Oakland housing project to meet a young drug dealer named Tyrone Robinson. Robinson was a member of the Black Guerrilla Family, the rival prison gang that claimed George Jackson as its founder. The younger man took advantage of the easy opportunity to shoot the forty-seven-year-old icon three times in the head and left him sprawled unconscious to die on the sidewalk, as fate would have it, in the same neighborhood as the early morning shootout with officers Frey and Heanes almost twenty-two years before. Robinson took off, thinking that he had just proved himself with the BGF, by killing a long-listed enemy. Police reported they had no idea who the perpetrator was when they first began investigating Newton's death as the latest Oakland homicide victim. The news was featured so quickly on television that the cameras caught the firemen hosing Newton's blood off the street. When Melvin Newton got notification, he said, "We always knew this was gonna happen. We just didn't know when."[32] Newton's penniless wife Fredrika was inundated with phone calls of folks offering assistance. By the time of his death, Newton had acquired so many enemies David Hilliard could imagine a whole host of possible assassins. He and Melvin started their own investigation.

The next day, as mourners covered with bouquets of flowers the street corner where he was shot, *The Oakland Tribune* ran a three-page spread on the life and death of Huey Newton. Charles Garry said that his long-time client "should be remembered as a 'tremendous contributor to the quality of black Americans.'" Prosecutor Tom Orloff expressed a decidedly different view: "The Newton I dealt with in the '70s was basically a gangster. There was nothing political about him."[33] African-American staff reporter Brenda Payton called Newton "the face of black defiance" whose admirers, including herself, arrogantly ignored lessons from the past in a brash show of militancy that ultimately amounted to "little more than immature adventurism."[34] One reporter noted that the Panthers' former headquarters was now a legal aid office. The change in tone of coverage of Newton was noticeable since the Knowland family had divested itself of the paper. For the past decade, *The Tribune* had been edited by renowned African-American journalist Robert Maynard, who became its owner in 1984.

Robinson saw the coverage on television and confided to a friend that he had killed Newton in self-defense. She went to the police. When arrested, the cocaine dealer claimed Newton had pulled a gun first. But this time police concluded that Newton had been an unarmed victim. Robinson was convicted of murder and received a 32-year sentence. Ironically, Robinson himself had participated as a child in a Panther free-breakfast program at a nearby Oakland housing project.

"Who killed Huey YO!? The same people he set out to feed, educate and free"? The self-proclaimed "Servant of the People" had an elaborate funeral paid for mostly by myriad small donations. Thousands of people attended the service at the Allen Temple Baptist Church—Oakland's largest black congregation, where Newton had become a member in his last years. Most of the crowd of over 2,000 people were black, but there were some whites and Latinos in the crowd. A caravan of white limousines accompanied the hearse carrying Newton's flower-bedecked wooden casket. The entourage passed through blocks of buildings whose walls were newly covered with Panther slogans and graffiti silhouettes of Newton. It then pulled up to the church decorated with Pan-African flags, Panther posters, and an enormous banner proclaiming "Huey Lives."

From the vehicles emerged Huey's widow Fredrika and son Kieron as well as a Who's Who of Panther stars in their heyday: Bobby Seale, Elaine Brown, Angela Davis, and H. Rap Brown (now an Islamic community leader in Atlanta renamed Imam Jamal Abdulla Al-Amin), David Hilliard, and Johnnie Spain, released from prison only the year before, after his conviction from the San Quentin Six trial was overturned. Upon word of this expected reunion, city officials feared violence might result. Television cameras and a flock of reporters swooped in like carrion to cover Newton's funeral procession, just as they had focused international attention on the even more elaborate funeral Newton himself had attended for drug czar Felix Mitchell in 1986.[35] Newshounds unabashedly shoved microphones in the faces of the celebrity attendees, including football star James Brown, snapped photos, and tape-recorded their responses. As it turned out, the only violence was an ugly sideshow that erupted when teenagers assaulted the cameramen.

Not surprisingly, Kwame Ture (the former Stokely Carmichael), who lived in exile in Guinea, did not show up. Nor did Eldridge Cleaver, who was now the darling of the Right. By the early 1980s, the Cleavers had separated (Kathleen divorced him in 1987). Eldridge flirted with joining Rev. Sun Myung Moon's Unification Church, but then rejected association with the "Moonies" and was baptized into the Mormon Church in 1984. Cleaver registered Republican and endorsed his old nemesis Ronald

Reagan for President. The former revolutionary then ran unsuccessfully in the Californian Republican Senate primary in 1986, seeking to unseat three-term incumbent Democrat Alan Cranston.

Though two black City Council members showed up to pay silent respects at Newton's funeral, noticeably absent was Oakland's Mayor, Lionel Wilson, then ending his third term. Changing his mind about retirement at age seventy-five, Wilson would soon face stiff competition (and fail against a field dominated by black candidates) in his quest for a fourth term, saddled with blame for an embarrassingly expensive and losing effort to bring the Raiders football team back to Oakland.

The overflow crowd listened from the street as specially set-up loudspeakers broadcasted the service, which wound up amplified by a bullhorn when the sound system failed. KPFA public radio in Berkeley covered the orations. Newton lay in the stylish casket, his beard shaved off, his legs festooned with roses and carnations. He was dressed in a gray suit, shirt, and red tie, for all to pass by and pay their respects. Bobby Seale, donning a trademark Panther black beret, led the eulogies in the three-hour service. With a clenched fist salute to his co-founder, Seale recounted the major community programs the Panthers instituted. He told his audience that they tested more people for sickle cell anemia than all state and federal programs combined. Congressman Ron Dellums, who had also spoken at the packed funerals of the Jackson brothers, mentioned that he first met Newton as a student at Merritt College before the Panthers were formed. Dellums pointed out the irony that "the very same streets that [Huey Newton] tried to make safe for the children are the streets that took his life."[36] Hilliard challenged the audience to deal with drug and alcohol dependency before it brought down their whole race as it bested Newton in the end, and almost killed Hilliard himself before he joined Alcoholics Anonymous. Elaine Brown called Newton "a hero who sparked a dream of freedom in all of us runaway slaves."[37] Newton's second wife, Fredrika, also spoke. Respecting his wishes not to be buried, after the funeral, she planned to have her husband cremated, with the intention of someday sprinkling his ashes across the city.

Father Earl Neil lambasted the mainstream press for focusing only on Newton's misdeeds. Neil urged his listeners to look past the skeletons in

Newton's closet and see his most famous congregant as he did: a brilliant visionary and courageous prophet, "our Moses" battling modern day pharaohs. Rev. Cecil Williams also lauded Newton's achievements for black communities, as did Allen Temple's own Reverend J. Alfred Smith, who quoted one of Newton's favorite lines in the Declaration of Independence: "When a long train of abuses and usurpations pursues and invariably evinces a design to reduce a people under absolute despotism, then it is the right of the People to alter or change that government and to provide New Guards for their future security and happiness." Rev. Smith ended by asking the congregation to repeat the old familiar chant from 1968: "Free Huey, Free Huey" and then added, "Well, let me tell you, he's free!! He's free!!!"[38]

All but drowned out for the time being were those in the black community who rejected this hero worship. One elderly woman reportedly shook her head in disbelief at all the lavish praise for a "plain old thug." "All these fools are trying to make him into a saint, but he was a real-life sinner. Comparing him to Dr. King or Malcolm [X] is downright blasphemy."[39]

* * * * *

Robinson's senseless act of political retribution mirrored that of another BGF wannabe, Edward Brooks, who had shot George Jackson's and Newton's former attorney Fay Stender in her home on Memorial Day weekend ten years before. The shocking home invasion left her wheelchair bound in fear of further attacks against herself and her family. The police located a copy of the BGF hit list, prompting them to provide Charles Garry temporary protection as another named target. By that time, Stender had not been handling any prisoner work for years. Disillusioned with black revolutionaries and particularly bitter about Newton's rejection of her after all she had done for him, she had turned to championing women's issues. Upon release from the hospital following the near-fatal shooting, Stender went into hiding with 24-hour police protection. She agreed to testify as the state's star witness against her would-be assassin. The riveting Oakland trial in early 1980 had spectators divided almost completely on racial lines, with white Leftists and Liberals rallying to lend Stender moral support and militant blacks and Latinos raising their fists in solidarity with Brooks. Soon after Brooks was sentenced to prison, Stender fled the country in self-imposed exile. Emotionally shattered and in constant pain, she committed suicide in May 1980.

There were almost no black faces amidst the hundreds of mourners at Stender's San Francisco funeral. Among those profoundly affected was journalist David Horowitz. He considered Stender a kindred disaffected spirit. With co-author Peter Collier, Horowitz published a lengthy, controversial article on Stender, "Requiem for a Radical," arguing that her death marked the end of an era. It later became chapter one in their book *Destructive Generation: Second Thoughts About the Sixties,* stirring up an angry backlash among Leftists.

7. A CLOSER LOOK AT THE COMPETITION

As you're grasping for that innocence
Sequestered in your mind
Was it guilt or were they blind
All this time.
LYRICS FROM "TRIAL OF THE CENTURY"
BY THE PUNK ROCK BAND "GOOD RIDDANCE"

For most of 1980, the nation followed with great fascination the arrest and trial of a headmistress of a private girls' academy for murdering her lover Herman Tarnower, best-selling author of *The Complete Scarsdale Medical Diet.* The story soon became the subject of two books about Jean Harris, a television docudrama starring Ellen Burstyn, and a movie in which Mrs. Harris was portrayed by Annette Bening. Starting in 1982, Americans were similarly captivated by the first of two high-profile attempted murder trials of Claus Von Bulow. The second husband of wealthy socialite Sunny von Bulow was accused of rendering his wife comatose with an overdose of insulin. In 1984, of far more lasting significance, Americans began hotly debating the propriety of an array of criminal charges against thirty-seven-year-old "subway vigilante" Bernhard Goetz. Trial Judge Stephen Crane called it the "most difficult case of our time."[1]

The willowy, bespectacled son of a Jewish mother and German Lutheran father had been severely beaten by three assailants on Canal Street in lower Manhattan in 1981. The assault left Goetz with a permanent injury to his knee and an abiding grudge because the one attacker police had caught faced only a criminal mischief charge. Since 1966, New York

City had experienced a tripling of violent crime, which occurred all too often on the city's poorly patrolled subways.[2] Over the next decade, the Big Apple's reported crimes would greatly exceed those of any other city in the country. Following the 1981 mugging, Goetz applied for a permit to carry a concealed weapon. His request was denied for insufficient need, apparently independent of a draft deferment Goetz had obtained by feigning mental illness during the Vietnam War. Goetz bought a revolver anyway and carried the Smith and Wesson every day concealed in a special quick-draw holster worn close to his body. From then on Goetz went gloveless no matter how cold it got in the winter so he would always be ready to pull his hidden weapon on any would-be mugger. At the time, the city was in the midst of an unprecedented explosion of crack cocaine usage which increased the homicide rate among teenage blacks nearly fivefold.

One afternoon a few days before Christmas 1984, Goetz entered the rear of a subway car at the 14th Street station in Manhattan. Most of the fifteen to twenty other passengers were seated toward the front, distancing themselves from four rowdy blacks in their late teens in the back. Troy Canty was sprawled across a bench; the other three were seated near him. Goetz chose to sit across from the youths. Within seconds Canty rose and demanded from Goetz, "Give me five dollars," while Canty's companion Barry Allen stood and joined Canty in an apparent effort to intimidate Goetz. None of the four teenagers showed any weapons. (Two carried sharpened screwdrivers they intended to use to pry open coin boxes at the video arcade where they were then headed. One later testified he had a crack cocaine habit since he was thirteen that cost $50 a day to support.)

On prior occasions Goetz had warded off potential attackers simply by showing his gun. Yet this time Goetz saw the smirk on Canty's face and felt all four were playing a cat and mouse game with him. Goetz snapped. He stood up, turned, and whisked out his revolver, faced Canty and his friends again and fired four shots in rapid succession aimed at the youths' midsections. Goetz then stood over Darrell Cabey, who was seated, and fired once more. All four were wounded, three critically. Luckily, none of the other petrified passengers was hurt by a bullet ricocheting off the wall.

Most of the other passengers fled. A few prostrated themselves on the floor in fear. When a conductor in the next car responded to the emergency, Goetz told the conductor that the youths had tried to rob him. As the train came to a screeching halt and the conductor went to the aid of the wounded, Goetz ran out, rented a car, and hid out in New England. Police circulated a likeness of the unknown perpetrator on wanted posters, which some locals decorated with halos. As one New York journalist put it, "In . . . telephone conversations and exchanges in bars, on street corners, in beauty parlors, in pool halls, and wherever . . . people met, from the too rich to the very poor, there was a collective emotion that cannot be described as anything other than jubilant."[3] After more than a week's manhunt, Goetz turned himself in and confessed that his intention was to "murder [the four youths], to hurt them, to make them suffer as much as possible."[4] Back in Manhattan, Goetz got a hero's welcome much like that accorded Sheriff Shipp in Chattanooga at the century's start after the sheriff completed his short jail term for facilitating the lynching of Ed Johnson in defiance of the U.S. Supreme Court. Many fans wore tee shirts picturing Goetz with the title "Thug Buster." The Guardian Angels helped furnish his $50,000 bail.

All but Darrell Cabey recovered. He was rendered paraplegic and brain-damaged. A *New York Times* poll the following month showed more than half those questioned supported Goetz. Most felt that crime was the worst feature of city life. Nearly a quarter reported a family member had been a victim of crime in the prior year and forty percent agreed that muggings and holdups had become so bad that New Yorkers "have a right to take matters into their own hands."[5] The frustration crossed color lines among law-abiding decent people fed up with "predators who roamed New York looking for people to bully and mug or rape. . . young, crude, obnoxious, sullen, elbowing people on the subway, making vile statements to women, cursing anywhere and as loudly as they could."[6] Yet many who championed Goetz had not yet become aware of his dark ambition; this subway confrontation had been for him an exercise in wish fulfillment. At a community meeting Goetz had argued that the crime problems in his neighborhood would only be resolved once they got "the niggers and the spics" out of there.[7] Meanwhile, radical lawyer William Kunstler—one of the famed Chicago Seven attorneys who also defended the Panther 21 and Attica inmates—filed suit against Goetz seeking $50 million in damages for his injured clients.

The first grand jury believed Goetz acted in self-defense, enraging African-American ministers in the pulpit and black politicians alike with the perceived double standard employed in indicting Goetz only for carrying a weapon without a permit. Many community leaders who came to the youths' defense accepted their account that they were just panhandling. Newspapers focused on the youths' criminal background. Most were unaware as well of prosecution evidence that Goetz had missed Cabey the first time and paused before getting off his fifth shot. A second grand jury was presented with the following sequence of events:

> The first shot hit Canty in the chest; the second struck Allen in the back; the third went through Ramseur's arm and into his left side; the fourth was fired at Cabey . . . but missed, deflecting instead off of a wall of the conductor's cab. After Goetz briefly surveyed the scene around him, he fired another shot at Cabey, who then was sitting on the end bench of the car. The bullet entered the rear of Cabey's side and severed his spinal cord.[8]

Police also played tapes of two post-arrest interviews. After firing four shots, Goetz saw Cabey sitting apparently unharmed: "I said 'You seem to be all right, here's another,'" and Goetz then fired the final shot. Goetz added that "if I was a little more under self-control . . . I would have put the barrel against his forehead and fired." He concluded that "if I had had more [bullets], I would have shot them again, and again, and again."[9] The second grand jury charged Goetz with thirteen counts, including attempted murder and reckless endangerment of other passengers. The lower courts then tossed all but the concealed weapon charge, based on the assumption the use of deadly force by a crime victim should not depend on whether a reasonable person would have reacted the way Goetz did, but whether Goetz believed he was acting in self-defense. New York's Court of Appeals reversed the dismissal of the serious charges and sent the case back for trial based on an objective standard of whether Goetz responded reasonably to the perceived threat.

It took two years to bring the headline case to trial. As the case progressed, Goetz relished the spotlight as the poster child for aggressive self-defense. As in the 1968 Newton murder trial, jury selection took several weeks of questioning. Ultimately the panel included ten whites and two blacks, some of whom had been victims of crime themselves. At trial, Goetz's attorneys Mark Baker and Gary Slotnick outmaneuvered the prosecutor Gregory Waples with dramatic tactics reminiscent of Charles Garry. First, the two portrayed Goetz as the victim. Slotnick called the injured youths from notorious Bronx projects "this gang of four . . . savages and vultures." At the time of the subway incident, though all four had criminal records, they were mostly for minor offenses. Slotnick objected when the prosecutor referred to the youths as "the four victims on the train" as a characterization for the jury to determine. Waples then retracted the label "victims" and instead called the four wounded passengers "young men."[10]

Goetz wisely exercised his right not to take the stand in his own defense, although the prosecution played his rambling two-hour confession. Barry Allen invoked the Fifth Amendment. Cabey did not testify and the other two alienated the jury. Some confusion was introduced as to whether Cabey was hit by the fourth or fifth bullet, whether they were all fired in quick succession, and whether Goetz actually said anything to Cabey before he shot him. One of the passengers who testified insisted that, after he heard the initial gunfire, the car cleared so he had an unimpeded view of Goetz standing over Cabey, who was then seated clutching the bench. The witness then watched Goetz fire the fifth bullet at Cabey from two to three feet away.

Most damaging to the case was the cross-examination of James Ramseur, who came to court in prison garb. (Recall that, though jailed during trial, Newton had been allowed to change from his regulation jumpsuit into respectable dress clothes when he sat in front of the jury.) By the time of trial, Ramseur had started serving a lengthy sentence for assisting in a subsequent gang rape of a pregnant woman. Ramseur displayed an argumentative attitude as Slotnick brought up Ramseur's conviction, which Ramseur claimed was unfounded. Until warned to stop by the judge, Slotnick then repeatedly called the jury's attention to this savage crime committed five months *after* Goetz shot the youths in the subway, to plant the seeds of justification for Goetz's action. Ramseur became even more insolent and refused to answer questions about his activities on the days leading up to the subway incident—a line of questioning that appears problematic. What was the relevance to the subway shooting of possible misconduct by Ramseur that Goetz knew nothing about? What about the risk of prejudicing the jury against Ramseur for engaging in totally unrelated incidents? Judge Crane directed Ramseur to answer the questions and then issued a contempt citation against Ramseur when he still refused to describe what he did during that week. At a later hearing, the judge castigated Ramseur for playing "right into the hands of Mr. Goetz's lawyer" by his conduct on the stand.[11]

After four days of deliberation the jury returned to the crowded courtroom. Spectators gasped as the foreperson rattled off verdict after verdict of "not guilty" through seventeen acquittals before a final "guilty" verdict only for the illegal possession of a firearm. The proceedings adjourned to loud applause. A contingent of Guardian Angels in red berets escorted Goetz through the hordes of onlookers outside the courtroom amid shouts of congratulations and a handwritten sign praising Goetz for winning one for "the good guys." There were also some competing angry cries. One African-American shouted "Goetz is a Nazi!"[12] Community leaders like Rev. Al Sharpton and Manhattan Borough President and future Mayor David Dinkins worried that it was now "open season" on young black men.[13] The head of the NAACP urged a federal civil rights prosecution, but Assistant U.S. Attorney Rudy Giuliani had already investigated the case in 1985 and determined Goetz was motivated by crime, not race. No federal charges were initiated.[14]

The illegal possession charge itself could have resulted in a seven-year sentence. Instead, Goetz's original sentence was six months jail time, plus one year of psychiatric treatment, a $5000 fine, 200 hours of community service, and five years of probation. His jail sentence later was increased on appeal to one year of which he wound up serving eight months. It was not until 1996, the year after Kunstler died, that his younger partner Ron Kuby finally succeeded in bringing the federal civil rights case in the Bronx to trial on behalf of Cabey. From the mostly minority jury pool, the lawyers picked a panel of six: four blacks and two Hispanics. Goetz took the stand and was vilified as a racist who deliberately sought the confrontation, with epithets Goetz had uttered as proof. In turn, Goetz's attorney called reporter Jimmy Breslin to help support the self-defense claim: when Breslin interviewed Cabey in 1985, the wheel-chair–bound youth had implicated the other three in attempting to rob Goetz.[15] The jury focused on the time Goetz took to reflect before he crippled Cabey with his fifth shot. At that point the seated youth—who denied ever menacing Goetz himself—could not credibly be characterized as posing any threat to Goetz whatsoever. The panel gave Cabey what turned out to be a largely symbolic award of $18 million in actual damages and $25 million in punitive damages. Goetz then filed for bankruptcy, but found that the judgment for the intentional tort could not be discharged. Yet, according to Goetz, he managed not to pay a dime of the award through at least 2004.[16]

Starting around 1990, New York City began dramatically reducing its crime rate as successive mayors—including Dinkins and Giuliani—made it their highest priority. In 2010 the city was listed as one of America's ten safest metropolises.[17] Goetz claimed a substantial role in that turn around. Others credit as significant factors the city's investment in many more police patrols, proactive law enforcement policies, a drop in the at-risk population, increased incarceration, and other factors like decline in crack cocaine usage and the advent of drug courts.[18]

Goetz has been interviewed periodically over the quarter century since the incident by talk show hosts and journalists. He ran as a protest candidate for Mayor in 2001 and four years later for the position of Public Advocate, seeking to draw attention to his championship of vigilantism. Several books about the trial include one by a juror providing insights into the role of reasonable doubt in their deliberations. Goetz became a cult figure woven into the fabric of American culture. The long-running television series *Law & Order* featured an episode that dramatized the incident; characters mirroring his vigilantism appeared in a number of television shows and movies, popular songs, and raps. Goetz also sparked a movement to relax state laws restricting concealed weapons.

In 2010, looking back on the *Goetz* case, one legal commentator observed:

> Of the many cases of racial injustice . . . few have sparked as little outcry as the case of Bernhard Goetz . . . This is a social misfortune because, in many ways, the Goetz case represents the epitome of society's racism and the dangerous consequences of the 'fight-violence-with-violence' mentality. Few have bothered looking deep at the case and what it says about our culture. . . . [T]he four young men [were not] innocent victims. . . . they indeed intended to rob or extort money out of Goetz and their criminal record speaks for itself. They were not nice kids. But the justice system doesn't defend nice people only. Our justice system is there for a reason. As egregiously flawed as it is, it is preferable to a self-righteous and emotionally unbalanced gunman taking the law into his own hands.[19]

Bloggers still debate whether the Goetz criminal case would play out similarly today. Most posting responses assume the country is just as polarized. In June 2011, Libertarian radio talk show host Neal Boortz went on a rant prompted by frustration with car jackers in Atlanta (a theft risk that many other cities then exceeded). Boortz urged his millions of listeners to arm themselves as vigilantes and "litter the landscape" with dead thugs.[20] Goetz said he would have kept shooting, too, had he not run out of bullets.

* * * * *

Overlapping the coverage of the criminal trial of Bernie Goetz from 1984 through 1987, national attention focused on sensational accusations of sexual abuse in a Manhattan Beach, California, preschool operated by the McMartin family. Following three years of investigation from 1983 to 1986, seven defendants faced a total of 321 charges of molesting 48 small children, whose inconsistent testimony may have been influenced by suggestive questioning that produced false memories. A new district attorney then reviewed the case and dismissed five of the seven defendants due to the paucity of evidence against them. Trial against the remaining two defendants, Peggy McMartin Buckey and her son Ray, took place over the next three years while Ray Buckey was denied bail and his mother only freed after posting $1 million. The jury deliberated for two full months in 1990 before acquitting Peggy Buckey on all counts and Ray Buckey of

52 of 65 counts, unable to reach agreement on the others. When the $15 million, thirty-month trial ended inconclusively in 1990 it earned the dubious distinction of the longest criminal trial in American history.[21] After Ray Buckey's retrial ended in another hung jury, the case was dropped. The results greatly embarrassed both the prosecutor and the media, which was accused of biased reporting of unprovable allegations of satanic rituals and sodomy, enraging the public against the defendants, none of whom was ever found guilty. Harvard Prof. Alan Dershowitz dubbed it "the Salem witch trial of the twentieth century."[22]

At the time the original charges in the McMartin case hit the news, Dershowitz was busy representing Claus Von Bulow on his successful appeal from the original 1982 conviction. Dershowitz later turned the mystery surrounding Sunny Von Bulow's vegetative state into a book which became the 1990, box office hit *Reversal of Fortune* for which Jeremy Irons won the Oscar for best actor. Yet Dershowitz himself states, "There is nothing extraordinary about the cast of characters, except that they were very rich."[23]

The same year of the McMartin verdict and Irons' Academy Award–winning portrayal of Von Bulow, television viewers found themselves riveted to the real-life soap-opera trial of Pamela Wojas Smith. It was the first such trial to be broadcast live "from start to finish." The ruthlessly ambitious blond wanted to be the next Barbara Walters. Instead she got a life sentence in prison as an accomplice to the murder of her husband by her under-aged lover, fifteen-year-old William Flynn, and three companions. Smith was later portrayed by Helen Hunt in the television drama "Murder in New Hampshire" and by actress Nicole Kidman in the 1995 movie *To Die For.* New Hampshire courts later clamped down on the availability of live television coverage of their trials. A Portsmouth, New Hampshire, reporter later bragged that, "before O. J., the Smith trial was 'THE' trial of the century." New Hampshire Police Captain Loring Jackson vehemently disagreed: "I think the case was blown way out of proportion by the news media. They seized on sex, drugs and rock 'n' roll. . . . To me, the press was nothing but a royal pain in the ass, and you can quote me on that."[24]

The list goes on.

In her book, *Headline Justice: Inside the Courtroom—The Country's Most Controversial Trials,* veteran reporter Theo Wilson wrote that memorable trials attract our collective interest because they dissect real people, unsparingly examining the skeletons in their closets in a way that "tell[s] us much about ourselves, our own facades and secrets behind them."[25] For that reason, such trials have the same impact as great theater, "filled as those trials are with revelations of human weakness and folly, with violence and sorrow and humor and pity and passion."[26] It is not surprising that, over the course of the last century, the headline grabbers focused mostly on rape, murder, and political assassination, treason, graft and corruption, and titillating glimpses into the sex lives of the rich and famous. What vaults some to a higher plane? Gilbert Geis and Leigh Beinen point out in *Crimes of the Century* that: "a crime truly becomes historic when like an eclipse, its timing brings into alignment many profound and often troubling questions about society. Acting as a prism the macabre crime has the power to show the spectrum of various ongoing struggles in the culture."[27]

In the past decade, professors Alan Dershowitz and Gerald Uelmen—both members of the O. J. Simpson "Dream Team"—each compiled a list of some forty famous trials from 1900 to 2000 that were either self-described as "trials of the century" or otherwise considered to be pivotal. Did they reach consensus on their choices? No, not even close. While the two legal experts agreed on the Thaw trial, the Leopold and Loeb proceedings, and the Hauptmann kidnap/murder case, they differed on roughly half of the other cases each included.[28] Theo Wilson's *Headline Justice* discusses yet several others, as does *Justice For All: Legendary Trials of the Twentieth Century.*[29] To add more disagreement to the mix, one also finds a few other 20th century cases included among those highlighted by Prof. Douglas Linder, a constitutional scholar who maintains a website summarizing famous trials through the ages. None of these sources featured *People v. Newton,* even though they included many trials that laid no claim to representing an epic struggle over America's soul. Linder's site does have a secondary list with more than two dozen "Other Famous Trials" of the 20th century. The Newton trial is not there either, but after scrolling down, one finds a further category called "Yet More

Trials—Links Only," which refers the reader to Wikipedia, including a citation to the 1968 Newton trial.

The encyclopedic *Great American Trials: From Salem Witchcraft to Rodney King,* later updated through 2001, chronicles more than two hundred trials since 1637. The Newton trial is listed among twenty-five entries in the 1960s alone, sandwiched chronologically between a domestic murder trial against a black Chicago doctor (John Marshal Branion) and the vandalism prosecution of former Roman Catholic priest Philip Berrigan and his brother Daniel for spilling vials of blood on Selective Service files in protest of the Vietnam War. Readers of that tome learn that disputes about the "potential jury's racial balance [were] central to the [Newton defense] trial strategy" and that the 1968 case represented "one of the most politically charged trials of its era."[30] But then the editors diminish the 1968 Newton trial's significance in describing the 1969 Chicago Seven Trial as "possibly the most divisive—certainly the most chaotic—political trial in American history."[31]

In January 1999, television, radio, and newspaper reporters began asking experts to share their views on what was "THE" trial of the century. NBC invited subscribers to cast their own votes from a list of sixteen famous trials and suggested that participants consider whether the answer should be based on "the gravity of the crime, its impact on society or merely the amount of publicity?" Twelve trials were listed as receiving at least one per cent of the vote. Only four won votes in the double digits: the Scopes "Monkey" trial (14 percent); the Nazi war crimes trials, which did not occur on American soil (21 percent); the O. J. Simpson trial (24 percent); and the impeachment trial of President Clinton (20 percent). The Lindbergh baby kidnapping and murder trial scored next highest with seven percent, the Leopold and Loeb case got one percent, and the all-but-forgotten trials of Harry Thaw and Fatty Arbuckle did not garner any votes at all.[32]

NBC followed the poll with a mini-debate. In a short segment of the "Today Show" aired in early February of 1999, Prof. Charles Ogletree of Harvard argued that the O. J. Simpson trial merited the distinction of "THE" trial of the century. His opponent, veteran trial attorney Jim Brosnahan of San Francisco, argued that the impeachment trial of

President Clinton then underway deserved that title. Certainly by allowing cameras in the courtroom in an age where almost everyone owned a television, those two proceedings attracted the most fascinated observers, but that should hardly be the test. Nor should the title be awarded simply based on the happenstance of a famous trial being recent and therefore in the public mind.

To be sure, the five-week Clinton impeachment trial in 1999 was only the second such trial in the nation's history and the only one to take place in the 20th century. Though the Senate trial was presided over by the Chief Justice, it paled in significance when compared to the 1974 congressional Watergate hearings that precipitated President Nixon's resignation without the necessity of a trial. (It also paled in comparison to the Watergate-related "Pentagon Papers" treason case against Daniel Ellsberg, which was dramatically dismissed for gross governmental misconduct.) The Clinton impeachment trial—which just beat the deadline for consideration as one of the 20th Century's most significant legal proceedings—also bore little resemblance to a true trial. Thirteen House Republicans took turns "prosecuting" the case, which involved only four videotaped witnesses. Chief Justice Rehnquist, in ornate robes he designed himself, looked like a character gone missing from a Gilbert and Sullivan operetta.

Though impeachment was designed to be a rare and presumptively grave matter of historical importance transcending mere politics, the predicate for this impeachment was widely viewed otherwise. The replacement of special prosecutor Robert Fiske with the more partisan Kenneth Starr led to accusations of a Right Wing witch hunt. Later, in his book *Blinded by the Right: The Conscience of an Ex-Conservative,* journalist David Brock revealed the inside story of the anti-Clinton "Arkansas Project," funded in large part by publisher Richard Mellon Scaife.[33] Brock's confession of the scandal-mongering behind the impeachment effort only reinforced most Americans' view, shared by Harvard Prof. Alan Dershowitz, that the prosecution smacked of "sexual McCarthyism." As Dershowitz put it, "The framers of our Constitution could hardly have imagined that the extraordinary power to impeach a duly elected president would have been invoked in response to a sex fib told under oath."[34]

By the time Clinton left office, the cost of independent-counsel probes into his administration totaled a record $70 million, not counting the money Congress allocated to the impeachment proceedings. Americans who had twice elected the still popular President made it abundantly clear that they would have preferred Congress to focus on more pressing matters, especially as some of Clinton's harshest Republican critics had their own marital infidelities exposed. (For example, one of Starr's married assistants who later ran for Senate was arrested in 2006 for stalking his own former mistress.) Concern for the misuse of government resources launched a new grassroots political organization—MoveOn.org. In acquitting Clinton, the Senate split almost entirely on party lines. No, the Monica Lewinsky scandal did not come close to qualifying as the legal battle of the century.

Focus on a trial involving the issue of abrupt termination of a President's term also makes one ask, why leave out assassinations? Indeed, Prof. Uelmen includes on his list the two-day virtually undefended 1901 trial of Leon Czolgosz for assassinating President McKinley; the 1964 trial of Jack Ruby for murdering Kennedy assassin Lee Harvey Oswald; the 1981 trial of John Hinckley, Jr. for the attempted assassination of President Reagan; and the 1969 trial of Sirhan Sirhan for assassinating presidential candidate Robert Kennedy. But none of them stand up under scrutiny as trials of the century.

Jack Ruby stunned the nation during televised coverage of pretrial proceedings against accused Kennedy assassin Lee Harvey Oswald. Despite Oswald's security escort, Ruby somehow emerged from a throng of reporters and photographers in the basement of the Dallas police department to shoot Oswald pointblank in the stomach. But Ruby's murder trial—which took place in the highly charged atmosphere in Dallas following the President's assassination—was no epic legal battle. Though legal giant Melvin Belli volunteered to represent Ruby for free, the famed personal injury lawyer was not at the top of his game, and his attempt to prove Ruby insane failed. Ruby was found guilty of murder in 1964 and sentenced to death. His conviction was later overturned on appeal (after Belli no longer represented Ruby) on the ground that a confession admitted into evidence had improperly been obtained while Ruby was in police custody, and on the separate ground that the trial judge should have granted a change of venue from Dallas.

The Texas Court of Criminal Appeals issued its opinion in October of 1966—four months after the landmark United States Supreme Court opinion vacating the 1954 murder conviction of Dr. Samuel Sheppard because of the circuslike atmosphere in which Sheppard's 1954 trial had taken place. Though ten of twelve jurors had seen television footage of Ruby killing Oswald, that fact alone was not disqualifying. Newspaper stories suggesting a Communist conspiracy between Ruby and Oswald may have influenced jurors, but of paramount concern was the huge stake the city was perceived to have in the outcome. The Dallas courthouse where Ruby's trial took place was so close to where President Kennedy had been assassinated that jurors likely saw visitors placing wreathes each day at the site. A concurring justice noted that "the citizenry of Dallas consciously and subconsciously felt their home city was itself on trial for allowing the tragedy to occur."[35] Two months later, as preparations for a new trial in Wichita Falls, Texas, were underway, Ruby died of complications from cancer at the same Dallas hospital where President Kennedy and Lee Harvey Oswald had been pronounced dead.

Whether Lee Harvey Oswald acted alone has been the subject of ongoing controversy, as is the related question whether Ruby acted as part of a conspiracy to prevent Oswald from implicating anyone else. Conspiracy theories include as suspects Fidel Castro, the Russians, the CIA, the Mafia, the FBI, the Pentagon, and the far right (who considered Kennedy a traitor for his promotion of civil rights). As crime journalist Michael Newton notes: "Hundreds of books and thousands of articles have been written about [the Kennedy assassination and Ruby's killing of Oswald two days later]. . . and virtually every detail remains a subject of heated debate . . . Despite three official investigations, two criminal trials, and 40-odd years of journalistic argument, a definitive verdict . . . remains elusive."[36]

* * * * *

The nation recoiled in shock and horror when Senator Robert Kennedy was shot just after the popular Democrat finished a presidential primary victory speech in the Los Angeles Ambassador Hotel. Witnesses said that an unidentified blonde woman in a polka dot dress fled the scene, yelling, "We killed the senator!"[37] While Kennedy lay dying, police interrogated the alleged shooter, Sirhan Sirhan, who confessed that he intended the act as retribution for Kennedy's support for Israel in the six-day war exactly a year before. The diary of the Jerusalem-born Palestinian also cited Kennedy's alleged promise to supply Israel with fifty fighter jets if elected. Sirhan later retracted the confession and pleaded not guilty. Sirhan's lawyers unsuccessfully sought a change of venue from Los Angeles. Judge Herbert Walker then rejected Sirhan's efforts to fire his attorneys, change his plea to guilty, and die a martyr. Judge Walker instead conducted a two-month trial during which Sirhan's outbursts against Zionists upset defense co-counsel Emile Berman so much that the Jewish attorney had to be talked out of resigning before the case was over.

Despite his bizarre behavior in court, Sirhan's attorneys also lost in their attempt to claim he acted with diminished capacity. Their star witness was Charlie Garry's favorite psychiatric expert, Prof. Bernard Diamond, who had proved so pivotal to the Newton defense the summer before. Though Sirhan was convicted, many questions remain unanswered. A number of legislative and judicial panels in the next decade revealed that the Los Angeles Police and FBI investigation into Kennedy's death had been severely compromised from the outset, including failure to pursue evidence indicating the presence of a second gunman. The Los Angeles coroner, Dr. Thomas Noguchi, determined that the bullet that killed Kennedy entered from several inches behind him, though witnesses placed Sirhan several feet in front of Kennedy. Photographs of the kitchen also appeared to show more bullets were fired than could have come from Sirhan's gun, but the LAPD later destroyed the evidence which would have clarified the question. A CBS news staffer in the kitchen with Kennedy swore that he saw a temporary security guard named Eugene Cesar pull his gun and shoot, which Cesar later denied.

Journalist Dan Moldea later researched the crime and found that Cesar had "motive, means and opportunity" to kill Senator Kennedy. Yet in his 1995 book, *The Killing Of Robert Kennedy—An Investigation into Motive, Means and Opportunity*, Moldea concluded that Sirhan acted alone. Several other authors have concluded otherwise, naming the Mafia or the CIA as prime suspects.[38] Sirhan's appellate lawyer subscribed to the CIA theory, asserting that Sirhan was hypnotized into firing his gun, like a real-life *Manchurian Candidate*, but was accompanied in the hotel kitchen by a CIA gunman to ensure the assassination occurred and that Sirhan was the fall guy to blame it on.[39] Though Sirhan was sentenced to death, his sentence was converted to life imprisonment following the California Supreme Court ruling three years later that invalidated the death penalty as cruel and unusual punishment under the state Constitution. He has been denied parole more than a dozen times for a crime he claims not to remember committing. In a renewed challenge to his conviction filed in federal court in April 2011, his lawyers submitted the results of numerous interviews of Sirhan while placed under hypnosis by an expert, along with other evidence that supports the theory of a second gunman who killed Kennedy. They seek to establish that Sirhan shot his gun only after being tricked into believing he was at target practice, acting under mind control triggered by a beautiful woman in a polka dot dress.[40] With all of the lingering uncertainties, it is no wonder that a number of crime journalists consider Robert Kennedy's assassination an unsolved crime despite Sirhan Sirhan's conviction.

* * * * *

The 1981 trial of attempted assassin John Hinckley, Jr. provided better theater, inspired as it was by the assassination attempt in the movie *Taxi Driver*, but the unsuccessful effort to kill President Reagan was devoid of any political message. Hinckley had become obsessed with actress Jodie Foster and tried to impress her by killing the President. Apparently any President would do. Hinckley had first planned to assassinate President Jimmy Carter, but did not complete his plans in time. The jury found Hinckley not guilty by reason of insanity.

* * * * *

One can see why Prof. Ogletree judged the O. J. Simpson case a more compelling candidate for "THE" trial of the century than other cases customarily put forth for that honor. It did engage more than a hundred million spectators around the world. The African-American Harvard professor pointed out that the Simpson trial had the key elements of "sex, violence and power."[41] He also hailed it as a pioneering trial for the prominence of a female prosecutor. The fact that the Newton trial almost thirty years earlier had featured a woman co-counsel was far more remarkable, given the rarity of women criminal defense lawyers at the time. To be sure, Fay Stender played a secondary role at trial, but her legal briefs were critical to Garry's success in defeating the murder charges, and Stender then became Newton's lead counsel in pursuing his equally challenging, successful appeal. Nor was Prof. Ogletree correct in assuming that the Simpson case marked "the first time in a major trial of [the 20th century] that you've seen a diverse trial, women and minorities able to serve as jurors."[42] The Newton trial not only had a majority of women, almost half the panel were minorities, with an African-American jury foreman at a time when that, too, was extraordinary in a high profile trial.

Prof. Ogletree homed in on the major breakthrough of the Simpson case. It forced national discourse on race relations as a key political issue of the American 20th century. Today, in retrospect, the evolving status of African-Americans during the last century takes on even greater significance: the remarkable one-hundred-year period began just four years after the United States Supreme Court declared "separate but equal" the law of the land and ended just eight years before American voters electrified the world in decisively electing their first African-American President. So the question whether the O. J. Simpson murder case acted as a prism for the many facets of societal turmoil over evolving race relations merits a serious look.

On June 12, 1994, the Los Angeles police reported the double murders of Nicole Simpson and her friend Ron Goldman outside her Brentwood condominium with her children inside asleep. Nicole's ex-husband, NFL football Hall-of-Famer O. J. Simpson, was sought as a suspect. Simpson's attorneys arranged for him to turn himself in voluntarily just before noon on June 17, but when Simpson failed to appear, the LAPD put out an all-points bulletin for his arrest. Two hours later, his friend Robert Kardashian read a letter to the media from Simpson that denied any involvement in the murder but sounded like a suicide note. The case then captured millions of viewers' attention when the charismatic athlete-turned-actor was spotted on a freeway in a friend's white Ford Bronco. O. J. led police on a slow, several hour, televised car chase before he was arrested for the brutal stabbing deaths.

Viewers were hooked by the jarring criminal charges against a familiar, trusted persona, a self-made man who seemed to have it all. Even before he retired from professional football as a record-breaking running back, "the Juice" had begun a successful career as a movie actor. Afterward, he was much sought after as a sports commentator and product endorser. How many Americans had not seen O. J., a broad grin on his face, effortlessly sprint through airports in Hertz Rent-A-Car commercials? National magazines immediately focused on racial issues. O. J.'s attorneys noticed that when *Time* magazine put Simpson's face on its cover, it darkened the color of his skin. *Newsweek* psychoanalyzed Simpson as a troubled black man who self-destructed when he "tried to be white."[43] Half of the country would eventually watch the reality show soap opera of one of the longest criminal trials ever conducted in the United States. The magnetic attraction of the televised Simpson trial was due to public fascination with the ugly reality underlying O. J.'s picture perfect marriage and Hollywood lifestyle, but also in large part because of Simpson's ability to afford a Dream Team of defense lawyers.

The team, which sometimes operated more like a pride of lions, started out headed by celebrity defense lawyer Robert Shapiro. He added law professors Dershowitz and Uelmen for their legal analysis and veteran defense lawyer F. Lee Bailey as a mentor to provide strategic advice. Because of the key role DNA evidence would play, the growing team recruited DNA experts Barry Scheck and Peter Neufeld of the pioneering Innocence Project. But, like the prosecution, the defense team had no credibility without an African-American lawyer. Shapiro brought in Johnnie "the Best in the West" Cochran. Cochran had made a name for himself as both a defense attorney and prosecutor, at different times handling cases charging police abuse in private practice and serving as the first African-American Assistant District Attorney in Los Angeles. Bailey and Shapiro wound up in a public feud to the point they stopped speaking to each other. Simpson's Dream Team questioned every aspect of the prosecutors' case, particularly focused on deficiencies in the crime lab and misconduct by the Los Angeles Police Department. These allegations had greater weight than might otherwise have been accorded them because public memory of the politically explosive Rodney King beating incident was still fresh.

Rodney King, an African-American in his mid-twenties, had been arrested in Los Angeles County late at night on March 2, 1991, for speeding and driving under the influence. A bystander videotaped the arresting officers beating King repeatedly with batons, footage which was replayed many times on television around the world. The incident fanned pre-existing outrage in poor black communities over decades of police mistreatment. When four of the policemen who beat Rodney King won a change of venue to a white suburb, the jury of ten whites, one Latino, and an Asian came back with three acquittals, deadlocking on the final officer's guilt. Mayor of Los Angeles Tom Bradley, himself an African-American, condemned the outcome; President George H.W. Bush said he was stunned, as were millions who had seen the sickening video. Los Angeles erupted in several days of race riots in which over fifty people died and thousands were arrested before order was restored with help from the Army, Marines, and National Guard. The riots following those acquittals caused more damage by far than the historic Watts riots.

* * * * *

The explosive reaction to a manifestly unjust outcome reminded many members of the public of the "White Night Riots" thirteen years earlier, sparked by the outrage of the San Francisco gay community to the Dan White jury verdict of voluntary manslaughter. Thirty-two-year old former supervisor White was a handsome "All-American boy"[44] from a large, working class family: valedictorian of his Catholic high school; a veteran of the Vietnam War; a former policeman and firefighter; married with a newborn son. As depicted in 2008's movie *Milk,* during his first year in office, the conservative Democrat increasingly clashed with Supervisor Harvey Milk, the city's first openly gay elected official, and with other Progressives on the Board aligned with Mayor George Moscone. Disillusioned by his inside look at city politics, on November 10, 1978, White quit his poorly paid elected post. White had not consulted supporters before making that decision. When the community members who had worked so hard to elect him begged White to reconsider, he changed his mind and asked Mayor George Moscone to reappoint him. Moscone refused. Two weeks later, White shocked the nation when, in retaliation, he shot and killed Moscone in the Mayor's office and then walked down the hall to assassinate Supervisor Milk as well.

The surprisingly lenient result of a verdict of voluntary manslaughter resulted from juror sympathy for the unbearably conflicting pressures on the overwhelmed political neophyte. The defense team also included in its presentation a much-ridiculed "Twinkie Defense"—that White suffered from diminished capacity from months of eating too much sugary junk food. When the jury verdict was announced, seething protesters from Milk's Castro District broke windows and doors at City Hall, burned police cruisers, and vandalized other vehicles and stores. Mobs then turned their rage against responding officers before order was restored. Still, the vandalism of the White Night Riots of May 1979 paled in comparison to the estimated billion dollars in damages wreaked in late April of 1992 by enraged protesters following the acquittal of the police who beat Rodney King.

* * * * *

After the state exonerated the Los Angeles policemen for the Rodney King beating, federal charges were brought to trial against the same four officers for violating King's civil rights. This time, two of the defendants were found guilty and sent to jail. King won over three million dollars in damages in a separate civil suit. The case also spawned numerous new organizations across the country to protect against future police abuse. One of King's attorneys in the damages case was civil rights attorney John Burris. In his 1999 book *Blue v. Black: Let's End The Conflict Between Cops and Minorities,* the Oakland lawyer described how African-American men had grown all too familiar over the years with the so-called suspicious conduct that got them pulled over. Burris explains:

> 'Driving While Black,' 'Walking While Black' . . . are situations where individuals are stopped without probable cause [largely] . . . because they fit a racial profile, a racial stereotype. Or, on freeways, they are stopped by police officers who see a black male driving a car . . . [whom the officers think] fit[s] the profile of a drug courier . . . Disrespecting [black suspects like Rodney King]. . . only heightens the fear and the concern in the African American community that the police are not there to serve and protect but actually are there to intrude into their daily lives and to treat them whenever they can in a hostile way.[45]

Memory of the publicity surrounding the Rodney King beating not only lent credibility to allegations of police misconduct in the 1995 Simpson trial, it also assured a rapt audience as the major networks hired experts like Burris to explain the trial issues on the nightly news. Legal pundits examined every aspect of how the Simpson case was tried by the defense and prosecution teams and by the trial judge, who did not keep a tight rein on the proceedings. The Dream Team scored big when it obtained a tape-recorded prior interview of a key prosecution witness, Detective Mark Fuhrman, which they used to expose his bigotry. Fuhrman needed to be thoroughly discredited by the defense because he claimed to have found incriminating bloody gloves at the crime scene. In a dramatic moment, prosecutor Chris Darden asked Simpson to try one of the blood-soaked gloves on in front of the jury. The gambit backfired when it appeared too tight, although that could have been explained by the glove's condition.

The defense never put O. J. on the stand to deny the killings, relying on the jury taking to heart Judge Lance Ito's instruction that O. J. had the right as a defendant to remain silent. What the jury never knew—but *The National Enquirer* spread to the world—was that O. J. had wanted to testify against his lawyers' advice, but was dissuaded after the team brought in two top-notch women criminal defense attorneys, Penny Cooper and Cris Arguedas, to put Simpson through grueling mock cross-examination. Presumably, Simpson was convinced by this experience that he would not bear up well if subjected to penetrating questions from prosecutor Marcia Clark. In his closing argument, Cochran famously pointed out that the bloody glove found at the scene had been too small for Simpson's hand: "if it doesn't fit, you must acquit." Cochran also gambled that the jury—nine blacks, two whites, and one Latino—would agree with his fulminations against Fuhrman. Cochran compared the detective to Hitler: "a genocidal racist, a perjurer, America's worst nightmare and the personification of evil."[46] Columnist George Will pointed out the negative impact of televising such highly charged cases: Cochran's attacks on Fuhrman might sway the twelve members of the jury panel, but inflame the nation as a whole. Will argued that the tactic Cochran employed made him "a good lawyer, but a bad citizen."[47] Most judges would instead blame the decision to air the criminal trial rather than the artful defense lawyer for any polarization of viewers on the underlying hot-button issue.

With race painted as the preeminent factor in the 1994–95 O. J. Simpson trial, concern escalated that the verdict might cause riots like those that occurred three years earlier after the state's exoneration of the policemen who beat Rodney King. Anticipating the jury's announcement of a guilty verdict, police officers surrounded the courthouse. Simpson's lawyers were also apprehensive. Although sports figures usually fared better than most defendants, the Dream Team had trouble reading the body language of the jury even after months of trial. They assumed that their best hope was a hung jury with one or two hold-outs against conviction. So they, too, were surprised when the jury came back with an acquittal.

With a result so deeply critical of the conduct of the Los Angeles Police Department, no race riots occurred. Still, with over a hundred million viewers ultimately bearing witness, polls revealed that reactions to the Simpson verdict divided along racial lines. A Gallup Poll found that 42 percent of whites who were interviewed agreed with the acquittal, while 49 percent thought he was guilty as charged. In contrast, 78 percent of blacks thought the acquittal was the right verdict and only 10 percent disagreed.[48] An NBC news poll ten years after the verdicts came in found that 87 percent of whites polled now thought Simpson was guilty of the murders, but only 29 percent of blacks.[49] In the meantime, the families of both victims won civil verdicts against Simpson and the rights to the proceeds of Simpson's controversial book, *If I Did It,* which became a best seller. Most of O. J.'s lawyers wrote books about the trial, and a former friend published his own account: *How I Helped O. J. Get Away with Murder: The Shocking Inside Story of Violence, Loyalty, Regret and Remorse.* In an unrelated incident in 2007, Simpson robbed a Las Vegas vendor of sports memorabilia and is now serving a nine-year-sentence for that crime.

* * * * *

The Simpson trial had been a major diversion for the nation from the carnage wreaked in the Oklahoma City Bombing—the country's worst terrorist act of the 20th century. The destruction of a federal office complex on April 19, 1995, by a powerful truck bomb killed 168 people and injured 800 others while causing extensive damage in several hundred other buildings in the vicinity.[50] The shocking explosion caused widespread fear. It was first speculated to be the work of Arab terrorists like those who bombed the World Trade Center in New York in February of 1993. But the FBI quickly focused on another possibility. As the *New York Times* wrote, "Before it happened in Oklahoma City, it happened in a book called 'The Turner Diaries,' an explicitly racist and anti-Semitic work of the political extremist right."[51]

The Turner Diaries was published in 1978 under the name Andrew Macdonald by white supremacist William Luther Pierce, a former member of the American Nazi party and leader of the white separatist National Alliance organization. It envisions the overthrow of the United States government, followed by nuclear war and the annihilation of every ethnic and racial group except whites. The book had a passage devoted to the bombing of the FBI building in Washington, D.C. Other tactics described in the book were known to have inspired a number of hate crimes before the explosion in Oklahoma City.

The FBI conducted a nationwide manhunt and literally collected tons of documentary evidence as well as completing 28,000 interviews. Within days, two men were in custody: Timothy McVeigh and Terry Nichols. In the hunt for co-conspirators, the bombing investigation dwarfed all other criminal cases ever prosecuted up to that time in America. The only other person prosecuted was Michael Fortier, who later cooperated with the police. Fortier, Nichols, and McVeigh had met in army basic training. All three strongly opposed gun control and the power of the federal government to interfere in any way with the stockpiling of weapons by survivalists. McVeigh was a decorated veteran of the Gulf War and a member of the National Rifle Association. In the army, when he saw black servicemen wearing "Black Power" tee shirts, he ordered his own "White Power" shirt from the Ku Klux Klan. A 2001 FBI report showed that McVeigh had possible links with the Aryan Republican Army. It also turned out that McVeigh had, in fact, read and recommended to his friends *The Turner Diaries.*

The stated purpose of bombing the federal complex in Oklahoma City was to commemorate the fiery death of seventy-six people, including more than twenty children, in an FBI siege in Waco, Texas, exactly two years before. The Waco group lived in an apocalyptic cult led by polygamist David Koresh. Koresh had split off from the Branch Davidians, a sect of Seventh Day Adventists, and considered himself the final prophet of his followers. Residents of the compound still identified themselves as Branch Davidians. Koresh had stockpiled weapons and was accused of sexual abuse of children. When the Bureau of Alcohol, Tobacco and Firearms attempted to exercise a search warrant, a gun battle resulted. Four agents and six members of the compound were killed. New Attorney General Janet Reno gave the go ahead to the FBI to conduct a siege, which lasted fifty-one days and ended tragically with a fire that destroyed the compound. How the fire started and what the federal agents might have done differently to avoid unnecessary loss of life were subjects of great controversy.

Before the siege ended, a television docudrama was complete, *In the Line of Duty: Ambush at Waco.* Critics assailed it as a propaganda piece told from the government's perspective. Within two months the controversial film *Waco: The Big Lie* instead blamed the siege and conflagration on the federal agents, though it was also heavily criticized for bias.[52] Both civil rights activists and right wing talk show hosts joined in with their own harsh words for the government's handling of its response. Observers saw a sudden rise in armed paramilitary groups over the next two years. The

Anti-Defamation League reported that, by the spring of 1995, the perception that the siege reflected a government conspiracy against survivalists had galvanized extremists to form militias in practically every state.[53]

In August 1993, twelve of the Branch Davidian survivors were indicted on charges including conspiring to murder federal officers and unlawful possession and use of firearms. One entered into a plea bargain, the rest were defended in a jury trial that lasted close to two months. All were acquitted of murder, eight were convicted on the firearms charges, and five of aiding and abetting voluntary manslaughter of the six federal agents who died. Lengthy sentences of up to forty years were imposed. Their appeals were still pending at the time of the Oklahoma City bombing.

McVeigh had seen *Waco: The Big Lie* and agreed with its conclusion. He defended the bombing as similar in his view to murders committed by abolitionist John Brown in the mid-19th century. Like a counterpart of his hero, McVeigh believed that he had righteously retaliated for egregious wrongs done by the government both in the Waco siege and an earlier siege in August 1992 in Ruby Ridge, Idaho. In June of 1994, the Department of Justice had itself severely criticized the FBI for storming the Idaho mountain home of former Green Beret Randy Weaver and killing Weaver's wife, one of his four children, and his dog. Weaver, like Koresh, was a survivalist who had stockpiled weapons in preparation for the apocalypse. At the time, the government was investigating Weaver's possible association with the Aryan Nation and accusations that he had made threats against the lives of public figures, which Weaver denied. The federal agents who converged on Weaver's property were found to have improperly used deadly force without giving the occupants a chance to surrender.

Many radical right-wing critics of the government who shared McVeigh's political views publicly disagreed with his chosen target in Oklahoma. The explosion killed many innocent people totally uninvolved in either siege, including a daycare center full of women and children. The former army sergeant had rationalized that he was at war, like President Truman, who never voiced regret for bombing civilians in Hiroshima and Nagasaki. On reflection, McVeigh later commented that it would have been more fitting had he instead targeted Attorney General Janet Reno for assassination, along with several other federal officials.[54]

Following appeals and a retrial of the Branch Davidians, the United States Supreme Court held that a jury should have decided whether the weapons the defendants used should be classified as machine guns, not the judge. As a result, when the case was sent back down yet again, most of their sentences were greatly reduced. All would be released from prison by 2007. In the meantime, over a hundred family members of the deceased Branch Davidians joined survivors in suing the federal government and state and federal officials for damages. Most of the claims were dismissed before trial. After hearing a month of evidence, the trial judge found that it was the Davidians who started the gun battle by firing upon federal officials who were lawfully serving search warrants. The court further found that agents only fired back to protect themselves and their colleagues; and that the Branch Davidians themselves caused the fire. The judge also held that the government was immune from suit for any errors in planning the siege and had not been negligent in its use of tear gas. On appeal, claims of bias against the judge were rejected and his judgment in favor of the government defendants affirmed.[55]

Both McVeigh and Nichols had very highly regarded teams of lawyers, who first got them a change of venue to Colorado based on the perceived inability to obtain a fair trial in Oklahoma. McVeigh was tried first. A month before potential jurors were impaneled, a damning interview surfaced in which the unapologetic bomber told defense investigators he chose the time of day for the explosion to "increase the body count."[56] Although McVeigh did not get the invalid political defense of "necessity" that he urged his lawyers to present, they did play *Waco: The Big Lie* for the jury. McVeigh was convicted and ultimately executed in 2001 for the mass murder. Nichols' lead counsel, Prof. Mike Tigar and Ronald Woods, a former FBI agent and United States Attorney, sought to convince a second jury that Nichols had distanced himself from McVeigh before the bombing, but were unable to create reasonable doubt. In the penalty phase, they did persuade the jury not to vote for Nichols' execution. Nichols is now serving 161 consecutive life sentences without possibility of parole. (Tigar later explained the needle-threading defense strategy in his 2008 book, *Trial Stories.*)[57] Fortier was released early for good behavior and given a new identity in a witness protection program. In 2009, FBI Director Robert Mueller and Homeland Security Secretary Janet Napolitano informed a Senate committee that they remained as concerned about "homegrown" terrorists as those from overseas.[58] Of the estimated 1,000 active hate groups in America today, watchdogs assume the KKK alone accounts for some 5,000 members[59]—equal to or greater than the total membership of the Black Panther Party in its prime. Yet armed right wing hate groups attract far less public focus or apparent concern than black militants. Among white extremists who treat *The Turner Diaries* as their bible, many no doubt still consider McVeigh the way he saw himself, a martyr to their cause.

* * * * *

So how is it possible to weigh each of these trials in the balance? Certainly one could argue that the devastating Oklahoma bombing—if it signals the likelihood of other such plots by domestic extremists—is of far greater significance than the O. J. Simpson trial or the Clinton impeachment trial. Indeed, looking back in 1999 at all the choices for "THE" trial of the century, Prof. Douglas Linder argued that the O. J. Simpson trial never merited serious consideration: "The OJ trial was a domestic murder, one of thousands that happen each year. The facts of the case had nothing, really to do with race. The main significance of the Simpson trial is as a lesson for a judge and prosecutors in how not to conduct a trial."[60]

Prof. Linder and others discount the media frenzy over the Simpson case, which was, at its core, a celebrity trial for an unfortunately commonplace act of brutality. Simpson had a previous record of domestic abuse before the violent stabbing deaths occurred. The prosecutor did not even ask for the death penalty, which would almost certainly have been sought on the grisly facts if the alleged perpetrator were a common criminal. The stakes were thus intentionally lowered in recognition that no jury was likely to impose the ultimate sanction if it convicted the former sports hero. The case did, however, have political significance because it brought intense public focus to questions of racism in the

American criminal justice system. It also demonstrated beyond doubt how enormous a difference money and fame can make in the quality of justice a criminal defendant receives.

If neither the Simpson trial nor the Clinton impeachment merited the distinction of being deemed "THE" trial of the century, was it, as many contend, the Scopes Trial? The Oklahoma City Bombing Trial? The Rosenberg Espionage Trial or the Trial of Big Bill Haywood? In 2005 Prof. Ogletree moderated a panel on the 1972 Angela Davis trial to inaugurate the Charles Hamilton Houston Institute for Race and Justice at the Harvard Law School. By then Ogletree had changed his mind about singling out the O. J. Simpson trial above all others, and instead called the Davis kidnap/murder trial "clearly the trial of the 20th century, and one that exemplified the vast and diverse talents of the true Dream Team of the legal profession."[61]

That conspiracy trial of a political pariah—which Prof. Dershowitz omits from his book of pivotal American trials and Prof. Linder relegates to his tertiary "yet more trials—links only" list—did merit recognition as a remarkable event in the history of our country. Although the black militants with whom Davis was closely aligned no longer were perceived to pose a threat to the nation's security, millions of people worldwide followed the case closely, skeptical that the dedicated Communist would get a fair trial. It showcased the innovative use of professional jury consultants and expert testimony on the unreliability of eyewitnesses. It also featured a rare woman on its Dream Team as well as a relatively uncommon woman foreperson of a high profile jury. Yet it was a circumstantial case of far less difficulty to defend than the O. J. Simpson trial. Ironically, when Charles Ogletree had originally considered the Davis trial of lesser significance, he did so with full knowledge of the comparison and contrasts between the two.

Ogletree suffered through repeated body searches to sit in on much of the Davis trial as a nineteen-year-old editor of the Stanford campus *Black Panther* newspaper, *The Real News.* Exposed to radical ideas in college, the farm lad had responded like so many alienated African-Americans his age. He became enthralled, as Angela Davis herself did, with Huey Newton and Bobby Seale for founding their own revolutionary party advocating the killing of racist "pigs." Not long before Angela Davis was transferred to the Palo Alto jail near his college campus, the young militant met one of his recently freed icons, Bobby Seale, on campus for a recruiting conference for black high school students. Seale's release presented living proof that black revolutionaries could get a fair trial somewhere in America. Yet Ogletree still so mistrusted the local populace that he fully expected Angela Davis to have no chance with an all-white Santa Clara County jury. Watching that legal drama unfold before his eyes had a few dull moments, but its overall impact was impressive. The experience convinced the skeptical youth that becoming a successful criminal defense lawyer might fulfill his own long-held ambition to battle racial injustice.[62]

In 1968, Ogletree was a high school student in rural Merced, still under his divorced mother's watchful eye and too young to travel to Oakland to witness the compelling theatrics of the Newton murder trial that caused journalist Gilbert Moore to quit his secure job at *Life* magazine and embark on a new career path. As a youth, Ogletree already had witnessed police tactics close at hand that he considered outrageous, which were undoubtedly a major catalyst for his magnetic attraction to the Panther Party when the seventeen-year-old arrived on the Stanford campus in the fall of 1970. Newton's hard-hitting defense at his 1968 trial strongly appealed to new Party recruits harboring similar anger to that smoldering within young Ogletree. It aggressively reinforced the Party's message by vilifying the homicide victim, Officer Frey, and by arguing that Frey instigated his own death by abusive behavior. In contrast, the state presented a weak circumstantial conspiracy case against activist Angela Davis, who did not in any way attack the character of the victims of the failed kidnap attempt. Rather, she claimed no advance knowledge of the misguided plot and then declined to take the stand and submit to vigorous cross-examination.

Unlike Newton, Davis did not play the dual role of victim/avenger; her jury had no power to impose a death sentence if she lost; and no "sky's the limit" national reprisals were anticipated if she were convicted. In fact, rather than being escorted back and forth from jail in chains as had occurred when she was first caught, by the time of her trial the college instructor was out on bail. Her Dream Team defense in the spring of 1972 was quite impressive, but it had a much easier set of facts to address and prior Movement successes to build upon. Indeed, the strategies employed to reduce the impact of racism at the 1968 Newton trial had already been issued three years before the Davis trial as a Lawyers Guild primer for criminal defense lawyers nationwide. Looking back in 1989, former *Ramparts* editors Peter Collier and David Horowitz pointed out that "the 'political defense' Garry and Fay conducted for Newton gave perfect expression to the radical viewpoint of the time and became a model for the trials of Angela Davis, the Chicago Seven, and others that followed."[63]

Isn't it about time to recognize *People v. Newton* on the short list of top contenders?

8. THE PRECARIOUS PATH TO A BI-RACIAL PRESIDENT

Let's face it, my presence on this stage is pretty unlikely. . . .
I owe a debt to all those who came before me and
in no other country on earth is my story even possible.

Excerpt from Barack Obama's Keynote Address,
2004 Democratic Convention

On July 27, 2004, an obscure senatorial candidate from Illinois electrified audiences with his keynote speech at the Democratic Presidential Convention. For older viewers, Barack Obama's performance brought to mind Texas Congresswoman Barbara Jordan—the first Southern black woman elected to the House—who wowed the nation in 1976 when she eloquently noted the special nature of her own presence on that same national platform. The historic invitation to the daughter of a Baptist preacher and domestic servant four years after she first gained national office was "one additional bit of evidence the American Dream need not forever be deferred."[1]

Commentator Gwen Ifill's 2009 book, *The Breakthrough: Politics and Race in the Age of Obama,* provides insight into the political evolution that produced the watershed election of 2008. In another best seller, *Game Change: Obama and the Clintons, McCain and Palin, and the Race of a Lifetime,* journalists Mark Halperin and John Heileman detail how Democrats wrangled over the historic opportunity to nominate either their first black or first woman at the top of the ticket, prompting Republicans to seek a momentum shift by picking a woman vice presidential candidate for the first time. These pioneering nominees emerged from a field that some pundits speculated included African-American Secretary of State Condoleezza Rice as a viable Republican candidate for either slot on the ticket.

Ifill profiles many of the black politicians a generation or two older, whose collective efforts made the "Age of Obama" possible by risking their positions, safety, or even their lives for desegregation, fair housing, voting rights, and educational and job opportunities. Among the most widely sold books of 1964 was Irving Wallace's novel *The Man*, which envisioned the harsh backlash if an African-American Senator accidentally succeeded to the Oval Office. One paperback cover enticed readers with the blurb "overnight a Negro becomes President of the United States."[2] While this imaginary scenario was still fresh in the public consciousness, at the fractious Democratic Convention of 1968, SNCC co-founder H. Julian Bond (who had quit SNCC in 1966 when Lewis was ousted) had his name put forward as a protest candidate for Vice President. (Bond's Georgian colleagues had to be forced to seat him in 1967 by decree of the Supreme Court that Bond's anti-war views were protected free speech, not evidence of disloyalty to the Constitution.) As head of the new Georgia Legislative Black Caucus, Bond quickly withdrew his name from consideration—at 28, the lightning rod for hawks and Dixiecrats was too young to serve as Vice President.

New York's Shirley Chisholm endured both ridicule from her black male colleagues in the House and multiple assassination attempts in her 1972 run as the first African-American to test the presidential campaign trail. That same year science fiction writer Rod Serling (famed for producing the television series *The Twilight Zone*) turned Irving Wallace's best seller into a low-budget movie featuring James Earl Jones as the Senate pro tem leader suddenly elevated by happenstance to Commander-in-Chief. Though no one at the time considered an African-American to have a genuine shot at election to the White House, mainstream political commentators began giving serious thought to the idea of a black vice presidential candidate and predicted that there would be a black governor in at least one of the fifty states by the decade's end.[3] Ten years later in 1982, most California gubernatorial polls showed Los Angeles Democratic Mayor Tom Bradley poised for that breakthrough. Bradley then surprised pundits by losing in a close race due to a surge of absentee ballots for his "law and order" Republican opponent George Deukmejian. A similar disparity between major polls and ballot results has since been observed in other high profile races pitting an African-American candidate against a traditional white male. The phenomenon came to be known as "the Bradley effect"—the tendency of a percentage of white voters to mask their true intentions for fear of being perceived as racist. (Actually, in Bradley's case the result could have been attributed to a strong push by the NRA to defeat a handgun control initiative on the same ballot.)

In 1983, Jesse Jackson debuted his Rainbow Coalition and surprisingly won five presidential primary contests. With a much stronger organization in the 1988 race, he won several million additional votes, more than doubling his primary and caucus victories of 1984 with his left-of-center challenge to the status quo. Retired General Colin Powell's very public contemplation in 1995 of his own presidential run as the more widely admired black "Ike" further paved the way for Senator Obama's campaign. (Though Powell was warned by the publisher of *Black Enterprise* that his popularity among white voters would likely fade behind closed doors.)

Obama launched his improbable bid for the presidency with a call to abandon the politics of division between Liberals and Conservatives, black America and white America, red states and blue states. Just the fifth black Senator ever sworn in (and only the third since Reconstruction), Obama skyrocketed to international celebrity status in 2006 following publication of his second autobiographical book, *The Audacity of Hope: Thoughts on Reclaiming the American Dream.* As he crisscrossed the nation making speeches, whites initially supported the appeal of the self-described "skinny guy with a funny name" to look beyond race more than skeptical African-Americans did. Senate Majority Leader Harry Reid privately noted that the prospects of the dynamic outsider in the 2008 race were enhanced by his light skin and absence of a Negro dialect. Meanwhile, a January 2008 poll showed African-Americans favoring ex–First Lady Hillary Clinton by a three-to-one margin. Some wondered out loud if the articulate Hawaiian Ivy Leaguer was "black enough" to champion their core issues; and, before his convincing victory in the Iowa caucus, whether his skin color would prevent him from prevailing in key primaries or succeeding in the then almost unimaginable task of winning the general election.

Back at the Democratic Convention in 1968, the effort to give the spotlight to anti-war activist Julian Bond was quickly stifled by turning off the sound on his nominator's microphone. In that year, most delegates who gathered in Chicago considered it sufficiently daring to feature a tame speech from Hawaiian Senator Daniel Inouye, a decorated hero of World War II and the first Japanese-American to serve in Congress. At the height of the Black Power Movement, African-American community organizers sent chills down the spines of leaders among the Democratic Party establishment. In 1968 the scent of revolution was in the air; it was late that very year when Charles Manson and his Family began plotting how to instigate and win an apocalyptic race war.

The following year, in the trial of what began as the Chicago Eight, Judge Julius Hoffman ordered Panther Party Chairman Bobby Seale bound and gagged, inadvertently turning Seale into a searing countercultural symbol. The only black among several unruly defendants was the lone man deprived of his voice and freedom of movement. Seale's treatment shocked observers throughout the world, but his forced silencing reflected a long-established color code. Calls for political empowerment were harshly suppressed, while black achievements were historically understated, if acknowledged at all. That was the lesson learned by the Negro soldiers of the 24th infantry who stormed San Juan Hill in the Spanish-American War, and by slave-born hero Big Jim Parker after he tackled President McKinley's assailant. Accounts of black victims of violent crime at best ended up buried deep in a local newspaper, while similar atrocities perpetrated against whites made above-the-fold, front-page news.

During the 1960s, when national media focused on milestones achieved in toppling Jim Crow laws, newspapers in Cotton Belt states ignored the momentous change happening before their eyes. In the summer of 2004, a telling page-one apology appeared in a metropolitan Kentucky daily: "It has come to the editor's attention that the *Herald-Leader* neglected to cover the civil rights movement . . . We regret the omission."[4] In 1968, two years before National Guardsmen shocked the nation by opening fire on white war protesters at Kent State in Ohio,

South Carolina police responded with lethal gunfire to an unruly crowd of student protesters at the mostly black Orangeburg campus of the state university. Three were killed and 28 wounded, some shot in the back. Eight policemen were later acquitted of using excessive force. Practically no national media coverage attended the Orangeburg Massacre. In an attempt to embarrass the United States, a petition to the United Nations signed by Huey Newton and Bobby Seale listed the Orangeburg killings as one of many examples of alleged racist persecution by the United States in violation of the Genocide Convention of 1948. It took until 2001 for a South Carolina governor to acknowledge the police response as "a great tragedy for our state" and to voice his "deep regret."[5]

Throughout the '60s and '70s more subtle discriminatory coverage also pervaded supposedly Liberal enclaves such as the San Francisco Bay Area and New York. *Ramparts* magazine editor Warren Hinckle recalled the rule of thumb he learned as an East Bay cub reporter: "Whether a homicide would be reported at all depended largely upon the neighborhood in which it was committed. Ghetto murders, being regarded as natural black events, were rarely considered newsworthy."[6] Journalist Bob Herbert still vividly remembers that double standard when he arrived as the first black deputy city editor at the *New York Daily News*: the editorial staff assigned breaking crime stories priority levels depending on the color of the victim's skin—even if the killing involved an innocent baby.[7]

In 1986 a detailed statistical analysis (the Baldus Study) was presented to the United States Supreme Court to prove that, in the state of Georgia, if a victim of homicide were white, the convicted defendant was four times as likely to be sentenced to die. By a five-to-four vote in *McCleskey v. Kemp*, the high court concluded that the remarkable disparity did not show a "constitutionally significant risk of racial bias affecting the Georgia capital sentencing process."[8] After he retired, Justice Lewis Powell, Jr.—who authored the majority opinion—wished he could take those words back and cast his swing vote the other way.[9] Not only might the Virginian have prevented McCleskey's execution, among many others, but that lone jurist's second thoughts could have dramatically changed the future course of equal protection jurisprudence.[10] Newark Mayor Cory Booker recently noted little progress even by 2008: "The reality is we're still in a place and a time where everybody knows who JonBenet Ramsey is [a six-year-old blonde beauty queen found strangled in her parents' basement in 1996], or who Natalee Holloway is [a blonde Alabama teenager who went missing in Aruba in 2005]. But so many people . . . cannot name a black child that died . . . in an unsolved murder. So you still see a world in which there [are sometimes] . . . different degrees of horror or response, or . . . persistent and insidious divisions between black and white."[11]

What thornier issue dominated the American 20th century? In 1915 black military veterans first dared lobby for a museum on the National Mall dedicated to African-Americans who defended their homeland with life and limb. At the time, the Ku Klux Klan was reemerging with renewed vigor, lynchings were common sights in the Cotton Belt, and *Birth of a Nation* broke box office records in cities where the controversial film was not banned. It took until the late 1990s for a "Spirit of Freedom" sculpture and museum to open elsewhere in Washington, D.C., memorializing more than 209,000 "Colored Troops" of Union soldiers and sailors, 40,000 of whom died in the Civil War. In early planning stages at that time was a separate thirty-foot statue honoring Dr. Martin Luther King, Jr. at 1964 Independence Avenue in West Potomac Park, near the Franklin Delano Roosevent Memorial. (Fifteen years after its authorization by President Clinton, the ceremonial opening of that new federal memorial took place in mid-October 2011, ironically postponed by hurricane warnings from the anniversary of the "I Have a Dream" speech to the anniversary of the 1995 Million Man March.)

In 2000 a powerful collection of photographs of early 20th century lynchings drew record crowds to a New York gallery. It prompted a traveling art show, numerous educational programs and websites and a haunting book, *Without Sanctuary: Lynching Photography in America.* The graphic reminder of largely forgotten, gruesome celebrations of white supremacy made its debut in a Southern venue in a temporary exhibit in the Martin Luther King, Jr. National Historical Site in Atlanta, Georgia. Accompanied by Billie Holiday's rendition of "Strange Fruit," the exhbit drew over 175,000 visitors. Amid great controversy, the collection was then acquired by the Atlanta Center for Civil and Human Rights which plans to display the photos as part of its permanent collection when the center opens to the public. As noted by African American Studies professor Leigh Raiford in *Imprisoned in a Luminous Glare,* "It is a strange century that opens and closes with images of dead black bodies at center stage."[12]

Not until 2003 did Congress finally overcome entrenched opposition led by white Southerners to fund a National Museum of African American History and Culture on the Mall itself, near the Washington Monument. The Smithsonian plans to cut the ribbon in 2015 on that ambitious project. In 2011, its director and board still have a controversial duty:

> grappling with fundamental questions about the museum's soul and message . . . What story will it tell? . . . the "official"—that is the government's—version of black history . . .[or] one of pain, focused on America's history of slavery and racial oppressions and memorializing black suffering? Or will it emphasize the uplifting part of the story, highlighting the richness of African-American culture, celebrating the bravery of civil rights heroes and documenting black "firsts" in fields like music, art, science and sports? Will the story end with the country's having overcome its shameful history and approaching a state of racial harmony and equality? Or will the museum argue that the legacy of racism is still dominant—and, if so, how will it make that case?

The Museum's Director, Dr. Lonnie Bunch III, envisions a unifying purpose: "to make sure people see this is not an ancillary story, but it's really the central story of the American experience."[13] Toward this end, in 2009 Dr. Bunch invited an inter-racial mix of nearly a thousand people to form numerous focus groups. His outreach included former Black Power activists. Undoubtedly among the key stories the museum will tell from various perspectives is that of the Black Panthers and Huey Newton. More than forty years ago Newton emerged as a master at commanding attention, starting with the spectacular gun-toting debut of his Party that he orchestrated in the California State Capitol building in Sacramento in May 1967. The Panthers quickly became the focus of international media, threatening traditional law and order. COINTELPRO infiltrated the Party ranks and systematically removed its leadership from the streets, killing members or throwing them in prison where many were forgotten. Eventually, Newton was dismissed as a gangster. But the official view of

Newton as a wrongly glorified thug does not explain his huge following. Even mainstream reporters acknowledged on his death that, by co-founding the Panthers, Newton gave birth to a "new era in American history" in which "expressions of rage spread across the nation . . . After his arrest at the height of the black power movement, the slogan 'Free Huey' became an emblem for a generation of revolutionaries."[14]

Why does the trial of Huey Newton merit consideration as a pivotal point in American history? It was not just avowed revolutionaries that the Movement hero inspired. By the time Newton went on trial for his life in 1968, he had given thousands upon thousands of young inner city blacks a sense of empowerment and pride in their cultural heritage. The Panther leader called attention to long neglected health and safety issues in black communities and started bold programs to do something about them. By aggressively asserting arrestees' rights and denouncing officers as "racist pigs," Newton also galvanized a grassroots movement for community control of police.

The Panthers were barely a blip on the FBI's radar screen when the spontaneous urban riots of 1967 prompted President Johnson to convene the Blue Ribbon Kerner Commission, which strongly urged integration of the nation's police forces. Just four years later most major cities had done so. One can assume the Panthers were a major catalyst to the speedy embrace of that recommendation. Huey Newton did not help his own legacy when he shifted in the early 1970s from a revolutionary spokesman for the people to a drugged-up imitation of a ruthless Mafia kingpin. But in spite of his own self-destructive course, Newton's influence continues. In 1994, Hugh Pearson predicted that the "Black Panther Party will remain a historical phenomenon . . . the quintessential intersection of all the confusion inherent in what it has meant to be African American for the past thirty years."[15] During that time Newton has been the subject of countless books, plays, and songs. On the right, "Red Diaper" baby David Horowitz repeatedly describes his own fascination in the late '60s and early '70s with Newton as a counterculture hero of mythic proportions, and credits his about-face embrace of Conservatism to disillusionment following discovery of the gruesome murder of Panther bookkeeper Betty Van Patter. Hugh Pearson also recognized

Newton as a Dr. Jeckyl and Mr. Hyde, who supplied both "proud black imagery" in a time of great need, and savage behavior that fulfilled a "racist's ultimate dream."[16] The late Rap artist Tupac Shakur (executed gangland style in 1995) dedicated "Fallen Star" to Huey Newton as a misunderstood and ridiculed visionary. (Both of Shakur's parents were Panther members; his mother was one of the Panther 21.)

In popular culture, Newton turns up in places like *The Boondocks* syndicated comic strip and television cartoon series, whose central character Huey Freeman was named for the Panther leader. Newton's appeal to later generations is also evident from the success of 1995's *Panther* and director Spike Lee's acclaimed 2001 movie remake of the 1996 one-man show *A Huey P. Newton Story*. Newton's and Seale's alma mater, Merritt College, which moved to the Oakland Hills in 1971, has a large painting of Newton on his wicker throne on display in its student lounge dedicated in 2001 to the college's most famous alumni for their pioneering role in organizing black students on campus. The Oakland Museum of California features a bronze replica of Newton's empty wicker throne, which it invites all visitors to try out for themselves. The Black Panther official website offers guided "legacy" tours of the location of the October 1967 shootout among other sites associated with the Party's history. In 2006, to celebrate the 40th anniversary of the Party's creation, San Francisco's Yerba Buena's Center for the Arts mounted a "Black Panther Rank and File" show that drew crowds for several months. At the same time, the Dr. Huey P. Newton Foundation marketed Panther clothing and a hot sauce called "Burn, Baby, Burn." Presumably, some consumers used it to spice up the authentic ribs they grilled from a recipe out of *Barbeque'n with Bobby Seale*, the popular cookbook by his estranged co-founder who dedicated the proceeds to charity. Rap artists like Paris, Public Enemy and the Fugitives, still sing of the life and death of Huey Newton the way Irish immigrants in Australia lionized the 19th century outlaw Ned Kelly. Huey Newton's name appears among the "Black People Who Changed The World" on a British Black History month website.[17]

As race and ethnic studies scholar Jane Rhodes observed in her 2007 book, *Framing the Black Panthers: The Spectacular Rise of a Black Power Icon*:

> Nearly forty years after Huey Newton and Bobby Seale founded the Black Panther Party for Self-Defense in Oakland, California, this organization and its leaders are lasting fixtures in mass culture and popular memory. The passage of time has not eroded the strength of their symbols and rhetoric—the gun, the snarling panther, the raised fist, and slogans such as "All power to the people" and "Off the pig." Today, representations of the Black Panthers linger in diverse arenas of commodity culture, from news stories to reality television to feature films and hip-hop, as they function as America's dominant icons of Black Nationalism.[18]

Radicals recognized Newton's symbolic value back when he was first arrested for murdering an Oakland cop. The perception that the Panther leader had audaciously acted on his clarion call for revolution signaled a "radical turn in the trajectory of black protest. What had begun to occur elsewhere as spontaneous rioting or disorder took the form of an organized political actor . . . [The Panthers] armed refusal to accept the boundaries of a racialized civil order gave voice to deeply held grievances in the black community, while their dramatic presence brought the issue of racial inequality of power forcibly into the public sphere."[19] By February 1968, when black militants gathered in Oakland for Newton's birthday rally, many of them knew he was worth much more to them dead than alive. On the center stage, the empty wicker throne was an apt symbol of the man Eldridge Cleaver called "our Jesus."[20]

The perception that Newton's execution could only help the Movement was one shared by earlier generations of radicals. In 1920, Eugene Debs ran as a Socialist candidate for President from his prison cell. When Debs grew seriously ill, Attorney General Palmer convinced new President Warren Harding to pardon Debs so the government would not be blamed for his death. Back in 1907, radicals had recognized that Big Bill Haywood's extraordinary popularity with labor would have made him a potent symbol, far larger than life, had he been condemned to die, a perception Clarence Darrow featured in his closing argument. Yet labor was then divided by race. Haywood himself had inflamed WFM members in Northern Idaho with lurid descriptions of black federal troops "ravishing their wives, mothers, sisters and sweethearts" while keeping union members corralled in a barn.[21] Unlike the appeal to racism employed in defense of Haywood and his colleagues by the WFM's long-time counsel Edmund Richardson, Newton and his counsel emphasized that the Panthers targeted both capitalism and racism. The Panthers also joined forces with a strong, diverse anti-war movement. Following the cascade of political crises America faced in 1968, Newton's murder conviction may well have had far more cataclysmic consequences than Haywood's potential martyrdom in 1907.

As more states adopted protective legislation, the work place restrictions faced repeated attacks under the 1905 *Lochner* doctrine upholding employers' and employees' freedom of contract. The forty-hour work week finally became the rule for non-exempt employees during the New Deal when the high court abandoned the *Lochner* doctrine. With time, popular appreciation of the high stakes for the social order involved in Haywood's murder trial diminished greatly. Yet, by using increased numbers of independent contractors and splitting work into part-time shifts, many blue and white collar employers today avoid statutory benefits like overtime pay. Others have shifted plants to states where they can operate non-union shops. Today one of the biggest political battles between capital and labor is over universal health care—with over fifty-two million of the nation's adults not covered by any health insurance in 2010. Most devastatingly for American workers over the past two decades, major industries have simply moved their base of operations and jobs overseas where cheap labor abounds with few, if any, worker protection restrictions.[22] Republican Governors and legislators have recently cited state budgetary woes to launch efforts to attack collective bargaining by public employees on any issue, economic or otherwise.

Ironically, the most dramatic confrontation came in the spring of 2011 in Fighting Bob La Follette's state of Wisconsin over the controversial legislative agenda of newly-elected Republican Gov. Scott Walker. As Republican governor of the state at the turn of the 20th century, La Follette was credited with creating the first workers' compensation system and the minimum wage, among other Progressive reforms aimed at enhancing the power of trade unions to counterbalance the power of corporations. In contrast, Gov. Walker sees himself as emulating

President Reagan's dramatic anti-union stance three decades ago in firing thousands of striking federal air traffic controllers in 1981. But the current nationwide attack on unions evidences a much broader design: it resembles *Los Angeles Times* owner Harry Otis's campaign a hundred years ago to break the back of all unions through the Merchants and Manufacturers Association. In Wisconsin, the public employees' unions acceded to economic demands, leaving Gov. Walker and his supporters to argue that the right to collective bargaining itself impeded the state's chances for fiscal recovery. The unions countercharged that Walker's true aim was to render public employees politically powerless on non-economic issues as well as wages and benefits, undoing many decades of hard-fought gains on issues from worker safety to grievance procedures. Threatened with loss of their collective bargaining rights, public employees across the nation have galvanized support from private sector unions fearing their own demise in pitched political battles that are expected to shape many local, state, and federal races in upcoming elections. Whichever side one favors, the recurrence of lines drawn in the sand gives us a greater appreciation of the impact of Haywood's 1907 trial and the 1911 trial of the McNamara brothers.

The competing labor versus capital approaches to shaping public policy are not the only early 20th century battles that have resurfaced to loom large in the 21st century. The cause espoused by another presidential aspirant, populist William Jennings Bryan, in the celebrated 1925 Scopes trial still sparks considerable interest today. In 1999—after a half century off the national radar screen—the Fundamentalist Christian battle against the teaching of evolution hit headlines once again when creationists on the Kansas state school board succeeded in temporarily removing the big bang theory from mandatory coverage in the state's science classes. When the religious right reemerged as a major political player at the turn of the 21st century the teaching of evolution faced increased opposition. In 2005, the *Scopes* trial had its sequel in a widely publicized Dover, Pennsylvania, case. The ACLU again played the lead role when several parents challenged the local school board's decision to require the teaching of intelligent design as an alternative to evolution. A six-week trial took place before District Judge John Jones, a recent Republican appointee who was himself a devout Lutheran. Judge Jones studied the evidence and concluded that intelligent design was clearly a religious belief, not a scientific principle, and that teaching it in public schools violated the First Amendment. In 2010 Tea Party Republican candidates continued to court Fundamentalists by challenging the separation of church and state.

The 1913 Leo Frank trial provides another example of an issue with multi-generational appeal. Mounting class resentment against exploitation of child labor in the impoverished city of Atlanta resulted in an outburst of misdirected wrath against a Jewish factory manager. Frank served as a proxy for all the carpet-bagging Northern industrialists whom nostalgic white Southerners blamed for the loss of the slave-based agrarian economy of the antebellum South. Look, too, at the international riots against Americans that followed Sacco and Vanzetti's execution and the lingering stain on the country's justice system that their trial represents. It coincided with the rise of the United States following World War I to an unparalleled world superpower and widespread fears around the globe of a future dominated by American capitalists and xenophobes. Within the United States, the Protestant establishment rebelled against foreign pressure, which only sealed the fate of the two anarchists. This played right into the game plan of the Soviet Union. Among the picketers at the final vigil was future Pulitzer Prize–winning writer Katherine Anne Porter, who naively confided to a Communist leader her hope for last minute clemency. "Saved?" the indignant organizer retorted, "Who wants them saved? What earthly good would they do us alive?"[23] Their martyrdom was far more effective in stirring up anti-American feelings on the world stage than if the pair had been successful on appeal and retried by a judge who did not have his thumb on the scales of justice. At home, the backlash among intellectuals, workers, and minorities also helped launch the Liberal coalition that gave rise to Roosevelt's New Deal.

Similarly, in the territory of Hawaii in 1931, convicting five islanders of gang-rape was so important to the white power elite that even an ironclad alibi and a transparent police frame-up left half the jury too intimidated to acquit the innocent men. The kidnapping and murder of defendant Joe Kahahawai turned the local boxer into an instant martyr. The heavy-handed efforts by the Navy, the press, President Hoover, and

Congress to treat Kahahawai's shooting as an honor killing nearly led to a military takeover of the territorial government. Instead, over time it helped galvanize a more peaceable, though difficult, transition of Hawai'i from control by a white oligarchy to a multi-ethnic democracy. In 1953, echoing the global support for Sacco and Vanzetti in 1927, hundreds of thousands of people around the world protested the impending execution of Julius and Ethel Rosenberg for treason, to no avail. McCarthy Era hysteria fueled this widely criticized trial against both husband and wife, orphaning their two young sons. If charges against Ethel had been dropped for insufficient evidence and Julius Rosenberg had been tried fairly, there would likely have been a far lesser outcry upon his conviction.

The spontaneous urban riots following Dr. King's assassination in April 1968 provide a closer model of what might have occurred if Newton were convicted of murder in September of that year. Immediately following Dr. King's death, President Johnson tried to quell unrest by declaring a national day of mourning. Most black community leaders heeded the government's urgings and told constituents to keep their cool; Panther leader Bobby Seale embraced this advice. But looting and firebombing still broke out in Chicago, Baltimore, Detroit, Kansas City, and Washington, D.C. and elsewhere, requiring more than sixty thousand National Guardsmen to keep the peace. Indeed, historian Curtis Austin points out that King's murder "helped fuel the party's expansion" as "more and more blacks came to believe non-violence died with King." Over the next twenty months, James Clark, a sociologist who specialized in the study of race and crime, noted a nearly five-fold increase in black/white violence which he attributed largely to "swelling black rage."[24]

One can assume that the violence black militants threatened if Newton were condemned to die might easily have had an equal or even greater impact. Just before Judge Friedman instructed the jury, ugly confrontations between nearly 12,000 Chicago police and thousands of activists had caused President Johnson to have 7500 more federal troops in readiness at army bases in the Southwest to mobilize to restore peace. At the last minute the pilloried Commander-in-Chief cancelled his own plans to attend a 60th birthday celebration at his Party's national convention. Mayor Daley reported recent death threats against the Vice

President and Eugene McCarthy; the Secret Service feared that more violence would erupt and put the President's life at high risk despite the extraordinary fortifications and military garrison surrounding the Convention Hall.[24] The debacle in Chicago exacerbated the cultural divide nationwide. It forced far more ordinary Americans into one of two warring camps: Liberals who questioned the sacrifice of so many youths in an unwinnable war, and hawks and Conservatives who demanded law and order. Presidential candidates Nixon and George Wallace advocated even tougher crackdowns on demonstrators, as then California Gov. Reagan was already doing at every opportunity to further his own presidential ambitions. As each side dug in its heels, the country was primed for violent confrontations to escalate.

The editor of the *San Francisco Examiner* held his tongue until the Newton trial was over, but could wait no longer to observe that the murder trial raised issues that "will long echo." The concerns raised were ironic, coming from the flagship paper run by the Hearst media conglomerate. Its editor-in-chief William Randolph Hearst, Jr. was the son of the man who built his empire on yellow journalism, sensationalizing "trials of the century" with sometimes tragic results. The central question raised in the September 10, 1968, editorial was: "Did the big 'Free Huey' demonstrations around the courthouse while the trial was in progress amount to attempted intimidation of the judge, jury and prosecution witnesses?" The editorial noted that, if the courthouse had been surrounded by a hanging mob (like that Hearst, Sr. helped arouse in the Lindbergh case, for instance?), the result would have been a mistrial—a conclusion only very recently reached by the Supreme Court after decades of circuslike national coverage of dramatic trials. The Hearst editorial concluded:

> [If] American justice is to be done, the judge and jury must be as free from attempted intimidation by those who want to free a defendant as those who want to hang him. . . . [S]ociety [must] maintain a system of justice functioning in an atmosphere of calm detachment, not one surrounded by demonstrators, bullhorns, paramilitary forces shouting allegiance to the defendant, armed sheriff's deputies at every courthouse door, physical searches of courtroom spectators, cries

> of 'pigs' yelled at police, and big banners proclaiming in fierce rhetoric that "the sky's the limit" if anything happens to the defendant.[26]

Though it represented a total turnabout for one of the nation's most ardent First Amendment rights' champions, the editorial had a point. Within two years the State Legislature would enact a criminal law to prevent a recurrence of potentially intimidating demonstrations circling courthouses. But heightened courthouse security heralded the new norm, and, as Hearst well knew, "Free Huey" rallies could be held at a nearby park with no repercussions. The editorial also failed to mention that, to the embarrassment of law enforcement, two drunken policemen had just committed the only violence by shooting up Panther headquarters. Most glaring in its absence from the editorial was its explosive context: an overwhelmingly white establishment in open confrontation with a broad coalition of anti-war activists who embraced Newton as an icon; a black community seething over decades of abuse; and skewed *Oakland Tribune* coverage of the shootout making the Panther leader's murder conviction look like an open and shut case before the trial had even started. These were only a few of the factors impeding "calm detachment"—an unattainable goal for a trial of a black revolutionary in 1968 in Oakland or anywhere else in America.

* * * * *

In a television interview with *60 Minutes* near the end of his life, Eldridge Cleaver confessed that "If people had listened to Huey Newton and me in the 1960s, there would have been a holocaust in this country."[27] How would American race relations have fared if "El Rage" had been instead killed in a bloody siege in Oakland like that which later occurred in Waco? Would Cleaver's death have been followed by widespread urban eruptions across the country? How different is the context today?

On early New Year's Day 2009, several cell phone videos captured a white Bay Area Rapid Transit (BART) police officer shooting an unarmed black man lying handcuffed on the platform of an Oakland BART station. Like the Rodney King videos seventeen years before, the clip of 27-year-old officer Johannes Mehserle killing Oscar Grant III was replayed over and over to a shocked public. Rioters caused more than $200,000 in damage to cars and Oakland businesses. Now in his seventies, Black Panther Bobby Seale (who had returned to Oakland in 1998 to act as campaign manager for David Hilliard in a losing Oakland City Council race) was among those who spoke out once again to condemn senseless violence.[28] As the black community erupted in anger, Mehserle claimed it was an innocent mistake; he only meant to use his Taser. The Alameda County District Attorney concluded otherwise and charged Mehserle with murder—the first law enforcement officer so accused in the State of California in several decades. Mehserle's lawyer then won a change of venue to Los Angeles after an opinion poll showed a sharp racial divide between whites and blacks in Alameda County over the presumption of Mehserle's guilt and the likelihood of violence if he were to be acquitted.

On March 21, 2009, Oakland again made grim national headlines when two policemen stopped an ex-felon in broad daylight for a routine traffic violation in a crime-ridden section of East Oakland's flatlands. Lovelle Mixon was armed with a semi-automatic hand gun and an AK47. Desperate, as "El Rage" had been, to avoid returning to prison for parole violations, the 26-year-old Mixon opened fire on the surprised motorcycle cops and fled the scene as a Good Samaritan offered futile aid to the dying officers. Cornered soon afterward, Mixon killed two members of a SWAT team before being gunned down himself. It set a chilling record—the worst single day of police fatalities in the violence-plagued city's history, adding an ironic and bitter coda to a year in which the number of police officers killed in the line of duty had reached a fifty-year low. Three days later, Oakland's Mayor, former long-time East Bay Congressman Ron Dellums, expressed the city's grief at an evening vigil. Hundreds of residents gathered at the site of the street shootings. The black community demonstrated its overwhelming support for the police and their families, drowning out the few housing project residents who cheered Mixon's senseless act.

Some four decades before, as most local officials mourned fallen police officer John Frey, Dellums had alienated members of the establishment when he criticized Newton's indictment by a grand jury with no black panelists. At that volatile time, Dellums was so identified with the

Panthers some people assumed he was himself a member. The Leftist Congressman later acknowledged that "the Oakland Police Department was then in more or less open warfare with the Black Panther Party."[29] But in the spring of 2009, a much more somber and reflective Mayor Dellums expressed the city's "shock and sadness at officers who paid the ultimate price in service to community. We come to thank them. We come here to mourn them. We come here to embrace them as community."[30]

Those paying their final respects to the four fallen officers gathered in the same 10,000-seat Oakland Arena where 41 years before revolutionary black leaders had pledged vengeance if Huey Newton were executed for killing the Oakland policeman who had stopped the Panther leader for outstanding traffic tickets. Dellums had then stood in apparent solidarity on the same platform as Forman shouted, "The sky's the limit." In 2009, half the overflow crowd watched the proceedings on screens set up at the adjacent Coliseum as the entire Oakland police force turned out alongside local, state, and national dignitaries and colleagues. Gov. Arnold Schwarzenegger, Senator Dianne Feinstein, and then California Attorney General (now Gov.) Jerry Brown addressed the crowd. Brown had been Oakland's immediate past mayor before Dellums. Though Mayor Dellums shared the stage with the other officials, he honored a request from two of the slain policemen's families that he not offer any eulogy; after all these years, they still regarded him as a controversial figure. President Obama sent his and his wife Michelle's somber thoughts and prayers to the families and the community, expressing the nation's gratitude "for the men and women in law enforcement who . . . risk their lives each day on our behalf" and condemning "the senseless violence that claimed so many of them."[30]

With all its ongoing problems, Oakland in 2009 was a decidedly different, much more integrated community than in 1968 when the Black Panther Party first rose up to challenge the historic police abuse of ghettoized blacks. Then, it was like so many other polarized American cities where white men held almost every position of power. Today, Oakland's municipal government, police force, and county judiciary are far more representative of its multi-cultural population. Like other urban areas Oakland still struggles with intractable issues associated with high levels of poverty, crime, and unemployment. Yet the city takes justifiable pride in its remarkable gains and the way it has assimilated many diverse cultures, which it celebrates each March with an annual "Unity Day Parade." In 2010, Oakland voted in its first woman and Asian-American mayor. Three out of four of her immediate predecessors were black men; another formidable candidate in the 2010 race was a lesbian City Council member endorsed by *The Oakland Tribune.* The election highlighted a sea change in the city's political structure and dominant culture over the four decades since the Panthers first erupted on the political scene. Yet even in such a different climate racial tension under the surface can quickly erupt in violence: witness the January 2009 rioting that followed Internet dissemination of footage of the killing of Oscar Grant III by BART officer Johannes Mehserle.

Shortly after Grant's death, Mehserle resigned from the BART force; the BART Board fired its police chief, retrained its police in the proper use of Tasers, and invited the Legislature to create a civilian police review board for BART officers. The case against Mehserle went to trial before a Los Angeles jury with no black panelists. In anticipation of Mehserle's possible acquittal, city officials worked with community leaders, churches, and nonprofit mediators coordinated by Fania Davis, to minimize the risk and severity of a violent reaction. Meanwhile, Oakland's black police chief enlisted diverse reinforcements from fifteen other agencies, all trained to effectuate by-the-book arrests of suspected vandals and other miscreants while giving broad scope to those exercising their First Amendment rights.[31]

None of those prophylactic steps to minimize violence were taken before the jury deliberated Newton's fate in September 1968. Had he been convicted of first degree murder, what forces could have held back the collective rage of inner city blacks? What if all the hordes of hidden—almost exclusively white—National Guardsmen and police had been deployed to bash heads as the Chicago police had done the week before at the Democratic National Convention? Would the resulting race violence have rivaled or surpassed that of the bloody 1919 Chicago riots? Black journalist Gilbert Moore, with his plum job at *Life* magazine, did not even know he carried that rage within him until he covered the Newton trial.

Rodney King was an unknown speeder before his beating was captured on tape; yet suppressed rage gave vent to a billion dollars in damages from the riots that broke out after four policemen won acquittal on charges of using excessive force in King's arrest. In contrast, by the time of Newton's trial, posters of the defiant Panther leader were plastered on many thousands of walls of Movement supporters across America. The 1992 Rodney King riots in Los Angeles sparked smaller riots in several cities across the country. One can easily imagine the nation's cities erupting in violence of far greater magnitude if Newton's followers had been incited to avenge his death sentence.

On October 3, 1995, six months after the horrific Oklahoma City bombing, the nation stood ready for urban riots in the wake of O. J. Simpson's anticipated conviction for the violent stabbing death of his ex-wife Nicole and her friend Ron Goldman. The Nation of Islam's Louis Farrakhan had already advertised a Million Man March on Washington, D.C. to take place in mid-October, expecting to draw far more followers than Dr. King's similarly named march back in November of 1963. On October 16, 1995, a broad coalition of several hundred thousand African-American men did assemble in the nation's capital with the controversial Black Muslim leader, to present a positive image of the black male, renew their commitment to their families, and protest the ongoing economic and social problems facing their communities: poverty; unemployment; truancy; high incarceration rates for drugs and crime; bitterness and rage.

Future President Obama, who attended that rally, recognized at the time that turning toward black nationalism and "cursing out white folks" was not going to solve anything.[32] Yet Farrakhan, Jesse Jackson, and other irate voices resonated with seething members of black communities. Perhaps urban violence might have broken out on the day of the Simpson verdict and at the time of the Farrakhan protest march if the jury had convicted the celebrity of homicide. But the prospect of O. J. Simpson doing time for murdering his ex-wife had to be far less a catalyst to urban riots than if the author of *To Die for the People* had faced execution in 1968 for killing an Oakland policeman labeled as a racist "pig."

Newton's followers had considered "sky's the limit" reprisals more than just a condemnation of his death sentence and execution; El Rage and other militants had already announced plans to start a revolution avenging four hundred years of abuse at the hands of racist law enforcement. As Bobby Seale feared, the government's response would have been brutal. Yet it was only much later that Seale realized that Cleaver had acted like a classic anarchist. Suppression of major uprisings in 1968 could only have polarized society far more than it already was. If Newton had been condemned to die, he would undoubtedly have rallied far more supporters to his cause while the appeals pended, just as Sacco and Vanzetti did over forty years before. In 1972, when the California Supreme Court outlawed the state's death penalty, Newton would have had his sentence converted to life imprisonment, just as that ruling benefited others then on death row, including Sirhan Sirhan and Charles Manson. Then, instead of heading into a downward tailspin leading to an ignoble end at the hands of a crack dealer, Newton could have remained a Movement star, an untarnished revolutionary hero for the rest of his life, as new generations of followers pressed for his release in numbers dwarfing Manson's less predictable fan club.

Perhaps Newton would have written more books from prison. Surely he would have become an even bigger cause célèbre than he was as a free man. To his admirers, Newton might have drawn comparisons to South African statesman Nelson Mandela, whose political influence grew exponentially in prison. Mandela is himself one of the leading international voices who supported the release of Geronimo Ji Jaga (Pratt) that was eventually won in 1999. Mandela also has lent his voice to the long list of protesters seeking the release of journalist Mumia Abu-Jamal, a former Black Panther on death row in Pennsylvania for more than a quarter century after being convicted in 1982 of killing a Philadelphia policeman. (In April of 2011, a panel on the federal Third Circuit vacated his death sentence and ordered a new sentencing hearing.)[33] Abu-Jamal's famous case bears eerie similarities to Newton's own, except for the fact that Newton enjoyed a much wider reputation as a counterculture hero and would undoubtedly have remained a far more potent icon. Recall that in 1968, Reverend Jesse Jackson wired Huey Newton a supportive message, proclaiming that the Black Panther leader, regardless of a verdict of guilty or innocent, represented "the disenchanted and degraded" against whom "unjust men" could not "render justice." Newton in prison all these years would have remained a polarizing figure. Would Jackson have been able to launch a national Rainbow Coalition in 1984 if he had endorsed an ongoing "Free Huey" campaign for a living, cop-killing revolutionary?

Since the '60s, the look of people in power has become far more diverse. Not only are women now more prominent in political life—including the 2006 election of the first female Speaker of the House—but as of 2009 the aging white majority constituted less than two-thirds of the total population. In 2010, Republicans won back decisive control of the House in part because their white constituents feared that the President and Democrats in Congress would respond disproportionately to the demands of minorities by increasing the size of government and moving America closer to a debt-ridden, socialized state. Though the speakership returned to a white male in that midterm election, one Republican rising star is the son of Cuban refugees: another who aspires to national office is the offspring of Hindu emigrants from India; and a conservative African-American businessman surprisingly threw his hat into the ring for the 2012 Republican presidential nomination. California, the most populous state, has been transformed into a decided majority of "minorities"—just forty percent of its population is white, a trend among preschoolers nationwide.

The societal and demographic evolution in the past forty years has unleashed a virulent white male reaction not just to black empowerment, but to that of other minorities and women.Underlying the vitriol of some displaced blue collar Caucasians against woman and minorities is a bitter truth: statistics show that the prolonged economic downturn that began in 2008 adversely affected middle-aged white men far more than any recession since World War II. By mid-2009, as jobs kept disappearing overseas, the unemployment rate for American men over 55 skyrocketed to twice its historical average in sixty years. Yet, from 2000 to 2007, black unemployment was two times the level of white unemployment, while fully a third of all black children lived in poverty.[34] As journalist Charles M. Blow observed in 2009, "Blacks are living a tale of two Americas—one of the ascension of the first black president . . .; the other of a collapsing quality of life and amplified racial tensions."[35]

Back in 1971, Archie Bunker of "All in the Family"—the most popular sitcom of its time—personified the angry white man whom television audiences either laughed at or identified with. In one episode Bunker tells his hippie son-in-law "Meathead" Mike Stivic (played by a young Rob Reiner): "If your spics and your spades want their rightful share of the American dream, let 'em get out there and hustle for it like I done."

Stivic responds: "So now you're going to tell me the black man has just as much chance as the white man to get a job?

Bunker retorts: "More, he has more . . . I didn't have no million people marchin' and protestin' to get me my job."

His guileless wife Edith then adds, "No, his uncle got it for him."[36]

Archie Bunker's rants against affirmative action were far less menacing than the anger manifested by his counterparts today—more than three decades after the nation's highest court decided *Bakke v. The Regents of the Univ. of California,* declaring racial preferences in school admissions unconstitutional, and fifteen years after former U.C. Regent Ward Connerly spearheaded passage of California Proposition 209. The California Civil Rights Initiative led to similar abolition of racial preferences in other states. Yet, even before Barack Obama won the 2008 Democratic nomination, he received Secret Service protection because he was the target of so many death threats. As President, despite his efforts to disassociate himself from controversial black activists, to take centrist positions and mediate between extremists of both major parties, Obama drew more assassination threats by far in his first several months of office than any other President, averaging over 30 per day—quadruple those recorded against his immediate predecessor.[37] Since then the White House has declined to comment on the number of threats against the nation's first African-American President. Historian Roger Wilkins, publisher of the NAACP's official magazine *The Crisis,* observed in 2008: "There has never been a change in the condition of blacks that has been as dramatic and consequential as the change from the time I was born [in 1932] to now. Never. Never."[38]

Conservative political commentator Pat Buchanan describes the current polarization as the return of the "Angry White Man." It coincides with increased gun sales and the continued growth of white hate groups and militias since the FBI's deadly 1993 siege of the survivalist compound in Waco, Texas, which triggered the catastrophic 1995 Oklahoma City Bombing. The powerful symbolism President Obama represents to African-American youth and to the world has become for many white extremists a renewed call to arms. The 1978 white supremacist book *The Turner Diaries* inspired not only Oklahoma City bomber Timothy McVeigh, but also white supremacist James Von Brunn, who, in December 1981, threatened the lives of the Federal Reserve Board. In 1999 Von Brunn authored *Kill The Best Gentiles,* arguing that "today on the world stage [one sees] a tragedy of enormous proportions: the calculated destruction of the White Race and the incomparable culture it represents. Europe, former fortress of the West, is now over-run by hordes of non-Whites and mongrels."[39] On June 10, 2009, 88-year-old Von Brunn picked up a rifle and joined a crowd of visitors entering the Holocaust Museum in Washington, D.C., where he killed a black security guard and was crippled by return gunfire. Found in his pocket was a list of Congressional leaders, fueling speculation they were also intended targets.

Von Brunn's act of terrorism came in the midst of what many Democrats perceived as an unrelenting effort from Republicans to delegitimize Obama's presidency. In August 2009, two investigative reporters wrote an in-depth analysis of the increasingly nasty health care debate (one Republican e-blast the month before ridiculed "Obama Care" as a Communist plot cooked up by the President, caricatured as a half-naked witch doctor). Other opponents likened President Obama to Hitler. The reporters concluded that these expressions of rage reflected deep-seated anger "brewing in the nation's troubled soul" for a long time.[40] In September 2009, Conservative South Carolina Congressman Joe Wilson shocked millions of observers when he rudely interrupted the President's speech to a joint session of Congress to call his Commander-in-Chief a liar. Though he grudgingly apologized, the next morning the former aide to Senator Strom Thurmond parlayed his outburst into a fund-raising gambit. Support for Wilson poured in from the Sons of Confederate Veterans—to which Wilson belongs—and from survivalist militia groups lauding the politician as a "Great American Hero" for giving vent before a national audience to his contempt for the country's bi-racial leader.

Accusations of thinly veiled appeals to bigotry and fear redoubled as both sides geared up for the 2012 election. On September 11, 2010, when Americans paused to remember the terrorist attack on the twin towers nine years before, challenger Newt Gingrich labeled President

Obama's foreign policy approach "Kenyan, anti-colonial." In professorial style, the former House Speaker was promoting a new book arguing that the Commander-in-Chief was a dangerous disciple of his African father, embracing revolutionary black nationalism as a world view.[41] In April 2011, a prominent California Republican circulated a doctored image of the President as a chimpanzee. Meanwhile, Republican legislators in over a dozen states rushed to introduce bills to deny ballot listing to any presidential candidates absent advance proof of their citizenship. Karl Rove criticized focus on the birther issue as disserving his Party, but flash-in-the-pan presidential hopeful Donald Trump wooed support from the birther movement by demanding additional evidence of the President's birth place. The Celebrity Apprentice television host helped create such a media distraction that the Commander-in-Chief felt compelled to request the state of Hawaii to release his certified long-form birth certificate in an effort to put the unprecedented query to rest.

Democrats denounced the birther "sideshow" as "just code for having problems dealing with Obama as an African American in the White House."[42] That did not stop Gov. Rick Perry from re-raising the moribund birther issue not long after the public learned that, for years, the Texan's family hunting camp had prominently displayed the name "Niggerhead." Tea Party members countered charges of racism by pointing to Herman Cain's brief surge in polls. Before Cain suspended his campaign, many party activists looking for a rival to Mitt Romney became intrigued by Cain's 9-9-9 tax plan. Former Party Chair Michael Steele immediately warned that Cain wouldn't cause black voters to suddenly forget that "ugly stripe" they see on the Republican Party from over four decades of a Southern Strategy in which it courted white males while doing "jack to empower them [African-Americans]."[43] Indeed, Cain's signature tax proposal was criticized for hitting the poor the hardest, and the middle class harder than the rich. Like Clarence Thomas, Cain won the Right's embrace by rejecting the politics of most African Americans. At the same time, the Right ridiculed Obama as an extremist—even as some of his former supporters on the Left, like Prof. Cornel West, lambasted the President for being too cozy with Wall Street.

During the 2008 presidential election campaign, Obama foes used Obama's acquaintanceship with University of Illinois Prof. Bill Ayers to link Obama with the former Weatherman's and his wife Bernardine Dohrn's radical activities in the late '60s. Back in 1995 Ayers had helped Obama with a political fund-raiser; the two men also served together on a community board.[44] But Obama was only eight when the underground Weathermen set bombs off. By the time the two met, Prof. Ayers had long since been named "Citizen of the Year" by Chicago officials for his achievements in school reform. Obama condemned the Weathermen's violent actions in the '60s as "despicable."[45] The smear campaign backfired. Congressman John Lewis labeled John McCain and running mate Sarah Palin race baiters who were "playing with fire" as George Wallace had done in the '60s. The ploy to demonize the Democratic candidate helped galvanize General Powell—the most trusted man in America on national security issues—to come off the sidelines to endorse Obama over the war hero in his own party who had been the general's longtime friend. The freshman Illinois Senator thus obtained Powell's much-coveted seal of approval on Obama's readiness to assume the role of Commander-in-Chief.

Yet Obama, as a teenager, voraciously read the works of dissident black writers and could easily picture himself, as so many young African-Americans then did, picking up the gauntlet of the fiery preacher Malcolm X, assassinated little more than a decade before. In his autobiography, *Dreams from My Father: A Story of Race and Inheritance*, Obama candidly described his freshman year at college when he felt most at home with the radical Left. He hung out with Marxists and militant blacks, including one whose older sister helped found the Los Angeles branch of the Black Panthers. Like Huey Newton and Bobby Seale, Obama and his friends found inspiration in the philosophical tracts of Algerian revolutionary Frantz Fanon, who railed against the evils of neocolonialism.

Obama moved to Chicago in 1985, two decades after the windy city had gained fame as the birthplace of community organizing and just a year after the National Rainbow Coalition became the emblem of Rev. Jesse Jackson's 1984 Presidential Campaign. By the time the ambitious college graduate accepted a job as director of the Developing Communities Project, Chicago was headed by its first African-American mayor. Harold Washington was a veteran of the Daley machine and a protégé of the late South Side Congressman Ralph Metcalfe, but likely owed his election more to the murder of Black Panther Fred Hampton. On Chicago's West Side, Obama could also see other evidence of Hampton's legacy.

From his first days as an NAACP organizer, Hampton had always been adept at building community support for local projects. In early 1969, Hampton enthusiastically embraced Huey Newton's directive to expand the Panthers' local food banks, medical clinics, and breakfast programs as J. Edgar Hoover warily observed the success of that effort. Throughout that volatile year, the FBI Chief harbored a siege mentality. The antennae of the FBI and CIA rose considerably in June of 1969 when fugitive Eldridge Cleaver left Cuba for Algeria and hooked up with representatives from various liberation movements around the world. The agencies feared radical groups were gaining ground in promoting global uprisings. President Nixon agreed that drastic action was necessary to protect both his domestic and foreign policies. Even hitherto staid Ivy League campuses were rocked by strikes and sit-ins; lawmen reported that radical groups were teaching inner city blacks how to make Molotov cocktails. The Broadway megahit *Hair* captured the "us v. them" bunker mindset in one four-letter word: a San Quentin guard was fired for refusing to trim his sideburns; Disneyland barred young men with ponytails from access to its amusement park.

In Chicago what worried the FBI most was the meteoric rise of Fred Hampton. Federal agents worked with local police to have the charismatic Black Panther arrested in the spring of 1969 as he was about to appear on television. Hampton was then convicted of two-year-old charges of a $71 ice cream truck robbery and sent to jail. In August 1969, his lawyers secured his release on bail pending appeal, challenging the conviction on the grounds that the police had improperly influenced the eyewitness who fingered Hampton as the perpetrator. On his release, the indomitable Panther undertook another series of speaking engagements and was expected by some to soon be named the Party's national spokesman. Locals started calling him "Chairman Fred," which caused friction with Party Chairman Bobby Seale in Oakland. Hampton was not even on the central committee, where Hilliard was next in line. By November, extreme measures were finalized by COINTELPRO to eliminate any prospect of

Hampton replacing King as the much-feared black messiah. Aided by an informer, on the early morning of December 4, 1969, the nation's top law enforcement agency collaborated with Chicago police, who invaded Hampton's apartment and engineered a gangland-type execution of the sleeping Panther leader in the presence of his pregnant fiancée.

By the time Obama came of age, Hampton was long since revered among civil rights activists as a martyr. His death had been the subject of a 1971 documentary, *The Murder of Fred Hampton*, and further exposed in a 1973 reinvestigation of his killing. The Commission of Inquiry into the Black Panthers and the Police, headed by NAACP executive director Roy Wilkins and Ramsey Clark, issued a scathing report that detailed a prior state and federal cover-up. In 1983—after more than a decade of legal wrangling—Hampton's family received an historic $2 million from the City of Chicago in compensation for his wrongful death.

As Obama began developing his own roots in Chicago's black community, Hampton remained a legendary role model among blacks for his efforts a generation earlier to transform Chicago's most impoverished areas. In 1987, PBS aired the first part of its award-winning miniseries *Eyes on the Prize,* reviewing the history of the Civil Rights Movement. It was instantly acclaimed by civil rights educators as "the principal film account of the most important American social justice movement of the 20th century."[46] Three years later, in 1990, PBS aired *Eyes on the Prize II: America at the Racial Crossroads 1965–1985.* Episode 12, "A Nation of Law? (1968–1971)," focused in large part on COINTELPRO's efforts to destroy the Black Panther Party in Chicago and murder Fred Hampton. In December 1990, the increased political clout of Chicago's black voters prompted a divided City Council to honor the slain Black Panther with a controversial Fred Hampton Day, loudly condemned by Conservatives who cited Hampton's criminal record (still being challenged on appeal when he died). Fourteen years later, just after Obama won his Senate seat, the Chicago City Council unanimously approved December 4, 2004, as another "Fred Hampton Day in Chicago." In 2006, local police blocked an attempt to name a Chicago street for Hampton, incensed that a national Panther leader, who demonized officers as "pigs" and called the establishment "motherfuckers," could be considered for such a permanent tribute.

Influential black pastors lobbied hard for the honors posthumously bestowed on Fred Hampton as a martyred community organizer. If Panther Party co-founder Huey Newton were still serving a life sentence in the 1980s and 1990s, one can easily imagine Rev. Jeremiah Wright, Jr. circulating "Free Huey" petitions at his Trinity Church of Christ in Chicago and Barack Obama, as Wright's then-protégé, signing such a petition, even though he harbored growing misgivings about the efficacy of black militants. By 1995 Obama would dismiss "the politics of black rage . . . which exhorts but does not organize ordinary folks or create realistic agendas for change."[47] In 1999, Obama bucked the local black political establishment by trying to unseat Chicago Congressman Bobby Rush, a veteran of SNCC who grew up on Chicago's streets and helped Fred Hampton found the Illinois Black Panther Party. Thrust into a more prominent role on Hampton's death, Rush became the local chapter's Minister of Defense and named his son after Huey Newton, before Rush quit the Party and went back to school. After Rush's son Huey was killed by robbers, Rush represented the authentic voice who shared the community's pain. The impeccably dressed Harvard graduate who ran against him was dismissed as just a "white man in black face."[48]

Gwen Ifill asserts that, when later running for President, "Obama somehow managed to escape one rite of passage for black politicians—the need to explain or distance himself from well-known but divisive leaders such as [Al] Sharpton, [Jesse] Jackson, and Louis Farrakhan."[49] But Obama had long since disassociated himself from all three men, whom critics accused of exacerbating race relations with anti-white and anti-Semitic rhetoric while failing to condemn black violence against other ethnic communities.[50] Even so, Rev. Wright almost derailed Obama's campaign in the spring of 2008 when some of Wright's extreme sermons condemning American domestic and foreign policy received national exposure in *Rolling Stone* magazine. The negative publicity prompted Obama to distance himself from his former mentor in a brilliant televised speech on race relations that some observers felt rivaled Dr. King's best oratory.

When ex-President Clinton then courted super delegates for his wife by suggesting the nation was not ready to elect a black Commander-in-Chief, the backlash stunned the Clinton camp. Obama took the offensive, noting that he didn't "look like all those other presidents on those dollar bills."[51] In mid-July 2008, *The New Yorker* created a storm of controversy with its cover cartoon labeled "The Politics of Fear." The lampoon purported to show the Obamas post-election, bumping fists in the Oval Office as they had famously done at a celebratory rally in June. Obama is dressed as a Muslim wearing a turban and sandals, standing under a portrait of Osama bin Laden—the face of global terrorism—as the American flag burns in the fireplace. His wife Michelle sports an Afro hair style and is dressed in military camouflage draped in a bullet belt, wearing combat boots and carrying a menacing AK-47. That caricature evoked memories of Angela Davis and Kathleen Cleaver. By the time the menacing cartoon appeared, Obama had already assured himself the nomination of his party as a transformational agent of change. The fear-mongering the cartoonist sought to mock had limited impact. Obama's acceptance speech at the Democratic Convention brought tears to the eyes of attendees when he invoked memories of Dr. King's dream.

Accusations that the Clintons had cynically played "the race card" prompted McCain to avoid a similar pitfall. He vetoed suggestions of his campaign team to tar Obama with his past closeness to Rev. Wright, but that did not stop his running mate Sarah Palin from going rogue and re-raising the issue. Not until the month before the election did McCain belatedly seek to rein in rabid supporters. The Republican presidential candidate endured a loud chorus of boos after he sought to reassure one rally attendee, petrified at the thought of an Obama presidency, by saying he "is a decent person and a person you don't have to be scared of as president."[52] Some doubters may have only become convinced after Obama dramatically announced on May Day 2011 that he had made good on his campaign promise to track down Al Qaeda leader Osama bin Laden and ordered the daring raid on his Pakistani compound in which the world's most infamous terrorist was killed. The President won bi-partisan praise and prompted spontaneous public gatherings in jubilation for accomplishing that mission nearly a decade after the confidence-rattling September 11 attack on New York's World Trade Center. But that sense of patriotic unity was fleeting. Other, more confirmed skeptics will never feel comfortable under Obama's leadership.

* * * * *

Assume that Huey Newton, like Mumia Abu-Jamal and Ruchell Cinque Magee, remained an aging radical prisoner in 2008. Obama's opponents would hardly have been deterred by a public denunciation of the Black Panther founder, like the way Obama distanced himself from Rev. Wright or emphatically rejected Louis Farrakhan in a debate with Senator Clinton. Rather, Obama's political enemies would have undoubtedly searched the many "Free Huey" petitions over the years looking for one with the future presidential candidate's signature. If such evidence existed, broadcasting Barack Hussein Obama's name endorsing a "Free Huey" petition would easily have frightened hordes of voters.

Indeed, twice during a key period of the presidential race in August and September of 2008, the Federal Bureau of Prisons publicly objected to another high-profile prisoner's request just *to read* Obama's two best-selling books, *Dreams from My Father* and *The Audacity of Hope.* At the time, Al Qaeda member Ahmed Omar Abu Ali was serving thirty years in a "super-maximum" security federal prison for attempting to assassinate President Bush. While vice-presidential candidate Sarah Palin repeatedly accused Obama of "pallin' around with terrorists," prison authorities bizarrely reported that the FBI considered some passages of Obama's widely disseminated autobiographies "potentially detrimental to national security." The Bureau of Prisons quietly withdrew this extraordinary attack on Obama's patriotism just after his election.[53]

This effort to derail the Democratic candidate failed to dispel what Ifill calls the "Obama effect"—the perception that whites are far more at ease with black candidates, like black entertainers, who do not seem to carry "that anger." Ifill credits the ready acceptance of "No Drama" Obama partly to the way already paved by superstar entertainers with broad, cross-racial appeal, such as Bill Cosby, Oprah Winfrey, and Denzel Washington. But Ifill also points out Obama's cultivation of a "supraracial" image that appealed to whites more than blacks. Despite his efforts to set himself apart from polarizing activists, "the shadows, links, and political equations to [black] leaders of previous generations never went away." In October of

2008, only four weeks before the election, forty percent of "swing voters" and, apparently not coincidentally, forty percent of whites responding to an NBC News/Wall Street Journal poll declared they were "bothered" that "Barack Obama has been supported by African American leaders such as Reverend Jeremiah Wright and Al Sharpton." Ifill observes: "This was the backlash risk the Obama campaign had been worried about." Such fears factored into his decision to quit Rev. Wright's congregation. Even so, doubts about Obama's identification with Wright's history of angry anti-white rhetoric persisted for months afterward.[54] But his charisma, centrist appeal, and unflappable demeanor—particularly during the economic crisis that unfolded in the fall—overcame those doubts to lead him to a lopsided victory in a record turnout of over 131 million voters. The historic victory prompted Wee Pal's creator Morrie Turner to circulate an exuberant new cartoon with the caption, "ROSA SAT . . . SO MARTIN COULD WALK . . . SO OBAMA COULD RUN . . . SO OUR KIDS COULD FLY!"

As civil rights advocates celebrated how far the nation had come since Dr. King's martyrdom in 1968, a backlash was already being mounted. On Election Day 2008, a Republican poll watcher in Philadelphia captured on video two black men in paramilitary dress accosting people at a mostly African-American polling place. The police ordered King Samir Shabazz to leave, and he did, taking his billy club with him; his unarmed companion Jerry Jackson had credentials as a poll watcher and was allowed to stay. The video circulated on the Internet, with a clip of Shabazz shouting death threats against white "crackers" at a different time and location. The pair represented a fringe hate group its members decided to call the New Black Panther Party. The copycat organization formed in 1989 in Dallas, Texas, the year Huey Newton died a political has-been on the streets of Oakland.

Less than two weeks before Obama's inauguration, the Department of Justice filed charges against the New Black Panther Party and its chairman, as well as Shabazz and Jackson, for voter intimidation, charges that a civil rights specialist claimed the Bush administration had rarely filed when presented with numerous other reported incidents. Hold-over attorneys from the Bush Department of Justice later dismissed most of the charges. The action prompted accusations of reverse racism against Obama's newly appointed African-American Attorney General Eric Holder. On the agenda of the Judiciary Committee of the new Republican majority in the House in 2011–12 is an investigation of Attorney General Holder's handling of voting rights cases. Its Chair Lamar Smith explained to the media: "We've already seen this administration dismiss one case against a political ally—the New Black Panther Party—for no apparent reason."[55] Had the Dallas group chosen a different name, the incident and any follow-up federal inquiry could be expected to draw far less public attention. The powerful negatives associated with the Black Panthers more than four decades ago still reverberate. Assuming Huey Newton remained an imprisoned revolutionary in 2008, of all the political efforts to discredit candidate Obama, proof he had signed a petition to free the co-founder of the Black Panther Party might very well have had the most traction. Any link—no matter how attenuated—with Newton and the Black Panther Party would presumably have been toxic.

Obama's chief rival Hillary Rodham Clinton would have provided an even more direct target. In the spring of her first year at Yale Law School, she was already a nationally known student anti-war activist and veteran of the 1968 Democratic National Convention. At the time, Hillary adopted the look of feminist icon Gloria Steinem, complete with tinted aviator sunglasses. That year marked the height of "radical chic," the term journalist Tom Wolfe coined for the cause du jour of Left-leaning high society after news spread of a cocktail party fund-raiser for the Panthers at composer Leonard Bernstein's Manhattan penthouse. Rodham then helped found the Yale Law School Review of Law and Social Action, which decided to devote an entire issue to cases involving the Panthers' civil rights. As national attention focused on the Bobby Seale murder trial, Rodham coordinated law students monitoring the headline-grabbing proceedings for potential constitutional violations.

After Charles Garry achieved a hung jury in New Haven in May 1971 before a courtroom packed with supporters, he rushed back to Oakland to prepare for the retrial of Panther leader Huey Newton. Meanwhile, fresh from her experience monitoring the Seale trial, Rodham secured a job that summer with Garry's long-time Lawyers Guild colleagues at the Treuhaft, Edises & Walker firm in Oakland, where one of her major assignments was to research California's gun laws for use in the defense of other Panther arrestees. At the time, name partner Dobby Walker was deeply involved in discovery proceedings in the sensationalized Angela Davis kidnap/murder case. The Treuhaft firm also represented a key witness in Newton's retrial for Officer Frey's death. Rodham and her new boyfriend from Arkansas, bearded Rhodes Scholar Bill Clinton, may have taken time to watch some of Garry's latest courtroom theatrics in Newton's retrial and meet the Movement icon. Had she won the nomination instead of Obama—as originally expected—her political enemies on the Right no doubt planned to recycle this ammunition to attack Clinton as a closet extremist, too.[56]

But connections to Obama would also not have been hard to draw and would have been magnified by a far larger fear factor. When Ron Dellums left his long congressional career, he was succeeded by his protegé Barbara Lee, a self-described renegade who got her start in politics as a staffer in Shirley Chisholm's grassroots 1972 presidential campaign. Representative Lee became Senator Obama's Western Regional Co-Chair for his 2008 presidential campaign. Long vilified for her strong Leftist views, Lee needed bodyguards in the aftermath of 9/11 when targeted with death threats as a traitor for casting the lone vote against the congressional resolution to give President Bush broad power to conduct a borderless war on terror. If Newton were still in prison, Lee would undoubtedly have been among the most vocal advocates for his release. She was his close associate in the early '70s and a key fund-raiser for Seale's unsuccessful 1973 Oakland mayoral campaign.

Obama's uphill victory over the seven other candidates in the 2008 Democratic primaries depended both on his appeal to moderate and Liberal whites and on winning over influential African-American politicians, many of whom had originally lined up behind Hillary Clinton as the party's 2008 standard bearer. That fall, the get-out-the-vote efforts of a supportive old guard became a key part of Obama's ability to turn out record numbers of voters. Many of these champions of Obama, like Barbara Lee, themselves would have been tarred by any connection to a campaign to free Huey Newton. If the aging revolutionary had remained incarcerated in 2008, it is difficult to imagine Democrats taking the risk of anointing Barack Obama as their candidate or, if he were nominated, how the

Obama Campaign could have persuaded swing voters to disregard qualms about electing a black community organizer as President.

* * * * *

Statehood for Hawai'i came two years before Obama was born, opening up previously unattainable political opportunities for the majority of non-whites. Since the '60s, much progress removing perceived racial barriers to success has been made in the rest of the country. To be sure, changed demographics following white flight to the suburbs laid the groundwork for many mayoral victories, but in 2010 African-Americans could count the presidency, several governorships, prominent posts in the Cabinet, and chair of the Republican Party among their achievements. Who could have predicted such progress so early in the 21st century? The martyrdom of Martin Luther King, Jr. undoubtedly helped galvanize major reforms. So, too, did black militants like Malcolm X and the Panthers.

Just as prosecutor Lowell Jensen noticed that Charles Garry's often outrageous positions induced judges to move from the middle ground toward Garry's direction, black militants made the more modest demands of mainstream African-Americans look all the more reasonable, while speeding up the timetable for progress. President Lyndon Johnson's 1968 Kerner Report directly linked white racism with urban unrest, but it had taken the riots of 1964, the 1965 Watts riots, and the riots of 1966 and the summer of 1967 to galvanize Johnson into action.

As momentum built toward the Civil War, Frederick Douglass provided early support for John Brown's efforts to create an army of fugitive slaves to free others in the South. Douglass rallied abolitionists by arguing that "power concedes nothing without a demand. It never did and it never will."[57] His famous observation applied equally to entrenched political control in the succeeding century. The threat of radical unions in Big Bill Haywood's day helped galvanize passage of Progressive workplace reforms. Without revolutionary threats by black power advocates, the procession of moderate black community and business leaders seeking bipartisan support for election to municipal, state, and national offices would undoubtedly have taken far longer to achieve.

Yet as factions battle over shrinking economic and social resources, the problems faced by so many poor African-American families remain largely unsolved. The authors of *The Black White Divide in America . . . Still* [2008] directly link the us/them dichotomy to entrenched resistance on the part of a large percentage of whites to the "declared intentions and the premise upon which this nation's constitution is structured."[58] While Neoconservative David Horowitz has criticized fellow Republicans for not doing enough to "[g]ive minorities and the poor a shot at the American Dream,"[59] many members of the new generation of black politicians have eschewed the angry rhetoric of civil rights leaders and declined to embrace their aggressive agendas. During the time black candidates increasingly wooed white voters by championing middle class priorities, America was in the midst of a nearly sixfold increase in incarceration rates, with its heaviest impact on young black men.

The dramatic national policy shift toward imprisoning far more citizens coincided with the War on Drugs, first declared by President Nixon in 1971 and later fueled by a huge increase in federal expenditures as a high priority of Reagan's presidency. Over the ensuing decades, Conservative politicians continued to use the specter of black militants, crack cocaine peddlers, and violent felons effectively to inflame the public. Vice President George H. W. Bush's infamous campaign ads featuring paroled rapist Willie Horton—who murdered a white woman after being released on work furlough—had a powerful impact on the 1988 presidential election. Similar tactics recurred with regularity in the years that followed, with Democrats like Bill Clinton acting as tough or tougher on crime than their Republican critics. As a result, voters and their representatives have criminalized far more behavior and required increasingly heavy sentences for violent and nonviolent convicts alike. In California, the mismatch between incarceration rates and capacity became so pronounced that in May 2011 the United States Supreme Court (by another five to four vote) upheld decisions in two long-pending class actions that declared state prisons unconstitutionally overcrowded. In an exceedingly unusual move, Justice Kennedy appended photographs to his majority opinion illustrating some of the inhumane conditions found to have violated the Eighth Amendment.[60]

Michelle Alexander, author of *The New Jim Crow: Mass Incarceration in the Age of Color Blindness*, points out that more African-Americans are now "in prison or jail, on probation or parole—than were enslaved in 1850, a decade before the Civil War began." She argues that convicted felons have become a "permanent undercaste . . . relegated by law to a second-class status." Among other restrictions, "they can be denied the right to vote, automatically excluded from juries, and legally discriminated against in employment, housing, access to education, and public benefits, much as their grandparents and great-grandparents were during the Jim Crow era."[61]

To be sure, the vast majority of convicted felons achieve that label through their own illegal conduct. The very word "felon" conjures up an image of a dangerous criminal: a murderer, rapist, armed robber, or kidnapper. Yet violent crimes have actually fallen off in recent years. The exponential increase in the American inmate population is primarily for possession of illegal drugs. Ironically, despite a prolonged War on Drugs, the United States reports the highest rate of illegal drug use in the world—most prevalent among those in higher income brackets, who studies show are least likely to be prosecuted.[62] In 2009 nearly 22 million Americans over the age of 12 were estimated to be current illegal drug users.[63] Apparently, there but for the grace of law enforcement go millions more potential "felons." The public likely also remains unaware that prosecutors have discretion to apply the felony label to a wide range of other circumstances. In California some years back, under the 1994 "Three Strikes and You're Out Law," the third conviction that put one recidivist away for life was for stealing a pizza. In Mississippi, it is a felony to walk away from a $25 bar tab.

One of the lasting symbols of discriminatory felonization of black men is heavyweight champion Jack Johnson, convicted nearly a hundred years ago of taking a white woman across state lines in violation of the new Mann Act. Yet even with bipartisan congressional support for a posthumous pardon and a groundswell of pressure from influential sports figures as the centennial of the historic Johnson-Jeffries 1910 fight approached, President Obama declined to risk any political capital by granting that request. As one commentator noted, "[Obama] would likely not be hailed for righting a historic wrong but for playing race with a deceased black man who in his day flaunted the law and the moral code of society. Race and politics simply can't be separated even when the recipient of justice is a dead man."[64]

The United States now posts the highest rate of incarceration in the world. In 2009, 7.2 million adults were under some form of criminal justice supervision. Over 5 million Americans are currently denied the right to vote because of felony convictions—one out of approximately every 43 adults.[65] This grim situation does not look to improve any time soon. As of 2009, 15 million children lived in poverty, many of whom our education systems are failing. Some states like California have for years been planning ahead for new prisons based on the illiteracy rates of third and fourth graders, earmarking billions of dollars for the prison system that critics point out are sorely needed for improving public education. In 2003, a *Christian Science Monitor* reporter noted that America's aggressive incarceration rates of minorities have "broad implications for everything from state fiscal crises to how other nations view the American experience." She predicted: "If current trends continue, it means that a black male in the United States would have about a 1 in 3 chance of going to prison during his lifetime. For a Hispanic male, it's 1 in 6; for a white male, 1 in 17."[66] As of 2010, Michelle Alexander confirmed that one out of three young black men was supervised in or out of prison by the justice system.[67]

Recently elected officials like California's new Attorney General Kamala Harris—the first woman and person of color to serve in that office—have begun promoting more finely tuned law enforcement that is "smart on crime" instead of just "tough on crime" to reduce the high cost to society of incarcerating nonviolent convicts. Reducing nonviolent prison populations is also a "right on crime" goal now shared by stalwart Republicans like Newt Gingrich, Grover Norquist, and Reagan's Attorney General Ed Meese.[68] Meanwhile, children of impoverished minorities continue to drop out of school and populate prisons at greatly disproportionate rates. That vicious circle remains the most visible reminder of chronic societal shortcomings in achieving the stated goals of our Declaration of Independence: a new republic "dedicated to the proposition that all men are created equal" and "endowed with unalienable rights" including "life, liberty and the pursuit of happiness."

* * * * *

Great American Trials: Trials from 1637 to 2001 notes that "many of the great turning points in America's history have occurred in courtrooms."[69] Among scores of pivotal 20th century criminal trials, only six juries who passed judgment on unpopular defendants appear to have searched their souls to question the legitimacy of a highly political prosecution—in the Haywood trial, the Sweet trials, the Massie rape trial, the Newton trial, the Chicago Seven trial, and the Angela Davis trial. Only two of these panels had life or death say over an accused enemy of the state challenging the social order: the gray-haired Caucasian farmers on the 1907 Haywood jury, and the 1968 Newton jury—seven whites and five minorities, seven women and five men of varying ages and backgrounds.

Both defendants were intimidating men who represented movements that the country's leaders perceived to menace the status quo. Unlike the *Haywood* case which incorporated *an appeal to race bias* into its defense strategy, the key issue confronting the Newton panel was whether the precipitating incident was *tainted by racism*—the cancer that has afflicted our proclaimed egalitarian democracy since birth. The black foreman at the helm of the Newton jury may well have been the very first to serve in that role in any major American criminal trial. Until the summer of 1968, it was quite unusual to see black jurors passing judgment in *any* death penalty case. The June 1968 Supreme Court ruling in *Witherspoon* created a new paradigm for capital cases. No longer would anyone with a general aversion to capital punishment be disqualified automatically from jury service. Nor, due to a recent local ruling, could Alameda County prosecutors dismiss all members of the defendant's race from a jury for fear they would identify with him. Lowell Jensen had no intention of violating that stricture and left some of his challenges unused.

David Harper certainly felt the weight of history on his shoulders. He and his fellow jurors were keenly aware of the angry crowd of protesters outside the Oakland courthouse, but made every effort to focus on the evidence and to shut from their minds the potential personal consequences. They listened closely to two seasoned lawyers' skillful arguments, weighed witness credibility, and tried to reach a just result. A freelance reporter saw the historic occasion for what it was: "The time spent deliberating, and the . . . nature of the ultimate decision, indicates profound turmoil on the part of 12 'ordinary' citizens suddenly thrown face to face with the complexities of a society in change."[70]

Looking back five years later, journalist Murray Kempton considered it remarkable that Newton's risky performance on the stand convinced the jury that their preconceived notions of good guys and bad guys had to be set aside: "a recognition by comfortable persons—unique then—that even policemen can be evil and that even notorious public nuisances can be victims with understandable provocations."[71] Kempton assumed that the members of the diverse, female-dominated jury were not among those increasingly uncomfortable with the nearly all-white male establishment, but that assumption seems unrealistic when discriminatory laws and practices made most of them less than fully empowered themselves. The diverse jurors that judged Huey Newton were thus likely to be more open to appreciating the defense's perspective. George Jackson's lawyer John Thorne had something similar in mind when he argued that jurors should be selected not just for "fairness of mind" but "understanding of soul." In Oakland in the tense summer of 1968 a dozen women and men more representative of a cross-section of county residents than the historic "twelve good men" were culled from a randomly selected list of voters and did their collective best to serve the American justice system. In the process, they disappointed both sides, but showcased why a jury of one's peers is a hallmark of our democracy.

Some might still argue that the outcome is the reason why the Newton trial has been almost completely overlooked as a candidate for "THE" trial of the century. After all, Newton was not convicted of first degree murder. No devastating riots occurred. But the Haywood trial, the Scopes trial, the Massie trials, the O. J. Simpson trial, and the Clinton impeachment trial all lead to the same conclusion: sometimes what does not happen, and an unexpected—even anticlimactic—outcome can change history. What did not happen in September 1968 is likely to have been just as pivotal to the future course of America as what did.

ENDNOTES

Abbreviations Used in Notes

AC	*The Atlanta Constitution*
BB	*The Berkeley Barb*
BG	*The Boston Globe*
BP	*The Black Panther* newspaper
HPN	Dr. Huey P. Newton Foundation, Inc. Collection, 1968–1994, M864, Green Library Special Collections, Stanford University, Series 1
LAT	*The Los Angeles Times*
NYT	*The New York Times*
OP	*The Oakland Post*
OT	*The Oakland Tribune*
SFC	*The San Francisco Chronicle*
SFE	*The San Francisco Examiner*

Foreword

1 Leigh Raiford, *Imprisoned in a Luminous Glare: Photography and the African-American Freedom Struggle* (Chapel Hill: North Carolina Univ. Press, 2011), 119.

2 Eldridge Cleaver, *Target Zero: A Life in Writing* (New York: Palgrave Macmillan, 2006), 13.

3 Bobby Seale, *Seize the Time: The Story of the Black Panther Party and Huey P. Newton* (New York: Random House, Black Classic Press, 1970, 1991), 222.

4 Clayborne Carson, *In Struggle: SNCC and the Black Awakening of the 1960s* (Cambridge: Harvard Univ. Press, 1981, 1995), 282 and note 51.

5 "Nation's Life at Stake," *BB,* July 19–25, 1968, 3.

6 Fred Hampton 1948–1969, http://www.hartford-hwp.com/archives/45a/715.html; see also "Today in Counterculture History, The Murder of Fred Hampton," http://www.shroomery.org/forums/showflat.php/Number/13580978.

7 Edward Jay Epstein, "The Black Panthers and the Police: A Pattern of Genocide?," *The New Yorker,* Feb. 13, 1971, http://www.edwardjayepstein.com/archived/panthers.htm.

8 Curtis J. Austin, *Up Against the Wall* (Fayetteville, Arkansas: Univ. of Arkansas Press, 2006), 92 and fn 8.

9 Eugene Rostow, Dean, Yale Law School, Introduction to Edward Bennett Williams, *One Man's Freedom* (New York: Atheneum, 1962) ix.

Introduction

1 J. Anthony Lukas, *Big Trouble* (New York: Simon & Schuster Touchstone Books, 1997), 634.

2 In the 200-meter Olympic medal awards ceremony in Mexico City, Smith and Carlos followed through individually on what had originated as a group protest by black U.S. athletes. Thirty-five years later, Carlos still had no regrets for bringing global attention to racism in the United States, despite the high personal price he paid in forfeiting any right to compete in future Olympics. Dave Zirin, "The Living Legacy of Mexico City:

Interview with John Carlos," Counterpunch, Oct. 31, 2003, http://www.counterpunch.org/zirin11012003.html.

3 Ekwueme Michael Thelwell, "To Die for the People?" Introduction to Gilbert Moore, *Rage* (New York: Carroll & Graff Publishers, Inc., 1993), xxvi–xxvii.

4 Jamil Abdullah Al-Amin (aka H. Rap Brown), "Discover the Networks.org, A Guide to the Political Left," http://www.discoverthenetworks.org/individualProfile.asp?indid=1308 JAMIL ABDULLAH AL-AMIN (A.K.A. H. RAP BROWN).

5 Carson, *In Struggle,* 256 and fn. 29.

6 Stokely Carmichael, "Let Another World Be Born," speech given on or about April 22, 1967, quoted in Terry Anderson, *The Movement and the Sixties* (New York: Oxford Univ. Press, 1995), 158–59 and fn. 22.

7 Huey Newton interview, *Eyes on the Prize: The American Civil Rights Movement 1954–1985,* "American Experience Blackside," http://www.pbs.org/wgbh/amex/eyesonthe prize/about/pt_203.html.

8 Thelwell, Introduction to Moore, *Rage,* xi.

9 Robert Kirsch, "Black Panther Assignment," *LAT,* May 17, 1971, E10.

10 Moore, *Rage,* back-cover quote.

11 Williams, *One Man's Freedom,* cited in Gerald Uelmen, *Lessons From the Trial: The People v. O. J. Simpson* (Kansas City: Andrews and McMeel, 1996), 205.

12 Mark Curriden and Leroy Phillips, Jr., *Contempt of Court: The Turn-of-the-Century Lynching that Launched a Hundred Years of Federalism* (New York: First Anchor Books Ed., 2001) xiv.

13 Uelmen, *Lessons From the Trial,* 208–209.

PART ONE, CHAPTER 1 — *The Playing Field*

1 Peter Carlson, "The (Last) Trial of the Century," *The Washington Post,* Jan. 4, 1999, C01.

2 Grant and Katz, *The Great Trials of the Twenties: The Watershed Decade in America's Courtrooms* (New York: Sarpedon, 1998), 91.

3 Wanda Felix, "The Trial of Fatty Arbuckle," *Ralph Magazine,* http://www.ralphmag.org/fatty.html.

4 Daniel Alef, "William Randolph Hearst: Media Myth and Mystique," *Titans of Fortune* (ISBN:9781608041596, Digital Edition, 2010), locations 134–137 and 188.

5 Denise Noe, "Fatty Arbuckle and the Death of Virginia Rappe: How Did She Die?" Tru TV, http://www.trutv.com/index.html.

6 "PLAIN WORDS," History Is a Weapon, http://www.historyisaweapon.com/defcon1/plainwords.html.

7 "Wilson Denounces Police Strike That Left Boston a Prey to Thugs," *NYT,* Sept. 12, 1919.

8 Lawrence, M. Salinger (ed.), *Encyclopedia of White-Collar and Corporate Crime* (Thousand Oaks: Sage Publication, Inc., 2005), Vol. 1, 868.

9 Baseball Almanac, http://www.baseball-almanac.com/prz_qwt.shtml.

10 Geoffrey C. Ward and Ken Burns, *Baseball: An Illustrated History* (New York: Alfred A. Knopf, 1994), 55.

11 "Ty Cobb," *The New Georgia Encyclopedia,* http://www.georgiaencyclopedia.org/nge/Home.jsp.

12 Don Rhodes, *Ty Cobb: Safe At Home* (Guilford, Ct: Lyons Press, 2008), 58.

13 Ken Burns, *Baseball: Second Inning Something Like A War, 1900 to 1910* (The Baseball Film Project, Inc., 1994), Vol. 2.

[14] Ward and Burns, *Baseball: An Illustrated History*, 109–110.

[15] Grant and Katz, *The Great Trials of the Twenties*, 65.

[16] John Stravinsky, "Hal Chase, Major League Baseball 1905–1919," June 8, 1999, http://www.villagevoice.com/1999-06-08/news/hal-chase-major-league-baseball-1905-1919/.

[17] "1919: Race Riots," Deaths, Disturbances, Disasters and Disorders in Chicago, Chicago Public Library, http://www.chipublib.org/cplbooksmovies/cplarchive/chidisasters/raceriots.php.

[18] Both quotes in this paragraph were obtained from "Gangs and the 1919 Race Riot," http://www.uic.edu/orgs/kbc/ganghistory/Industrial%20Era/Riotbegins.htmlhtm.

[19] Douglas O. Linder, "Before *Brown*: Charles H. Houston and the *Gaines* Case," http://www.law.umkc.edu/faculty/projects/ftrials/conlaw/houstonessay.html.

[20] Ward and Burns, *Baseball: An Illustrated History*, 56.

[21] *Ibid.*, 139.

[22] Lowell Blaisdell, "Mystery and Tragedy: The O'Connell-Dolan Scandal," SABR Research Journal Archive, http://research.sabr.org/journals/oconnell-dolan-scandal.

[23] Ward and Burns, *Baseball: An Illustrated History*, 142.

[24] Harvey Frommer, *Shoeless Joe and Ragtime Baseball* (Univ. of Nebraska, 2008), 140.

[25] Linder, "Famous Trials: The Black Sox Trial: An Account of the 1919 Black Sox Scandal and the 1921 Trial," http://www.law.umkc.edu/faculty/projects/ftrials/blacksox/blacksoxaccount.html.

[26] Grant and Katz, *The Great Trials of the Twenties*, 62.

[27] Ward and Burns, *Baseball: An Illustrated History*, 142.

[28] Scott Deveney, "Did the 1918 Cubs throw the World Series?," *The Sporting News*, April 19, 2008, http://www.soundopinions.org/forum/index.php?showtopic=16355.

[29] "Kenesaw Mountain Landis," Baseball Statistics, http://www.baseball-statistics.com/HOF/Landis.html.

[30] "Landis Quits Bench for Baseball Job," *NYT*, Feb. 18, 1922, 1.

[31] James Kirby, "The Year They Fixed the World Series," *ABA Journal*, Feb. 1, 1988, 65; Joe Jackson as told to Furman Fisher, "This is the Truth," *SPORT* magazine, October 1949, http://www.blackbetsy.com/theTruth.html.

[32] Grant and Katz, *The Great Trials of The Twenties*, 68.

[33] Bruce Lowitt, "Black Sox scandal: Chicago throws 1919 World Series," *St. Petersburg Times*, Dec. 22, 1999, http://www.sptimes.com/News/122299/news_pf/Sports /Black_Sox_scandal_Ch.shtml.

[34] Grant and Katz, *The Great Trials of the Twenties*, 53.

[35] Daniel J. Voelker and Paul A. Duffy, "Black Sox: 'It ain't so, kid, it just ain't so,'" *Chicago Lawyer*, Sept. 1, 2009, http://www.chicagolawyermagazine.com/2009/09/01/black-sox-it-aint-so-kid-it-just-aint-so/.

[36] Shoeless Joe Jackson official site, http://www.shoelessjoejackson.com/about/quotes.html.

[37] Alan M. Dershowitz, *America on Trial: Inside The Legal Battles That Transformed Our Nation* (New York: Warner Books, 2004), 239.

[38] *Ibid.*

[39] Timothy M. Gay, *Tris Speaker, The Rough-And-Tumble Life Of A Baseball Legend* (Kearney, Nebraska: Morris Book Publishing, 2007) 227–33.

[40] Rhodes, *Ty Cobb: Safe At Home*, 102–103.

[41] Mark Alvarez, "Say It Ain't So, Ty," *Mr. Baseball*, http://www.mrbaseball.com/index

.php?option=com_content&task=view&id=43&Itemid=61.

42 Both quotes are from Gay, *Tris Speaker, The Rough-and-Tumble Life Of A Baseball Legend,* 243.

43 Rhodes, *Ty Cobb: Safe At Home,* 63, 67.

44 Patrick Butters, "Meet the Unknown Slugger," *Insight on the News,* Vol. 14, Sept. 21, 1998, http://www.encyclopedia.com/doc/1G1-21157150.html.

45 Josh Gibson, Baseball Library, http://www.baseballlibrary.com/ballplayers/player .php ?name=Josh_Gibson_1911.

46 John Drebinger, "Cox Retracts Admissions on Betting . . . OWNERS HEAR ROBESON Organized Baseball Urged to Admit Negro Players — Up to Each Club, Lardis Replies," *NYT,* Dec. 4, 1943, 17. Landis, of course, did not add gender to the list. In 1931, a Tennessee farm team had signed a teen-aged pitcher named Jackie Mitchell. She faced the Yankees in an exhibition game and made news when she struck out both Babe Ruth and Lou Gehrig. The following day Landis nullified Mitchell's contract, asserting baseball was "too strenuous" for females. http://www.baseball-almanac.com/articles /kenesaw_landis_biography.shtml.

47 Paul Robeson and Philip Sheldon Foner, *Paul Robeson Speaks: Writings, Speeches, Interviews 1918–1974* (New York: Kensington Pub. Corp. Citadel Press Books, 1978), 152.

48 Drebinger, *NYT,* Dec. 4, 1943, 17.

49 Peter Golenbock, "Breaking Baseball's Color Barrier," excerpt from *Bums: An Oral History of the Brooklyn Dodgers* (New York: Putnam Adult Books, 1984), http://thatsbaseball1 .tripod.com/id147.htm.

50 *Ibid.*

51 Ward and Burns, *Baseball: An Illustrated History,* 44.

52 James D. Robenalt, *The Harding Affair, Love and Espionage During the Great War* (New York: Palgrave Macmillan, 2009).

53 Rich Cohen, *Tough Jews: Fathers, Sons, and Gangster Dreams* (London: Vintage Books, 1999), 53; see also Linda Grant, "Defenders of the faith," *The Guardian,* July 6, 2002 http://www.guardian.ca.uk/books/2002/jul/06/.featuresreviews.guardianreview10.

Part One, Chapter 2 — *Dementia Americana: The Murder of Stanford White*

1 Paula Uruburu, *American Eve: Evelyn Nesbit, Stanford White, The Birth of the "It" Girl and the Crime of the Century* (New York: Riverhead Books, 2008) 11.

2 Linder, "Famous Trials: The Trials of Harry Thaw," http://www.law.umkc.edu/faculty /projects/ftrials/thaw/Thawaccount.html.

3 Uruburu, *American Eve,* 191.

4 *Ibid.,* 282.

5 The quotes from Evelyn and Harry Thaw the night of the killing are from a front page story, "THAW MURDERS STANFORD WHITE: Shoots Him on the Madison Square Garden Roof," *NYT,* June 26, 1906, 1–2.

6 Uruburu, *American Eve,* 287.

7 "THE NEW YORK JOURNAL AND THE ASSASSINATION OF WILLIAM MCKINLEY," novelguide.com, http://www.novelguide.com/a/discover/adec_0001_0001_0 /adec _0001_0001_0_00202.html.

8 Eric Rauchway, *Murdering McKinley: The Making of Theodore Roosevelt's America* (New York: Hill and Wang Div. of Farrar, Straus & Giroux, 2003), 61.

9 Jane Addams, *Twenty Years at Hull House* (New York: The MacMillan Co., 1910), 403.

[10] Eric Rauchway, *Murdering McKinley*, 171.

[11] Emma Goldman, "The Tragedy at Buffalo," *Free Society*, October 6, 1901, 1.

[12] The term was already in use in the late 19th century. Historians Gilbert Geis and Leigh Bienen point out that, in 1898, author Henry Hunt published *The Crime of the Century: Or the Assassination of Dr. Patrick Henry Cronin*, which described the physician's ambush murder in Chicago in 1889 by members of his Irish secret society. Dr. Cronin had created a political maelstrom by publicly accusing leaders of the radical political group of embezzling funds solicited for Irish freedom fighters. *Crimes of the Century* (Boston: Northeastern Univ. Press, 1998), 4. The 1906 Stanford White case was the first known to have been hyped contemporaneously by journalists as "the crime of the century," staking a claim to superiority against all future contenders that journalists would repeat as they covered the latest sensational trial in each of the ensuing nine decades.

[13] Linder, "Famous Trials: The Trials of Harry Thaw," http://www.law.umkc.edu/faculty/projects/ftrials/thaw/Thawnewspapers2707.html, quoting reporter Irvin S. Cobb.

[14] 198 U.S. 45, 56 (1905).

[15] "D. Delmas, Legal Napoleon of San Francisco: Character sketch of the Californian who's conducting the Thaw Defense and will settle in New York," *NYT*, Feb. 10, 1907.

[16] "EVELYN THAW TELLS HER STORY; Accuses Stanford White of Causing Her Fall; CONFESSED IT TO THAW; Lays Bare Her Life in Court to Save Husband; HE SOBS AS HE LISTENS; She Will Tell More Today—Then Cross-Examination—Letters of Thaw's Love Read," *NYT*, Feb. 6, 1907, 1.

[17] Linder, "Famous Trials: The Trials of Harry Thaw for the Murder of Stanford White," http://www.law.umkc.edu/faculty/projects/ftrials/thaw/Thawaccount.html.

[18] Francis Russell, *Sacco and Vanzetti: The Case Resolved* (New York: Harper & Row, 1986), 210, fn. 20, citing Louis Adams, *Dynamite: The Story of Class Violence in America*, 149–50.

Part One, Chapter 3 — *Undesirable Citizens: The Murder Trial of Big Bill Haywood*

[1] "Rioting and Bloodshed in the Streets of Chicago," *NYT*, May 4, 1886.

[2] Peter Carlson, *Roughneck: The Life and Times of Big Bill Haywood* (New York: W.W. Norton, 1983), 48.

[3] Lukas, *Big Trouble*, 226.

[4] Linder, Famous Trials: "Big Bill Haywood," http://www.law.umkc.edu/faculty/proects/ftrials/haywood/HAY_BHAY.HTM.

[5] Lukas, *Big Trouble*, 150.

[6] *Ibid.*, 145.

[7] William Cahn, *A Pictorial History of American Labor* (New York: Crown Publishers, 1972), 126.

[8] James D. Horan and Howard Swiggett, *The Pinkerton Story* (New York: G.P. Putnam's Sons, 1951), 126.

[9] Joseph G. Rayback, *A History of American Labor* (New York: The Free Press, 1966), 133.

[10] Carlson, *Roughneck*, 96.

[11] Elizabeth Gage, *The Day Wall Street Exploded: A Story of America in its First Age of Terror* (Oxford: Oxford Univ. Press, 2009), 79, fn. 19.

[12] Lukas, *Big Trouble*, 278.

[13] Carlson, *Roughneck*, 98.

[14] Kevin Boyle, *Arc of Justice: A Saga of Race, Civil Rights and Murder in the Jazz Age* (New York: Henry Holt & Co., 2004), 231.

15 Irving Stone, *Clarence Darrow for the Defense* (New York: Doubleday & Co. Signet Books, 1941, 1969), 220–221.
16 Carlson, *Roughneck*, 109.
17 *Ibid.*, 108.
18 Lukas, *Big Trouble*, 387.
19 *Ibid.*, 521.
20 *Ibid.*
21 *Ibid.*, 524.
22 Stone, *Clarence Darrow for the Defense*, 191.
23 Carlson, *Roughneck*, 112.
24 Stone, *Clarence Darrow for the Defense*, 191.
25 Gage, *The Day Wall Street Exploded*, 81 and fn. 24.
26 John E. Nevins, Scripps-McRae News Service, *Milwaukee Journal*, June 6, 1907, 1.
27 Linder, "Famous Trials: The Trial of William 'Big Bill' Haywood," http://www.law.umkc.edu/faculty/projects/ftrials/haywood/HAY_ACCT.HTMT.
28 Oscar King Davis, "Orchard Tells About Murders," *NYT*, June 6, 1907.
29 Stone, *Clarence Darrow for the Defense*, 280.
30 Lukas, *Big Trouble*, 703 citing *The Boston Globe*, July 20, 1907.
31 *Ibid.*, 704.
32 *Ibid.*, 705.
33 "Darrow's Speech in the Haywood Case," *Wayland's Monthly*, No. 90, 110, Oct. 1907 (Girard, Kansas; J. A. Wayland, Oct. 1907) http://darrow.law.umn.edu/documents/Darrow_Speech_Haywood_Case.pdf.
34 Stone, *Clarence Darrow for the Defense*, 274.
35 Carlson, *Roughneck*, 139.
36 *Ibid.*

Part One, Chapter 4 — ***Showdown with the Supreme Court: The Contempt Trial of Sheriff Joseph Shipp***

1 Edmund Morris, *Theodore Rex* (Random House: New York, 2001), 55.
2 Thomas Dixon, Jr., "Booker T. Washington and the Negro," *Saturday Evening Post*, Aug. 19, 1905, 1.
3 Glenda Elizabeth Gilmore, *Gender and Jim Crow: Women and the Politics of White Supremacy in North Carolina, 1896–1920* (Durham, Univ. of North Carolina Press, 1996), 66–70.
4 James M. Dormon, "Shaping the Popular Image of Post-Reconstruction American Blacks: The 'Coon Song' Phenomenon of the Gilded Age," *American Quarterly* 40: 450–471 (1988); Richard A. Reublin and Robert L. Maine, "Question of the Month: What Were Coon Songs?" Jim Crow Museum of Racist Memorabilia website, Ferris State Univ. (May 2005), http://www.ferris.edu/jimcrow/.
5 Samuel K. Roberts, "Kelly Miller and Thomas Dixon, Jr., on Blacks in American Civilization," *Phylon* (1960), Vol. 41, No. 2 (Clark: Atlanta Univ., 1980), 202.
6 Eric Foner, *Reconstruction: America's Unfinished Revolution* (New York: Harper & Row, 1988), 608.
7 Curriden and Phillips, *Contempt of Court*, 36.
8 Linder, "Famous Trials: The Trial of Sheriff Shipp," http://www.law.umkc.edu/faculty/projects/ftrials/shipp/chronology.html.
9 Curriden and Phillips, *Contempt of Court*, 39.

10 *Ibid.*, 48.

11 *Ibid.*, 49.

12 *Coffin v. United States*, 156 U. S. 432, 15 Supreme Ct. Rptr. 394, 403 (1895).

13 Linder, "Famous Trials, The Trial of Sheriff Shipp," http://www.law.umkc.edu/faculty/projects/ftrials/shipp/chronology.html.

14 Curriden and Phillips, *Contempt of Court*, 76.

15 *Ibid.*

16 *Ibid.*, 83.

17 Linder, "Famous Trials: The Trial of Sheriff Shipp," http://www.law.umkc.edu/faculty/projects/ftrials/shipp/chronology.html.

18 Curriden and Phillips, *Contempt of Court*, 109.

19 *Ibid.*, 118.

20 *Ibid.*, 192, citing an article in *The Chattanooga Times*, March 19, 1906.

21 Curriden and Phillips, *Contempt of Court*, 214.

22 Leigh Reiford, *Imprisoned in a Luminous Glare: Photography and the African American Freedom Struggle* (Chappel Hill: Univ. of North Carolina Press, 2011) 38-39, 46 (quoted language at 46, citing historian Winfield H. Collins' 1918 pamphlet, *The Truth About Lynching and the Negro in the South.*

23 Curriden and Phillips, *Contempt of Court*, 231.

24 *Ibid.*, 232-233.

25 "Sheriff Shipp Talks of Government Action," *AC*, May 29, 1906, 3.

26 *United States v. Cruikshank*, 92 U.S. 542 (1876).

27 The five consolidated civil rights cases were *United States v. Stanley; United States v. Ryan; United States v. Nichols; United States v. Singleton; Robinson et ux. v. Memphis & Charleston R.R. Co.*, 109 U.S. 3 (1883).

28 Douglas A. Blackmon, *Slavery by Another Name: The Re-enslavement of Black Americans from the Civil War to World War II* (New York: Anchor Books, 2009), 93.

29 See, eg, Judge L. H. Perez, "The 14th Amendment Is Unconstitutional," http://www.sweetliberty.org/fourteenth.amend.htm.

30 *United States v. Shipp*, 214 U.S. 386, 29 Supreme Ct. Rpr. 637, 644 (1909).

31 Curriden and Phillips, *Contempt of Court*, 318.

32 *United States v. Wade*, 388 U.S. 218, 229 (1967) quoting Wall, *Eye-Witness Identification in Criminal Cases.*

33 Kevin Johnson, "States change police lineups after wrongful convictions," Sept. 19, 2009, *USA Today*, http://www.usatoday.com/news/nation/2009-09-16-police-lineups_N.htm.

34 Charles J. Ogletree, Jr. and Austin Sarat, *From Lynch Mobs to the Killing State: Race and the Death Penalty in America* (New York: New York Univ. Press, 2006), 3. See also Charles J. Ogletree, Jr., ed., *When Law Fails: Making Sense of Miscarriage of Justice* (New York: New York Univ. Press, 2009).

Part One Chapter 5 — *Labor v. Capital Redux: The* Lost Angeles Times *Bombing Case*

1 Howard Blum, *American Lightning: Terror, Mystery, the Birth of Hollywood, and the Crime of the Century* (New York: Crown Publishers, 2008), 20.

2 Stone, *Clarence Darrow for the Defense*, 329.

3 Gage, *The Day Wall Street Exploded*, 71.

4 Maria Pascualy, "Witness to History: The Life and Times of Ralph Chaplin," *Columbia: Summer 2001;* Vol. 15, No. 2, http://columbia.washingtonhistory.org/magazine /

articles/2001/0201/0201-a2.aspx.

5 Jack Phillips [pseudonym of Carl Sandburg],"HAYWOOD OF THE I. W. W.," *International Socialist Review*, 18.7 (Jan. 1918), 343.

6 Murray B. Levin, *Political Hysteria in America: The Democratic Capacity for Repression* (New York: Basic Books, 1971), 29.

7 Lukas, *Big Trouble*, 753–754.

PART ONE, CHAPTER 6 — *Murder Begets Murder: The Tragic Deaths of Mary Phagan and Leo Frank*

1 Steve Oney, *And the Dead Shall Rise: The Murder of Mary Phagan and the Lynching of Leo Frank* (New York: Pantheon, 2003), 7.

2 *Ibid.*, 15–16, citing C. Vann Woodward, *Origins of the New South* (Baton Rouge: Louisiana State Univ. Press, 1951), 418.

3 *Ibid.*, 6.

4 History Place: Child Labor: Newsboys, http://peachtree-online.com/printer/newsboys.htm http://www.historyplace.com/unitedstates/childlabor/.

5 Oney, *And the Dead Shall Rise*, 42, citing Herbert Asbury, "Hearst Comes to Atlanta," *American Mercury*, Jan. 1926.

6 "Race Voting Rights and Segregation Techniques of Direct Disfranchisement," http://www.umich.edu/~lawrace/disenfranchise1.htm.

7 "Atlanta Race Riot of 1906," *New Georgia Encyclopedia*, http://www.georgiaencyclopedia.org/nge/Article.jsp?id=h-3033.

8 James C. Cobb, *Georgia Odyssey: A Short History of the State* (Univ. of Georgia Press, 2d ed. 2008) 43–44.

9 Michael Perman, *Struggle for Mastery: Disfranchisement in the South, 1888–1908* (Univ. of North Carolina Press, 2001). The issue of black disenfranchisement became a major focal point again in the 2000 election. On its review, the Civil Rights Commission found that many thousands of African-Americans in that close contest were improperly disenfranchised in Florida, Missouri, and Ohio. http://www.usccr.gov/pubs/vote2000/report/ch9.htm.

10 "Glover Not Affected: Failure of Intervention by Supreme Court Does Not Affect Him," *AC*, Dec. 22, 1907, C9.

11 Peter N. Carroll and David W. Noble, *The Free and the Unfree: A Progressive History of the United States* (New York: Penguin Books, 3d rev. ed., 2001), 294.

12 Ken Burns, *Unforgivable Blackness: The Fight of the Century*, PBS, www.pbs.org/unforgivableblackness/fight/.

13 See Dr. Renford R. Reese, "The Socio-Political Context of the Integration of Sport in America," Cal Poly Pomona, *Journal of African American Men* (vol. 4, no. 3, Spring 1999) http://www.csupomona.edu/~rrreese/INTEGRATION.HTML.

14 Michael Walsh, "Great Expectations," *Smithsonian*, June 2010, 54.

15 Colin Linneweber, "The Black Boxer No White Could Beat Fairly," Bleacher Report, April 7, 2009, http://bleacherreport.com/articles/152523-the-black-man-no-white-fighter-could-beat-fairly.

16 In his appeal to Congress, Roddenberry argued that: "Intermarriage between whites and blacks is repulsive and averse to every sentiment of pure American spirit. It is abhorrent and repugnant. It is subversive to social peace. It is destructive of moral supremacy, and ultimately this slavery to black beasts will bring this nation to a fatal conflict," quoted at http://www.nbjcoalition.org/news/interracial-marriage-bans-vs.html.

17 Leonard Dinnerstein, *The Leo Frank Case* (Atlanta: Univ. of Georgia Press, 1987), 9 and fn. 27, citing *Atlanta Georgian*, April 28, 1913, 3.

18 *Ibid.*, 16 and fn. 60, citing Charles and Louise Samuels, *Night Fell On Georgia* (New York: Dell Publishing Co., 1956), 20.

19 *Ibid.*, 3, citing Henry A. Alexander, "Some Facts about the Murder Notes in the Phagan Case (privately published pamphlet, 1914), 5, 7.

20 Oney, *And The Dead Shall Rise*, 97–98.

21 *Ibid.*, 617.

22 *AC*, July 27, 1913, 1.

23 Dinnerstein, *The Leo Frank Case*, 151 and fn. 10.

24 *Ibid.*, 60.

25 Dershowitz, *America on Trial*, 220.

26 Oney, *And The Dead Shall Rise*, 381.

27 Dinnerstein, *The Leo Frank Case*, 97.

28 Carroll and Noble, *The Free and the Unfree: A Progressive History of the United States*, 294.

29 Thomas Clough, "Hoodwinked: The Legacy of Robert Byrd, The Birth & Rebirth of the Ku Klux Klan," August 29, 2010, http://www.weirdrepublic.com/episode114.htm.

30 *Leo Frank v. C. Wheeler Magnum* (1915) 237 U.S. 309, 347 (Justice Holmes dissenting).

31 Dinnerstein, *The Leo Frank Case*, 129 and fn. 37.

32 "CRIES OF LYNCH HIM HURLED AT SLATON AS HE QUITS OFFICE," photo of contemporaneous newspaper headline, http://upload.wikimedia.org/wikipedia/en/c/ce/Leo-frank-slaton-headline.jpg.

33 Oney, *And the Dead Shall Rise*, 508.

34 *Ibid.*, 520.

35 Video accompanying City of Marietta news release, "Leo Frank lynching site recognized with historical marker," 3/7/2008, http://marietta.granicus.com/MediaPlayer.php?publish_id=45.

36 Oney, *And The Dead Shall Rise*, 574.

37 Dinnerstein, *The Leo Frank Case*, 145.

38 Dershowitz, *America on Trial*, 221.

39 Oney, *And The Dead Shall Rise*, 643.

Part One, Chapter 7 — *Anarchist Scare: The Trial of Sacco and Vanzetti*

1 Clyde Haberman, "New Yorkers Speaking Softly," http://cityroom.blog.nytimes.com/2011/07/12/new-yorkers-speaking-softly/. In July of 2011 Republican Congressional candidate Bob Turner invoked Roosevelt's 100 percent American speech in his successful campaign for Democrat Anthony Weiner's former seat in New York's Ninth District.

2 Russell, *Sacco and Vanzetti*, 80.

3 Grant and Katz, *The Great Trials of the Twenties*, 50.

4 Gage, *The Day Wall Street Exploded*, caption and photograph of flyer following page 150.

5 "Vanzetti Files Plea in Fight to Cheat Death," *The Lima News*, May 5, 1927, 7.

6 "Radicals' Cause May be Assisted," *The North Adams Transcript*, July 11, 1927, 1; Moshik Temkin, *The Sacco-Vanzetti Affair: America on Trial* (New Haven: Yale Univ. Press, 2009), Kindle location 203–205, ISBN 978-0-300-12484-2.

7 Russell, *Sacco and Vanzetti: The Case Resolved*, 116.

8 See, e.g., Isa Engleberg, *Working in Groups: Communication Principles and Strategies* (My Communication Kit Series, 2006) 133.

9 Grant and Katz, *The Great Trials of the Twenties*, 42.

10 Felix Frankfurter, "The Case of Sacco and Vanzetti," *The Atlantic Monthly*, March 1927. In Francis Russell's otherwise highly credible account, *Sacco and Vanzetti: The Case Resolved* at pages 110–116, Russell dubiously defends Thayer's fairness, based primarily on two biased sources: interviews of the jurors, with their own verdict to defend, and court personnel who might likewise be presumed to support their presiding judge from attacks on his performance. Russell states that both groups believed Thayer ran a very fair trial and dismisses without discussion Thayer's prejudicial out-of-court statements sworn to by reputable disinterested parties, who later submitted similar affidavits to the Lowell Commission. Most troubling of all, Russell rejects veteran attorney Thompson's testimony before the Lowell Commission that Thayer used a sarcastic and abrupt tone of voice and dismissive body language to convey his intense dislike for the defendants and their lead counsel. Russell fails to address the substantial impact of nonverbal cues from tone of voice and body language. Words used by a speaker—all that is left in a written record—generally account for 30 to 40 percent of communication. (See note 7, above.)

11 "Sacco Vanzetti Ordeal Haunts Longtime Advocate," *Boston Globe*, June 18, 1998, http://www.highbeam.com/doc/1p2–8487281.htm).

12 Gage, *The Day Wall Street Exploded*, 312–313, citing Louis Post, "The Deportations Delirium of Nineteen-Twenty: A Personal Narrative of an Historic Official Experience" (1923), 307.

13 *Ibid.*, 322–323.

14 *Ibid.*

15 Temkin, *The Sacco-Vanzetti Affair*, Kindle location 575–79.

16 *Ibid.*, location 590–92.

17 *Ibid.*, location 608–10.

18 Grant and Katz, *The Great Trials of the Twenties*, 48-49.

19 *Ibid.*, 49.

20 Leslie Burdick, "Sacco and Vanzetti—The Jury is Still Out," *The Sun*, Lowell Massachusetts, Aug. 2, 1977, 30.

21 Paul Avrich, *Sacco and Vanzetti: The Anarchist Background* (Princeton: Princeton Univ. Press, 1991), 204–207.

Part One. Chapter 8 — *Leopold and Loeb: Murder for the Thrill of It*

1 Simon Baatz, *For the Thrill of It: Leopold, Loeb and the Murder that Shocked Chicago* (New York: Harper Collins, 2008), 70 (reproduction of ransom note).

2 Clarence Darrow, *The Story of My Life* (New York: DaCapo Press, 1996), 232.

3 *Ibid.*, 233.

4 Stone, *Clarence Darrow for the Defense*, 450.

5 Hal Higdon, *Leopold and Loeb, The Crime of the Century* (Illinois: G. P. Putnam's Sons, 1996), 138.

6 *Ibid.*, 140.

7 *Ibid.*, 159.

8 Linder, "Famous Trials: Leopold and Loeb," http://www.law.umkc.edu/faculty/projects/ftrials/leoploeb/BIO_CAVE.HTM.

9 "Weird and Haunted Chicago: A Guide to the Ghosts, Local Legends and Unsolved Mysteries of the Windy City: Leopold and Loeb, Chicago's Thrill Killers," http://www.prairieghosts.com/leopold.html.

[10] Darrow, *The Story of My Life*, 242.

[11] Grant and Katz, *The Great Trials of the Twenties*, 190–91.

[12] *Ibid.*

[13] Baatz, *For the Thrill of It*, 401.

[14] *Ibid.*, 402.

[15] *Ibid.*, 406.

[16] Dershowitz, *America on Trial*, 261.

[17] Linder, "Famous Trials: Leopold and Loeb," http://www.law.umkc.edu/faculty/projects/ftrials/leoploeb/BIO_CAVE.HTM.

[18] Baatz, *For the Thrill of It*, 462.

[19] "Governor Ryan Declares Moratorium On Executions, Will Appoint Commission To Review Capital Punishment System," press release, Jan. 31, 2000, http://www.illinois.gov/PressReleases/ShowPressRelease.cfm?.

[20] *Roper v. Simmons* (1995) 543 U.S. 551, 575.

Part One, Chapter 9 — ***Scopes: The Staged Battle of Evolution v. Creationism***

[1] Edward J. Larson, *Summer for the Gods: The Scopes Trial and America's Continuing Debate over Science and Religion* (New York: Basic Books, Perseus Book Group, 1997), 265.

[2] Larson, *Summer for the Gods*, 83.

[3] *Ibid.*, 12–13.

[4] *Ibid.*, 15.

[5] *Ibid.* 40–41.

[6] The Butler Act as reprinted in *NYT*, July 18, 1925, 1.

[7] Larson, *Summer for the Gods*, 71 and fn. 28, citing Darrow biographer Kevin Tierney.

[8] George W. Hunter, *A Civic Biology Presented in Problems* (New York: American Book Co., 1914), 195–196, reproduced at Google Books, http://books.google.com/books?id=-ylCAAAAIAAJ&pg=PA200&dq=intitle:civic+intitle:biology+inauthor:hunter&lr=&num=30&as_brr=0&output=text#c_top.

[9] *Ibid.*, 196, 261, 263. See also Joe Resnick, "The Dark Side of Darwinism," http://www.nmidnet.org/JUNE%20%202010.pdf.

[10] Larson, *Summer for the Gods*, 140.

[11] Stone, *Clarence Darrow for the Defense*, 486.

[12] Larson, *Summer for the Gods*, 142 and fn. 100.

[13] Stone, *Clarence Darrow for the Defense*, 493.

[14] Larson, *Summer for the Gods*, 150.

[15] *Ibid.*, 154 and fn. 18.

[16] Linder, "What is THE trial of the century?" Jan. 28, 1999, http://www.law.umkc.edu/faculty/projects/ftrials/century.html.

[17] *Ibid.*

[18] Edward McGlynn Gaffney, Jr., "How the Scopes Trial Framed the Modern Debate Over Science and Religion," *LAT*, July 12, 1998, http://articles.latimes.com/1998/jul/12/books/bk-2824.

[19] Although the ACLU attacked the statute under which Scopes was convicted on several constitutional grounds, the only argument that persuaded the Tennessee Supreme Court was that the state constitution then prohibited judges from setting fines over $50, i.e., the Scopes jury should have decided to award the $100 minimum fine, not the trial judge. The high court then went further and recommended that the prosecutor decline to retry

the case since Scopes was no longer teaching in Tennessee. (*Scopes v. State*, 154 Tenn. 105 (1927).) The prosecutor followed that recommendation and dropped the case.

20 George William Hunter, *New Civic Biology: Presented In Problems* (New York: American Book Co., 1926), 250–51, 411–12.

21 *Epperson v. Arkansas*, 393 U.S. 97 (1968).

PART ONE, CHAPTER 10 — *Even a Black Man's Home Is His Castle: Pyrrhic Victory in the Sweet Murder Trials*

1 Boyle, *Arc of Justice*, 118.

2 *Ibid.*, 155.

3 Linder, "Famous Trials: The Sweet Trials," http://www.law.umkc.edu/faculty/projects/ftrials/sweet/sweetaccount.HTM; Marcet Haldeman-Julius, "Clarence Darrow's Two Great Trials" (Girard, Kansas: Haldeman-Julius Company, 1927), 45.

4 Linder, "Famous Trials: The Sweet Trials," http://www.law.umkc.edu/faculty/projects/ftrials/sweet/sweetaccount.HTM.

5 Boyle, *Arc of Justice*, 32, 37.

6 *Ibid.*, 196.

7 *Ibid.*, 225.

8 *Ibid.*, 139.

9 *Ibid.*, 245–246.

10 Linder, "Famous Trials: The Sweet Trials," Opening Statement of Arthur Garfield Hays, http://law2.umkc.edu/faculty/projects/ftrials/sweet/transcriptexcerpts.HTM # Opening Statement.

11 "Stephenson Sentenced," *Indianapolis News*, Nov. 16, 1925, 1.

12 Boyle, *Arc of Justice*, 289.

13 Linder, "Famous Trials: The Sweet Trials, Transcript Excerpts," http://www.law.umkc.edu/faculty/projects/ftrials/sweet/transcriptexcerpts.HTM.

14 Haldeman-Julius, "Clarence Darrow's Two Great Trials," 54.

15 "Sweet Trial Is Race Issue, Darrow Insists," *Detroit Free Press*, April 21, 1926.

16 Haldeman-Julius, "Clarence Darrow's Two Great Trials," 55.

17 Boyle, *Arc of Justice*, 329. Additional excerpts from the closing argument of Thomas Chawke are set forth in Linder, "Famous Trials: The Sweet Trials," http://law2.umkc.edu/faculty/projects/ftrials/sweet/chawkespeech.html.

18 Linder, "Famous Trials: The Sweet Trials, Darrow Summation," http://www.law.umkc.edu/faculty/projects/ftrials/sweet/darrowsummation.html.

19 "Charge to the jury in the case of MICHIGAN v. HENRY SWEET Detroit, Michigan by Judge Frank Murphy," May 13, 1926, http://law2.umkc.edu/faculty/projects/ftrials/sweet/chargetojury.html.

20 "The Law of Love," This Case is Close to My Heart: American History Feature, History Net.Com, August 2000, http://www.historynet.com/this-case-is-close-to-my-heart-page-1-august-2000-american-history-feature.htm/6.

21 Linder, "Famous Trials: The Sweet Trials, Darrow Summation," http://www.law.umkc.edu/faculty/projects/ftrials/sweet/darrowsummation.html.

22 Boyle, *Arc of Justice*, 344 and fn. 14.

23 Darrow, *The Story of My Life*, 311.

24 "Active U.S. Hate Groups," Intelligence Report, Southern Poverty Law Center, http://www.splcenter.org/get-informed/hate-map; "About the Ku Klux Klan—Extremism in

America," Anti-Defamation League, http://www.adl.org/learn/ext_us/kkk/default.asp.

25 323 U.S.214, 65 S. Ct. 193, 240, Justice Murphy dissenting (1944).

Part One, Chapter 11 — *Southern Justice Revisited: The Railroading of the Scottsboro Boys*

1 Maria Weston Chapman, (ed.), *The Liberty Bell: Testimony against Slavery* (Kessinger Publishing: Whitefish, Montana, 2007), 29–30; quoting a letter from Alexis de Tocqueville.

2 "The Scottsboro Boys: Jim Crow on Trial," *Crime Magazine, An Encyclopedia of Crime*, July 13, 2009, http://www.crimemagazine.com/scottsboro_boys.htm.

3 James Goodman, *Stories of Scottsboro* (New York: Pantheon Books, 1994), 16.

4 James R. Acker, *Scottsboro and Its Legacy* (Westport, Ct.: Praeger Publishing, 2008), 26; see also David Aretha, *The Trial of the Scottsboro Boys* (Greensboro, North Carolina: Morgan Reynolds Publishing, 2008).

5 Stone, *Clarence Darrow for the Defense*, 559.

6 *Weems et al. v. State* (1932) 224 Ala. 524, 141 So. 215.

7 *Powell v. State of Alabama* 287 U.S. 45, 71 (1932).

8 Goodman, *Stories of Scottsboro*, 211.

9 Linder, "Famous Trials: The Scottsboro Boys," "EXCERPTS FROM THE SUMMATION OF WADE WRIGHT," http://www.law.umkc.edu/faculty/projects/FTrials/scottsboro/wr-summations.html.

10 Linder, "Famous Trials," "Judge Horton Orders a New Trial in the Case of Haywood Patterson," June 22, 1933, http://law2.umkc.edu/faculty/project FTrials/scottsboro/Exhorton.htm.

11 F. Raymond Daniell, *NYT*, Nov. 20, 1933, 1.

12 "The Best of the Century," *Time*, Dec. 31, 1999, http://www.time.com/time / magazine/article/0, 9171, 993039, 00.html.

13 See Mary L. Dudziak, *Cold War Civil Rights* (Princeton: Princeton Univ. Press, 2000).

14 See Jack Epstein, "Baseball's conscience finally gets his due," *SFC*, July 10, 2005, A1, 13, citing Irwin Silber, *Press Box Red: The Story of Lester Rodney, the Communist Who Helped Break the Color Line in American Sports* (Philadelphia: Temple Univ. Press, 2003).

15 "Desegregation of the Armed Forces: Chronology," Truman Library, http://www.trumanlibrary.org/whistlestop/studycollections/desegregation/large/indexphp?action=chronology.

16 Thomas B. Edsall, "Lott Decried For Part of Salute to Thurmond: GOP Senate Leader Hails Colleague's Run As Segregationist," Common Dreams.org, Dec. 7, 2003, http://www.commondreams.org/headlines02/1207-01.htm.

17 "Alabama Anything But Gentlemanly," *Time*, May 10, 1948, http://www.time.com/time/magazine/article/0, 9171, 804636, 00.html.

18 Jessica Mitford, *A Fine Old Conflict* (New York: Vintage Books 1956, 1977), 193.

19 Leslie Brody, *Irrepressible: The Life and Times of Jessica Mitford* (Berkeley, California: Counterpoint, 2010), 174.

20 David E. Stannard, *Honor Killing: How the Infamous "Massie Affair" Transformed Hawai'i* (New York: Viking Penguin Books, 2005), 305.

Part One, Chapter 12 — *The Explosive Massie Affair: Truth Battles Raw Power*

1 John F. Galliher, Larry W. Koch, David Patrick Keys, Teresa J. Guess, *America Without the Death Penalty: States Lead The Way* (Boston: Northeastern Univ. Press, 2005), 159.

2 Stannard, *Honor Killing: How the Infamous "Massie Affair" Transformed Hawai'i* (New York: Viking Penguin Books, 2005), 55.

3 Uelmen, *Lessons From the Trial: The People v. O. J. Simpson*, 114.

4 Stannard, *Honor Killing*, 103.

5 "American Experience: The Massie Affair," PBS, http://www.pbs.org/wgbh/amexmassie/peopleevents/p_suspects.html.

6 Linder, "Famous Trials: The Massie Trials: A Commentary," 2007, http://law2.umkc.edu/faculty/projects/ftrials/massie/massietrialsaccount.html.

7 *Ibid.*

8 Uelmen, *Lessons From the Trial*, 129.

9 Stannard, *Honor Killing*, 212.

10 *Ibid.*, 212–215.

11 *Ibid.*, 222.

12 Galliher et al., *America Without the Death Penalty*, 161 and fn. 54.

13 *Personal Justice Denied, Report of the Commission on Wartime Relocation and Internment of Civilians* (Univ. of Washington Press, 1982) Chapter 11, Military Rule, fn. 31, http://www.nps.gov/history/history/online_books/personal_justice_denied/chap11.htm.

14 Linder, "Famous Trials: The Massie Affair," http://www.law.umkc.edu/faculty/projects/FTRIALS/massie/massietrialsaccount.htm.

15 Peter Van Slingerland, *Something Terrible Has Happened: The account of the sensational Thalia Massie affair which burst from prewar Hawaii to incense a nation* (New York: Harper & Row, 1966) "Confession of the Killer of Joe Kahahawai, Deacon Jones," 316–322, quote at 319.

16 Stannard, *Honor Killing*, 267.

17 Linder, "Famous Trials: The Massie Affair," http://www.law.umkc.edu/faculty/projects/FTRIALS/massie/massietrialsaccount.htm.

18 "Races: Lust in Paradise," *Time*, Dec. 28, 1931, http://www.time.com/time/magazine/article/0,9171,753207,00.html. In. 161, fn. 53.

19 Stone, *Clarence Darrow for the Defense*, 565.

20 Stannard, *Honor Killing*, 400.

21 Darrow, *The Story of My Life*, 458.

22 Stannard, *Honor Killing*, 301.

23 *Ibid.*, 322.

24 *Ibid.*, 321.

25 Van Slingerland, *Something Terrible Has Happened,* 318.

26 Darrow, *The Story of My Life*, 467.

27 Van Slingerland, *Something Terrible Has Happened,* 316–322.

28 Linder, "Famous Trials: The Massie Affair," http://www.law.umkc.edu/faculty/projects/FTRIALS/massie/massietrialsaccount.html.

29 Richard A. Hawkins, "Princess Abigail Kawananakoa: The Forgotten Territorial Native Hawaiian Leader," *Hawai'i Journal of History*, Vol. 37 (2003) 163, http://www.evols.library.manoa .hawaii.edu/bitstream/10524/354/2/JL37167.pdf.

30 Linder, "Famous Trials: The Massie Affair," http://www.law.umkc.edu/faculty/projects/FTRIALS/massie/massietrialsaccount.html.

Part One, Chapter 13 — *National Frenzy: The Lindbergh Baby Killing*

1 Edward W. Knappman et al., ed., *Great American Trials: From the Salem Witch Trials to Rod-*

ney King (Detroit: Visible Ink Press, 1994), 320.

2 Fisher, *FBI Summary Report; The Lindbergh Case* (New Brunswick, New Jersey: Rutgers Univ. Press 1987, 1994), 129.

3 *Ibid.*, 129 and fn. 7, citing Al Dunlap, "Why No Lie Detector for the Lindbergh Case?," *The Detective,* Sept. 1932.

4 *Ibid.*, 437, fn. 13.

5 Lloyd Gardner, *The Case That Never Dies: The Lindbergh Kidnapping* (New Brunswick, New Jersey: Rutgers Univ. Press, 2004), 107–108.

6 *Ibid.*, 220, fn. 60.

7 Ludovic Kennedy, *The Airman and the Carpenter: The Lindbergh Kidnapping and the Framing of Richard Hauptmann* (New York: Viking Penguin, Inc., 1985), 240, fn. 2.

8 Gregory Ahlgren and Stephen Monier, *Crime of the Century: The Lindbergh Kidnapping Hoax* (Boston: Brandon Books, 1993), 140.

9 373 U.S. 83 (1963).

10 Fisher, in *The Lindbergh Case,* 249–250, relies on a police diary notation, but acknowledges that the FBI was quite skeptical at the time of the voice identification by Lindbergh of such few words spoken two-and-a-half years earlier. Lloyd Gardner in *The Case that Never Dies,* 188–191 and 202, questions the reliability of Fisher's source, noting that the contemporaneous reports were that Lindbergh could not identify Hauptmann when asked to do so before trial. Ahlgren and Monier in the *Crime of the Century: The Lindbergh Kidnapping Hoax,* 165–166, criticize the inherent unreliability of the method by which Lindbergh was asked to identify Hauptmann's voice both before and at trial.

11 Gardner, *The Case That Never Dies,* 162–163 and fn. 48.

12 Kennedy, *The Airman and the Carpenter,* 179.

13 Gardner, *The Case That Never Dies,* 161.

14 *Ibid.*, 344 and fn. 45.

15 Dershowitz, *America on Trial,* 274, citing Sidney P. Whipple, *The Trial of Bruno Richard Hauptmann* (Birmingham: The Notable Trials Library, 1989), 561–563.

16 Kennedy, *The Airman and the Carpenter,* 342.

17 "Darrow Urges Delay," *NYT,* April 2, 1936, 2.

18 Ahlgren and Monier, *The Lindbergh Kidnapping Hoax,* 272–275.

19 Fisher, *The Lindbergh Case,* 5.

20 Hugo Adam Bedau and Michael L. Radelet, "Miscarriages of Justice in Potentially Capital Cases," 40 *Stanford Law Review* 21 (1987) 124–25 and fn. 582. The two professors noted that the Hauptmann trial featured an "atmosphere of near-hysteria" and a "grossly incompetent defense attorney." In addition, review of a number of independent analyses of the proceedings led them to conclude: "There is no doubt that the conviction rested in part on corrupt prosecutorial practices, suppression of evidence, intimidation of witnesses, perjured testimony, and Hauptmann's prior record." See also Mary E. Williams, ed., *Is the Death Penalty Fair?* (Farmington Hills, Minn.: Greenhaven Press, 2003), 48, ["Doubt about the guilt of the condemned man is a common thread in some of the most celebrated murder trials in this nation's history. Bruno Richard Hauptmann's chances for a fair trial in the Lindbergh kidnapping—and the ability truly to ascertain his guilt or innocence—were compromised by perjured testimony, tampering with exhibits, and the suppression by the New Jersey state police of exculpatory evidence."]

21 C. Ronald Huff, "Wrongful Conviction: Causes and Public Policy Issues," 18 *Crim. Just.* 15 (Spring 2003), 18.

22 Kennedy, *The Airman and the Carpenter*, 6.

23 "The Lindbergh Kidnapping Hoax," http://www.lindberghkidnappinghoax.com/.

24 See discussion in Geis and Bienen, *Crimes of the Century: From Leopold and Loeb to O. J. Simpson*, 116–120, "Bruno Richard Hauptmann (1932), Public Outrage, and Criminal Justice."

25 Michael Newton, *The Encyclopedia of Unsolved Crimes* (New York: Checkmark Books, 2004), 257.

26 Gardner, *The Case That Never Dies*, 344.

27 Robert R. Bryan, "The Execution of the Innocent: The Tragedy of the Hauptmann-Lindbergh and Bigelow Cases," 18 *NYU Review of Law and Social Change* (1990–91), 831, 833; see also authorities cited in fn. 20, *supra*.

28 Geis and Bienen, *Crimes of the Century: From Leopold and Loeb to O. J. Simpson*, 116.

PART ONE, CHAPTER 14 — *Shameless Haste: The Rosenberg Espionage Trial*

1 Harry S. Truman, *Year of Decisions* (Garden City, NY: Doubleday and Co. 1955) 416; see Gene Dannen, World War II Documents, The Atomic Bomb Decision, http://www.dannen.com/decision/index.html.

2 Howard Gest, "The July 1945 Szilard Petition on the Atomic Bomb, Memoir by a Signer in Oak Ridge," Indiana Univ., Bloomington, Indiana 47405, http://sites.bio.indiana.edu/~gest/hgSzilard.pdf.

3 Richard B. Frank, *Downfall: The End of the Imperial Japanese Empire* (New York: Random House, 1999).

4 Robert H. Ferrell, *Off the Record: The Private Papers of Harry S. Truman* (New York: Harper & Row, 1980), 55–56.

5 "Britain and US to keep atomic bomb secret," *The Guardian*, August 10, 1945, reprinted August 10, 2009, http://www.guardian.co.uk/theguardian/2009/aug/10/truman-japan-atomic-surrender.

6 The American Experience: "President Harry S. Truman, Foreign Policy," http://www.pbs.org/wgbh/amex/presidents/33_truman/truman_foreign.html.

7 Sanderson Beck, "Einstein and Schweitzer on Peace in the Atomic Age," http://www.san.beck.org/GPJ23-Einstein.html.

8 *Ibid.*

9 Michael Steven Smith, "About the Smith Act Trials," http://www.english.illinois.edu/maps/poets/g-l/jerome,smithact.htm.

10 Geis and Bienen, *Crimes of the Century*, 128.

11 See, e.g., David J. Garrow, "From Russia with Love," *Newsweek*, May 16, 2009, http://www.newsweek.com/2009/05/15/from-russia-with-love.html, citing John Earl Haynes, Harvey Klehr, and Alexander Vassiliev, *Spies: The Rise and Fall of the KGB in America* (New Haven: Yale Univ. Press, 2009).

12 Linder, "Famous Trials: The Rosenbergs," http://www.law.umkc.edu/faculty/projects/FTrials/Rosenb/ROS_ACCT.HTM.

13 Ronald Radosh and Joyce Milton, *The Rosenberg File* (New Haven: Yale Univ. Press, 2d. ed., 1997), 4.

14 *Ibid.*, 323.

15 Jason Briker, "The Rosenberg Executions: Atomic Spies or Victims of Communist Hysteria," Facts on File: Issues & Controversies in American History, Facts on File News Service, http://2facts.es.vrc.scoolaid.net/icah_story.aspx?PIN=haa00001190.

[16] Michael Powell, "Anatomy of a Counter-Bar Association: The Chicago Council of Lawyers" *Law & Social Inquiry*, Vol. 4, 3: 501–541. July 28, 2006, doi: 10.1111/j.1747-4469.1979.tb01027.x.

[17] Radosh and Milton, *The Rosenberg File*, 411.

[18] *Ibid.*, xxx and 329–30.

[19] Dershowitz, *America on Trial*, 334, citing Gary May, *Un-American Activities: The Trials of William Remington*, (New York: The Notable Trials Library, 1999), 182.

[20] *Time Capsule: 1954—The Year in Review*, (Time Inc., 1954, 2004), 13.

[21] "Have You No Sense of Decency": The Army-McCarthy Hearings, History Matters, http://historymatters.gmu.edu/d/6444.

[22] FBI Chief J. Edgar Hoover testified annually before Congress with precise, if unverifiable, figures his office had developed for Communist Party membership. See Neil Middleton, *The I. F. Stone's Weekly Reader* (New York: Vintage Books, 1953), 29.

[23] Robert McFadden, "Khrushchev on Rosenbergs: Stoking Old Embers" *NYT*, Sept. 25, 2008.

[24] Radosh and Milton, *The Rosenberg File*, xxx.

[25] Richard Pyle, The Associated Press, Dec. 6, 2001, "50 years later Rosenberg brother admits lie," *The Berkeley Daily Planet*, http://www.berkeleydailyplanet.com/issue/2001-12-06/article/8732?headline=50-years-later-Rosenberg-brother-admits-lie.

[26] Radosh and Milton, *The Rosenberg File*, 417.

[27] Morgan Cloud, "The Bugs in Our System," *NYT*, Jan. 13, 2006, A23.

Part One, Chapter 15 — *The Death of Innocence: Hate Crimes and the Civil Rights Movement*

[1] Doug McAdam, *Freedom Summer*, (New York: Oxford Univ. Press, 1988), 25–26.

[2] Dwight D. Eisenhower, "Radio and Television Address to the American People on the Situation in Little Rock," September 24, 1957, *Public Papers of the Presidents of the United States: Dwight D. Eisenhower, 1957*, 690–694, cited in Dudziak, *Cold War Civil Rights*, 133, fn. 45.

[3] The other three were Republican judges John Minor Wisdom and John Robert Brown and Democrat Richard Rives, who was reportedly a close friend of Justice Hugo Black on the Supreme Court. Jack Bass, *Unlikely Heroes: The Dramatic Story of the Southern Judges of the Fifth Circuit Who Translated the Supreme Court's Brown Decision Into a Revolution for Equality* (New York: Simon and Schuster, 1981).

[4] Robert Brown, Jr. and Allison Herren Lee, Esq., "The Neutral Assignment of Judges at the Court of Appeals," 78 Texas Law Review 1037 (April 2000) at 1051 and fn. 76. In 1963, after Judge Benjamin Franklin Cameron charged that the Chief Judge had deliberately skewed assignments, a random assignment policy was adopted.

[5] Millie J. McGhee, *Secrets Uncovered: J. Edgar Hoover, the Relative* (Rancho Cucamonga, Ca.: Allen Morris, 2002, 2d ed.).

[6] George Ott, "Secrets Uncovered . . . The Research Discoveries," Appendix to McGhee, *Secrets Uncovered*, 217, and back cover quote from Prof. Robert Stuckert.

[7] Kenneth D. Ackerman, *Young J. Edgar: Hoover, The Red Scare and the Assault on Civil Liberties* (New York: Carroll & Graf Publishers, 2007), 5.

[8] David R. Davies, ed., *The Press and Race* (Jackson: Univ. Press of Mississippi, 2001), 41, quoting the *Jackson Daily News* and *The Meridian Star*.

[9] Clayborne Carson, David J. Garrow, Gerald Gill, Vincent Harding, Darlene Clark Hine, gen. editors, *The Eyes on the Prize Civil Rights Reader, Interim Report of the United States Com-*

mission on Civil Rights, April 16, 1963 (New York: Penguin Books, 1991), 179–80.

10 Dershowitz, *America on Trial*, 358.

11 *Detroit Free Press* interview of George Crockett, http://www.freep.com/news/obituaries/qcrock8.htm, 2.

12 Paul Harris, "'We are Family:' The Not-So-Bloody History of Resolving Internal Conflicts in the National Lawyers Guild," http://www.guerillalaw.com/guildarticle.html, 3.

13 Ward Churchill and Jim Vander Wall, The COINTELPRO Papers, Cambridge: South End Press,1990, 2002), 95-99, quoting from internal FBI memos. In 1975, the Select Committee to Study Governmental Operations with respect to Intelligence Activities United States Senate, chaired by Senator Frank Church, undertook extensive hearings and issued reports ("Church Committee Report"). The Church Committee found to its astonishment that Hoover instructed all the FBI's branch offices to treat the nonviolent Southern Christian Leadership Conference led by Dr. King as a "Black Nationalist 'Hate Group.'"(See the Church Committee's Final Report , Book III, COINTELPRO: The FBI's Covert Action Programs Against American Citizens (Washington, D.C: U.S. Gov't Printing Office, April 23, 1976), 4 (citing a memo from headquarters to all SACs dated 8/25/67, p.2.) The Committee further found that: "From December 1963 until his death in 1968, Martin Luther King, Jr. was the target of an intensive campaign by the Federal Bureau of Investigation to 'neutralize' him as an effective civil rights leader. In the words of the man in charge of the FBI's 'war' against Dr. King: 'No holds were barred. We have used [similar] techniques against Soviet agents.'" Church Committee Final Report, Dr. Martin Luther King, Jr.: A Case Study, Intro., 1. At Hoover's request, atty. Gen. Robert Kennedy approved wiretaps on Dr. King's home. The SCLC headquarters and Dr. King's associates were also bugged as were motel rooms where Dr. King stayed. Hoover was outraged when the Nobel Committee announced that King would be the recipient of its 1964 Peace Prize. In response, the FBI tried heavy-handed blackmail. Within days of the announcement, the FBI sent King a package featuring a string of "highlights" from illegal audiotapes of his sex life, and an an anonymous threat to go public and reveal him as an "evil, abnormal beast." The letter warned "you are done" and gave him 34 days to do the "one thing left "for you to do. You know what it is . . . There is but one way out for you. You better take it before your filthy, abnormal fraudulent self is bared to the nation." Churchill and Vander Wall, The COINTELPRO Papers, 99. The Senate Committee heard conflicting testimony on this episode. Its report notes, "According to the Chief of the FBI's Domestic Intelligence Division, the tape was intended to precipitate a separation between Dr. King and his wife in the belief that the separation would reduce Dr. King's stature . . . . Dr. King and his advisers interpreted [the note] as a threat to release the tape recording unless Dr. King committed suicide." *Ibid.*, 2.

14 Davies, ed., *The Press and Race*, 88, 91, 100, 102.

15 Sheila Byrd, Associated Press, *The Sun Herald, South Mississippi's Newspaper,* "Barbour apologizes to activists arrested in 1961," May 24, 2011, 1.

16 Clay Risen, "How the South was won," *BG*, March 5, 2003, http://www.boston.com/news/globe/ideas/articles/2006/03/05/how_the_south_was_won/.

17 Thomas B. Edsall, "Lott Decried for Part of Salute to Thurmond: GOP Senate Leader Hails Colleague's Run as Segregationist," *The Washington Post,* Dec. 7, 2002, http://222.commondreams.org/headlines02/1207-01.htm.

PART ONE, CHAPTER 16 — *Beyond Civil Rights: Movement Cases*

1 Stephen J. Whitfield, *The Culture of the Cold War* (Baltimore: The Johns Hopkins Univ. Press, 1996).

2 Jo Freeman, "Remembering SLATE," Sixties Protest, May 28, 2000, http://www.jofreeman.com/sixtiesprotest/sixties.htm.

3 Irving Hall, "The Meisenbach case: The FBI and HUAC Convicted," *The Californian*, June 1961 (2nd ed.), www.notinkansas.us/Library/Meisenbach.pdf.

4 "Operation Abolition & Operation Correction," The Miscellanarian, http://miscellanarian.wordpress.com/2011/05/14/operation-abolition-operation-correction/.

5 Charles Garry and Arthur Goldberg, *Streetfighter in the Courtroom: The People's Advocate* (New York: E. P. Dutton, 1977), 72.

6 Rob Nagle, "Demonstrators commemorate 50th anniversary of historic protest," *SFE*, May 13, 2010, http://www.sfexaminer.com/local/demonstrators-commemorate-50th-anniversary-historic-protest#ixzz1EG1qWBGI.

7 Grace Hechinger, "Clark Kerr, Leading Public Educator and Former Head of California's University, Dies at 92," *NYT*, Dec. 2, 2003, A28.

8 Free Speech Movement Chronology: *California Monthly, February 1965: "Three Months of Crisis: Chronology of Events,"* http://www.bancroft.berkeley.edu/FSM/chron.html.

9 Jeffery Kahn, "Ronald Reagan launched political career using the Berkeley campus as a target," News Center, U.C. Berkeley News, June 8, 2004, http://www.berkeley.edu/news/media/releases/2004/06/08_reagan.shtml.

10 "UC legend Clark Kerr dies," *OT*, Dec. 2, 2003, 1.

11 Shirl Pleskan and Matt Marsh, "It's Not How You Draw; It's What You Draw: An Interview with David Lance Goines," *Pressing Times*, Vol. 7, No. 2 (Berkeley: Alternative Press, 2006), 22.

12 *The Whole World's Watching: Peace and Social Justice Movements of the 1960s & 1970s* (Berkeley: Berkeley Art Center Association, 2001), 37.

13 King's ground-breaking "Beyond Vietnam" speech was given at New York's Riverside Church on April 4, 1967. See Marilyn Young, *The Vietnam Wars 1945–1990,* cited at Oakland Museum of California.org, http://www.museumca.org/picturethis/5_4.html.

Part Two, Chapter 1 — *"Free Huey"*

1 Ginger, *The Relevant Lawyers: Conversations out of court on their clients, their practice, their politics, their life style* (New York: Simon & Schuster, 1973), 69.

2 "Oakland Policeman Slain: 2 Hurt in Panther Shootout," *SFE*, Oct. 28, 1967, 1.

3 David Hilliard and Lewis Cole, *This Side of Glory* (Boston: Little, Brown & Co., 1993), 147–148.

4 David Hilliard, *Huey: Spirit of the Panther* (New York: Thunder's Mouth Press, 2006), 32–33.

5 Thelwell, Introduction to Moore, *Rage*, xvi.

6 Raiford, *Imprisoned in a Luminous Glare,* 144–145, 153.

7 Austin, *Up Against the Wall,* 35.

Part Two, Chapter 2 — *The Panther's Roots*

1 Thomas Fleming, "'Raincoat' Jones, black businessman extraordinaire," The Columbus Free Press—Reflections on Black History, March 17, 1999, http://www/freepress.org/fleming/flemg72.html; Lloyd Boyles, 'Raincoat' Jones—A Man Who Outlived His Heyday," *OT*, Jan. 16, 1968, 1.

2 Harry Johanesen, "California Negro History: War Brought Negro Influx To S.F. and Changing Status," *SFE*, August 2, 1968, 52.

3 Broussard, *Black San Francisco: The Struggle for Racial Equality in the West, 1900–1954*

(Lawrence: University Press of Kansas, 1993) 50–51, 134. By 1945, there were 37,327 blacks counted in the official Oakland census.

4 Don Hausler, unpublished manuscript, *Blacks in Oakland 1852–1987*, Vol. 3, 113, 116. Oakland Public Library History Room.

5 *Ibid.*, Vol. 3, 174.

6 *Report of the National Advisory Commission on Civil Disorders* (New York: Bantam Books, 1968) 10 [aka "the Kerner Report," after its chair, Illinois Gov. Otto Kerner].

7 Dudziak, *Cold War Civil Rights*, 12.

8 Pamphlet distributed at memorial service for Thelma Traylor Seale, Oakland, Feb. 1, 2008, author's collection.

9 Pearson, *The Shadow of the Panther* (New York: Perseus Books, 1995), 330.

10 Hilliard, *Huey: Spirit of the Panther*, 9.

11 *Ibid.*, 21.

12 HPN Box 14, Folder 11. Probation Report, 9. Letter of Deputy Probation Officer Thomas Broome.

13 Huey Newton and J. Herman Blake, *Revolutionary Suicide* (New York: Harcourt, Brace, Jovanovich, 1973), chapter 14.

14 Hilliard, *Huey: Spirit of the Panther*, 46.

Part Two, Chapter 3 — *Takin' Care of Business*

1 Mitford, *A Fine Old Conflict*, 108.

2 *People v. Newson* (1951) 37 Cal. 2d. 34, 38.

3 John Burris, *Blue v. Black: Let's End The Conflict Between Cops and Minorities* (New York: St. Martin's Press, 1999), 210.

4 Kate Coleman, with Paul Avery, "The Party's Over: How Huey Newton created a street gang at the center of the Black Panther Party," *NYT*, July 10, 1978, 23, 25.

5 Raiford, *Imprisoned in a Luminous Glare*, 149.

6 Philip S. Foner, *The Black Panthers Speak* (Cambridge: Da Capo Press, 1970), 5–6.

7 Jones, ed., *The Black Panther Party [Reconsidered]*, 33, fn. 35.

8 Thelwell, "Afterword," to Gilbert Moore, *Rage*, 288.

9 Fonor, ed., *The Black Panthers Speak*, 40.

10 Raiford, *Imprisoned in a Luminous Glare*, 153–154. The term came from the Japanese likely by way of Richard Aoki.

11 David Hilliard and Lewis Cole, *This Side of Glory*, (Boston: Little, Brown & Co., 1993) 123.

12 Bobby Seale, *Seize the Time*, 129.

13 Terry Anderson, *The Movement and the Sixties: Protest in America from Greensboro to Wounded Knee* (New York: Oxford Univ. Press, 1995), 11 and fn. 35.

14 Clayborne Carson, *In Struggle*, 254, fn. 23.

15 Declaration of Jessica Mitford, July 14, 1977, *People v. Newton*, Oakland Municipal Court, Alameda County No. 64624A and 65919, HPN Series 1, Box 15, folder 5.

Part Two, Chapter 4 — *The Defense Team*

1 Garry and Goldberg, *Streetfighter in the Courtroom*, 146.

2 Ginger, *The Relevant Lawyers*, 69.

3 Ann Fagan Ginger, ed., *Minimizing Racism in Jury Trials* (National Lawyers Guild, 1969), xv.

4 Jerold S. Auerbach, *Unequal Justice: Lawyers and Social Change in Modern America* (New York: Oxford University Press, 1976), 284.

[5] Susan Berman, "Meet Fay: Huey Newton's Attorney," Stender newspaper collection, circa Nov. 1970, 1C.

[6] Tribute by Justice Matthew Tobriner to Barney Dreyfus, June 3, 1979, Testimonial Dinner, Lawyers Guild program private collection of Marvin Stender.

[7] HPN, Box 11, Grand Jury Transcript.

[8] Eldridge Cleaver, *Target Zero,* 77–78 [manuscript for "Uptight in Babylon"].

[9] *The Black Panther,* Vol. I, No. 6, Nov. 25, 1967, 1.

[10] Jessica Mitford, foreword to Garry and Goldberg *Streetfighter in the Courtroom,* ix.

[11] "Incompetent, Irrelevant and Immaterial," *Inter-City Express,* undated news clipping, HPN Box 11, folder 8.

[12] Jahna Berry, "Legal World Says Farewell to White," *The Recorder,* June 29, 2001, 1, quoting then San Francisco Mayor, Willie Brown.

Part Two, Chapter 5 — *Who Do You Trust?*

[1] Stokely Carmichael, "Black Power Speech" (1967), http://balrog.sdsu.edu/~putman/410b/blackpower.htm.

[2] Cleaver, *Target Zero,* 77–78 [quoting from "Uptight in Babylon"].

[3] Hilliard and Cole, *This Side of Glory,* 148–149.

[4] Cleaver, *Target Zero,* "Bunchy," 130.

[5] Seale, *Seize the Time,* 204.

[6] Garry and Goldberg, *Streetfighter in the Courtroom,* 25.

[7] "Charles Garry Closing Argument," Ann Ginger, ed., *Minimizing Racism in Jury Trials,* 203.

[8] Seale, *Seize the Time,* 204.

Part Two, Chapter 6 — *"Honkies for Huey"*

[1] At the time, attorneys who shared royalties with clients did not automatically raise eyebrows. Under current California Rules of Professional Conduct, a fee agreement granting the attorney a percentage of a client's literary rights would be permissible only if first reviewed for fairness by independent counsel on the client's behalf. See Cal. Rule 3-300.

[2] "Panther Calls For Violence," *The Richmond Independent,* Dec. 23, 1967, HPN Box 19, Folder 12.

[3] "Incompetent, Irrelevant and Immaterial," *The Inter-City Express,* HPN Box 19, Folder 12.

[4] HPN Box 11, Folder 7, telephone message.

Part Two, Chapter 7 — *The Smell of Revolution*

[1] Newton, *To Die for the People,* 10, Executive Mandate No. 2, June 29, 1967.

[2] Newton and Blake, *Revolutionary Suicide,* 195.

[3] Seale, *Seize the Time,* 222.

[3] David Hill and Lewis Cole, *This Side of Glory* (Boston: Little, Brown & Co., 1993) 148-149.

[4] Seale, *Seize the Time,* 182.

[5] Thelwell, "To Die For the People?" Introduction to Gilbert Moore, *Rage,* xxvi–xxvii.

[6] Carson, *In Struggle,* 283 and note 51.

[7] *Ibid.,* 283 and note 52.

Part Two, Chapter 8 — *Client or Comrade?*

[1] California Constitution, Article 1, Section 6.

2 Newton, *To Die for the People,* 11–13, Executive Mandate No. 3, March 1, 1968.

3 HPN, Box 11, File 8, Grand Jury Testimony of Dell Ross.

4 *Ibid., Newsweek* clipping.

PART TWO, CHAPTER 9 — *Power to the People*

1 Foner, ed., *The Black Panthers Speak,* 62, quoting Huey Newton, "Huey Newton Talks to the Movement About the Black Panther Party, Cultural Nationalism, SNCC, Liberals and White Revolutionaries."

2 *OP,* Editorial, April 17, 1968.

3 "1st Negro to Have Flag At Half Staff," *SFE*, April 8, 1968, 2.

4 "King's Dream Is Not Dead—LBJ," *SFE,* April 5, 1968, 4. At the same time, the FBI stepped up its efforts to discredit King. As noted by the Church Committee: "The depth of Director Hoover's bitterness toward Dr. King . . . was apparent from the FBI's attempts to sully Dr. King's reputation long after his death. Plans were made to 'brief' congressional leaders in 1969 to prevent the passage of a 'Martin Luther King Day.' In 1970, Director Hoover told reporters that Dr. King was the 'last one in the world who should ever have received" the Nobel Peace Prize.' Church Committee Final Report, *Dr. Martin Luther King, Jr. Case Study,* (Washington, D.C. U.S. Printing Office, April 23, 1976), Intro. 1. The Justice Department cleared the FBI of any role in King's assassination, but failed to convince skeptics. Investigative reporter Michael Newton notes in his book, *The Encyclopedia of Unsolved Crimes* (New York: Checkmark Books, 2004) that: "There was evidence of an accomplice in King's murder from the beginning . . . . There is persuasive evidence that G-men never seriously looked for evidence of a conspiracy in King's death [and] . . .were actively discouraged from reporting conspiracy leads." *Ibid.*, 164-165. See also Ward Churchill and Jim Van der Wall, *Agents of Repression: The FBI's Secret Wars Against the Black Panther Partyand the American Indian Movement* (Boston: South End Press, 1988, 1990), 395, fn. 53 and cited sources).

5 See, e.g, "6000 at King Memorial in Civic Center Plaza; Whites Get Blame for Race Crisis,'" *SFE*, April 5, 1968, 1, 14; Harry Johanesen, "Grieving City Deplores 'Senseless' Murder," *Ibid.*

6 The award bested Anne Bancroft's stellar performance as the mother in *The Graduate,* Audrey Hepburn as the blind protagonist in the thriller *Wait Until Dark,* and Faye Dunaway's unforgettable gun moll in *Bonnie and Clyde.*

7 "Carmichael Reaction to King's Murder, *SFE*, April 5, 1968, 5.

8 Cleaver, *Target Zero,* 78–79, quoting from "Uptight in Babylon."

9 Hilliard and Cole, *This Side of Glory,* 195.

10 "Eldridge Cleaver, 'Recalled to Life,' Plans Huey March," *OP,* Vol. 5 No. 10, Wed., July 10, 1968, 1.

11 *Witherspoon v. Illinois* (1968) 391 U.S.510, 520–21.

12 United Press International, "Screams of Joy on Death Rows" *OT,* June 4, 1968, 1.

13 The California Supreme Court was then considering an ACLU and NAACP Legal Defense Fund suit challenging the death penalty as cruel and unusual punishment. In the interim, it had stayed all executions. On November 18, 1968, the California high court upheld the constitutionality of the death penalty, but followed *Witherspoon* to uphold the right to new penalty trials for defendants in cases where potential jurors opposed to the death penalty had been improperly dismissed. (*In re Anderson* 69 Cal. 2d. 613 (1968).) The California Supreme Court would revisit the constitutional argument in 1972.

14 H. Zeisel, "Some Insights Into the Operation of Criminal Juries," 42 (Confidential First

Draft, Univ. of Chicago, Nov. 1957), cited in fn. 10, 391 U.S. 510.

15 *Witherspoon v. Illinois*, 391 U.S. 510, 523, fn. 21 (1968). By week's end, the California Attorney General sent a letter to district attorneys throughout the state interpreting the new mandate's impact on capital cases as follows: "We conclude from the opinion that no prospective juror should be challenged and excused for cause on account of his views in opposition to the death penalty unless he answers affirmatively one or more of the following three questions:

1. Are your views on the death penalty such as would prevent you from making an impartial decision as to the defendant's guilt?
2. Are your views such that you could never vote to impose the death penalty?
3. Are your views such that you would refuse even to consider imposing the death penalty in this case?"

"Each Death Row Case to Get Reviewed," *OT*, June 7, 1968, 1.

16 Moore, *Rage*, 118, quoting Defendant's Memo in support of Motion to Quash Jury Panel.

17 Blacks in Berkeley and Oakland had been divided. Senator Kennedy, in a debate the week before with Senator McCarthy, had alienated some of them with comments indicating that suburban integration should proceed slowly. John George, who was running for Congress, had endorsed Eugene McCarthy. George later attributed his failure to win the Democratic nomination, which would have assured his election to Congress in a decidedly Democratic district, to write-in votes urged by the Peace and Freedom Party for his former client Huey Newton.

18 Quoted in *OT*, June 6, 1968, 1.

19 See, e.g., Joseph L. Myler, Washington UPI "The American Way — Is It??" *OT*, June 8, 1968, 1.

20 Robert Scheer, "Eldridge Cleaver Defense," letter to the editors of *The New York Review of Books*, Vol. 11, No. 9, Nov. 21, 1968.

21 "Superior Court Orders Eldridge Cleaver Freed," *OT*, June 12, 1968, 1–2, quoting Arlo Smith, Chief Assistant Attorney General.

22 The trial dates for the April shootout still had not been set. In June, while the Garry, Dreyfus firm handled Eldridge Cleaver's probation revocation hearing, another attorney, R. J. Engel, undertook the representation of Bobby Seale in a hearing before Judge Staats in Alameda County, seeking a stay of execution of a three-year probation sentence from his recent conviction for possessing a loaded shotgun outside the Oakland city jail in the spring of 1967. The stay of the probation sentence pending appeal was denied. Instead, Judge Staats added to the conditions of probation to specifically prohibit Seale from encouraging or inciting others "to use or carry guns" in addition to refraining from carrying guns himself or associating with persons carrying weapons.

Part Two, Chapter 10 — *The Quest for a Jury of His Peers*

1 Hugh Pearson, *The Shadow of the Panther* (New York: Perseus Books, 1995), 166.

2 Editorial, *OP*, April 17, 1968.

3 Frank Piazzi, East Bay Bureau, "Oakland Mayor Disenchanted, May Bow Out," *SFE*, July 21, 1968, 6.

4 Justice Shenk dissenting in *Perez v. Sharp*, 32 Cal. 2d 711 (1948), 743–44, 750.

5 David Greenberg, "Civil Rights: Let Em Wiretap!" George Mason Univ. History News Network, July 6, 2002, http://www/hnn.us/articles/366.html.

6 Carolyn Anspacher,"A Landmark Ruling on Juries' Racial Composition," *SFC*, July 10, 1968, 11. The United States Supreme Court would not reach the same conclusion for

almost another two decades in *Batson v. Kentucky*, 476 U.S. 79 (1986). In practice, after Batson, prosecutors retained wide latitude to excuse any and all black jurors by giving the court a race-neutral explanation. See study cited in Michelle Alexander, *The New Jim Crow: Mass Incarceration in the Age of Color Blindness* (New York: New Press, 2010), Kindle location 1620, fn. 72.

7 Despite being labeled a "pinko," Bob Treuhaft had garnered thirty percent of the votes in his race for Alameda County District Attorney, largely from Berkeley and Oakland's flatlands. His wife Decca Mitford was his amused campaign manager. On learning the vote count, Coakley had quipped: "I didn't realize there were that many Commies in Alameda County." Jessica Mitford, *A Fine Old Conflict*, 125.

8 Moore, *Rage*, 95.

9 "As Aid to Newton—Lysistrata '68," *SFE*, July 21, 1968, A 23.

10 Thelwell, Introduction to Moore, *Rage*, "TO DIE FOR THE PEOPLE?," xxxi, citing the files of Prof. C. E. "Bud" Schultz, Trinity College, Hartford, Connecticut.

11 "Decks Cleared for Newton Trial: Both Sides Expect to Go to Trial," *OP*, July 10, 1968, 1.

12 Moore, *Rage*, 118.

13 "Newton Attorneys Seek New Delays," *OT*, July 12, 1968, 14.

14 Moore, *Rage*, 79.

15 *Ibid.*, 27.

16 *Ibid.*, 97.

17 *Ibid.*, 108.

18 "Newton Attorneys Seek New Delays," *OT*, July 12, 1968, 14.

19 *OT*, July 16, 1968, 1.

20 "Bombs and Bombast," *OP*, Vol. 5. No. 11, July 17, 1968, 1.

21 Moore, *Rage*, 120, 153.

22 Newton Trial Starts, Then Hits Delay," *OT*, July 15, 1968, 1, 6.

23 Moore, *Rage*, 192.

24 Almea Lomax, "Newton Trial Gets Down to Cases; Guard Tighter—Defense Sobered as Eyewitness Claimed," *OP*, August 7, 1968, 1.

25 "Pst-st-st . . . UC Student Sours on Panthers," *OP*, Aug. 14, 1968, 1, 6, quoting an Aug. 2, 1968 editorial column by Thomas Brom in *The Daily Californian*.

26 *BB*, July 19–25, 1968, 3.

27 "U.S. Supreme Court Plea for Newton," *OT*, July 16, 1968, 1.

28 Carson, *In Struggle*, 160.

29 "Negro Joins Newton Jury; Another Dismissed," *SFE*, July 18, 1968, 1, 16.

30 "Challenge to Newton Jury" *OT*, July 17, 1968, 6.

31 Fay Stender, letter dated July 24, 1968, to Prof. Hans Zeisel, HPN, Box 11, Folder 7.

32 *OP*, July 22, 1968, 1.

33 "Jacks Is Black," *OT*, July 18, 1968, TV page.

34 "Report from Black America," *Newsweek*, June 30, 1969, 20.

35 "Newton On Stand, Says He's Broke," *OT*, July 17, 1968, 1.

36 Moore, *Rage*, 153.

37 William O'Brien, "Only Hope: Courtroom Revolution—Newton," *SFE*, July 17, 1968, 8.

Part Two Chapter 11 — *A Minority of One*

1 Sam Blumenfeld, "1st Negro Joins Newton Jurors," *SFE*, July 18, 1968, 1, 16.

2 Pearson, *The Shadow of the Panther*, 166.

3 Sam Blumenfeld, "Newton Defense Will Charge Plot," *SFE,* July 25, 1968, 1.
4 Sam Blumenfeld, "Newton's Challenge List Empty," *SFE,* July 29, 1968, 1.
5 Charles Garry, Introduction, Ann Ginger, ed., *Minimizing Racism in Jury Trials,* xxii.
6 Moore, *Rage,* 138.
7 *OP,* August 7, 1968, 6.
8 Moore, *Rage,* 140–141.
9 *Ibid.,* 145.
10 *Ibid.,* 142.
11 Robert Blauner, "Sociology in the Courtroom: The Search for White Racism," Ginger, ed., *Minimizing Racism in Jury Trials,* 59.
12 *Ibid.*
13 Excerpt from transcript, Huey P. Newton testimony, HPN, Box 11, Folder 3.
14 *OP,* July 24, 1968, 1.
15 Moore, *Rage,* 134.
16 "Newton Jury Selection Goes On," *OT,* July 19, 1968, 6.
17 Ginger, *Minimizing Racism in Jury Trials,* 93–94.
18 Moore, *Rage,* 139.
19 Garry and Goldberg, *Streetfighter in the Courtroom,* 109.
20 Ginger, *Minimizing Racism in Jury Trials,* xxi.
21 In 1947, the United States Supreme Court had (by a bare majority) upheld that practice against a challenge that systematic discouragement of female participation deprived criminal defendants of a jury of their peers. The dissent would have found that such practice denied the accused an "impartially drawn jury from a cross-section of the community." *Fay v. New York,* 332 U.S. 261, 296 (1947) (Justice Murphy dissenting, joined by Justice Black, Douglas, and Rutledge).
22 See Marissa N. Batt, "Just Verdicts? A Prosecutor Extols Jury Service for Women," *Ms. Magazine,* Summer 2004, http://www.msmagazine.com/summer2004/justverdicts.asp.
23 In *Taylor v. Louisiana,* 419 U.S. 522, 537, the high court—which would not include its first woman justice for another six years—concluded: "If there was ever the case that women were unqualified to sit on juries or were so situated that none of them should be required to perform jury service, that time has long since passed."
24 Sam Blumenfeld, "Opening Newton Trial Arguments Today,"*SFE,* July 31, 1968,3.
25 Sam Blumenfeld, "New Panel Called in Newton Trial," *SFE,* July 23, 1968, 1, 14.

PART TWO, CHAPTER 12 — *On Trial — Newton or American Society?*

1 "Cleaver Warns on Huey Trial," *OT,* July 24, 1968, 8. As noted in the text, earlier that month Eldridge had held a press conference in New York predicting the likelihood of open warfare in the streets of California if Huey Newton were sentenced to death and that the carnage would spread quickly across the country.
2 Rush Greenlee, "Newton's Dad: Guilty? That's a Fool Question," *SFE,* Aug. 6, 1968, 6.
3 Moore, *Rage,* 154.
4 Greenlee, "Newton's Dad: Guilty? That's a Fool Question," *SFE,* Aug. 6, 1968, 6.
5 "Newton Trial Defense: 'Police Radio Tapes Prove Bias,'" *SFE,* Aug. 6, 1968, 1, 6.
6 Jeff Morgan, "Re-Enactment of Officer's Murder," *OT,* Aug. 7, 1968, 7.
7 *Ibid.*
8 Morgan, "'Gun Under Pillow,' Newton Jury Told," *OT,* Aug. 7, 1968, 3.
9 Morgan, "Re-Enactment of Officer's Murder, *OT,* Aug. 7, 1968, 7.

10 "Witness Saw Frey Killed," *OT*, Aug. 8, 1968, 2.

11 Morgan, "Defense in Newton Trial Fires Back," *OT*, Aug. 8, 1968, 1.

12 Garry and Goldberg, *Streetfighter in the Courtroom*, 121.

13 "Ross Defies the Court—Won't Talk," *OT*, Aug. 13, 1968, 1.6.

14 "Threatened Deadlock in Newton Trial Broken: See No Evil, Tell None 'Try' Fails," *OP*, August 14, 1968, 4.

15 *Ibid.*

16 *Ibid.*

17 "Ross Defies The Court—Won't Talk," *OT*, Aug. 13, 1968, 1, 6.

18 *Ibid.*

19 "Newton Jury Hears Ballistics Expert," *OT*, Aug. 14, 1968, 1, 6.

20 *Ibid.*

21 *Ibid.*

22 Blumenfeld and Greenlee, "Newton May Go on Stand Last—in Next Week?" *SFE*, Aug. 16, 1968, 8.

23 Unpublished manuscript and notes of Prof. Robert Blauner.

24 *Ibid.*

Part Two, Chapter 13 — *The Day of Reckoning Arrives*

1 The "Dear Nigger Lover" letter (HPN, Box 11, File 10) quoted in part at the beginning of the chapter had commenced:

> I guess you will get that murdering coon off because the judge, jury and witnesses have all been intimidated to the extent that nobody would dare convict him. I hope he will be gunned down in the street by some friends of the poor policeman he killed . . . It's too bad we ever stopped lynching. At least the damn niggers knew their place in those days and didn't cause any trouble. I remember reading about how one time they strung up coons and pulled out pieces of their flesh with corkscrews. That must have been a lot of fun. I wish I'd been there to take part in the good work.

2 "Witnesses Recall a Happy Newton, " *OT*, Aug. 21, 1968, 7.

3 Edward M. Keating, *Free Huey!* (Berkeley: Ramparts Press, 1971), 129–30.

4 Garry and Goldberg, *Streetfighter in the Courtroom*, ix.

5 The Secretary of State had refused to accept Cleaver's name on the ballot because Cleaver was only 33, two years below the minimum age specified in the Constitution to serve as President. The Peace and Freedom Party planned to sue for a court order to require Cleaver's name to be listed on the ballot, on the argument that it was only service as President and not ballot listing that had a minimum age requirement. No one expected him to win, after all. The suit was rejBocted and his name excluded from the ballot.

6 Hilliard, *Huey: Spirit of the Panther*, 156.

7 Moore, *Rage*, 191.

8 Newton and Blake, *Revolutionary Suicide*, 292.

9 Almena Lomar, "Newton Talks Peace as Panthers Shout Defiance," *OP*, Aug. 28, 1968, 3.

10 "40 Whites Parade at Newton Trial," *SFE*, Aug. 22, 1968, 8.

11 "Stokely at Newton Trial—'Political,'" *SFE*, Aug. 22, 1968, 8.

12 Sam Blumenfeld and Rush Greenlee, "D.A. Ends Newton Grilling," *SFE*, Aug. 26, 1968, 1.

13 "Huey Relates His Story of Shooting," *OT*, Aug. 23, 1968, 1, 9.

14 Foner, *The Black Panthers Speak*, 41–42.

15 Garry and Goldberg, *Streetfighter in the Courtroom*, 141.
16 *OT,* Aug. 27, 1968, 3.
17 Eldridge Cleaver, "Newton On Trial," *Ramparts*, Fall 1968, 23.
18 Rush Greenlee, "Newton Casts a Long Shadow," *SFE*, Aug. 27, 1968, 16.
19 HPN, Series 1, Box 11, File 9 [letter, dated Aug. 28, 1968, from J. Herman Blake to Huey Newton].
20 Moore, *Rage*, 204.
21 Greenlee, "Newton Casts a Long Shadow," *SFE*, Aug. 27, 1968, 16.
22 HPN Box 19, Folder 1, transcript direct examination of Dr. Diamond, 3397 at 3405–3407.
23 *Ibid.* at 3401–3403.
24 "Defense Winds Up Case in Newton Murder Trial," *OT,* Aug. 27, 1968, 3.
25 "Huey Newton Trial Enters Final Phase," *OT,* Sept. 3, 1968, 1.
26 *Ibid.*
27 "Newton Case to Jury," *OT,* Sept. 3, 1968.
28 "Huey Newton Trial Enters Final Phase," *OT,* Sept. 3, 1968, 5.
29 Jeff Morgan, "Jury Given Newton Murder Case: Jurors Select Negro Foreman," *OT,* Sept. 5, 1968, 1.
30 Ginger, ed., *Minimizing Racism in Jury Trials,* 216 (excerpt from defense closing argument, *People v. Newton*).
31 *Ibid.*, 199.
32 *Ibid.*, 200.
33 *Ibid.*, 201.
34 *Ibid.*, 204.
35 Blumenfield, "Newton Attorney: Witness a Liar—Or Psychopath," *SFE,* Sept. 3, 1968, 1.
36 Blumenfeld and Greenlee, "Newton Jury Hears Closing Arguments," *SFE,* Sept. 4, 1968, 1.
37 Blumenfeld and Greenlee, "Newton Fate Up To Jury," *SFE,* Sept. 5, 1968, 1, 4.
38 Greenlee, "Row on Newton Evidence: Judge Refuses Defense Plea," *SFE,* Sept. 6, 1968, 1, 4.
39 *Ibid.*
40 Anderson, *The Movement and the Sixties*, 225 and n. 32, quoting one gleeful yippie calling the Chicago debacle "a revolutionary wet dream come true."
41 Blauner, unpublished manuscript, Chapter Two, 10.
42 Greenlee, "How the Jury Decided; Puzzling Newton Verdict," *SFE,* Sept. 9, 1968.
43 Moore, *Rage*, 229.
44 Gayle Montgomery, "Newton Is Guilty Of Manslaughter," *OT,* Sept. 9, 1968, 1.
45 "Huey Says He Ordered 'Keep Cool'," *OT,* Sept. 12, 1968, 7.
46 Austin, *Up Against the Wall*, 115 and fn 8 citing Cox's unpublished manuscript.
47 Moore, *Rage*, 231.
48 Montgomery, "Newton Is Guilty Of Manslaughter," *OT,* Sept. 9, 1968, 1.

Part Two, Chapter 14 — *Aftermath*

1 Gaile Russ, "Juror in Newton Trial Talks," *OT,* Sept. 10, 1968, 1, 5.
2 Sam Blumenfeld and Rush Lee, "Oakland Reaction Parallels Race," *SFE,* Sept. 10. 1968, 6.
3 Moore, *Rage*, 268.
4 *Ibid.*, 236.
5 *Ibid.*, 246.
6 Daryl E. Lembke, "Newton Case Strains Nerves of Police," *The Vallejo Times Herald,* Sept.

25, 1968, HPN, Series 1, Box 23 [publicity clipping].

7 Celia Rosebury, "In the aftermath of the Newton trial, Huey, Panthers Keep it Cool," *The People's World*, Sept. 21, 1968.

8 Terry A. Reim, "Cops' Panther Shoot Blows 1000-year Cover," *BB*, Sept. 19, 1968, 1.

9 "Panther HQ Shot Up: 2 Police Fired," *SFE*, Sept. 10, 1968, 1.

PART THREE, CHAPTER 1 — *The "Free Huey" Campaign Expands to Bursting*

1 HPN, Series 1, Box 11, Folder 5, Probation Report 4.

2 Ronald Stevenson, "Black Community Reacts to Verdict, HPN Box 23, Folder 1 [undated clipping].

3 "Tensions, Martyrdom and Where Causes Lie," *San Raphael Independent Journal* editorial, HPN, Series 1, Box 23, Folder 1 [clipping of editorial].

4 Terry Ryan, "Mrs. Cleaver criticizes white men," *The Redwood City Gazette*, Oct. 2, 1968, newsclipping, HPN Box 23, Folder 1 [clipping].

5 "Hoffer Rows with Negro at Hearing," Washington, D.C., Oct. 26, 1968, Allen News Service, HPN, Box 23, Folder 1 [clipping].

6 "Newton Predicts Bloodshed," *The Redwood City Tribune*, Oct. 25, 1968, HPN Box 23, folder 1 [clipping].

7 Lawrence J. Kirshbaum, "Militant Head of New Left Moves HQ Here," *The San Francisco Sunday Examiner and Chronicle*, Sept. 29, 1968, Section A, 10 [*Newsweek* Service].

8 Horowitz, *The New Left*, 76.

9 The San Francisco State College Strike Collection, http://www.library.sfsu.edu/about/collections/strike/chronology.html.

10 Horowitz, *Left Illusions: An Intellectual Odyssey*, 76.

11 "Races: Professor on Ice," *Time*, Sept. 27, 1968, http://www.time.com/time/magazine/article/0,9171,902310,00.html.

12 The course at Cal, Social Analysis 139X, "Dehumanization and Regeneration in the American Social Order," was offered for five units of credit by Prof. Jan Dizard, who had testified for the defense in the jury selection phase of the Newton trial.

13 "At State: That Ole Cleaver Rhythm," *BB*, Oct. 17, 1968, HPN, Box 23, Folder 1.

14 Cleaver, *Target Zero*, 146, 148–49.

15 Anderson, *The Movement and the Sixties*, 325.

16 P. Mathers, "Radical change to aid justice for blacks urged by Newton lawyer," Jan. 17, 1969, *SFC*, May 15, 1969, 1.

17 "Bloodbath 'Figure of Speech,'" *OT*, April 8, 1970, 1.

18 Today, People's Park occupies the same location near Telegraph Avenue as it did in April 1969. It is overseen by a volunteer council. A mural memorializes the killing of student James Rector on May 15, 1969. There is a stage for rallies. The park sports two basketball courts and includes community gardens and public toilets. Mostly it is occupied by homeless people.

19 Eldridge Cleaver, *Post Prison Writings and Speeches* (New York: Vantage Press, 1969), 38.

20 Hilliard, *Huey: Spirit of the Panther*, 126.

21 "COUNTERINTELLIGENCE PROGRAM BLACK NATIONALIST—*HATE GROUPS RACIAL INTELLIGENCE 3/4/68, COINTELPRO: FBI Domestic Intelligence Activities, COINTELPRO Revisited—Spying & Disruption, IN BLACK AND WHITE: THE F.B.I. PAPERS,*" What Really Happened, http://whatreallyhappened.com/RANCHO/POLITICS/COINTELPRO/COINTELPRO-FBI.docs.html. The memo is reproduced

in Churchill and Vander Wall, *The COINTELPRO Papers*, 108–11.

22 Churchill and Vander Wall, *Agents of Repression*, 63, quoting Noam Chomsky and a June 1970 special report to President Nixon.

23 *Ibid.*, 68, fn. 42, quoting May 15, 1969, internal FBI memorandum.

24 L. F. Palmer, "Out to Get the Panthers," *The Nation*, July 28, 1969, 80.

25 J. Edgar Hoover, letter to the head of the San Francisco FBI office, June 9, 1969. Counterintelligence and Special Operations (1970), http://www.icdc.com/~paulwolf /cointelpro/specialops.htm.

26 "Supplementary Detailed Staff Reports on Intelligence Activities and the Rights of Americans Book II Final Report April 23, 1976," www.icdc.com/~paulwolf /churchfinalreportIIIb.htm. The Committee staff noted "little or no apparent evidence of violations [by the targets] of state or Federal Law." *Id.*, Book II p. 220 fn. 156 p. 128.

27 Hilliard and Cole, *This Side of Glory*, 264-265.

28 Cecil Levinson, "Huey is My BROTHER TOO!," *BP*, Jan. 25, 1969, 7.

29 Roland Young, "Huey's Appeal," *BP*, Feb. 28, 1970, 2.

30 Defendant's Proposed Instructions, *People v. Newton*, Alameda County Superior Ct. No. 41266, HPN Box 15, Folder 5.

31 *People v. Newton* (1970) 8 Cal. App. 3d. 359, 375.

32 Robert J. Minton, Jr. (ed.), *Inside: Prison American Style* (New York: Random House, 1971), Introduction, xv; "Racism II" by Micha Maguire [pseudonym for George Jackson's Marxist friend and fellow inmate Michael McCarthy], 84.

33 Jo Durden-Smith, *Who Killed George Jackson? Fantasies, Paranoia and the Revolution* (New York: Knopf, 1976), 174.

34 *Ibid.*, 175.

35 *Ibid.*, 177.

36 *Ibid.*, 184.

37 "3 Charged with Soledad Murder," *Monterey Peninsula Herald*, January 27, 1970, 3. The apparent source of this inflammatory misstatement was a summary of one of the many official interviews of prisoners after the killing. A prisoner allegedly told an investigator that he overheard such a boast from a black inmate when word of Mill's death circulated in Y wing. But the Monterey District Attorney's office never substantiated any such statement, written or oral.

38 Fay Stender, Introduction to Eve Pell, ed., *Maximum Security: Letters from Prison* (New York: E. P. Dutton, 1972), 11.

39 George Jackson, *Soledad Brother: The Prison Letters of George Jackson* (Chicago: Lawrence Hill Books, 1994), 212 [letter addressed "Dear Fay," dated March 9, 1970].

40 *Ibid.*, 10 [letter dated June 10, 1970, to Gregory Armstrong].

41 Quoted from March 1970 flyer in personal collection of Hon Richard Silver, (ret.).

42 Eric C. Brazil, "Long Trial Foreseen in Soledad Prison Slaying," *Salinas Californian*, Feb. 25, 1970, 1.

43 Fred Sorri, "Attorneys Hit Grand Jury Plan," *Monterey Peninsula Herald*, March 17, 1970, 2.

44 Helen Manning, "Judge Enters Pleas for Soledad Inmates," *Salinas Californian*, March 18, 1970, 2.

45 Ann Ginger, *The Relevant Lawyers*, 284–85.

46 Mark Lane, "Exclusive: Mark Lane interviews Huey Newton in jail," *Los Angeles Free Press*, July 24, 1970, 4, 18.

47 *OT*, Aug. 5, 1970, 1; *SFC*, Aug. 4, 1970, 1; *SFC*, Aug. 5, 1970, 1.

48 Branning, "Newton Warns Establishment: Free 'Political Captives,'" *SFE*, Aug. 6, 1970, 1.

49 "Alameda Sheriff on Panthers and OEO," *SFC*, Oct. 16, 1970, 3.

50 Branning, *supra*, 1.

51 Durden-Smith, *Who Killed George Jackson?*, 142–44; Liberatore, *The Road to Hell*, 93–94. Newton's older brother Sonny Boy told him a similar account. Newton was so skeptical of Pratt that Hilliard had Pratt submit to an injection of truth serum to prove he was not an undercover agent. Newton remained unsatisfied, assuming that Pratt had been trained by the Army to pass that type of test. Hillard and Cole, *This Side of Glory*, 310–312.

52 Citizens Research and Investigation Committee and Louis Tackwood, *The Glasshouse Tapes*, 114; Durden-Smith, *Who Killed George Jackson?*, 153–56.

53 Stephen Cook, "Marin Judge, 2 Cons Die in Marin Court Kidnapping," *SFE*, Aug. 7, 1970, 1, 8.

54 "Eyewitness Story of Terror: Young Couple, Baby Escape Kidnap," *SFE*, August 7, 1970, 1, 9.

55 "Nation: Justice: A Bad Week for the Good Guys," *Time*, August 17, 1970, http://www.time.com/time/magazine/article/0,9171,909547-1,00.html. Durden-Smith, *Who Killed George Jackson?*, 142.

56 Gregory Armstrong, *The Dragon Has Come* (New York: Harper & Row, 1974), 130.

57 Christopher De La Torre, "The interviews/John Knoebel," July 2, 2009, http://christopherdelatorre.com/2009/07/02/40-years-after-stonewall-part-3-john-knoebel. Author Leigh Reiford reports that at the final session the attendees ambitiously voted to demand "an international bill of rights, international reparations, the abolition of capitalism, the renunciation of U.S. nationhood, the destruction of nuclear weapons and the United States army, support for gay and women's liberation, a demand for socialized medicine, and an end to genocide." Reiford, *Imprisoned in a Luminous Glare*, 204.

58 *In Search of Common Ground* (W.W. Norton, 1973), 47, 50. In "A Surprisingly Gentle Confrontation," reviewer Philip Rosenberg noted that the book severely edited Newton's opening remarks. Rosenberg assumed that abridgement was a disservice to Newton that made him sound less than fully coherent. *NYT* on the Web, http://www.nytimes.com/books/99/08/22/specials/erikson-common.html.

59 Hilliard, *Huey: Spirit of the Panther*, 175.

60 Durden-Smith, *Who Killed George Jackson?*, 155. The journalist presumed this happened in August, but according to Hilliard, Newton reluctantly okayed Pratt's move underground to Alabama and did not banish his group from the Party until several months later, at the same time as the Panther 21. Hilliard and Cole, *This Side of Glory*, 320.

61 Earl Caldwell, "Is Panther Party Dying? Or Regrouping?," *The Sacramento Observer*, March 18, 1971, B-3.

62 Associated Press Chief 'Was Astonished' By Indictment of Seale," April 4, 1972, *SFC*, 1.

63 Garry and Goldberg, *Streetfighter in the Courtroom*, 216. Donald Freed published his book the following year, *Agony at New Haven: The Trial of Bobby Seale and Ericka Huggins* (New York: Simon & Schuster, 1973).

64 Newton and Blake, *Revolutionary Suicide*, Kindle ed. E185.97.N48A3, 2009, Kindle location 3450–3460.

65 Hilliard and Cole, *This Side of Glory*, 130. McKinney's contempt citation was overturned on appeal because Judge Friedman had no jurisdiction over McKinney at the time he ordered the sanction.

66 Hilliard and Lewis Cole, *This Side of Glory*, 131–33.

67 "House Probers Split on Panther Study," *OT*, Aug. 24, 1971, 36 E.

68 See, Pearson, *The Shadow of the Panther*, 292, quoting Newton's Ph.D. advisor Bob Trivors

interviewed after Newton's death.

69 These book reviews are quoted in Armstrong, *The Dragon Has Come*, 172–173.

70 Jackson, *Soledad Brother*, 232 [letter to Fay Stender, April 1970].

71 Peter Collier and David Horowitz, *Destructive Generation: A Second Look at the Sixties* (New York: Summit Books, 1989), 38.

72 George Jackson, *Blood in My Eye* (Baltimore: Black Classic Press, 1990), 32.

73 Paul Liberatore, *The Road to Hell: The True Story of George Jackson, Stephen Bingham, and the San Quentin Massacre* (New York: The Atlantic Monthly Press, 1996), 115.

74 Armstrong, *The Dragon Has Come*, Author's Note, x.

75 Collier and Horowitz, *Destructive Generation*, 22.

76 Durden-Smith, *Who Killed George Jackson?*, 165.

77 Liberatore, *The Road to Hell*, 81.

78 *Ibid.*, 98.

79 Durden-Smith, *Who Killed George Jackson?*, 35–36.

80 Liberatore, *The Road to Hell*, 148.

81 Durden-Smith, *Who Killed George Jackson?*, 86. See also Eric Mann, *Comrade George; an Investigation into the Life, Political Thought, and Assassination of George Jackson* (New York: Harper & Row, 1972, 1974), 81–82, detailing the failed experiment conducted by staff of *SFC*. This skepticism was not shared by the judge at Stephen Bingham's preliminary hearing. *The Road to Hell, supra*, 228. Reporter Paul Liberatore's book mistakenly attributes *Judge Stephen*'s assessment of the case following the preliminary hearing to *defendant Stephen Bingham*, stating that "Steve provided his lawyers with an analysis of the incident" that matched the prosecution's theory. To the contrary, Bingham maintained his innocence throughout the proceedings that resulted in his acquittal—and demanded a correction, which the publisher printed, but failed to ensure was pasted in the books.

82 Durden-Smith, *Who Killed George Jackson?*, 243, fn. 5.

83 Victor Riesel, *OT*, Sept. 28, 1971.

84 "Brutality At Attica, Doctor Says," *SFC*, April 28, 1972, 2.

85 "Newton: 'Panthers Have Put Down Their Guns,'" *Berkeley Daily Gazette*, Jan. 13, 1972, 1.

86 Tim Findley, "A Grim Finale for Prison Inmates," *SFC*, May 25, 1973, 6.

87 "Cruel Isolation," *NYT*, Aug. 2, 2011, A20. The editorial was prompted by a recent hunger strike by maximum security inmates at California's Pelican Bay prison.

PART THREE, CHAPTER 2 — *Eclipsed*

1 Anderson, *The Movement and the Sixties*, 219–21.

2 Randal B. Woods, *LBJ: Architect of American Ambition* (New York: Free Press, 2006), 864.

3 "Jerry Rubin's Happy Day of Fulfillment: *SFC*, March 22, 1969, HPN, Box 23, folder 3 [clipping].

4 *United States v. Dellinger et al.* (7th Cir. 1972) 472 F.2d 340.

5 Jason Epstein, "A Special Supplement: The Trial of Bobby Seale," *New York Review of Books*, Dec. 4, 1969, http://www.nybooks.com/articles/archives/1969/dec/04/a-special-supplement-the-trial-of-bobby-seale/.

6 L. F. Palmer, "Out to Get the Panthers," *The Nation*, July 28, 1969, 78.

7 In 1999, allegations were made that Chief Justice Rehnquist deliberately picked a skewed judicial panel that then selected Kenneth Starr as replacement Independent Counsel to pursue the impeachment allegations against President Clinton. In response, Republican Senator Arlen Spector introduced a bill known as The Blind Justice Act.

It would have mandated random selection of judges nationwide for both federal trial courts and appellate panels. The bill was defeated. For the background and strong rationale for such a requirement, see *Neutral Assignment of Judges*, Univ. of Denver, Sturm College of Law, http://www.law .du.edu/index.php/neutral-assignment-of-judges.

8 Dershowitz, *America on Trial*, 392.

9 Linder, "Famous Trials: The Chicago 7 Trial," http://www.law.umkc.edu/faculty /projects/ftrials/Chicago7/Account.html.

10 Mark Levine, George McNamee, Daniel Greenberg, *The Tales of Hoffman* (New York: Bantam Books, 1970), quote from the cover.

11 Its illegality was determined in *Bucher v. Selective Service Local Boards* (1970) 421 F. 2d 24.

12 Quoted in *The New Yorker*, http://www.newyorker.com/archive/196809/07/1968_09_ 07_038_TNY_CARDS_000287941#ixzz1SOPK0611.

13 Levine et al., *The Tales of Hoffman*, xix.

14 Mitford, *The Trial of Dr. Spock* (New York: Alfred A. Knopf, 1969).

15 Garry and Goldberg, *Streetfighter in the Courtroom*, 178.

16 *Ibid.*, 176.

17 Levine et al., *The Tales of Hoffman*, 55–57, 62, 68–69.

18 Abbie Hoffman, "Conspiracy in the Streets," http://www.haymarketbooks.org/product _info.php?products_id=1187.

19 Levine et al., *The Tales of Hoffman*, 285.

20 "On This Day: Jury Convicts Five of Chicago Seven," Feb. 18, 2011 quoting Herbert Ehrmann, http://www.findingdulcinea.com/news/on-this-day/Feb/On-this-Day—Jury -Convicts-Five-of-Chicago-Seven.html.

21 Robert W. Meserve, "The Pace of Criminal Justice," President's Page, *ABA Journal*, Nov. 1972, Vol. 58, 1129. Some of the contempt charges against the Chicago Seven and their counsel were retried before a different judge and upheld, but limited to time served, putting an abrupt end to one of the most embarrassing prosecutions in the country's history.

22 *United States v. Dellinger et al.* (7th Cir. 1972) 472 F.2d 340.

23 Joel Tlumak, "The New Reality Walks Out on Jerry Rubin," *SFC & SFE*, May 31, 1970, Section A,7.

24 Monica Davey, "In Court, AIM Members Are Depicted as Killers," *NYT*, Feb. 5, 2004, http://www.nytimes.com/2004/02/05 national/05TRIB.html.

25 Vincent Bugliosi, Jury Summation, quoted in *Crimes of the Century: The Manson Murder Case*: "On the hot summer night of Aug. 8, 1969, Charles Manson, the Mephistophelean guru who raped and bastardized the minds of all those who gave themselves so totally to him, sent out from the fires of hell at Spahn Ranch three, heartless, blood-thirsty robots." http://investigation.discovery.com/investigation/history/crimes-century/crimes -article-manson.html.

PART THREE, CHAPTER 3 — *Visions of Apocalyptic Race War*

1 Linder, "Famous Trials: The Manson Trial," http://www.law.umkc.edu/faculty/projects /ftrials/manson/mansonchrono.html.

2 Vincent Bugliosi and Curt Gentry, *Helter Skelter: The True Story of The Manson Murders* (New York: W.W. Norton & Co., 1974 [afterword 1994]), 336.

3 *Ibid.*

4 *Ibid.*

5 See Book III, *Church Committee Report, The FBI's covert action program to destroy the Black*

Panther Party, section A.1. The Effort to Promote Violence Between the Black Panther Party and the United Slaves (US), Inc., http://www.icdc.com/~paulwolf/cointelpro/churchfinalreportIIIc.htm. In November of 1968, Hoover informed FBI branch offices that "a serious struggle is taking place between the Black Panther Party (BPP) and the US organization . . . taking on the aura of gang warfare with attendant threats of murder and reprisals. ¶In order to fully capitalize upon BPP and US differences as well as to exploit all avenues of creating further dissension in the ranks of the BPP, recipient offices are instructed to submit imaginative and hard-hitting counterintelligence measures aimed at crippling the BPP." To that end, Hoover directed field offices to report to him every two weeks what measures they proposed and what was accomplished. All counterintelligence actions required his approval. (*Ibid.,* memo dated 11/25/68 re "Counterintelligence program, Black Nationalist Hate Groups, Racial Intelligence (Black Panther Party)" In response, Special Agent Richard Held of the L.A. field office proposed fake threats to exacerbate tension between the two militant groups. After Held implemented that plan, two US members ambushed and killed Carter and Huggins, which prompted the San Diego FBI office to circulate more anonymous derogatory cartoons aimed at promoting reciprocal violence between the BPP and US. (Reproduced in Churchill and Vander Wall's The COINTELPRO Papers, 130-133.) Pleased at the results, Hoover soon promoted Held to run the FBI's San Francisco office.

6 Bugliosi and Gentry, *Helter Skelter,* 329.

7 Ray Hoekstra, *Will You Die For Me? The Man Who Killed for Charles Manson Tells His Own Story: Tex Watson as told to Chaplain Ray* (Cross Roads Publications, 1978) Chap. 13, "You Were Only Waiting for This Moment," http://www.aboundinglove.org/sensational/wydfm/wydfm-013.php.

8 Bugliosi and Gentry, *Helter Skelter,* 134.

8 Wilson, *Headline Justice,* 165.

10 Bugliosi and Gentry, *Helter Skelter,* 44–45.

11 "Death and Drugs" *LAT,* August 24, 1969, F5.

12 Bugliosi and Gentry, *Helter Skelter,* 337.

13 *Ibid.,* 298.

14 *Ibid.,* 429, 432.

15 Linder, "Famous Trials: The Manson Trial," http://www.law.umkc.edu/faculty/projects/ftrials/manson/mansonchrono.html.

Part Three, Chapter 4 — *"Triple Jeopardy—Black, Female, and Communist"*

1 Aileen C. Hernandez, Introduction to Mary Timothy, *Jury Woman: The Story of the Trial of Angela Y. Davis—Written by a Member of the Jury* (San Francisco: Glide Pub., 1974, 1975), ix.

2 Robert Popp, "Convict Stalls Arraignment: Court Hearing in Marin Shootout," *SFC,* Sept. 11, 1970, 13.

3 Robert Kaufman, "Ruchell Magee;" Ruchell Magee, "Letters to Angela Y. Davis," Angela Davis, ed, *If They Come In The Morning: Voices of Resistance* (New York: Third Press, 1971), 174, 175.

4 Paul Avery, "How the Angela Furor Was Fanned," *SFC,* May 13, 1972, 4.

5 Mick Jagger, "Sweet Black Angel," Keno's ROLLING STONES Web Site, http://www.keno.org/stones_lyrics/blackangel.html.

6 Excerpt from Chisholm's announcement speech, Jan. 25, 1972, http://www.essortment.com/all/shirleychisholm_ruol.htm. (Republican Sen. Margaret Chase Smith had been the first woman to have her name placed in consideration by either party eight years before.)

7 Avery, "How the Angela Furor was Fanned," *SFC*, May 13, 1972, 4.

8 Sol Stern, "The Campaign to Free Angela Davis and Ruchell Magee," *NYT*, June 27, 1971, http://www.nytimes.com/books/98/03/08/home/davis-campaign.html.

9 Angela Davis, ed., *If They Come In The Morning*, Dedication.

10 *Ibid.*, 60 [introduction to "Prison Where Is Thy Victory?" by Huey P. Newton].

11 *Ibid.*, Howard Moore, Jr., "Angela—Symbol of Resistance," 203.

12 Audrey Cleary, "Scientific Jury Selection: History, Practice, and Controversy," Villa Nova University, 2005, http://www.publications.villanova.edu/Concept/2005/jury_selection.pdf.

13 The HistoryMakers Biography, http://www.thehistorymakers.com/biography/biography.asp?bioindex=96.

14 Cal. Penal Code S. 169 added by statutes 1970, c. 1411, p. 2679, eff. Sept. 18, 1970.

15 Nine percent were undecided. Among non-whites the death penalty was disfavored by a wide margin (24 percent in favor and 64 percent against). George Gallup, "Gallup Poll on Death Penalty," *SFC*, March 16, 1972, 17.

16 Franklin H. Williams, "The Death Penalty and the Negro," *The Crisis*, Oct. 1960, 3, HPN Box 14, Folder 1.

17 *Ibid.*

18 *People of the State of California v. Anderson*, 6 Cal. 3d 628, 493 P.2d 880 (Cal. 1972). A few months later in a contentious five-to-four decision, a bare majority of the United States Supreme Court spawned a nationwide moratorium on the death penalty. Its decision in *Furman v. Georgia*, 408 U.S. 238 (1972), required consistency in the application of capital punishment. The high court found that most state capital statutes violated the Constitution, but did not categorically outlaw executions under more carefully tailored laws. Four years later—after John Stevens replaced the more liberal Justice William Douglas on the high court—the Supreme Court upheld a series of death penalty sentences as not violating the Eighth Amendment. The lead case was *Gregg v. Georgia*, 428 U.S. 153 (1976). That same year, Robert Page Anderson, the convicted murderer in the 1972 California case, won release on parole unaffected by these later events.

19 "Death Penalty Abolished by State Supreme Court: Reagan Calls It a 'Mockery,'" *SFC*, Feb. 19, 1972, 1.

20 Caroline Williams, "Death penalty costs California $184 million a year, study says," *LAT*, June 20, 2011, http://articles.latimes.com/2011/jun/20/local/la-me-adv-death-penalty-costs-20110620.

21 Michael Harris, "2 Judges Assail Top State Court," *SFC*, March 9, 1972, 4.

22 "TRIALS: Freed Angela," *Time*, March 5, 1972, http://www.time.com/time/magazine/article/0,9171,910206,00.html. The California Supreme Court soon clarified that bail could still be denied those accused of murder if there was sufficient likelihood of guilt. See *People v. Anderson*, 6 Cal. 3d. 628, 657 fn. 45 ["The issue of the right to bail in cases in which the law has heretofore provided for the death penalty has been raised for the first time by the People and amici curiae on petition for rehearing. . . . The underlying gravity of those offenses endures and the determination of their gravity for the purpose of bail continues unaffected by this decision. Accordingly, to subserve such purpose and subject to our future consideration of this issue in an appropriate proceeding, we hold that they remain as offenses for which bail should be denied in conformity with article I, section 6, of the Constitution and Penal Code section 1270 when the proof of guilt is evident or the presumption thereof great."]

23 "More Threats: Angela Backer Has To Hide Out," *SFC*, March 4, 1972, 2; "Angela's Friend Goes Home," *SFC*, March 9, 1972, 2.

24 Stephen Cook, "Angela Trial Finally Starts Tomorrow," *SFC*, March 27, 1972, 22.

25 In 1970, draftees who opposed the war had successfully lobbied Congress to lower the voting age, arguing that if they were deemed old enough to die for their country in Vietnam, they should also have a say in electing the officeholders whose policies were being defended. Later that year in *Oregon v. Mitchell*, 400 U.S.112 (1970), the Supreme Court held that the new lowered age only applied in federal elections, leaving states free to keep a higher age for state elections. In response, Congress overwhelmingly ratified the 26th Amendment, which granted all eighteen–year-olds the right to vote in both state and federal elections. State legislatures rushed through their own ratification, so the amendment was signed into law in July 1971.

26 Caroline Anspacher, "Search for Angela Jurors Continues," *SFC*, March 9, 1972, 2.

27 Anspacher, "Angela Accepts All-White Jury: Four Men, 8 Women to Try Her," *SFC*, March 16, 1972, 1, 16.

28 "No Delay On Death Penalty Ban," *SFC*, March 21, 1972, 20. See *People v. Anderson*, 6 Cal. 3d. 628, 657 fn. 45, quoted in note 18, above.

29 Keith Power, "A Not Guilty Verdict for the Soledad Brothers: Trial in Slaying of Guard," *SFC*, March 28, 1972, 1, 22.

30 Reginald Major, *Justice in the Round: The Trial of Angela Davis* (New York: The Third Press, 1973), 174.

31 Joy James, "Opening Defense Statement Presented by Angela Y. Davis in Santa Clara County Superior Court," March 29, 1972, *The Angela Y. Davis Reader* (Malden, MA: Blackwell Publishers, 1998), Appendix, 334.

32 Durden-Smith, *Who Killed George Jackson?*, 142.

33 James, ed., *The Angela Y. Davis Reader*, Appendix, 335.

34 *Ibid.*, 337.

35 Bettina Aptheker, *The Morning Breaks: The Trial of Angela Davis* (New York: International Publishers, 1975), 196.

36 Major, *Justice in the Round: The Trial of Angela Davis* (New York: The Third Press, 1973), 226.

37 Durden-Smith, *Who Killed George Jackson?*, 133.

38 "Trial of 2 Suspects in Carr Slaying," *SFC*, April 27, 1972, 4. The men were former Black Panthers and were later tried and convicted without evidence of who hired them. In prison, David Hilliard heard accusations from Betsy Carr and others that Huey Newton ordered the hit (*This Side of Glory*, 362, 380), but the widow later acknowledged that the two gunmen could have been secret police agents, agreeing with investigative journalist Jo Durden-Smith that "The whole American left scene of the 60s and early 70s was so riddled with informers and agents provocateurs that [it was impossible to tell]." (James Carr, *Bad: The Autobiography of James Carr* (Oakland: Nabat/AK Press, 2000), Afterword by Betsy Carr, 234).

39 Durden-Smith, *Who Killed George Jackson?*, 122.

40 Carolyn Anspacher, "'Love' Motive Pressed," *SFC*, April 27, 1972, 4; Bettina Aptheker, *The Morning Breaks, The Trial of Angela Davis* (Ithaca, N.Y.: Cornell Univ. Press, 1976), 236.

41 "A Witness's Poor Memory," *SFC*, May 12, 1972, 16.

42 "The Angela Davis Trial," *SFC*, June 2, 1972, 1, 18.

43 "Witness Tells of Angela In Tears," *SFC*, May 24, 1972, 2.

44 Timothy, *Jury Woman*, 230.

45 Major, *Justice in the Round*, 297.

46 Aptheker, *The Morning Breaks*, 273.
47 Major, *Justice in the Round*, 295; "Reagan on the Angela verdict," *SFC*, June 6, 1972, 6.
48 *Ibid.*, 310.
49 Elsie Milne, "A Bitter Reaction by the Marin DA," *SFC*, June 5, 1972.
50 Aptheker, *The Morning Breaks*, 194–195.
51 Kate Coleman, "Elmer 'Geronimo' Pratt: The Untold Story of the Black Panther Leader, Dead At 63," *The New Republic*, June 27, 2011, http://www.tnr.com/article/politics/90735/black-panther-geronimo-pratt-murder-conviction-prison-huey-newton. See also Austin, *Up Against the Wall*, 245.
52 *In re Pratt*, 69 Cal. App. 4th 1294 (1999).
53 Durden-Smith, *Who Killed George Jackson?*, 133.
54 "Ramsey Clark's Plea for Magee," *SFC*, March 24, 1973, 3.
55 "Another Shout: Magee's Case Goes to the Jury," *SFC*, March 27, 1973, 3.
56 "Magee Gets Life Term," *The Milwaukee Journal*, Jan. 23, 1975 (San Jose); "The Men Whose Lives are Worse Than Death," *SFC*, March 23, 1972, 36.
57 Curtis Mullins, "RUCHELL CINQUE MAGEE POLITICAL PRISONER," http://www.itsabouttimebpp.com/political_prisoners/ruchell_cinque_magee-political_prisoner.html; Hans Bennett, Update on Political Prisoner Ruchell Cinque Magee, Nov. 6, 2008, OpEd News, http://www.opednews.com/populum/diarypage.php?did=10653.
58 "Western and Red Press Differ on Angela Verdict," *SFC*, June 6, 1972, 6.
59 *Ibid.*

Part Three, Chapter 5 — *Watergate Overshadows the Cobra*

1 Ronald Garay, "Watergate," Museum of Broadcast Communications, http://www.museum.tv/eotvsection.php?entrycode=watergate.
2 Carroll Kilpatrick, "Nixon Tells Editors 'I am not a crook,'" *Washington Post*, Nov. 18, 1973, AO1, http://www.washingtonpost.com/wp-srv/national/longterm/watergate/articles/111873-1.htm.
3 "American Rhetoric Top 100 Speeches," Barbara Jordan Judiciary Speech, www.americanrhetoric.com/speeches/barbarajordanjudiciarystatement.htm.
4 The History Place: Presidential Impeachment Proceedings http://www.historyplace.com/unitedstates/impeachments/nixon.htm.
5 Keith W. Olson, *Watergate: The Presidential Scandal That Shook America* (Lawrence: Univ. of Kansas Press, 2003).
6 *Sheppard v. Maxwell*, 384 U.S. 333, 348, 357 (1966).
7 165 Ohio St. 293, 294, 135 N.E.2d 340, 342.
8 *Sheppard v. State of Ohio*, 352 US 910 (1956).
9 *Sheppard v. Maxwell*, 384 U.S. 333, 350 (1966).
10 *Sheppard v. Maxwell*, 384 U.S. 333, 355, 360, 362 (1966).
11 *Sheppard v. Maxwell*, 384 U.S. 333, 363 (1966).

Part Three, Chapter 6 — *Downward Spiral*

1 Newton, *To Die For The People* (New York: Random House, 1972), 179.
2 Murray Kempton, *NYT Book Review*, May 20, 1973, 35, 42.
3 Flores Forbes, *Will You Die With Me?: My Life and The Black Panther Party* (New York: Random House, 2006), 76.
4 *Ibid.* 67–68.

5 Robert McG. Thomas, Jr., "Lionel Wilson, 82, A Mayor of Oakland for Three Terms," *NYT*, Jan. 31, 1998, http://www.nytimes.com/1998/01/31/us/lionel-wilson-82-a-mayor-of-oakland-for-three-terms.html.

6 Kate Coleman with Paul Avery, "The Party's Over: How Huey Newton created a street gang at the center of the Black Panther Party," *New Times*, July 10, 1978, 29–30. See also Flores Forbes, *Will You Die with Me? My Life in the Black Panther Party*.

7 Hugh Pearson, *The Shadow of the Panther: Huey Newton and the Price of Black Power in America* (Reading, Mass.: Addison-Wesley, 1994), 264.

8 Dan Flynn, "Panther Leader Seale Confesses," *Front Page*, Front Page Magazine.com, April 23, 2002, http://archive.frontpagemag.com/readArticle.aspx?ARTID=24216.

9 Pearson, *The Shadow of the Panther*, 265.

10 Coleman with Avery, "The Party's Over," 35.

11 *Ibid.* These charges were confirmed in Elaine Brown's and Flores Forbes' autobiographies.

12 The head of the Center for Cuban Studies, who coordinated the visits of many Leftists to Cuba during this time, was Sandra Levinson, a friend of Marvin Stender who first met Charles Garry when she became a witness for the defense in the 1961 "Black Friday" trial of Robert Meisenbach. As mentioned in Part Two, Levinson later co-chaired Eldridge Cleaver's 1968 international fund-raising committee; her apartment in Greenwich Village became the headquarters of *Ramparts'* New York office. Charles Garry often stayed with Levinson during Bobby Seale's New Haven trial. After *Ramparts* folded in 1972, Levinson's apartment remained a gathering place for Panthers.

13 Elaine Brown, *A Taste of Power: A Black Woman's Story* (New York: Anchor Books, 1992), 359.

14 Hilliard, *Huey: Spirit of the Panther*, 157.

15 Liberatore, *The Road to Hell*, 225.

16 At Bingham's trial, neither side called double agent Louis Tackwood, though the defense had apparently planned to do so. (Liberatore, *The Road to Hell*, 224–25). Bingham took the stand before a packed courtroom, denied supplying Jackson with the 9-mm gun, and explained his flight as fear of being wrongly blamed, not evidence of guilt. In key cross-examination, Bingham's lawyer Gerry Schwartzbach got San Quentin guard Bernard Betts to admit that, before letting Bingham take the tape recorder Vanita Anderson had handed to him to take through security to his interview with Jackson, Betts had inspected the machine "fairly closely," including removal of its battery plate cover and saw nothing hidden inside. (Liberatore, *The Road to Hell*, 250–51.) In his closing argument, the prosecutor insisted that Bingham had the only opportunity to supply Jackson with the gun that day. Schwartztbach argued that Bingham was framed, and queried why investigator Vanita Anderson had not been prosecuted. The jury took five days to deliberate upon the circumstantial evidence. Bingham's exoneration left the bloody incident in which George Jackson died still shrouded in mystery. (See Robert Lindsey, "Bingham Case Trial Yields No Answers," *NYT*, July 3, 1986, A18.)

17 Durden-Smith, *Who Killed George Jackson?*, 240.

18 Elaine Brown, *A Taste of Power*, 364.

19 *Ibid.*, 430. As part of his affirmative action plan for changing the face of Oakland's city officials, Wilson did soon institute a nationwide search for a new city manager, looking for a qualified black candidate, but ultimately picked the white city attorney for that role. Contrary to Elaine Brown's expectation, Wilson made no move to oust the white police chief, George Hart, who had replaced Chief Gain in 1973. Hart would serve for

nearly two decades before Wilson's successor appointed the first black chief of police.

20 The source of this observation is EBMUD Director Bill Patterson (not Communist lawyer William Patterson). Bill Patterson was very familiar with the Panthers as the Director of Recreation at De Fremery Park. At the time Wilson first ran for Mayor, Bill Patterson had just stepped down as long-time chair of Alameda County's Juvenile Delinquency Prevention Commission. He later became President of the local NAACP and was later honored as Oakland's Citizen of the Year, among other accolades.

21 Austin, *Up Against the Wall*, 327.

22 "Wilson Pledges to Listen," *OT*, May 18, 1977, 12.

23 "Forward With New Mayor," *OT*, May 18, 1977, 20.

24 Lance Williams, "A Two-Week Wait for Newton," *OT*, July 4, 1973, 1.

25 HPN Foundation, Box 15, Folder 5, Affidavits of David Horowitz and Ericka Huggins in Support of Release on Own Recognizance, July 14, 1977. *People v. Newton*, Oakland Municipal Court, No. 64624A and 65919.

26 The details are included in the autobiography of Flores Forbes, *Will You Die With Me?*, 150, 163 et seq.

27 Kate Coleman, "The Party's Over," *New Times*, July 11, 1978, http://centerforinvestigativereporting.org/articles/thepartysover.

28 "Nation: The Odyssey of Huey Newton" *Time*, Nov. 13, 1978, http://www.time.com/time/magazine/article/0,9171,946144,00.htmlh.

29 Lance Williams, "Newton mistrial declared," *OT*, Sept 26, 1979, 1, A20.

30 Forbes, *Will You Die With Me?*, 214–215.

31 Pearson, *The Shadow of the Panther*, 286, 288. The thesis was republished with a foreword by his widow several years after his death: Huey Newton, *War Against the Panthers: A Study of Repression in America* (New York & London: Harlem River Press, 1996).

32 Hilliard, *This Side of Glory*, 1.

33 Wiliam Brand and Larry Spears, "Friends and foes remember Newton 'visionary,' 'thug,'" *OT*, Aug. 23, 1989, 2.

34 Brenda Payton "Black Panthers failed to learn lessons of history," *OT*, Aug. 23, 1989, 1, 2.

35 Unperturbed by Newton's boast in July 1977 that he intended to rid Oakland of drug dealers, Mitchell presided over a growing Oakland-based empire for several more years before he was convicted in federal court in 1985 and knifed to death at Leavenworth Prison the following year. Like Newton, Mitchell had generously supported community projects. Astounded television viewers worldwide watched clips of Mitchell's horse-drawn funeral carriage and more than a dozen limousines caravanning—with proper city permits—from the 69th Avenue housing project where the "Robin Hood of the Hood" grew up to the Baptist Church where his services were held in nearby Emeryville.

36 Pearson, *The Shadow of the Panther*, 322–324.

37 Bill Snyder and Michael Collier, "Newton laid to rest: Many former Black Panthers attend rites," *OT*, Aug. 29, 1989, 1.

38 Pacifica radio KPFA, Huey P. Newton funeral transcripts, http://www.lib.berkeley.edu/MRC/netwonfuneraltranscripts.html.

39 *Ibid.*, 327–328.

PART THREE CHAPTER 7 — *A Closer Look at the Competition*

1 Otto Friedrich, Roger Kaplan and Raji Samgaba, "Not Guilty," *Time*, June 29, 1987, http://www.time.com/time/magazine/article/0,9171,964773,00.

2 Mark S. Felton, "The New York City Transit Authority in the 1980s" (2005), http://www.nycsubway.org/articles/history-nycta1980s.html.

3 Stanley Crouch, "The Joy of Goetz: There Was A Moment In Bullied-By-Thugs, Pre-Rudy New York When Even This Creep Was A Hero," http://nymag.com/nymetro/news/anniversary/35th/n_8601/.

4 *The People of the State of New York v. Bernhard Goetz*, 68 N.Y. 2d 96, 101 (July 8, 1986).

5 Robert McFadden, "POLL INDICATES HALF OF NEW YORKERS SEE CRIME AS CITY'S CHIEF PROBLEM," *NYT*, January 14, 1985, 1.

6 Stanley Crouch, "The Joy of Goetz: There Was A Moment In Bullied-By-Thugs, Pre-Rudy New York When Even This Creep Was A Hero," http://nymag.com/nymetro/news/anniversary/35th/n_8601/.

7 *Ibid.*

8 *The People of the State of New York v. Bernhard Goetz*, 68 N.Y. 2d 96, 102 (July 8, 1986).

9 *Ibid.*

10 Knappman, *Great American Trials*, 751.

11 *Ibid.*, 753.

12 Otto Friedrich, Roger Kaplan and Raji Samgaba, "Not Guilty," *Time*, June 29, 1987.

13 http://www.time.com/time/magazine/article/0,9171,964773-1,00.html. "Goetz Verdict Will Endanger Young Black Males, Leaders Say," *Jet Magazine*, Vol. 72, No. 15, July 6, 1987, 18; see also David Pitt, "Blacks See Goetz Verdict as Blow to Race Relations," *NYT*, June 18, 1987, A1, 33.

14 Sarah Lyall, "N.A.A.C.P. LEADER SEEKS FEDERAL CASE ON GOETZ," *NYT*, June 20, 1987, http://query.nytimes.com/gst/fullpage.html?res=9B0DE0DC1E31F933A15755C0A961948260.

15 Jan Hoffman, "Goetz Defense Opens, Calls Jimmy Breslin and a Psychiatrist, Then Closes," *NYT*, April 18, 1996, http://query.nytimes.com/gst/fullpage.html?res=9800E6DA1E39F93BA25757C0A960958260.

16 Nancy Grace, "Larry King Live," "Interview with 'Subway Vigilante' Bernhard Goetz," aired Dec. 17, 2004, http://transcripts.cnn.com/TRANSCRIPTS/0412/17lkl.01 .html.

17 "Top and Bottom 25 Cities Overall" 2010, http://www.morganquitno.com/cit05pop.htm.

18 Janet Gilmore, "New research reveals historic 1990s US crime decline," Feb. 16, 2007, citing to Frank Zimring, *The Great American Crime Decline*, http://www.eurekalert.org/pub_releases/2007-02/uoc—nrr021207.php.

19 *The Austin Criminal Defense Lawyer*, "The Bernie Goetz Story: 25 Years Later April 7, 2010, http://www.austincriminaldefenselawyer.com/2010/04/07/the-bernie-goetz-story-25-years-later.html.

20 "[W]e got too damn many urban thugs, yo, ruining the quality of life for everybody. And I'll tell you what it's gonna take. You people, you are—you need to have a gun. You need to have training. You need to know how to use that gun. You need to get a permit to carry that gun. And you do in fact need to carry that gun and we need to see some dead thugs littering the landscape in Atlanta. We need to see the next guy that tries to carjack you shot dead right where he stands. We need more dead thugs in this city. And let their —let their mommas—let their mommas say, 'He was a good boy. He just fell in with the good [sic] crowd.' And then lock her ass up." Neal Boortz, "We Got Too Damn Many Urban Thugs, Yo . . . We Need More Dead Thugs [in Atlanta]. Cox Radio Syndicated, "Neal Boortz Show," June 14, 2011, http://mediamatters.org/mmtv/201106140022.

[21] Robert Reinhold, "The Longest Trial—A Post-Mortem; Collapse of Child-Abuse Case: So Much Agony for So Little," *NYT*, Jan. 24, 1990, 1.

[22] Dershowitz, *America on Trial*, 486.

[23] *Ibid.*, 462.

[24] Amanda Milkovits "Before O. J. It Was 'THE' Trial of the Century," http://www.hampton.lib.nh.us/hampton/biog/pamsmart/beforeoj.htm.

[25] Theo Wilson, *Headline Justice: Inside the Courtroom—The Country's Most Controversial Trials* (New York: Thunder's Mouth Press 1996), 4.

[26] Wilson, *Headline Justice*, 4.

[27] Geis and Bienen, *Crimes of the Century: From Leopold and Loeb to O. J. Simpson*, 6, quoting journalist Ralph Frammolino.

[28] Gerald Uelmen, "The Lawyer of the Century" (Jan. 2000), Dershowitz, *America on Trial*, Appendix I, The Trials of The Century.

[29] Daniel J. Lanahan, *Justice For All: Legendary Trials of the Twentieth Century* (Bloomington, IN: Author House, 2006).

[30] Lisa Paddock, Introduction to Knappman, ed., *Great American Trials From Salem Witchcraft to Rodney King*, xlvi.

[31] *Ibid.*, 586.

[32] Linder, "Famous Trials: The Scopes Trial, Today Survey," http://www.law.umkc.edu/faculty/projects/trials/scopes/Todaysurvey.html, Appendix A.

[33] David Brock, *Blinded by the Right: The Conscience of an Ex-Conservative* (New York: Crown Publishers, 2002).

[34] Dershowitz, *America on Trial*, The Clinton Impeachment Trial, 522–23.

[35] *Rubenstein (aka Ruby) v. State of Texas* (1966) 407 S. W. 2d. 793, 796.

[36] Michael Newton, *The Encyclopedia of Unsolved Crimes*, 153.

[37] *Ibid.*, 160.

[38] Among books espousing conspiracy theories are Philip Melanson and William Klaber, *Shadow Play—The Untold Story of the Robert F. Kennedy Assassination* (New York: St. Martin's Press, 1997); James DiEugenio and Lisa Pease, *The Assassinations—Probe Magazine on JFK, MLK, RFK and Malcolm X* (Los Angeles: Feral House, 2003); William Turner, *Rearview Mirror—Looking Back At The FBI, The CIA and Other Tails* (New York: Penmarin Books, 2001); Peter Evans, *Nemesis: Aristotle Onassis, Jackie O, And The Love Triangle That Brought Down The Kennedys* (New York: Harper Collins, 2004); and Shane O'Sullivan, *Who Killed Bobby?: The Unsolved Murder of Robert F. Kennedy* (New York: Union Square Press, 2008).

[39] Robert Jablon, "Attorney Says Sirhan Didn't Kill Robert Kennedy," *Daily Breeze*, June 6, 2003, Daily Breeze.com, http://nl.newsbank.com/.

[40] Linda Deutsch, "Sirhan says he was under mind control," Assoc. Press, *OT*, April 29, 2011, 1–2.

[41] "NBC Today Show," transcript of broadcast of debate on "THE" Trial of the Century, National Broadcast Co., Inc., Feb. 2, 1999, 29.

[42] *Ibid.*

[43] Uelmen, *Lessons Learned From the Trial*, 55.

[44] Robert Lindsey, "Dan White, Killer of San Francisco Mayor, A Suicide" *NYT*, Oct. 22, 1985.

[45] John L. Burris, "This is America: You Deserve Justice," http://www.johnburrislaw.com/CM/Custom/Commentary.asp, summarizing his 1999 book, *Blue v. Black: Let's End The Conflict Between Cops and Minorities*.

[46] Analysis of the O. J. Simpson Murder Trial: Time to Go Home, http://www.trutv.com/li

brary/crime/notorious_murders/famous/simpson/home_15.html. Prof. Uelmen was the proud author of "if it doesn't fit, you must acquit."

47 Uelmen, *Lessons Learned From the Trial,* 2.

48 Linder, "Famous Trials: The O. J. Simpson Trial," http://www.law.umkc.edu/faculty/projects/ftrials/Simpson/polls.html.

49 "NBC News Poll 10 Years after Simpson verdict: Issue of Race still figures prominently in public opinion," http://www.msnbc.msn.com/id/5139346/.

50 The Oklahoma City Police Department official "After Action Report" on the Alfred P. Murrah Federal Building Bombing states that the bomb destroyed or damaged 324 buildings and 86 cars within a sixteen-block radius and shattered glass in 258 nearby buildings, http://replay.waybackmachine.org/20070703233435/http://www.terrorisminfo.mipt.org/pdf/okcfr_App_C.pdf.

51 Peter Applebome, "TERROR IN OKLAHOMA: THE BACKGROUND; A Bombing Foretold, In Extreme-Right 'Bible,'" *NYT,* April 26, 1995, http://nytimes.com/gst/fullpage.html?res=990CE7D7143CF935A15757C0A963958260.

52 See "Waco Siege the Final Assault," Museum Stuff.com, citing Michael McNulty,"Waco: An Apparent Deviation," criticized the editing in "Waco: The Big Lie" for serious distortions of the event, http://www.museumstuff.com/learn/topics/Waco_Siege::sub::The_Final_Assault.

53 Anti-Defamation League, "The Militia Movement—Extremism in America—ADL," http://www.adl.org/learn/ext_us/militia_m.asp?xpicked=4&item=19.

54 "McVeigh Considered Assassination of Reno, Other Officials," *Fox News,* April 27, 2001,http://www.foxnews.com/story/0,2933,17501,00.html.

55 *Andrade v. Chojnacki,* 338 F.3d 448 (5th Cir. 2003), cert. denied (2004).

56 Linder, "Famous Trials: The Oklahoma City Bombing & The Trial of Timothy McVeigh," 2006, http://law2.umkc.edu/faculty/projects/ftrials/mcveigh/mcveighaccount.html.

57 Michael Tigar and Angela J. Davis, ed., *Trial Stories* (New York: Foundation Press, 2008).

58 Meredith Simons, "FBI watching for 'homegrown' terrorists," *Houston Chronicle,* Washington Bureau, Sept. 30, 2009, http://www.chron.com/disp/story.mpl/metropolitan/6645914.html.

59 "Active U.S. Hate Groups," Intelligence Report, Southern Poverty Law Center, http://www.splcenter.org/get-informed/hate-map; "About the Ku Klux Klan—Extremism in America," Anti-Defamation League, http://www.adl.org/learn/ext_us/kkk/default.asp.

60 Linder, "Famous Trials: What is THE trial of the Century?," http://www.law.umkc.edu/faculty/projects/ftrials/century.html.

61 Marjorie Cohn, "Legendary Lawyer Doris Brin Walker Dies; Represented Angela Davis, Smith Act Defendants," August 16, 2009, http://www.marjoriecohn.com/2009/08/legendary-lawyer-doris-brin-walker-dies.html.

62 Sara Lawrence Lightfoot, *I've Known Rivers: Lives of Loss and Liberation* (Reading, Mass.: Addison-Wesley Pub., 1994),147–148, 158.

63 Peter Collier and David Horowitz, *Destructive Generation: Second Thoughts About the Sixties* (New York: Summit Books, 1989) 30.

PART THREE, CHAPTER 8 — *The Precarious Path to a Bi-Racial President*

1 "American Rhetoric, Barbara Jordan 1976 Speech at Democratic Convention," http://www.americanrhetoric.com/speeches/barbarajordan1976dnc.html. The prime time speaking slot offered to Barack Obama in 2004—which insiders dubbed the "Barbara

Jordan Project"—resulted from the efforts of three highly influential black Democrats, including Al Gore's 2000 Campaign Director Donna Brazile, to catapult another rising star to national attention just as former President Lyndon Johnson had engineered that of Jordan as his protégée.

2 Irving Wallace, *The Man*, paperback (Fawcett Crest, 1969).

3 Hanes Walton, Jr., *Black Political Parties: An Historical and Political Analysis* (New York: The Free Press, 1972) publisher's note, inside jacket cover.

4 Editorial Insert to the Lexington, Kentucky, *Herald Leader*, July 4, 2004, 1.

5 Jack Bass, "Documenting the Orangeburg Massacre," http://www.orangeburgmassacre 1968.com/docs/NiemanReport.pdf.

6 Warren Hinckle, *If You Have A Lemon, Make Lemonade* (New York: W.W. Norton, 1973), 30.

7 Bob Herbert,"What Color Is That Baby?," *NYT* editorial page, May 11, 2009.

8 481 U.S. 279 at 313 (1987).

9 Adam Liptak, "David C. Baldus,75, Dies; Studied Race and the Law,"*NYT*, June 15, 2011, A23, referencing John C. Jeffries, Jr.'s *Justice Lewis F. Powell, Jr.: A Biography*, 451 (1994).

10 See, e.g., Anthony Amsterdam, "Race and the Death Penalty Before and After *McCleskey*," *Columbia Human Rights Law Review* 39: 34 (2007); Steven Graines and Justin Wyatt, "The Rehnquist Court, Legal Process Theory, and *McCleskey v. Kemp*," *American Journal of Criminal Law* 28: 1 (2000).

11 Gwen Ifill, *The Breakthrough: Politics and Race in the Age of Obama* (New York: Random House, Anchor Books, 2009), 148.

12 Raiford, *Imprisoned in a Luminous Glare*, 210.

13 Kate Taylor, "The Thorny Path to a National Black Museum," *NYT*, Jan. 23, 2011, 1, 22.

14 Lori Olszewski and Rick Delvecchio, "Huey Newton Shot Dead on West Oakland Street: Black Panther Co-Founder Slain at 47," *SFC*, August 23, 1989, 1.

15 Pearson, *The Shadow of the Panther*, 340.

16 *Ibid.*

17 See "Black People who Changed the World," Norfolk Black History Month.org, http://www.norfolkblackhistorymonth.org.uk/contact.html.

18 Jane Rhodes, *Framing the Black Panthers: The Spectacular Rise of a Black Power Icon* (New York: The New Press, 2007), 3.

19 Chris Rhomberg, *No There There: Race, Class, and Political Community in Oakland* (Berkeley: University of California Press, 2004), 155.

20 Eldridge Cleaver, "Newton on trial," *Ramparts*, Fall 1968, 23, "Yes Huey is our Jesus, but we want him down from the cross."

21 Lucas, *Big Trouble*, 151. Yet the WFM did not take an extreme racist position. Other unions of that era had racial exclusion as a fundamental provision in their charters or developed racist strategies to keep African-Americans or Asian-Americans from competing in their labor markets. In contrast, the International Workers of the World that Haywood helped found adopted an express policy of inclusion of all workers as did a handful of other Progressive unions. But the WFM was not among them.

22 Palavi Gogoi, "Where are the jobs? For many companies, overseas," Associated Press, http://www.usatoday.com/money/economy/2010-12-28-jobs-overseas_N.htm. As the article notes, the chief economist at Standard & Poor's pointed out that half of the recent revenue for companies listed in the top 500 in 2009 and 2010 came from outside the country.

23 Russell, *Sacco and Vanzetti: The Case Resolved*, 139.

24 Austin, *Up Against the Wall*, 168.

[25] Anderson, *The Movement and the Sixties*, 225; Robert Dallek, *Flawed Giant* (New York: Oxford Univ. Press, 1998), 573; White, *The Making of the President 1968*, 305.

[26] Editorial, "The 'Free Huey' Demonstrations," *SFE*, September 10, 1968, 32.

[27] David Horowitz, *hating whitey and other progressive causes* (Dallas: Spence Pub. Co., 1999), 213.

[28] Kristin Bender, "Black Panther Party co-founder Bobby Seale speaks in Berkeley," *OT*, Feb. 2, 2009.

[29] Ronald V. Dellums and H. Lee Halterman, *Lying Down with the Lions* (Boston, Beacon Press, 2000), 50.

[30] *SFC*, March 28, 2009, A11.

[31] It made front-page news again in Oakland when Mehserle was released on June 13, 2011 (with credit for time served on his two-year term). At his attorneys' request, Mehserle had remained in the Los Angeles County Jail and in isolation for safety reasons. The federal civil suit for damages remains pending, as does his appeal. Paul T. Rosynsky, "Mehserle now a free man," *OT*, June 14, 2011, 1, 7.

[32] David Remnick, *THE BRIDGE: The Life and Rise of Barack Obama* (New York: Random House, Knopf, Borzoi Books, 2010), 285.

[33] *Mumia Abu-Jamal a/k/a Wesley Cook v. Sec'y, PA Dept of Corrections et al.* (3d. Cir. April 27, 2011) No. 01-9014, http://www.ca3.uscourts.gov/opinarch/01-9014p2.pdf.

[34] Barbara Ehrenreich and Dedrick Muhammad, "The Recession's Racial Divide," *NYT*, Sept. 13, 2009, *The Week In Review*, 17.

[35] Charles M. Blow, "Black in the Age of Obama," *NYT*, Dec. 5, 2009, A 19.

[36] Norman Lear (creator), "All in the Family" (1971) Memorable Quotes, Internet Movie Database http://www.imdb.com/title/tt0066626/quotes.

[37] Toby Harnden, "Barack Obama faces 30 death threats a day, stretching US Secret Service," *The Telegraph*, Aug. 3, 2009, http://www.telegraph.co.uk/news/worldnews/barackobama/5967942/Barack-Obama-faces-30-death-threats-a-day-stretching-US-Secret-Service.html.

[38] Ifill, *The Breakthrough*, 17, quoting a 2008 personal interview.

[39] John Wojcik, COMMENTARY Holocaust Museum, "Dr. Tiller: Janet Napolitano saw it coming," June 12, 2009, www.peoplesworld.org/commentary-holocaust-museum-drtiller-janet-napolitano-saw-it-coming/.

[40] Ehrenreich and Muhammad, "The Recession's Racial Divide," *NYT*, Sept. 13, 2009, *The Week In Review*, 17.

[41] Robert Costa "Gingrich: "Obama's Kenyan, anticolonial world view," September 11, 2010, The Corner, http://www.nationalreview.com/corner/246302/gingrich-obamas-kenyan-anti-colonial-worldview-robert-costa. Gingrich used his platform on the anniversary of 9/11 to call attention to the thesis of conservative educator Dinesh D'Souza's controversial new book published later that month, *The Roots of Obama's Rage* (Washington, D.C.: Regnery Pub., 2010) attacking Obama as a dangerous reincarnation of his father and calling for the election of a new President.

[42] Steven Harmon, "State Democrats rage over GOP's treatment of Obama," *OT*, May 2, 2011, A11.

[43] David Weigel,"Black Swan: 'The surprise rise of Herman Cain has the Tea Party asking: "Who's racist now?"," Oct. 14, 2011 http://www.slate.com/articles/news_and_politics/politics/2011/10/herman_cain_campaign_does_it_prove_the_tea_party_isn_t_racist_.html. Steele added, "People [in the Republican Party] need to be careful, not to come at this [Cain candidacy] with the attitude that it's going to fix their image.

It's offensive to Herman. It's offensive to me as an African-American." *Ibid.* See also http://wonkette.com/414991/michael-steele-admits-gop-has-been-strategically-racist-for-40-years-hooray.

44 Joanna Weiss, "How Obama and the Radical Became News," *BG*, April 18, 2008, http://www.boston.com/news/nation/articles/2008/04/18/how_obama_and_the_radical_became_news/.

45 Remnick, *THE BRIDGE*, 281.

46 This is a frequently cited quote from Stanford Univ. History Professor Clayborne Carson, general editor of *The Eyes on the Prize Civil Rights Reader: Documents, Speeches, and Firsthand Accounts from the Black Freedom Struggle.* See, e.g., DocuWatch, "America: Eyes on the Prize," http://america.docuwat.ch/videos/eyes-on-the-prize/eyes-on-the-prize-02-fighting-back-1957-1962.

47 Hank De Zutter, "What Makes Obama Run?" *Chicago Reader*, Dec. 8, 1995, http://www.chicagoreader.com/chicago/what-makes-obama-run/Content?oid=889221.

48 Michael Weisskopf, "Obama: How He Learned to Win," *Time*, May 8, 2008, http://www.time.com/time/magazine/article/0,9171,1738494,00.html.

49 Ifill, *The Breakthrough*, 45.

50 See, e.g., Horowitz, *hating whitey and other progressive causes*, 6.

51 Mark Mooney, ABC News, "Obama Aide Concedes 'Dollar Bill' Remark Referred to His Race: Obama Strategist Calls McCain's Attack Ad Insulting; McCain Camp Defends It," Aug. 1, 2008, http://abcnews.go.com/GMA/Politics/story?id=5495348&page=1.

52 Ben Smith, "McCain calls Obama decent person, is booed," Politico.com, Oct. 10, 2008, http://www.politico.com/blogs/bensmith/1008/McCain_calls_Obama_decent_person_is_booed.htmlPolitico.

53 Matthew Barakat, "Al-Qaida inmate gets access to Obama's books," Associated Press, July 20, 2009, http://hosted.ap.org/dynamic/stories/U/US_SUPERMAX_OBAMAS_BOOKS_COOL-?; "Obama books OK'd for inmates," *Los Angeles Times*, July 11, 1990, A14.

54 Ifill, *The Breakthrough*, 30, 35, 45, 69. Ifill attributes coinage of the term "supraracial" to Obama's mentor Dean Christopher Edley of U.C. Berkeley's Boalt Hall. Obama critic Dinesh D'Souza applauded the supraracial approach. D'Souza, a longtime opponent of affirmative action, authored *T-he End of Racism* (New York: Free Press Paperbacks, 1995) to rebut Cornel West's new book, *Race Matters* (New York: Vintage Books, 1994).

55 Lou Dubose, ed., "BlackPanthergate?," *The Washington Spectator*, Feb. 1, 2011, Vol. 37, No. 2, 4.

56 See, e.g., Josh Gerstein, "Hillary Clinton's Radical Summer: A Season of Love and Leftists," *The New York Sun*, Nov. 26, 2007, www.mysun.com/national/hillary-clintons-radical-summer/66933/.

57 "Frederick Douglass, the Accurate 'Without Struggle/No Freedom' Quote, "http://www.buildingequality.us/Quotes/Frederick_Douglass.htm. For discussion of Douglass's close ties with John Brown, see Julius Thompson, James L. Conyers, Jr., and Nancy J, Dawson, eds, *The Frederick Douglass Encyclopedia* (Santa Barbara: Greenwood Press, 2010), 4.

58 Marlin Foxworth, Ph.D. and Ralph Gordon, *The Black/White Divide in America . . . Still: The Inherent Contradiction in Partial Equality* (Berkeley: Regent Press, 2008), 26.

59 David Horowitz, *Left Illusions: An Intellectual Odyssey*, IV Reflections on Race, Chapter 18, "Racism and Free Speech" (Dallas: Spence Publishing Co., 2003), 187, fn. 14.

60 *Brown v. Plata*, 563 U.S.___ (2011), 1313 Sup. Ct. 1910. The court was bitterly divided, with the dissent especially criticizing the decision to uphold the lower court's requirement that California reduce the number of prisoners to 137.5% of design capacity

within two years or house the excess inmates in new construction.

61 Michelle Alexander, *The New Jim Crow: Mass Incarceration in the Age of Color Blindness* (New Press, 2010), ISBN 978-1-59558103-7, Kindle location 2355–2361; http://www.disinfo.com/2011/04/more-black-men-now-in-prison-system-than-were-enslaved-before-the-civil-war-began/; "Obama's America and the New Jim Crow: The Recurring Racial Nightmare, The Cyclical Rebirth of Caste," quoted at http://nathanielturner.com/obamasamericaandnewjimcrow.htm.

62 "U.S. Leads The World In Illegal Drug Use: Survey Says People With Higher Incomes More Likely To Use Legal And Illegal Drugs, Marijuana Use Widely Reported," "CBS News," July 1, 2008, http://www.cbsnews.com/stories/2008/07/01/health/webmd/main4222322.shtml. See Michelle Alexander's *The New Jim Crow, supra*, Chapter Three, "The Color of Justice." Alexander summarizes a number of studies that evidence extraordinary percentages of African-Americans imprisoned for drug crimes in recent decades. Human Rights Watch reported that in 2000 blacks comprised 80 to 90 percent of imprisoned drug offenders in several states and were incarcerated at rates far exceeding their percentage of the offending population in many more. That same year, the National Institute on Drug Abuse reported that white students used both cocaine and heroin at seven times the rate of black students; another study showed that white teenagers were significantly more likely to sell drugs than black students.

63 "Current Drug Use Statistics in America," An Initiative of the Foundation for Social Improvement, 2011, Drug-Free Alliance, http://www.drug-freealliance.org/drug-information.html.

64 Earl Ofari Hutchinson, "Why Obama Won't Pardon Jack Johnson," *Friendly Fire*, The Daily News Opinion Blog, Feb. 13, 2010, http://www.insidesocal.com/friendlyfire/2010/02/why-obama-wont-pardon-jack-joh.html.

65 The Sentencing Project: Research and Advocacy for Reform, http://www.sentencingproject.org/template/page.cfm?id=133.

66 Gail Russell Chaddock, "U.S. Notches World's Highest Incarceration Rate," *The Christian Science Monitor*, Aug. 18, 2003. Chaddock adds, quoting Marc Mauer as spokesman for The Sentencing Project in Washington, D.C.: "These new [incarceration] numbers are shocking enough, but what we don't see are the ripple effects of what they mean." http://www.csmonitor.com/2003/0818/p02s01-usju.html.

67 Alexander, *The New Jim Crow*, Kindle location 161.

68 Newt Gingrich and Pat Nolan, "Prison reform: A smart way for states to save money and lives," *The Washington Post*, Jan. 7, 2011, http://www.washingtonpost.com/wp-dyn/content/article/2011/01/06/AR2011010604386.html.

69 Knappman, ed., *Great American Trials*, Introduction by editor Lisa Paddock, xli.

70 Celia Rosebury, "Black Liberation on Trial: The Case of Huey Newton," reprint by the Bay Area Committee to Defend Political Freedom, Berkeley, CA, 1968, from articles originally appearing during the summer of 1968 in *The People's World*, 19. Archives of the Oakland, CA, African-American Museum and Library, Black Panther Collection.

71 Murray Kempton, "Revolutionary Suicide," *NYT Book Review*, May 20, 1973, 35, 39.

SOURCES

INDIVIDUALS:

Among those who graciously gave of their time for interviews and background information in person, by telephone and via e-mail were Anthony Amsterdam, Hon. Richard Arnason, Ed Bell, Bernhard E. Bergeson, III, Stephen Bingham, Robert Blauner, Bergliot Bornholdt, Thomas Broome, Allan Brotsky, Malcolm Burnstein, Deborah Chase, Kathleen Cleaver, Kate Coleman, Penny Cooper, Steve and Bari Cornet, Fania Davis, Joan De La Sceaux, Henry and Evelyn Elson, Peter Franck, Gordon Gaines, Ann Fagan Ginger, David Lance Goines, Brian Gluss, David Greenberg, Dag Hamilton, Milton Hare, Hon. Thelton Henderson, Hilde Stern Hein, Ezra Herndon, Jonathan Hiatt, David Hilliard, Alex Hoffmann, David Horowitz, Howard Janssen, Don Jelinek, Hon. D. Lowell Jensen, Don Kerson, Ying Lee Kelley, Kumasi, Sandra Levinson, Michael Magbie, Marling Mast, Michael McCarthy, Jerrie Meadows, Hon. Marilyn Patel, William B. Patterson, Sheriff Charles Plummer, Dru Stender Ramey, Robert Richter, Jae Scharlin, Bobby Seale, Dan Siegel, Hon. Richard Silver, Damon Silvers, Marvin Stender, Elise Stone, Peter Sussman, Hon. John Sutter (ret.), Hon. Jacqueline Taber, Michael Tigar, Morrie Turner, Karen Lee Wald, Doris Brin Walker, Doron Weinberg, David Wellman, John Wells, Jayne Williams, Laura X, and Philip Ziegler.

SPECIAL COLLECTIONS:

Black Panther Collection, archives of the African American Museum and Library, Oakland, California.

Department of Justice FBI FOIA Files: The Black Panther Party, Huey Newton, Fay Stender, Student Nonviolent Coordinating Committee.

Don Hausler, unpublished manuscript, *Blacks in Oakland 1852–1987,* Vol. 3, 113, 116. Oakland Public Library History Room.

Dr. Huey P. Newton Foundation, Inc. Collection 1968–1994, M864. California: Green Library Special Collections, Stanford University.

U.C. Berkeley Bancroft Library: Meiklejohn Civil Liberties Archives; Elsa Knight Thompson papers.

PRIVATE COLLECTIONS:

Trial notes of Prof. Robert Blauner from *People v. Newton,* 1968; files of Hon. Richard Silver from his representation of Soledad Brother Fleeta Drumgo; correspondence, documents, and magazine and newspaper clippings of Bergliot Bornholdt, Priscilla Camp, Marvin Stender, Elise Stone, and Laura X; Peter Sussman collection of unpublished letters of Jessica Mitford; newspaper clippings and notes of freelance reporter Karen Wald.

PRINCIPAL NEWSPAPER AND PERIODICAL SOURCES:

American Civil Liberties Northern California News, Atlanta Constitution, Berkeley Barb, Black Panther newspaper, *New York Times, Oakland Post, Oakland Tribune, Ramparts* magazine, *San Francisco Chronicle, San Francisco Examiner, Time* magazine.

BOOKS:

Acker, James R., *Scottsboro and Its Legacy* (Westport, Ct.: Praeger Publishing, 2008).

Addams, Jane, *Twenty Years at Hull House* (New York: The MacMillan Co., 1910).

Ahlgren, G., and Monier, S., *The Crime of the Century: The Lindbergh Kidnapping Hoax* (Boston: Brandon Books, 1993).

Alef, D., "William Randolph Hearst: Media Myth and Mystique," *Titans of Fortune*, ISBN:9781608041596, 2010.

Alexander, M., *The New Jim Crow: Mass Incarceration in the Age of Color Blindness* (New York: New Press, 2010).

Armstrong, Gregory, *The Dragon Has Come.* New York: Harper & Row, 1974.

Anderson, T., *The Movement and the Sixties: Protest in America from Greensboro to Wounded Knee* (New York: Oxford University Press, 1995).

Aptheker, Bettina, *The Morning Breaks: The Trial of Angela Davis* (New York: International Publishers, Co. Inc., 1975).

Armstrong, Gregory, *The Dragon Has Come* (New York: Harper & Row, 1974).

Auerbach, Jerold S., *Unequal Justice: Lawyers and Social Change in Modern America* (New York: Oxford Univ. Press, 1976).

Austin, Curtis, J., *Up Against the Wall* (Fayetteville: Univ. of Arkansas Press, 2006).

Avrich, Paul, *Sacco and Vanzetti: The Anarchist Background* (Princeton: Princeton Univ. Press, 1991).

Baatz, S., *For the Thrill of It: Leopold, Loeb and the Murder that Shocked Chicago* (New York: Harper Collins, 2008).

Blackmon, Douglas A., *Slavery by Another Name: The Re-Enslavement of Black Americans from the Civil War to World War II* (New York: Anchor Books, 2009).

Blum, H., *American Lightning: Terror, Mystery, the Birth of Hollywood and the Crime of the Century* (New York: Crown Publishers, 2008).

Boyle, K., *Arc of Justice: A Saga of Race, Civil Rights and Murder in the Jazz Age* (New York: Henry Holt & Co., 2004).

Brock, David, *Blinded by the Right: The Conscience of an Ex-Conservative* (New York: Crown Publishers, 2002).

Broussard, A. S., *Black San Francisco: The Struggle for Racial Equality In the West, 1900–1954* (Lawrence, Kansas: University Press of Kansas, 1993).

Brown, Elaine, *A Taste of Power: A Black Woman's Story* (New York: Anchor Books, Doubleday, 1992).

Bugliosi, Vincent, and Gentry, Curt, *Helter Skelter: The True Story of The Manson*

Murders (New York: W.W. Norton & Co., 1974).

Burris, John, *Blue v. Black: Let's End The Conflict Between Cops and Minorities* (New York: St. Martin's Press, 1997).

Cahn, William, *A Pictorial History of American Labor* (New York: Crown Publishers, 1972).

Carlson, P., *Roughneck: The Life and Times of Big Bill Haywood* (New York: W.W. Norton & Co., 1983).

Carr, James, *Bad: The Autobiography of James Carr* (Oakland: Nabat/AK Press, 2000).

Carroll, P. N., and Noble, D. W., *The Free and the Unfree: A Progressive History of the United States* (New York: Penguin Books, 2001, 3d rev. ed.).

Carson, Clayborne, *In Struggle: SNCC and the Black Awakening of the 1960s* (Cambridge, Massachusetts: Harvard Univ. Press, 1981, 1995).

Carson, C., Garrow, D. J., Gill, G., Harding, V., and Hine, D. C., *The Eyes on the Prize Civil Rights Reader* (New York: Penguin Books, 1991).

Chapman, Maria, *The Liberty Bell: Testimony against Slavery* (Whitefish, Montana: Kessinger Publishing, 2007).

Churchill, W. and Vanderwall, J., *Agents of Repression: The FBI's Secret Wars Against the Black Panther Party and the American Indian Movement* (Boston: South End Press, 1988, 1990).

Churchill, W., and Vanderwall, J., *The COINTELPRO Papers: Documents from the FBI's Secret War Against Dissidents* (Boston: South End Press, 1980).

Cleaver, Eldridge, *Target Zero: A Life In Writing* (New York: Palgrave Macmillan, 2006).

Clinton, Bill, *My Life* (New York: Alfred A. Knopf, 2004).

Cobb, James C., *Georgia Odyssey: A Short History of the State* (Atlanta: Univ. of Georgia Press, 2008).

Cohen, R., *Tough Jews: Fathers, Sons, and Gangster Dreams* (London: Vintage Books, 1999).

Collier, Peter, and Horowitz, David, *Destructive Generation: A Second Look at the Sixties* (New York: Summit Books, 1989).

Curriden, M., and Phillips, J. L., *Contempt of Court: The Turn-of-the-Century Lynching that Launched a Hundred Years of Federalism* (New York: Anchor Books, 2001).

Dallek, Robert, *Flawed Giant* (New York: Oxford Univ. Press, 1998).

Darrow, Clarence, *The Story of My Life* (New York: Da Capo, 1996).

Davies, David R. (ed.), *The Press and Race* (Jackson, Mississippi: Univ. Press of Mississippi, 2001).

Dellums, R. V., and Halterman, H. L., *Lying Down with the Lions* (Boston: Beacon Press, 2000).

Dershowitz, A. M., *America on Trial: Inside The Legal Battles That Transformed Our Nation* (New York: Warner Books, 2004).

Dinnerstein, Leonard, *The Leo Frank Case* (Atlanta: The Univ. of Georgia Press, 2008).

D'Souza, Dinesh, *The Roots of Obama's Rage* (Washington, D.C.: Regnery Pub., 2010).

Dudziak, M. L., *Cold War Civil Rights* (Princeton, New Jersey: Princeton Univ. Press, 2000).

Durden-Smith, Jo, *Who Killed George Jackson? Fantasies, Paranoia and the Revolution* (New York: Alfred A. Knopf, 1976).

Engleberg, I., *Working in Groups: Communication Principles and Strategies* (My Communication Kit Series, 2006).

Ferrell, Robert H., *Off the Record: The Private Papers of Harry S. Truman* (New York: Harper & Row, 1988).

Fisher, Jim, *The Lindbergh Case* (New Brunswick, New Jersey: Rutgers Univ. Press, 1988).

Foner, Eric, *Reconstruction: America's Unfinished Revolution* (New York: Harper & Row, 1988).

Foner, P. S., *The Black Panthers Speak* (Cambridge, Massachusetts: Da Capo Press, 1970).

Forbes, Flores, *Will You Die With Me? My Life in the Black Panther Party* (New York: Washington Square Press, Simon & Schuster, 2006).

Foxworth, Marlin and Ralph Gordon, *The Black/White Divide . . . Still* (Berkeley: Regent Press, 2008).

Frommer, Harvey, *Shoeless Joe and Ragtime Baseball* (Omaha, Nebraska: Univ. of Nebraska, 2008).

Frank, Richard B. Frank, *Downfall: The End of the Imperial Japanese Empire* (New York: Random House, 1999).

Gage, Elizabeth, *The Day Wall Street Exploded: A Story of America in its First Age of Terror* (Oxford: Oxford Univ. Press, 2009).

Galliher, J. F., Loch, L. W., Keys, D. P., and Guess, T. J., *America Without the Death Penalty: States Lead The Way* (Boston: Northeastern University Press, 2005).

Gardner, Lloyd, *The Case That Never Dies: The Lindbergh Kidnapping* (New Brunswick, New Jersey: Rutgers Univ. Press, 2004).

Garry, Charles, and Goldberg, Arthur, *Streetfighter in the Courtroom: The People's Advocate* (New York: E. P. Dutton, 1977).

Gay, T. M., *Tris Speaker, The Rough-And-Tumble Life Of A Baseball Legend* (Kearney, Nebraska: Morris Book Publishing, 2007).

Geis, Gilbert, and Beinen, Leigh, *Crimes of the Century* (Boston: Northeastern Univ. Press, 1998)

Gilmore, Glenda Elizabeth, *Gender and Jim Crow: Women and the Politics of White Supremacy in North Carolina, 1896–1920* (Durham, North Carolina: Univ. of North Carolina Press, 1996).

Ginger, Ann Fagan, *Minimizing Racism in Jury Trials* (National Lawyers Guild, 1969).

__________, *The Relevant Lawyers: Conversations out of court on their clients, their practice, their politics, their life style* (New York: Simon & Schuster, 1973).

Goodman, James, *Stories of Scottsboro* (New York: Pantheon Books, 1994).

Grant, Robert, and Katz, Joseph, *The Great Trials of the Twenties: The Watershed Decade in America's Courtrooms* (New York: Sarpedon, 1998).

Grossman, M., *Political Corruption in America: An Encyclopedia of Scandals, Power, and Greed* (ABC–Clio, 2003).

Haldeman-Julius, M., *ClarenceDarrow's Two Great Trials* (Girard, Kansas: Haldeman-Julius Company, 1927).

Halperin, Mark, and Heileman, John, *Game Change: Obama and the Clintons, McCain and Palin, and the Race of a Lifetime* (Harper Collins E–books, 2010).

Higdon, H., *Leopold and Loeb, The Crime of the Century* (New York: G. P. Putnam's Sons, 1975).

Hilliard, D., *Huey: Spirit of the Panther* (New York: Thunder's Mouth Press, 2006).

Hilliard, D., and Cole, L., *This Side of Glory* (New York: Little, Brown & Co, 1993).

Hinckle, W., *If You Have A Lemon, Make Lemonade* (New York: W.W. Norton & Co, 1973).

Horan, James D., and Swiggett, Howard, *The Pinkerton Story* (New York: G.P. Putnam's Sons, 1972).

Horowitz, David, *hating whitey and other progressive causes* (Dallas: Spence Publishing Co., 1999).

__________, *Left Illusions: An Intellectual Odyssey* (Dallas: Spence Publishing Co., 2003).

__________, *Radical Son: A Generational Odyssey* (New York: Touchstone, 1997).

Hunter, George W., *A Civic Biology Presented in Problems* (New York: American Book Co., 1914).

__________, *New Civic Biology: Presented In Problems* (New York: American Book Co., 1926).

Ifill, G., *The Breakthrough: Politics and Race in the Age of Obama* (New York: Random House Anchor Books, 2009).

James, Joy, *The Angela Y. Davis Reader* (Malden, Massachusetts: Blackwell Publishers, 1998).

Jerome, Fred, *The Einstein File: J. Edgar Hoover's Secret War Against the World's Most Famous Scientist* (New York: Macmillan, 2003).

Jackson, George, *Blood in My Eye* (Baltimore: Black Classic Press, 1990).

__________, *Soledad Brother: The Prison Letters of George Jackson* (Chicago: Lawrence Hill Books, 1994).

Jones, Charles E. (ed.), *The Black Panther Party [Reconsidered]* (Baltimore: Black Classic Press, 1998).

Keating, Edward M., *Free Huey!* (Palo Alto, California: Ramparts Press, 1971).

Kennedy, Ludovic, *The Airman and the Carpenter: The Lindbergh Kidnapping and the Framing of Richard Hauptmann* (New York: Viking Press, 1985).

Kerr, Clark, *The Gold and the Blue: A Personal Memoir of the University of California 1949–67* (Berkeley: Univ. of California Press, 2001).

Knappman, E. W., *Great American Trials* (Detroit: Visible Ink Press, 1994).

Lanahan, D. J., *Justice For All: Legendary Trials of the Twentieth Century* (Bloomington, Indiana: Author House, 2006).

Larson, E. J., *Summer for the Gods: The Scopes Trial and America's Continuing Debate over Science and Religion* (New York: Basic Books, Perseus Book Group, 1997).

Lee, Barbara, *Renegade for Peace and Justice: Barbara Lee Speaks for Me* (Landham, Maryland: Rowman & Littlefield Publishers, Inc., 2008).

Lerner, Michael, and West, Cornel, *Jews & Blacks: A Dialogue on Race, Religion, and Culture in America* (New York: Penguin Books, 1995, 1996).

Levin, Murray B., *Political Hysteria in America: The Democratic Capacity for Repression* (New York: Basic Books, 1971).

Levine, M., McNamee, G., and Greenberg, D., *The Tales of Hoffman* (New York: Bantam Books, 1970).

Liberatore, Paul, *The Road to Hell: The True Story of George Jackson, Stephen Bingham, and the San Quentin Massacre* (New York: The Atlantic Monthly Press, 1996).

Lukas, J. Anthony, *Big Trouble* (New York: Simon & Schuster Touchstone Books, 1997).

Major, Reginald, *Justice in the Round: The Trial of Angela Davis* (New York: Joseph Okpaku Publishing Co., Inc., 1973).

Mann, Eric, *Comrade George; an Investigation into the Life, Political Thought, and Assassination of George Jackson* (New York; Harper & Row, 1972, 1974).

McAdam, D., *Freedom Summer* (New York: Oxford Univ. Press, 1988).

McGhee, Millie M., *Secrets Uncovered: J. Edgar Hoover, the Relative* (Rancho Cucamonga, California: Allen Morris, 2002).

Middleton, N., *The I.F. Stone's Weekly Reader* (New York: Vintage Books, 1953).

Minton, Robert, Jr. (ed.), *Inside: Prison American Style* (New York: Random House, 1971).

Mitford, Jessica, *A Fine Old Conflict* (New York: Vintage Books, 1956, 1977).

Moore, Gilbert, *Rage* (New York: Carroll & Graf Publishers, Inc., 1993).

__________, *A Special Rage* (New York: Harper & Row, 1971).

Morris, E., *Theodore Rex* (New York: Random House, 2001).

Nash, J. R., *The Great Pictorial History of World Crime* (Lanham, Maryland: Rowman & Littlefield, 2004).

Newton, Huey, *To Die For the People* (New York: Random House, 1972).

Newton, H., and Blake, J. H., *Revolutionary Suicide* (New York: Harcourt, Brace, Jovanovich, 1973).

Newton, Michael, *The Encyclopedia of Unsolved Crimes* (New York: Checkmark Books, 2004).

Obama, Barack, *Dreams from My Father: A Story of Race and Inheritance* (New York: Three Rivers Press, 1995, 2004).

Ogletree, Charles J., Jr., and Sarat, Austin (eds.), *From Lynch Mobs to the Killing State: Race and the Death Penalty in America* (New York: New York Univ. Press, 2006)

Ogletree, Charles J., Jr. (ed.), *When Law Fails: Making Sense of Miscarriages of Justice* (New York: New York Univ., Press, 2009).

Olson, Keith W., *Watergate: The Presidential Scandal That Shook America* (Lawrence, Kansas: Univ. of Kansas Press, 2003).

Oney, S., *And the Dead Shall Rise: The Murder of Mary Phagan and the Lynching of Leo Frank* (New York: Pantheon, 2003).

Pearson, Hugh, *The Shadow of the Panther* (New York: Perseus Books, 1995).

Pell, Eve (ed.), *Maximum Security: Letters from Prison* (New York: E. P. Dutton & Co., 1972).

Perman, Michael, *Struggle for Mastery: Disfranchisement in the South, 1888–1908* (Chapel Hill: Univ. of North Carolina Press, 2001).

Radosh, Ronald, and Milton, Joyce, *The Rosenberg File* (New Haven: Yale Univ. Press, 2003).

Raiford, Leigh, *Imprisoned in a Luminous Glare: Photography and the African-American Freedom Struggle* (Chapel Hill: Univ. of North Carolina Press, 2011).

Rauchway, E., *Murdering McKinley: The Making of Theodore Roosevelt's America* (New York: Hill and Wang, Div. of Farrar, Straus, Giroux, 2003).

Rayback, J. G., *A History of American Labor* (New York: The Free Press, 1966).

Remnick, David, *THE BRIDGE: The Life and Rise of Barack Obama* (New York: Random House, Alfred Knopf, 2010).

Rhodes, D., *Ty Cobb: Safe At Home* (Guilford, Connecticut: Lyons Press, 2008).

Rhodes, Jayne, *Framing The Black Panthers: The Spectacular Rise of a Black Power Icon* (New York: The New Press, 2008).

Rhomberg, Chris, *No There There: Race, Class, and Political Community in Oakland* (Berkeley: Univ. of California Press, 2004).

Robenalt, James D., *The Harding Affair, Love and Espionage During the Great War* (New York: Palgrave Macmillan, 2009).

Robeson, Paul, and Foner, Philip S., *Paul Robeson Speaks: Writings, Speeches, Interviews 1918–1974* (New York: Kensington Pub. Corp. Citadel Press Books, 1978).

Russell, F., *Sacco and Vanzetti: The Case Resolved.* (New York: Harper & Row, 1986).

Scheck, Barry, Neufeld, Peter, and Dwyer, Jim, *Actual Innocence: Five Days to Execution, and Other Dispatches From the Wrongly Convicted* (New York: Doubleday, 2000).

Seale, Bobby, *Seize the Time: The Story of the Black Panther Party and Huey P. Newton* (New York: Random House, Black Classic Press, 1970, 1991).

Stannard, D. E., *Honor Killing: How the Infamous "Massie Affair" Transformed Hawai'i* (New York: Viking Penguin Books, 2005).

Stone, Irving, *Clarence Darrow for the Defense* (New York: Doubleday & Co., Signet Books, 1941, 1969).

Sussman, P. Y. (ed.), *Decca: The Letters of Jessica Mitford* (New York: Alfred A. Knopf, 2006).

Temkin, Moshik, *The Sacco-Vanzetti Affair* (Kindle ed., 2009).

Time Capsule: 1954—The Year in Review. (New York: Time, Inc., 1954, 2004).

Timothy, Mary, *Jury Woman: The Story of the Trial of Angela Y. Davis—written by a member of the jury* (San Francisco: Glide Publications, 1974,1975).

Uelmen, G., *Lessons From the Trial: The People v. O. J. Simpson* (Kansas City: Andrews and McMeel, 1996).

Uruburu, P., *American Eve: Evelyn Nesbit, Stanford White, the Birth of the "It" Girl and the Crime of the Century* (New York: Riverhead Books, 2008).

Van Slingerland, P., *Something Terrible Has Happened: The account of the sensational Thalia Massie affair which burst from prewar Hawaii to incense a nation* (New York: Harper & Row, 1966).

Walton, Hanes, Jr., *Black Political Parties: An Historical and Political Analysis* (New York: The Free Press, 1972).

Ward, G. C., and Burns, K., *Baseball: An Illustrated History* (New York: Alfred A. Knopf, 1994).

Wellman, David, *Portraits of White Racism* (New York: Cambridge University Press, 1977).

White, Theodore H., *The Making of the President 1968* (New York: Atheneum Publishers, 1969).

Whitfield, Stephen J.,*The Culture of the Cold War* (Baltimore: The Johns Hopkins University Press, 1996).

Wilson, T., *Headline Justice: Inside the Courtroom—The Country's Most Controversial Trials* (New York: Thunder's Mouth Press, 1996).

Woods, Randal B., *LBJ: Architect of American Ambition* (New York: Free Press, 2006).

The Whole World's Watching: Peace and Social Justice Movements of the 1960s & 1970s (Berkeley: Berkeley Art Center Association, 2001).

Web Sources:

(Unless otherwise noted, all web sources were accessible as of June 14–15, 2011.)

"1919: Race Riots – Chicago Public Library." Home – Chicago Public Library. http://www.chipublib.org/cplbooksmovies/cplarchive/chidisasters/raceriots.php.

Alvarez, Mark. "MrBaseball.com – Say It Ain't So, Ty – By Mark Alvarez." MrBaseball.com – Home. http://www.mrbaseball.com/index.php?option=com_content&task=view&id=43&Itemid=61

"Analysis of the O. J. Simpson Murder Trial: Time To Go Home " Crime Library on truTV.com." truTV.com: Not Reality. Actuality.http://www.trutv.com/library/crime/notorious_murders/famous/simpson/home_15.html.

"Austin Criminal Defense Lawyer" www.austincriminaldefenselawyer.com.Austin Criminal Defense Lawyer; www.austincriminaldefenselawyer.com. http://www.austincriminaldefenselawyer.com/2010/04/07/the-bernie-goetz-story-25-years-later.html.

Bass, Jack. "Documenting the Orangeburg Massacre," Nieman Report. http://www.orangeburgmassacre1968.com/docs/NiemanReport.pdf.

Batt, Marissa N. "*Ms. Magazine* | Just Verdicts? History of Women and Jury Service." Ms. Magazine Online | More Than A Magazine – A Movement. http://www.msmagazine.com/summer2004/justverdicts.asp.

Beck, Sanderson. "Einstein and Schweitzer on Peace in the Atomic Age by Sanderson Beck." Literary Works of Sanderson Beck. http://www.san.beck.org/GPJ23-Einstein.html.

Bennett, Hans. "OpEdNews – Diary: Update on political prisoner Ruchell Cinque Magee." Opednews.com Progressive, Liberal United States and International News, Opinion, Op-Eds and Politics. http://www.opednews.com/populum / diarypage.php?did=10653.

Bisher, Furman [and Jackson, Joe]. "This is The Truth!" by Shoeless Joe Jackson as told to Furman Bisher, http://law2.umkc.edu/faculty/projects/&trials/blacksox/jacksonstory.html.

Blaisdell, Lowell. "Mystery and Tragedy: The O'Connell-Dolan Scandal." SABR redirect. http://research.sabr.org/journals/oconnell-dolan-scandal.

Briker, Jason. "Rosenberg Executions." Facts On File Online Databases. http://2facts.es.vrc.scoolaid.net/icah_story.aspx?PIN=haa00001190.

Bugliosi, Vincent. "Manson's Legacy : Crimes of the Century:Investigation Discovery." ID – Investigation Discovery: Hollywood Crimes, Forensics, Murders. http://investigation.discovery.com/investigation/history/crimes-century/crimes-article-manson.html.

Burris, John L. *Blue vs. Black.* http://www.johnburrislaw.com/CM/Custom/Comen tary.asp.

Butters, Patrick. "Meet the unknown slugger. (baseball player Josh Gibson) (Brief Article) Insight on the News | HighBeam Research." Encyclopedia – Online Dictionary | Encyclopedia.com: Get facts, articles, pictures, video. http://www.encyclopedia.com/doc/1G1-21157150.html.

CBS. "U.S. Leads The World In Illegal Drug Use," CBS News. http://www.cbsnews.com/stories/2008/07/01/health/webmd/main4222322.shtml.

Chaddock, Gail Russell. "US notches world's highest incarceration rate." The Christian Science Monitor – CSMonitor.com. The Christian Science Monitor – CSMonitor.com. http://www.csmonitor.com/2003/0818/p02s01-usju.html.

"City Crime Rankings by Population Group." Morgan Quitno Press. http://www.morganquitno.com/cit05pop.htm.

Clough, Thomas. "Hoodwinked: The Legacy of Robert Byrd." Weird Republic – Conservatism's Best Kept Secret. http://www.weirdrepublic.com/episode114.htm.

CNN. "CNN.com – Transcripts." CNN.com – Breaking News, U.S., World, Weather, Entertainment & Video News. http://www.csmonitor.com/2003/0818/p02s01-usju.html.

"Cobb and Those Outside Baseball." http://wso.williams.edu/~jkossuth/cobb/race.htm.

Cohn, Marjorie. "Legendary Lawyer Doris Brin Walker Dies; Represented Angela Davis, Smith Act Defendants." Marjorie Cohn. http://www.marjoriecohn.com/2009/08/legendary-lawyer-doris-brin-walker-dies.html.

Coleman, Kate. "Elmer 'Geronimo' Pratt: The Untold Story of the Black Panther Leader, Dead At 63," *The New Republic*, June 27, 2011. http://www.tnr.com/article/politics/90735/black-panther-geronimo-pratt-murder-conviction-prison-huey-newton.

Coleman, Kate. "The Party's Over | Center for Investigative Reporting." CIR | Journalism revealing injustice since 1977 | Center for Investigative Reporting. http://centerforinvestigativereporting.org/articles/thepartysover.

Costa, Robert. "Gingrich: Obama's 'Kenyan, anti-colonial' worldview – By Robert Costa – The Corner – National Review Online." National Review Online. http://www.nationalreview.com/corner/246302/gingrich-obamaskenyan-anti-colonial-worldview-robert-costa.

Crime Magazine. "The Scottsboro Boys: Jim Crow on Trial," Crime Magazine, An Encyclopedia of Crime. http://crimemagazine.com/scottsboro-boys-jim-crow-trial.

Crouch, Stanley. "The Joy of Goetz." New York Magazine — NYC Guide to Restaurants, Fashion, Nightlife, Shopping, Politics, Movies. http://nymag.com/nymetro/news/anniversary/35th/n_8601/.

Davey, Monica. "In Court, AIM Members Are Depicted as Killers – NYTimes.com." The New York Times – Breaking News, World News & Multimedia. http://www.nytimes.com/2004/02/05/national/05TRIB.html.

Dannen, Gene. "ATOMIC BOMB: DECISION (Hiroshima–Nagasaki)." Gene Dannen's Home Page. http://www.dannen.com/decision/index.html.

Deveney, Scott. "Did the 1918 Cubs Throw the World Series???" – Sound Opinions Message Board." Sound Opinions from WBEZ Chicago. http://www.soundopinions.org/forum/index.php?showtopic=16355.

De Zutter, Hank. "What Makes Obama Run? | Feature | Chicago Reader." Chicago Reader | Chicago's guide to music, movies, arts, theater, restaurants, and politics. http://www.chicagoreader.com/chicago/what-makes-obama-run/Content?oid=889221.

Douglas, Frederick. "Frederick Douglass, Canandaigua, New York." *Building Equality,* http://www.buildingequality.us/Quotes/Frederick_Douglass.htm.

"Drug information and drug use statistics in America." Drug-Free Alliance – Sensible drug policy for America. http://www.buildingequality.us/Quotes/Frederick_Douglass.htm.

Edsall, Thomas B. "Lott Decried For Part Of Salute to Thurmond: GOP Senate Leader Hails Colleague's Run As Segregationist." www.commondreams.org www.commondreams.org/headlines02/1207-01.htm.

Essortment.com. "Shirley Chisholm Biography." Shirley Chisholm. http://www.essortment.com/all/shirleychisholm_ruol.htm.

"FBI Counterintelligence and Special Operations." ICDC – Internet Connect – Internet Access – Web Hosting. http://www.icdc.com/~paulwolf/cointelpro/specialops.htm.

FBI. "COINTELPRO." WHAT REALLY HAPPENED | The History The US Government HOPES You Never Learn! http://whatreallyhappened.com/RANCHO/POLITICS/COINTELPRO/COINTELPRO-FBI.docs.html.

Feinman, Mark S. "The New York City Transit Authority in the 1980s." www.nycsubway.org – New York City Subway History, Photos & More. http://www.nycsubway.org/articles/history-nycta1980s.html.

Felix, Wanda. "The Trial of Fatty Arbuckle." Krishnamurti | Pictures of the American Revolution | Stanley Cavell | Combat Trauma John Lardner | Pluto | Train Dreams | Chickens in the City. http://www.ralphmag.org/fatty.html.

Flynn, Dan. "Panther Leader Seale Confesses," *Front Page* magazine, Front Page Magazine.com, April 23, 2002. http://archive.frontpagemag.com/read Article.aspx?ARTID=24216.

Fox News. "McVeigh Considered Assassination of Reno, Other Officials." www.foxnews.com. http://www.foxnews.com/story/0,2933,17501,00.html.

Freeman, Jo. "Social Protest in the Sixties." Jo Freeman: Feminist Scholar and Author. http://www.jofreeman.com/sixtiesprotest/sixties.htm.

"Gangs and the 1919 Race Riot." University of Illinois at Chicago – UIC. http://www.uic.edu/orgs/kbc/ganghistory/Industrial%20Era/Riotbegins.html.

Garay, Ronald. "WATERGATE – The Museum of Broadcast Communications." The Museum of Broadcast Communications. http://www.museum.tv/eotvsection.php?entrycode=watergate.

Garrow, David J. "From Russia with Love" (citing John Earl Haynes, Harvey Klehr, and Alexander Vassiliev)." www.newsweek.com. http://www.newsweek.com/2009/05/15/from-russia-with-love.html.

Gerstein, Josh. "Hillary Clinton's Radical Summer: A Season Love and Leftists,"

The New York Sun, Nov. 26, 2007, www.nysun.com/national/hillary-clintons-radical-summer/66933/.

Gest, Howard. "The July 1945 Szilard Petition." The July 1945 Szilard Petition. http://sites.bio.indiana.edu/~gest/hgSzilard.pdf.

Golenbock, Peter. "Breaking Baseball's Color Barrier, Peter Golenbock." That's Baseball. http://thatsbaseball1.tripod.com/id147.htm.

Hall, Irving W. "The Meisenbach Case: The FBI and HUAC Convicted" (*The Californian*, June 1967, 2d. ed). http://www.notinkansas.us/Library/Meisenbach.pdf.

Harnden, Toby. "Barack Obama faces 30 death threats a day, stretching US Secret Service – Telegraph." The *Telegraph* online, http://www.telegraph.co.uk/news/worldnews/barackobama/5967942/Barack-Obama-faces-30-death-threats-a-day-stretching-US-Secret-Service.html.

Hine, Lewis W. "The History Place – Child Labor in America: Investigative Photos of Lewis Hine." The History Place. http://www.historyplace.com/unitedstates/childlabor/.

Historynet.com. "The Law of Love." This Case is Close to My Heart: American History Feature. http://www.historynet.com/this-case-is-close-to-my-heart-page-1-august-2000-american-history-feature.htm/6.

Hoffman, Abbie. "Conspiracy in the Streets | Haymarket Books." Haymarket Books. http://www.haymarketbooks.org/product_info.php?products_id=1187.

Hoffman, Jan. "Goetz Defense Opens, Calls Jimmy Breslin and a Psychiatrist, Then Closes – New York Times." The New York Times – Breaking News, World News & Multimedia. http://query.nytimes.com/gst/fullpage.html?res=9800E6DA1E39F93BA25757C0A960958260.

Hutchinson, Earl Ofari. "Why Obama Won't Pardon Jack Johnson – Friendly Fire." Los Angeles Newspaper Group. http://www.insidesocal.com/friendlyfire/2010/02/why-obama-wont-pardon-jack-joh.html.

Internet Movie Data Base. "Memorable quotes for 'All in the Family,' 1971." www.imdb.com. http://www.imdb.com/title/tt0066626/quotes.

"Interracial Marriage Bans vs. Bans on Marriage Between Same-Sex Couples." National Black Justice Coalition. http://www.nbjcoalition.org/news/interracial-marriage-bans-vs.html.

Jagger, Mick. "Sweet Black Angel," aka "Black Angel," keno.org. http://www.keno.org/stones_lyrics/blackangel.html.

Johnson, Kevin. "States change police lineups after wrongful convictions – USA TODAY.com." News, Travel, Weather, Entertainment, Sports, Technology, U.S. & World – USATODAY.com. http://www.usatoday.com/news/nation/2009-09-16-police-lineups_N.htm.

Jordan, Barbara. "American Rhetoric: Barbara Jordan." http://www.american

rhetoric.com.

Kahn, Jeffery. "Ronald Reagan launched political career using the Berkeley campus as a political target." University of California, Berkeley. http://www.berkeley.edu/news/media/releases/2004/06/08_reagan.shtml.

"Kenesaw Mountain Landis." Baseball-statistics.com. http://www.baseball-statistics.com/HOF/Landis.html.

Kilpatrick, Carroll. "Nixon Tells Editors 'I am not a crook.'" www.washingtonpost.com. http://www.washingtonpost.com/wpsrv/national/longterm/watergate/articles/111873-1.htm.

Koppleman, Alex. "When James Von Brunn Tried to Arrest the FED." www.salon.com, War Room. http://www.salon.com/politics/war_room/2009/06/10/vonbrunn_fed/.

"Leo Frank lynching site recognized with historical marker." Video. http://marietta.granicus.com/MediaPlayer.php?publish_id=45.

"LEOPOLD & LOEB: CHICAGO'S THRILL KILLERS." AMERICAN HAUNTINGS: WHERE DEAD MEN STILL TELL TALES. http://www.prairieghosts.com/leopold.html.

Linder, Douglas O. "Famous Trials." School of Law | University of Missouri–Kansas City. http://law2.umkc.edu/faculty/projects/FTrials/ftrials.htm.

Lowitt, Bruce. "Black Sox scandal: Chicago throws 1919 World Series." www.sptimes.com. http://www.sptimes.com/News/122299/news_pf/Sports_Black_Sox_scandal__Ch.shtml.

Lyall, Sarah. "N.A.A.C.P. LEADER SEEKS FEDERAL CASE ON GOETZ – New York Times." The New York Times – Breaking News, World News & Multimedia. http://query.nytimes.com/gst/fullpage.html?res=9B0DE0DC1E31F933A15755C0A961948260.

Milkovits, Amanda. "Before O.J., it was the trial of the century." Lane Memorial Library, Hampton, NH. http://www.hampton.lib.nh.us/hampton/biog/pamsmart/beforeoj.htm.

Mooney, Mark. "Obama Aide Concedes 'Dollar Bill.'" ABC News. http://abcnews.go.com/GMA/Politics/story?id=5495348&page=1.

"More Black Men Now In Prison System Than Were Enslaved Before the Civil War Began." www.disinfo.com. http://www.disinfo.com/2011/04/more-black-men-now-in-prison-system-than-were-enslaved-before-the-civil-war-began/.

Mullins, Curtis. "Ruchell Cinque Magee – Political Prisoner." It's About Time – Black Panther Party Legacy & Alumni 45th Year Reunion. http://www.itsabouttimebpp.com/political_prisoners/ruchell_cinque_magee-political_prisoner.html.

Nagle, Rob. "Demonstrators commemorate 50th anniversary of historic protest." sfexaminer.com. http://www.sfexaminer.com/local/demonstrators-commem

orate-50th-anniversary-historic-protest#ixzz1EG1qWBGI.

"NBC News Poll: 10 years after Simpson verdict – Dateline NBC – msnbc.com." msnbc.com – Breaking news, science and tech news, world news, US news, local news. msnbc.com. http://www.msnbc.msn.com/id/5139346/.

"New Georgia Encyclopedia." New Georgia Encyclopedia. http://www.georgiaencyclopedia.org/.

"New York Baseball Team | Dave Adams Card World | Discount Display Cases at Baseballalmanac.com." Baseball Teams | Basball Almanac Roster | Cash Advance at Baseballalmanac.com. http://www.baseballalmanac.com/articles/kenesaw_landis_biography.shtml.

Noe, Denise. "Fatty Arbuckle and the Death of Virginia Rappe: How Did She Die?" Crime Library on truTV.com." truTV.com: Not Reality. Actuality. http://www.trutv.com/library/crime/notorious_murders/classics/fatty_arbuckle/7.html.

"Obama's America and the New Jim Crow: The Recurring Racial Nightmare, The Cyclical Rebirth of Caste." Obama's America and the New Jim Crow: The Recurring Racial Nightmare, The Cyclical Rebirth of Caste. http://nathanielturner.com/obamasamericaandnewjimcrow.htm.

"Oklahoma City Police Department Alfred Pi Murrah Building Bombing After Action Report." Oklahoma City Police Dept., Alfred Pi Murrah Building Bombing After Action Report. http://replay.waybackmachine.org/20070703233435/. http://www.terrorisminfo.mipt.org/pdf/okcfr_App_C.pdf.

Pacifica radio KPFA Huey P. Newton funeral transcripts http://www.lib.berkeley.edu/MRC/newtonfuneraltranscripts.html.

"Picture This: Vietnam/Civil Rights Era." Oakland Museum of California. http://www.museumca.org/picturethis/5_4.html.

"Plain Words." History Is A Weapon. http://www.historyisaweapon.com/defcon1/plainwords.html.

"President William Taft Baseball Related Quotations by Baseball Almanac." Baseball Almanac – The Official Baseball History Site. http://www.baseball-almanac.com/prz_qwt.shtml.

Pyle, Richard. "50 years later Rosenberg brother admits lie." Category: Page One from The Berkeley Daily Planet. Local News and Opinion from The Berkeley Daily Planet. http://www.berkeleydailyplanet.com/issue/2001-12-06/article/8732?headline=50-years-later-Rosenberg-brother-admits-lie.

Reese, Dr. Renford R. "Dr. Renford R. Reese's Homepage." Cal Poly Pomona. http://www.csupomona.edu/~rrreese/INTEGRATION.HTML.

Reublin, Richard A., and Robert L. Maine. "Question of the Month – Jim Crow Museum at Ferris State University." Ferris State University: Michigan College Campuses in Big Rapids MI, Grand Rapids MI, Off Campus Locations Across

Michigan. http://www.ferris.edu/jimcrow/question/may05/.

"Revolutions in Communication: Media history from Gutenberg to the Digital Age." http://revolutionsincommunication.wordpress.com/.

Risen, Clay. "How the South was won – The Boston Globe." Boston.com – Boston, MA news, breaking news, sports, video. http://www.boston.com/news/globe/ideas/articles/2006/03/05/how_the_south_was_won/.

Rosenberg, Philip. "A Surprisingly Gentle Confrontation." New York Times on the Web. http://www.nytimes.com/books/99/08/22/specials/erikson-common.html.

Select Committee to Study Governmental Operations with respect to Intelligence Activities United States Senate ("The Church Committee Report"), http://www.icdc.com/~paulwolf/cointelpro/churchfinalreport.htm.

"Shoeless" Joe Jackson – The Official Web Site. http://www.shoelessjoejackson.com/about/quotes.html.

Smith, Ben. "McCain calls Obama 'decent person,' is booed – Ben Smith – POLITICO.com." Politics, Political News – POLITICO.com. http://www.politico.com/blogs/bensmith/1008/McCain_calls_Obama_decent_person_is_booed.html.

Stravinsky, John. "Hal Chase, Major League Baseball 1905–1919 – Page 1 – News – New York – Village Voice." New York News, Events, Restaurants, Music, Village Voice. http://www.villagevoice.com/1999-06-08/news/hal-chase-major-league-baseball-1905-1919/.

"Techniques of Direct Disenfranchisement, 1880–1965." University of Michigan. http://www.umich.edu/~lawrace/disenfranchise1.htm.

The Guardian. "Britain and US to keep atomic bomb secret" The Guardian. http://www.guardian.co.uk/theguardian/2009/aug/10/truman-.

"The History Place – Impeachment: Richard Nixon." The History Place. http://www.historyplace.com/unitedstates/impeachments/nixon.htm.

"The History Makers." The HistoryMakers.com – African American history archive. http://www.thehistorymakers.com/biography/biography.asp?bioindex=96.

"The Law of Love – Clarence Darrow 1926." World History for the Relaxed Historian. http://www.emersonkent.com/speeches/the_law_of_love.htm.

"THE LINDBERGH KIDNAPPING HOAX – Bruno Richard Hauptmann: Wrongly Executed April 3, 1936." http://www.lindberghkidnappinghoax.com/.

"The Militia Movement – Extremism in America." ADL: Fighting Anti-Semitism, Bigotry and Extremism. http://www.adl.org/learn/ext_us/militia_m.asp?xpicked=4&item=19.

"The National Black Bacchus Caucus: Soul on Rice. . . ." The National Black Bacchus Caucus. http://blackbacchus.com/2007/10/soul-on-rice.html.

"The San Francisco State College Strike Collection." J. Paul Leonard Library Home

Page. http://www.library.sfsu.edu/about/collections/strike/chronology.html.

"The Sentencing Project News – Voting Rights." The Sentencing Project Home. http://www.sentencingproject.org/template/page.cfm?id=133.

Thomas, Robert McG., Jr., "Lionel Wilson, 82, A Mayor of Oakland for Three Terms," *The New York Times*, Jan. 31, 1998. http://www.nytimes.com/1998/01/31/us/lionel-wilson-82-a-mayor-of-oakland-for-three-terms.html.

Time magazine. "Races: Professor on Ice," Sept. 27, 1968. http://www.time.com/time/magazine/article/0,9171,902310,00.html.

__________. "Nation: The Odyssey of Huey Newton" Time Magazine, Nov. 13, 1978. http://www.time.com/time/magazine/article/0,9171,946144,00.html.

"Today in counterculture history (12/04) – The Pub – Shroomery Message Board." Shroomery – Magic Mushrooms (Shrooms) Demystified. http://www.shroomery.org/forums/showflat.php/Number/13580978.

"Truman Library: Desegregation of the Armed Forces Online Research File." Harry S. Truman Library and Museum. http://www.trumanlibrary.org/whistlestop /study_collections/desegregation/large/index.php?action=chronology. (Univ. of Washington Press 1982). "Personal Justice Denied, Report of the Commission on Wartime Relocation and Internment of Civilians," Chapter 11, Military Rule, fn.31. http://www.nps.gov/history/history/online_books/personal_justice_denied/chap11.htm.

Voelker, Daniel J., and Paul A. Duffy. "Chicago Lawyer Magazine – We keep you in the loop about Chicago's legal community." Chicago Lawyer Magazine – We keep you in the loop about Chicago's legal community. http://chicagolawyermagazine.com/Archives/2009/09/01/092009sox.aspx.

"Waco Siege : The Final Assault." 1000s Of Museums Online : MuseumStuff.com. http://www.museumstuff.com/learn/topics/Waco_Siege::sub::The_Final_Assault.

Weiss, Joanna. "How Obama and the radical became news – The Boston Globe." Boston.com – Boston, MA news, breaking news, sports, video. http://www.boston.com/news/nation/articles/2008/04/18/how_obama_and_the_radical_became_news/.

Wikimedia. "Cries of Lynch Him Hurled at Slaton as He Quits Office." Wikimedia.org. http://upload.wikimedia.org/wikipedia/en/c/ce/Leo-frank-slaton-headline.jpg.

Wikipedia. www.wikipedia.org

Wojcik, John. "COMMENTARY Holocaust Museum, Dr. Tiller: Janet Napolitano saw it coming." Home peoplesworld. http://www.peoplesworld.org/commentary-holocaust-museum-dr-tiller-janet-napolitano-saw-it-coming/.

Zirin, Dave. "Dave Zirin: An Interview with John Carlos." CounterPunch: Tells the Facts, Names the Names. http://www.counterpunch.org/zirin11012003.html.

Journal Articles and Pamphlets:

Bedau, Hugo Adam, and Michael L. Radelet. "Miscarriages of Justice in Potentially Capital Cases." *Stanford Law Review* 40, no. 21 (1987): 124, 125.

Brown, J. Robert, Jr., and Lee, Allison Herren, "The Neutral Assignment of Judges at the Court of Appeals," 78 *Texas Law Review* 1037 (April 2000).

Bryan, Robert R. "The Execution of the Innocent: The Tragedy of the Hauptmann-Lindbergh and Bigelow Cases." *NYU Review of Law and Social Change* 18 (1990).

Cleaver, Eldridge. "Newton On Trial." *Ramparts*, Fall 1968.

Dixon, Thomas, Jr. "Booker T. Washington and the Negro." *Saturday Evening Post*, August 19, 1905.

Frankfurter, Felix. "The Case of Sacco and Vanzetti." *The Atlantic Monthly*, March 1927.

Goldman, Emma. "The Tragedy at Buffalo." *Free Society*, October 6, 1901.

Palmer, L. F. "Out to Get the Panthers." *The Nation*, July 28, 1969, 80.

Phillips, Jack [pseudonym of Carl Sandburg]. "HAYWOOD OF THE I. W. W." *International Socialist Review* 18, no. 7 (1918).

Pleskan, Shirl, and Matt Marsh. "It's Not How You Draw; It's What You Draw: An Interview with David Lance Goines." *Pressing Times* 7, no. 2 (2006).

Powell, Michael. "Anatomy of a Counter-Bar Association: The Chicago Council of Lawyers." *Law and Social Inquiry* 4, no. 3 (2006).

"Report from Black America." *Newsweek*, June–July 1969.

Rosebury, Celia. "Black Liberation on Trial: The Case of Huey Newton." *The People's World*, Summer 1968. Reprint by the Bay Area Committee to Defend Political Freedom, Berkeley, CA, 1968, from articles originally appearing during the summer of 1968 in *The People's World*. Archives of the Oakland, CA African-American Museum and Library, Black Panther Collection.

Time, Inc. "Time Capsule: 1954—"The Year in Review." (*Time*, Summer 1954.)

INDEX

A

A Huey P. Newton Story 684
Abbott, Burton 338
Abbott, Robert 20
Abernathy, Ralph 285
Abt, John 564
Abu-Jamal, Mumia 696, 706
Actual Innocence 261, *see* Innocence Project
Adams, John Quincy 601
Adams, Steve 70, 73
Addams, Jane 44, 718
African Black Brotherhood 186
Agnew, Spiro 607
Agnos, Art 295
Ahakuelo, Benny 220
Ahlgren, Gregory 262
Al-Amin, Imam Jamal Abdullah 642 (*see* H. Rap Brown)
Al Qaeda 705, 706
Alexander II 43
Alexander, Michelle 711–713
Allen, Barry 647, 650
Allen Temple Baptist Church 642, 644
Allen, William 251
American Civil Liberties Union ("ACLU") and Black Panther Party ("BPP") 496; and Civil Rights cases 290–291; and Dover, PA "Scopes" trial 687; and Free Speech Movement 296, 299; and HUAC 291–294; and Geronimo Pratt 600; and Rosenberg appeal 276; and prisoners' rights 530, 600; and Scopes trial Part I, Chap. 9 *passim*; and Scottsboro Boys 207–208; and first Sweet trial 192
American Communist Party
Baseball integration role 32, 211; Cleaver endorsement for President 5, 392; Angela Davis trial, Part Three, Chap. 4 *passim*; decline 278, 291; Dreyfus and Garry membership 4, 307; lobbying for McGee case 212, 307; Newton trial funding 307; William Patterson as President 307, 616; Rosenberg Espionage case and McCarthy Era, Part One, Chap. 14 *passim*, 217; Sacco and Vanzetti case, Part One, Chap. 7 *passim*; Treuhafts' membership 307; United Nations petition 210
American Constitution *passim*
American Federation of Labor ("AFL") 59, 100
American Indian Movement ("AIM") 548, 640
Amsterdam, Anthony
Anderson appeal 572; Angela Davis case 572; Pratt appeal 600; Soledad Brothers case 573
Anarchist Fighters, The 14, 132
Anderson, Maxwell 143
Anderson, Robert Page 572
Andrews, Harry 99
Andrews, Ronald 423
Angelou, Maya 406
Angels in America 280

Anti-Defamation League
formation 106; report re growth of militias 670; role in Leo Frank pardon 128
Aoki, Richard 311, 323
Arbuckle, Roscoe "Fatty" 10–12, 656
Arguedas, Cris 666
Armstrong, Gregory 487, 530
Arnason, Richard Part Three, Chap. 4 *passim*
Aryan Brotherhood 506
Aryan Republican Army 669
Asbury, Herbert 109
Asinof, Eliot 29
Attica uprising 536–537
Audacity of Hope, The 678, 706
August 7th Movement 529, 534
Austrian, Alfred 24, 25, 27, 29, 39
Autobiography of Malcolm X 529
Avakian, Bob 351, 358, 398
Avakian, Spurgeon
father of Bob Avakian 351; discovery request from District Attorney 388; IQ test case 569–370, 382, 403
Avrich, Paul 144
Axelrod, Beverly
and Black Panther Party 309, 327, 348; Civil Rights cases 308; Eldridge Cleaver 307–309, 345–348; 352, 361, 373, 508; membership in CORE 308; membership in Lawyers Guild 308; and Reggie Majors 345; Huey Newton's attorney 307–309, 337, 337, 351–352, 345, 527; defense attorney Stop the Draft Week 350; attorney for Reies Lopez Tijerina 471
Ayers, Bill 699–700

B

Baatz, Simon 159
Bachrach, Benjamin 150–154
Baez, Joan 297
Bailey, F. Lee 9, 612, 614, 663
Baker, Mark 650
Bakke v. The Regents of the Univ. of California 698
Baldus Study 680
Baldwin, James 319
Bales, Bruce 598
Balin, Albert 138
Barbarella 521
Barbie, Klaus 9
Barbour, Haley 288
Barry, Joan 13
Barrymore, John 39, 51
Bates, Ruby 205–206, 208
Baxter, Carolyn 616
Bayonet Constitution 215
Beach Boys, The 551–552, 556
Beatles, The 520, 549, 552
Beinen, Leigh 264, 655
Bell, Alexander Graham 219
Belli, Melvin 658
Bening, Annette 646
Bennett, Fred 528
Benton, Claude 222, 226
Bergen, Candice 536
Berkeley Barb The formation 299; and Black Panther Party 342; Newton case 354, 414
Berkley, Thomas 370, 386, 393
Berlin Wall 291
Berman, Emile 660
Bernstein, Carl 606
Bernstein, Leonard 707
Berrigan, Daniel 543
Berrigan, Philip 569, 656
Besig, Ernist 294

Big Five 215– 216, 222, 224–225, 235
Big Strike 271, 313
Bill of Rights 87, 92
 1st Amendment 101, 170, 178, 292, 296, 356, 541, 562, 613, 688, 691; 2nd Amendment 310; 4th Amendment 362; 5th Amendment 273, 292, 338, 439–440, 444, 452, 650; 6th Amendment 88, 95, 422, 545; 8th Amendment 580, 711
Bingham, Stephen
 attorney for George Jackson 534–535; trial of 628
Bin Laden, Osama 705
Birth of a Nation, The 77, 121, 681
Black Bottom 182, 201–202
Black, Cobey 240
Black/White Divide in America . . . Still 711
Black August 536
Black Friday 291, 293–295, 333
Black Guerrilla Family ("BGF") 625, 640–641, 644
Black Metropolis 19
Blackmon, Doug 94
Black Muslims 319, 549–550, 694
Black Nationalists 496
Black Panther newspaper
 and Elaine Brown 527, 621; Emory Douglas artwork for 310; Free Huey campaign 341, 469; launching 327, 347; Newton trial prosecution evidence 456–457; Ogletree, editor Stanford student paper 673; Seale as editor 621; van used in robbery 493;
Black Panther Party
 Foreword, Introduction, Part Two, Part Three, Chap. 1, 2, 6, 8 *passim*
"Black Panther Rank and File" 684
Black Power 289, 346, 412–413, 418, 623, 669, 679, 682, 684
Black Sox scandal Part One Chap. 1, 14–34
Black Thursday 61
Blackman, Doug 94
Blake, Herman 451, 490, 617, 634
Blauner, Robert
 and views of BPP 451; and Communist Party 451; jury consultant 411–413, 418, 421; and Huey Newton 418; pretrial work 369, 378, 387; trial witness 398–399, 404–405.
Block, Emanuel 275
Blood in My Eye 529
Bloody Thursday 271
Blow, Charles M. 697
Boda, Mike (*see* Mario Buda) 144
Bolsheviks 133, 137
Bond, H. Julian 677, 679
Booker, Cory 680
Book of Daniel, The 279
Boondocks, The 683
Borah, William 66–68, 72–74
Bork, Robert 607
Bortz, Neal 653
Boston Brahmins (*see* Brahmins) 143
Boston Five 542
Bowles, Charles 183, 193
Boyle, Kay 426
Boyle, Kevin 201, 720
Bradley Effect 678
Bradley, Tom 664, 677–678
Brady, Matthew 10
Brady v. Maryland 255, 337
Brahmins 143
Branch Davidians 669, 671
Brandeis, Louis 142
Branton, Leo, Jr. Part Three, Chap.

4 *passim*
Breakthrough, The 676
Breckinridge, Henry 248
Breiner, Leon 189, 196, 198–199
Breslin, Jimmy 652
Bridges, Harry 271, 292, 525
Brock, David 657
Brooks, Edward 644, 645
Brosnahan, James 656
Brotherhood of Sleeping Car Porters 313
Brother, The: The Untold Story of Atomic Spy David Greenglass 279
Brotsky, Al 350, 452
Brown, Elaine 527–528, 617–626, 628–635, 638, 642–643
Brown, Gov. Edmund G., Jr. ("Jerry") 12, 630–632, 693
Brown, Gov. Edmund G., Sr. ("Pat") 12, 297, 326, 367, 561, 571, 631
Brown, H. Rap
SNCC leader 3–4, 330, 356–357, 488, 492; at Newton's funeral as Jamil Abdullah Al-Amin 642
Brown, James 323, 642
Brown v. Board of Educ. 281, 283–284
Brown, Willie 330, 344, 633
Brownell, Herbert 273, 276
Bryan, Robert R. 264
Bryant, Roy 282
Buchanan, Pat 698
Buckey, Peggy McMartin 653
Buckey, Ray 653–654
Buckhout, Robert 592
Buda, Mario 144
Buddha Samurai 634
Bunch, Lonnie, III 682
Bunker, Archie 697–698
Burnham, Margaret 565, 583
Burns, Ken 112
Burris, John 665–666
Burstyn, Ellen 646
Bush, George H. W. 664, 711
Bush, George W. 664, 705–706, 708, 710
Butler Act 167, 174– 178
Butler, Marian 422
Bye, Charles 657–658

C

Cabey, Darrell 647–648
Cain, Herman 700
California Civil Rights Initiative 697
Calles, Plutarco 244
Calley, William, Jr. 614
Callins, Preston 624, 636
Campbell, Gordon 510–511, 571
Canovas del Castillo, Antonio 43
Canty, Troy 647, 649
Capone, Al 150, 153, 249
Carmichael, Stokely
And BPP 5, 356–359, 455, 495, 524, 642; Black Power viii, 346; and Eldridge Cleaver 346, 379; FBI target 392, 496; and MLK 346, 372–373; Lowndes County Freedom Org. 311; SNCC rift 357, 453; Vietnam War 5, 299; see also Student Nonviolent Coordinating Committee ("SNCC")
Carnegie Foundation 210
Carnot, Sadi 43
Carpetbaggers 110
Carr, Betsy Hammer 29, 585, 589
Carr, Jimmy 516, 528–530, 584, 589, 627
Carroll, Lewis 425
Carter, Alprentice "Bunchy" 362, 552
Carter, Jimmy 614, 661
Castro, Fidel 291, 415, 491, 541,

626–627, 659, 665
Catonsville Nine 543, 546, 569
Causey, Clarence 504
Caverly, John 153, 155, 157–158, 194
Ceausescu, Nicolae 9
Cemetery John 250, 252–253, 255–256
Chambers, Whittaker 272, 274
Chandler, Happy 29, 32
Chaney, James 286–287
Chang, Henry 220, 223
Chaplin, Charlie 11, 13
Chase, Hal 18
Chavez, Cesar 299, 309, 471
Chawke, Thomas 197, 199–200, 213
Che-Lumumba Black Communist Party Club 532
Chessman, Caryl 308, 571
Chesterton, G. K. 597
Chicago Eight 545, 679
Chicago Riots 1919 184, 694
Chicago Seven, Part Three, Chap. 2, *passim*, 563–564, 566, 648, 656, 675, 714
Chinese Exclusion Act of 1882 215
Chisholm, Shirley 564, 590, 677, 709
Christian Science Monitor, The 713
Christmas, William 517, 598
Church, Frank 630
Churchill, Winston 267–268, 270
CIA 542, 604, 606, 630–631, 659, 661, 702
Cicotte, Eddie 23, 25–27
Cinque 601, see also Ruchell Magee
Cinque, General Field Marshall 608
Civil Rights Act 1964 287, 289
Civil Rights Act of 1875 94
Civil War 48–49, 57, 63, 79, 87, 89, 94, 109, 110–111, 122, 125, 215, 536, 681, 709, 711
Clansman, The 77, 121–122
Clark, James 689
Clark, Marcia 667
Clark, Mark 498
Clark, Ramsey 569–570, 601, 634, 703
Cleaver, Eldridge
Foreword, Introduction, Part Two, Part Three, Chap. 1, 2, 6, 8 *passim*
Cleaver, Kathleen Neal
candidate for California Assembly 391; and Free Huey Campaign 353, 394, 419, 453, 488, 494; and Eldridge Cleaver 347–348, 374, 453, 642; and BPP split 523; on Pratt appellate team 600; posed with rifle 488, 705
Clinton, Hillary Rodham 678, 704–708
Clinton, William Jefferson 215, 615, 656–657, 681, 704–705, 709, 711
Clutchette, John 503, 506, 508, 580, 583, 593
Clutchette v. Procunier 504
Cobb, Ty 16–17, 30–31, 46, 129, 186, 304
Cochran, Johnnie 564, 600, 663, 667
Cochran, Todd "Bayete" 564
Coffin, William Sloane, Jr. 542
Cohen, Richard 33
Cohn, Roy 275, 280
COINTELPRO 3, 496, 498, 512, 516, 520, 528, 553, 601, 621, 628, 639, 682, 702
Cold War 178, 212, 266, 270–271, 273–275, 280, 290–291, 451
Coleman, Kate 636
Collier, Peter 645, 675
Collins, Eddie 22
Colorado Labor Wars 57, 60
Comiskey, Charles 19, 22–30

Communist Party Part Three Chap. 4 *passim*; 137–138, 280, 283, 291, 319, 451, 491; *see also* American Communist Party; Castro, Fidel; Che Lumumba Club; Khrushchev, Nikita; Stalin, Vladimir
Condon, John 250, 256
Confederacy 91, 110–111
Congress of Racial Equality ("CORE") 296, 308
Conley, Jim 117–123, 128
Connor, Theophilus Eugene "Bull" 211–212, 281, 285
Coolidge, Calvin 12, 139, 142, 243–244
coon songs 76
Cooper, Penny 369, 387, 424, 495, 666
Coplon, Judith 272
Cosby, Bill 406, 705
Council for Justice 299, 502
Cox, Archibald 606, 611
Cox, Donald 498
Cox, James 33
Cox, William 88
Crane, Stephen 646
Cranston, Sen. Alan 643
Cristy, Albert 232, 234, 238
Crockett, George 286, 732
Cronaca Sovversiva 131–132
Cronkite, Walter 543
Crowe, Bernard "Lotsapoppa" 553
Crowe, Robert 151
Curriden, Mark 7, 97, 716
Czolgosz, Leon 44–45, 658

D

d'Adesky, Anna Christine 411
Daley, Richard 22, 466, 539, 541, 546, 689, 700
Darden, Christopher 666
Darrow, Amirus 64
Darrow, Clarence
Part One, Chap. 3, 5, 8–10, 12 *passim;* 5, 259, 264, 594, 685.
Darrow, Emily 64
Darrow, Jessie 65
Darrow, Paul 65
Darrow, Ruby Hamerstrom 65, 99–101, 151, 191, 195, 213, 239
Darwin, Charles or Darwinian theory of evolution, Part One Chap. 9 *passim,* 687–688
Daugherty, Harry 12, 33, 139
Davies, Marion 11
Davis, Angela
acquittal 622; flight 532–534, 536; at Newton's funeral 642; Nixon enemies' list 606; symbol in 2008 political campaign 705; Trial of, Part Three, Chap. 4, *passim;* suggested as "THE" trial of the century 673–675, 709, 714
Davis, Charles 234
Davis, Fania (*see* Fania Davis Jordan) 563, 694
Davis, O. K. 69
Davis, Rennie 541
Davis, Sammy, Jr. 371, 563
Dean, Dizzy 31
Death of Innocence 282
Debs, Eugene 54, 62–66, 101, 103–105, 685
Declaration of Independence 644, 713
Dee, Henry 286
Deep Throat 606
DeFreeze, Donald 608, 611
Dellinger, David 541

Dellums, C. L. 330
Dellums, Ron
on Berkeley City Council 330, 341, 358, 391–392, 692; as Congressman 330, 634, 643, 709; as Mayor of Oakland 330, 692
Delmas, Delphin 49
Delmont, Maude 10, 11
Dementia Americana 35, 49, 51
Depression (*see* Great Depression) 195, 202, 218, 242, 271, 273
DePriest, Oscar 233
Dershowitz, Alan 29, 127, 286, 542, 654, 655, 657, 663, 673
Destructive Generation 645
de Tocqueville, Alexis 203
Deukmejian, George 580, 678
Diamond, Bernard 378, 405, 431, 461, 501, 660
DiFalco, S. Samuel 278
Dillingham, Walter 218, 222, 230, 234–235, 239, 240
Dinkins, David 651, 652
Dixiecrats 211–212, 281, 283, 288–289, 677
Dixon, Thomas 76–77, 122
Doctorow, E. L. 53, 279
Dohrn, Bernardine 508, 700
Dole, Sanford 215
Dorsey, Hugh 116–124, 127
Douglas, Emory 310
Douglas, William 277
Douglass, Frederick 403, 565, 709
Dreams from My Father 701, 706
Dred Scott decision 63
Dreyfus Affair, The 129, 139
Dreyfus, Barney 4, 293, 307, 334–338, 362, 375–378
Drumgo, Fleeta 506, 580, 583, 592, 628
D'Souza, Dinesh 759 n. 41, 760 n. 54
DuBois, W. E. B. 77, 192, 319, 346, 465
Dukakis, Michael 144
Durden-Smith, Jo 515, 587, 599, 628
Dylan, Bob 290, 536
Dymally, Melvin 330

E

Easy Rider 520
Edison, Thomas 46
Edley, Christopher 760 n. 54
Edmund Richardson 685
Ehrmann, Herbert 547
Eichmann, Adolf 9, 448
Einstein, Albert 33, 270, 276
Eisenhower, Dwight David 265, 276–277, 282–283
Ellsberg, Daniel 605–606, 657
Empress Elizabeth of Austria 43
Epstein, Edward J. 524
Equal Rights Amendment 564
Erikson, Erik 522
Erikson, Kai 522
Ernst, Morris 276
Espionage Act 104, 133, 274, 605
Evolution, Theory of 163, 166, 169, 171, 178
Eyes on the Prize 703
Eyes on the Prize II 703

F

Fabio, Sarah Webster 366
Fall, Albert 12
Fanon, Frantz 2, 321, 360, 465, 700
Farrakhan, Louis 694–695, 704, 706
Faubus, Orval 283
Fawcett, James 253
FDR 278
Federal Bureau of Investigation ("FBI") *passim*

Feinstein, Diane 294, 692
Felt, Mark 606
Fernandez, Raymond 277
Finch, Thomas 355, 443
Fisher, C. Lloyd 254–255
Fisher, James 263–264
Fiske, Robert 657
Flack, Roberta 563
Flynn, William 654
Fonda, Henry 422
Fonda, Jane 520, 535, 590, 620, 632
Foner, Eric 77
Forbes, Flores 619, 623, 633, 635–636, 639
Ford, Gerald 559, 612
Ford, Henry 182–183
Fortescue, Grace 219, 231, 233–235
Fortescue, Granville Roland 218
Foster, Marcus 607, 608, 615
Fountaine, Gwen (*see* Gwen Fountaine Newton) 521, 624–625
France, Anatole 139
Franck, Peter 299, 439, 501, 508
Frankfurter, Felix 136–137, 140–141, 276
Frank, Leo Part One Chap. 6 *passim*, 145, 156, 208, 259, 262, 614, 688
Franklin, Aretha 563
Frank, Lucille Selig 115
Franks, Bobby 144, 148–150, 157, 217
Freed, Donald 496, 521, 637
Freedom Summer 284, 288, 295, 368
Freeman, Huey 683
Free Speech Movement ("FSM") 295–300; 321, 338, 351, 368, 378, 494, 501
Freud, Sigmund 153, 522
Frey, John Part Two *passim*, 7, 500–501, 526, 640, 674, 692–693
Friedman, Monroe Part Two *passim*, 500–501, 689
Friends of SNCC 311, 357, 368
Froines, John 541, 547
Fromme, Lynette 558–559
Frost, David 524–525
Fuchs, Klaus 273
Fuhrman, Mark 221, 227, 666–667
Fukunaga, Myles 217, 224
Fuller, Alvan Tufts 141–143
Fuller, Chief Justice Melville W. 90, 92, 96
Fullerton, Hugh 15, 23–24, 27
Fundamentalism Part One Chap. 9 *passim*, 182, 687
Furman, Mark 273

G

Gaffney, Edward 177
Gain, Charles 309, 351, 357, 378, 386, 479–480, 625
Galleani, Luigi 130–133
Game Change 676
Gandhi, Mahatma 283
Gardner, Lloyd 262
Garry, Charles
as attorney for Huey Newton and BPP, Part Two *passim*, 569, 575, 595, 621, 625, 633, 639, 650, 662, 675; Black Guerilla family hit list 644; and expert Dr. Bernard Diamond 650; as attorney for Rev. Jim Jones at Jonestown 637; Oakland Seven case 293–294, 544–545; Seale trial 524–527, 708–709; as attorney for San Quentin Six defendant Johnnie Spain 627–628;

as John Thorne's attorney 588
Gary, Raphael *see* Grey, Crystal
Gay Rights Movement 519–520
Geis, Gilbert 264, 655
Genet, Jean 497, 508, 519
George, John
as Alameda County Supervisor 631; candidate for Congress 391; as attorney for Huey Newton 344, 348, 395; as attorney for Laverne Williams 306
Gibbons, Jenevie 417, 475, 478
Gibson, Josh 31
Gideon v. Wainwright 209
Gilded Age 35, 53
Gingrich, Newt 699–700, 713
Ginsberg, Allen 346, 546
Giuliani, Rudy 651–652
Glover, Arthur 111, 124
Goetz, Bernhard 646–653
Goines, David Lance 296, 298,
Goldman, Emma 44, 54, 73
Goldman, Ron 662, 695
Goldwater, Barry 296
Gomon, Josephine 195
Gompers, Samuel 59, 100–102
Gooding, Frank 67, 71
Goodlett, Carlton 307, 314, 342
Goodman, Andrew 286–287
Goodman, Robert 287
Good Riddance 646
Gow, Betty 246, 249, 251
Grant, Oscar, III 691, 693
Grant, Robert 28, 137
Great American Trials 656, 714
Great Depression 195, 202, 218, 242, 271, 273
Great Migration 20
Greenglass, David 273–275, 278–279
Greenglass, Ruth 279
Greenlee, Rush 399, 431, 459–460, 472, 475
Grey, Crystal 625, 635, 639
Grier, Henry 429, 431, 436–438, 447, 462, 464–470, 476–478, 500, 526–527
Griffiths, D. W. 121–122
Gropman, Donald 29
Guevara, Che 2, 5, 319, 332, 350, 541, 610, 629
Guthrie, Arlo 546
Guthrie, Woody 143, 210

H

Hair 702
Haley, Harold 517
Hallinan, Vincent 525
Halperin, Mark 676, 763
Hamburg Athletic Club 22
Hamerstrom, Ruby (*see* Ruby Darrow) 65
Hammer, Joan 585, 589
Hampton, Fred 498, 523–524, 567, 634, 701–704
Hand, Learned 276
Hansberry v. Lee 201
Hapgood, Norman 55
Harding, Warren 12, 33, 203, 685
Harlan, John 76, 89–91, 94
Harper, David 423–424, 453–454, 468, 472, 475–479, 481, 714
Harper's Ferry 64
Harris, Albert Part Three, Chap 4, *passim*
Harns, Billie "Buzzard" 506
Harris, George 505
Harris, Jean 646
Harris, Kamala 713
Harrisburg Seven, The 569, 601
Harrison, Benjamin 57

Harry Reid 678
Hart, Helen 423
Hauptmann, Anna 253
Hawley, James 66
Hayden, Tom 491, 497, 539, 541, 632
Haymarket Square Riot/Massacre 56, 63, 66, 105, 131, 639
Hays, Arthur Scopes trial 173, Sweet trial 192–194, 197
Hays, Samuel 59
Haywood, Big Bill
Part One, Chap. 3 *passim*, candidate for "THE" trial of the century 673, 68– 687, 710, 714–715; political activities 101–106, 130, 133, 135, 138, 391
Heanes, Herbert Part Two *passim*, appellate decision in *People v. Newton* 501, 640
Hearst, Patti 609–610, 612, 615
Hearst, William Randolph 11–13, 43–48, 107-109, 113–116, 121–123, 153, 189, 232, 253–254, 609
Hearst, William Randolph, Jr. 690–691
Heavens Fall 209
Heen, William 223, 227–228
Heileman, John 676
Heir to an Execution 280
Hemphill, Janie 576–577
Henson, Larry 626, 637
Hepburn, Katherine 371
Herbert, Bob 680
Hershey Directive, The 542
Hewitt, Ray "Masai" 618, 620
Hewlett, Emanuel 89
Heydler, John 19
Hilliard, David
BPP Chief of Staff, Part Two and Part Three Chap. 1, 6 *passim*, 5, 701; candidate for Oakland City Council 691; trial 707
Hilliard, June 623
Hinckle, Warren 680
Hinckley, John, Jr. 45, 658, 661
Hinman, Gary 554
Hiss, Alger 271–274, 277
Hitchcock, Alfred 159
Hitler, Adolph 265, 268, 286, 385, 415, 667, 699
Hixson, Will 80–81, 85
Hochmuth, Amandus 256, 259
Hoffman, Abbie x, 392, 471, Part Three Chap. 2, *passim*
Hoffman, Harold 259
Hoffman, Julius 541, 679
Hoffman, Thomas 423
Hoffmann, Alex
as attorney for BPP, Eldridge Cleaver and Huey Newton, Part Two and Part Three, Chap. 1, *passim*, 621; as attorney for Cesar Chavez 299, 309; as attorney for Civil Rights Auto Row and Sheraton Palace picketers 295, 308; as attorney for "Stop the Draft week" Oakland Seven defendants 351
Holder, Eric 707
Holiday, Billie 209–210, 681
Holloway, Natalee 681
Holmes, Oliver Wendell 91, 96, 121–122, 142
Holocaust 286, 698
Honkies for Huey 351
Hoover, Herbert 143, 238, 622, 688
Hoover, Ivery 285
Hoover, J. Edgar
abuse of power 289, 496–497, 622; Black Friday 293–294; focus on BPP ix, 3, 385, 496–497,

521, 524, 622, 688, 701; focus on Harry Bridges 271; Civil Rights Era 280, 285, 287–288; COINTELPRO 3, 496, 498, 528, 553, 639, 682, 701; focus on suspected Communists 3–4, 138–139; death 622; tenure as FBI Director 139, 249, 274, 622; Fred Hampton murder 702; Alger Hiss case 272–273; collaboration with HUAC 272–273, 293–294; focus on Martin Luther King, Jr. 284–285, 496; Lindbergh case 248–249, 252, 256, 263; and Richard Nixon, 271–272; Attorney General Palmer's protégé 132; Palmer Raids 139, 496; prosecution of Public Enemies 550; focus on Paul Robeson 284; and President Franklin Roosevelt 139; Rosenberg Espionage case and other McCarthy Era prosecutions 272–274, 280; focus on Sacco and Vanzetti and other anarchists 132, 139; secrets of 285; Smith Act 272; and President Truman 272; See COINTELPRO, Palmer Raids

Horowitz, David 621, 629, 634, 636, 645, 675, 683, 711

Horsley, Albert (*see* Harry Orchard) 69

Horton, Willie 711

House Un-American Activities Committee ("HUAC") 270–274, 291–295, 338

How I Helped O.J. get Away With Murder 668

Howard, Elbert "Big Man" 498

Howell, Robert E. Lee 126

Hudson, Erastus Mead 258, 277, 450

Huff, C. Ronald 261

Huggins, Ericka 522–524, 568, 583, 620–621, 634–635

Huggins, John 552, 620

Hughes, Charles Evans 122

Hughes, Langston 305

Hughes, Ronald 558

Humphrey, Hubert 211, 382, 689–690

Hunter, George William 170, 726

Huston Plan, The 606

Hutchins, Styles Part One, Chap. 4 *passim*

Hutton, Bobby
Black Panther Party first recruit 323, 325; and Defremery Park 396, 515; memorial poster 493, shooting death 5, 373–375, 379–380, 386, 391, 525, 567

I

Ida, Horace 220

If I Did It 668

Ifill, Gwen 676–677, 704

Il Gruppo Autonomo 133–134, 143

Immigration Restriction League 141

Ince, Thomas 11

Innis, Carlton 338–339

Innocence Project 98, 261, 663

Inouye, Daniel 679

International Labor Defense Committee ("ILD") 140, 207

International Workers of the Worlds ("IWW" aka "The Wobblies") 54, 60, 74, 103–105, 130, 135, 496

In the Line of Duty: Ambush at Waco 669

Invisible Empire (*see* Ku Klux Klan) 189, 192

Iron Curtain 270, 382
Iron Workers Union 101
Ito, Lance 666

J

Jackson, George
 Part Three, Chap 1, and 4 *passim*, 608, 715 and Black Guerilla Family 625, 640; death 628, 640; death of attorney Fay Stender, 644
Jackson, Jesse 406, 678, 695–696, 701, 704
Jackson, Jonathan
 Part Three, Chap. 4 *passim;* Marin County Courthouse kidnapping 517–519, 532, 534; death and August 7 Movement 529, 534–535
Jackson, Jonathan, Jr. 590
Jackson, Lester 511, 593
Jackson, Reggie 632
Jackson, "Shoeless" Joe 23–29
Jaworski, Leon 611
Jeffersonian Magazine 109
Jefferson, Rendell 635
Jenkins, Michelle 637
Jennings, Hughie "Eeyah" 17
Jensen, D. Lowell
 District Attorney 297, 638; Federal Judge 297; Free Speech Movement prosecutor 297; Prosecutor Huey Newton trial for death of Officer Frey, Part Two *passim*, 6, 526–527, 710, 714; Oakland Seven prosecutor 300, 544; SLA prosecutor 610, 615
Jerome, William Travers 48
Jet 282
Ji Jaga, Geronimo (*see* Geronimo Pratt) 513, 600–601, 620, 696
Jim Crow Laws 77–78, 211, 272, 287, 290, 317, 679
Johnson, Byron ("Ban") 15
Johnson, Ed Part One, Chap. 4 *passim*, 122, 126, 202, 204, 648
Johnson, Jack 28, 112, 639, 712
Johnson, Louis "Tex" 635
Johnson, Lyndon 4, 240, 289, 316, 371, 382, 389, 412–413, 539–544, 683, 689, 710
Johnson, Walter 31
Jones, Deacon 231
Jones, Howard 92
Jones, James Earl 677
Jones, Rev. Jim 637
Jones, District Judge John 687–688
Jonestown, murder-suicide 637
Jordan, Barbara 611, 676
Jordan, Fania Davis 563
Judd, Lawrence 217, 238

K

Kahahawai, Joe Part One, Chap. 12 *passim*, 688–689
Kalakaua, King 215
Kamehameha I 214
Kamehameha II 214
Kardashian, Robert 662
Karenga, Maulana Ron viii, 358, 512
Karpis, Alvin 550
Kasabian, Linda 557
Katz, Joseph 28, 137
Katzmann, Frederick 134–137
Kaufman, Irving 275, 276
Kawananakoa, Princess 223, 239, 728
Keating, Ed 399, 402, 404, 411, 469, 526
Keker, John 627
Kelley, John 235–237, 239
Kempton, Murray 617, 715
Kennedy, Judge Anthony 161, 711

Kennedy, John Fitzgerald 265, 320, 382, 512, 659
Kennedy, Ludovic 262–263, 729
Kennedy, Michael 637–638
Kennedy, Robert 284, 658–661
Kent State Shootings 499, 679
Kerner Report 4, 412–413, 465, 710
Kerr, Clark 296, 298
Key, Francis Scott 20, 49
Khrushchev, Nikita 278, 291
Kill the Best Gentiles 699
Killen, Edgar Ray 288
Kind and Unusual Punishment 531
King, Coretta Scott 622
King, Martin Luther, Jr.
assassination 4, 370, 383, 424, 597, 619, 707, 710; BPP view 6, 457; Leader of SCLC 283–285, 346; memorials 326, 644, 681; opposition to Vietnam War 299, 457
King, Rodney 644–667, 691, 694–695
Kirschke, Jack 562
Kline, Tony 630
Knights of Mary Phagan 125–127
Knowland, Joseph 618, 632–633
Knowland, William 618, 633, 641
Koehler, Arthur 257
Kokka, Harvey 422
Korean War 274–275
Korematsu v. United States 201
Koresh, David 669–670
KPFA 333, 368, 374, 471, 517, 643
Krause, Marshall 449
Ku Klux Klan
Part One Chap. 10 *passim*; and William Jennings Bryan 172; Colfax massacre 94; and Angela Davis family 583; Leopold and Loeb case 152; new version of KKK and Timothy McVeigh 669; and Neo-Nazis 201; resurgence after death of Mary Phagan 106, 121–122, 127, 681; KKK in South in the 1960s 288, 325, 583
Kunstler, William 543, 545–547, 648, 651
Kwanzaa 358

L

LaBianca, Leno 555
LaBianca, Rosemary 555–556
La Follette, Robert 12, 686
Landis, Kenesaw Mountain 18, 27, 104
Lane, Mark 368, 513, 520–521
Larson, Edward 163
League of Nations 13, 268
Leary, Timothy 546
Lee, Barbara 709
Lee, George W. 282
Lee, Newt 114, 127
Lee, Odell 320, 458
Lee, Spike 684
Leibowitz, Samuel 208
Leisure, George 233
Lenin, Vladimir 105, 138, 406
Lennon, John 598
Leonard, Corinne 306
Leonard, Dutch 30
Leopold, Nathan Part One, Chap. 8 *passim*, 144, 165, 169, 174, 194, 213, 217, 555, 655–656
Lewis, John 284, 677, 701
Lewis, Sinclair 143
Life 393–394, 476, 529, 674
Liliuokalani, Queen 215
Lindbergh, Anne Morrow 251, 262, 265
Lindbergh, Charles Part One, Chap. 13, *passim*

Lindbergh, Charles Jr. 242, 255
Lindbergh Law 252
Linder, Douglas 655, 672
Little Rock crisis 283
Little, Russell 609, 615
Littleton, Martin 52
Lochner v. New York 47, 60
Loeb, Jacob 147, 151
Loeb, Richard Part One, Chap 8 *passim*; 165, 169, 174, 194, 213, 217, 555, 655–656
London, Jack 112, 508
Long, Huey Pierce 2, 318
Look 282, 528
Lord, Edward 231
Los Angeles Criminal Conspiracy Section ("CCS" or "Red Squad") 516
Lott, Trent 289
Lowell, A. Lawrence 141
Lowell Commission 141, 143
Lueker, Claude 17
Lukas, George 619
Lukas, J. Anthony 1, 105
lumpenproletariat 2, 320, 322, 495, 522
Lupica, Ben 249, 256–260
Lutesinger, Kitty 557

M

Mack, Connie 16, 29
Madigan, Frank 332, 515
Magee, Ruchell "Cinque" Part Three, Chap 4 *passim*, 517–518, 533, 608, 706
Magers, Mabel "Mickey" 589
Mailer, Norman 308, 379, 546
Majors, Reggie 345
Malloy, Nelson 635, 639
Man, The 677
Mandela, Nelson 695
Manhattan Project, The 267–268, 273
Mann Act 13, 112–113, 205, 639, 712
Mann, Alonzo 128
Manson, Charles, Part Three, Chap. 3 *passim*, 559, 561, 573, 608, 696
March, Frederic 164
Marcos, Ferdinand 9
Marcos, Imelda 9
Marin County Courthouse incident 516–519, Part Three, Chap. 4, *passim*
Markle, Arnold 524
Marshall, Thurgood 6, 289, 316, 358, 614
Marxist 299, 361, 378, 502, 505, 522, 532, 563, 583, 608, 621
Massie Affair, The Part One, Chap 12, *passim*, 213, 263, 714–715
Massie, Thalia Part One, Chap. 12 *passim*
Massie, Tommie Part One, Chap 12 *passim*
Mathewson, Christy 18
Matthews, Connie 522
Maximum Security 531
Maynard, Robert 641
McAnarney, Jeremiah 135–137, 139
McCain, John 676, 701, 705
McCarran-Walter Act 276
McCarthy Era 275, 287, 570, 689
McCarthy, Eugene 382, 389, 690
McCarthy, Joseph 278, 307, 640
McClain, James 516–518, 584, 593, 598–599
McClellan, George 48, 228
McCleskey v. Kemp 680
McConnell, Harvey 85, 437
McCord, James 587, 604
McDonough, Big Joe 21–22
McFadden, Robert 279

McGee, Willie 212, 307, 565
McGhee, Millie 285
McIntosh, John 227
McKinley, William 43, 47, 57–58, 138, 658, 679
McKinney, Gene 451–452, 456, 460, 467, 475, 526, 623
McNamara, James 101–103, 106, 159, 564, 687
McNamara, John 101–102, 564, 687
McParland, James 60–63, 67, 69, 70–71
McQueen, Steve 553
McReynolds, Samuel Part One, Chap. 4 *passim*, 194, 204
McTernan, Francis 307, 400, 402
McVeigh, Timothy (Oklahoma Bombing Case) 668–672, 698
Medina, Ernest 614
Meeropol, Abel 203–204
Meese, Ed 297, 361, 426, 713
Mehserle, Johannes 691–693, 756
Meisenbach, Robert 291–295, 333
Mencken, H. L. 175
Merchants and Manufacturers Association 100, 686
Merriam, Frank 271
Merritt College 299, 311, 319, 324, 368, 423, 494, 643, 684
Metcalfe, Ralph 265, 701
Milam, J. W. 282
Milk, Harvey 474, 664
Millay, Edna St. Vincent 143
Miller, Opie 505
Miller, Tommy 439, 447, 465
Million Man March 681, 694
Mills, John 504, 506, 580
Milosevic, Slobodan 9
Milton, Joyce 279
Minh, Ho Chi 535
Miranda v. Arizona 566
Mississippi Freedom Democratic Party 284
Mississippi Summer Project (*see* Freedom Summer) 284
Mitchell, Billy 243
Mitchell, Felix 633, 642
Mitford, Jessica ("Decca") *see also* Treuhaft, Jessica
BP supporter 330, 497, 622, 634; book on American prisons 531; book on Dr. Spock trial 543; civil rights investigation of Oakland police practices 324; member of Old Left 307; daughter Dinky Romilly and SNCC 357
Mixon, Lovelle 691–692
Moldea, Dan 660
Moll, Lester 190, 200
Molly Maguires 60–61, 66
Monier, Stephen 262
Moody, William H. 92–93, 95
Moon, Rev. Sun Myung 642
Mooney, Tom 131
Moore, Charles 286
Moore, Fred 135
Moore, Gilbert 5–7, Part Two, Chap. 10–14 *passim*, 674, 694
Moore, Harry 248
Moore, Howard 565, 568
Moore, William Henry 634
Morelli gang 140
Morgan, J. P. 105, 133, 244
Morris, Newt 126
Morrow, Constance 249
Morrow, Dwight 244–245
Morrow, Elisabeth 245
Moscone, George 474, 665
Most, Johann 131
Motley, Constance Baker 289

Moyer, Charles 62
Mueller, Robert 672
Muhammad, Elijah 112, 319, 496, 549, 550
Murakami, Robert 224, 227
The Murder of Fred Hampton 703
Murphy, Frank, Part One, Chap. 10 *passim*
Murray, George Mason 490–491, 532
Murrow, Edward R. 278
Mussolini, Benito 140, 268
My Lai massacre 605, 614
Myrdal, Gunnar 210–211

N

Napolitano, Janet 672
Nash, Graham 539
National Association for the Advancement of Colored People ("NAACP") *The Crisis* 698; Civil Rights cases Part One Chap. 15, *passim*; Angela Davis trial team member Margaret Burnham 565; W. E. B. DuBois co-founder 346; death penalty 380; Goetz case 651; Fred Hampton and 701; Thurgood Marshall 316; Donald McCullum 638; Port Chicago defense 316; Scopes trial 172; Scottsboro Boys 203, 207, 209–210, 213; Sweet trial 178 and Part One, Chap 10, *passim*; Clinton White 344; Roger Wilkins 698; Roy Wilkins 702
National Civil Liberties Bureau (*see* Amer. Civil Liberties Union) 167
National Guard x, 1, 21, 58, 81, 90–92, 120, 205, 271, 283, 397, 469, 471, 479–480, 500, 537–538, 664, 679, 689, 694
National Guardian 276
National Lawyers Guild
and Beverly Axelrod 307; Civil Rights cases and Freedom Summer 286, 288, 290; Communist Party alleged ties 276, 288, 290; George Crockett 290; Barney Dreyfus 336; Charles Garry 300; government target 276, 288; Hiss trial 276; how-to manual for addressing race bias in jury cases based on Newton defense 675; HUAC and 272; Treuhaft firm 707; Doris Walker 565
National Museum of African American History and Culture 681
National Rifle Ass'n ("NRA") 329, 669, 678
National United Committee to Free Angela Davis and All Political Prisoners ("NUCFAD") 563–564, 567, 573–574, 585
Nation of Islam 2, 311, 496, 549–550, 694
Neal, Kathleen (*see* Kathleen Cleaver) 347–348
Neil, Earl 372, 411, 431, 643
Nesbit, Evelyn, Part One, Chap. 2 *passim*
Neufeld, Peter 261, 663, *see* Innocence Project, Barry Scheck
New Black Panther Party 707–708
New Deal 272, 314, 389, 685, 688
New Jim Crow, The 712
New Left 6, 290, 491, 541
New Times 636
New York Times 3, 42, 46, 69–70, 78, 121, 176, 232, 234, 260, 278, 359,

393, 497, 529, 534, 542, 564, 574, 605, 617, 622, 648, 668
New Yorker, The 524, 705
Newsweek 498
Newson, Jerry 324–325
Newton, Armelia 317, 358, 431
Newton, Fredrika Slaughter 640–643
Newton, Gwen Fountaine 521, 624–625
Newton, Huey
  Foreword, Introduction, Part Two, Part Three Chap. 1, 2, 4 & 8 *passim,* 104, 235, 549, 557, 663, 673–675
Newton, Leander ("Lee") 318
Newton, Melvin 308–309, 374, 462, 641
Newton, Michael 659
Newton, Walter 317–318, 431
Newton, Walter, Jr. ("Sonny Man") 318
Nicholson, Jack 521
Nichols, Terry 668–669, 671–721
Nietzsche, Frederich 145, 165, 169
Nixon, Richard
  and anti-war activists 523; BPP 495, 498; Cambodian invasion 500; campaign in 1968 389, 690, 701; China diplomatic relations 527, 590; Davis trial 561; enemies list xi; and David Frost 525; Alger Hiss and 271, 277; Manson trial 558; New Haven demonstrations x; Weathermen 523; War on Drugs 711; Watergate, Part Three, Chap. 5 *passim* and 657
Nobel, Alfred 56
Noe, Denise 11
Noguchi, Thomas 660
Nolan, Nick 95–96
Nolen, W. L. 505
Norquist, Grover 713
Norris, Clarence 206, 209
Norton v. Alabama 209
NRA 328, 678
Nunes, John 300–301
Nuremberg Principles 9, 300

O

Oakland A's 622, 632
Oakland Citizens Police Review Board 617, 639, 693
Oakland Community School 621, 629, 631, 633–635, 640
Oakland Museum of California 469, 684
Oakland Raiders 643
Oakland Seven 300–301, 351–352, 489, 544, 546
Oakland Tribune, The 332, 343, 354, 368, 389, 396, 412, 475, 618, 632, 634, 636, 638, 641, 691, 694
Obama, Barack, Part Three Chap. 8, *passim*
Obama, Michelle 578, 637, 693, 704, 710, 712
Oberholtzer, Madge 194
Occupy Wall Street 539
Ochs, Adolph 46, 78, 90, 121, 126
O'Donnell gang 160
Ogletree, Charles 656, 661–674
Oklahoma City Bombing 668, 673, 695, 698–699
Olson, Sara Jane 615
On Doing Time 278
Oney, Steve 125–126, 128
Ono, Yoko 598
Operation Abolition 293–294
Operation Correction 294
Operation Downfall 269
Orangeburg Massacre 680

Orchard, Harry (aka Thomas Hogan) Part One Chap 3, *passim*
Orloff, Thomas 633, 635, 637–638, 641
Oswald, Lee Harvey 658–659
Otis, Harry 100–101, 686
Owen, Russell 234

P

Pacifica Foundation 287
Paige, Satchel 31
Palin, Sarah 676, 701, 705
Palmer, Alexander 132–133, 137–138, 496, 639, 685
Palmer Raids 132–133, 496, 639
Pan-Africanism 495
Panther 684
Panther 21 512, 522–524, 583, 648, 683
Parden, Noah 83–84, 87– 95
Parker, James ("Big Jim") 45, 679
Park, Jim 534
Patterson, Haywood 208
Patterson, William (American Communist Party) 4, 140, 210, 307, 616,
Patterson, William B. (Advisor to Lionel Wilson) 632
Payton, Brenda 641
Peace and Freedom Party Bob Avakian 352, 358; BPP alliance viii, 350–352, 356–358, 376, 387, 391–392, 414, 467, 490; Eldridge Cleaver for President 5, 350, 391, 453, 467, 617; Kathleen Cleaver for State Assembly 291; leadership 351; Newton for Congress 376, Oakland 7 Trial 300; Mario Savio 351; Bob Scheer for Congress 322, 391; Jack Weinberg 351
Pearson, Hugh 623, 683
Peeples, Agnes 220– 223
Pell, Eve 531
Pelosi, Nancy 697
Peltier, Leonard 548 (See also "AIM")
Pentagon Papers, The 605, 657
People's Park 494–495, 533, 542, 608
People's Temple 637
People v. Anderson 572, 575
Perry, Harold 451
Perry, Julian 197
Perry, Gov. Rick 700
Pershing, John 27, 244
Pettibone, George Part One Chap. 3, *passim*
Phagan, Mary Part One, Chap 6 *passim*
Phillips, George 389, 544
Phillips, Leroy Jr. 97
Piltdown man 165–166
Pinell, Hugo 625
Pinkerton Detective Agency, Part One, Chap 3 *passim*, 101, 117, 239–241
Pinkerton report 239–240
Pittman, William 223, 227
Pius XII, Pope 276
Place, Martha 277
Plessy v. Ferguson 77, 89, 281
Polansky, Roman 551, 554, 556
Populist Party 109
Port Chicago 316
Porter, Katherine Anne 688
Port Huron Statement 491
Posey, Cum 31
Post, Louis 138
Powell, Colin 678
Powell, Lewis, Jr. 680

Powell v. Alabama 207

Powell, William 504–505

Pratt, Elmer "Geronimo" Ji Jaga, banishment from BPP 523; civil rights suit 696; alliance with Eldridge Cleaver 600; flight 516–517; and Los Angeles branch of BPP 517, 620; and Marin Civic Center kidnap plot, 516, 601; murder trial, 600–601; at Newton's release 513–514; release following appeal 696

Prelli, Eda 423, 475, 478

Price, Victoria 205, 208

Prison Law Collective 531

Prison Law Project 530–531, 538

Progressive Party 12, 212, 525

Prohibition 10, 12–13, 33, 44, 150, 168

Pulitzer, Joseph 43

Puzo, Mario 636

Q

Quintana, Joseph 422, 478

R

Rackley, Alex x, 498, 524, 620

Radosh, Ronald 279

Rainbow Coalition 678, 697, 701

Ramparts magazine

BPP support viii, 329; employment of Eldridge Cleaver 308–309, 328, 346, 368, 375, 379, 458; Kathleen Cleaver article and photo with gun 388; Peter Collier 675; Warren Hinckle, editor 680; David Horowitz 621, 675; Ed Keating as publisher 399, 526; Mark Lane 512; Sandra Levinson 375; Bob Scheer 391; Betty Louise Van Patter 629

Ramseur, James 649–651

Ramsey, JonBenet 264, 681

Rappe, Virginia 10

Raulston, John 167, 176

Rayback, Joseph 61

Reading, John 372, 617, 631

Reagan, Nancy 599

Reagan, Ronald ix, 7, 45, 288, 297–298, 328, 534–538, 642–643, 658, 661, 686, 690, 711, 713

Reconstruction Era and Amendments 91, 94–95, 122, 678

Red Squad 516–517, 532, 599, 627

Red Summer 22, 184, 316, 495

Reid, Sen. Harry 678

Reilly, Edward 254–255

Remington, William 274, 278

Remiro, Joseph 609, 615

Reno, Janet 669, 671

Revolutionary Action Movement ("RAM") 319

Rhodes, Don 31

Rhodes, Jane 684

Rice, Condoleezza 677

Richardson, Edmund 70–71, 685

Richardson, Elliot 607

Richardson Report, The 234–235

Rivera, Geraldo 559

Roan, Leonard 119

Robeson, Paul

background 31; meeting with baseball owners and Commissioner Kenesaw Mountain Landis 31–32; FBI target 285; genocide claim 210, 307; and William Patterson 210, 307; and Bob and Decca Treuhaft 307

Robinson, Jackie 211

Robinson, Tyrone 640–641

Rockefeller, John D. 110

Rockerfeller, Nelson 537
Rodham, Hillary (*see* Hillary Rodham Clinton) 708–709
Rogers, Earl 103
Rolling Stone 704
Rolling Stones, The 563
Romilly, Dinky 357, 403
Romney, Willard Mitt 700
Roosevelt, Franklin 139, 201, 267, 688
Roosevelt, Theodore,
and "Great Detective" William Burns 101; appointment of Kenesaw Mountain Landis as federal judge 18; governor of New York 48; Rough Riders 58; Ruef prosecution for San Francisco political scandal 101; Sheriff Shipp contempt prosecution 74–76; 91–96; Unification Speech 131; and Booker T. Washington 77; and WFM leaders' prosecution 57, 62–63, 66–67, 73–74
Roper v. Simmons 161
Rosenberg, Ethel Part One Chap. 14 *passim*; 563, 639, 689
Rosenberg, Julius Part One Chap. 14, *passim*, 639, 689
Rosewood 184, 195
Ross, Dell
grand jury testimony 340, 364, 500; Doug Hill as attorney for 439–502; Newton trial appearance 439–442, 444, 502, 636
Rosser, Luther 116, 120, 123
Rothstein, Arnold 24–27, 33
Rough Riders 58
Rove, Karl 700
Rubin, Jerry Part Three, Chap. 2, *passim*; Vietnam Day Committee 299; Yippie leader x, 539, 541, 544, 546–547
Ruby, Jack 658
Ruckelshaus, William 607
Ruef, Abraham 101
Rush, Bobby 703
Rustin, Bayard 283–285
Ruth, George Herman "Babe" 20, 23, 26, 28, 31, 243
Ryan, George 160

S

Sacco, Nicola
Part One, Chap. 7 *passim*; Herbert Ehrmann as counsel for 547; Felix Frankfurter article 276; martyr 207, 351, 399, 489, 639, 696; miscarriage of justice 129, 245, 259, 275, 399, 603, 614; John MacAnarney as counsel for 139–143; Fred Moore as counsel for 135; William Patterson and 307; William Thomson as counsel for 139–143; *see* also Vanzetti, Bartolomeo
Salsedo, Andrea 133
Sandburg, Carl 105, 130, 143
San Francisco Chronicle, The 538, 607
San Francisco Examiner 42, 399, 406, 475–476, 515, 690
San Francisco Human Rights Commission 295
San Quentin Six 535, 585, 593, 625, 627, 642
Sartre, Jean Paul 319
Saturday Night Massacre, The 607
Savio, Mario 295, 298, 351
Saypol, Irving 274, 277
Scheck, Barry 261, 663, *see* Innocence Project, Peter Neufeld
Scheer, Robert 322, 391

Scherr, Max 299
Schmitz, Eugene 101
Schneider, Bert 520, 536, 621, 623–624
Schwarzenegger, Arnold 693
Schwarzkopf, Norman 248–250, 252, 257, 259
Schwerner, Michael 286–287, 296, 375
Science of Revolutionary Warfare, The 131
Scopes, John, Part One, Chap 9 *passim*; Clarence Darrow as attorney for 192; Arthur Hays as attorney for 192; trial significance 542, 656, 673, 687, 715
Scott, George C. 164
Scottsboro Boys Part One, Chap. 11, *passim*; 233, 275, 283, 307, 489
Seale, Artie 312
Seale, Bobby Foreword, Introduction, Part Two, Part Three, Chap. 1, 2, 4, 6 & 8 *passim,* 299, 547, 643, 673–674, 692
Seale, George 316
Seale, Thelma 316
Sedition Act 104, 133
Seeger, Pete 143
Serling, Rod 677
Serra, Tony 638
Shabazz, Betty 329
Shabazz, Samir 707
Shakur, Tupac 684
Shapiro, Robert 663
Sharpton, Rev. Al 651, 704, 707
Sharp, Violet 251
Shepherd, Lewis 82–87, 90, 93–94
Sheppard, Sam 612–613
Shipp, Joseph, Part One, Chap. 4 *passim,* 648
Shipp, Thomas 204
Shuttlesworth v. City of Birmingham 286
Sickles, Daniel 49
Siegel, Dan 495
Silliman, Floyd 508, 581
"Silver" Republicans 58
Silver, Richard 508, 581
Simpson, Nicole 662, 695
Simpson, O. J. 8, 221, 227, 261, 655–656, 661–662, 667, 672–673, 694–695, 715
Sinatra, Frank 553
Sinclair, Upton 143
Sirhan, Sirhan 658, 660–661, 696
60 Minutes 691
SLATE 292, 299, 532
Slaton, John ("Jack") 107, 120, 123–124, 259
Slaughter, Arlene 621, 640
Slotnick, Gary 650
Smith, Abram 204
Smith Act, Smith Loyalty Act 272, 286, 293, 338
Smith, Hoke 111, 121, 124, 127
Smith, Rev. J. Alfred 644
Smith, Jess 12
Smith, Johnny 183
Smith, Kathleen 624, 633, 635, 637
Smith, Rep. Lamar 708
Smith, Pamela Wojas 654
Smith, Robert 30
Smith, William 118, 122, 128
Snyder, Ruth 277
Sobell, Martin 274, 278
Social Darwinism 145, 163, 170
Socialist Party 54, 63
Soledad Brothers Defense Committee 565, 586, 589, 608
Soledad Brothers, The
Steven Bingham and 628; Angela Davis and 532–533, 562–563, 568, 593, 596; Joan Hammer and 589;

Marin Courthouse invasion and 584, 601; murder charges 506; Newton and 515; Salinas pretrial hearing 510–512, 573, 593, 596; trial 519, 526, 571, 580–582
Soliah, Kathleen 615
Soltysik, Patricia Mizmoon 608
Southern Christian Leadership Conference ("SCLC") 283, 288, 383; see also Martin Luther King, Jr.
Spain, Johnnie 628, 642
Spanish-American War 43, 58, 215, 314, 679
Spock, Dr. Benjamin 542–543, 546, 563
Staats, Redmond 342, 352–353, 362
Stalin, Joseph 140, 267–268, 270, 274, 278, 280, 283, 291, 451
Stannard, David 240
Stanwyck, Barbara 277
Starr, Kenneth 657
Star Wars 619
Steadman, Alva 224
Steele, Michael 700
Steffens, Lincoln 103, 229
Steinem, Gloria 708
Stender, Fay
Part Two and Part Three Chap. 1 *passim,* 569, 625; Council for Justice 299, 501; death 644–647; attorney for George Jackson and Soledad Brothers defense commttee 502–512, 528–630, 563, 625; attorney for Huey Newton 4; Prison Law Project and Prisoners Rights Movement 630–532, 538; husband Marvin Stender 299, 334, 591
Stender, Marvin 361, 381, 469, 591
Stephenson, David 193–194, 201
Steunenberg, Frank 57–62, 65, 67–72, 74, 106
Stewart, Lynne 531–532
Stimson, Henry 269
Stirling, Yates, Jr. Part One, Chap. 12 *passim*
Stone, Irving 33, 65
Stop the Draft Week 300, 351, 544
"Strange Fruit" 209–210, 681
Stuckert, Robert 285, 731
Student Nonviolent Coordinating Committee ("SNCC")
and BPP 5, 311, 322, 356–359, 403, 519, 703; Black Power 329, 391; and Communist party 286, 288; FBI target 3, 288; founding 283, 677; Freedom Summer 284, 368; Free Speech Movement 296; Howard Moore as General Counsel 565; Nashville Conference and riots 346–348, 375; Vietnam War 299.
Students for a Democratic Society ("SDS") 300, 491, 497, 539
SWAT Team 516, 610, 635, 692
Sweet, Henry 190, 196, 198, 200, 714
Sweet, Gladys Part One, Chap. 10, *passim*
Sweet, Marguerite ("Iva") 180–181, 184–185, 187, 196, 200
Sweet, Ossian Part One, Chap. 10, *passim,* 714
Symbionese Liberation Army ("SLA") 607–608
Szilard, Leo 268, 269
Szilard Petition 269

T

Tackwood, Louis 516–518, 521, 532, 599, 601, 606, 627–628

Taft, William Howard 14–15, 27, 126
Takai, David Part One, Chap. 12, *passim*
Tammany Hall 47–48
Tarnower, Herman 646
Tate, Sharon 551, 554
Taylor, Elizabeth 553
Taylor, Glen 212
Taylor, Johnnie 623
Taylor, Nevada 78, 81, 85
Tea Party 541 (Boston), 688, 700
Teapot Dome Scandal 12
Thaw, Harry Part One, Chap 2, *passim*, 68, 145, 153, 655–656
Thaw, Mother (Mrs. William) 40, 46
Thayerism 140
Thayer, Webster 134, 194, 259
Thelwell, Ekwueme Michael 312
Thirteenth Amendment 94, *see also* Reconstruction Amendments
Thomas, Clarence 700
Thomas, Gary 518–519, 568, 584, 602
Thomas, W. G. 82
Thompson, Big Bill 21
Thompson, Clifford 561, 565, 570, 597
Thompson, Elsa Knight 368, 374, 471, 517, 621
Thompson, William 136, 139
Thorne, John 319, 509–511, 534, 583, 588–590, 715
Thorne, Richard (William Brumfield) 319
Three Strikes and You're Out 712
Thurmond, Strom 211–212, 289, 389, 699
Tigar, Michael 531–532, 565, 671
Tijerina, Reies Lopez 471
Till, Emmett 281–282
Tillman, Benjamin 76
Till-Mobley, Mamie 282
Time 210–211, 233, 243, 529, 663
Timothy, Mary 579, 582, 584, 590, 593, 595
Tolson, Clyde 289
Toms, Robert 191, 200–201
Tracy, Spencer 164, 371
Treaty of Versailles 13
Trenchard, Thomas 259
Treuhaft, Robert 307, 324–325, 344, 364, 378, 390, 565, 708–709; *see* also Jessica Mitford (Decca Treuhaft)
Triangle Shirtwaist Factory Fire 47
Truman, Harry S. 210–212, 266–272, 278, 291, 367, 670
Trump, Donald 700
Tse-Tung, Mao 323, 494, 508, 527
Tucker, Dave 632
Ture, Kwame (*see* Stokely Carmichael) 642
Turner Diaries, The 668–669, 672, 698
Turner, Morrie 707
Tuttle, Elbert 284
Twenty-fourth Infantry (24th Infantry) 58
Twilight Zone, The 677

U

Umberto I, King of Italy 43, 130
United Farm Workers 640
United Nations Commission on Human Rights 210
United Slaves ("US") 552; *see* US
Unruh, Jesse 495
Up 266
Uprising of 20,000 47
Uruburu, Paula 53
US, viii, 358, 512, *see* also Maulana Ron Karenga

V

Vahey, James 134
Van Beethoven, Camper 605
Vanderbilt, Gloria 13
Van Ingen, Philip 251
Van Patter, Betty Louise 629–630, 640, 683
Van Slingerland, Peter 240
Vanzetti, Bartolomeo
Part One, Chap. 7 *passim*; Felix Frankfurter article 276; martyr 207, 351, 399, 489, 639; miscarriage of justice 129, 245, 259, 275, 399, 603, 614, 619, 647, 656, 664; John MacAnarney as attorney for 139–143; William Patterson and 307; William Thompson as attorney for 135, 139–143; James Vahey as attorney for 134; *see Il Gruppo Autonomo* and Sacco, Nicola
Veeck, Bill 25
Vietnam Day Committee 300
Vietnam Veterans Against the War 521
Vietnam War ix, 5–6, 104, 291, 295, 299–300, 318, 321, 356, 371, 385, 389, 392, 457, 493, 497, 508, 521, 528, 543–544, 546, 548, 570, 590, 605, 614, 619, 632, 647, 656, 664
Volstead Act 12, 150
Von Brunn, James 699
Von Bulow, Claus 646, 654
Von Bulow, Sunny 646, 654

W

Waco Siege 669, 691
Waco: The Big Lie 669–670, 671, 754
Walker, Doris "Dobby" Brin 565, 708–709
Walker, Herbert 660
Walker, Gov. Scott 686–687
Wall Street Journal 12, 94, 707
Wallace, George 209, 389, 590, 690, 701
Wallace, Henry 212
Wallace, Irving 677
Walter, Francis 293
War Against the Panthers 639–640
War on Drugs, The 711–712
Warden, Donald 348, 350, 534
Warren, Earl 12, 33, 203, 281, 290, 389, 414, 680, 685
Washington, Booker T. 45, 76–77
Washington, Denzel 706
Washington, Essie May 211
Washington, Harold 701
Wasserman, Zach 633
Watergate 605–607, 611–612, 622, 657
Watson, Charles "Tex" 553–554, 557
Watson, Thomas 109–113, 120–121, 123–124, 127
Weathermen 104, 131, 497, 508, 523, 536, 700–701
Weaver, Randy 670
Weaver shooting stance 528
Weinberg, Jack 296, 351
Weiner, Lee 541, 547
Weinglass, Leonard 547
Welch, Joe 278
Welles, Orson 159
Wellman, David 368–369, 378, 387, 409, 413, 421
Wells, Bob 349
Wells-Gorshen rule 349
Wells, H. G. 139, 168
West, Cornel 700, 760 n. 54
West, Joanne 638
Western Federation of Miners ("WFM") Part One, Chap. 3 *passim*, 101, 103, 106, 685

Westfield, Floyd 78, 82
Whitaker, Matt 83, 85–86, 90, 92–93
White Citizens Council 283
White, Clinton 344, 348, 376, 476, 566
White, Dan 474, 664
Whited, Millard 256, 259
White, Edward D. 122
White Night Riots 664–665
White, Stanford Part One, Chap. 3 *passim,* 153
Who Killed George Jackson? 628
Wight, Griffith 225, 227, 232
Wilentz, David 256–258
Wilkins, Roger 698
Wilkins, Roy 703
Will, George 136, 667
Williams, Cecil 634, 644
Williams, Edward Bennett 7
Williams, Eugene 21
Williams, LaVerne 306, 339, 341, 400, 431–433
Williams, Luther 96
Williams, Robert 319
Wilson, Dennis 551, 553, 556
Wilson, Joe 699
Wilson, Lionel 326, 366, 622, 631, 638–639, 643
Wilson, Theo 655
Wilson, Woodrow 122
Winfrey, Oprah 706
Witherspoon v. Illinois 366, 380, 714
Without Sanctuary 681
Wobblies (*See* "IWW") 54, 104, 639
Wofford, Julia 95–96
Wolfe, Tom 708
Wolfe, Willie 608, 610
Women's Liberation Movement 422, 519, 564
Wood, Fremont 67
Woods, Ronald 671
Woodward, Robert 606
World's Christian Fundamentals Association ("WCFA") 166
World War I 13, 18, 20, 27, 104, 130–132, 167, 169, 216, 243–244, 252, 274, 314, 687
World War II 20, 94, 139, 210, 230, 240, 266–268, 270–273, 282, 294, 311, 313–314, 316, 326, 465, 471, 542, 571, 631, 679, 697
Wounded Knee 548
Wright, Donald 572
Wright, Fielding 211
Wright, Jeremiah 704, 707
Wright, Roy 206

X

X, Malcolm 289, 308, 319, 321, 329, 360, 465, 489, 495, 506, 528, 549–550, 617, 644, 701, 710

Y

Yat-sen, Sun 631
Yellow journalism 11, 43, 113, 614, 689
Yippies x, 392, 471, 539, 548
Young, Bertram 506
Young Communist League 273
Young, Cy 15
Younger, Evelle 572, 580

Z

Zeisel, Hans 381, 387, 405–406

ACKNOWLEDGMENTS

My deep thanks go to all those who gave me access to private collections and those who shared personal knowledge of events (most, if not all, listed in sources). I am particularly grateful to the encouragement and skillful assistance of two highly talented editors of my early drafts, authors Sara Houghteling (Pictures at an Exhibition) *and Dan White* (The Cactus Eaters). *Both Sara and Dan tried their best to cure me of writing like a lawyer—lessons in plain English that I sorely needed and did not always heed. A special thanks to Mark Weiman of Regent Press for believing in this project. My thanks also go to Christopher Bernard for his proofreading talents. Among the extraordinary resources now available on the web, I am especially beholden to Prof. Douglas Linder of the Univ. of Missouri at Kansas City School of Law for the impressive collection of original source material accessible at his site,* Famous Trials. *I am very grateful as well to experts who read and gave me early feedback on the book as a whole, particularly Judges D. Lowell Jensen and Thelton Henderson, and attorney Penny Cooper. I am enormously thankful as well to my friends Morrie Turner and Rosie Lee Allen, who served as sounding boards for my thesis, and those who reviewed individual chapters in their respective fields: Giants pregame host and baseball historian Marty Lurie for reviewing the section on early professional baseball; AFL-CIO Chief of Staff Jon Hiatt and Assistant General Counsel Damon Silvers for reviewing sections on labor history; Rutgers history professor Lloyd Gardner and New Jersey State Police museum archivist Mark Falzini for reviewing the chapter on the Lindbergh case; Fania Davis, who read an earlier version of the chapter on her sister's trial; and Karen Lee Wald for various suggested edits, especially on life in Cuba in the mid-1970s. None of these fine people are responsible for any mistakes I may have incorporated into the final version or any opinions expressed in the book. Thanks most of all to my family: my daughter Anna Benvenutti Hoffmann for editing suggestions, daughters Jamie and Mali Benvenutti for their research assistance and feedback, my sister Leslie Pearlman for additional proofreading, and my husband Peter Benvenutti—for support in every way, without whom this project would never have come to fruition.*